The Diary of George Templeton Strong

POST-WAR YEARS
1865–1875

The DIARY of
George Templeton Strong

★ ★ ★ ★

POST-WAR YEARS

1865—1875

———✧———

EDITED BY

ALLAN NEVINS

AND

MILTON HALSEY THOMAS

THE MACMILLAN COMPANY

New York : 1952

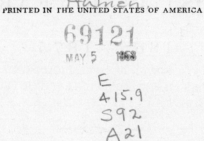

CONTENTS

ILLUSTRATIONS

DRAMATIS PERSONAE

GEORGE C. ANTHON.   This nephew of Professor Charles ("Bull") Anthon, for many years one of Strong's intimates, ruptured the friendship in a fit of pique. A highly temperamental man, he long refused to repair the breach. When Strong sent him a friendly message, he disregarded it for three years on the excuse that the bearer had made some untactful remarks about waterproof overshoes when delivering it! As for Charles Anthon, his death on July 29, 1867, was a blow to all sons of Columbia.

ADAM BADEAU.   The clever military secretary on Grant's staff retained his position until Grant became President, then leaving the army to devote himself to writing and diplomacy. Strong, who saw a good deal of him, thought him "sensible and observant."

FREDERICK A. P. BARNARD.   President of Columbia throughout this period, and the best head it had thus far had. Although the diarist suffered under Barnard's endless flow of talk, more otiose he thought than Mendelssohn's Introduction to the *Lobgesäng*, he delighted in the man's progressive ideas. "But for his two infirmities, deafness and prolixity, he would be very near perfection as president of Columbia College," wrote Strong.

HENRY WARD BEECHER.   In the years 1872–1875 the Woodhull-Tilton charges of adultery made Beecher the center of a resounding scandal. Beecher admitted that he had been indiscreet—"there never was a bigger ass, nor a deeper pit." But Strong was reluctant to believe him guilty of anything worse than folly. "Though most erratic and unsound, Beecher is manly, able, and eloquent."

HORACE BINNEY, JR.   The eldest son of the eminent Philadelphia attorney and statesman, himself a brilliant attorney practicing with his father and active in municipal affairs, was related to Strong by marriage to his cousin, Eliza Johnson. For ten years before his death in 1870, he had been on intimate terms with the diarist, who recorded that he "never knew anyone who came nearer to the ideal of a churchman and a gentleman."

CHARLES F. CHANDLER. Born in Massachusetts, trained at Harvard and Göttingen, and given his first teaching experience at Union College, Chandler had come to Columbia as professor of chemistry. In 1864 Egleston invited him to help establish the School of Mines, and his splendid work for this institution endeared him to Strong. A man of tremendous industry, Chandler was also a great industrial chemist and a most valuable head of the city board of health 1873–1883.

RICHARD HENRY DERBY. Strong's nephew ("Dickon," Harvard 1864) came to New York in 1870 and began practice as an ophthalmologist and ophthalmic surgeon. Trained by the best men in Boston, Dresden, Vienna, Berlin, Paris, and London, he won distinction in his profession in which he was active until his death in 1907. Strong took the young man into his family circle, introduced him proudly to his friends, brought him into the Century Club, and rejoiced in his success. A son, Dr. Richard Derby (Harvard 1903), married Ethel, the daughter of President Theodore Roosevelt.

CHARLES DICKENS. The death of the great novelist in 1870 seemed to Strong and to countless other Americans "as that of a personal friend." His genius had its flaws; but since 1837 he had "reigned by popular vote as monarch of prose fiction," and Strong thought that in some ways he might be compared with Shakespeare.

JOHN A. DIX. The general, nearly sixty-seven when the war ended, made a good minister to France 1866–1869, and an excellent governor of New York 1873–1875.

MORGAN DIX. News of the Rector's engagement, at the age of forty-five, to a woman more than twenty years his junior struck the diarist almost speechless. He could not believe the report until it was confirmed by the young lady's family; however, he disagreed with those who took a pessimistic view of the union. Describing the wedding, Strong wrote that "Morgan Dix looked like a beatified saint and, as it were, phosphoresced from brow to boots." The bride, whom he found intelligent and interesting rather than pretty, was soon included in Strong's approval of all the Dixes.

THEODORE WILLIAM DWIGHT. First professor and then Warden of the Columbia Law School, Dwight throughout this period performed most of its work singlehanded. While Strong had nothing but admiration for his forceful personality, learning, and forensic power, he could not but wish to see the School placed on a broader basis.

THOMAS EGLESTON.   Founder and informing spirit of the School of Mines, and builder of its fine mineralogical collections; a sensitive and brooding man and a warm friend as well as stalwart co-worker of Strong's.

HAMILTON FISH.   As ex-governor and ex-senator, Fish had more public prestige than any other Columbia trustee. His services to the college were many and great, though he had a tendency to be "perturbed and dissatisfied about everything." In 1869 he took the Secretaryship of State for what he thought would be a few weeks, and remained eight years, making one of the ablest records in the history of the office.

JAMES FISK, Jr.   As a director of the Erie Railroad, he helped Jay Gould and Daniel Drew loot that line; and later he and Gould carried out the infamous attempt to corner the gold market which ended in Black Friday. His murder in January, 1872, by the dissolute Edward Stokes, with whom he had quarrelled over the possession of the actress Josie Mansfield, exploded what Strong termed "a special stink-pot."

ULYSSES S. GRANT.   The general dined at Strong's house soon after Appomattox, and they had other meetings. Strong wrote in 1868: "Grant's chance for the White House is worth tenfold that of any other man. This is due partly to the general faith in his honesty and capacity, and partly to his genius for silence."

HORACE GREELEY.   Having been disgusted by Greeley's erratic course during the Civil War, Strong regarded his campaign for the presidency in 1872 with sharp hostility. Indeed, he pronounced the great editor a foolish old philanthropic gander, whose "weakness, gullibility, and capacity for folly are unlimited."

A. OAKEY HALL.   The "elegant Oakey" (New York University 1844), who had brilliant talents but no principles, furnished an imposing façade for the operations of the Tweed Ring throughout most of his four years as mayor, 1868–1872. Brought to trial, he defended himself and won an acquittal (December, 1872).

JOHN T. HOFFMAN.   This capable lawyer, who as a city judge had done good service in punishing participants in the Draft Riots, was elected mayor in 1865 and reëlected two years later. He was also grand sachem of Tammany, 1866–1868. As mayor he appointed Peter B. Sweeney city comptroller, while he was intimate with the other leaders of the Tweed Ring. When he was elected governor in 1868 Strong felt certain he would use his high office to abet the Ring thieves. So he did; but as the revolt against Tweed rose he moved toward repudiation of the Ring, and Strong gives a stirring account of his use of militia to support the Orange parade in 1871 that Tammany had tried to suppress. Once men had talked of him for the presidency; but he left the governorship politically ruined.

FRANCIS LIEBER. When the Civil War ended, this distinguished political scientist had reached the age of sixty-five, and his powers were flagging. Unable to interest Columbia students or maintain discipline, he was saved from dismissal by being transferred to the School of Law. Here again he was so useless that only his death in 1872 forestalled compulsory retirement. Strong credited him with learning, ability, and dignity, but thought he lacked common sense. "He is such an *owl*, so wise and lazy, and so puffy with self-importance. . . ."

DANIEL LORD. The death of this eminent lawyer, who had practised in New York since Madison was President, took place in 1868, and left a great gap in the Bar.

JAMES PECH. One of the most extraordinary figures to appear in the diary. As a musician and conductor he had great talent, and Strong was gratified to obtain his services for the Church Music Association. When he gave the first C.M.A. concert at Steinway Hall in January, 1870, he made an excellent impression. For two years he gave efficient service in both choral and orchestral training. Then dissension arose; when dismissed, he brought suit against the C.M.A.; and it turned out that he was a bigamist of scabrous record named Peck.

SAMUEL B. RUGGLES. Strong's father-in-law, still the most useful member of the Columbia board of trustees, was American delegate to the International Monetary Conference at Paris in 1867, and to the International Statistical Congress at Berlin in 1869. On October 22, 1872, he suffered a paralytic stroke of which Strong gives a vivid account. But he recovered and continued his public labors, surviving Strong, and doing more than any other trustee to make Columbia great. It was he who cabled Professor John W. Burgess, when the trustees approved the new School of Political Science on June 7, 1880: "Thank God, the University is born."

PHILIP H. SHERIDAN. His course as military governor of the Louisiana-Texas district during military reconstruction was subject to criticism, and Strong was disgusted by his later activities in New Orleans. But his Civil War services were such that the diarist was proud to entertain him. "The General is a stumpy, quadrangular little man, with a forehead of no promise and hair so short that it looks like a coat of black paint. But his eye and mouth shew force. . . ."

CHARLES E. STRONG. Cousin, law-partner, confidant, "Charley" shared with George Anthon the diarist's most intimate friendship. His daughter Kate ("little Miss Puss") was Strong's god-daughter; she came close to filling the place of his own daughter lost at birth. When, in 1866, Mrs. Eleanor Strong and little Kate went to Europe to live and Charles sold the home on East 22nd Street that he had built in 1852, George Strong was full of sadness and foreboding. Charles's trips abroad to visit his wife and daughter in the following years, Mrs. Eleanor's long illness, the growing up of Kate and her engagement to an English captain all caused the diarist anxiety and unhappiness.

ELLEN RUGGLES STRONG. The diarist often indulged in praise of his wife. Once he wrote: "Her social faculty is great. She acts on people of diverse temperaments and tastes just as a bit of platinum sponge acts on a current of mixed oxygen and hydrogen—makes them react on each other and become luminous—by a special unaccountable gift of catalysis." The Church Music Association could hardly have been the success it was without her skillful rallying of New York society to its support.

WILLIAM MARCY TWEED. Here called His Scoundrelism. The boss was fully exposed in 1871–1872. But his stubborn impudence in demanding "What are you going to do about it?" and holding on to the last elicited a dubious tribute from Strong: "The basalt columns of the Giant's Causeway are not more rigid than Boss Tweed's backbone. It has been reserved to this age to produce a hero in the department of Larceny and Peculation, corresponding in grade with the Heroes of the Greek Tragedy in their departments."

GULIAN C. VERPLANCK. His death in 1870, at the age of nearly eighty-six, removed one of the landmarks of New York life. "He is a great loss to our Vestry," wrote Strong, "and to sundry other boards and trusts, and to what *literate* society we have in New York. Had he only lived in Boston, he would have been famous."

JUNE–DECEMBER
1865

DR. LIEBER UNDER ATTACK · TRIAL OF LINCOLN'S ASSASSINS ·
RECONSTRUCTION DIFFICULTIES · GRANT VISITS
NEW YORK · THEODORE THOMAS

———————❦———————

When the war ended, Strong was still only forty-five years old; but the heavy burden he had carried during the conflict—the fourfold burden of the Sanitary Commission, his law office, the Columbia trusteeship, and the Trinity vestry—had weakened his constitution. He had only ten years to live, and henceforth we find frequent mention of ailing health in his diary. Nevertheless, he tried to labor as hard as ever, and neglected none of his responsibilities. In the Wall Street office he not only carried his full share of the routine legal work, but undertook important and arduous cases, such as the suit (1866) of the Bank for Savings v. Field, in which his argument before the Supreme Court was specially praised by Justice Nelson; the argument (1867) of the Seamen's Savings Bank against hostile legislation proposed at Albany, which involved an elaborate address before a subcommittee of the Assembly Committee of the Whole; and the partition (1868) of the many properties held in common by the Schermerhorn family, a "formidable job." He took time to prepare a full and exact financial history of the Sanitary Commission, which was published in 1866. His enthusiasm for the Columbia Law School and the School of Mines showed no abatement, and he was as ready as ever to put his shoulder to the wheel for their benefit and the general improvement of the college. To Trinity Church he gave endless hours of unrequited toil. And in this decade he performed his greatest services to music, assuming the presidency of the Philharmonic Society, and founding an organization to offer the best in sacred compositions, the Church Music Association—a body which scored an unexpected success.

[1]

It was with heartfelt thanksgiving for the victory of the Union cause, and with profound relief that the bloodshed, destruction, and demoralization of the conflict were over, that Strong turned his face towards the days of peace. Neither he nor any other American fully appreciated the debit accounts still to be settled by the nation, or the magnitude of the tasks of reconstruction both North and South.

June 1, THURSDAY.   Most shops and offices closed, this being the national day of mourning for the President's murder. Attended service in Trinity Church awhile. . . .

After dinner to Union League Club. General Hooker expected there to receive a sword presented by California. Rooms crowded, gas-lights many, carbonic acid and caloric predominant. So after a couple of hours spent investigating a volume or two of the Townsend *opus magnus*, the great corpus of newspaper cuttings, I came off. The excerpts preserved in these folios from the *World*, *News*, and *Express* of the summer of 1863 are stupendous monuments of the Northern treason that was trying to paralyze us by riot and arson in concert with Lee's invasion of Pennsylvania. There has seldom been a much baser exhibition of dirt-eating scoundrelism.

Yesterday afternoon our financial subcommittee (*in re* School of Mines) met at the Law School. There were Delano, Howard Potter, W. E. Dodge, Jr., George Cabot Ward, and I.' Decided to put off our $250,000 enterprise until next fall, wisely, I think. It is too late in the season. Many have left town. Those who remain will be languid and unimpressible until they have recovered from the succession of shocks and excitements that they have undergone since the first of April last. The people has (I think) just been bringing forth a new American republic—an amazingly big baby—after a terribly protracted and severe labor, without chloroform. It is too weary and prostrate as yet to listen to appeals on behalf of crystallography and "stochiometry." We can conjure no money out of it in the name of science just now. It will be a tough job in the best of times. . . .

Jefferson Davis, "yeoman," as his indictment presumes to style him, is, or soon will be, at Washington awaiting arraignment and trial in due course of law. He is reported to say that "the United States will never hang him," but his past mistakes should make him hesitate about any more predictions. His prophesyings of four years ago have proved disastrous to himself and to all who put faith in him. He told his people that the North would never undertake a war against secession and that France and England would have to become active allies of the South or perish for want of cotton. His people believed this flattering tale and rebelled. Most of them regret it just now!

Southern statesmanship is among the ancient delusions this war has blown away. Southern leaders have displayed energy, activity, audacity, intense purpose, perseverance under discouragement—all the virtues of the belligerent, carnivorous animal. No grizzly bear ever shewed greater ferocity or less rational forethought. Their administration of affairs has been most plucky and resolute, but without a trace of science, except in military strategic engineering work learned at West Point years ago. It has been a series of blunders worthy to succeed their first great blunder of rebellion. All the calculations on which that fatal move was founded, after thirty years of preparatory study and intrigue, have proved untrustworthy. Their most extreme and desperate measures have reacted against their course; that is, starving their prisoners. Any intelligent child could have told them that whatever they thereby gained in the course of exchanges would be far more than counterbalanced by the invigoration this atrocity gave Northern war-feeling and by the trouble it inflicted on Northern allies of rebellion. . . . Another gross blunder was their perseverance to the last in swaggering about death before reunion with the hated Yankees. Had they made anything like a show (however fraudulent and illusory) of willingness to talk about "reconstruction" on any terms—the conservation or restoration of slavery, for instance—at any time before Lincoln's reëlection, they would have enabled Northern traitors to make a fearfully damaging diversion in their favor. There would have been ruinous division here. Lincoln would have been defeated. The national government would have passed into the hands of friends of the South. Buchanan would have come back to life in the person of that unhappy McClellan, bringing with him Southern independence on easy terms and a continental chaos. . . .

Although the diarist says nothing about it, at the end of May President Johnson launched his reconstruction policy with two proclamations, one of limited amnesty and one laying down the mild conditions under which North Carolina might remodel her government in a way satisfactory to the executive. Throughout the summer and fall reconstruction went forward under the very moderate Lincoln-Johnson plan, while such radical Republicans as Sumner and Thaddeus Stevens chafed angrily. The absence of comment in Strong's record is evidence that, like most sensible Northerners, he was satisfied with the scheme. Meanwhile, the Sanitary Commission was nearing the close of its heavy labors. Its heads ordered that the manufacture and procurement of supplies be stopped on July 4, and followed this step by issuing a farewell address to their agents throughout the nation. Strong still had accounts to supervise, and the stores on hand still had to be distributed, but his hard work was finished. In New York, public-spirited citizens were awakening to the need for municipal reform, for during the war the evils of overcrowded slums, foul streets, inadequate sewage disposal, and endemic disease had grown to horrible magnitude.

June 3. . . . Bellows, Agnew, and Blatchford here last night. Blatchford reports 225,000 men camped around Washington and in special need of Sanitary Commission supplies, signs of scurvy being prevalent. During this process of mustering out, it is specially difficult to get requisitions duly honored. Hospital population on the 30th was 89,000, of which not much less than half is within sight of the dome of the capitol.

There is a score or so of paroled pauper rebel colonels and captains at the New York Hotel, sponging on Copperhead Cranston for rooms and meals, and negotiating with their Northern friends the subsidies that give them pocket money and one good solid drunk per diem. Certain people caress them, ask them to dinner, and give them old clothes. Mr. George Deas is there, who resigned his commission in April, 1861. He hailed Willy Cutting the other day in front of this rebel hotel. "Willy! Willy! How are you? Don't you remember me? I'm George Deas!" Cutting bowed, said he knew nobody of that name, and walked on. It's Deas that tells this. Good for Cutting. The world has moved since the New York Club squabble four years ago, when he was furious against any formal club censure of Deas. Deas and his colleagues—haughty, high-toned, superior, aristocratic creatures all—consent to pocket eleemosynary five-dollar greenbacks and to put on cast-off Yankee breeches, without perceptible pain or struggle and without much expression of thankfulness.

June 4, SUNDAY. Mr. Ruggles dined with us. He recovers slowly from his recent illness. He was here again this evening; also, Dr. Peters and his wife, Miss Lily Clymer, Charley Strong, George Anthon, Graham, and Dr. Duncan, who kept us entertained with reminiscences of Georgia and South Carolina for just four hours. He is very queer and quaint. "As to the fellows that had charge of our prisoners," says the gracious Duncan,

"Hell is too cool for them anyhow. I'd have it heated up hotter than Nebuchadnezzar's fiery furnace when he got up that Jew-bake, and then I'd put an extension on to Eternity." He thinks South Carolinians the loudest talkers and poorest fighters in rebeldom; Wade Hampton a mere braggart and bully. Description of Sherman on the march through South Carolina, looking about him at columns of smoke rising near and far and farther, five, ten, and twenty miles away: "That's Slocum; *that* must be Howard; that's probably so and so. Boy! If you can find a deserted house anywhere around just set it on fire, and let them know where we are." Georgia woman watching the progress of a cavalry regiment past her door, *loquitur*: "Why-y! Did you-uns come all the way down hee-ah, critter-back?"

June 5. Long session of College trustees this afternoon. Preliminary session of Law School Committee, and recommendations that [John] Ordronaux be given certain duties among undergraduates of the Senior class—lectures on physiology as a foundation for his Medical Jurisprudence course in the Law School. The Committee on Honors also met—the Bishop, Rutherfurd, Betts, and I. We decided *not* to recommend that Professor Silliman of Yale, Frederick DePeyster of the Historical Society, and Charles Edward Anthon of the Free Academy be made LL.Ds. Silliman has lost caste, more or less, with certain of his scientific fraternity by reports about California petroleum. I know nothing of the merits of the case. But if we confer these honorary degrees at all, we should do so only where they are plainly fit and proper.

Barnard read an elaborate and valuable report on the inner life of the College for the last year, which was well received and ordered printed. He gave us also copies of the new catalogue of alumni. It's full of errors. I brought up the appropriation for the School of Mines next year—$27,000 (from which must be deducted estimated fees of students, say $16,000), *and it was carried*, Barnard and Mr. Ruggles fighting for it with great spirit. That dogmatic donkey, Mr. Zabriskie, opposed (he has lately restored his name by act of legislature or in some other way to its original Slavonic Zbrowski) and so did Bradford—smart, keen, and fluent, and always wrong on every question. Just before we adjourned, Haight surprised us with resolutions that a committee enquire and report whether the professorships of history (Lieber) and higher mathematics (Davies) should not be abolished, and that there be a special meeting on the 19th instant. This move is extraordinary and will probably produce a shindy. It has not been made without consultation and grounds for expecting it to succeed, but I do not understand its motive.[1] Davies is a mere fifth wheel to our academic coach. He is rich and independent of his salary, and that is not a full salary. It would seem to be a move against Lieber, Davies being joined to give the move an aspect of impersonality and general retrenchment in the undergraduate course. Lieber is fairly vulnerable only because the discipline of his lecture room is abominable. But it cannot be worse than that of Renwick's in my day and of McVickar's afterwards. He has done great public service during the last four years. That fact would dispose certain members of the board—Betts, Beadle, and Zabriskie—to decapitate him, but Haight seems a loyal man, and unlikely to have moved his resolutions on that ground. A committee of five was appointed.

June 8. At 823 today was an Andersonville prisoner, who said he had seen his brethren there on their hands and knees around the latrines of that infernal pen, grubbing among faeces for undigested beans and grains of corn wherewith to mitigate the pains of slow starvation.

The movement against Lieber is even more formidable than I supposed. Mr. Ruggles came in to talk of it at breakfast time. Haight's committee (of which Mr. Ruggles is a member) met yesterday. Haight and Barnard are bitterly bent on legislating Lieber out of office on two grounds. He has but four hours' work a week and doesn't earn his salary; and, secondly, and mainly, his lecture room is in chronic scandalous disorder, insubordination, and row. I suppose this latter averment quite true. The most audacious pranks are said to be played in that room, and the intercourse between the Professor and his classes, as reported, is often conducted in a dialect nearly allied to that of Billingsgate and Mackerelville. Lieber's mode of dealing with his mutinous boys is doubtless very bad indeed. He has no tact at all. But he has been backed by no exercise of legitimate college discipline. President Barnard has made no visits to his room. He might thereby have stopped its disorders. It is

[1] President Barnard, who felt personal hostility for Lieber, was anxious to bring about his dismissal. The two had long distrusted each other. Lieber, a strong Unionist, remembered that Barnard, as head of the University of Mississippi, had defended slavery and just after Sumter had even justified the Confederate cause. Lieber was now a Radical Republican; Barnard believed in moderate policies. Lieber held liberal ideas on religion. Barnard attacked the German theological seminaries as schools of atheism. Lieber lectured to his students on history; Barnard, who criticized Lieber's methods of instruction in sweeping terms, thought lectures unsuited to undergraduates. The need for more money to support the new School of Mines gave Barnard an opening for his proposal that Lieber be removed, and his chair of history and political economy be consolidated with the chair of English and philosophy.

quite certain that two or three sentences of dismissal would have made this cowardly crew of undergraduate Fifth Avenue blackguard boys as still as mice. But only last Monday Barnard informed us in his elaborate report on the state of the college that he has not been obliged to order a single student before "the Board" [faculty] during the past year. . . .

Lieber's activity in public affairs since 1860 will tell against him in the board. Copperhead old Verplanck has been growling to me and to others about the political heresies Lieber is teaching in the College and the Law School. Lieber upholds the nation and cares little for state rights in comparison. I fear all clerical trustees will follow the lead of Haight and Barnard. If so, Lieber must go overboard.

June 9.   Hotter. Tonight showery. Visit from Lieber this morning to talk of the college attack on him. He is more phlegmatic than I expected to find him, and proposes to see no other trustee, except Mr. Ruggles, Charles King (to whom he has written), and possibly the Bishop. He says he is too old for lobbying and that this move is, in his opinion, wholly on political grounds. Of course, he would like to go out, if he must go, in the capacity of martyr. . . .

June 10. . . . The *World* and other papers publish letters from Southern correspondents stating that Southern Niggerdom refuses to work for wages, holding freedom to mean the right to support by government, or by somebody, without labor. I suppose these statements true as to the course adopted and the theory held by some of our Africo-Americans. We cannot wonder that they should take up any delusion whatever, after being studiously and systematically assimilated to brutes by the legislation of their masters, generation after generation, for so many years. There are predictions of a social or servile war, a war of races, but it is unlikely. If the Negroes go to work and earn their living, they will fall naturally into their proper place, and hold it to the great advantage of all parties. If they decline to do so, they will starve and perish and disappear, and emigration will supply the labor needed to develop the wealth of secession soil.

June 12, MONDAY.   With William Schermerhorn to Columbia College this afternoon by the Third Avenue Railroad for a meeting of the Library Committee. Barnard with us, and the spasmodic librarian Mr. Jones. I like Barnard so much that I cannot believe he is behaving ill in this matter of Lieber's, but it would seem he is. After getting through with what very little we found to do, Schermerhorn and I adjourned to the School of Mines, and Chandler shewed us casts, recently acquired, of paleontological forms. . . . Also, we inspected the new building; that is, the old paper factory which the School is to occupy next session. A most dirty, dilapidated, disreputable structure. If our cabinets become very heavy, they will certainly break it down. . . .

June 13. . . . Newspapers report that society in certain regions of Georgia and Alabama has gone to chaos and disintegration—all asthenic, passive, dry gangrene and death. Most property there, public and private, is destroyed. The bare soil is left. That soil could support ten times its population, but it is left untilled. Cuffee will not work because Mass'r has no money to pay him. Cuffee is distrustful and suspicious, and gives no credit. Mass'r belongs to a First Family, was not born to work, and would rather starve than work; and he and his house seem to be starving, partly for the sake of spiting the Yankees. If Mass'r have any money put away at the North or in London, he means to leave the country. "It is not our country any more. You d——d Yankees have conquered it, and we are aliens. Take your country, and let us get out of it, leaving our curse behind us." Parts of Secessia may have to pass through a period of absolute anarchy and barbarism, longer or shorter, before they become Christianized and civilized.

Per contra, Gouverneur M. Wilkins read me a letter from one Trumbull, a nephew of his in Mississippi, stating the measures in progress in his district to reëstablish order, and they seemed healthy and hopeful. But very many Southern aristocrats, probably a majority of them, are utterly broken and ruined and incapable of any resolute effort to recover their lost position. . . .

June 16. . . . Strolled sweatily tonight on the east of the town, in the obscure region of First Avenue and Allen Street. The population of that district is prolific and its nursery is the sidewalk. Poor little children— what a blight and misfortune to them to have been born in a city! Brought to awhile at Union League Club, where was George Anthon, and so home. A Galveston newspaper announces that "it 'pears like subjugation,"—and wonders whether a (*soi-disant*) nation of so many millions was ever subjugated so suddenly. Southern papers and correspondents of Northern papers tell a dismal story of social disorganization and of probable famine in the chivalric states. Everything has been carried away from Southern plantations, except their mortgages. The Southern white race can do nothing for itself, being used so long to make niggers attend to its work.

June 17. . . . Proof given on the assassination trial that "Honorable" Ben Wood, Fernandy Wood's brother, the traitorous proprietor of the *Daily News,* received a check for $25,000 from the treason fund of the rebel refugees and plotters in Canada. I do not perceive the relevancy of this fact to the issues on trial, but it is valuable as a contribution to put in histories. Mr. Ruggles seems not to have returned from Washington. Very unfortunate. The special committee on Lieber was to meet today and the College Board meets Mondays. Lieber continues to pepper me with notes and memoranda. He writes today that he inclines to think Barnard sympathizes somewhat with the move to displace him. The unsuspicious Teuton! Barnard got it up. . . .

Texan newspapers are frank, naïve, and funny. "It seems unaccountable," they say, "but we are actually subjugated. Let us do the best we can under the circumstances." Shall we get through the next year without a social war in the Carolinas and the Gulf States?

June 19, MONDAY. Columbia College trustees met specially at two o'clock to consider the case of Lieber and Davies. Haight's committee reported resolutions abolishing the chairs of both, and that Lieber be continued in the Law School at his present salary of $4,000 till next May. This would be very well, were it not apparent that he will then be cut off altogether, or his salary made nominal. No reasons reported. Haight did not wish to assign reasons. Mr. Ruggles made a speech on both sides of the question. He has misgivings as to Lieber's capacity to manage our unruly undergraduates and thinks we may secure him better terms in the Law School by not opposing too strongly his excision from the College. Barnard favored us with a characteristic specimen of his copious, viscid oratory, letting out that the main reason for the movement was disorder in Lieber's room. I made a brief, dull argumentation against the report, but it was evident I stood alone. Bradford moved postponement, a motion almost always carried unanimously in this board. King supported it in his usual bungling, jolly way, but it was carried *by Fish's casting vote,* 7 to 7, Dr. Hutton and perhaps Anderson not voting. It was delightful to see the promptitude with which Ogden and Copperhead Betts and Zabriskie rose on a division being called for. Dix voted to postpone. Then there was a question whether the postponement be to the 6th of July or to the 20th of September. The former day was adopted by Fish's casting vote again. They mean to make quick work of it, and it is clear that the board has been privily manipulated so as to secure an abundant working majority. John Astor and the Bishop were not present.

Lieber has made enemies of many trustees by his silly, sensitive vanity. He has been offended with Fish ever since Barnard's inauguration and has not spoken to him because there was no mention, in some little address delivered by Fish on that occasion, of the honor and dignity the College and its new President derived from official connection with him, Lieber. When Mr. Ruggles was preparing some report or resolution for the Chamber of Commerce in which Agassiz, Guyot, and Lieber were to be mentioned as representing physiological, ethnological, and political science, Lieber actually wrote him several letters begging that he might be named *first* of the three. Isn't it amazing? I have no doubt he has affronted and alienated Barnard, who seems a kindly disposed man, by some offensive display of vanity. According to Fish, Governor Aiken of South Carolina says Lieber taught pure Calhounism while a citizen of that state. I believe this statement untrue. But Lieber is to all practical intents and purposes *dismissed* with his present salary continued till next May. There is no saving him. Stanton and Seward may be stimulated to raise a breeze about it in the newspapers, but it would be useless.[2]

Tonight Agnew, Blatchford, and Parrish were here for a Sanitary Commission conference. We decide to draw in our tentacles, dismiss agents, close relief stations, curtail work and expenditure everywhere and at once, and to be diligent in gathering and arranging material for a final report, the last dying speech and confession of the Sanitary Commission. Thank God the time for the Sanitary Commission's release and disembodiment seems so near at hand at last!

June 20.   This evening young Lee here, and a very agreeable Major Nichols of Sherman's staff, full of anecdotes of the great march from

[2] Barnard had written Hamilton Fish that Lieber's instruction was practically thrown away. Lieber himself had constantly complained "of the listlessness, inattention, imperfect performance, and general ill behavior of his classes," yet these same students were attentive, diligent, and interested auditors of the other courses. An incipient student revolt against him had been barely prevented. Inasmuch as he taught only four hours a week, declared Barnard, his chair could easily be abolished or merged with another. Lieber made no formal answer to the president's charges, though he was full of private complaints. With the help of his friends in the board, Fish, Strong, Ruggles, and King, he was transferred to the Law School, where henceforth he was to occupy the chair of constitutional history and public law at an undiminished salary of $4,000 a year. Lieber was doubtless a failure as a teacher of undergraduates; as a teacher of the whole nation through his books, pamphlets, articles, and lectures, he was a distinct success, and Columbia University has never ceased to cherish his memory. Strong appreciated his best qualities.

Atlanta to Raleigh.[3] He confirms the story told by all Sherman's officers that the braggarts of South Carolina were the slowest fighters, and are the most abjectly whipped rebels in all Rebeldom. They did nothing but whine, he says, as Sherman's column marched over their plantations. (N.B. A rebel prisoner who called at 823 today to ask after a little tobacco, observed to Collins that if he'd known New York was such a hell of a big place he wouldn't never have fit agin it.)

Joe Dukes, *ci-devant* South Carolinian, now New York lawyer, and always opposed to secession, tells Charley Strong of letters he receives from the South on which he prophesies a war of extermination by the white race on the black, or else vice versa, and more probably the latter. He holds that the two races cannot long remain in peaceful contact under their altered relations, and that a struggle must soon begin which will wipe out one or the other. It does not seem likely, but no one can form an opinion on the question without intimate knowledge of the South as it was and as it is. Secessia has no more hope from her present population than our Southwest frontiers have from the Comanches. They are alike incapable of civilization and progress and must be displaced to make room for a better breed. It is to be hoped that the displacement may be through a peaceful process of immigration, gradually changing the stock by intermarriage; but it may be destined to come with tragical abruptness, and bring with it all the horrors of San Domingo. . . .

I rather expect a depopulation of the South by pestilence. The vital forces of men and women are lowered by a profound sense of failure, defeat, mortification, and subjugation, especially damaging to so arrogant a race. Add to this a very general privation of the means of living, and in many regions (as reported), destitution and starvation, even unto death, and there seems abundant provocation for an epidemic of the deadliest type.

The political pots of Washington are simmering ominously and are not unlikely to reach boiling heat before long. Advanced Republicans grumble over President Andrew Johnson's reconstruction policy, and say he is selling his party, after the manner of dirty old Tyler, twenty-five years ago. I do not "see it in that light," and have faith in the President's judgment and honesty. But a split in the party seems certainly coming,

---

[3] Brevet Major George Ward Nichols, one of Sherman's aides, had kept a diary of the campaigns in Georgia and the Carolinas, from which he extracted this year material for a capital book, *The Story of the Great March.*

and Copperheads chuckle over the prospect, to my serious aggravation.[4] Next winter will probably find Sumner, Wilson & Co., organized as an opposition, and "conservative" Republicans sustaining the Administration, in alliance with Northern "democrats" and malignants and restored penitent Congressmen from the Carolinas, with bowie knives about their persons. Next session of Congress will be an anxious time. "Darkey Suffrage" is a dark and troublesome question, and it must be met. That freedmen, who have as a class always helped the national cause to the utmost of their ability, at risk of their lives, should have political rights at least equal to those of the bitter enemies of the country who are about to resume those rights, sullenly and under protest, only because they are crushed, coerced, and subjugated, is (abstractly considered) in the highest degree just and right. But the average field hand would use political power as intelligently as would the mule he drives. The current phrase that "those who have helped the country with bullets should be permitted to help it with ballots" is mere nonsense. . . . Were I President, I should aim at securing political rights to property-holding Ethiopians and to such as could read and write.[5]

June 22. Mr. Ruggles gave a dinner at Delmonico's to jolly old Charles King, who sails for Europe tomorrow in a French steamer. That Anglophile of other days vows he will not pass under the British flag. His wife and daughters may go and see England if they like, but he will stay on the Continent. . . . Lieber is down upon Barnard. I fear my first estimate of Barnard was too high. . . .

June 27. . . . Gibbs is interested in Lieber's case, and I think understands its pros and cons.

At Union League Club tonight, looking into the pamphlets of three years ago, especially at half a dozen fat volumes I had bound up and gave the club when its library was first launched. Two lamentable diatribes entitled "American Bastilles," or some such thing, I found particularly refreshing. They are detailed personal narratives by disloyal Marylanders bagged in September, 1861, and detained near six months in Fortress Monroe, Fort Lafayette, and Fort Warren. They had mere army rations

---

[4] An acute prophecy; Henry Winter Davis, Ben Wade, Charles Sumner, and Thaddeus Stevens were already publicly denouncing the President's policy, while the old-time abolitionists were full of wrath.

[5] This had been substantially Lincoln's policy. In his letter to Michael Hahn, the free-state governor of Louisiana, on March 13, 1864, Lincoln had suggested that the suffrage might be extended to some of the colored people—"as, for instance, the very intelligent, and especially those who have fought gallantly in our ranks."

to eat—their coffee was not good—they had no liquor except what they bought and paid for and except the baskets of champagne sent them by New York and Boston sympathizers. "Tadpoles" (query: mosquito larvae?) occurred in their drinking water, and worst of all, they were mixed up with mere common men from North Carolina, captured at Fort Hatteras! Their pork was intolerably fat and their soup thin, poor fellows. Their pamphlets are well-defined specimens of Slave-ownia Secesh literature, which embodies the characteristics of (1) the Northern gent, who tries to mask his vulgarity by deportment and swagger and much talk about his own exalted gentility; (2) the Swashbuckler, Alsatian, "bully-ruffian" or "Mohock" of 160 years ago; and (3) the sharp attorney of the present day, whose clients are found in the Tombs, and whose vocation it is to keep thieves and burglars from being consigned to Black-well's Island by invoking law in their behalf. The typical Southerner is a snob—a bully, a "shyster," and (I fear) an assassin.

June 28. To Columbia College Commencement at the Academy of Music. Discoursed with sundry agreeable people in the reception room, and then marched in august procession down the parquet with Barnard and the faculty and Fish and Governor Morgan, and the other fashion-ables, to the sound of soft music, and took my seat on the stage. Sat through six or eight orations and poems. I will not answer for the Greek and Latin salutatories, but all the rest were very small trash, and the efforts of the poets to be smart and funny would have given a cassowary the dyspepsia. . . . There should be a stern censorship of Commencement speeches. The only decent thing I heard was Mendelssohn's exquisite little melody, "Ich wollt' mein Lieb ergöss sich," rendered by a most respectable orchestra—an improvement on the Commencement brass bands of my college days. As each orator made his final bow, there came a concentric fire of bouquets from all parts of the house. The fair artil-lerists sometimes made bad practice. A four-pound bouquet hit me on the leg, and a ten-pounder took the Rev. Morgan Dix in the eye, producing a contusion of the left spectacle. When the cannonade ceased, the orators gathered up these graceful tributes and carried them off, and then came back for a second armful, looking like "Posy John," the peripatetic florist of Broadway. This absurd practice ought to be stopped somehow. The graduating class appeared in academic head-gear, "Oxford caps," for the first time. On the whole, I thought what I heard of these "com-mencement exercises" no credit to the College, but rather a lamentable proof that we, the trustees, are doing our duty most imperfectly. . . .

June 29. Nothing very notable. Parke Godwin and Major Nichols
here this evening. I like Godwin, and differ therein from the majority of
the human race.[6] The *Daily News*, the organ of Seceshdom in this city,
making hardly a decent pretense of loyalty to government (which the
World tries to do) prints an elaborate editorial earnestly advocating
Negro suffrage! This was, of course, dictated south of the Potomac, and
it shews that some, at least, among the leaders of Secessia propose changing their base. But the move is inexplicable to me. It is possible, though
improbable, that they think the change sure to be made and are, therefore, hastening to make friends among the Ethiopian voters of the future.
Perhaps they want to embarrass and bother the Administration or to
promote schism in the Republican party. Whatever may be the politic
purpose they have in view, the "progress of human events" since 1860
is bewildering. Never did human events make such news before. Southern
newspaper articles of three or four years ago make me feel very old.
They seem medieval relics. When I remember having read them on their
first appearance, my sensations are those of the Wandering Jew refreshing his recollections of political literature under Commodus. Centuries
seem to have elapsed since the Richmond papers went into spasms about
the invasion of Virginia and the occupation of Alexandria, and proclaimed
no quarter to any black man allowed to shoulder a musket in the national
army. . . .

June 30. . . . Bellows and I decided to call the Commission together
ten days hence at Washington.

Dipping into the *Rebellion Record.*[7] We begin now to be able to look
at the Union war as a whole. Of course, we shall have a better view of it
as we get further off, but from our present position, July 4th, 1863,
stands out as the critical day that determined its result. Gettysburg seems
to have been the turning point of the four years' struggle. I believe,
moreover, that Lee's failure on that field saved us from an organized
Copperhead rising in New York, headed by sneaking Horatio Seymour's
underlings—traitors, bolder but not baser than their chief. That the plot
was matured is certain. Meade's victory and the fall of Vicksburg dis-

[6] Son-in-law of William Cullen Bryant, and in time Bryant's successor as editor of
the *Evening Post*, Parke Godwin combined marked talents with somewhat bearish
manners.
[7] Frank Moore (1828–1904), an indefatigable compiler and editor, issued the
eleven volumes of the *Rebellion Record*, a vast scrapbook of newspaper stories, official
documents, military reports, and what not, in the years 1861–1868. A supplementary
volume completed the work.

heartened the conspirators, but the Draft Riots of July were a partial deflagration and explosion of the combustible ruffianism that had been stored away for yet worse mischief on a larger scale. Had Meade been routed at Gettysburg, Seymour would have screwed his courage up to a *coup d'état* backed by the mayor and aldermen of this city and all the rest of its rascaldom in office and out. With Lee riding in triumph over Pennsylvania and New York arrayed against government, the national cause would have been nearly hopeless. . . .

Copperheadism is not dead, to be sure, any more than original sin, but it sleeps just now or, rather, lies comatose and senseless, stunned by blows that have smashed its cranium. Its only sign of life is an incoherent bubbling now and then about the sufferings of Sambo as freedman, the dreadful consequences of hanging Mr. J. Davis, the virtues of General Lee, and the "New England fanatics who brought about the late war."

July 3. . . . The *Herald* still clamors for Ethiopian suffrage. Very few even of the Southerners who will be allowed to vote under A. Johnson's Reconstruction system will see the question in that light. The freedman is in their eyes merely a domesticated animal that used to be docile and valuable, but which, having got loose and escaped to the woods, has certainly become worthless and is probably a rank nuisance and is a breed of mischievous vermin. Perhaps they are right, but I think they are fearfully wrong. They must work out their own destiny.

July 5. . . . Reading tonight the first part of Dickens's unfinished serial, *Our Mutual Friend.* . . . I am interested in the future of "Lizzie Hexam." Mr. Dickens's young women (dear little Dora excepted) are generally as uninteresting as an algebraic symbol. But "Lizzie Hexam," though an absurd, impossible conception, is rather agreeable and attractive, and I hope Mr. Dickens means to treat her well and to make her happy all her days in his last number.

July 6. . . . Result of the assassination trial announced this evening; Payne, Herold, Atzerodt, and Mrs. Surratt sentenced to death. Sentence approved, and execution ordered for tomorrow. Dr. Mudd and one O'Laughlin to be imprisoned for life. Spangler, who probably helped Booth to get out of Ford's Theatre and possibly knew of his design, to be imprisoned six months. The guilt of Payne and Herold is manifest. But I fear the evidence on which the other five are convicted will not bear scrutiny, and that their punishment will enable Copperheads to get up a howl against government. No justice of the peace in the most benighted rural district has judicial capacity much below that of the average military court. "Crowner's 'quest law" is sounder than that of most major-generals. I have read the testimony as it has been published from day to day—not very critically, to be sure—but I remember nothing that establishes more than a strong suspicion that Mrs. Surratt was privy to the plot, or that Dr. Mudd had any connection with it or with any of the conspirators, except that when Booth called on him with a broken leg, he did his professional duty, set the leg, and asked no questions. I do not like the look of this. It will do us harm. Better to have erred on the other side and spared the lives even of Herold and Payne— and that is saying much. Reaction against this will save Jeff Davis's worthless neck. Major Nichols, who was here this evening, heartily endorses my estimate of military courts—"only more so." The most unusual promptness with which execution follows judgment in this case will shock public feeling; perhaps unreasonably, but it will hurt and weaken the Administration.[8] The philanthropes of the *Tribune* will give us interesting matter to read tomorrow. So will the rebel sympathizers of the *World*.

July 7. Piping hot. Have just been perspiring copiously for two hours in the Rev. Bellows's study with him, Agnew, and Blatchford. We settled, among other things, the draft of a Sanitary Commission vale-dictory to the branches and aid societies, and directed a telegram to San Francisco, in substance: "You need not trouble us with any more money, unless you particularly wish it." A remarkable change of base!

Extr-r-r-y *Times* this afternoon (our first extra for two months, I think) announced that Payne & Co., Mrs. Surratt included, had been duly and decorously hanged. That word *extra* has been a word of power all through these four years. How many scores or hundreds of times has the suspicion of its distant sound started me up from this very desk, at mid-night or later, and sent me down stairs to unlock the front door and stand outside, in hope of waylaying a circumambient newsboy. How often have

---

[8] Strong's caustic comment does credit both to his head and to his heart. The prosecution of John Wilkes Booth and other conspirators against Lincoln, as conducted by Judge Advocate-General Holt, had some flagrantly objectionable features. Though the use of a military commission to try civilians was generally approved, it was wrong in principle. The government's witnesses indulged in gross perjury. The prosecution was deplorably willing to rake in all kinds of testimony. Holt was later accused of suppressing adverse material, including Booth's diary. The question whether he was to blame for the failure to bring the military commission's recommendation of clem-ency for Mrs. Surratt before President Johnson precipitated a memorable controversy, which raged for years. The trial was not one on which fair-minded Americans could look with complacency.

I jumped up spasmodically, saying to Ellie, "There's an extra," and rushed off to secure it. And what a bad article of news I often got. . . .

People seem better satisfied with the findings of the Military Commission than I thought they would be. The feeling seems general that the four who were capitally convicted and whose sentence is now executed got no more than they deserved. There are a few to whom hanging a woman (Mrs. Mary E. Surratt) is rather distasteful, but it troubles them little. Killing women is certainly an unpleasant office, but if a man and a woman be both guilty of a murder, the woman deserves the severer punishment. The depravity that produced the crime must be presumed greater in her case, because it had to overcome and outweigh the instincts of her womanly nature. . . .

July 8. . . . Stroll after dinner and inspected newspapers at the Society Library. The *Daily News* (rebel organ in New York) screeches itself into danger of sore throat over the hanging of Payne and the rest by sentence of a military court and wants "the people" to organize and subscribe and agitate till all members of the Court and the Judge Advocate and the Provost Marshal shall have been duly indicted for murder. The nasty *Express* whines the same tune—*pianissimo* and *sotto voce*. The *News* has always done what it could to damage the national cause manfully and openly, but the *Express* has been for the last five years the basest, meanest, dirtiest periodical within my knowledge. Had they been the hundredth part as tender and scrupulous about violations of law when their friends of the woman-flogging oligarchy were threatening to "secede," there would have been no secession and no war. But they and the "democracy" in general tempted our poor Southern brethren into rebellion and ruin by the assurance that at least half the North sympathized with their seditious purposes and would tolerate no attempt to "coerce" them.

July 13. Lovely weather. A vigorous northwest wind made the tedious railroad ride from Washington less prostrating than usual. Reached home at five P.M. Lonely house, for Ellie marched on Long Branch yesterday at the head of her column, leaving two of the women behind her. I'm dusty and grimy. In default of any "Scabbi-fugic" (a new patent medicine stenciled on Baltimore fences), I shall presently try what Croton water will do. On reaching Broadway from the Jersey City ferry boat, I perceived a crowd of bipeds and a great convocation of steam fire engines puffing and shrieking. A big fire that began at noon had just ended. Barnum's show shop and several buildings of less note on Broadway, Ann Street, and Fulton Street were burned up. Alas, for the "Happy

Family" and the inmates of scores of Aquaria, and for the stuffed monkey riding on the stuffed yellow dog, which my childhood venerated. Alas, for the huge quartz crystal I have so often coveted for the School of Mines!

Barnum's was an ancient institution. The museum building dates back (I think) to 1830. It has long been an eyesore, with its huge pictures of the fat woman, the "What-Is-It?," the albino children, and the tableau from the reigning "Moral Spectacular Drama." The horrible little brass band that was always tooting in its balcony must have produced or aggravated many cases of nervous disease, for it tormented all passengers at the very junction of our two most crowded downtown thoroughfares. May the sins of those six cruel artists be forgiven them. May they henceforth play less hideously false, and may they all find remunerative engagements in some situation where people will not be forced to hear them notwithstanding all they can do. . . .

With Barnum's famous museum were burned an assemblage of rarities which, the showman later wrote, "a half million of dollars could not restore, and a quarter of a century could not collect." Among the animals killed were two white whales recently placed in the basement tank. The insurance was only $40,000. Horace Greeley advised Barnum to accept the fire as a notice to quit and go fishing; but, reflecting that New York needed a museum, and that two hundred and fifty employees depended on him for wages, the showman leased a new building on the west side of Broadway at Spring Street, sent agents throughout Europe and Asia to collect curiosities, bought out several smaller museums, and in November of this year proudly reopened his doors. At the same time he laid plans for making his establishment the nucleus of a great national museum—plans disrupted by a new fire in March, 1868.

The Sanitary Commission had a new General Secretary in John S. Blatchford, previously superintendent of the relief work of the Boston Associates, who this spring succeeded Dr. J. Foster Jenkins. The work of the great organization was being steadily wound up. E. L. Godkin wrote in the newly founded Nation *(July 20) that "it is indeed marvelous that a scheme of benevolence so extensive and efficient as we know the Commission to have been should have been sustained without ostentation, without bustle, and with so much certainty. . . ." No word of official thanks, however, ever came from the government. For its own part, the Commission was more generous; and much*

WALL STREET IN STRONG'S LATER YEARS

NO. 68 IS THE THIRD BUILDING FROM THE RIGHT

MRS. STRONG AND LEWIS

*as it had suffered from official neglect, its officers in July formally expressed
their deep gratitude to Quartermaster-General Meigs for his invaluable
services.*

*Three topics this summer dominated national attention: Reconstruction,
which was proceeding rapidly as Southern states prepared to call conventions
to act on President Johnson's plan; relations with France, for Napoleon III
still had an army in Mexico, and the United States had collected one on the
Rio Grande; and the first disclosures of war-time corruption, for a wealthy
New York banking house, Ketchum, Son & Co., suddenly failed in August as
a result of forgeries.*

Our Sanitary Commission session has been far shorter than I expected.
Our new General Secretary is, unlike either of his predecessors, a man of
business. He brings forward every subject in a clear, compact form, so
that we can dispose of it in the minimum of time, and he is a man of
greater administrative ability and decision than he has seemed to me. I
took him for a formal soft-spoken, red-tapy Miss Nancy.

Ride to Washington Monday, eight A.M. to six P.M. Day overcast
and cool, but with heroic storms of dust. Devoted myself to Miss Yonge's
last novel, *The Clever Woman of the Family*; her best, I think, since *Heartsease*. She has no great creative or constructive power; she can produce
but two finished portraits of woman-kind (Amy and Laura in *The Heir
of Redcliffe*, Lady Temple and Rachel Curtis in this last book, Violet and
her sister-in-law in *Heartsease*), but all she writes is pure, refined, womanly,
healthy, and wholesome beyond the work of any living novelist. Anthony
Trollope comes next. . . .

Blatchford had provided us quarters far better than have ever been
secured us at Washington. "Mrs. Dull's" boarding house, No. 248 F
Street, is close to No. 244, and entirely unoccupied during this summer
vacation. Each of us had a most eligible bedroom (barring a few mosquitoes
and a bull-rooster in the back yard possessed of a magnificent barytone
organ, who began roaring soon after midnight) and our table was luxurious. "Goodwife Dull" was away, but represented by a couple of
pleasant-mannered daughters.

Only Bellows, Agnew, Binney, Stillé, and I were at this meeting.
Newberry's default unaccountable. We needed his counsels, but being
without them, went on according to our best judgment, and took order
for winding up of our affairs and publication of a final report. There was

no substantial disagreement in our long discussion of these two questions and especially of the former. Dr. Bellows rather favored a slow and gradual closing up. Agnew and I preferred a more expeditious and less costly process. Binney and Stillé, on the whole, inclined the same way. Knapp and Dr. Parrish, who were with us, would, of course, prefer a longer lease of power to expend a few thousand every month. We shall probably devolve the duty of preparing our final report, the History of the Sanitary Commission, on Stillé, a man of leisure and culture. Drove yesterday afternoon through beautiful woods to the scene of the last of our battles with rebellion in the immediate neighborhood of Washington, just a year ago—Forts Slocum, Massachusetts, Reno. Saw a burial ground in which lie forty-eight national soldiers, killed in repelling that raid. Had Ewell, the rebel, known how weak we were on that line, he could *probably* have marched into Washington, could *possibly* have secured a triumph for rebeldom.

July 15. . . . No political news. Professor McCulloh in durance at Washington. If he is tried for arson, convicted, and hanged, does etiquette require me as an acquaintance and a trustee of Columbia College to attend the execution?

The South is quiet and passive. But there are abundant signs that the old plantation spirit ("Plantation Bitters"?) of truculence and lawlessness is not dead but sleeping, or rather shamming dead. It takes more than one licking to cure a bully. The *World* and the *News* and their rapidly diminishing train of followers continue wailing over a violated constitution. There has been only outrage after outrage for the last four years, and the series continues. What fools they are! Of course, subordination of government to the Constitution and to law is good—very good—among the very best things. But it's not the only good thing. To save the country is also good. To prevent Jeff Davis from chasing Lincoln out of Washington in 1861 was an object of some public importance. Emergencies are certainly conceivable that justify a little unconstitutionality. Perhaps our recent experiences are of that class. The only people I know that maintain their constitution absolutely inviolate no matter what happens are the Chinese. Poland did so, too, with her *Liberum Veto* and her Right of Confederation, "constitutional" rights too sacred for interference. They made her a nuisance to her neighbours, and too weak to prevent them from abating her and using her to manure their own estates. Respect for written law and constitutions may be excessive and no less deadly than hypertrophy of the heart. A nation (or a church) that has finally crystallized into permanent, definite form and become incapable of developing new organs or agencies to meet new conditions is *dead*, and will begin to decompose whenever time brings the new conditions. *Anno Domini* 1861 brought us a batch of new conditions, and Abraham Lincoln met them wisely and well. He saved the country. If learned counsel prove by word-splitting that he saved it unconstitutionally, I shall honor his memory still more reverently than I do now. In A.D. 1865, the situation is wholly changed once more. The whole South is in a state of subjugation, indignation, emancipation, ruination, and starvation. It's a chaos of hostile elements mitigated and quieted by bayonets, a collection of acids and bases hardly restrained from fizzing into furious disastrous reaction at any moment. Our constitution-framers never dreamed of this state of affairs and made no provision for it. One would think it most desirable to get the South into good order again without delay. But our Chinese conservatives protest against any step that way, unless chapter and verse of the Constitution can be cited for it. They are political Pharisees, who would let government perish (government being not in the hands of "our party"), rather than see it saved "on the Sabbath Day."

It must be admitted, though, that the present and the late administrations are responsible for violations of law that can be justified by no plea of public necessity. The last of these misdemeanors is the closing of Ford's Theatre by order of the Secretary of War. Of course, the performance of plays suited to the taste of a Washington audience in the very building in which Abraham Lincoln, our martyr President, was so recently murdered, would have been unseemly and shocking. But what right has the Secretary of War to tell the owner of a place of public amusement that his capital must be unemployed because there are sentimental objections to its lawful employment?

Stanton has done the country great service and will take high place in history. But he is a born tyrant. He likes to use official power to crush and destroy rebels and sympathizers with rebellion and anybody else who may happen to stand inconveniently in his way. And I think he likes this use of his power best when it has the "game flavor" of illegality. Some of his acts (for example at West Point) have been most abominable. He is wholly "incorruptible" in the ordinary sense, but most corruptible by prejudice and passion. If this able, unscrupulous, arbitrary man leave his office at last, and surrender the great and ill-defined power he has been necessarily allowed to assume, without permanent damage to public liberty, it will prove that the people has little to fear from usurpation.

July 19. . . . *Died,* old Mme. Jumel, or more strictly, Mrs. Aaron Burr. She was very old.[9] When I was a boy she was spoken of mysteriously as a very wonderful, wealthy, wicked old lady, living in great seclusion. *Also,* old Thomas N. Stanford, for many years the meekest of bibliophiles and of men. He was of Swords & Stanford, church booksellers. *Also,* old Ambrose L. Jordan, long the most accomplished master of Billingsgate at the New York bar. *Also,* old Richard D. Arden, at 88, who made such an unfortunate display when examined in the Shedden case six years ago. Quite a little group of luminaries snuffed out together. . . .

Reports from the South are of diverse quality. We have stories of sullenness, and reluctant submission to force, with mutterings about trying it again hereafter; of bitter hatred of all Northmen, especially among Secesh women; of infamous cruelties and outrages upon freedmen, and so on. On the other hand, Southern orators and editors confess the South thoroughly beaten, preach the duty and the advantage of loyalty to the reëstablished government, and prophesy a comfortable increase of profit from free labor. On the whole, the symptoms seem to me far more favorable than we had any right to hope. Universal acquiescence in failure, enthusiasm for the Star-Spangled Banner, approval of Emancipation, could not be expected. Soreness, and wrath ill suppressed, and spite expended in maltreatment of niggers, are inevitable. It's only four months since Rebeldom was, or professed itself, full of truculent life, protesting that it never, never, never would or could endure the thought of recognizing Yankees as fellow countrymen. When a man is cured of delirium tremens, I suppose his nerves do not quite recover their tone, and his mental powers continue shakey for some little time. The progress of the drunken South toward complete convalescence seems to me quite remarkable.

July 21. Mr. Ruggles goes to Hamilton Fish's (opposite West

[9] This was indeed an echo from the past. Mme. Jumel, originally Eliza Brown or Betsey Bowen, had lived with Stephen Jumel, wealthy merchant, for several years before they were married in 1804. Six years later he bought for her the Roger Morris house, which had been built in 1765 and used by Washington as headquarters, and which is now preserved as a monument. Jumel died in 1832, and the following year Aaron Burr, then nearly eighty, married the widow. This match lasted only a year, though Burr lived until 1836. Mme. Jumel was buried in the uptown cemetery of Trinity Church.

Point) with Lieber to talk over the reorganization of the Law School. Lieber's laziness is a sore impediment to his friends' efforts in his behalf. He is unwilling to undertake work enough to justify us in asking the trustees to keep him in the School on a full salary.

Mrs. John Sherwood has found a young Mr. Eugene Schuyler who will become historiographer of the Great Metropolitan Fair for a consideration.[10] He came to see me this morning, and we arranged and agreed on certain questions touching the report. But he was not prepared to state what would be his charge for his services as editor, so final action was postponed. Agnew and Bellows are out of town, so I am the Sanitary Commission at present, under a resolution passed at its last Washington session. . . .

Rebel generals, Congressmen, officials, and leaders of every class are flooding Washington with prayers for leave to take the oath and be thereby whitewashed and restored to citizenship. This morning's *Times* notes the fact as significant of a great deal, and so it is. The cause these penitent traitors worked and fought for is simply destroyed by force, without any treaty or compromise or concession wherewith to justify their submission or soften its pang, doubly humiliating when they remember their savage swagger and bluster of bygone days. The nation rides rough-shod over state rights and abolishes slavery!!! Cavaliers of 1650, Puritans of ten years later, Jacobites any time after 1688, Tories after our Revolution, Legitimists after the French Revolution, Red Republicans of our own day, have chosen death or civil disabilities or exile before allegiance to the new order against which they had struggled in vain. Our rebels are elbowing each other as they crowd up to the office where the oath is administered. A few special caitiffs, such as Magruder, Breckinridge, and Kirby Smith, have run away. One man, "the venerable E. Ruffin," has blown out his addled old brains. But these cases are exceptional. Subjugated Rebeldom is generally eager to conform itself to its state of subjugation.

July 24, MONDAY. . . . No special Southern news. Of course, there are plenty of cases there of the most cantankerous carryings on by returned rebel soldiers and officers. But a parole and an amnesty and the oath cannot be expected to transmute ruffians and bullies into civilized Christians and gentlemen all at once.

July 27. . . . At 823 this afternoon. Agnew and I were so moved by the

[10] Eugene Schuyler (1840–1890), a graduate of Yale, did much miscellaneous literary work, and became minister to Greece, Rumania, and Serbia.

reports of scurvy in the Texan army of occupation that we nullified the resolution adopted at our last Washington session stopping the purchase of army supplies and ordered a large consignment of onions to go south by Saturday's steamer. We are to have 100,000 men on the Rio Grande, and tonight's papers report that Louis Napoleon is to send heavy reinforcements into Mexico. Another war is clearly on the cards. Louis Napoleon cannot afford to back out, and I think our government does not intend to tolerate a Franco-Austrian emperor in Mexico. War on that issue will be popular, strange to say—except perhaps with capitalists and importers. I think it will be upon us within three months. It will be madness, but we must stand by the government. One thing is certain. We have lots of fighting material lying about loose just now, South as well as North—in the hungry South especially; and six months of campaigning by Virginians and Mississippians and Texans, shoulder to shoulder with New Englanders and Western men and "dam Dutch and Niggers," might be wonderfully reconstructive in its effect and reunite our fractured young national bones faster than any other treatment could possibly do.

Charley tells *me* that George Boker tells *him* that General Meade tells *him* that the *ci-devant* General Lee tells *him*, that Rebeldom came very near a disastrous defeat at Fredericksburg, and that if Franklin had heartily supported a certain move on Lee's right, the whole rebel army must have been doubled up and disorganized. This confirms what Burnside told me not very long after that battle. This was one of the blessings in disguise which we owe to McClellan and to the disloyal McClellanist spirit with which the Army of the Potomac was narcotized many a month after he ceased to command it. Had the eastern rebel army been thoroughly beaten and destroyed at Fair Oaks or Malvern Hill or Antietam or Fredericksburg, or even at Chancellorsville or Gettysburg, we should be worse off today. The interests of the country required that Secessia be ground down to an impalpable powder, and that process has been necessarily slow.

July 28. . . . Mr. Ruggles looked in awhile this evening. He tells me Miss Kenzua has all but "struck ile." The boring tools in Well No. 1 at 265 feet come up greasy and smelly and unpleasant, and the indications are first-class. Curious that the old divining-rod superstition should reappear in the wild lands of northwest Pennsylvania, and that this respectable instrument, heretofore used to dealings with precious metals and springs of living water, should consent to indicate a subterranean current of stinking hydrocarbonous oil. The point at which this well was sunk was selected by a necromantic expert with a witchhazel wand in his left hand. He transferred the magic rod to one of Miss Kenzua's servants, a fat New Haven Yankee, who tells Mr. Ruggles, "I walked all round, and the rod didn't move any more than any stick would. But when I come to that place, something or other pulled the *other* end of it right down toward the ground, and I could not keep it straight, all I could do." The tough, shrewd, unbelieving Yankee generally develops a taste for marvels —for infinitesimal homeopathy, magnetism, spiritualism, *et id genus omne.*

August 1. . . . Pleasant evening at Union League Club . . . , where Mr. Superintendent Kennedy tells me that there were killed, during the riots of 1863, 1,155 persons, exclusive of those who were supposed to have been smuggled to their graves. He thinks there were many deaths besides from injuries received in the course of that performance, because the number of deaths by sunstroke reported during August and the latter half of July, 1863, was more than double the number of deaths from that cause during all the twenty-one summer months of the next preceding seven years. He supposes that many of our Celtic fellow citizens returned to their hod-carrying too soon after their heads had been broken by the locusts of his myrmidons.

Cholera reported in England. Then we shall doubtless have it here. This stinking town is ripe for its sickle, and if it invade the South, there will be a fearful harvest. All classes at the South, black and white, are in a condition to explode into death on the first spark of pestilence. —The so-called Liberals seem to have gained ground in the late Parliamentary elections. Who cares? —The election at Richmond coolly and summarily nullified by military order because the Union ticket (so-called) was defeated. Very good. It's a step toward the only reconstruction that will last, though the constitutionality of the proceeding does not protrude so far as to be conspicuous. The New York *World* notices this fact. . . .

We daily expect news of the *Great Eastern* with Atlantic telegraph cable No. 2. I expect a failure like that of 1858, or a success that will endure but for a season. I shall feel no disappointment now. I have ceased to love England since 1858, and wish she were thirty thousand miles off instead of three—the sordid, heartless, money-grubbing old Babylon. Heaven give her Pharisees all prosperity, but I do desire we may be better strangers.

Meeting of scoundrels in Broad Street to devise ways and means for getting Jeff Davis out of jail. About a dozen present (so Kennedy tells me); Peter Y. Cutler and Mr. Surrogate Gideon J. Tucker among them. May mangy dogs defile the tombs of their ancestors! May Heaven prolong my life beyond this surrogate's official term, and spare me the indignity of being admitted to probate by so uncommonly disreputable an official! Benedict Arnold was a Hampden compared with these caitiffs and reptiles.

St. Thomas Church sold and its congregation is to emigrate uptown, so we shall lose an old landmark.

August 4. Little news. Signs of peace and amity and loyalty and reconstruction do *not* multiply. Healthy granulations form slowly in the lacerated tissues of the South; perhaps because the patient is still in a state of "shock," prostration, and collapse, everybody being ruined, society disorganized, and the old-established relations between labor and capital destroyed, and the greater part of the country in a transition stage between the old regime and the new. Planters cannot get laborers. They could probably get plenty of them by the exercise of a little common sense, but that article is rare south of the Potomac. When affairs settle down and Southerners see their way to making a little money once more, reaction will set in and the wounds of war will begin to heal rapidly. It is to be remembered that this is the only great Civil War ever undertaken without any substantial wrong or grievance, political, social, religious, or personal, to justify it.

August 7. Wade Hampton publishes a cheeky letter to his fellow countrymen of South Carolina. Tells them not to think of emigrating, though he fully admits the universal prevalence of ruin. Advises them to stay at home and do what they can toward rebuilding society, though the job does seem nearly hopeless, and above all to elect to office (whenever they get a chance to elect anybody) only rebels of undoubted genuineness who have given their proofs. Politicians who didn't fight, Unionists and lukewarm friends of rebellion, and men who might have stayed at home and made money out of the war should, in his judgment, be excluded from office by the nation of South Carolina. All of which is refreshingly plain-spoken and cool.

August 9. Reports from the South continue to be mixed, but on the whole, not discouraging. Newspapers generally say, in substance: "We are thoroughly whipped; only a lunatic would dream of further struggle against government. We cannot be expected to be jolly and jubilant over our defeat and suppression, but we must take things as they come and make the best of them. The best thing for us is to acquiesce in our failure, save what we can out of the general wreck, try to reorganize the ruins of society, and submit in good faith and without reservation to the national rule imposed on us by the chances of war, and get ourselves restored to our normal place in the national system as soon as may be." Some of these newspapers devote themselves to long, dreary articles of the true Virginia type, on questions of constitutional interpretation. I suppose there must be Virginians who read these ingenuous lucubrations and like them, which is bad for Virginia. But there are wiser editors who dwell rather on the advantages of free immigration, the importance of encouraging it, the undeveloped resources of every Southern State, the value of skilled mechanics to the community and the dignity of labor!!! The world moves indeed! Of course, there are signs of gall and bitterness, breaking out sometimes into overt acts of ruffianism. But the wonder is they are so few.

August 15. Let us confess human life . . . the heaviest failure on record. Among the failures that come near it in magnitude is that of Morris Ketchum & Co., this day proclaimed abroad. "I saw the tents of Wall Street in affliction," as the prophet Habbakuk would have remarked had he happened to be downtown today. . . . I cannot think it possible that he would have used his prophetic gift to take advantage of future fluctuations in the stock market. However that may be, Morris Ketchum has come to grief by reason of forged certificates of gold deposits generally estimated at $2,500,000. It's said that his son, Edward Ketchum, is the forger, and that the ingenious young man has run away. Of course, G. W. Blunt remarked to a select circle at the Club tonight [Union League Club], "I always knew it, sir. Spent last Sunday at Edward Minturn's, sir, and we were talking about things, and I said now you mark my words; that young man won't come to good. You stand from under. I'd never seen him in my life, you know. Hadn't heard anything special against him. But I knew his gen-e-ral style of work, sir—his gen-e-ral style of work." Hushed pause of wonder. This great fraud and failure coming on the heels of the amazing defalcation of one Jenkins, a dirty little subordinate in the Phenix Bank, which has given the penny-a-liners so much work of late, looks as if the crash and fall of much that is rotten and hollow were nearer than we thought. . . .

Simeon Draper is "with sighing sent" from his pleasant place in the Collectorship, and fat Preston King reigns in his stead.

August 18, FRIDAY. . . . Definite news from the cable. It parted and went overboard in 1900 fathoms. The *Great Eastern* began forthwith dredging for the lost thread and Cyrus W. Field says it was grappled and raised three several times. But the rope always broke. So they anchored a buoy and returned home to get some more rope and try again. . . .

Bishop Elliott[11] of Georgia publishes a letter about the reunion of the Church, North and South—a fine example of Southern arrogance. "Still in their ashes live their wonted fires." He admits that the schismatic dioceses must come back sooner or later, now that the Rebellion (which he and his Rt. Reverend and Reverend Brethren instigated for the sake of their right to flog women, sell children, and grind the faces of the poor) is put down. But he is uneasy lest they should seem to come back as penitents and prodigals and without recognition as a separate ecclesiastical body. It does not suit him that Southern bishops should present themselves at the General Convention next fall and claim their seats in the upper house. He prefers that the Convention appoint a "committee with power" to wait on the "Council" of the Secession Church in November and humbly beg that the past may be forgotten and our old relations restored. He is uneasy lest somebody say something to the disadvantage of that gunpowder prelate, Bishop-Major General Polk—"our beloved Polk"—at whose funeral the same Elliott preached a remarkably infamous sermon. I humbly trust the next Convention will maintain a masterly inactivity upon the Southern schism, silently admitting those bishops who ask to be received again, and passing over the Southern Council and all its works without a word of notice.

August 21. Nothing special at 823 or at the Union League Club tonight. Ketchum, Jr., continues to outrun the constable, and there are two or three new defalcations, but they are paltry affairs, not one reported to exceed $100,000—mere petty larcenies.

Curious effect of war in changing the flora of a district. Throughout Virginia the Canada thistle is springing up abundantly in the track of every Northern column and cavalry raid, or in other words, all over the state. It used to be nearly unknown there. But its seeds were mingled with Northern oats and passed undigested through the bowels of myriad Northern horses. The appearance of our Eastern milkweed in abundance along the lines of wagon travel over the great Western plains is not so easily accounted for. Horses and cattle eat no milkweed seeds, and the

[11] Stephen Elliott (1806–1866), first Protestant Episcopal Bishop of Georgia. A warm friend of Leonidas Polk's, Elliott had been associated with him in the effort to raise funds for the University of the South at Sewanee. Strong is needlessly harsh toward a prelate who had many Northern friends and admirers.

only animals that specially affect it, so far as I have noticed, are certain slim, longicorn coleoptera. . . .

August 24, THURSDAY. . . . Nothing special in Wall Street or at 823. The London *Index*—Rebel "organ"—a smart, reckless, lying paper, writes its own obituary, drops a tear on the dead Confederacy, and declares itself defunct. Why have not the New York *World, News, Freeman's Journal,* and *Express* grace to follow its good example?

Joe Johnston writes a short plain letter to somebody who wanted his opinion on things in general to the effect that the South is beaten and must make the best of it, and that it is every Southern man's duty to recognize the fact and to do what he can toward restoring general prosperity and putting himself *rectus in curia* with the government of the United States. Like indications of the temper of Southern leaders appear every day. I distrust them, and fear that Southerners will talk in another tone as soon as their sham humility has restored them to their old places of power. They will then have a formidable force of Northern scoundrelism to help them in mischief—repudiation of the war debt, reëstablishment of slavery under new forms, or something else. But I may give them too much credit for subtlety and policy. Their hearts are false but their brains may be shallower than I suppose them to be. Their talk about submission to facts and to the fortunes of war may be sincere.

August 28, MONDAY.   Went to West Point (Roe's, not Cozzens's) Friday afternoon on the *Mary Powell*. Half-past three to half-past six of a summer afternoon can hardly be spent more agreeably than on the river between this and West Point. Daniel Huntington and I agreed that we had never seen the river's landscape series look lovelier. We watched that noble modulation into a new key, the grand shifting of the scenery as you pass Caldwell's Landing, and pronounced it very good. . . . My sojourn at West Point was most satisfactory. That annoying insomnia its only drawback. Ellie and her boys thrive. She has her horse, and if there be no other available cavalier, Master Johnny or the faithful John Nolan is on hand. Johnny likes the honor of squiring Mamma. . . . That glorious view from the north piazza took me back years and years, to the summer when I fearfully watched her unsteady convalescence from that all but fatal shock of April, 1849, and to the summer of 1851, when I was expecting Johnny's birth and shuddering for fear of a tragedy like that of two years before, and to that of 1852, Johnny's "first summer," when he was in permanent stomach-ache, and poor Mrs. Professor Bailey was so kind with her supplies of milk from her own cow, and all manner of helpfulness, and when Mrs. Bailey and her bright, lovely little Miss Kitty were murdered together on that fatal steamboat the *Henry Clay*.

The official residents of the Point have changed sadly since those days. We miss poor Bailey—dead; Fitz-John Porter, disgraced; Kirby Smith, D. H. Maury, Colonel (*soi-disant* General) Lee, superintendent in 1852, false to their oaths and their flag. So were Ives, Gustavus Smith, and many others who were flourishing on the Point thirteen to sixteen years ago. McClellan was there in those days—"Capt. McClellan." "Such a splendid fellow!" I suppose his diluted loyalty has been far more costly to the country than any treason of which he was capable. We should all be better off this day had he followed Lee to Richmond. I charge twenty per cent of the income tax I must pay before the month is out against McClellan, and ten per cent against Fitz-John Porter.

Old General G. W. Cullum is superintendent now.[12] He talked much of the Sanitary Commission, from which he resigned, as I suppose, under orders from Stanton. That tyrannical old Turk was hourly expected at the Point while I was there. But he did not appear. He would have been received with all manner of salutes and military honors, of course. But he is most bitterly hated by all the army. . . .

August 29. . . . The distinguished Ketchum consigned to the Tombs.

August 30. . . . Union League Club tonight. George W. Blunt, George Gibbs, and others. Report that Olmsted is about leaving Mariposa and the Rocky Mountains to become executive officer of some "Freedmen's Bureau." Mariposa stock was at fifty, two years ago. It is now at ten or thereabouts. I guess Olmsted mistook the matter when he undertook gold-digging.

August 31. . . . No political news. From what I hear, it seems likely that the Southern bishops will all come back with a few wry faces. I should do nothing to hurry them. Their room is better than their company. A couple of years ago (September 10, 1863), I wrote in this book my conviction that the late war was a religious war, a struggle between Christianity (more or less corrupted and diluted) and another religion at the South. Two years have strengthened that opinion. . . .

September 4, MONDAY. Heat, steamy, sickly heat, of the most muggy, repulsive, aggravating brand. Even the *Mary Powell's* forward deck was

[12] The before-mentioned George Washington Cullum, who had left Halleck's staff in the summer of 1864, then served as superintendent of the Military Academy for two years.

breezeless and sultry Friday afternoon. All well at West Point, except
the weather. I did not venture beyond the plain, hardly off the piazza,
where I sat and sweated over Mendelssohn's Letters and Anthony Trollope's *Can You Forgive Her?* Trollope is surely the most prolific of novelists, except perhaps the elder Dumas. But Dumas is said to employ a large
staff of clerks for his heavy work or routine business, reserving only the
intense and critical points of his story for his own personal manipulation,
whereas Trollope manifestly writes out his own stories from Chapter I
to Finale. He is also the most realistic of all novelists, exceeding Thackeray
in that particular. His novels seem photographs of Mr. A. and Miss B.
and Lady C., as they live and talk and do and leave undone, this day, in
the aristocratic and the upper middle castes of England. There is nothing
ideal in any of them. "Lady Glencora" (in this last novel) is a wilful,
foolish, pretty blonde woman, hardly saved from sacrificing herself and
her most respectable husband to a handsome, disreputable lover. I rather
like the pretty golden-haired young lady, and should prefer to see her at
her husband's feet in a passion of penitence and loyalty and good resolutions. But Mr. Trollope presents her at the end as likely to get along
comfortably with her husband for the future because she has borne him a
baby at last. *Sitch* is life, I suppose. Analysis of the moods, caprices, and
mental processes of young women seems Trollope's special gift.

My main comfort at West Point was that noble up-river view from the
north piazza. Looked at evening parades with Ellie. Called on Grandma
Cullum (General Cullum, the Superintendent) and spent last evening with
Professor Bartlett. Bartlett's highly distinguished son-in-law, General
Schofield (a most distinguished lieutenant of Sherman's), seems a brick.[13]
Gave Bartlett some magnesium wire. He had never seen it before. He thinks
it may be made most useful in our signal service—naval and military.

September 7. . . . Handsome Phil Lydig, who served with credit as one
of Burnside's aids, married to Miss Pauline Heckscher, a pretty brunette.
Clarence Cram's marriage also announced to some young woman nobody
ever heard of, from Elmira or thereabouts. . . .

State Convention of the wicked old pseudo-Democratic party in session
at Albany. I fear it will carry the state in November. That ancient institution is a great public misfortune.

[13] John M. Schofield had married Professor W. H. C. Bartlett's daughter Harriet in
1857. He had commanded the Union forces in the battle of Franklin, which severely
crippled Hood, and a little later shared with Thomas the honors of the battle of Nashville. He was now about to go to France as a confidential agent of the State Department.

September 8. . . . The Democracy (so-called), by the resolution of its Albany witenagemot, implicitly excommunicates and casts out the Woods, Barlows, Seymours, and other Copperhead caitiffs of the "Peace" faction—or professes so to do. That these politic, astute wire-pullers and professional observers of the public pulse think it judicious to do so, is an encouraging symptom. Their ticket points the same way; for example, they nominate Lucius Robinson for comptroller.[14] It would not be easy now to draw a line between Democrats and Republicans, Conservatives, and Radicals, unless in regard to Negro suffrage—and that's a question to be left to the Southern States themselves, and not a national issue. Were it national, I think the Radicals, so-called, would be beat on it.

News from the South continues contradictory. The South has made up its mind most fully to submit. The South is hushed in grim repose and only waiting a chance to rebel again. Niggers are generally fairly treated when they engage to work and keep their bargains. Niggers are being flogged, hanged, and shot by their late masters everywhere, no matter how they behave—and so on. Probably there are abundant facts to support each of these statements. But the refusal of the Mississippi Constitutional Convention to repeal the ordinance for the secession of that state, and its adoption (six to one) of a resolution declaring that ordinance null and void *ab initio* is a controlling and significant fact. If that cut-throat state have undergone so radical a change of heart, we may hope that all the wayward sisterhood will bring forth fruit meet for repentance. No Southern State seemed more irreclaimably given over to a reprobate mind than Mississippi only a year ago, unless possibly South Carolina. And South Carolina is today the worst-whipped state of them all. She lies stunned and passive, without energy enough to get on her legs and try to resume her place in the ranks.

I forgot to note the other evening a part of that wicked little Mrs. LeRoy's recent experiences. Major–General C. had been making fierce love to her and supposed himself accepted, though the position to which he aspired had been vacated by the death of poor Bob hardly six months ago. So he proceeded to Point Judith, bringing with him cases of champagne, baskets of fruit, and no end of pâtés and the like from Duncan's. The first evening after his arrival at Anthony's, the lovely widow committed

---

[14] Democratic party leadership in the state was changing. Dean Richmond and John Van Buren were to die before the end of 1866; new men of ability were coming forward—Samuel J. Tilden took Richmond's place as state chairman, and Lucius Robinson, who had joined the Lincoln forces during the war, was nominated for high office. Both Tilden and Robinson were eventually chosen governor.

some little sin against the conventionalities that rather offended the general's nice sense of propriety. He told his beloved not to do *so* any more, and the lady responded by denying his right to any control over her conduct. This led to an explanation, and a disillusionation, and a treaty of mutual secession. One of its clauses provided for the destruction by fire of all the general's amatory epistles—a rather bulky mass of MS. They thought it would attract attention if they went into Anthony's kitchen and poked the bundle of letters into the range, and decided to burn them in some out-of-the-way place on the beach—"by the sad sea-waves"—next morning. So off they went, after breakfast (the general in white pantaloons and lemon-colored kids, with his pockets full of locofoco matches), selected a convenient locality for the holocaust, and proceeded to inaugurate that ceremonial. But the wind was high and the sea air damp. They scraped match after match, but not one would ignite, or keep ignited long enough to do its office. The general, however, found a newspaper in his pocket, and they went into a bathing house, whence they emerged, each with a paper torch lit up within its shelter. They fired their pile of amatory epistolography and watched its burning. While it burned, a lot of boys and men came down to go a-clamming or a-fishing and asked whether that was a clam-bake, and two ladies appeared and took possession of the bathing house, proposing to disrobe themselves for a saltwater dip. The lovers—or ex-lovers—watched the blazing pyre till it burned out. Then they suddenly perceived that they had set the beach grass on fire and that the conflagration was fast approaching the bathing house and its disrobing inmates. Mrs. LeRoy tried to put it out. She couldn't do it. She invoked the aid of her adorer. He said, "I can't. I shall black my pantaloons." So the lady rushed into the bathing house and borrowed a pail and invoked the assistance of the clam-diggers. Between them they put out the fire. Her lover watched the process and said, "Good God, what a position for a major-general of the U.S.A.!" and went off by the next train. So Charley Strong and Tappan and Mrs. LeRoy had a good time together over his champagne and peaches and pâtés that evening, and this little female devil told the story with the keenest gusto and the most wonderful mimicry, and they all nearly choked with laughing. Poor General C. has had a lucky narrow escape.

September 11. Nothing new in town. The Hon. Henry A. Wise publishes a letter stating that he had become an Abolitionist long before the war was over. Solidified carbonic acid is not cooler than this. We shall have Lee claiming the credit of taking Richmond in April, and J. Davis producing certificates of his unqualified loyalty during the last four years, I suppose. Bully Wise is in many of his qualities a typical Southerner. Being thoroughly flogged, he avers that a flogging was the object for which he had been biting and gouging, and that his doctor had told him that his health would be permanently improved by a few bruises and gashes. Woe to us when these impudent copper captains return to their old place in Congress and begin caballing with their old pals of the "Democracy." . . .

September 13. Exhibition of bull frogs at Dodworth's building. A catchpenny concern, but some of them are colossal frogs—as big as babies almost.

I devoutly hope the so-called Democrats will regain no power at the fall elections. But the law of political oscillation and reaction is in their favor everywhere, and the squabble between Weed and Greeley will help them in New York. We have yet to see whether their record for the last four years will be remembered against them. It probably will be. The Federalists died because they were factious in opposition to government during the war of 1812. England never forgave the Whigs for the part they played during her anti-Napoleonic struggles. Neither party displayed a tenth part of the malignity that characterized our Democracy from 1862 to the end, and neither dared so impudently to avow its sympathy with the public enemy and its wish to hinder and embarrass government. May the people have wisdom enough to consign the men who backed J. Buchanan and G. B. McClellan to the outer darkness of a life gladdened by no office—a fortune without salaries, jobs, or stealings.

September 16. Poor Jem Suydam dead of dysentery at North Conway. . . . He devoted himself to landscape art some years ago, first as amateur and then professionally, and was represented at every academy by pictures that embodied no sentiment of any kind, but that shewed he had made himself a very good painter. An excellent fellow, with a streak of the Dutchiness that belongs to his race.

Professor Mahan tells me that little Dabney H. Maury is to open a classical and mathematical school at Fredericksburg. If all the dismounted Southern brigadiers follow his sensible precedent and take to peaceful, useful pursuits, it will be well for the country.

Old John Austin Stevens (always most gracious to me of late) tells me that the prospects of Southern trade are brilliant, that far more specie has been hoarded at the South than we suppose, and that Southern merchants are ordering largely and (wonderful to relate) paying off their old debts. As president of the Bank of Commerce, Stevens ought to know, and what he says is colored by no Southern partialities.

September 22.   With Ellie tonight to one of the series of Parepa[15] concerts at Irving Hall. The lady's voice is voluminous, flexible, cultivated, and of large compass, so people crowd her concerts and applaud her most inartistic and meaningless *tours de force*. She is entitled to credit for appreciating real music, for of her four pieces tonight, "Batti, batti," and "With verdure clad" were two. But she delivered both these noble, exquisite melodies with a coarse vehemence that would have better suited a screaming hurdy-gurdy aria by Verdi, much as Edwin Forrest would, I suppose, recite "To be, or not to be." There was a satisfactory little orchestra, and its last performance was remarkable—a *Quadrille* by Strauss. It was a canto of little bits or gems from Mendelssohn's Wedding March, the *Zauberflöte*, *Robert le Diable*, *Lucrezia*, *Freischütz*, *Oberon*, Beethoven's Sonatas, and so on; very scrappy and absurd, of course, but not at all disagreeable. Each scrap was delicious *per se*, and the mosaic was skilfully put together. . . .

The Republican Convention has put up its platform. Nearly identical with that of the "Democrats." I gravely fear that the Democrats will carry the state in November. If they do not, it will be through the defection of the *Daily News* and its gang, the unalloyed traitors of the party. The fall elections will give us an important observation of the orbit in which Northern opinion is moving. Straws shew which way the wind blows, so it may be worth while to note the talk of Ned Bell. That foolish, garrulous Copperhead confesses that he has been all wrong for the last four years, though guided by conscientious conviction all the time. He now finds fault with government only because it will keep pardoning rampant rebels who ought to be hanged.

September 24, SUNDAY.   Charles H. Marshall, President of the Union League Club, died last night at seventy-four. Gout, or rheumatism, "misplaced," attacked the heart or some other vital organ. Few men have done the country as much volunteer, unofficial, unpaid service during these last five years. He upheld the national cause through good report and evil report, even in the dark days of November, 1862, and May and June, 1863, and his geniality, personal influence, and activity contributed a great deal toward keeping New York capitalists firm in the support of government.

The Bishop requests the Standing Committee to meet at Trinity Church tomorrow, at two o'clock, as his "council of advice." So I shall

[15] Euphrosyne P. de B. Parepa-Rosa (1836–1874), Scottish singer.

have to make default at the meeting of trustees of Columbia College. I understand that our "advice" is to be asked on questions arising from the subject of the Bishop's pastoral letter of a few months ago, whereby he condemned the novel practice of certain Low Church presbyters who invite dissenters to their pulpits Sunday evenings. I believe the younger Tyng—S. H. Tyng, Jr.—has been thus fraternizing with outsiders, and has had a peppery correspondence with the Bishop about it. It looks like a case calling for active treatment, which I hope the Rt. Rev. Horatio may have courage to administer. If he have it not, I shall insist on Vinton's (or the Rector's) inviting Bellows to preach in Trinity now and then. Bellows's fluency and originality would be a delightful change, a refreshing alternation with Vinton's dull commonplaces and orthodoxy. (He was very shallow this morning.) Why should we not occasionally listen to a Jewish rabbi, a Methodist class-leader, or a Congregationalist deacon?

September 26. . . . Two long conferences with Blatchford today. There's a nasty embroilment in the affairs of the Sanitary Commission. I won't go into details and record how Blatchford's chief executive officer at Washington, Mr. S—d, a young man of excellent social position and great moral worth, who was superintendent of his church's Sunday School at Utica, was tempted to sin as was King David, but by a black Bathsheba; how her husband, a very reputable nigger in our employ, found it out and imparted his discovery to all the employees of the Washington office; how Collins got the story from Captain Harris, and imparted it to Blatchford three weeks ago; how he was dissatisfied with Blatchford's treatment of the case (very kind and judicious treatment, by the by), and being aggravated and incensed thereby and by sundry other misconstructions as unreasonable, "sasses" Blatchford and sends me his resignation as assistant treasurer. Bellows and I agreed this afternoon that S—d must be dismissed and he will be, or rather is. Collins has made a sort of blunt amend to Blatchford, so the bother may be patched up. . . .

At the Union League Club tonight, "reception" of an Honorable Englisher, Cosham, by name, I think, an Anglican Americanophile. Mr. Ruggles in the chair; much crowd. I arrived late and when the speeches were over. No great loss probably. After Cosham had let off his oration full of sympathy with our national cause, that blockhead G. W. Blunt got up and begged the gentleman to tell the meeting why the Neutrality Proclamation was issued and how *Alabamas* and other rebel privateers were allowed to sail from British ports. Very stupid, silly, and ill-bred.

September 28.   Talk with Phil Lydig this morning. He worships Burnside and not without reason. Union League Club awhile tonight.

Reports of Southern feeling are still contradictory. One set of correspondents reports all the secesh talk, cases of cruelty to freedmen and relics of plantation arrogance that it can pick up, and reports nothing else. Another set sends its newspapers only professions of loyalty, civilities to Yankees, and fair bargains between *ci-devant* master and *ci-devant* slave. The former writes for the *Tribune*, the latter for the *World*, and both for the *Herald*. Probably each furnishes about the same percentage of truth and of fiction. I incline to think that most Southerners are fast becoming reconciled to the downfall of slavery; that many of them have long seen the economic disadvantages of the system, but have been afraid to say so. But the old spirit of braggart insolence that claimed the title of a "master-race," "descendants of Cavaliers," and so on, is still unbroken. Many of these people, doubtless, still regard the war as a *jacquerie* in which Southern gentlemen ought to have ridden down and dispersed the Northern mob of tradesmen and cobblers and snobs of every species, as Froissart's knights and princes squelched the weavers of Ghent at Rosebecque—and would have done it had not the *canaille* been too strong for them.

September 30. . . . At 823. We are selling off what surplus stores the Sanitary Commission has on hand here and at Washington. . . .

Major-General Robert B. Potter was married Thursday to that beautiful Miss Abby Stevens. He has been among the best and bravest of our volunteer generals, and she is among the loveliest young women of the land. He marries into a troubled household, for I suppose Pete Strong's matrimonial—or divortial—caldron will be actively simmering again within a month. . . .

October 1, SUNDAY.   Bishop McCoskry[16] bullied us outrageously from the pulpit of Trinity Church this morning and gave judgment of final condemnation against nearly every human creature I have ever known. His sermon would account for Johnny's attack of sick headache (slight but much to be regretted, for Johnny is to begin school tomorrow), were it possible Johnny could have understood the sermon. Music was poor and mean.

October 2.   Law School Committee at the School, at one o'clock. Settled details of Lieber's duties as "Professor of Constitutional History and Public Law." . . .

[16] Samuel Allen McCoskry (1804–1886), Protestant Episcopal Bishop of Michigan.

As Ellie wanted to hear the new prima donna (Bosisio or Bossissieri —what matters the name of a woman whose vocation is to sing such drivel as she sang tonight?), we walked to the Academy of Music and took seats in the balcony. House overcrowded with an enthusiastic and enlightened public. Heaven help the public wits! Opera was *Ione*, by one Petrelli. Libretto supposed to be related to Bulwer's novel, *The Last Days of Pompeii*. People behind the footlights seemed to be having a dreadful time, I don't know about what, nor did I care; and the audience neither knew nor cared. Enough for them that it was lyric drama and high art and a masterpiece of a great composer, with whom it would be simply absurd to compare such an obsolete bewigged old pedant as, e.g., Mozart. We sat through three acts of twaddle and twiddlings and inane vocalization, and just as I had made up my mind to offer Ellie a *douceur* of fifty dollars if she would spare me the *fourth*, she spontaneously announced that she had had enough and we came off. One should be very thankful for getting off with only three-fourths of an *Ione*.

October 4. Union League Club tonight. We received Governor Fenton and fat Preston King. Introduced to the governor, who is gracious to the Sanitary Commissioners. Didn't hear his feeble remarks, but King talked some twenty minutes in a simple, homely, honest, sensible way that gave me a high opinion of him.

The Great Britons are in a blaze over their plotting, rebellious Fenians, and have discovered that domiciliary visits, arbitrary arrests, and the shutting up of seditious newspaper offices *may* be right and proper sometimes, after all. Very natural Irishmen should incline to a little secession after the talk of most organs of English opinion for the last four years about the iniquity of attempting to coerce a people that desires independence and the impossibility of doing it. This Fenian movement is nothing but froth, which may become streaked with a little blood, but that is unlikely. If it grew to large dimensions, we should follow the example of England. We should proclaim ourselves neutral as between the two "belligerent powers," and proceed with due caution to prevent by process of law the sailing of "Irish Rams" from any American port. Also, there would be an "Irish Independence Association" and large subscriptions to an Irish loan secured by a pledge of potatoes. Mr. Foster would proclaim in the Senate that Phelim O'Toole "had created a nation," and the Connaught correspondent of the New York *Times* would draw picturesque contrasts between the brutality, inefficiency, and cowardice of British colonels and the chivalrous energy, the self-denying patriotism, the generous devotion to the cause, displayed by even the common soldiers of the liberating army. Michael Cooney, representative of the Fenian Republic, though not formally recognized in his diplomatic capacity, would be fêted and lionized in Washington and Fifth Avenue. We should unanimously pronounce the O'Mulligan Lieutenant-General of the Fenian hosts the most high-minded and valiant captain named in modern history. We should be unable, of course, to prevent reckless speculators from trying to run the blockade with cargoes of Springfield rifles, and privateers would get out of our ports, in spite of all we could do, and burn British merchantmen by the hundred.

October 5.   Thirty years ago tonight, *Egomet Ipse* George T. Strong, a Columbia College Sophomore, began this journal, kept up since that date with few considerable lapses of continuity. Would that every duty of mine had been as faithfully fulfilled. I remember nothing at all about making my first entry, but I perfectly recollect the night before—a Sunday night —when I conceived the project of a diary. It was under the stimulus of a cup or cups of strong coffee, a Sunday evening tea-table indulgence then recently introduced among the domestic institutions of 108 Greenwich Street. I perfectly remember my cogitating intensely over the project and considering what manner of book I should use. Vague aspirations were floating through my mind, I think, toward some huge folio volume like a bank ledger. While I was thus exercised, I suppose Mamma and Mary were reading by the light of an Argand lamp. My father had gone up to the library and was deep in the Septuagint or the Greek Testament. Perhaps Aunt Olivia and poor dear Aunt Jane had looked in from next door, "No. 110." I was deploring our recent return home from the pleasant places of Whitestone, or rather, "Powell's Cove," where I had spent August and part of September at Mrs. Whitney's with two sweet children for playmates: Lothian Whitney (dead I think), a gem of a little brunette, and Mary Powell, who was, as I first remember her two years before, an ideal specimen of childish beauty. What nice times we had together picking up apples in the orchard and looking for hens' eggs in the barn!

When I began this journal thirty years ago, "Uncle Johnson" in Murray Street was our great authority. Next to him was "Uncle Benjamin" in Leonard Street. At St. Paul's Chapel I used to hear Bishop Onderdonk and Dr. Schroeder every Sunday. Bond Street was the Northern boundary of New York. George C. Anthon lived in Lispenard Street!!! Giles Hillyer, the most distinguished and illustrious of my acquaintances, in Liberty Street!! William H. Aspinwall's house in College Place was probably the most luxurious and magnificent in all the city. These memories make me feel very old.

October 6.   Long meeting of the School of Mines Committee at the Law School. Barnard brought forward a long series of recommendations to the trustees, all judicious and some of them important. He's a valuable man, or would be if he could hear. "Have you seen anything of Rood?" bellowed Rutherfurd, with his mouth close to the presidential ear. "No," said the President blandly, "I don't hear anything new." Prospects of the School of Mines are sunshiny just now. How long will this last?

Standing Committee of the Sanitary Commission at Bellows's tonight. Bellows, Stillé, Blatchford, and I. We dropped Dr. Parrish. Dr. Blake, our whilom Newbern inspector, is the subject of ugly charges, and brings no accounts and few vouchers to Washington for an expenditure of several thousand dollars. Edge, released from prison, writes Bellows and me.

October 7. . . . I am heartily glad England is squelching Irish "Fenianism" so thoroughly and promptly. She treats Irishmen as they treat niggers, and she is serving her Celts just as they deserve. They are cruel and merciless toward their inferiors, and are entitled to no favor from their superiors. The small majority by which niggers were denied suffrage in Connecticut was doubtless Irish.

October 8, SUNDAY.   We had one of our returning prodigals at Trinity. After the gospel, Dr. Ogilby announced that the sermon was to be by the Rev. Dr. Crane of Jackson, Mississippi, rector of St. Andrew's Church there, which sacred edifice had been casually burned by certain circumambient soldiers of Slocum's corps. Also, that the collection would be for the rebuilding of that particular rest-place of the Southern Zion. He went on to read certain certificates from Bishop Potter, Bishop Coxe, and *Barnard*, and one from Hawks (which he might better have left unread) as to the character of the reverend doctor. That subjugated rebel, thus endorsed, ascended the pulpit stairs and preached a commonplace old sermon with a few sentences tagged on to its peroration. These were, in substance, that his region was devastated, and its people ruined; that we had got that country and its people back into the Union, and that it was to our interest as well as theirs that they should not sink into heathenism. On the whole, a logical statement, which impressed me five dollars' worth, at last, though I intended, when he began, to give nothing. I noted with interest the phenomena of my usual plate-carrying tour down the middle aisle. In a few pews everybody sat still and declined to see the great silver salver I poked under their noses. But there was generally a liberal contribution of bills ($1 and upwards) along with "currency" and pennies, and I think the collection must have been unusually large for that congregation.

October 9.   Columbia College trustees, Rutherfurd in the chair; agreed to lease the restored block on Fifth Avenue, which was wise. We brought in a long string of recommendations from the School of Mines Committee. Zabriskie . . . was a little less vicious, but he can do us great mischief. Barnard brought in a plan for fellowships and scholarships. Ordered printed. Jones may leave the librarianship; a good riddance. . . .

October 12. . . . General commotion in full cry over that uncanonically consecrated prelate, Wilmer of Alabama; a very crooked stick.[17] Little to be hoped for from a convention in which sit Washington Hunt, Horatio Seymour, and Chambers of Maryland. Mr. Ruggles has had his say, but one can't discover (from the newspaper report of his speech) on which side. I hope Wilmer may be handsomely and emphatically snubbed. That's the only way to make a Southerner respect you. It was Northern hyper-aesthesia of brotherly love and respectful tenderness toward our slave-holding countrymen that produced secession and war. There is great danger that this old ingrained habit may return. But the fall elections thus far shew no sign of it, or of a "Democratic" reaction, though the slightness of the vote indicates general languor and apathy. The Republicans have just elected a mayor for the Copperhead city of Newark by a majority that amazes everybody, themselves included. This promises well for the important state election next month, and for that good and true man, Marcus L. Ward. But the conversion of benighted old New Jersey would be classed—and properly—among miracles.

The Protestant Episcopal Church held a memorable convention this fall in Philadelphia. It had its happier aspect in witnessing a restoration of its national fabric. The main body of the church had never recognized the withdrawal of the Southern element. The roll as called in 1865, like that at the previous General Convention in 1862, therefore included the names of the Southern bishops. These men, after some hesitation, resumed their old places in the organization, and unity became complete. As the church had never declared

[17] Richard Hooker Wilmer (1816–1900), a Virginian by birth and a graduate of Yale, had become bishop of Alabama after secession in 1861. He was strongly devoted to the Confederate cause—hence Strong's condemnation. After the war ended he got into trouble with the military authorities by ordering the clergy not to pray for the President until civil authority should be restored.

itself before the war on the slavery question, no old antagonisms remained to be overcome.

In other respects, however, the convention was less enlightened. Much debate was held on such questions as ritual etiquette, the proper ordination of a bishop, and textual changes in the Prayer Book and book of hymns. But the bishops refused to discuss more practical matters, or to express any gratification over the preservation of the nation; while their indifference to the needs of the freedmen drew down upon them a weighty rebuke from the New York Nation.

October 13.   Tonight Bellows here. We were the Standing Committee of the Sanitary Commission, and this was our weekly evening session. Bellows is just from Philadelphia. He and Bishop Clark of Rhode Island were guests of C. J. Stillé's. Clark says the House of Bishops is all one way as to the question of receiving back into full communion the rebel prelates and dioceses of the South. Any clamp or chain that connects North and South, Rebeldom and Loyalty, is useful just now. The Anglo-American Church has not been so conspicuous for zeal in the cause of nationality and freedom during the last five years as to disqualify it for service in reuniting the fractured bones of the country. As Clark says, it's sometimes convenient that one's clothes be dirty; it enables one to undertake without annoyance or damage jobs that are necessary, but very dirty indeed.

October 16, MONDAY.   General Convention tabled a resolution offered by Binney, asking the House of Bishops to appoint a day of thanksgiving for the restoration of national authority, and for the removal of the great cause of national discord. This was done after an angry debate. I am becoming ashamed of the church, or at least of her leaders and chief ministers. Their servility to Southern slaveholding potentates will long be remembered against them and compared with that of English prelates to the Stuarts, and such comparison will be much to our disadvantage. The New York delegation (including Mr. Ruggles) is said to have voted right on this question.

October 18.   Another effort to get a resolution for a day of thanksgiving through the Lower House of General Convention at Philadelphia has failed signally. Will the majority, led by Chambers of Maryland, be consistent and propose a day of fasting and humiliation for the downfall of slavery and rebellion? (Perhaps I should rather say their temporary eclipse.) It's by no means clear that such a resolution could not be carried.

It is lamentable that one should have reason to feel ashamed of belonging to the Anglo-American Church. Dr. Vinton seems to have behaved well and shewn pluck; Dr. Higby to have failed, this once, in backbone. But he has "given his proofs" of loyalty heretofore, and I will not condemn him unheard.

October 21. Republican ratification meeting at Cooper Institute last night was lively and hopeful. There is naturally much apathy and a full vote will not be polled, but the prospects of the pseudo-democracy, the party of Buchanan and the Chicago Platform, of H. Seymour, Toucey, Vallandigham, and the anti-draft riots of 1863, are bad in this state and in New Jersey—thank God! I am no party man, but I vote henceforth with any party that is in opposition to that party.

October 23. This afternoon to School of Mines to meet Robert Hone, who brought with him his eldest son, a handsome, gentlemanlike boy of seventeen, whom he proposes to confide to the School. George Anthon also there, introducing Cambridge Livingston, who brought with him his son, another nice, promising young fellow. We spent an hour or so inspecting rooms, collections, and so on, with Chandler and Egleston. Everything is still semi-chaotic, but dim signs of order begin to appear. Hone and Livingston seemed satisfied and pleased, and so did the two young embryo engineers. Considerable additions have been made to the collections by purchases in Germany. Among them are specimens of the insects (or rather impressions of insects) from rocks of the Tertiary Age, dragon-flies, and grasshoppers. Had read of them, but never saw them before. Geology can shew few things more profoundly impressive and suggestive than these permanent records of the existence of fragile, ephemeral insect life in so remote an era but in forms so nearly the same with those of our own familiar insect friends.

Dr. Torrey[18] has brought back with him from California some fine things for the cabinet of the School. But Egleston says his quarters are so contracted that he is afraid to ask after them. We are fearfully cramped, no doubt, but our present development would have been held an impracticable dream two years ago. Never has New York had such an opportunity of securing a great, influential school of science. Every accident has favored us thus far. If the trustees of Columbia College felt any lively interest in the doing of their duties, they could readily make their School of Mines a

[18] Dr. John Torrey, for thirty years a faculty member of the College of Physicians and Surgeons, also taught botany at Princeton and served for many years as trustee of Columbia College.

most important institution. But our (or their) misfortune is that only two or three of them—or of us—care twopence about the matter. Were we earnest in our work, we should soon find this wealthy and free-handed community backing us up with all the money we need.

October 29, SUNDAY. . . . A sad and murderous "accident" was committed on board the splendid N.R. steamer, *St. John*, this morning. She is probably the longest river boat ever built, and the most gorgeously decorated, with gilding and ormolu, rosewood and brocade. Her saloons were like Fifth Avenue drawing-rooms. But they put cheap iron ("sand-iron") into her boilers. So one of them blew up. A dozen people were steamed or boiled to death, and many others injured, more or less gravely. Among the killed were a young couple married last Thursday. The husband had gone through certain campaigns and survived several months in Andersonville to be flayed alive by red-hot steam in this magnificent mantrap, with its sumptuous upholstering and its cheap boilers. A peculiar feature of this homicide was the instantaneous flooding of the saloon into which the state-rooms opened with several inches of scalding water. . . . But nobody will be punished for it.

November 2. . . . The *Freeman's Journal* says the "Democracy" is disorganized and demoralized and in a bad way. That the party of Buchanan and of the Chicago Platform should have the impudence to survive at all is indecent. But its chief scoundrels will perhaps do less mischief hereafter under their own disgraced label of Democrat than in some new organization and under some political alias. Let them, by all means, keep their old banner flying.

November 5, SUNDAY. . . . Mr. and Mrs. D. Colden Murray have returned from Europe, and are lying in the lower bay, quarantined till Wednesday, as being possibly choleriferous. No quarantine precautions against this disease will prevail. What we need is practical sanitary reformation of back streets, tenement houses, and pestiferous bone-boiling establishments. Thereby, and by nothing else, can the inevitable epidemic be mitigated. The city government will not do this, or any other good work, honestly and thoroughly, for it is rotten to the core. The "Citizens' Association" will do what it can. It is free from corruption, I believe. If it have, or can raise, sufficient means, it will doubtless take prophylactic measures, to the great benefit of the community. The *Evening Post* invites the Sanitary Commission to undertake that work. But that work is far outside the duties the government assigned to the Sanitary Commission in 1861. When the rebellion was squelched and peace returned to us, the Sanitary Commission became *functus officio.* We now exist only in liquidation, for the winding-up of our affairs. I sacrificed four years to the public service, because the country, in deadly grapple with a malignant rebellion, demanded every sacrifice of private interest from every loyal American.

November 6. Rather interesting meeting of the College trustees at two o'clock. Ogden read his treasurer's report, which had been printed in advance and laid on the table. It shews a probable surplus of income for the next financial year, likely to go on increasing. A good special committee of seven appointed to settle a financial policy for amount of current expenditure and to consider the question of creating a building fund wherewith to give the College gradually a better abiding place than its present inconvenient, rambling, rickety "asylum." . . .

Election of librarian. As a clergyman was in nomination, though without an opposing candidate, the white cravats attended in force. The clergyman was Betts's son, the Rev. Beverley Robinson Betts, rector of a little parish at Maspeth, Long Island. I had learned within a day or two that he is a virulent Copperhead. Fish says he omitted the prayer for the President during the war, and the special prayers put forth by the bishop. I did not vote, therefore, nor did Mr. Ruggles, but the election went by default. Barnard brought up a curious correspondence about a contumacious Hebrew Sophomore, named Isaac Adler (I think); Isaac of New York, whose conscience compels him to decline standing up with the rest during service in chapel, and who wants to be a martyr like his forebears in *Maccabees.* Barnard offered certain resolutions affirming the College to be a Christian institution, and there was much shallow talk around the edges of certain deep and difficult questions. But somebody, Betts, I believe (let him alone for adroitness in dodging a question of principle) proposed a substitute, which was carried—in substance that inasmuch as the rules and practice of the College are generally known, every student must be presumed to have matriculated with intent to conform to them—and bound to such conformity.

Barnard had a very long string of resolutions about points of detail in the administration of the College. He attends to his work most thoroughly and closely, and I think wisely. I know very little about Dr. Harris, who died some thirty-six years ago, and of whom ancient graduates talk largely. But since his day, at least, the College has been governed by no president so alive and wide awake as Barnard. His resolutions, offered at a former meeting and presented in print at this, for the establishment of scholarships and fellowships, were tabled, but in no unfriendly spirit and only because this board can never decline any motion to postpone a proposition for development and progress. They were made the special order for the next meeting and will be carried.

The scholarship scheme is unexceptionable. But I think that of fellowships can be improved. It proposes merely to give the "fellows" $— per annum for three years after taking the degree of B.A., as a prize to be attained by a special "class" examination, and assigns them no duties. I would prefer, therefore, a single fellowship held for one year with say $1,000 income, and the obligation to spend that year in attendance on postgraduate studies in letters or science or both. College symptoms are hopeful for the first time during the twelve years I have had the honor to sit on that stolid board. It would be a great gain if Mr. Zbrowski and Dr. Beadle would emigrate to California, and if Dr. Haight were made Bishop of the Guano Islands, for he is an embodiment of all that is unpleasant in the clergyman as such—of every clerical foible.... The board would be stronger if rid of all its white-cravated members, save and except Morgan Dix. Dr. Jay and Robert Ray are mere cyphers, but in spite of these drawbacks, positive and negative, the prospects of the College are improving.

November 7, TUESDAY. Voted a clean Republican and Union ticket, though with misgivings as to the judiciary. . . .

November 8. Morning papers brought good news. Democrats have lost New York by 24,000 majority, and marvelous to relate, New Jersey besides. Marcus L. Ward is elected governor and the Unionists have both branches of the legislature.

The result of the fall elections was a crushing defeat for the Democratic Party. Interest specially centered in the outcome in New Jersey and New York, for in both states the chief Democratic leaders had opposed the Thirteenth Amendment for the abolition of slavery. The New Jersey legislature had rejected the amendment; Representative S. S. Cox of New York had voted against it; Horatio Seymour had asserted that it would be better to sacrifice the Union than to preserve it by means of emancipation. The Republican triumph was taken as marking the final collapse of the Copperheads. To some extent the election was also a warning to the South; the conventions sitting this summer and fall were reluctant to recognize the new status of the Negro, and the North was serving notice that the era of freedom must be accepted.

November 9. A vigorous campaign is to be opened against the Medical Bureau in Congress. Most of the leading volunteer surgeons mustered out of service are organizing for a combined assault. Many of the best officers of the Bureau say they wish they were well out of the service that they might speak what they know. Lyman is a type of the former class, Cuyler of the latter. The Bureau is in lower degradation under Barnes than it was under Finley. We shall probably do a little to help this movement, either by an open statement and appeal to Congress or by contributing to the expenses of the movers. No application of our funds can be more proper or more useful.

R. M. Blatchford has just returned from Washington. He claims to be intimate with Johnson and the government.[19] He tells Bellows that the Administration is relieved from grave concern by the result of the New York and New Jersey elections. It was feared that those elections would shew a reflux of feeling or apathy, at the North, and that would encourage Democrats to league themselves with Congressmen from "reconstructed" rebel states, and undo all the good the war has done. But Northern Democrats must be satisfied now that their constituents desire to see no such alliance, and that the Democratic party must be in a bad way when New Jersey elects a Republican governor and legislature.

November 10.   Wirz of Andersonville memory was hanged at Washington this morning. It was very meet, right, and our bounden duty to hang somebody for that deepest and most damnable crime of the late Confederacy —the politic murder of thousands of its prisoners by slow torture; and Winder having died a natural death,[20] Wirz was the most prominent agent in the homicide, and a proper subject for the execution of national justice. But I suppose his moral guilt was not of special intensity. He seems to have been merely a man without feeling or compassion, who did as he was ordered, without compunction.

November 11.   Thomas's first concert this evening.[21] Not a full house.

[19] The lawyer Richard M. Blatchford had certainly long been intimate with Seward. Always an active, public-spirited man, he had done first-rate war work in the New York area, and in 1862–1863 had represented the United States at the Vatican. He was now commissioner of Central Park.

[20] Brigadier-General John H. Winder, a West Point man, was in charge of Union prisoners in the Confederacy from Bull Run until his death in 1865. His offenses and those of Major Henry Wirz were much exaggerated.

[21] Theodore Thomas was coming into full prominence as a conductor. He had organized an orchestra of his own in 1862, while in the same year he became associated with Theodore Eisfeld as alternate conductor of the Brooklyn Philharmonic. Already he was exercising a great spell over music-lovers in the metropolitan area, though his career in the national field remained before him. In the winter of 1864–1865 he had used his own orchestra for a series of symphony soirées.

We heard Liszt's hysterical "Mazeppa," and Weber's "Invitation to the Waltz," arranged for orchestra by Berlioz. The arrangement is effective, but it wants something—delicacy, refinement, or elegance. Also, Beethoven's Fourth Symphony. It has comparatively few salient points and takes away one's breath only once or twice—as, for instance, in its noble, joyous trio. So it seems tame beside most of its eight sisters. But it is a grand work. It smells strongly of Mozart and of Haydn by turns. Only its first movement is at all characteristic of Beethoven. As a whole, it reminds one of Haydn's greatest symphony (or rather the greatest of his symphonies that I have the happiness to know), that which the Philharmonic people have played twice or thrice—in F, I think. The sentiment of the two compositions is nearly the same, though Beethoven, of course, intensifies Haydn, and this relationship between the two compositions seems especially visible in their third movements.

November 14. . . . Very sad news about honest old Preston King. Its present form is this. He was at the Astor House Saturday evening and has not been seen alive since he left it, when his disappearance caused inquiry. Those who were last with him remembered symptoms of aberration in his talk and manner. His body was picked up today near Hoboken, it's said. He was a most respectable and valuable man, and a close friend, ally, and counselor of Johnson's. Bidwell tells me that in 1839 or thereabout he made a great effort to repress "sympathizing" demonstrations in aid of the abortive Canadian insurrection—visited a post established opposite Ogdensburg, having got a license to do so from the provincial authorities, and that this work and its excitement produced a fit of insanity, and that he was under restraint for a month or two.[22]

November 15. To Columbia College at two o'clock for the opening of the second year of the School of Mines. (Seventy students on the rolls and more coming.) We met in the president's room. There were a dozen trustees, as many of the College and School faculties, and twenty or thirty outsiders, including the Bishop of Honolulu. We proceeded to the chapel. Chaplain Duffie opened with a brief service. Barnard made a sensible address, with certain points admirably put, as to the progress and the wants of the School. Egleston, as senior professor, followed with certain details. Chandler read the programme of lectures, and so on. Mr. Ruggles

[22] Ex-Senator Preston King, a loyal supporter of Lincoln's policies, had been active in Andrew Johnson's nomination for the vice-presidency. Johnson appointed him collector of the port of New York, and the pressure of office-seekers and anxieties of the unfamiliar post proved too much for the obese, excessively conscientious politician. Becoming mentally affected, King dropped from a Hoboken ferry-boat.

followed with a most brilliant little offhand speech on the mineral wealth
of the land, the Pacific Railroad, the Rocky Mountains, the Sierra Nevada,
and the application of science to the development of this great national
estate. He contrasted it effectively with the mines of Fribourg, worked for
more than half a thousand years and producing but $700,000 a year, but
held important enough to demand a special school of science—a school
that produced Werner and Humboldt. He referred to the action of the last
general convention which established three missionary bishoprics for the
emigrant miners that are soon to people the region of silver and of gold,
and delivered as telling and effective a little oration as any I ever heard.
Bishop Potter, who has been, as Mr. Ruggles thinks, a little miffed with
him for voting in the general convention against killing the fatted calf
before the Southern prodigal has committed himself to penitence—Bishop
Potter, the "Doctor Invertebratus" of some future hagiology—applauded
"with effusion."

Gouverneur Ogden, thinking the president had not done justice in his
address to the liberality of the trustees toward the School of Mines, privily
asked the president to call on him as treasurer for a financial statement. He
was called upon and made it, and a very dull, incomprehensible statement
it was.

Then we adjourned to inspect the cabinets and laboratories and to eat
oysters and drink coffee in one of the lecture rooms. This little performance
was most successful. Barnard understands his work, and wants to do it.
The College has a live president for the first time in near forty years.

Archie Pell dined here and went to the opera with Ellie and Miss
Kitty Dix and McMahon. Pell is a brick—has served through the war, and
leaves the service with the grade of colonel. He's a handsome young
fellow, too. He told several good stories; for example, a certain Southern
Rajah dining with Alfred Pell enunciates this query: "Now, do you not
really think, Mr. Pell, that the Southern gentleman is, on the whole, much
superior to those you call gentlemen at the North?" Alfred Pell responds,
"Well, as you put this question to me at my own table, I should say it
answered itself." Very good for Alfred Pell.

November 17. . . . After dinner to Standing Committee of the Sanitary
Commission at 21 West 12th Street, henceforth our place of meeting. So
that long series of pleasant weekly evening sessions at Van Buren's,
Agnew's, Bellows's, Gibbs's, and on these premises that began in 1861
and were devoted to business from eight to ten, and to a simple supper from
ten to twelve (at which the lady or ladies of the house commonly assisted)

is over and done with. They were always comfortable and hopeful, even when our prospects were darkest. I think those symposia did the state some service by keeping the Sanitary Commission in good heart and up to its work. . . .

General Grant is to dine here tomorrow with his staff, and I feel quite nervous about so august a transaction.

November 18.   Our symposium did not go into operation till half-past six, for the Lieutenant-General and his staff were behind time like Grouchy at Waterloo. Grant appeared at last, however, with Mrs. Grant and with General Comstock, Colonel Badeau, and Colonel Babcock of his staff. I made it a point to have Johnny, Temple, and Louis present, and to bring them severally up to shake hands with the General. They will remember it fifty years hence, if they live so long, and tell their children of it, if they ever have any. Mrs. Ellie had organized her dinner table thus:

Mrs. George T. Strong

Gen. Grant	Sen. Foster of Conn.
Mex. Gen. or Señor Romero	Mrs. Morgan
Mrs. Gen. Grant	Henry J. Raymond
Mr. S. B. Ruggles	Col. Babcock
Gov. Morgan	Mrs. Dix
Gen. Dix	Col. Badeau
Mrs. Ruggles	Chas. Bristed
Gen. Comstock	Mrs. Foster

Egomet Ipsissimus

It was a brilliant, distinguished, or "nobby" assemblage, and they all seemed to have a pleasant time, as people always do at any party organized by Mistress Ellen. I must say that I think it a great honor and privilege to have received Grant here, and there is no element of snobbishness in my feeling about it. We owe the privilege to Ellie's attractions and tact: Foster took her to call on Mrs. Grant, who was much delighted with her, and asked her to lend her aid and countenance to the reception at the Fifth Avenue Hotel Monday night. Ellie slipped in an invitation to dinner, and it was cordially accepted. William B. Astor's was declined, but I am verging on snobbery. I had a pleasant session with Mrs. Foster and [Charles Astor] Bristed. After the ladies withdrew, Bristed, Comstock, Mr. Ruggles, Foster, and others got together and chewed a certain amount of clear, compact talk out of the Lieutenant-General. Dr. Peters joined us, and

COLUMBIA COLLEGE AT FORTY-NINTH STREET, 1860
MADISON AVENUE AT THE LEFT

SCHOOL OF MINES, 7 MAY 1866

JOHN ADAMS DIX

MORGAN DIX

Macdonough and Bininger, a committee from the Century Club. The Lieutenant-General thinks black regiments trustworthy if they have good officers, but not otherwise. He holds General Lee in high respect.

Mrs. Grant is the plainest of country women, but a lady, inasmuch as she shews no trace of affectation or assumption, and frankly admits herself wholly ignorant of the social usages of New York. After dinner, Mrs. Paran Stevens and Miss Fanny Reed came in, Miss Helen Stanly, John Sherwood, Mrs. Murray, Miss Kitty Dix, and Mrs. Blake, with others. Miss Fanny allowed me to take her to the piano and sang Mrs. Julia Ward Howe's version of the John Brown song with immense spirit and effect.

New York gave Grant an imposing and tumultuous reception on the evening of November 20. "Ovation to General Grant"—"The Hero Carried by Storm"—"Vast Assemblage of the Celebrities of the Metropolis"—such were the headlines carried by the press next morning. A crowd of ten thousand gathered at an early hour in the evening about the Fifth Avenue Hotel. Various civic committees assembled at seven o'clock. Among the guests of honor invited and present were a galaxy of generals—Winfield Scott, John C. Frémont, John A. Dix, Hooker, Meade, Burnside, Slocum, Anderson, Wool, Lew Wallace, and Kilpatrick, with others. Admirals Farragut and Wilkes were there; five Senators, including W. M. Stewart of Nevada, who is mentioned below; and such prominent citizens as Bryant, Greeley, Manton Marble, Thurlow Weed, and Samuel J. Tilden. When Grant entered the hotel, escorted by General Hooker and William B. Astor, he was the center of an irresistible rush. Hooker had to bellow "Halt!" at the top of his lungs. Three thousand persons jammed themselves into the supper room in an effort to get some oysters and champagne; and soon those who were in could not get out, and those who were out could not get in. At ten o'clock an elaborate pyrotechnic display took place (amid a cold rain) in front of the hotel. But the whole affair was described by the Tribune *as "one of the most imposing ceremonies ever witnessed in this city," and one which "will be remembered for a lifetime by all who were present." Next day the hero, escorted to the Cortlandt Street Ferry by the Seventh Regiment, took the train to Washington.*

November 20, MONDAY. . . . After dinner I took Ellie down to the Metropolitan Hotel. She had promised Mrs. Grant to stand by her during tonight's august and solemn "reception" at the Fifth Avenue Hotel, of which ceremonial that simple Western lady stood in great awe. As I could not attend in person, I left her in the General's parlor, after bidding Grant and his staff goodbye. They were very polite and kind. Our little dinner of Saturday seems to be considered a most "brilliant" and "distinguished" transaction. I believe the people enjoyed themselves reasonably well, and that is all there is to say about it, except that I am gratified to have had Grant here. . . .

November 24. . . . To No. 21 West Twelfth Street. Olmsted with us, returned from California day before yesterday by the Nicaragua route. He has given up Mariposa. After our Committee meeting we adjourned to Delmonico's and had a very nice little supper. Olmsted had much to tell us. He looks well and is as bright as ever.

November 26, SUNDAY. This evening Mr. Ruggles brought Senator Stewart of Nevada here.[23] I had taken measures to bring him into contact with the School of Mines, so we had also Egleston, Vinton, Rood, and Peck. Vinton's reverend uncle, Dr. Frank Vinton, came in, and David A. Wells of the United States Revenue Commission, Mr. Derby, Dr. Carmichael, D'Oremieulx, and others, not forgetting General Frank Barlow, who looks as he did when I last saw him before the war—like a boy of eighteen—though he has fought his way up during these five years from private to major-general, was desperately wounded at Antietam, and left for dead on the field of Gettysburg. He married Miss Arabella Griffith in those hurrying days of April, 1861, in his volunteer's uniform, bade his bride goodbye at the church door, and went off to Washington. She died about eight months ago of typhoid fever contracted while working for the Sanitary Commission in the hospitals of Fredericksburg.

Stewart sees the national importance of the School of Mines, and may possibly do it great service. The supper-table talk of Stewart, Mr. Ruggles, Egleston, Wells, and Mr. Derby was weighty. They demonstrated the country's ability to pay its debts—and also that California, Nevada, Arizona, etc., are producing gold and silver enough to account for the rise in prices (independently of a paper currency) and that this rise of prices, or change of values, is therefore permanent and progressive. That's very bad for me, a holder of mortgages and a receiver of a fixed income. I shall probably die a pauper. But inflation is a great fact for Trinity Church and

<hr>

[23] William M. Stewart (1827–1909), a New Yorker by birth and a lawyer, was elected Republican Senator from Nevada in 1862, holding his seat until 1875, and again 1887–1905. He was long a pillar of silverite interests.

Columbia College. They are leasing for long terms. The Church is letting the 300 lots covered by the expiring Burr lease, and the College is letting the "Botanic Garden" property on Fifth Avenue. Both are rented at rates that would have seemed fabulous ten years ago. There is much consolation in that fact. If I can only comfort and provide for poor Ellie and give her boys an education that will qualify them to make their own way in the world, I shall be satisfied and thankful. My appetite for book buying, my lust for Alduses and MSS, and Sweynheyms and Pannartzes, my ambition to own a Caxton, my dream of possessing a copy of the Mazarin Bible, the Mainz Psalter, and the Complutensian Polyglot—all these fancies have passed away. My utmost hope is that I may be able to provide bread and butter, beef and mutton, for my wife and my babies.

Strong's unhappy cousin, Peter R. Strong, had been forced into a lawsuit which at once became a public sensation, and which throughout December powerfully agitated the diarist. Its roots ran far back into the past. Peter Strong had been married in May, 1853, to Mary E. Stevens, daughter of the wealthy and prominent banker and littérateur, John Austin Stevens. They at first lived happily together, and three children were born to them. But Peter Strong's brother, Edward, a man of "religious inclinations," lost his wife and came to live with them. An illicit intimacy sprang up between him and Mrs. Peter Strong in 1860, and was repeatedly renewed. Finally, in January, 1862, the wife, in a fit of remorse, confessed it to her husband. Thereafter the two lived separately, but Peter Strong did not at first sue for a divorce. All that he asked was to have full rights to the oversight and care of his children. When the wife demanded full and exclusive custody of one child, the difficulties between them reached a crisis. She was upheld in her position by the powerful Stevens family; and in June, 1865, defying a habeas corpus which Peter Strong had obtained for the daughter Alice, she fled with the child to parts unknown. It was possible for the husband to communicate with her through the Stevens family, but not to find out where she and his daughter lived. He therefore brought suit for divorce, and for the care and custody of the children.

The trial opened on Friday, November 25, before a jammed courtroom, Peter Strong's attorney, Cram, making a long plea. On the following Monday, a governess gave the first important testimony against the defendant. The

case was front-page news from that time forward; and one "painful revelation,"
as the newspapers called it, followed another. Mrs. Peter Strong was never
in the courtroom; but her aged father and her brother, John A. Stevens, Jr.,
were there nearly every day.

December 1. The town is ringing with denunciations of the Stevens
people for forcing the hateful details of this divorce suit into public view
and refusing the liberal offers of the plaintiff and of their counsel
for the brutality with which such women as Mrs. Bedell and Mrs. Ben
Strong are treated. Old Stevens and his amiable son stink in our nostrils
just now. Such impressions on this community are ephemeral. But for
the time being the whole household is talked of as leprous and outcast.
The developments of this trial have been all in Pete's favor, thus far, but
the other side is yet to have its innings, and we must wait to see what it
can do. Probably it will do little but throw dirt, but John Graham can
scatter filth as effectively as any one of Gulliver's Yahoos. . . .

This morning's *Times* refers to the case editorially; says that if its
publicity has been caused by the "conceit and presumption" of one of the
defendant's kinsfolk (meaning John A. Stevens, Jr.,) he has committed a
criminal blunder. This editorial comes from Thurlow Weed, of course.
He has political reasons for hating John A. Stevens, Jr. The *Herald* says
it's a horrid case, and indicates deep social demoralization, which is due
to the influence of the Academy of Music and the theatres which no
longer advertise in its columns. That is funny, but this contest is founded
on the darkest tragedy. I have meant to go into the Superior Court every
day, but I have been unable to do it. The memory has always appeared to
me of that beautiful bride of twelve years ago in her pearls and white
lace, and I have been forced to run away from the court room in which
that noble creature is being dragged through the mud by her vindictive,
senseless father and brother. Noble, even, in her penitence and contrition,
till her own people had moulded her into wickedness deeper than sexual
sin—into renunciation of penitence, and therefore hostility and hate
toward the husband she had wronged.

December 2. . . . Dined at Delmonico's on Stillé's invitation. There
were Mr. and Mrs. Stillé, one Strong (!), a kinsman of that lady's, Bellows, Olmsted, Van Buren, Agnew, Godkin, Blatchford, and I. Very
pleasant. . . .

December 4. . . . At Society Library and Club tonight. Much talk of
tomorrow's charter election, and of the Strong divorce suit. Every one

seems to understand that it is the Stevenses, *père et fils*, who bring its demoralizing details before every breakfast table in the state every morning, by their mulish hatefulness and perverseness in refusing to entertain the plaintiff's extravagantly generous offers, and everyone seems to appreciate the responsibility whereof those two men have recklessly and wilfully undertaken the burthen. . . .

Congress organized today, very harmoniously. Its Republican majority shews no sign of the split Copperheads have been predicting. Southern members are to be kept out in the cold a little longer. And there are already steps toward most important legislation. Bills are introduced to prevent the practical restoration of slavery by the *ci-devant* slave states.

The Thirty-ninth Congress opened on Monday, December 4, for a momentous session; for battle was at once to be joined between President Johnson and the Radicals over the issue of Reconstruction. Thaddeus Stevens, stern, grim, and impassive, ruled the House with a rod of iron. At his behest and that of the other Radicals, the clerk, in calling the roll of the House, ignored the entire Southern delegation. When he passed over Tennessee a protest was heard, but it was instantly crushed. The Republican caucus had determined to take Reconstruction out of the hands of the President. On Tuesday, President Johnson's message was read in both chambers. Its moderate tone and its literary merit (George Bancroft had assisted Johnson in writing it) were generally commended. It was in fact a state paper of very unusual ability, marked by honest frankness, good nature, and sagacity. It contained no reference to the existing condition of affairs in the South; and though it did offer a candid explanation of the President's views on Reconstruction, it did not urge them upon Congress.

But the Radical leaders were determined to have their own way. Without loss of time they passed a resolution creating a joint committee on reconstruction; a body which it was intended should take the whole Southern problem out of Andrew Johnson's hands. The dominant spirit in this committee was Thaddeus Stevens, who meant to deal harshly with the hated "rebels," and who was earnestly supported by Ben Wade and Charles Sumner in the Senate. "The Stevens Committee will have a wide field of operation," rejoiced the New York *Tribune. On December 11 the morning papers announced that the Thirteenth Amendment, abolishing slavery, had been ratified by the requisite number of states—including South Carolina and Virginia.*

December 7. The President's Message seems to me a paper of great power. It will produce an impression abroad. This is what our *tailors* can do. Is it much inferior to the average work of hereditary statesmen, of peers who were first classmen at their university? Stanton's report, McCulloch's,[24] and General Grant's, are each in its way of great merit and value. Mr. Ruggles thinks it "mean" in Stanton to have said nothing about the Sanitary Commission, but I don't see it. The Secretary of War was not officially called upon to report as to the work of the Commission. Had its operations been an hundredfold more important, they would still have been outside his official sphere. As Secretary, he could know nothing of any voluntary effort by the people to supplement the work of government and provide relief in frequent instances of inevitable failure. I do not love Stanton, but he is right in ignoring the Sanitary Commission, when he is reporting on the work of the War Department.

Since the first Thanksgiving sermon was preached in New England, this people has seen no such Thanksgiving Day. What country has ever passed through like peril and come out with like gain? . . .

These four years have reduced me to something like pauperism. But I am profoundly thankful for them, nevertheless. They have given me— and my wife and my boys—a country worth living in and living for, and to be proud of. Up to April, 1861, it was a mean, sordid, money-worshiping country, in my judgment at least, and I think I was not far wrong.

The legislature of South Carolina, meekly making haste to ratify a Constitutional Amendment abolishing slavery in 1865, is a phenomenon which her legislators of 1860 did not think very likely to occur in their day and generation! Indeed, anyone who should have predicted December 7, 1860, the political status of today, would have been held to be without foresight, judgment, and common sense, and laughed at as a madman, by North and South alike. Only a year ago, victory seemed but a shadow in the dim distance. Thorough pacification through all the length and breadth of the land, and a frank admission by all Rebeldom of its defeat and subjugation, were not among the contingencies talked of as belonging to our day.

December 13. School of Mines meeting at the College at half past three o'clock. Present of the Committee: Barnard, Betts, Edward Jones, Rutherfurd, Torrey, and I. Associates: Agnew, Delafield, Osten-Sacken, Dodge. Faculty: Vinton, Egleston, Chandler, Rood, Peck, Joy, and Van

[24] Hugh McCulloch, Indiana financier, had become Secretary of the Treasury at the beginning of Lincoln's second Administration.

Amringe. We agreed on certain recommendations to the board, of which the most important was the establishment of a chair of geology and paleontology. May the board take our advice! We then adjourned to the School and inspected laboratories and cabinets. A satisfactory meeting. How much has been done by the energy of Egleston and his colleagues, and how much remains to do!

Tonight at meeting of trustees of Lincoln Home. Evidence collected by Dr. Bellows from all parts of the country shews that the demand for establishments of this class is small and grows daily smaller, and that people everywhere begin to see its smallness. It would be hard to collect a corporal's guard of disabled *native* soldiers willing to live on public charity or without reliances and resources of their own. Had we a new *Hôtel des Invalides* now open, its only inmates would be Celts and Teutons, with a few natives, who may just as well be cared for in the alms house on Blackwell's Island, because they would be there if they had never enlisted. . . .

December 18, MONDAY. . . . General Barlow last evening discoursed much of the absence of strategy in our battles. He holds the overthrow of the Rebellion due to the rank and file and to regimental officers, and above all to our overwhelming superiority of resources, but not to general-ship, and thinks that the nature of the country we fought over made combinations and changes such as Frederick, Napoleon, and Marlborough conceived on the battlefield, under the inspiration of actual conflict, absolute impossibilities. He says that when Pope, Burnside, Hooker, or Grant found himself obliged to deliver a battle, the corps commanders were assembled and told to "go in" and do the best they could; and whether they succeeded or failed, to act on their own judgment. They gave like instructions to generals of divisions, and so downwards, and each colonel took in his own regiment to fight on its own front without concert or system. This is exaggerated, but there is some truth in it. Barlow overstates the case a little—in a half-affected spirit of self-depre-ciation pardonable in a man who fought his own way from the ranks to the grade of major-general, and was left for dead on two such fields as Antietam and Gettysburg. No doubt the rebel practice was primitive or Homeric, no less than ours. . . .

December 20. . . . In Congress, Thaddeus Stevens and Charles Sumner seem inclined toward open war on the President's "reconstruction" policy, as perilously lenient. They may be right. There is room for diverse opinion pro and con. But Sumner was wrong in denouncing the

President's report or communication on Southern affairs as "a white-washing message, like Pierce's on Kansas." It was certainly an indecorum, and he was rebuked for it by his own friends.

December 28. Professor Joy came in last evening to consult about a meeting to be got up next week as to the Paris Exposition of 1867 in the collection of material for which, illustrating the mineral resources of this country, he evidently meant that the School of Mines should take the lead. It seemed a politic plan. But today came a long letter from Barnard throwing ice water on the project, and declining to have anything to do with the proposed meeting. There are signs of some little discord between president and professor. I shall walk warily and keep outside the squabble if there be any.

December 30. George Anthon came in with last reports from the Superior Court room—disgusted and furious—at eight o'clock. The discordant jury called for instructions several times during the day, last time at five o'clock. Then they asked for certain documentary evidence which was given them, and it looked as if this documentary evidence were called for to justify the minority in consenting to a verdict. But [Judge Samuel B.] Garvin spoiled this hopeful prospect by telling the jury that he would come downtown at nine this evening to ascertain whether they had agreed, and that perhaps he would discharge them if then still discordant. Of course, the two or three stupid or bribed jurors will hold out for so short a space, and I dare say the jury is discharged before this, and there is no verdict. Cram is much mortified and disappointed. But he has fought this fight most splendidly. George Anthon and Charley Strong admit now that they have undervalued his ability. Pete is not likely to push this suit any farther, and it therefore results in a triumph of noisy and unscrupulous vindictiveness over the plainest right. But the Stevens people will stand worse with this quasi-victory than they would if Pete Strong had got a verdict.

On December 31, the Strong divorce case ended in a hung jury. It was understood that the jurors agreed in favor of the plaintiff, Peter R. Strong, on all points but one—the recriminatory charge that he had been guilty of adultery himself. Bribery of two jurors was vehemently alleged, and vehemently denied. The Tribune *summed up the general verdict on this "nauseous exposé of domestic depravity." "Everyone is wondering," it remarked, "what must have possessed the parties and their influential friends that they did not somehow keep the matter out of court."*

December 31, SUNDAY.   I'd give fifty dollars, though I can ill afford even fifty cents for any personal luxury, to have been in the Superior Court at nine this morning to see the dénouement of this memorable trial. The jury came in and declared they could not agree; unanimous on the issue as to defendant's guilt and on that of condonation, but ten to two on the issue of recrimination. The two were James Rufus Smith and J. J. Sigler. Cram moved that their verdict as far as it went be received and recorded. Garvin denied the motion. He was probably right, but had I been in his place I should have granted it. It could have done no one any hurt. Then (the Court having declared the jury discharged) one of them (Worstall) "asked leave to make a statement." Garvin rather discouraged him. But another of them made the same demand, and then it appeared that this wretched fellow Sigler had been seen by his fellows leaving the Court room in company with one of J. A. Stevens, Jr.'s, detectives, "Arthur Jones" by name, and had declared immediately after that interview that he never would agree to a verdict for the plaintiff. Another juror declared against Smith as obstinate and probably bought. Cram made a brief speech about the power of money to buy jurors as well as witnesses, and the ten responded, "That's so." Robinson was getting their signatures this afternoon to a certificate of the facts for publication. The Stevens side will claim this as a victory, but it's like Fredericksburg and Chancellorsville, an attack repulsed with terrible loss. Pete has failed to get his verdict, so his wife retains her dower estate in his property, but her family is disgraced and her guilt is proclaimed at every point on earth reached by a New York newspaper. Were ever people so maddened and blinded by sheer vindictiveness and pugnacity? I am glad to find that Cram is inclined to go on. He should serve a notice of trial before the week is over.

1866

A WASHINGTON VISIT · WAR BETWEEN JOHNSON AND
CONGRESS · CHOLERA INVADES NEW YORK ·
FENIANS ROUTED IN CANADA · TRIUMPH
OF RADICALS IN FALL ELECTIONS

❦

*The year 1866 opened with all the political barometers predicting a storm,
for the quarrel between President Johnson and the Radicals over Reconstruction was about to become violent. Strong continued to be much engrossed
by duties outside his law office; that is, by Columbia, Trinity, the Bank for
Savings, and the Sanitary Commission, now fast winding up its affairs. At
last, however, he had some time for social relaxation. On January 7 he and
Mrs. Strong went to a musical party at Professor Joy's on Forty-ninth
Street, where the guests included President Barnard, the astronomer Lewis
Rutherfurd, the sculptor John Rogers (of the well-known statuette groups),
and Bayard Taylor. "Would there were more houses in the city like Joy's!"
exclaimed Strong. "Its elegant, refined appointments are a standing protest
against the barbaric costliness of our Fifth Avenue drawing-rooms." Four
days later the Strongs themselves gave a reception. "It's so long since I have
attended upon any large fashionable gathering," wrote the diarist, "that I
felt like an owl in daylight. I recognized scores of faces, but could not recall
the names that went with them, and went about asking everybody in a whisper
who everybody else was." Music was furnished by Karl Wehli, the Austrian
composer and pianist, who sent up his own Chickering for his selections. Among
those present was Anson Burlingame, the American minister to China. Later
in the month came a reception by President and Mrs. Barnard, their Forty-
ninth Street rooms well filled. "Barnard and his wife 'entertain' with a
simple, agreeable heartiness of manner. I esteem him more and more highly."
But the noise during the music annoyed Strong. "Our civilization is still of*

low grade. An assemblage of average New Yorkers will gossip and cackle during one of Mozart's melodies or Beethoven's symphonies."

Inflation gripped the nation, causing great distress among middle-class folk like the Strongs. At Columbia College, the faculty suffered so much from the rise in the cost of living that a special committee of the trustees on salaries decided, on January 15, to give the whole academic staff permanent increases, and also to make a temporary 25 per cent addition to salary for the next two years. Strong thought this bare justice in view of "the present ruinous pauperizing cost of everything." He also thought that Chandler, as head of the School of Mines, ought to have an increase of $1,000 a year. "He is the most self-sacrificing and earnest of men, to say nothing of his scientific ability and attainments." Despite his busy life, the diarist maintained his own scientific tastes, attending meetings of a small Microscopical Society at Clinton Hall. Early in the year we find him still deeply distressed by the divorce case which involved his cousin Peter. He was meanwhile much interested in a lawsuit which the Bank for Savings had carried to the Supreme Court—one concerning a clause of the internal revenue laws; and he presently journeyed to Washington to argue the case before Chief Justice Chase.

January 11, THURSDAY. Dined at seven. Accompanied Johnny through another stage of Caesar's campaign in Gaul (I suspect that great captain of lying horribly as to the magnitude of the forces opposed to him), and then went to the annual meeting of the Union League Club, which adjourned at half-past ten. Did not wait to learn the result of annual election. John Jay is doubtless elected president. I voted against him, as did others. . . .

January 12. Standing Committee of the Sanitary Commission at Twelfth Street tonight. . . . We decided this day to publish the evidence of Andersonville prisoners collected by our Second Commission or Committee of Investigation at Annapolis. It has been asleep these ten months in the hands of the Rev. Walden of Philadelphia, and I had forgotten all about it when I received a letter from William Henry Rawle offering to prepare it for publication and to write a report to be published with it. We accepted his offer *nem. con.* Of course, we shall be blamed for opening an old sore, for not letting bygones be bygones, and so forth. But I see little sign of fraternal feeling south of the Potomac, so little that it is not worth considering. The truth of our former report (which was, by the way, a rather weighty and memorable paper) was denied by Richmond papers, by rebel representatives on the floor of their so-called Congress at Richmond, and by the Honorable Mason in the London *Times.* So we are fully entitled to confirm it by another batch of depositions, even if we thereby offend the sensibilities of Rebeldom. The treatment of national prisoners at Libby and Andersonville is an important historical question. ... .

R. B. Minturn's funeral is tomorrow afternoon at two at the Church of Holy Communion. I would attend, but a meeting of the Law School Committee is called for that hour. The services will be most fully attended. No man in New York will be so missed by the charitable and public-spirited people of the community and by the poor and needy.

We were allies in 1854, in the cause of St. Luke's Hospital. In 1857 he became party to an attack on the corporate rights of Trinity Church, and I rather withdrew myself from his acquaintance till 1861, when a common feeling about rebellion and treason had brought us heartily together again. For Minturn was not only a most generous giver to every worthy object, private and public, but a patriotic supporter of the national cause with his money and his personal influence. Whatever faculty of hating was in his kindly temper was bestowed on rebels and their sympathizers.

January 19. The House has passed the bill for Negro suffrage in the District of Columbia, and by a two-thirds vote. I think the Senate will pass it, and I do not expect a veto from Johnson. The whole question is full of difficulties and conflicting rights. No statesman ever had a more knotty problem set him by destiny. But whatever doubts there may be as to South Carolina and Mississippi, I approve of Negro suffrage in the District, for it will de-Southernize and nationalize the atmosphere of the national capital.

The cleavage between the Radical Republican extremists in Congress and President Johnson was steadily growing wider. As yet, however, no open and irreconcilable break had occurred, and most Republicans still hoped to stand behind the Chief Executive. A majority of them, as Rhodes says in his history of this sad era, were down to mid-February nearer to the policy of Johnson than to that of Charles Sumner and Thaddeus Stevens. But the course taken by the Southern States made it difficult for the President to rally the popular support that he needed. During the period from October, 1865, to

March, 1866, the Southern legislatures passed a series of laws dealing with the freedmen—the so-called "black codes"—which seemed to Northern observers very unfair. They gave the black man a grudging and partial measure of civil rights; while they applied to him a variety of harsh criminal provisions. The new laws on vagrants and contract labor seemed likely, in various parts of the South, to permit the establishment of a system of peonage in place of slavery. Negroes were forbidden to hold public meetings, their movements were restricted, and in some states they were not allowed to bear arms. Their position in the courts was also generally made inferior to that of the whites. These "black codes" were in general well meant, for the Southerners had a problem of frightful complexity with which to deal. But the North, which failed to understand this complexity, viewed them as cruel and malignant. The observations of Strong were typical of those of a host of other observers.

January 25. . . . *How* shall we deal with our Southern malignants? What shall we do with them? We cannot afford to let them back into the Congressional seats they left so unceremoniously and defiantly and truculently five years ago. We cannot leave our black soldiers, now mustered out, to the mercy of their late masters. We have the Southern wolf or hyena by the ears. Letting go would be ruinous. Holding on awhile is inconvenient. I prefer to hold on awhile, as the less of two evils, and belong (I suppose) to the Radical Party. It seems clear that no Northern man, no Yankee, can live at the South in any moderate safety yet. Negroes are oppressed, tortured, and murdered by their *ci-devant* owners. We may have to undertake another civil war. If we do, it will be waged in most grim and bitter earnest, with no scruple about the summary hanging of rebels and traitors. Troubles and taxes have taught us much. We disincline to hang J. Davis because he and we were equally untaught as to the value of civil order and the criminality of rebellion, five years ago. We know better now. Woe to the next gentleman that sets up a rebellion.

January 27, SATURDAY. . . . To Philharmonic concert. Mozart's Symphony No. 1 in D, and the *Melusina* overture were delightful. Mr. Wehli's piano was very good. But for *finale* we had Berlioz's overture or symphony entitled "Episode in the Life of an Artist," with a page of printed programme setting forth that the artist must be supposed to have fallen in love, to have become much worried, nervous, and bothered thereby, to have taken a narcotic, to have passed a restless night, and to have dreamed that he saw the beloved object at a ball (second movement), that he went into the country and heard shepherds tootle pastoral melodies (third movement), and that he murdered his beloved object and was about to be hanged (fourth movement). (I hope his dream came true and he was hanged.)

> " 'S death, this would make a man spew!"
> Mr. Smith, in *The Rehearsal*. . . .

February 1. Every symptom of Southern temper is bad. It seems to grow worse rather than better. The South is crushed for the time, but the more bitter and vindictive for its humiliation, and fuller than ever, even, of sectional, anti-national, traitorous impulses. Nothing but physical exhaustion keeps the Southern Hyena from instantly flying at our throats again. The beast is whipped into temporary submission, but utterly untamed. It will not be domesticated in our day, if ever.

> "Stern looks the Fiend, as frustrate of his Will,
> Not half sufficed, and greedy yet to kill."

There is a quarrel among his keepers, much to be regretted. The Republican party is cracked, and the crack is spreading and widening. Andrew Johnson seems more and more inclined toward what is called conservatism, and Raymond leads a "Conservative" party in the House. His party is small, but will grow in the sunshine of executive favor. The "Radicals" are firm. I am sure their doctrine is gaining ground with the people. Every change I notice in anyone's political sympathies is that way. Almost every one has changed a little during the last six months, and become a little more Radical or Conservative. The constitutional amendment (as to the basis of representation) passed the House yesterday, 120 to 46.[1] Expediency, abstract right, and common sense agree in calling for some amendment of the Constitution there anent, and this seems a judicious amendment. The President is said to disapprove it. The Hon. Thaddeus Stevens belabored the President in debate yesterday, loudly, coarsely, and unwisely. Brooks, Win Chanler, and the Devil chuckled over Stevens's oratory, no doubt.

February 3. . . . Bidwell and Charley keep tormenting me to go to Washington for this Savings Bank case on Monday. . . .

February 10, SATURDAY. I have seen the face of the Supreme Court

[1] That is, the Fourteenth Amendment, defining citizenship, declaring that no state might abridge the privileges or immunities of citizens, and stipulating that any state which denied the ballot to male citizens over twenty-one should have its representation in Congress proportionately reduced.

of the United States, and yet live (though with a slight headache). Got home last night at six-thirty, too tired to journalize.

To Washington *Monday*, 5th inst., by seven-thirty train. Severely cold. River so ice-blocked that the ferry boat had to back into her dock when half way across, and take a fresh start. She reached Jersey City at last, crashing her way through a great ice field that stretched northward without visible boundary. Railroad ride was arctic. Everything sealed up with clear frost all the way to Washington; every little water-course dead, Gunpowder Creek and other streams sheets of ice.[2] Washington itself for once in a state neither of dust nor of mud, but of congelation. People said to be skating on the Potomac, and that river frozen nearly across. Comfortable room at Willard's, but in a corner of that caravansary so remote that I was two days learning the way to it. Came near providing myself a hatchet wherewith to "blaze" the corners of the multiplex corridors.

Discoursed with Judge [William F.] Allen (whom I like much and find worthy of all regard and respect), Benjamin Silliman, William E. Dodge (who is likely to oust Jem Brooks from his seat in the House); Maclure (just from New Orleans), Sam E. Lyon, [William M.] Evarts, Burrill, and others.

Tuesday was clear and growing mild. Washington streets, and Pennsylvania Avenue in particular, began assuming one of their two normal conditions, namely, that of mud. After breakfast, Judge Allen told me I must take part in the argument of our case, and must *reply*, because (relying on Bidwell to reply) he had prepared himself for the opening. My hair stood on end at the suggestion. But he reminded me that the Supreme Court allows counsel only two hours each, and will hear two counsel on the same side. If he alone were heard for the plaintiff, he would be compelled to confine himself to one of his two hours in opening, and the other in reply, while the defendant, represented by Mr. Attorney-General Speed and the Assistant Attorney-General (Ashton of Philadelphia, a very respectable fellow), would be entitled to the attention of the Court for four hours between them. Whereas, if I consented to take part in the argument, he could open, and I could reply, for two hours each. So I thought it my duty to give a despairing assent. With Judge Allen to the Capitol and Supreme Court room.

---

[2] Strong had recorded on January 8 "the coldest day for sixty years," with a wind that "blows lancets and razors." His house that day, with both furnaces in full blast and fires in every story, had an interior temperature of 38.

At eleven o'clock, there was the voice of one crying: "The Honorable the Chief Justice and the Associate Justices of the Supreme Court of the United States!" Mr. Chief Justice Chase and his associates in their judicial robes marched solemnly into the courtroom, everyone rising. The Court bowed to the Bar, and *vice-versa*, and the crier "made an oyez," finishing it off with "God save the United States of America and this Honorable Court!" I wish more of these Old World formalities survived among us. Judge Allen then moved my admission as attorney and counselor of the Court, and "introduced me." I bowed, and was bowed to by the Bench, took the usual oath in the courtroom (that I would demean myself decently as an officer of the Court and obey its directions), and then went to the Clerk's office and took the special "iron-clad" oath that I had never designedly given Rebellion any aid or comfort, which oath I took most honestly and heartily, with no mental reservation whatever—thank God.

Then the Court proceeded to hear the "Bankers and Brokers Cases" under the Internal Revenue Act.[3] Mr. Attorney-General opened and closed for the Collector; Judge Allen, John Burrill, and Evarts *in contra*. All three acquitted themselves well, Evarts *very* well. I have heretofore thought him overrated. This case was disposed of sooner than was expected. Our case was called a little after two. Judge Allen opened, with great ability, and the Court adjourned at three.

Wednesday (cloudy, dull, and drizzly). Judge Allen resumed and finished his opening. Ashton thereupon argued for the defendant at great length. His argument was clever and lawyer-like though disingenuous, and his manner and delivery forcible and impressive. Not more than one-fifth of it was devoted to the merits; all the rest was on the question of jurisdiction. Then the Attorney-General took up his parable, and made a good, effective stump or platform speech, mainly on the question of jurisdiction, maintaining the propositions of his printed brief (as did

[3] Now generally referred to as the Bank Tax Cases, and others. The issues concerned the constitutionality of the national banking system established in 1862, and the validity of the various state laws which laid taxes on the notes and business of the national banks, and on the federal securities held by state banks as part of their capital. At least nine cases dealt with these general issues, of which Strong's was The Society for Savings *vs.* Coite (6 Wall 611). The Supreme Court took a firm position in defense of national power. It held that the notes, operations, and shares of national banks could not be taxed without explicit Congressional permission, for such banks were an agency of the national government. It also held that investments by state banks (or others) in federal securities could not be taxed by the states. Attorney-General James Speed of Kentucky (1812-1887), who had been appointed by Lincoln in 1864, delivered the principal argument for the government.

Ashton) and reminding me strongly of the arguments of the Crown lawyers under Charles I and James II, when questions of Prerogative and Dispensing Power were discussed in Westminster Hall. They had the audacity to insist that the Internal Revenue Act, giving authority to the Commissioner of Internal Revenue to decide "on appeal" questions as to taxes levied by his subordinates, *ousted* all courts of law and equity, state and federal, of all jurisdiction over those subordinates, and their official head, and subjected all the business and all the property of the country to the discretion of an irresponsible executive officer. I could not have believed my ears had not this monstrous proposition been clearly enounced in the Attorney-General's brief and maintained in all its atrocity in twenty printed pages of "black on white." I could not but remember what Macaulay says of the Solicitor-General's argument (Sir William Williams) in the *Trial of the Seven Bishops*. "The audience stood aghast at the effrontery of the venal turncoats." I have no reason to suppose Mr. Attorney-General Speed a "turncoat," but his effrontery is unmatched within the last hundred years.

I hoped the defense would keep the Court occupied till the hour of adjournment. But I saw the Attorney-General was beginning to run emptiness and would soon dry up. I was sickening for a lunch after my early breakfast; was faint and heart-sunken. My hopes were in vain. The Attorney-General sat down at two o'clock, the Chief Justice bowed toward me, by way of invocation, and I got on my legs as one gets into a cold plunge bath. Once up—the ice broken—I was self-possessed and comfortable, and trotted out my little notions and lectured the Supreme Court "like a Dutch uncle" (why Dutch?). I was heard with the utmost courtesy and attention. Court adjourned at three P.M. On the Capitol stairs I crossed Judge Nelson diagonally and took off my hat. He stopped me most kindly, shook hands, introduced me to Judge Clifford, said sundry civil things, and as we parted remarked *sotto voce*, "I think you were a little nervous when you *began* your argument, Mr. Strong, but you will be all right tomorrow morning."

In fact, I was not nervous or alarmed. I was merely suffering physical depression for want of an oyster or two. But how kind this was of old Nelson; how good in the learned old judge to think of an encouraging word for the goose and greenhorn of an advocate! We generally forget the importance and value of such kind offices. This makes me Nelson's backer and supporter to my life's end!

Next morning (*Thursday*) I took up my parable once more. I had expatiated the day before on the distinction between banks and savings banks and tried to shew that they differed generically, and not as species of the same genus. (This was the best part of my argument, and perhaps presented certain considerations that Allen had not brought home to the Court. Judge Wayne was struck by a point I made on the construction of paragraph 79 and asked me to read the section again. It is a decisive point. Allen had made it when opening, but he had so much matter on his hands that he was obliged to talk very fast, and it had made no impression.) When Court opened I spent a little time on the verbal construction of the act, and then took up the question of jurisdiction. I think I treated both decently well. I had made some little progress in discussing the Attorney-General's atrocious position that all courts of law and equity are ousted of jurisdiction over assessors and collectors by the Internal Revenue Act, when Chase, C.J., and Nelson, J., laid their heads together a moment, and the former said, "I don't think we need hear you any further on this branch of the case, Mr. Strong."!!! Was ever Attorney-General so snubbed? But it was a blow to me, for I had meant to say a great many fine things about Charles I and James II, Dispensing Power, Strafford, Courts of High Commission, centralized despotism, and the like. So I had nothing left to do but prose a little on the quite unimportant question of our right to an injunction as "provisional remedy against which Ashton had told the Court the Internal Revenue Department had always objected." I suggested that such "objections" were an unpleasant novelty, and that we were entitled, anyhow, to directions from a court of equity as to the administration of our trust—with its 50,000 *cestuis que trust*. And there the case stands. The Court is with us on the question of jurisdiction. Nelson, the weightiest member of the Court, on the merits, and I think Wayne, too. But we shall be beat, of course. It's my luck. . . .

Went with Allen to the Congressional Library and spent an hour looking over Gould's gorgeous monograph of the *Trochilidae* with a sense of great relief and comfort, such as one feels when set free from the hands of his dentist. To the Sanitary Commission office, looking into affairs which need action by the Committee. . . .

Congress was faced with the question whether enlarged measures for the protection of the liberated Negroes in the South were necessary. Deciding that they were, it passed early in February a bill greatly increasing the authority of the chief protective agency, the Freedmen's Bureau, and extending its life for one year. When this came before the President, he gave it careful study and took expert advice. Then he vetoed it on the ground that it was unconstitutional, adding as "another very grave objection" the fact that it had been passed by a Congress in which eleven states of the Union still had no representation. He avowed, however, that he shared the desire of Congress to give the Negro adequate protection. The veto message was very strong and made a deep impression. When the Radicals in Congress attempted to repass the bill over the veto, they failed of the necessary two-thirds.

February 20. Today's sensation was Johnson's veto of the *Freedmen's Bureau* Bill. It seems a tough paper, not easily to be answered. It goes far toward demonstrating certain provisions of the bill not only impolitic and open to most mischievous abuse, but plainly repugnant to the Constitution. Johnson states his objections clearly and cogently. Had he contented himself with stating them, all but a few extremists would heartily approve this message (though the New York *World's* delectation over it disgusts all who love the nation more than they love the South). But after giving his sufficient reasons for this veto, in statesmanlike style, Johnson goes out of his way to lecture Congress for not letting in Southern Representatives, wherein I think he shews himself impertinent, and what's worse, radically unsound. I am sorry, for I do not want to lose my faith in Andy Johnson.

February 22, THURSDAY. A "legal holiday" now, so all banks are closed; Custom House, Treasury, and many stores. Wall Street is left as a lodge in a garden of cucumbers. After an hour or two there, I walked uptown. Weather genial, with the least little trace of spring flavor, and I found my overcoat a burthen. Broadway so packed with people who wanted to see the sojers that I had to work my way home by side streets.

Tonight is the grand reception of Lieutenant-General Grant at the Union League Club. Ellie was to have gone, escorted by Frank Howe and his wife. I would not have been squeezed in the crowd for fifty dollars. But she was feeling out of order at dinner time, and gave up the reception. I went off after dinner for a Standing Committee meeting of Trinity Church. But I found at Madison Square an almost impenetrable crowd watching the most brilliant beautiful fireworks. Stopped with the crowd till it was evident either that the Committee had got a quorum and did not want me, or that its members, if less than a quorum, had dispersed.

The "Freedmen's Bureau" bill failed of a two-thirds vote in the

Senate (30–18), so the "Radicals" are defeated, and you can distinguish a Copperhead a hundred yards off by the light that beams from his countenance. Confounded be their breed! The veto was wise, but I wish it did not give these caitiffs such keen enjoyment. H. W. Beecher says in the course of a long lecture or address defending it and the President's general policy, that an executive officer declining power and patronage so immense as Congress offered Johnson by this bill is something new under the sun. It's quite true. But the more extreme Republicans in both Houses are furious. Senator Anthony of Rhode Island writes Mrs. Charley Strong in depths of despair. "The party is broken up," he says. "No such scene in the Senate since Buchanan's time, when Senators from seceding states were going out." But he is an easy man to scare. It is clear, however, that moderation and temper are needed to keep the party from a split, and that "Radical" leaders have shewn little sign of either, since this bombshell burst among them.

February 23 . . .

Affairs of state look stormy. The vital force of government has for some time been decomposing into negative and positive, and these hostile electricities have now so accumulated apart, and intensified each other by mutual reaction, that their flash and crackle begins to be alarming, and there may well be a grand detonating discharge before equilibrium is restored. God grant the discharge may not smash the apparatus!

There was a "Conservative" meeting at Cooper Institute last night to "sustain the President." It was large and enthusiastic, and got up by men of weight, political purity, and unquestioned loyalty, Republicans and War Democrats. An important move. Seward was chief speaker, and his speech reminds one of his "ninety day" prophesyings five years ago. "All is just as it should be. Everything is serene. The Ship of State has weathered the storm and is as good as safe in harbor. To be sure, there is a little debate between her officers whether she should proceed to her anchorage on this tack or the other, but nobody will be hurt whichever way they settle it. Don't worry yourselves, my friends and fellow citizens! Our safety, comfort, and prosperity are *res judicata*. The universe is estopped from disturbing us in their enjoyment." Three cheers for Seward!

This meeting was significant. It shewed that discord in the National or Union party (i.e., the North, *minus* Copperheads) is beginning to formulate itself. But far more significant was Mr. President Johnson's long speech yesterday at the White House addressed to a mob that waited on him and asked for a few remarks. It is a very long speech and full of repetitions. Its bouquet seems to me (as to others) to be that of Old Bourbon, largely imbibed by the orator just before taking the rostrum. Anyhow it is bad, egotistical, diffuse, undignified, intemperate, unwise, and sure to do great mischief. He avowed himself at war with radicalism, and denounced Sumner of the Senate and Stevens of the House and Wendell Phillips, who is a mere private lecturer and sophist (if you will), as disunionists and traitors. He talked of Senators going about "with assassination in their hearts," and of his own indifference to such hypothetical designs; of the exceedingly moderate sum he needed for food and raiment, and talked much bosh beside.

This speech is a national calamity. It hurts us badly, and it will disgrace us abroad. The *Saturday Review* will make it the subject of an entertaining and scholarly leading article. Johnson made several good points, for the "Radical" policy he assailed is plainly open to grave objections. But so is his own. The problem is most difficult. Those who disagree about its solution ought to meet and confer with the utmost candor, forbearance, and temper. Neither party has shewn a trace of temperance or conciliatory disposition. And war being now declared, I fear it is manifest that the "Radicals" of Congress first drew the sword. This may result in an impeachment of the President within thirty days!!! The possibility had occurred to me, but I had not entertained it till a word from Blatchford this evening shewed that the same possibility or conceivability (remote enough to be sure) had occurred to him. Imagine it!!!!! Agnew says he would testify if called upon, as a professional expert, that the inspiration of this speech came from alcohol and from no other exciting cause. His acquaintance with toxicology satisfies him that Andrew Johnson was more or less *drunk* on inspection of what A. Johnson said. *Eheu!*

Johnson had made a most unfortunate speech, as Strong notes, on Washington's Birthday—though it was not made without provocation. When the Radicals in Congress failed to obtain a two-thirds vote for the Freedmen's Bureau Bill, they resentfully carried a joint resolution which declared that no Senator or Representative should be admitted from any state of the former Confederacy until Congress had declared that state entitled to representation. This gratuitous resolution was a slap at the President. It passed the House on February 20. Congress then adjourned over Washington's Birthday. On the

*night of the 22nd, a mass-meeting of the President's supporters proceeded to
the White House to congratulate him. Secretary Hugh McCulloch advised
Johnson not to make an address, and the President said: "I shall thank them
and that's all." But his old liking for a stump speech overcame him. He was
soon delivering a wildly irresponsible harangue, in which he called the Joint
Reconstruction Committee "an irresponsible central directory"; charged that
it had "usurped all the powers of Congress"; asserted that Sumner, Stevens,
and Wendell Phillips were trying to destroy "the fundamental principles of
this government"; and even intimated that some of his enemies would like to
have him assassinated. The speech did him infinite harm, although the charges
of his enemies that he was drunk when he made it had no foundation whatever.
S. B. Ruggles placed his finger on the real source of Johnson's error: he was
always a little intoxicated by a crowd.*

*How great was the change in public sentiment became evident when
Johnson found it necessary to veto another Congressional measure. This was
the Civil Rights Bill, which made the freed Negroes citizens of the United
States, with all civil rights, prohibited anyone from interfering with such
rights under color of a state law, and set up a firm national machinery for
dealing with any interferences. Johnson on March 27, as Strong notes below,
vetoed the bill as unconstitutional, inexpedient, and generally objectionable.
His reasons were for the most part sound. But some moderate men who had
formerly supported him now deserted his cause. The bill was easily repassed
by a two-thirds vote in both houses. So high did feeling now run that the
announcement of the vote provoked an excited tumult of applause in the Senate.
A deep gulf had opened between the President and the Congressional majority.*

March 1. All indications are that Johnson's policy gains ground
with the people, and that the extreme Left in Congress is losing heart.
But Southern representatives will have to "stand disconsolate," like
Tommy Moore's *Peri,* at the gates of the Congressional Paradise, a
little longer. There is still a working majority to keep them "out in the
cold." Sooner or later the gates must open, I suppose, for we cannot
always hold these barbarians as a conquered people. Their representatives
will have to be admitted, and the wolves swarm in to help the dogs guard
the sheepfold. What will happen then? . . .

All England is in great trepidation over the "bare-armed" (query:
legged?) Fenians, and doing all we shocked her by doing a year or two

since, and even more than that. Habeas corpus suspended! Military rule!! Domiciliary visits!!! Patriots by the score actually sentenced to imprisonment at hard labor!!! and all these wrongs done upon a people suspected of designing to assert their independence!!! O John Pecksniff Bull, what a diaphanous old humbug you are! Meanwhile, there is stir, no doubt, among the Fenians here and in Oireland, too. "Brian Boru's body lies a-moulderin' in the ground, but his sowl's a-marching on!"

March 2, FRIDAY. Suppose Andy Johnson, President of the United States, return to Congress the next bill Congress may send him for approval, with a message to this effect: "Gentlemen of the Senate and the House. I must decline signing this bill, because it has been passed by Senators and Representatives from a certain number of the states that form the political entity known as the United States, while the Senators and Representatives of certain other of those states were not allowed to sit with you. Had you refused to receive them as colleagues because they had been rebels, I should have no right to take their exclusion into account, for you are sole judges of the qualifications of members of your own Houses. But you have undertaken to exclude from his seat in Congress every man who professes to represent Virginia or Alabama, because the state he professes to represent was in rebellion a year ago. This you cannot do. Virginia and Alabama and South Carolina have been whipped into recognition of their proper relation toward the nation. While those states are unrepresented in the national Congress, I hold the acts of the body that calls itself a national Congress to be nullities. I ignore them and I ignore you. Go on with your debating club if you like. Your debates do not concern me. I hold that the nation is for the present without a Congress, and I shall, therefore, proceed to execute my own proper official duties to the best of my ability, acting on the theory that no Congress is now in session." I do not see why Andrew Johnson is not bound in logical consistency to take this ground, and I fear a majority of Northern people would sustain him in doing it—so anxious are we to have affairs settled, however illusory and temporary such settlement may be, and however dangerous and disastrous.

Mr. Ruggles says A. Johnson's violent, unbecoming speech to the Copperhead mob that swarmed around the White House February 22nd reminds him of the *Fille du Régiment*. The heroine of that opera is recovered from her low estate of *vivandière* by her noble relatives and trained in all the convenances of gentility, and she dutifully walks in that path till she hears one day the regimental drums as the regiment marches by the hotel in the faubourg. Then she breaks out into demonstrations of affection for her old friends and companions, and outrages all the usages of aristocratic life. So A. Johnson, stump orator by profession, accidentally made President, and stirred up by sharp collision with Congress on a grave political question, forgets the demands of official dignity, goes back to his old habits, and makes a vehement, reckless, stump speech, being stimulated thereto, at the moment, by the clamor of a rabble demanding an allocution or (what we call) "a few remarks."

Extreme Republicans denounce A. Johnson most savagely. "When he dies," quoth ———, "there will be one comfort. Judas Iscariot will not be quite so lonesome"!!! Another says, "It's bad enough to have a tailor for President, but a drunken tailor, and a drunken Democratic tailor, is beyond endurance." I see nothing to justify such extravagant bitterness.

March 5. College trustees at two o'clock; Barnard absent. He has narrowly escaped a severe inflammation of the bowels, and is still in bed. The "special order," namely, consideration of report on financial policy and establishment of a sinking fund and building fund, was laid over on account of his illness. My term and Anderson's on the Library Committee having expired, we tried to introduce the principle of rotation in office. I electioneered for Morgan Dix as my successor, but was badly beat and reëlected. Mr. Ruggles got through a resolution directing that committee to enquire and report what sum is necessary to make the library tolerably complete as a working library in language, mathematics, and science. Zabriskie made a prosing speech and got a committee appointed to consider the expediency of purchasing land for a permanent College site. He expatiated on the superior value of land on the west side of the town as compared with that of land on the east side. Told him he had thereby stirred up a hornets' nest, and after adjournment, Hamilton Fish, Lewis Rutherfurd, Edward Jones, William Schermerhorn, great landholders on the east side, mauled him mercilessly. I got the year for raising our outside subscription of $250,000 for the School of Mines, to be duplicated by the College, extended to March, 1867. Dr. Jay told me formally—and authorized me to state—that he would turn over to the College his splendid library of natural history and his collection of shells (among the finest in the world), whenever the College may have a fire-proof building to receive them. O were I William B. Astor or A. T. Stewart for a single hour!

March 13. . . . The Supreme Court of the United States decides against us in the Savings Bank Case!!! Nelson and Grier dissented, however, so that the weight of the Court is with us. The decision is amazing. Section 79 of the Internal Revenue Act defines banks and bankers and banking business. If we are within that definition I'll eat my head. . . .

March 23. . . . Library Committee—Barnard, Schermerhorn, and I— with the Rev. Beverley R. Betts, librarian, met at my office at three. Resolved to ask the trustees for a little more money; $2,000 a year for the next three years, in addition to the permanent appropriation contemplated by the "Financial Scheme." I wish we may get it. The Rev. Beverley is certainly the meekest and softest and least masculine of male mankind. Were a sea anemone or a jellyfish endowed with the faculty of speech, it would talk as he does.

Prices and gold seem settling downward a little, thank Heaven! Gold is at 128. Unless they shew much alacrity in sinking, I shall be forced to sell out, emigrate, and make Florence or Karlsruhe a city of refuge till better and cheaper times come (if they ever come), and this tyranny be overpast. That's a pet project of Ellie's. But the mere suggestion of it is as a pint of ice water poured under my coat collar and down my back. I may have to come to it, or to something worse. But I have no right to complain, for my belongings (such as they are) infinitely exceed my deserts, or rather my undeservings.

Johnson and Congress do not seem coming together again. Another veto is said to be expected. English papers are loud in Johnson's praise, which fact disposes me to instinctive distrust of his policy. It is the more strictly constitutional policy, no doubt—but it was no strict adherence to the English Constitution that saved England in 1688. No nation can live and prosper that is absolutely bound—in every emergency—by constitutional forms. The best thing old Eldon ever said was that "political liberty could not be durable unless the system of its administration permitted it to be occasionally parted with in order to secure it forever. Otherwise, liberty contained the seeds of its own destruction." We must not be too nice and scrupulous about the Constitution in dealing with these barbaric, half-subdued rebel communities, or we shall soon find that there is no Constitution left for Reverdy Johnson to analyze in the Senate, and Mr. Marble to glorify and exalt in the columns of the New York *World*.

March 26.   Spent most of this morning at the *Evening Post* office correcting proofs of Savings Bank Memorial to Congress. Gold 125. The Savings Bank Memorial is a respectable paper, but far unworthy its subject, which certainly involves first principles of political economy and may involve the worst consequences of legislative stolidity.

March 28. . . . Another veto! A. Johnson has put his foot on the Civil Rights Bill. So the crack spreads and widens. His message is less strong than that against the Freedmen's Bureau, but very able, perhaps sound, possibly a little disingenuous. I fear that these vetoes shew Johnson's sympathies and prejudices to be wrong and dangerous. I am losing my faith in him, by no logical process, but by instinctive distrust of any one who is commended by the *Express* and *Daily News* and *World*, the London *Times*, and the Richmond papers. The "restoration" he wants will crush the National Party just as that of the Stuarts suppressed all Commonwealth men. Seward, Stanton, and Sumner will have to look sharp lest they share the fate of the regicide judges as unconstitutional, bloody, murderous devastators of the South, and Lincoln's bones may be dug up like Cromwell's. There should be no "restoration" till all possible safeguards have been set up. The question "would you make the South a Poland?" causes me no shudder. I reply, by all means, if it be expedient.

April 2, MONDAY. Session of College Trustees from two to six this afternoon. Time spent mostly in skirmishing over Gouverneur Ogden's financial "ordinance" to create an "accumulating and sinking fund." . . .

Connecticut election is decided before this. Its result is waited for with anxiety. Marshall O. Roberts tells Mr. Ruggles that the current of feeling at the West sets strongly against the President. Maybe so. The loose, reckless denunciations of the President as without personal honesty and integrity which I hear uttered by "Radicals" (with whom I, on the whole, sympathize) tempts me to wish it may not be so. They are chargeable with most bitter intolerance and uncharitableness. But the opposing party, the Democrats and Copperheads of the *World* and the *Express* and *Daily News,* sin against charity no less, and are, moreover, utterly dead (and rotten) in all the trespasses and sins of political profligacy. Their peculiar boast is that Christian morals and the Christian religion have nothing to do with their schemes of public policy.

April 5. . . . They are jawing away at the veto in Congress and making much use of the *argumentum ad hominem* founded on Mr. President Johnson's talk when a Senator and disgusted with old Buchanan's exercise of the veto power. This is small business. The "Radicals" are strong on the merits, but they will fail to override the veto.

April 6. . . . This evening Rev. J. F. Young of St. John's came in to introduce Dr. James Pech, graduate of New College, Oxon., and Music Doctor, pupil of Chopin and Czerny, and a most agreeable man, who is to be nominated Monday night as organist of St. John's. After a couple of hours' talk . . . I took them into the parlor, where was Dame Ellen, and he sat down to the piano and gave us specimens of Pergolesi and of Chopin and of his own handiwork. . . . He seems so unexceptionable and admirable, of so high a grade of thought and culture and of accomplishments so various, that he must have some grave faults that will appear in time. If not, he will be worth his weight in gold, or even in greenbacks, to the music of the parish. . . .

April 9. With William Schermerhorn to Columbia College this afternoon; Library Committee. Nothing important. . . . We nearly burned up the College Friday night. Fire broke out in the assay room of the School of Mines (on the ground floor), owing to defect in a flue connected with the assay furnaces. . . . Damage about $2,000, covered by insurance.

April 11. Savings Bank trustees this afternoon. Sundry civil things said about the memorial to Congress, and a solemn vote of thanks passed. Walked up thence with Hamilton Fish and suggested to him the rather wild notion of putting up a long shanty—a rope-walk or park barracks—on the College grounds, parallel with Fourth Avenue, for the benefit of the School of Mines. Its rooms are overcrowded already, and the faculty declare there is no place to put the class that will enter next fall.

April 13, FRIDAY. The railroad-car drivers have struck, so omnibusses are overcrowded, and getting uptown and down is harder than ever. They held a mass-meeting this afternoon around the Washington statue on Union Square and afterwards marched in procession up Fourth Avenue. I heard one of their orators, an unwashed loon. He spoke grammatically, fluently, and sensibly, and with good manner and action. Would that I enjoyed the same gift! I hear of no rioting yet and of but few cases of assault on newly enlisted drivers. The police seem wide-awake.

Standing Committee of Trinity Church last night at Trinity Chapel schoolhouse. The irrepressible descendants of Anneke Jans are organizing another campaign against the church. One of them writes Dunscomb that she understands the church is buying up the claims of the heirs, and that she, being a church woman, would like to settle her claim without controversy, and is prepared to deal with the church liberally and generously. Some talk about Nelson J. Waterbury,[4] whom G. M. Ogden had retained for the church or for Columbia College, to lobby against the tax bill pending before the legislature of the state, which, if passed, would confiscate three-sevenths of the income of both institutions. General Dix said that Waterbury called at his house during the riots of July, 1863, to tell him that the draft could not be enforced, and that the Governor (Seymour) would order the New York militia regiments to resist its enforcement and to fire on any Federal forces employed to enforce it, or to suppress the riots. Dix ordered the caitiff out of his house. Pity he had not sent him before a drumhead court-martial and hanged him. The city would have been rid of one scoundrel.

After committee meeting to the Union League Club. The Copperhead papers, in despair and anguish, advise the President to summon Southern senators and representatives to Washington and to put them into their seats and keep them there by military force. They feel their party dissolving for want of office, and therefore advise the desperate remedy of a *coup d'état*. The suggestion will be remembered against them. May it speed the dissolution of that wicked, corrupt old party organization. Its decomposition would be great public gain.

April 19. . . . Committee on School of Mines sat nearly three hours yesterday at the Law School, reading and discussing the testimonials of Sterry Hunt, Kimball, and Newberry, candidates for the chair of geology and paleontology. Hunt's are very strong and include letters from Sir Roderick Murchison, Sir Charles Lyell, Professors Dana and Silliman, and others. He had had them printed and sent them to Barnard with a letter in which he said that understanding there would certainly be an election this spring, and inasmuch as he could not suppose there could be any one whose claims to the place were equal to his own, he had declined several advantageous offers from the West. This damaged him badly. Then Barnard, who abominates him, as do all the faculty, remarked quite casually and by way of parenthesis that he understood Hunt proposed, when elected, to procure a division of the chair, keeping geology as his own department, Hall to take paleontology. This settled Hunt's case, as far as the Committee is concerned. Barnard is a very sagacious old practitioner, and his opposition to Hunt is founded on most sufficient reasons. . . .

---

[4] Waterbury was a Tammany leader. He had been judge-advocate during the war, and had prepared a report on the enrollment of troops (1863) which upheld Governor Seymour's contention that New York's draft quota was excessive.

April 23. . . . There has been a scare about "Nitro-glycerine," alias "Glonoine," alias "blasting oil," a pestilent new compound, unstable like most nitrogen compounds and equaled by few of them in the mischief it can do by decomposing. Some small quantity of it exploded spontaneously last fall in Greenwich Street near Duane or Nassau Street and made much work for glaziers. Quite recently, there was another explosion at San Francisco. This was on a much larger scale. It destroyed many lives and a quarter of a million in property. Friday morning came news that the English steamer *European*, her tackle, apparel, and furniture, master, mates, and mariners, had been blown into little bits by this same devilish invention, as she was unloading at the pier at Aspinwall. Pier and Panama Railroad freight house were smashed at the same time. As this perilous stuff was known to be in the city, on storage and on sale, this news caused some uneasiness and much talk. People professed to be informed that there were "ten tons of it in a single store in John Street," enough I suppose to make a clean sweep of everything from Canal Street to the Battery. The Mayor (John T. Hoffman) acted promptly. Several parcels large enough to be dangerous were seized and were reverently carried, with fear and trembling, outside the city limits. Three hundred pounds were taken out of a bonded warehouse in Greenwich Street below Rector. Their spontaneous explosion would probably have wiped away the First Ward.

April 26. . . . Committee on School of Mines met yesterday at the Law School, Lafayette Place; present, Barnard, Torrey, and I. Also, by invitation, Professors Egleston, Vinton, and Chandler. The "Rump Committee" (for there was no quorum) agreed to recommend that Egleston have leave of absence during next month to do certain work for the Pacific Railroad that will give the School credit—taking a small, select party of students with him. Also, that tuition fees be raised to $200. Also, that a two-story brick building, 100 feet by 30, to cost not more than $12,000 (estimates about $10,300) be put up on the College grounds between the School and the President's house, fronting Fourth Avenue. This measure will be opposed in the board, but it is indispensably necessary. Without it, there will be no room for the fifty or sixty new students who will be applying for admission next fall.

People look daily, almost hourly, for news that the cholera has come, and of another epidemic probably more severe than those of 1832, 1834, and 1849. The new Board of Health is trying to clean the city, rooting up ancient nuisances, and using its great powers with energy, but also with moderation and sense. But the time is too short. To purify "Macker-elville" alone is a year's work. And that district, however scrubbed and deodorized, will never be fit for human creatures to live in till its long lines of huge, many-storied tenement houses are razed to the ground. This is true of many other districts of the town. Since the epidemic of 1849, New York has grown and extended not only in a superficial area but in vertical depth and height. A new town has been built on top of the old one, and another excavated under it. The cellars of stores on Broadway and its lower cross streets are two or three stories deep. Tenement houses tower upward, story above story. Hence, more crowding, less air-space, more of whatever fosters pestilence. There will be a violent explosion of cholera in the city the moment the spark lights.

April 28, SATURDAY. Discoursed with Mr. Derby next door this evening. He thinks the scale on which our naval armament is kept up, now that the rebellion is over, indicates that Seward means to call England to account for the depredations of the *Alabama.*

Pleasant "reception" at Governor Fish's last night, to meet the president and faculty of the College. The president was there and the faculty and trustees, or most of them. There were also Hoffman, the Mayor, Schultz, the very truculent-looking head of the new Health Board (a man of sense and energy),[5] Daniel Lord, George Bancroft, R. C. Winthrop of Boston, General Van Vliet, Charles Bristed, Brodhead, James W. Beekman, Gouverneur Kemble, Dr. Fordyce Barker, Judge Clerke, and Judge Bosworth; our *ci-devant* Professor and President N. F. Moore, now a very ancient, white-bearded man, but bright and genial still; Judge Pierrepont, Dr. Frank Vinton, and others. The ladies of the house did not honor us with their presence. After supper George Anthon walked home with me, sat awhile in a felicitous frame of mind, smoked, took a little something, and talked of *the Finn.* Fish's house is magnificent. He has much statuary, but none that I covet. . . .

May 3. Clear, but a disagreeable day. The north wind seems to

[5] Jackson Schultz, leather merchant, philanthropist, and leader in the movement for sanitary reform. The legislature in February had created a metropolitan sanitary district under a Board of Health. A few sporadic cases of cholera appeared in May, and the disease reached epidemic proportions in July and August. Before frost checked it, it had cost the city a total of more than twelve hundred deaths. The toll would have been much larger but for the exertions of the new board. As Strong writes, the overcrowded tenements, full of typhus and typhoid, the dirty streets, the inadequate sewerage system, the polluted milk and water supply, and other unsanitary conditions gave New York an outrageously high death rate.

come to us after passing over some great tract of half-thawed snow, it is so raw, sour, and penetrating. A second case of cholera is reported. It occurred yesterday in a Mulberry Street tenement house, a nasty, over-crowded Irish pigsty. The disease has, therefore, got foothold in the city, and is likely to make wild work before it leaves us, in spite of all that Schultz and Willard Parker and our friend [Elisha] Harris can do. People take the news very coolly. There is not the least sign of panic. Everybody professes faith in the Board of Health and says these are "sporadic cases." Sporadic cases of cholera seldom occur but during the fervor of summer heat. It is possible, however, that some scores of well-defined cases may appear, as in 1854, without a general pestilence. But I feel like sending Ellie and the children off to Brattleboro at once, though winter seems hardly over even yet. . . .

May 4. To School of Mines this afternoon. Saw Rood and Chandler, and went a few moments to Rood's nice little house in Fifty-second Street. I learn that there is reason for anxiety about Newberry's election, which the faculty desires. . . . Tonight Miss Kitty Dix and Rice (her avowed adorer) dined here. I went thereafter to 21 West Twelfth Street; Bellows, Van Buren, Blatchford, and I. Bellows had much to tell of his late visit to Washington and of long confabulations with the President and Seward.

May 7. Went with misgivings to our College session at two o'clock. It was full beyond precedent. Every trustee was in his place, except Charles King (who's in Europe) and A. W. Bradford. Even old half-blind Dr. Spring appeared for the first time in two years. He seems to retain all his vigorous faculties. I think Agnew had secured his attendance to vote for Newberry. But before we came to a vote on the professorship [of geology and paleontology], he had to go away and attend a funeral. One more was obliged to depart and twenty were left for the shock of battle. The preliminary skirmishing was long and sharp. Our pigheaded friend Mr. Zabriskie (alias Zbrowski) called pertinaciously for the reading of *all* the testimonials for the several candidates, and then for the reading of one-fourth of them, to be taken at random, and refused to waive this demand till Dr. Torrey withdrew [T. Sterry] Hunt's name and declared that he should vote for [John S.] Newberry, Hunt having no shew at all.

Before this, as afterwards, the discussion was mainly as to the relative merits of Newberry and Kimball. Of the latter no one spoke but in commendation. Rutherfurd, Barnard, and Mr. Ruggles pronounced distinctly for the former. I fired my popgun on the same side. The Bishop came out for Kimball, very strongly. He has personal relations with Kimball. The Rev. Haight, who, I am told, had promised Barnard to vote for Barnard's choice, thereupon conformed his policy *ad exemplar episcopi*, and declared that a man without scientific name and standing was preferable to one of the highest reputation, because the College stood too high (!) to be strengthened by any professor, however distinguished, and because the nameless professor would work harder to secure reputation than the professor who had already secured it. Was ever such nonsense? It elicited a broad grin from several of Haight's special friends, and a damaging reply from Barnard and Mr. Ruggles. Haight defended his position with vehemence and the Bishop supported him. I think the episcopal temper was lost for a little while. Betts seemed converted and convinced by this palpable sophism, and voted, I believe, for Kimball. At last, Dr. Haight and I were appointed tellers, and the ballots, being counted, stood Newberry 11, Kimball 8. . . .

Then we came to reports from the Committee on the School of Mines. Students' fees were raised, and so forth, whereupon we reached the critical question of a new building. The committee had recommended a two-story building, for the erection of which we must incur a debt of $12,000. Their recommendation was unlikely to be well received. But it was received without apparent shock, so I had the impudence to move that the appropriation be $15,000, and the building three stories high. It was carried *nem. con.* I could hardly credit my senses. A very good afternoon's work. Adjourned a little before six, and I then telegraphed Newberry, at Cleveland, from the Everett House.

The School of Mines was growing. Egleston, the founder, had at the beginning associated with himself Professors Francis L. Vinton and Charles F. Chandler, who were towers of strength. In 1864 three of the Columbia College faculty had also volunteered their services, which were gladly accepted: William Guy Peck, Charles A. Joy, and J. H. Van Amringe. Now, as Strong records, the chair of geology and paleontology was created and was filled by John S. Newberry. He had studied for two years in Paris, and had gained a considerable reputation. Though forty-six years old this year, he was destined to serve Columbia until his death in 1892. He was also state geologist of Ohio after 1869 and published nine volumes of reports upon the geological survey of Ohio. One of his distinctions was the Murchison gold medal awarded by the

Geological Society of London. His principal rival for the chair, Thomas Sterry Hunt, became a professor in the Massachusetts Institute of Technology. The School of Mines was expanding its curriculum, and though its original course of study was only three years, was soon to add a fourth. In fact, the tendency toward converting it into a general school of applied science, which it presently became, was already strong.

Old Gurowski, alias Goggleowski, alias Giglamps, died the other day at Charles Eames's house in Washington, of enteritis. Senator Foster of Connecticut writes Ellie that when this old Turk's physician told him he had but twenty-four hours at most to live, the patient replied: "A New York doctor told me the same thing seventeen years ago, and then he wanted to send me a priest. I told my doctor, seventeen years ago, that if any d—d priest came into my room, he should be kicked out. I'll kick out any priest *now* if you send him here." The poor old savage Ishmael-itish count was a man of talent, experience, and culture, but universally abominated for his bearishness and his petty malignities.

May 11, FRIDAY. Wednesday, Thursday, and today from half-past two to near six, and then from eight till after ten, at Law School examina-tion. Besides Professor Dwight, Mr. Ruggles, Ogden, and myself, the only members of the committee who troubled themselves to attend—a bare quorum. One day of this work is most interesting. After that it becomes a bore. I have attended every examination thus far and sat patiently through each. This is the best examination yet. There is no one in this class so brilliant and full of promise as poor young Vanderpoel of the class of 1865, but the average standard is very high. All are fairly entitled to pass. For the first time, the committee decided without being obliged to retire and consult over the case of two or three dull or lazy candidates. Mr. Ruggles announced this in a little speech, very well framed and highly eulogistic, which the young men received with en-thusiastic applause. A nice lot of ingenuous-looking, intelligent, culti-vated young fellows they are, with few exceptions. And it is pleasant to notice their cordial, affectionate relations with Dwight, who seems the ideal of a teacher. Was told tonight as a great secret that the class is to present him with some testimonial of regard on Monday afternoon, and was asked to attend, which I can't do. Perhaps the most promising of these boys is Nicholas Murray of Elizabeth City, New Jersey, son of a certain reverend Presbyterian who distinguished himself years ago by

certain polemical papers published over the signature of "Kirwan." . . .[6]
The School thrives. There are 117 in the Junior class. Among them are a
lot of Southerners, including a *ci-devant* Confederate colonel.

May 13. . . . Binney writes me that A. Johnson is known in Philadelphia as *Sartor Resartus*, that is to say, *The Reconstructed Tailor*. But A.
Johnson can survive even a better joke than that. Foster has lost his
renomination to the Senate. The Senatoress is probably disgusted. The
white surplices of the men and boys now introduced into the choir of
Trinity Chapel look more ecclesiastical than the pink bonnets that used
to adorn it.

May 14. Talked to Bradford about College affairs, and Mr. Ruggles
came in five minutes ago to discourse thereof. Dwight wants Charles
O'Conor made an LL.D. at the next Law School commencement, because
O'Conor is a learned lawyer and skillful advocate, and because he has
reason to believe that O'Conor designs giving or bequeathing his valuable library to the Law School. Dwight is a most true and loyal man, but
I think this cannot be done. Bradford disapproved the proposition strongly.
He is biassed, doubtless, by O'Conor's course in the great Jumel case,
now pending, which course Bradford thinks (rightly or wrongly) altogether outrageous. Bradford is on the other side. I care nothing for his
objections to O'Conor founded on O'Conor's conduct of this controversy.
But Mr. Ruggles and Hamilton Fish, with whom Mr. Ruggles has just
been consulting, seem unwilling that the College confer any academic
honor on any man who has been using his great talent and learning to
weaken the national cause and to uphold the cause of secession and of
slave-breeding, all through these years of war. It's said that O'Conor is
to be Jeff Davis's leading counsel on his trial for treason.[7] Davis has
been duly indicted by a grand jury of Virginia. (A great mistake, I think.)
O'Conor has asked government to send J. Davis to New York for free
conference with his counsel. So says Hamilton Fish. I think Columbia
College cannot confer academic honor on so maleficent a Copperhead as

[6] The elder Nicholas Murray (1802–1861), Irish-born Catholic but converted to
Protestantism, was sent through Williams College by friends and his employers, Harper
& Brothers, and became a divine of such power that many called him "the Presbyterian
Pope." His daughter, sister of the boy here mentioned, was mother of Nicholas
Murray Butler.

[7] An arrangement to this end was already being made, and O'Conor in a letter of
June 2, 1865, to Davis, formally volunteered his services as counsel. He prepared an
argument; but all proceedings in the case were cut short by President Johnson's
proclamation of amnesty, December 25, 1868, which included Davis.

O'Conor, not even for the bribe of a cart-load of law books. I will not vote for it, anyhow.

May 15. . . . The Bishop has done me the honor to name me as one of a commission to consider and report to him the best form for some memorial of *Keble*, which he designs to get up, if possible. So I went to Dr. Haight's (46 West Twenty-sixth Street) after dinner. There were Doctors Haight, Washburn of Calvary (nice person), Montgomery (who enjoys the gift of gab), Houghton, Dix, Professor Seymour of the Seminary, Professor Drisler, Thomas W. Ogden, and one or two more. We spent a couple of hours in talk, on the whole sensible. The first question, whether we should unite with the movement to get up a Keble College or Hall at Oxford, was negatived; that is to say, I objected that no money could be raised here for that purpose, and every one seemed to acquiesce. Then a Free Church in this city was proposed, a fellowship in the Seminary for the study of "exegesis," or of Christian Art (in its widest sense), and a lectureship on the latter subject, a "Keble Lectureship," nominally connected, perhaps, with Columbia College, but without academic functions; its lectures to be public and printed at the expense of the fund. I incline to this last. We decided on nothing and are to meet again.

Poor old Preston King is found at last. He was picked up at the Atlantic Docks yesterday, and seems identified beyond doubt, though after six months' submersion. They wanted me to be treasurer of this Keble fund, but I begged off. I think I must underrate Keble. Horace Binney accords him an exalted place among poets, and they spoke of him tonight as one would speak, not of George Herbert, but of an Anglo-Catholic Pindar. *The Christian Year* has always seemed to me the work of a cultivated, scholarly man, with pure tastes and keen poetic sensibility, but not of a poet in the highest sense of the word. Its moral and religious beauty, of course, are beyond controversy.

May 16. Ominous news from beyond seas. Cotton and American securities falling, for European war seems surely at hand. Moreover, cholera is developing in Northern Europe and has appeared at Liverpool. Have just made my way home from Law School commencement at the Historical Society room in Second Avenue, through a brisk thundershower. . . .

May 21. Much pulling down and building up in progress on Broadway. There have been four considerable fires during the last year, leaving damage as yet not fully repaired; among them the fire in Barnum's

Museum. A costly white marble edifice is fast rising on its site, destined to be the printing office of the New York *Herald*, a conspicuous monument, proof of the profit that can be made out of this people by unprincipled, demoralizing journalism. This structure is even worse, as an example to the public, than its predecessor. That represented the triumph of claptrap and humbug, of Feejee Mermaids, Joyce Heths, and Woolly Horses. This is the fruit of a systematic immorality, equally dishonest and infinitely more maleficent. I suppose that no one man can be named who has done as much to blunt the moral sense of the people on public questions as J. G. Bennett has done during the last thirty years. When I say Bennett, I mean the *Herald*. I do not charge all the profligacy of that paper on its chief editor and proprietor, personally. His editorial staff may be responsible for much of it. But his paper has been, and is, a national curse.

St. Thomas's Church is going down. So is the Stuyvesant Institute, opposite Bond Street, which Ellie graced as a school girl years ago. So is the "Apollo building" on the West side of Broadway just below Canal Street, where I first heard Beethoven's symphonies and much good music besides, 1842–48. So is a long front of small buildings on the West Side just below Thirteenth Street, and so on. There is much building in progress on Fifth Avenue above Forty-second Street. May Gouverneur Ogden, treasurer of Columbia College, soon have a large lot of leases to seal! The Law School wants $2,500 at once to complete its series of American reports, to say nothing of foreign books.

May 22, TUESDAY. Was waked at half-past one this morning to be told of a great fire at the Academy of Music.[8] Up forthwith, dressed, and trotted down to Irving Place. Found the Academy gutted but still blazing, and all the north side of Fourteenth Street from Irving Place to Third Avenue (including the Medical College) in ruins. So was about half the west side of Third Avenue between Fourteenth and Fifteenth Streets—a Dutch Reformed or Lutheran Meeting House on the South side of Fifteenth Street, east of Third Avenue, had caught fire, the wind setting strongly from the west, and was burning fiercely. Mrs. Christine Griffin's house is next door to it on this side. The wooden spire of this meeting-house was a most brilliant spectacle for near half an hour. When its outer cuticle, sheathing, or clapboarding burned away, its internal anatomy was revealed—a compact network of timbers, braces, trusses,

[8] The first structure of the Academy, at the corner of Irving Place, had been erected in 1854; it was rebuilt in 1868.

and what not. Every inch of this timber was a glowing live coal. The structure looked like a slender pyramid built wholly of rubies. It crumbled noiselessly down at last, in a great whirlwind of sparks and flaming fragments. Firemen and policemen seemed to work like experts. There were few spectators to bother them. A multitude of small birds was attracted to this fire, as moths to a candle. Many of them lost their presence of mind in the smoke and the smother, and perished miserably. In bed again at four. Have felt owlish all day, for I got no sleep till after daylight. . . .

There are long faces in Wall Street. Ill news from abroad. Financial panic in London, the wildest since 1825, it's said. Sundry great City houses have foundered. A Continental war, Austria *vs.* Prussia and Italy, seems certainly close at hand.

May 29. . . . Old General Scott died this morning at West Point. Did ever man with foibles so many and so ridiculous do his country so much service? Superficially regarded, he seemed all compact of vanity, irritability, egotism, pomposity, and prosiness; but till his faculties failed with advancing age, he was a very strong man. No one ever dared question his honesty. And there was a large stratum of generosity and goodness underlying his weaknesses.

To Trinity Church at half-past three through heavy rain for Mrs. Mary Cunard's funeral. "Everybody" was there. I never saw so many people at a private funeral. I heard this large attendance remarked as I came out of church, and always with the comment in substance, "Well, she deserves it. There never was a better woman." The choir was full. It did more than justice to its dreary, unmeaning music. Dix officiated, with Dutton, Dr. Hawks, and Washburn of Calvary. Hawks read the lesson with his usual rhetorical effect. I hear that poor Mrs. Cunard was killed by an *emeute* among the Irishry of her numerous household. She went down to her kitchen Monday to suppress a shindy, and suppressed it. But an old and valued servant, implicated in the squabble, I suppose, tendered her resignation. Poor Mrs. Cunard went upstairs and had a "good cry," and then a fit of hysterics, and then a visitation of puerperal convulsion.

June 1. Cholera rumors revive. A case reported in Cherry Street. Also we have a story this afternoon that the Fenians are invading Canada, by way of Buffalo. The donkeys may do serious mischief by embroiling us with Great Britain, which is probably one of their objects. To the College this afternoon; Committee on School of Mines—Barnard, Dr.

Torrey, Betts, Chandler, Vinton. Disgusted to discover that the new building will cost twice our original estimate, and that we shall have to ask the trustees to borrow $30,000 instead of $15,000.

The Fenian movement had originated in the United States just before the Civil War under the leadership of John O'Mahoney, who banded a large body of militant Irish-Americans together to supply money and equipment for a contemplated uprising in Ireland. His organization grew until it boasted of 250,000 members. At a great gathering at Philadelphia in October, 1865, they set up a "republic," with a Congress, a Secretary of War, a Secretary of the Treasury, and other officers. Each state was to have its Senators. They sold bonds, good "ninety days after the establishment of the Irish republic," and poor servant-girls and hod-carriers bought according to their means. But internal quarrels developed. O'Mahoney was astute enough to see that it was impossible to conquer Great Britain by an invasion of Canada. Some of his followers were not; and General Thomas W. Sweeny, the so-called Secretary of War, joined with the so-called Vice-President in a movement for the immediate capture of the British provinces. These "men of action" now conducted a series of nefarious raids. One body crossed the border at Fort Erie, fought with a body of Canadian troops, and hurriedly returned to Buffalo. Other groups, which intended to execute border raids at St. Albans, Vt., and Malone, New York, were held in check by United States troops. Strong's attitude, as the Fenian invasion thus broke down, was much that held by the generality of his fellow citizens.

Europe was about to witness far graver troubles. Bismarck, intent upon carrying through a Prussian unification of Germany, had made astute preparations for a war with jealous Austria. He had taken care to secure France's neutrality in the struggle, hinting at compensation; in April, 1866, he had effected an alliance with Italy, offering Victor Emmanuel the Austrian province of Venetia; and he had armed Prussia heavily. So well had he managed affairs that sentiment in Europe was generally on his side. It remained only to provoke Austria to combat. This proved easy; he sent Prussian troops to occupy Holstein, long held by Austria, and he proposed to remodel the German Confederation, excluding Austria from it. The brief Seven Weeks' War was about to begin.

June 4. College meeting this afternoon. Rather slim attendance. Barnard read a long report on the state and prospects of the College. Diffuse, certainly, but valuable, and full of magnificent visions of our future. He thinks he foresees a splendid and nobly endowed university with schools for every branch of science and learning. Report ordered printed. If these dreams ever come true, it will be Barnard's doing. He is the first *live* president the College has enjoyed in my time, and the first that has shewn an earnest desire to expand its work. Then he had a long string of small matters beside, which were tedious. Prolixity is his only fault, and he is very prolix. So we did not reach the really important business of the new building for the School of Mines, and adjourned late for a special meeting to be held a week from tomorrow. This increase in our estimates annoys several members of the board very seriously, and no wonder. I'm more annoyed myself than all of them together. But what can we do? There must be some place wherein to put the class that will enter next fall. . . .

The "Fenian" invasion of Canada was not wholly a farce. Real powder has been burned and real blood drawn. There was a skrimmage at "Ridgway." The Canuck volunteers seem to have been repulsed, but the telegrams are confused and contradictory. The invaders at any rate faced about immediately thereafter, and made remarkably good time for the border. Some gained the American shore, some were bagged by a neutrality-preserving gunboat of ours, and some by the minions of Saxon tyranny. These last are in some danger of being hanged, as I think they deserve to be. The fright and worry and expense that Fenianism is inflicting on our Northern neighbors are a just retribution for their treatment of us during the war—for their harboring and petting the vilest conspirators, assassins, and poisoners of Secessia, for the St. Albans Raid and the Coursol decision. A specially comforting feature of the case is that this "invading army" of outlaws and land-pirates appears to have been officered by ruffians formerly in the Confederate service, and therefore beloved of all Canadians two years ago.

There goes an "Extra" howling up the street. " 'Ere's the Extry— got the great fight in Canady!" "Extry! Great battle at Montreal!" I invest no five-pence in its purchase, being skeptical as to any such battle, and philosophically indifferent as to its result, admitting that it has come off.

June 6. . . . News from Europe not unfavorable. Italy, Prussia, and Austria may yet keep the peace. Fenians still on the war-path, in Vermont now, and formidable in number, it's said. Government is doing its utmost to enforce the neutrality laws, and thus returning good for evil. The Attorney-General directs all district attorneys to arrest all persons engaged in the Fenian movement. The *Tribune* thinks government is going too far. It objects to any effort to check anti-British feeling, beyond what is demanded by the strictest letter of international law. This seems a dirty attempt to make capital (and Celtic capital!!) against the Administration. It is at least a feeler that way. Very many of these Fenian filibusters have seen hard service under Longstreet and Lee. Canadian volunteers will find them ugly customers unless the sturdy ragamuffins be kept from crossing the frontier. It's said there is sympathy with them among our rank and file. If government would only practice neutrality according to British precedent, I think Canada would be in hot water for a season! . . .

June 8. Weather continues steamy, with dull, thunderless showers. Two cases of cholera in Broome Street. One was fatal, a lawyer named Frazer, with whom I was lately in rapport. . . .

A "Fenian Army"—minus artillery, baggage, commissariat, and transportation—has invaded Canada from St. Albans, Vt., or thereabouts. The President has opened fire on its rear with a vigorous and honest proclamation. General Sweeny and "President" Roberts are arrested. If Lord John Russell, etc., had done their international duty as loyally three years ago, the name of England would be less hateful on this side of the Atlantic. Sweeny has heretofore shewn himself an officer of as much conduct and sagacity as of spirit. Strange he should be mixed up with such a piece of folly as this invasion. The Canadian Irish do not rise. Their priests are all bitter anti-Fenians.

June 11, MONDAY. . . . After dinner to a vestry meeting. . . . We put restrictions on interments in Trinity cemetery, pursuant to hints from Dr. Harris and the Board of Health, and agreed to set up a strong iron railing (instead of our present wire fence) along the west and south sides of Trinity Church, so as to prevent little boys from playing leap-frog in the churchyard in church time, and demolishing tombstones.

Home. General Vinton here. Cigars and glass of whiskey.

Cholera in Hester Street and in West Twentieth Street. An epidemic seems sure. The Board of Health is acting with decision and vigor.

Fenianism has collapsed most pitifully. *Parturient Celtae, nascetur ridiculous Muss.* Their raid into Canada is a most ridiculous failure. The raiders, or patriots, are running away as fast as they can, and asking government for transportation to their homes. They must comfort themselves by remembering the prodigious scare they gave the Canadians. Had there been an Old John Brown among them they would have failed less ignominiously, at least. But there are no Celtic John Browns, and there never will be, I think.

June 12. . . . Went to special meeting of College Trustees at Law School at two o'clock. Not a full meeting. Mr. Ruggles absent, also William Schermerhorn, the Bishop, and Dr. Haight. Barnard made a rather prosy speech and moved to increase the appropriation for the new School of Mines building from $15,000 to $35,000. Mr. Zabriskie . . . made certain frivolous, captious objections to the shape in which the question came up; the report of the committee should have been fuller and more formal. These objections were fully disposed of at once by a word or two from Betts, Rutherfurd, and myself. Then this Wild Bore of Slavonia let off an elaborate speech against the motions, carefully prepared and delivered from written notes.

I never heard so much idiocy talked in the course of twenty minutes. For example, "The College was created one hundred years ago to teach 'the humanities' and not to teach applied science" (as if Oxford and Cambridge were precluded from teaching Greek because they were endowed in the middle ages to teach Scholastic Theology). "In 1832 there was a furor in England about Mexican mines. England sunk a vast amount of capital in Mexican mines. Great attention was paid just now to our mineral resources. It was a new fashion that would soon pass away. The mineral resources of the Pacific Coast were exhausted." (He said nothing about the iron, coal, copper, and so on, of the rest of the country.) "The School was an experiment and delusion—a year or two hence we should find it without students. It was said at first that it would cost the college nothing" (which is true, but the trustees found it growing so vigorously as to be worth the outlay of a little money). Then came the stereotyped fogy formulas about expenditure and debt. I do believe this stolid but doubtless well-meaning Zbrowski thinks it the vocation of an endowed college to save money out of its endowment, just as if it were a private capitalist.

Barnard replied with great effect and with more animation than I ever saw him shew. He put Zbrowski down—squelched him, disembowelled him, howked out his brains and displayed them, amid a general grin, and what's still higher proof of power, silenced him. Zbrowski had not a word by way of rejoinder. . . .

Colonel Badeau dined here and gave us many most interesting reminiscences of Grant's campaigns and Lee's surrender. Badeau's narratives are always perfectly modest, simple, and free from egotism. Being on Grant's staff, he naturally thinks his chief the best and greatest of men, and I certainly do not feel called on to dispute that proposition. . . .

June 16. Fine weather. Four cases of cholera yesterday. First, war —then, famine prices—next, pestilence. . . .

June 22. . . . "Keble Commission" at Dr. Haight's tonight. He is out of town. There were only the Rev. Houghton and Seymour, Mead of Albany, Professor Drisler, and I. We did nothing, and the undertaking will probably die out quietly. Last night at Standing Committee of Trinity Church. Drisler tells me ground is broken for the new School of Mines building. Barnard and Chandler lose no time. Ogden, by the way, spoke to me last night of Chandler's admirable accuracy in details of business. The professor, being dean of the faculty, is brought into frequent contact with the treasurer of the College.

July 2, MONDAY. . . . Europe is entering on a time of trouble. But our affairs are in no comfortable state. "Reconstruction" makes little headway, and party discords grow more and more bitter. No Congress was ever so berated as this. There are special backers of Johnson who think he has failed and thrown away his chances for want of decision at the right moment. Do they mean that he should have taken the advice of the *Daily News* and followed the example of Cromwell? They decline to say. There is to be a formal bolt from the Republican party. A convention is called for August 14th in which "every state" is to be represented. It will probably generate an intermediate anti-radical, semi-Copperhead faction, styling itself "Conservative"; in fact, the party of "the King's friends." Meanwhile, Southern arrogance and brutality have revived, lifted up their ugly heads, and seem nearly as rank as ever. The First Southern War may prove not the last. These blind barbarians are actually protesting against immigration of Northern capital. They fear the debasement of "their people." Free speech is hardly less perilous among them today than it was six years ago. Slavery being dead (we may hope it is), improvement in Southern manners is now possible. But it has not yet begun.

July 9. European news interesting. Austria and Italy fought 24th June, on a rather large scale at Castrozzi near Villa Franca. Victor Emmanuel was badly beaten, with loss of guns and prisoners. . . .

Mr. Ruggles is a little ill—not seriously, I hope, but any ailment seems perilous when its subject is sixty-six years old. This is "bronchitis," or a severe cold. . . . Vague report of a revolt in Cuba. Like enough to be true. So mean and cruel a power as Spain will get little sympathy in any trouble.

July 16, MONDAY. . . . News from Europe very important. After a series of minor defeats, Austria seems to have found her Waterloo "near Sadowa." Her army is reported demoralized or destroyed, with loss of more than one hundred guns and 14,000 prisoners. The success of Prussia is attributed to her new breech-loading rifle, which made the Prussian fire sixfold more rapid and effective than that of Austria. It is said that Austria asks the mediation of Napoleon, and agrees to surrender Venetia, and that there will be a Congress.

July 18. . . . Dawdling feebly over books of the class last to be understood by feeble men. Strange *Peter Wilkins* is so little known. Its author is almost equal to Defoe in Defoe's special knack of so describing details as to make them seem veritable. He is far beyond Defoe in fancy, and still further in purity of feeling. Poor "Robert Paltock of Clement's Inn" ought to have become a great name in English literature. It's preserved now only in a single scrap of accidentally preserved bookseller's MS and was unknown till 1835. What was Robert Paltock's difficulty? Did he take to drink?

July 24. . . . A very clever story or novel by Charles Reade is appearing by instalments in the *Atlantic Monthly*. *Griffith Gaunt* is its title. I am interested in its plot. I've felt no interest in the plot of any novel for twenty years, at least. All the parties to this plot are (at its present stage) in a very bad way. I cannot guess how Mr. Charles Reade will disentangle them. But he is a clever novelist.

Cholera prevalent. Bought twenty pounds of sulphate of iron and diffused it in water-closets and wash-hand basins. N.B. Sadowa was among the most terrible battles in modern history.

The exceptionally hot, stifling summer of 1866 found Strong in wretched health, complaining of weakness and languor. Probably one cause of this was overwork. Beside his law business and labors for Columbia and Trinity, he was much concerned with the issuance of an official history of the Sanitary Commission. The principal author was Charles J. Stillé of Philadelphia; but Dr. Bellows was to write on California's effort, Dr. B. A. Gould on vital statistics, and Strong himself on the financial history of the Commission. They ran into difficulties when Bellows turned in a chapter of "slovenly slip-slop of the lowest grade," done in haste, and they made him rewrite it. Stillé's own work, "a ton of MS," was too diffuse. As for Strong's chapter, he toiled upon it until he was sick of the sight of paper and ink. The whole city, as the heat grew worse, was in fear and trembling over the expected visitation of cholera. It duly arrived, and by the end of July had both Brooklyn and Manhattan in its grip. Mrs. Strong early in the summer visited Mrs. Paran Stevens in Newport, coming home pleased with her entertainment, but vowing that she would not be bothered by Mrs. Stevens's fourteen servants for all that lady's wealth. Strong was relieved when Ellen and the three boys departed for the cool and salubrious town of Brattleboro.

A variety of matters helped fill up the diary during the summer. Strong comments occasionally on the European war. Most Americans, he remarks, did not care a rap whether Austria or Prussia was in the right, and did not give a fig which won. But there was general sympathy for Italy and her desire to gain Venetia. A poignant paragraph on July 12 deals with the death of Willy Alston, Strong being present at his bedside. He was killed, as Strong puts it, by the breaking of the Mason will in 1853; for that misfortune compelled him to go to South Carolina to look after his plantation; he then naturally enlisted when the war began, and in service on Magruder's staff he lost his health. Early in July General Dix came to Strong to talk of a disagreeable business. A special money collection had passed into the hands of an assistant minister at Trinity; he had failed to give it to the church; and when inquiry was made, he confessed he had forgotten it. Now another special collection was missing. The assistant minister had forgotten again! Strong was much interested in Dr. H. von Haurowitz's book on the Militärsanitätswesen of the United States in the Civil War. But he could not compliment the German author on his accuracy. Haurowitz asserted that General Pope had been a bishop, and he placed Richmond on the Potomac.

The all-absorbing topic of the summer was the fast-intensifying struggle between President Johnson and the Radicals of Congress. The political crisis became more ominous every day. Behind Johnson were rallying the moderate Republicans, and the Democrats; but they were unable to form an effective coalition. The President's cause was badly injured when, late in July, a convention of Radicals in New Orleans was attacked by a mob, and some of its members, together with a number of Negroes in the neighborhood, were killed.

Johnson sent a dispatch to the Attorney-General of Louisiana which contained no reprobation of the "massacre," and which the Nation *therefore pronounced infamous. Nor was the President's cause particularly helped by the great gathering of conservative men of both parties which met in Philadelphia in mid-August. Though Ben Wood and C. L. Vallandigham were excluded, the body seemed to many observers to have a strong Copperhead seasoning. The able and disinterested men there—John A. Dix, Henry J. Raymond, Samuel J. Randall, Orville H. Browning—were overlooked. When the Massachusetts and South Carolina delegates entered arm in arm, the spectacle was derided as hypocritical. No proper effort was made by the President's followers to nominate candidates for Congress on a basis which would combine Democrats and magnanimous Republicans. And the mismanagement of Johnson's battle reached its climax when, late in the summer, he departed on his famous "swing around the circle" (August 28 to September 15), visiting a dozen great northern cities. His rough-and-ready speeches, and his general public demeanor before audiences which rudely heckled him, seemed to the country a humiliating spectacle.*

July 26.   Cholera has taken root at last and grows rankly. It is severe in certain districts of New York and Brooklyn, inhabited by the unwashed, and very severe, indeed, among soldiers at Governor's Island and Hart's Island, and among paupers at Bellevue Hospital and Ward's Island. *"Susurrat obscurior fama"* that there are many cases in the city beside those registered by the Board of Health. . . .

The town is very dull. People are interested only in the foreign news and in the Philadelphia Convention that is to be held next month. This convention will be a "bolt" from the Republican party in the interest of the President's peculiar policy. Some say it will be controlled by Copperheads, and that it is a Copperhead movement. Vallandigham, Fernando Wood, and my reconstructed client, "Vernon K. Stevenson," are nominated, or talked of, as delegates from the "Democracy." Will the convention receive those vermin? If it reject them, and if its members be mostly moderate, fair-minded patriotic men, from North and South, their conference can hardly fail to do good, though it may result in no definite action. But if a single well-known Northern Copperhead Peace-Democrat be prominent in the convention, it will surely come to naught.

July 30, MONDAY. . . . Atlantic cable laid and working. Not the least symptom of any tendency to jubilation over this closer alliance with

England; nothing like the cordial, exuberant demonstrations of Anglo-philism that were called out so spontaneously, from Maine to Minnesota, by the cable of 1858. There is ample reason for our change of feeling. Wonder how long this cable will last. Thirty days? I do not care if its wire be burned up tomorrow by the heavy currents it must require. The first news it brings is of peace between Prussia and Austria! Steamers bring us earlier news of fight. Austria beat, as usual. The map of Europe is going to be largely changed.

Congress has adjourned. Whether its "Radical" majority has done the country good or ill will be more apparent twenty years hence. But Andrew Johnson has played his cards badly. He might, I think, have prevented this split in the national party to which, as I hope and believe, he belongs. . . .

August 1. . . . The people of New Orleans have been cutting up rough. There was a "Convention" dispersed by rioters. Some forty people were killed. It was almost a rebellion. A. Johnson's course in the premises seems to have been unwise. I begin to fear that Sumner and Stevens may be right about him. A few more outrages like this will teach all Northern men (Copperheads excepted) that these Southern wolves are not yet so humanized as to be fit to share the government of the sheepfold. Will this generation of Southerners ever be fit for it, brought up as they have been under the ruffianizing influence of slavery? . . .

August 3. Cholera increases in the city, and is very virulent "on the islands." I hear there were sixty cases among the women of Black-well's Island yesterday. The Magic Cable has sent us no foreign news for three days past. There are people who whisper that it never will send any foreign news! that it does not *work*, and that its signals are irregular, and often so faint that the attending hierophants have to guess at them. . . .

August 6, MONDAY. Cholera multiplies. Cases are confined as yet to our disgraceful tenement houses and foul side streets—filthy as pigsties and even less wholesome. The epidemic is God's judgment on the poor for neglecting His sanitary laws. It will soon appear as His judgment on the rich for tolerating that neglect—on landlords for poisoning the tenants of their unventilated, undrained, sunless rookeries, poisoning them as directly as if the landlord had put a little ratsbane into the daily bread of each of the hundred families crowded within the four walls of his pest-house. And the judgment will be not on the owners of tenement houses alone, but on the whole community. It is shameful that men, women, and children should be permitted to live in such holes as thousands of them occupy this night in this city. We are letting them perish of cholera and then (as Carlyle suggests somewhere) they will prove their brotherhood and common humanity by killing us with the same disease—that capacity of infection being the only tie between us that we could not protest against and decline to recognize.

Another material change in the aspect of Broadway. Taylor's showy restaurant becomes the office of an Express Company. Chapin's Universalist or Unitarian Church (east side of Broadway between Prince and Spring streets, built some twenty years ago, used of late as a picture gallery) is being demolished. So things go. Let 'em go!

August 7. . . . The feud between Johnson and the "Radicals" grows more and more deadly every day, and threatens grave public mischief. His "Philadelphia Convention" seems likely to receive into brotherhood and full communion the Woods and Vallandighams of the North, and also any and every bitter rebel from the South who may call himself half-converted to a toleration of the national government, though avowedly so half-converted by the *vis major* and by nothing else. I am becoming an anti-Johnsonite, though with slow, unwilling steps. His policy seems to me wrong, and his practices bad. I fear the memories of his boyhood, when he was a Southern "poor-white," are ineradicable, and that he stands in awe of the chivalry. Yet his course from 1860 to 1865 does not look like it.

August 13. . . . Cholera decreases in New York, but seems to hold its own in Brooklyn. Dr. Peters has looked through the "Battery Hospital" and thinks it well managed.

Cable news important. Louis Napoleon tells Prussia that the changes in North Germany brought about by this war make it necessary that the boundaries of France be "rectified." This indicates another war at hand—France *vs.* Prussia, in which case, Heaven prosper the needle-gun!

August 14. . . . Philadelphia Convention met this morning. Rebels and Copperheads mostly. General Dix is in bad company.

August 15. . . . Philadelphia Convention in session. Fernandy Wood and Vallandigham decline to take their seats, lest they should thereby diminish and weaken the moral influence of the Convention. A good and hopeful sign. But if the Convention do its work, the Woods and Vallandighams and Seymours will be our chief rulers next year. All the patronage and power of Johnson's administration will be used against the Republican party, to which (and to John Wilkes Booth) Johnson owes his great place.

August 19, SUNDAY. The Philadelphia Convention has adjourned, after a smooth session. All debate was discouraged and suppressed. It would have been dangerous and revealed deep latent elements of discord between the South and the country. Southern gentlemen were politic enough to sit mute and bide their time. The Convention has put forth a strong, well-written address. Not a difficult thing to do, for the constitutional argument of the Johnsonists is unanswerable, except by the proposition that *Salus Populi Suprema Lex*. I predict that the fall elections will sustain the President. He has a strong case on the merits; the Radical project of Negro suffrage must find little favor with any but theorists, and the great law of reaction will tell in his favor. Perhaps it may prove best that the President's policy prevail. But I find my faith in A. Johnson growing daily weaker.

Cholera, by the by, now a little stronger. . . .

August 20. . . . Morning papers full of political bitterness. The *Tribune* calls A. Johnson "Judas"—"Judas Johnson." That is mere Billingsgate, I think. Were he a politic scoundrel, he would make fewer speeches (imitating Grant's most popular talent for silence) and would not have declined by his veto the vast power and patronage offered him by the Freedmen's Bureau Bill. The Philadelphia Convention was clearly a most important transaction. If the so-called Radicals go into the fall campaign as advocates of Negro suffrage, they will be badly beaten. Their only true ground is a change in the basis of Congressional representation such as will put the voter of South Carolina on equal ground with the voter of New York. On that position they may succeed.

August 22. To Columbia College this afternoon with a box of specimens for the School of Mines; New England and Nova Scotia gold and copper sent me by Nelson Derby. Found Chandler there, at work as usual, superintending the new building and its fixtures. It's nearly under roof now, about half its roof finished. When the whole is finished, the flooring and fitting up of the interior will advance fast.

I hear of Newberry at Buffalo, attending the American Association for the Advancement of Science and taking high ground for and against sundry glacial theories. Why don't he come here and advise with Chandler, Barnard, Egleston, and others about the details of this new building?

To Union League Club this evening in desperation. Looked through sundry stupid periodicals, and listened awhile to a dozen old codgers (G. W. Blunt and his congeners) who were prosing vehemently about A. Johnson and the Philadelphia Convention. I had read all their talk in the newspapers every day for the last month, so I soon tired and came home.

August 29. Sultry and lowering. The city upside down, looking for the advent of A. Johnson, who is making a progress to Chicago.⁹ All vehicles ordered out of Broadway. My omnibus broke down in Center Street, and I had to walk home through ill-flavored side streets. Turned into Broadway at Bleecker Street. Broadway full of people, sidewalks lined by a continuous crowd. Windows and housetops fully occupied. I saw no shops closed, however. Johnson came along at last, preceded and followed by a large militia-escort. With him were Seward and Welles, Grant and Meade and Farragut, and a lot of notables besides. There was much cheering and waving of hats and handkerchiefs. It was what is called in newspaper English "an ovation." I did not quite like the President's bearing as he stood in his barouche. His bows were a little too assiduous and too lowly, like those of a basso called before the curtain, not such as to become the Chief Magistrate of a great nation. But that may be hyper-criticism.

Surprised to find John Astor so strongly anti-Johnsonian—though he holds (as I do) that the controversy turns mainly on a question of fact, namely, whether the inclinations of our Southern brethren be good or evil. It's a very ugly quarrel as it stands. There may well be another sectional war within three years, or even a strictly civil war that will ravage both North and South.

August 30. From Ellie's letters all seems well at Brattleboro, except that the poor little woman herself has suffered from sick headache. Temple's poor little lacerated leg is slowly healing, and Johnny has been riding out with a young damsel of fourteen! Ellie purrs over her three kittens in almost every letter, and I honestly think one seldom sees three finer specimens, thank God, and may He preserve them! They will have to fight the battle of life for themselves, and to open their campaign in pauperism, unless things change very soon. Perhaps that may be best for them.

At Union League Club tonight. Special meeting to decide whether the Club should send delegates to the Philadelphia Convention No. 2. It meets on the 3rd, and the South is to be represented by anti-Secessionists. The *World* and its congeners style this the "Mean-White Convention"— a most "democratic" epithet! It was resolved to send delegates. There was much spouting, and all on the same side, it seemed. I did not listen to it all. The temper of the club seems most decidedly radical, and of an

⁹ The beginning of the swing around the circle, the ostensible purpose of which was the dedication of a monument to Douglas in Chicago.

extreme radical type. Many foolish extravagant things were said against
the President and applauded with enthusiasm. It seems to me senseless
to call him a usurper—wicked and cowardly to speak of him as having
been elevated to the Presidency by the late J. Wilkes Booth. But his
dealings with this New Orleans "Convention" are certainly prima facie
against him. I hope and believe—or incline to believe—they were a mere
mistake or blunder. Why does he not neutralize their effect by vigorous
action there or elsewhere, in Texas, for instance, where *ci-devant* rebel
soldiers are shooting a score of suspected Union men every week?

September 3. Visit from Murray Hoffman, very fervently anti-
Johnsonian, but agreeing with me that Stevens and Sumner will probably
do better with a smaller majority in Congress. The Club did me the
honor to make me one of their delegates to the Convention that met at
Philadelphia this morning.[10] Had I gone, I should have gone in very good
company; that is, Agnew, George Cabot Ward, Kennedy, John Weeks,
John Astor, and *sitch.* But it is quite out of my line. I should have done
no service. And though on the whole I prefer the policy of Congress to
that of the President, I do not want to take part in proceedings that will
doubtless endorse an extreme "radical" policy. It seems from the evening
papers that the Convention assembled and got under way amid signs of
great popular approval. This will be unlike the Convention of August 14,
which will be known in history as the "Silent Convention," because it
was held unsafe to allow any one of its members to "make a few remarks"
about anything. It was unique among American witenagemots. Johnson
is letting off one or two stump speeches every day as he travels westward.
He makes himself too cheap thereby, and he says, moreover, many things
that are not convenient. He descends to abuse of Congress, and suggests
the most dangerous notion that this is not legally a Congress, because
certain states are not represented therein. If so, *he* is no legal President,
for the same states cast no electoral votes in 1864. All this will do him
no good. *Demos* rejects any one who presents himself as agitator without
decent disguise.

Meeting in Union Square tonight—to support the presidential
policy. When I passed by at half-past eight, the meeting seemed very
small and utterly apathetic. There were more rockets and Roman candles

[10] A double convention was meeting in Philadelphia as an answer to the arm-in-
arm assemblage. A number of Southern Unionists hostile to the President, headed by
Governor Wm. G. Brownlow of Tennessee and former Attorney-General James Speed,
sat there; and prominent Republicans met at the same time. A great mass-meeting
brought the two groups together.

than bipeds. But it may have gained strength at a later hour. Whether it did or did not, tomorrow's *World* will report it as an immense uprising of the people. Henry Ward Beecher has published a letter announcing his adhesion to the President as against Congress. The *Tribune* raves over it and calls it a hideous apostasy.

Saved from an immortality of ridicule. Dr. Peters has published a book on cholera, which seems (so far as a layman can form an opinion) clear, sensible, and exhaustive of our present knowledge on that subject. This book he proposed to dedicate to *Me*. I told him he could do so if he pleased, and that I was grateful for the compliment, but that I thought he might better dedicate it to some member of his own profession—that is, Van Buren, or Parker, or Hammond. The dedication was excluded, because the preface filled up the page the dedication should have occupied, thank Heaven. He sent me a copy of the dedication concocted by himself and R. G. White, and its perusal made me shudder at the danger I had so narrowly escaped. It was a series of flourishes about my "cultivated literary taste" and "well-trained legal mind," my "knowledge of chemistry," and so on, "superior to that of most physicians," and my connection with the Sanitary Commission. This last was the only ground on which my name could be connected with any medical publication. Peters's personal partiality came near making me utterly ridiculous. He overestimates me most fearfully, and any such overestimate, publicly promulgated, reacts against its subject. . . .

September 4. . . . Talked with Verplanck about the Centennial Celebration of the opening of St. Paul's, which is to be solemnized next month. He suggests a "dole" of turkeys and the like to the pensioners of the parish.

Here is a bad business at Cleveland (Ohio), disgraceful to the country and an omen of evil. The President harangued the mob there as usual, and a most weak, egotistical harangue he seems to have delivered. The mob, or part of it, interrupted and insulted him with cheers for Congress and the like. The President lost his temper, scolded, abused those who interrupted him as cowards who had stayed at home during the war, and pretenders to patriotism, talked about hanging Thaddeus Stevens, and so on, and disgraced himself profoundly. So reports tonight's *Post*, which is on the President's side, but I hope it is untrue. If true, it is nearly as bad as the memorable Inauguration speech a year and a half ago, which the *World* and other papers insisted was delivered by the "boorish tailor" under the inspiration of strong waters. The *World* has revolved since that day, or, rather has made a half revolution.

September 5. . . . The President "progresses" and speechifies. Every speech costs "my policy" many votes, I think. No orator has used the first personal pronoun in all its cases (I—me—my) so freely since the days of Erskine, the "Counselor Ego" of the *Anti-Jacobin*. It is an unhappy mistake and may paralyze all his efforts to do the country service. I believe his intentions honest, whether his policy be wise or unwise, but this exuberance of egotism will surely weaken his influence. Seward helps him little. His auxiliary harangues are smart and plausible, but very shallow. Seward is a clever politician and has often secured many votes, but he has never secured any deep general faith in his sincerity and single-mindedness.

September 9, SUNDAY. . . . Went to Brattleboro Thursday by eight A.M. train. Lovely day and the country gorgeous to behold. . . .

No news in town. The temper of Brattleboro very decidedly radical, and so is that of all Vermont, it seems. The late election shews a heavy Republican or "radical" gain—five thousand at least. It is a weighty indication. . . . If the fall elections sustain Congress, the President will have his own unruly tongue to blame for the result. I think he had the inside track three months ago, but he has lost it by his exhibitions of petulance and egotism during this stump pilgrimage. *Per contra*, the last Philadelphia Convention did his opponents little good. The Rev. S. H. Tyng comes out against them, following Beecher's example, but neither of those reverend gentlemen has much weight on a strictly political question, though they were formidable in any controversy involving considerations of religion and morality, such as was that about slavery. The honors they won in that great battle against anti-Christian ethics have turned their heads and tempted them to enlist in another campaign with which, as clergymen, they have nothing to do. The *Herald* and its congeners have denounced them for years as "political parsons." They have now, for the first time, become "political parsons" indeed, putting themselves prominently forward on a mere question of state policy, and the *Herald* and all Copperheads caress and applaud them. Wonder if the Rev. Beecher does not feel a little uncomfortable when he reads the eulogies with which the New York *World* disgraces him.

Talked with Governor [John A.] Andrew at Brattleboro (he made an address at the Fair) and found him apparently a backer of Congress. John Schermerhorn, at the Lawrence, is fervent in extreme "Radicalism," and though he is of no great account, "straws shew—and so on and so on." . . . There is reason to think that Grant and Sherman do not enjoy this stumping tour, and Sherman slipped a little sentence into one of the speeches he had to make at some town or other which intimated, very quietly, that he was traveling with the President *by order*. And one of the presidential papers—either the *Times* or *Herald*—publishes in the report of its "own correspondence" an alleged remark of Grant's that this progress was not to his taste: "He didn't like attending a man who was making speeches at his own funeral." Possibly true, probably false, but rather smart. I cannot yet stir myself up to any earnestness on either side of this great dispute, though I incline to uphold Congress. Its merits depend on an issue of fact, namely, whether the temper of the late rebels be or be not such that they can safely be restored to their old places in the national councils. . . .

September 12. . . . The Republicans have carried Maine by 30,000 majority, gaining largely on the vote of 1864, in spite of the office-holder influence. This recalls the times of "Tippecanoe and Tyler, too."

> O have you heard from Maine-Maine-Maine-
> Have you heard from Maine?
> She went hell-bent for Governor Kent (bis)
> And with him we'll beat little Van.
> Van-Van-Van! Van is a used up man—and so on.

This most unexpected result, coming on the heels of the Vermont election, perplexes Democrats and Johnsonizing Republicans. The *World* says it is of no importance, because Maine is only a New England State. But the *Herald* thinks otherwise and seems getting ready to change front. It announced a day or two since, very distinctly, that IT would support no Democratic candidate for governor of this state except General Dix. Now the nominating convention has thrown Dix overboard, for Copperheads of the Seymour type could vote for no man who had shewn himself actively and efficiently patriotic during the war. John T. Hoffman, mayor of New York, is Democratic candidate for governor. He is a respectable person, but I shall vote against him with a clear conscience, which I could not have done against General Dix, for Dix, though not a great man, and without a perfectly consistent political record, means always right. On the whole, I think I am a "Radical." I have wavered between the President's policy and that of Congress. But A. Johnson's stump-philippics have uprooted all my faith in him. He is doubtless honest, but he wants common sense, to say nothing of statesmanship and decency.

September 13. . . . To Union League Club. Monthly meeting. Crowd. Sundry loyal Southerners present (the New York *World* calls them "mean whites"). Charles Butler was slowly delivering a long speech on the political situation. It was not a lively speech and the atmosphere was asphyxiating, so I did not stay to hear his peroration. I fear the Club is degenerating. Few of the first-rate men who used to attend its meetings in 1863 attend them now. The meetings are larger, but they are made up mostly of people who look and talk like low politicians and wire-pullers.

September 14. Went to a German bookseller's in North William Street, among canary birds and lager-bier saloons, to order a copy of certain numbers of *Unsere Zeit* (Brockhaus, Leipsic), which Lieber writes me contain an account of the Sanitary Commission. "No. 4," said the shopman, "why that's the number of which Secretary Stanton has ordered ten copies." Wonder whether he thinks we wrote the article—as he thought in 1864 that we had written everything that had appeared in foreign medical journals on the same subject. Lieber and I are in correspondence on things in general. Though a place-holder, he denounces the President, whom he calls "Moses" Johnson.

Visit from Dr. Peters this evening. He says that French physicians recognize a disease which they call the "malady of forty years." It attacks, Dr. Peters says, men who have led a dull, monotonous-lifed routine. They suddenly or gradually lose vital force and get somehow all wrong. This disease is partly physical, partly moral. Its only remedy is total change of scene and atmosphere. So Peters says I *must* go abroad, or go somewhere out of New York for a few months. He guarantees that I will come back fresh as a daisy, and as good as new. His prescription is pleasant, but he might as well advise me to jump over the City Hall. I am not in funds for a foreign tour.

September 17, MONDAY.   A sultry evening. Have just inspected the grand Democratic or Conservative meeting in Union Square. It was got up regardless of expense, particularly in the way of pyrotechny. There was an uninterrupted succession of rockets, Roman candles, "flower-pots" and "bombs," and there were sundry great elaborate "pieces" besides, which I did not wait to see fired. One was blinded by calcium lights (as they call them) and by the most refulgent red Bengolas and white Bengolas blazing in permanence at a dozen points. Chinese lanterns by the hundred were quenched and killed by these fervent fires. The principal platform (which looked down Broadway) was elaborately canopied. Brass bands were playing. People had been hired to sing and sang very badly. "The" cannon boomed at intervals. There was a great assemblage of all sorts and conditions of men. It would not have been so very much smaller had it been convoked to bear witness to the respect and affection of the American people for the memory of Christopher Columbus or Captain Hendrick Hudson. For the show was really brilliant and fine. The scenery of *The Black Crook*, at Niblo's, which is so highly commended, can hardly be more brilliant than was the view from the south side of Fourteenth Street in front of the Maison Dorée. I doubt if half as much money has ever been laid out upon the apparatus and accessories of any mass-meeting in New York. . . .

Today's cable news is that Austria and Prussia are like to come to blows again. . . . By the by, what a wonderful achievement is the dredging and dragging up from the depths of ocean the lost cable of last year, splicing it and establishing it as a second nerve of sensation between Europe and America! This looks as if cable communication would last.

Peters, who came and saw and prescribed last evening, tells me that many Democrats and Copperheads are disposed to give up the game. They think the Vermont and Maine elections the first blasts of a great northern gale that will sweep the whole country in November. I hear the same story from many other quarters. The *Herald* has changed front, and wonders Johnson does not see that he ought to adopt the "Congressional policy." The Hon. H. J. Raymond wavers. An editorial in this morning's *Times* assails the Albany Convention for forcing on "conservative Republicans" a Peace Democrat as candidate for governor, namely, Mr. John T. Hoffman, mayor, and so on, and personally entitled to all respect. Newsboys on railroad trains say they sell three copies of the *Tribune* for one copy of any other paper. This morning's *Tribune* certifies that its circulation is increased by near 60,000 since August 1. But, of course, any such certificate is of little value.

Visit from Stephen P. Nash about a question submitted to the Standing Committee of the diocese and referred to a subcommittee (Nash, old G. C. Verplanck, and myself); namely, whether a new parish should be set up in Morrisania (Westchester County) without the consent of one Appleton, now rector there. After reading the voluminous papers pro and con, I answer the question in the negative. So does Nash. Have read also two or three hundred MS pages of Knapp's Report on the Special Relief Service of the Sanitary Commission. It's a most slovenly, cacographic MS.

September 18. . . . Ellie is to come home next Monday. Thank God. It is not good for a man to be alone.

Bellows thinks national affairs very hopeful. He tells me things that indicate great wrath throughout the rural districts east and west called forth by Johnson's appointment of Copperheads to post offices and collectorships. . . .

September 24. . . . Barnard is in great glory over the new School of Mines building.

All political signs are hopeful now. Very many Democrats say their game is lost. But let us see what Pennsylvania says October 9th. If there be Republican gain there, it will be nearly decisive as to the result of the November elections.

September 25. After Wall Street to School of Mines; Barnard, Chandler, Egleston. All looks well there. . . . I am told Governor Hunt (Washington Hunt) is fatally stricken with some cancerous affection; also, that the Rev. [Francis L.] Hawks is very ill with what's supposed to be Bright's disease. Secessia will lose in them two backers who "gave it all, they could no more, though poor the offering be." Hunt gave his friends a grin like that of a galvanized corpse. Nobody ever cared much for him. Hawks's elocution has endeared him to many New Yorkers. But I suppose him a humbug. His information on any subject was malleable and ductile; he could spread out a pennyweight of gold into a square rood of gold leaf. But even I, George T. Strong, could see the utter shallowness and folly of his discourse about Mexican antiquities, and about certain MSS he knew of, and meant to secure, ten years ago. His talk proved that he knew nothing about its subject, that he was merely "blowing" at random. But he was very clever and keen when discussing his clerical colleagues —Dr. Anthon, Dr. Taylor, Dr. Berrian, and others.

September 30, SUNDAY. . . . Tonight General Dix here, Graham, Mr. Ruggles, Dr. Peters. What choice Dix would make among the several good things offered him by the Administration has been much debated in the newspapers. He takes the mission to Paris, sails in the latter days of October, and holds the naval office and its emoluments provisionally, meanwhile. Dr. Hawks died Thursday morning. His funeral yesterday at Calvary Church was attended by crowds.

With Ellie and General Vinton to Theodore Thomas's "open-air concert" Friday evening. Very respectable. Mendelssohn's A Symphony and the *William Tell* Overture among the pieces produced.

It seems admitted by everyone that the President's indiscretions have blighted his "policy" and mired his party. We shall see how that is next November. I fear the "President's party" is the old malignant "Democracy," most falsely so-called. He is certainly active in displacing Lincoln's appointees and putting very bad Copperheads into office as postmasters, collectors, and the like. I want to think well of Johnson. The statements on which one's opinion of him must be founded are obscure and conflicting. But I begin to fear that his name is destined to infamy.

October 9. . . . No news yet from Pennsylvania or from any of the state elections of today. We shall know something of their result tomorrow morning. God send us good news. If the country would avoid ruin it must sternly repudiate A. Johnson and his "policy." To that conclusion have I come, with slow, reluctant, amorous delay, for until this summer I held A. Johnson among the greatest and best of men. The carmagnoles of this recent stumping tour of his, the indecent demagogical blather he let off at every railroad station throughout the West, satisfied me that he was no statesman and that the people could not trust him as a leader. But I still believed him honest. He has so used his appointing power of late that I begin to believe him in dishonest league with rebels, and with rebel sympathizers. Loyal men (like George P. Putnam) who stood by the national cause in its darkest days are displaced, and the vilest Copperheads succeed them. This is exasperating. Mr. Ruggles thinks these state elections will prove a great cataclysm drowning A. Johnson and his "policy." God grant it!

October 10. Election news from Pennsylvania and other places is good. The national majorities fall off a little in large cities like Philadelphia and Cincinnati, for they have to contend against the Administration. The post office and the custom house and the navy yard have always been formidable reservoirs of ballots. They are reinforced now by an army of internal revenue assessors, collectors, cashiers, clerks, and detectives. These officials are the semi-Johnson party. The old Democratic Copperhead party seems a little numerically stronger from the alliance of these hirelings. But I guess the country sees the case aright and understands it.

The result of the October elections in 1866 was awaited throughout the country with the keenest interest. Four important states voted on the 8th, and they elected one-third of the membership of Congress. Moreover, the moral effect of their action upon the remaining thirty-two states would be very great. The battle between the Radical Republicans and the Johnsonian Conservatives and Democrats had been fought with a desperate intensity and had steadily grown more exciting. In Ohio and Iowa, the followers of President Johnson knew that they had no chance of carrying the state as a whole; but they hoped to win a few new Congressional seats, or at any rate hold their own. In

Indiana, their chances were better. As matters stood, the Republicans had eight Congressional seats there, the Democrats three; and the Democrats cherished expectations of a substantial gain. But the fiercest struggle was in Pennsylvania. Great mass-meetings, vociferous processions, and countless street affrays had marked the campaign. The Johnson Administration was charged with filling the Philadelphia navy yard, custom house, mint, and other offices with its adherents. Fenian discontent was expected to help it, for the Administration had displayed sympathy with the Irish.

But the vote revealed a sweeping victory for the Radical Republicans. They carried Pennsylvania by about 16,000 majority, Indiana by about 13,000, and Ohio by about 40,000. Iowa was almost unanimously with them. Their representation in Congress was strengthened. The result filled men like Strong with exultation. It was evident that the voters (who had been fed some highly misleading arguments by the Radical propagandists) had rejected Johnson's policy. "They have decided that massacre and insurrection shall not be tolerated as part of our political machinery," trumpeted the Nation. The Fourteenth Amendment, the main purpose of which was to guarantee equal civil rights to the Negro, had been placed before the legislatures of the country by Congress in June. Several of its provisions—notably its disqualification of large numbers of former Confederates from office-holding—were repugnant to the South. The great question now was whether the Southern States would accept the amendment, and so escape some worse penalties. Already various Radical leaders were talking of impeaching Johnson. One, Ben Butler, had in fact announced that he would go into Congress for the special purpose of pushing impeachment forward; and this would place one of the Radical leaders, Ben Wade, in the White House.

Cisco tells me that the Vestry (at its meeting 8th inst., which I failed to attend) resolved to sell St. John's Park to Vanderbilt. Consideration $1,000,000, of which the church gets $400,000, and the lot-owners $600,-000. I fear this will stir up a perilous storm of abuse and misrepresentation against us. "A bloated corporation"—"adding another to its untold millions, by destroying an old landmark, the garden spot of downtown, one of the few breathing places left to the city poor"—somehow "intriguing with the lot-owners to secure their concurrence"—"no reasonable man can doubt that members of the vestry pocket at least half the money," and so forth. Forty flagrant lies will be told about the transaction and

thirty-nine of them will be firmly believed except by a minority of rational
people. It is in fact a dangerous step for a wealthy corporation to take.
Our only safety is in keeping every dollar of the $400,000 out of our own
treasury, and applying that sum forthwith to some church-object outside
Trinity Church; as for example, to the erection and endowment of a Free
Church or two, over which we might retain some nominal control, or the
establishment of scholarships with stipends in Columbia College, the right
of nomination to be given to all the New York parishes. No one would
more gladly apply this money to the extinction of our debt than I, if it
could safely be done.

October 15, MONDAY.   On Thursday at six o'clock in the evening I
left the foot of Canal Street on the *Dean Richmond*. This boat and her
colleague the *St. John* are, I suppose, the most spacious and costly boats
ever built for river navigation. This boat is like four stories cut off the
Fifth Avenue Hotel and set afloat on the Hudson. There was no one I
knew on board; the night was dreary; so after tea and a cigar, I took to
my stateroom and woke at Albany, after a series of uneasy cat-naps.
Breakfast at Delavan House. Central Railroad for Utica at seven-thirty,
then north by the Black River Railroad, and at Trenton Falls at twelve-
forty. The solemn splendor of the autumn woods all the way from Albany,
and at Trenton Falls, was a spectacle to be thankful for. The grass in
every field and meadow looked as fresh and green as last June, and the
pines and hemlocks retained their dark verdure quite undimmed, and both
helped bring out and intensify the gold and orange, scarlet and purple of
the deciduous foliage. . . .

Explored the ravine of the Falls after dinner, with an intelligent
contraband, "William," a professional guide over those perilous paths
for twenty-two years. I should not have ventured on them without his
watchful aid and care, for I was shaky as to my knees, and notwithstanding
the chains fixed in the rocks for pedestrians to hold on by, I felt nervous
and almost dizzy at more points than one. The "Narrows," for example,
where the waters of West Canada Creek rush down, boiling and furious
and all alive with destructive power, through a narrow gorge which a
desperate man running for his life would try to leap, and so close to the
wet slippery pathway that you could dip your hand or foot into the
torrent. You feel that if you touched it with a finger you would surely
be dragged in and ground to powder. It is, I dare say, far more fearful than
"The Strid," on Wharfe, commemorated by Wordsworth and Samuel
Rogers. Back to my inn through lovely woodland paths. Visited one

Borden, who collects fossils and minerals, and bought $20 worth for the School of Mines cabinet. Saturday morning I turned my face homeward. . . .

This has been a fine fall day. Felt perfectly well when I went downtown, but that wretched sensation at the pit of the stomach returned soon after I entered Wall Street. Still it was so mitigated that I am sure this little spree has done me good. At three o'clock to School of Mines with that nice young fellow Charley Post. Inspected all the premises with Chandler and Egleston. Very satisfactory. Chandler commended my contributions from Trenton Falls, especially a big trilobite, and a specimen of well-formed quartz crystal growing out of semicrystalline lemon-colored carbonate of lime, mixed up with flakes of what seems to be black asphaltum. I had taken it for granted that Borden shaved me horribly in the sale of these specimens, but Chandler says they are worth more than I paid for them.

October 16. . . . John Van Buren died on the *Scotia* last Sunday. "Debility," following a slight touch of paralysis experienced at Alexander Duncan's place in Scotland; and also, it would seem, some disease of the kidneys.

October 18. . . . Yesterday with Ellie to School of Mines at two o'clock. There was a little celebration of the opening of its third year. Barnard made a little speech, so did Newberry (who appeared very well), and Egleston pronounced a brief eulogium on the undergraduate corps. This was in the chapel. Then we looked through the rooms, and partook of oysters and coffee.

October 26. . . . Ellie has just come in from a farewell visit to the Dixes. Mrs. Dix and Miss Kitty sail tomorrow. The Ambassador is to join them in Paris a month hence. This is a grave loss to poor Ellie; the two houses so near and so pleasantly intimate.

But I think General Dix's appointment to the naval office in New York and to the French Embassy have not raised him in public esteem, coupled, as they are, with his endorsement of the President's "policy" of surrender to the South. I like him much and respect him highly, but he has been too much in office. He has held high positions under Buchanan, Lincoln, Johnson. Official existence under conditions so diverse proves tact and sensibility. But it furnishes no evidence of faith in any political principle. I fear Dix, much as I like him, has none at all. He was a "Free-Soiler" in 1848, a proslavery Democrat in 1860, an administration man in 1861, noncommittal as between Lincoln and McClellan in 1864, and now, in 1866, a servant of A. Johnson.

October 31. . . . Meeting of Committee on School of Mines. Only Barnard, Edward Jones, and I with Egleston, Chandler, and Newberry. We must call on the trustees for some $4,500 more to fit up our geological room with cases and so on. A painful necessity.

November 1. . . . Thank Heaven, Mr. Zabriskie (alias Zbrowski) has gone to Europe! May his stay there be pleasant, prosperous, profitable, and above all, *protracted.* I wish he could be made king of Poland. His exodus is a great blessing to the College.

Very sudden death of Charles A. Heckscher. Little Gallatin married to Miss Amy Gerry. . . .

November 5, MONDAY. . . . At Union League Club tonight. An extemporized meeting, and an oration by John Jay, Esq., which I did not hear. People seem hopeful as to tomorrow's election, though it will probably be very close. The only bad symptom is that the *Herald* supports Fenton. Its candidates are apt to be beat. Home; General Vinton here, as lively and clever as usual.

I am more annoyed than need be, perhaps, by this stolid inaction of the College Board, and feel myself tempted to have nothing more to do with College concerns. Our corporate disease is deep-seated and incurable. The board undertakes to do a great deal that should be left to the faculty, but two-thirds of the trustees care nothing for the College and are disinclined to do any work for it. They have not the least inclination to push its interests actively and keep its affairs in public view. To attend our monthly meetings, when attendance is perfectly convenient, is to them the whole duty of a trustee. At these meetings they are always disposed to vote down or postpone any movement toward extension or invigoration, on any objection, however frivolous and unsubstantial. For they are not in earnest about the expansion and development of the College and its schools. I'm a conservative, but I believe the College would gain ground if its charter were annulled and its trustees elected annually by its alumni.

November 10. Miss Helen Stanly spent last evening here. The young lady goes to Europe with her invalid mamma on the 24th. Everybody is going to Europe. The tide of emigration and immigration has turned. She says Governor Curtin tells her the Senate will not confirm General Dix as Minister, which must afflict the young lady. I predict the General will be confirmed, though Congress will doubtless meet in a bitter bad humor.

Tuesday's elections were a victory, thank God. We were routed in the city, of course, but Fenton is reëlected by a majority of near 15,000. All the states that voted on that day (New Jersey included, Maryland and Delaware excepted), voted a condemnation of the President's "policy." Another Congress will be controlled by a two-thirds majority of so-called Radicals, and competent to override any presidential veto. May it use its great power with discretion and moderation. The ex-rebel states seem utterly to repudiate the "Constitutional Amendment." Rather than ratify it, they will remain without representation. That is bad, and full of peril. But it would be far worse and more dangerous to open the doors of Congress to Wade Hampton and Robert Lee.

November 12. College Library Committee met this afternoon; Schermerhorn, Barnard, Anderson, and I. Used up about half our annual appropriation of $1,000 for the College and $1,000 for School of Mines, and then walked through the School with Chandler. I took care that Anderson and Schermerhorn saw the desolation of the geological room.

As the October elections had foreshadowed, the campaign of 1866 ended in a decisive victory by the Radicals, and an irretrievable defeat for the President. His program was now dead; the extremists were in the saddle, and meant to ride hard. The Republicans carried every state outside the old Confederacy except three along the border—Maryland, Delaware, and Kentucky. They obtained more than a two-thirds majority in both houses. Thaddeus Stevens, Ben Wade, and Charles Sumner could pass what legislation they pleased over Johnson's veto. News was already coming in which indicated that enough of the Southern and Border States would defeat the fourteenth amendment to cause its rejection. In the end, in fact, twelve states refused to ratify it, and ten would have sufficed to set it aside. When Congress gathered at the beginning of December, it was therefore in an angry mood. The Radical leaders agreed that the South must be placed under military control and required to accept Negro suffrage; and legislation to that end was rapidly whipped into shape. As Strong writes below, the Congressional majority was ready to "cut up Southern institutions, root and branch." Thaddeus Stevens meanwhile introduced the Tenure of Office Act, the main purpose of which, as it shortly appeared, was to furnish a basis for the impeachment of the President.

One of the books of the autumn in which Strong was particularly interested was C. J. Stillé's History of the Sanitary Commission, *which received favorable reviews on all hands. It was praised as lucid, interesting, and comprehensive. What was more, it afforded an opportunity for eulogies of the Commission. "We are satisfied it will be admitted, and perhaps a hundred years hence more readily than now," stated the* Nation, *"that the Sanitary Commission, from the very first hour of its conception, represented the American people more fully and fairly in its best and noblest mood . . . than either the government or the politicians." Strong's full account of the finances of the agency was mentioned with credit. He had reason to feel pleased, too, by the continued steady progress of the School of Mines, the assured success of which was greatly encouraging the progressive group among the Columbia College trustees. No member of the board had taken a keener or more intelligent interest in the School than Strong.*

November 14. . . . The Chicago *Times,* the chief Copperhead organ of the Northwest, extreme in its antipathy to Niggers and its tenderness for treason, a most fetid and poisonous ally of Rebeldom, declares editorially that the Democratic party, whereof it is a well-deserving pillar, must change front or perish. It must repudiate A. Johnson & Co., and proclaim as its first principle "Impartial Suffrage in the Southern States," or die and decompose and become extinct like the megatherium. Thus and thus only can it extinguish and annihilate Radicalism. This is funny. . . . But there will be much kicking and swearing in the "Democratic" ranks before they are aligned on this new position, if they ever can be. The editorial deserves notice only as shewing how badly their leaders are scared by the fall elections, and for the cynicism with which it avows that if any one set of principles fail to secure the party place and power, it must try another.

November 18. . . . "The South" more and more mulish against the Constitutional Amendment.[11] Its newspaper editors bray and brag and bluster and write blatant fustian "leading articles" that remind one of 1860. The Democratic party (so-called) is in perplexity. Its politic leaders seem taking kindly to the suggestion of adopting black suffrage as a "Democratic" war-cry. . . . But this move would be risky, *periculosae plenum opus aleae.* It would alienate many Southern swashbucklers, and many of the nigger-haters whose votes swell the anti-national majorities of New York and Brooklyn. All the brutal Irishry—all the great multitude of low corner-grocers, of brothel-bullies, of professional gamblers, and their decoy ducks—will care little for a Democratic Party that advocates nigger suf-

---

[11] Only one of the states of the old Confederacy, Tennessee, ratified the Fourteenth Amendment in 1866. The other ten, angered by the third section, which was intended to make all former Confederate leaders ineligible for office, rejected the Amendment. This meant that it could not become part of the Constitution until they were forced to reverse their action.

frage. On the other hand, Northern votes will no longer sustain a party that seeks to excommunicate black men from civil rights, and has been a most abject flunkey of Rebeldom all through the war. Democracy seems in a bad way.

November 24, SATURDAY. General Vinton dined here and we went to Theodore Thomas's second concert at Steinway's new music hall. William Schermerhorn sat with us. We had the pretty *Nozze di Figaro* Overture, an inane piano concerto by Schumann (*pereat iste*), and then Beethoven's Ninth Symphony, for which precious gift to mankind let all who love music thank God. I never heard it so well performed. Ellie had heard it, but without seeing much in it or remembering much of it. To Vinton and Schermerhorn it was new. I feared this roughest and toughest of all Beethoven's symphonies would rather bore them, as I am sure it bored me on my first experience of it, and my second. But all three were enthusiastic over every movement of the symphony, and I suppose their sympathy magnetized me into special clairvoyance of its manifold beauties. It is less fresh—more labored—than the C Minor Symphony, the A Major, and the *Eroica,* but surely among the greatest of musical works. I tingle all over, this minute, as I think of some of its phrases. . . .

November 26. . . . Political affairs seem troubled. The Constitutional Amendment will not be adopted. It is dead, and its death is generally recognized. A. Johnson shews no disposition to conciliate Congress or to make any concession. He is refractory and lavishes his official patronage on Copperheads of the worst and most "septic" type. Congress will meet in bad humor. Its extreme "Radicals" will get up an impeachment if they can. A. Johnson disgraces his high place and deserves to be impeached, but these ultraists, as, for example, B. F. Butler, are no less violent in talk and revolutionary in aspiration than A. Johnson himself. They must be careful not to bring on a popular reaction. To retain public favor they should be most studiously moderate and dignified in all their action. If they undertake to out-scold or out-babble A. Johnson or to put him down by extreme measures, our popular weathercock will soon be pointing the other way.

November 28. . . . Our movements on the frontier of Mexico look as if we might be mixing ourselves up with the affairs of that rotten cadaver, without reason and at risk of war with France. I fear A. Johnson wants a foreign war. Perhaps L. Napoleon will not be forced into it, but he must be sulky and sore-headed since Sadowa, and will probably not stand a great deal of kicking.

December 1. Frosty. Long council with Mr. Derby this morning. He has just brought Mary home from a visit to Boston. At three o'clock with Jem Ruggles to Philharmonic rehearsal at Steinway Hall. Beethoven's Fourth Symphony is the most radiant and joyous of all his symphonies. Nos. 1, 2, and 8 are sunshiny, but none of them so bright as this. Its final movement is as full of healthy fun and high spirits as anything Haydn ever wrote. . . .

After dinner to Century Club. . . . Large assemblage. Macdonough was absent, so I was made secretary pro tem. Newberry was unanimously elected a member. Then we went downstairs to our oysters. I discoursed with sundry people—Dr. Barnard, Mr. Ruggles, Joy, Rood, W. E. Dodge, Jr., H. R. Winthrop, Henry C. Dorr, George Cabot Ward, Silliman of Merchants' Bank, Jem Dwight, Kirkland, Kensett, Stone, the Harrisse (?) of Thursday evening, Bellows, the illustrious 'Bancroft, Jack Ehninger, S. P. Nash, Edward Slosson, Wolcott Gibbs, Lucius Tuckerman, Isaac G. Pearson, and so forth. The bivalves were in good condition; so was a great bowl of sauterne punch. . . .

December 3, MONDAY. . . . Ellie has gone with Mrs. Wallack to witness her husband's debut for the season in *She Stoops to Conquer*.[12] Last night there were here Murray Hoffman, Mr. E. H. Derby, Mr. Ruggles, General Barlow, with a brother of his, Dr. Peters, and others.

"Extras" at two o'clock with President's message. It urges admission of Southern Congressmen temperately and fairly. The Congressional majority seems ready to go all lengths against the President. The temper of its caucus at Washington last Saturday was bad and ominous. I trust they may remember that it is excellent for the Republican or Radical Party to have a giant's strength, but tyrannous to "use it like a giant," and (what will touch them more nearly) that such use thereof may bring about a calamitous revulsion of public feeling.

December 13. . . . Congress seems going ahead with vigor. It is quite clear that the Southern States (so-called) spurn and repudiate the Constitutional Amendment, and Congress seems disposed to try another method of reconstruction, which will cut up Southern institutions, root and branch.

December 15, SATURDAY. . . . This has been a day of refreshing—a gracious season of good music. Heard the Fourth Symphony rehearsed (with Ellie) at Steinway Hall at ten o'clock in the morning. The room was scarcely half-full and Beethoven's sparkling music came out perfectly clear and bright, none of it being absorbed or muffled by a great area of

[12] This was Lester Wallack (1820–1888), who had opened Wallack's Theatre at Broadway and Thirteenth in 1861, and who there appeared in many parts.

skirts and shawls and furs and all sorts of feminine fixings. The Phil-harmonic orchestra seems in very good condition this season. Tonight with Ellie, Temple (!), and Mrs. Ruggles to the Philharmonic concert. Full house. Fourth Symphony. Violin concerto in F, op. 64, Mendelssohn. Violin by Mlle. Camilla Urso. A good-looking young lady violinist apparently of the first force is a novelty. I could detect no feminine short-comings in her work. She seemed to me to play admirably well, but then I'm no judge of execution on any instrument. Ellie's judgment of her execu-tion agreed with mine and affirmed it. The composition was—*me judice*—refined and elegant, but nothing more.

Then (Part II) came Wagner's "Introduction to the Opera *Lohengrin.*" I heard its opening movement at the rehearsal of a fortnight ago, supposed it was Hector Berlioz's *Carnival* Overture, and inferred that Hector Berlioz was experimenting on a new mechanical method. I did Hector B. injustice. This "Introduction" was as bad as anything he ever wrote and vastly less entertaining. Wagner writes like an "intoxified" pig, Berlioz like a tipsy chimpanzee. Then we had a concert for the piano (Mozart), by Miss Sophie Groeschel—well played, but not up to the Mozart standard; a polonaise by Miss Urso, and then Overture *Le Carnival Romain*, op. 7 in A by Berlioz. This was the finale. I can compare it to nothing but the caperings and gibberings of a big baboon, over-excited by a dose of alco-holic stimulus.

December 24. Monday and Christmas Eve. . . . Presents came in, were unpacked and arranged in the middle room, the boys being sent off to bed. But they were hallooing till near nine o'clock in high excitement. Then, or an hour later, we had our traditional roast oysters. . . .

December 28. At 21 West Twelfth Street tonight; Bellows, Blatch-ford, and I. Chief subject of discourse our incubus of a claim agency at Washington. There are still some sixteen thousand claims on hand, which we have undertaken to see through the Pension Bureau, and so forth, to collect gratuitously. We work them off at the rate of about twelve hundred a month, but by this process the plain and easy cases are being sifted out. In the course of a few months, we shall come down to a nearly insoluble residuum of hard cases, some of which may take ten years to settle from the difficulty of securing the necessary papers and vouchers. . . . Binney's hesitating, modest doubts as to the prudence of undertaking this claim business on any large scale, or at all, are abundantly justified. The record of the Commission is thus far decent and creditable, but its career may close in disgrace from the failure of its work in this subordinate and altogether supererogatory department of its relief service.

Mr. Ruggles has just happened in at eleven-thirty this evening. Spent an hour and smoked a cigar in the library. Talked of the Paris Exposition, and so on. Were I not a vestryman but a mere average Christian, I should say d— the "Exposition." It is a skillful operation of Louis Napoleon's (that imperial Barnum) designed to bring people from all the nations of the earth to his imperial capital to spend money in the shops and the lodging houses of that infamous city. The device will succeed. Paris is all "engaged" already. Its citizens are preparing to abandon their homes for a time that they may let them to Englishers and Yankees, Russians, Turks, Jews, and dwellers in Mesopotamia. On the whole, I am rather glad I have not money enough to go to Paris this spring. I should like well enough to visit Paris or any other ancient capital, but I do not want to see Paris in days of joy and jubilation and profit. I know a little of the record of Paris in the day of Marat and Couthon and Barère, and nowhere in Europe for a thousand years of war and revolution and insurrection did the great central fire of hate and murder and all abominations ever break through the crust of social charity and humane instincts so violently and so cruelly as in Paris seventy years ago. That city has been a maleficent blow-hole of poisonous gas over all Europe and over all the world since the days of Henry IV. Louis IX seems to have been the last Christian ruler of France. *He* was a soldier and a gentleman (*vide* Joinville). This Louis Napoleon seems to be neither.

December 31, MONDAY. . . . Nothing very notable in Wall Street. A.D. 1866 is just in *articulo mortis*. It will be midnight, and another day and another year will begin within five minutes. God bless Ellie and my boys through 1867, and may His mercy rescue me from the depression and paralysis that has made 1866 so barren of good works and enable me to try to do my duty.

1867

CORRUPTION AT ALBANY · MILITARY RECONSTRUCTION
INSTITUTED · DEATH OF ANTHON · ANDREW JOHNSON
UNDER FIRE · DICKENS'S SECOND VISIT

———————————— ❧ ————————————

*S*trong felt depressed as the year 1867 opened, and with reason. Not only did his health continue poor, for he was sometimes briefly prostrated by some illness that both he and his physician found mysterious, but he was increasingly worried about his finances as inflation drove up the cost of living. "Thoroughly blue," he had written on December 20, "and as to my exchequer, fearfully* lean." *Gold that day had stood at* 135½. *"They say prices begin to fall. Unless they fall fast and far, I must emigrate from New York. Yesterday I ordered some clothes at Derby's, my wardrobe being reduced to one nearly disintegrated suit for Sundays and weekdays, and a dress coat and so on now nearly six years old. I find a frock coat costs* $95!" *His doctor kept urging him to take a vacation, but he could not afford it. "I cannot work and I cannot play." Had his straitened circumstances not forbidden it, he would have liked to send his wife to Europe with her father, for S. B. Ruggles left early in March as a Commissioner to the Paris Exposition. Strong even feared that he might have to sell his house and library.*

He found consolation in music, for he attended concerts as assiduously as ever; in reading; and in the perceptible progress that Columbia College was now making under Barnard's sagacious administration. National affairs were not of a kind to hearten anybody, for the contest between Johnson and the Radicals was coming to a disgraceful climax. Thad Stevens, Ben Wade, and their associates were taking steps to erect something near a Congressional dictatorship. They were now able to repass any bill over a presidential veto. Using their power, they rapidly enacted a law for Negro suffrage in the District of Colum-

*bia; a Tenure of Office Act, making it a misdemeanor for the President to remove
high civil officers without the consent of Congress; and a Military Reconstruction Act, dividing the South into five military districts with a general in
charge of each. Representative Ashley brought in a resolution for an inquiry
into President Johnson's conduct, and although public opinion was as yet
decidedly against any humiliation of the President, signs multiplied that the
Radical leaders were contemplating his impeachment and removal. The new
Congressional plan of reconstruction was based upon Negro suffrage, and involved the establishment of mixed black-and-white governments in the Southern
States.*

January 7, MONDAY. . . . Columbia College trustees met at two o'clock
and sat till half-past four. Barnard, being one of the American Commissioners to the Paris Exposition, asked for leave of absence from March to
November. But on motion of the Bishop, warmly supported by Mr.
Ruggles, leave was granted with good nature and unanimity. Barnard
reported one thousand dollars given by Charles T. Cromwell for two gold
medals to be awarded in the School of Mines, one in Chandler's department
and the other in Vinton's. Also that a Mr. Brower offers to deposit in the
cabinet a valuable collection of Chilian minerals (now lodged with Union
College) provided we agree to keep them insured. We consented, though
with some little demur. This demur is a symptom of the corporate disease
that has so long excluded the College from public sympathy and from the
private benefactions by which every other college in the country is steadily
strengthened. Under Barnard's enlightened administration we make some
progress toward a cure of this disease.

January 8. . . . George Anthon looked in a moment this evening. His
uncle, Professor Charles Anthon, alias Bull Anthon, Professor in Columbia
College near half a century, was attacked yesterday by cerebral disturbance.
He could not call his roll, gibbered Greek at his classes, and was carried
home in a hack, half unconscious. He now lies prostrate and nearly senseless. This is probably the beginning of the end. I fear he cannot serve as
acting-president in Barnard's absence.

January 10. . . . Professor Bull Anthon is better. He was quite low and
wandering yesterday, lecturing an imaginary class on Greek prosody, I'm
told. His attack seems to have been something like apoplexy or paralysis,
but he may get up again, for his vitality is great. His temperament is much
mitigated since my college days, when he was our ideal of a ferocious

tyrant. The undergraduates are attached to him, and subscribe to send flowers to his sick room daily.

This movement in the House for the impeachment of A. Johnson seems to me certainly useless and probably mischievous. If it be serious, it will keep the country in confusion to the end of Johnson's term at least. It is disapproved here even by earnest Radicals.

January 12. A very frosty day. To Steinway Hall tonight for Theodore Thomas's concert. "Suite op. 101. Raff." Rather pretty-ish. A "Suite" seems to mean a twelve-minute symphony. I never saw the word on a programme before. This composition was nowise original or brilliant, but the composer had honestly tried to write something agreeable and graceful, wherefor he is to be commended. This is the last thing our Wagners and Volkmanns and Rubinsteins think of. They want to be stunning and fearful. . . . Went to Century Club (annual meeting) and spent an hour there. Discoursed with Barnard, Newberry, Egleston, George Bancroft, Choate, William E. Dodge, Jr., and others. Barnard tells me Bull Anthon is much better, quite himself again. . . .

January 13, SUNDAY. . . . Mr. Ruggles here tonight. He had a long talk with me in the dining room after supper, when Ellie had gone up to bed, urging me to go to Europe with him next March and offering me the most generous facilities. But it cannot be done. No use talking of it.

January 14. My old classmate Isaac Fowler in the omnibus this afternoon. Had not seen him since his abrupt departure from New York (he was postmaster) some seven years ago. He has been living in Western Mexico since then, and was lately pardoned, but will not resume his residence here till he can make good what was lost by him. He is here only for a brief visit. . . . Profoundly unhappy about this proposed expedition to Paris for the "Exposition." Not at all for my own sake (whatever Dr. Peters, Dr. Agnew, Charley, and George Anthon may predict) but because I fear I *cannot* send Ellie to Paris with her father. She would go with him so comfortably and would enjoy the visit so intensely. She says nothing about the matter, but my decision must have been a severe disappointment. I should feel ashamed to go off to Paris and leave her in Twenty-first Street. It's a dark time generally, but I suppose that "behind the clouds the sun is shining."

January 16. Nothing new in Wall Street. Am just from a dinner at John Astor's. There were President Barnard, Dr. Vinton, William J. Hoppin, Schroeder of the Astor Library, Charles H. Russell, Tuckerman, Mayor Hoffman, Bishop Potter, Hamilton Fish, Henry Brevoort, Dr.

Markoe, Henry Day, old James Gallatin, and myself. Also Astor's only son, who has shot up too fast and looks delicate and fragile. He seems a nice, well-mannered boy of eighteen, more or less. . . .[1] The dinner was sumptuous and splendid, of course, but apart from the viands and the marvelous wines, Astor's dinner parties are always pleasant. He receives his guests with perfect cordiality and simplicity, and his wife's graceful manner is worthy of a duchess. Neither of them seems conscious of the splendor of their drawing-rooms and their dinner-table. I have a great respect for them both, perhaps because they always treat me—I don't know why—with so much kindness and consideration. Walked down Fifth Avenue from Thirty-third Street with Hoppin. He is rapturous about Barnard and Egleston, being mixed up with them in sundry business connected with that confounded Paris Exposition. The College (which includes the School of Mines and the Law School) is certainly beginning to make itself perceptible to the community at large. It has allowed itself to be forgotten and ignored for the last fifty years. Better days seem coming—thanks to Barnard, Professor Dwight, and the faculty of the School of Mines.

January 17. . . . The late decisions of the Supreme Court of the United States are much talked of.[2] The doctrine of the majority of the Court seems sound, but the argument contra is weighty. The immediate effect of these decisions will be bad, whether they are right or wrong. They have stimulated and strengthened the impeachment movement in Congress, and an impeachment will be a public calamity. It's curious to see the New York *Herald* preaching extremest Radicalism, declaring that A. Johnson deserves to be impeached and degraded, that he certainly will be, and that his trial and conviction will cause no disturbance or mischief whatever. . . .

January 21. . . . John Astor tells me N. P. Willis is dead.

January 23. . . . It's a cruel winter. People were crossing the East River

[1] This was William Waldorf Astor (1848–1919), who inherited an immense fortune, wrote some light fiction, built part of what became the Waldorf-Astoria Hotel in New York, removed to England, and finally died as Viscount Astor. He was a graduate of the Columbia Law School.

[2] The Supreme Court judges had just delivered their decisions in full on the case of *ex parte Milligan*, declaring that neither Congress nor President had power to hold trials by military tribunal except in a theatre of war where the civil courts were not open. This decision, a memorable stroke in behalf of civil liberty, was angrily assailed by some Radical Republicans. Two other Supreme Court decisions handed down January 14, 1867, held that neither a state nor Congress could require any person to take what was then known as a test oath—that is, an oath declaring that the affiant had not supported the Confederacy—as a prerequisite to office. The reason given was that the Constitution forbade *ex post facto* laws. This again provoked much Radical indignation.

on ice this morning. The ice-bridge broke up without warning, and some of the pedestrians escaped drowning very narrowly. The ice flashed into fragments all at once like a Prince Rupert's drop. The streets are very bad. I have not yet been made seasick by an omnibus ride, as some have been, but yesterday afternoon, as I was entering an omnibus in motion, the horses were suddenly whipped up, the vehicle gave a sudden side-long lurch, and I was flung off the step and into a snowbank, describing the arc of a parabola. It was as when a two hundred pound Parrott shell strikes a sand-bag battery. The populace jeered, and I got up from a fine intaglio cast of myself in dirty snow and walked off, trying to look complacent, as if I had tried to do it and had succeeded.

January 26, SATURDAY. . . . Perils by flood and fire. When I got up this morning, I found great blotches of water-stain on all the paper-hangings of the stairs from front hall to garret. The womankind who sleep in the garret had left the Croton water running. It had overflowed its basin and done serious mischief. But our womanservants are so good and trustworthy that this oversight should be forgotten.

After dinner I was filling my cup of coffee, lighting a cigar, and unfolding the *Evening Post*—Ellie had just adjourned from the dining room to the front parlor—when there came a prolonged vehement ringing at the doorbell. Two or three people rushed in when the door was opened, and proclaimed, "The house is on fire!" Ran upstairs with them and with Peter the waiter, and found that a gas burner had lit up the lace and muslin curtains of the east window of the third story front room. They or their fallen debris were blazing fiercely. So was the window frame. The room felt like a furnace when I entered it. We suppressed the fire with basins of Croton water. It had caught the woodwork at the top of the window, which was burning freely. This is a repetition of the casualty that befell us in the spring of 1860. Gas and hot-air furnaces are convenient but perilous. . . .

January 28. . . . Charles A. Davis died last night after a very short illness—pneumonia, it's said—at seventy-two. He was author of the "Jack Downing Papers" that were famous thirty years ago; a prosperous merchant (Davis & Brooks), retired from business, I believe, of late years; and a notable story-teller (that is, a *raconteur*). His stories were good, but many and long. He was always pleasant to meet, nevertheless. Perhaps there were tendencies to tuft-hunting, and I think that during the war he despaired of the republic (as did Sidney Brooks) and was counted among Copperheads.

January 30. . . . The following extraordinary event I have mentioned to no one, for by mentioning it, I should only damage my character for veracity. But true it is that when I paid for my lunch of lager and oysters at Hampe's cellar this afternoon, I received in change a real silver five-cent piece of 1853!!!! Had it been a specimen of the coinage of Athens or Cyrene, or a silver penny of an Anglo-Saxon king, it would not have surprised me more.

When I got home, I found . . . Colonel [Adam] Badeau, of General Grant's staff, just from Washington. He is sensible and observant, and his talk has additional value as probably reflecting unconsciously the views of his chief and of headquarters. His sympathies are with Congress rather than with the President. He thinks the latter well-meaning, but mulish or pig-headed; the former (or its extreme Radical element) a little violent; impeachment probable, and probably leading to grave complications. Grant says (*teste* Badeau) that he has never felt so anxious about the country as at this time. He may well feel anxious. The majority of the House seems bent on impeaching A. Johnson. (N.B. His proper classical parallel seems to be R. Spurius Furius, whose name occurs in Roman history, somewhere during the Samnite War or the First Punic War, I think. But my Roman history is very rusty.) This impeachment will be regular and constitutional. But the House may be so deluded as to take the untenable ground that a President impeached is *ipso facto* suspended from all official functions before conviction and even before trial. Should it take this ground, A. Johnson will recalcitrate. The general-in-chief will have to choose whom he and his staff and subordinates will serve, Congress or President. A. Johnson will invoke the army and navy of the United States to sustain him in his place, and Grant must take one side or the other in our "Second Civil War." On this question, A. Johnson would be right. Badeau says that the South is as cantankerous as it was in 1860 and grows more vitriolic every day. Only remedy, martial law from the Potomac to the Rio Grande; a heroic remedy that may destroy republican institutions. But Badeau thinks the people bent on preserving national unity at any cost whatever; "republican institutions," the axiomatic democratic truths of seventy years ago, are losing credit in A.D. eighteen-sixty-seven. *Teste* the Albany "Commissions" that tend to save this city from utter destruction by the votes of an ignorant, corrupt mob of brute Irish voters, bought up, systematically, by the blackguards and swindlers who infest the City Hall. We do not hold certain political "truths" quite so self-evident as we did ninety years ago; as between Thomas Jefferson and Thomas Carlyle, I'm not sure but I prefer the latter!

February 4.   Columbia College, two o'clock. (Law School.) A quorum secured, which I hardly expected. Letter from Dr. Hinton about Professor Taurus Anthon. Taurus being nearly convalescent, wants to go to work again. Dr. Hinton thinks it won't do and wrote this letter to George Anthon, which I saw yesterday. Fish brought the subject forward, and we tendered the professor a six months' leave of absence in a very complimentary resolution, which compliment that old Turk has well earned by near half a century of diligent service.

Drisler is to be acting-president while Barnard is absent, with a little augmentation of salary, and is to attend meetings of the board. The resolution that he attend our meetings shocked one or two of our colleagues profoundly, but his attendance was plainly necessary. We raised salaries of two assistants in the School of Mines from $500 to $1,000, made provision for instruction in Greek, and so on.

February 9, SATURDAY. . . . Yesterday dined here Newberry, Egleston, and Chandler of School of Mines; also Agnew, George Anthon, Charley Strong, and Mr. Ruggles. The little convivium seemed comfortable, as convivia are apt to be when organized by Mrs. George T. Strong. She makes the atmosphere of this house genial to everybody, I think. Under her influence men as reserved as Newberry and Chandler become discursive and talk unrestrained. Her social faculty is great. She acts on people of diverse temperaments and tastes just as a bit of platinum sponge acts on a current of mixed oxygen and hydrogen; makes them react on each other and become luminous, by a special, unaccountable gift of "catalysis." Mrs. George T. Strong is a very great little woman.

February 14, THURSDAY. . . . Coming downtown Tuesday I found the great warehouse of Chittenden & Co. (southeast corner Broadway and Leonard Street) burned up, only the front wall standing. It was a rather ancient, venerable landmark, having been built for the Society Library no less than twenty-seven years ago. Few Broadway stores below Canal Street can boast of like antiquity. When the Society Library sold the building (to the great disgust of many of its shareholders) and moved into University Place, it became the Appleton bookstore. Then the Appletons moved above Canal Street, and it became a notable dry goods establishment, wholesale, of course, a palace of a "merchant prince." This "merchant prince" is probably fully insured. Some of our weaker insurance companies will surely go down if fires continue as frequent and as disastrous as they have been for several months. The loss by this fire was a million and a half. . . .

February 23. General Vinton dined here and went with us to Stein-way Hall for one of Theodore Thomas's concerts. There was a "suite" by one Grimm . . . not brilliant but clear, honest, and quite free from clap-trap. Chorus from Beethoven's "Ruins of Athens"—very grand. Something about Faust by Liszt, rubbish that gave one a sensation like that produced by eating sour apples or chokecherries. The second part of the concert was the noble *Eroica* symphony, which we enjoyed most keenly. . . .

February 26. . . . Meeting of School of Mines Committee at Betts's office: Betts, Edward Jones, and I. Action, or rather inaction, of the com-mittee disgusted me. . . . We are most astute in discovering "how *not* to do" anything. Perhaps somebody can suggest something better to be done, so we'll let this or that proposition lie over a month or two longer, though conceded to be good and certain to fail if postponed. Perhaps the faculty do not quite understand what they really do want, so we will sit still and leave them to their own reflections. They may conclude at some future period that they have changed their minds. Perhaps Dr. Torrey could tell us something about it, but he is not here, so we will adjourn, *re infecta*, and it's quite possible Dr. Torrey may casually meet the committee some of these days and give it the benefit of his judgment in the premises. Trustee-ship of Columbia College is to me a penance, a hair-shirt, and a spiky iron girdle next the skin. In my pilgrimage through life the College is as unboiled peas in my shoes. It is bitter to see so hopeful and so nobly endowed an institution paralyzed and atrophied instead of growing daily in power of public beneficence, as it would grow under any earnest and energetic administration. Its Fifth Avenue lots that were worth next to nothing forty years ago are worth thousands now. My excellent colleagues seem to think themselves entitled to the credit of this increase in our resources, whereas they have simply sat still like any old Dutch farmer and watched their cabbage garden develop into city lots. One or two of us made a little effort three or four years ago, and secured some six thousand dollars for equipment of our new-born School of Mines. To the best of my knowl-edge and belief, no trustee has done as much for the College during the last half century; that is, got as much money out of the community—the public.

March 2, SATURDAY. . . . Century Club tonight. It seems growing cold, half-clear and windy. A fine landscape presented to the Club by certain of its members. It is a Kensett, cost five thousand dollars. Seems to me dear at the money, but I am no judge. It is a nice, large, pretty picture anyhow. I moved that a plate be affixed to its frame recording the names of the artist and the donors. A lovely picture of Gifford's was on exhibition. Line of sand beach on which a quiet, gentle surf is breaking, then a wide area of ocean, and then the horizon, above which is a low-lying stratum of cloudy haze through which a full-orbed moon, just rising, throws loveliest gleams of light on the curves of the surf and on the water sliding up the beach.

March 9, SATURDAY. . . . Tonight with Ellie to Philharmonic concert, Steinway Hall. Mrs. D. C. Murray and Mrs. Ruggles sat with us. Overture to *Zauberflöte*. I have known it for years, but am only just beginning to see its wonderful power and beauty. . . . For finale, Liszt's "Poème Symphonique—Lamento e Trionfo." The Lamento was expressed by dreary phrases on the celli and double basses that seemed suggestive of a cow in a strange lane seeking an abducted calf and seeking it in vain. The Trionfo, by crashing brass chords, illustrated by fantasias on the triangle, apparently descriptive of the triumphant hero with his hands in his pockets, jingling his pennies and his bunch of keys. A long rigmarole on fourth page of the programme informed mankind that all this rubbish meant something about Tasso! The production of this trash on the same evening with works of Beethoven and of Mozart disgraced the Philharmonic Society, and its endurance without audible protest disgraced the audience. It was so utterly worthless and vulgar! . . . The Abbé Liszt has evidently studied the resources of the orchestra much more carefully than Verdi has condescended to study them. But his study has only made his malfeasances more painful to his hearers. Neither can be called a composer. Each is entitled to a certain place of degradation in the abyss as an anti-musician, or as a producer of work not merely alien, but positively hostile, to music. . . .

March 13.   Very busy. Fear I must go to Albany tomorrow on this Seamen's Bank for Savings business. Writing out a "brief" tonight, but I trust I may not be called on to harangue the "Grinding Committee" of the House. This nefarious, unconstitutional, dirty project of confiscating the sixpenny savings of near half a million sempstresses, mechanics, day-laborers, minors, and others, is a subject to which I cannot pretend to do justice. Though this pick-pocketing plan does not yet embrace all the half-million savings bank depositors throughout the state, it will soon do so. It is growing. The first bill proposed to grab all deposits in Seamen's Bank not acted on since January, 1865. This is already followed by another bill grabbing all such deposits in all the city savings banks. Its passage would produce financial crisis and collapse. Millions of government and state stock would be thrown on the market to be sold at any price. Millions of mortgage debt would have to be called in without mercy or reprieve. There would be a black time in Wall Street!

This infamous scheme is of naked, unblushing confiscation, and that of the meanest sort. The "Empire State" proposes to set out on the "kinchin-lay" like Noah Claypole in *Oliver Twist*, feeling itself unequal to the role of Fagin. If the people of this state must be introduced to the dangerous luxury of confiscation, in God's name (or in whatever other name may be more fitting) let their first essay be made with some degree of evil dignity, as burglars or highway robbers, rather than as area-sneaks. Let them boldly attack and sequestrate a few surplus millions of accumulated private and corporate wealth, rather than adopt this paltry thieving scheme by which a lot of poor people are to be "done" of their little savings without notice or warning, and left to recover them only by a special act of the legislature. Wish Mr. Ruggles were here. He would give me a few pungent phrases off-hand that would concentrate into ten words what I shall have to say against this larcenous project.

March 16, SATURDAY. To Albany Thursday at eleven A.M. by Harlem Railroad. Pleasant day. . . . At Albany. Congress Hall. Marshall (of the Seamen's Bank) had secured us good bedrooms and a sumptuous private parlor. The hotel seems well administered. It is soon to be pulled down to make place for a new State Capitol. Charley Strong came up late that night.

Next morning, Friday, we looked about a little. "Geological Rooms," and so forth. Mastodon bones recently disinterred from a peat bog near Cohoes, and the like. State collections seem no great affair.

At three o'clock in the afternoon to the "Grinding Committee" which sits in the Court of Appeals Room. More properly the "sub-committee of the House Committee of the Whole." Havens of Essex chairman. He is a sensible, intelligent man.

"House Bill No—" was called up after a little discussion of other matters, and then I proceeded to harangue the committee. I dwelt at some length on the unconstitutionality of the proposed act, and was going on to expatiate on its most perilous consequences, when I was interrupted by one Wyeth, a committeeman from Richmond County, I believe. He moved that the committee report against the bill as clearly unconstitutional. After much talk, the bill was tabled. It was tabled for the sake of courtesy to its mover, one Halsey, who told Charley that he did not attend the committee because he did not care a d—— about the matter.

This is a most corrupt and profligate legislature. A legislator who is asked to oppose a lawless and mischievous measure, and who responds by putting his open palm behind him—wide open—inviting a little honorarium of greenbacks, is a bad fruit of our prevalent political theories. . . .

March 19. . . . What a dreary time this is! Ellie shews me some little gimcrack I gave her ten or fifteen years ago, and casually remarks, "How rich we were *then*"—! Very true. We are very poor now. But she takes whatever comes, like an honest, true-hearted Christian woman. If she bewailed herself, and deplored prices and the currency, as many women would, I think I should blow out my brains.

March 21. . . . N.B. This house has changed its number. It has been No. 74 East Twenty-first Street ever since it has been inhabited—that is, since October, 1849. It is now No. 113 East 21st Street, re-numbered by order of the Common Council. Some tinman, influential among the blackguards and loafers of his ward, coveted the job of furnishing these new tin tickets. Our civic government, and I fear our state government, too, is utterly profligate and corrupt.

March 23, SATURDAY. Took Johnny and Temple to Theodore Thomas's concert tonight, which they enjoyed. . . . Concert was very good. "Two Entr'actes to Rosamunde," by Schubert, were satisfactory. The second seemed really genial and melodic, not unworthy the author of the Serenade and scores of loveliest songs beside. His orchestral work has always seemed to me far below those compositions. A movement from a piano concerto of Chopin's (Op. 11) was very pleasant to hear. . . .

April 2. . . . Looked in at the New Court House this morning while waiting to keep an appointment at surrogate's office. One of its rooms fitted up and Court of Appeals sitting therein. Sorry to see that this building is not fireproof, though it is so costly a swindle.[3]

General George Ruggles dined here yesterday. Miss Rosalie Ruggles here till this morning.

Connecticut has been carried by the Copperheads. Their majority about seven hundred. Phineas T. Barnum, the showman, prince of professional humbugs, was a burthen the Republicans could not carry into Congress. I do not at all regret the result. If the Republicans will adopt

[3] Already the County Court Building, which had been started in 1861, was in evil odor. The Tweed Ring had so manipulated the contracts that it was costing New York twelve million dollars. This plain white marble building, completed in 1872, still stands as a monument to one of the city's worst pieces of graft.

charlatans as their candidates, I am thankful for their defeat. Would that the voters of this city had a like sense of decency. With it, they would not have elected Ben Wood, the lottery dealer, and Morrissey, the pugilist and gambling-house keeper, as their representatives in our national council.

It would seem that the Administration is buying Russian America for seven million! What can the country gain by ownership of that desolate, dreary, starved region? It produces a few furs steadily diminishing in quantity, as the otters and seals and so forth are yearly persecuted toward extermination, and it produces nothing else I know of. But the acquisition of territory is an achievement on which any administration can rely as endearing it to the people. *Semble* that "the people" are fools.

Heard Mozart's noble *Jupiter Symphony* rehearsed by the Philharmonic Saturday afternoon. Rehearsal was open to criticism. I thought the third and fourth movements taken much too slow. But I doubt if there be anything in all music so perfectly pure, perfect, and translucent; especially the second and third movements. The symphony is less intense than some of Beethoven's, but is "one entire and perfect chrysolite." . . .

April 5. An April day. Am honored by a flourishing letter from John Jay, president of the Union League Club, notifying me of my election as an honorary member thereof. As the only honorary members that have been elected are Mr. Lincoln and about a dozen high-caste military and naval men, such as Grant and Farragut, this is a notable compliment, and the more gratifying because unanimous. But it is founded merely on my having been one of the four originators of the club, and on the impression entertained by many of its members that I was uncivilly treated in being dropped off the Committee on Admissions at the election of 1866. Jay's very kind flights of fancy about "public services" in Sanitary Commission, and so on, are bosh.

I'm bedeviled with invitations "to meet the Judges of the Court of Appeals." Evarts tonight, Bidwell Monday, Stoughton (E. W.), Ben Silliman, and I suppose Edwards Pierrepont's dinner party Wednesday to be an act of homage to the same august body. I suppose I must go to Bidwell's, but I "regret" that I cannot attend the others. I go willingly to no gathering intended to honor such a set of scrubs. Just think of Kent, Spencer, Samuel Jones, Oakley, and others, and then of these third- and fourth-rate men, who now represent the judiciary of this state! . . .

April 6. Busy downtown. Tried to see Travers (son-in-law of Reverdy Johnson, who is chief counselor of our admirable President) about Egleston's wish to go to Europe under government authority to investigate European process of metallurgy. Did not succeed. . . .

April 8. . . . Library Committee at Columbia College this afternoon. Only Drisler, the librarian, and myself. Then spent an hour in School of Mines, with Egleston and Chandler. Every sign of activity, prosperity, and steady acquisition. A collection of Chilian minerals deposited there by one Brower is valuable and splendid. The specimens of native silver are very fine; those of "ruby silver" can hardly be matched, I suppose. Egleston tells me the Free Academy contemplates setting up a rival School of Mines.[4] What business has the city to tax us for any such purpose? And what folly it is to multiply colleges and rival institutions, instead of two or three that are strong, endowed, and well appointed, and useful. . . .

Randolph Robinson called to tell me of his engagement to Miss Jay, one of John Jay's daughters, and a beauty. He is called a handsome man, but I never thought him so before. This alliance of a semi-Southerner by birth, a full-blooded Southerner in feeling, with the daughter of an Abolitionist, who talked Abolitionism twenty years ago, is an encouraging event.

April 12. Usual routine in Wall Street, and paralyzing depression. . . . As the country seems likely to buy Russian America for a summer resort, I suppose (consideration money $7,200,000), I shall apply to our excellent President for some little place in the new Territory of Sitka. I would make a good superintendent of walruses—a very efficient and disinterested head of a Polar Bears' Bureau—an admirable military governor of Oonalaska. . . .

Letters from Mr. Ruggles, who is in high feather at Paris. But there are symptoms of a European war. . . .

April 15, MONDAY. Talked with Skidmore about this plaguy question of the Reverend Vinton's demand for $10,000 per annum salary. His highest aspiration was $8,000, till he heard of A. W. Bradford's indiscreet motion at the last vestry meeting, whereupon he wrote me to say that he could be "solvent" on no less, and seemed to take it for granted that I was to support Bradford's $10,000 motion. I wrote him word that I was not prepared to say how I should vote on this question, that I sincerely desired to serve him every way, but that heads of departments at Washington receive an official income of $8,000, the Chief

[4] The Free Academy, founded in 1849, had been renamed in 1866 as the College of the City of New York.

Justice of the Supreme Court of the United States $6,500, Judges of the Court of Appeals of this state $3,500. It is unfortunate that our clergymen are informed, in some inscrutable way, of the vote of every member of the vestry on every question affecting their interests. . . .

Walked over the Broadway and Fulton Street bridge this afternoon for the first time. It is not yet quite finished. The Macneven monument in St. Paul's churchyard, on Broadway just north of the church, seems nearly complete. It offsets the Emmet obelisk on the south side of the church, which was set up thirty-five years ago. We should now authorize the erection of a monument in honor of some eminent Fenian martyr or confessor, whenever such personage shall turn up.

April 18.   Our special Trinity Church vestry meeting tonight was the saddest that I have attended during the very near twenty years that I have belonged to that body. The Rector brought its subject before us with frankness and decision, but with the utmost delicacy and tenderness toward the unfortunate gentleman on whose frailties we had to pass— the Rev. Mr. Higby. He has been an assistant minister more than thirty years. The most eloquent orator I ever heard in the pulpit, at the bar, or on the platform. Sermons of his have seemed to me unmatched and unsurpassable. He has been losing his efficiency and energies of late, from ill health, as I had supposed. But I learned the other day, with consternation, that he had *taken to drink*, and came near disgracing himself at morning service last Sunday in the chancel of Trinity Chapel. He seems to have been stupid drunk. God help us! Who can think himself safe?

There was some little conversational discussion—nothing that could be called a debate. Every member of the vestry was in his place, except John A. Dix and John Swift, who are beyond seas. Our action was a resolution forbidding poor Dr. Higby to officiate in the parish church or its chapels without special license from the rector or the vestry. I begged the question of a reduction of salary might lie over for the present, and so it does. . . .

Death of Henry D. Cruger announced, at Saugerties, at sixty-seven, having lived for twenty years on "alimony" extorted by process of law from a wife he hated and whom he had married for her money. Miss Harriet Douglas was a prodigy of an heiress in 1830. Never was a worse-matched pair. He was as arrogant, as grasping, and as mean as bad specimens of South Carolina chivalry are apt to be. Her obstinacy, her crotchets, her literary enthusiasms, and her pious Presbyterian exaltations were enough to madden Job or Socrates. This poor lady always meant right, but some people make everything a matter of conscience and principle with so uncompromising a sense of duty that they render life a torment to themselves and to all who are so unfortunate as to have any relations with them. Cruger *v.* Cruger gave the court of chancery much business years ago. She was mad and he was bad, and the legal muddle they brought about between them was very deep and formidable. I have not called at this lady's Fourteenth Street palazzo for two or three New Year's Days. She is so voluble and so unconventional that she frightens me a little, and bores me a great deal. . . .

But I can think of no one but poor Dr. Higby, my ideal of a preacher these thirty years, of whose eloquence I have so often spoken as incomparable, worthless for parochial work, but matchless in the pulpit. Yet his name will not be remembered as it deserves. He leaves next to nothing in print, to my knowledge, and his sermons were doubtless made doubly effective by his voice and delivery and his personal magnetism. But they were in themselves most admirable, free from the least taint of affectation, unreality, conventionalism, or sanctimoniousness, always deep, thoughtful, and earnest, often imaginative and poetical, without effort or even a flavor of fine writing. His English was perfect. I have heard sentences from him as grand and as massive as any in Coleridge's prose, or Milton's. I shall never forget two sermons I heard of his on Christmas and Easter eight or nine years ago. The text of one of them was "The Young Child and His Mother." Both were most lovely specimens of the purest and simplest religious eloquence. Charles Dickens never wrote anything more pathetic and touching about young children, and they were somehow made the special subjects of both sermons.

April 20. Philharmonic Concert tonight with Ellie and her mother. Dr. Markoe sat near us and we exchanged notions about the music. *Jupiter Symphony* grandly rendered. . . . After this noble, translucent, transcendant work, we were favored with a piano concerto in E-flat by Mr. Liszt, which was very dreary, and then with two movements (only two, thank Heaven) from the *Symphony Romeo et Juliette* by that ingenious Frenchman, M. Hector Berlioz. Is it not a shame that we cannot hear Mozart and Beethoven at a Philharmonic concert without having our stomachs turned by a dose of Berlioz, Liszt, or Schumann? I'll set about getting up an opposition Philharmonic for the culture and propagation of music in the true sense of that great word. Concert wound up with Wagner's *Tannhäuser* Overture. It is so clever and effective that it seems a work of genius, and not of mere talent; perhaps it is. . . .

April 25. . . . Election of members of convention to revise the state constitution went off quietly last Tuesday. It will be a Republican convention. May we hope to be relieved from the curse of an elective judiciary and for protection against the murderous taxation inflicted on us by corruption in this city and at Albany? Certainly we may hope, but I think we shall hope in vain.

April 29. . . . After dinner went to Law School, 37 Lafayette Place. Young Harry Schermerhorn, Mrs. R. A. Schermerhorn's youngest son, a member of the graduating class of this year, had asked the favor of a private examination a fortnight in advance of the regular examination, so that he could go out of town, being somewhat out of health. I am sorry to say that this nice, modest, gentlemanlike boy looks bad. His father died of consumption. Professor Dwight and Ogden were in attendance and the examination was duly administered and fairly passed, though the examinee was unnecessarily nervous and anxious.

May 1. . . . War cloud in Europe seems breaking away. There is anxiety about the decision of the Supreme Court of the United States on these States' Injunction Bills. If for complainants, it may complicate affairs very badly, and on counting noses it looks not unlikely.

May 2. News of the death of old "Black Jake" LeRoy at Hudson, where he lived these last few years on the debris of his once splendid fortune, squandered in the worst way. I should say rather of his late wife's fortune, which belonged *in foro conscientiae* to their two children after his death. But I fear there will be little or nothing for Mrs. DeKoven and for Bob LeRoy's little widow.

Standing Committee of diocese this evening at Dr. McVickar's, 21 West Thirty-second Street; the doctor, Eigenbrodt, Higby, Nash, Floyd Smith, and myself. Dr. Higby perfectly cool, clear, and intelligent. He took part in our little discussions with his characteristic fluency of speech and dignity of manners, and I walked downtown with him and Nash. We passed on a long series of our usual routine applications. . . . Then came a letter from the bishop asking the counsel of the committee whether he should attend the proposed meeting of a "Pan-Anglican" council at Lambeth in September, and what he should do about the meeting of the diocesan convention on the 26th of that month. We advised him to attend the council, and to issue a recommendation to the convention to organize on the 26th and then adjourn to some day in November. Where did the Archbishop of Canterbury (who convokes this council) and his brethren of

the Episcopal bench, all I suppose university men, pick up so barbarous
a word as "Pan-Anglican"? . . .

This "Pan-Anglican" council, if it contemplate decrees, will have
two great questions to deal with. First, *Essays and Reviews* and Darwinism; secondly, Ritualism. It will have to decide whether the followers
of Colenso and Strauss and the *Anthropological Review* believe too little,
and whether Morgan Dix and Vinton and our poor little spectacular
"Church of St. Alban's" believe too much. A decision against the former
would be like the "Pope's bull against the comet," quoted by poor dear
old A. Lincoln. (I guess A. Lincoln invented that apocryphal bull.) It
would be laughed at by mankind, and damage the church during this
generation, at least. As to ritualism, against which the majority of a
council composed of English, Scot, Colonial, and American bishops
would surely pronounce, I think the question should be laid on the
table. . . .

May 4. . . . Long Sanitary Commission meeting last night in Twelfth
Street. There were Bellows, Agnew, Van Buren, Blatchford, Harris,
Gibbs, Horace Binney, Newberry, Stillé, and Professor Gould. We
cleared away much rubbish, and then the hospitable Blatchford gave us a
little supper, which was enforced by certain flasks of Steinberger, the
best Rhine wine I ever tasted. Harris was hauled over the coals by Gibbs
and Agnew for dilatoriness in getting up a certain report on military
hygiene, which we proposed to publish. Anxious and unhappy all today
about our financial future. The treasury of the Commission is nearing
low-water mark, and we have large outstanding engagements to meet. . . .

General Vinton dined here. Then with him and Ellie, Johnny, and
Temple to Steinway Hall for the extra Philharmonic concert; the twenty-
fifth anniversary of the organization of that Society, its Silver Wedding.
How well I remember its first concert in November or December, 1842!
—Programme was the C Minor Symphony. An "oration" by a Rev.
Franklin Johnson, which was brief and unpretending. He told us how
ignorant this community was of first-class music in 1842, how the nascent
Philharmonic Society had to import its scores from Europe, and so on.
Then we were afflicted by "Preludes: Poème Symphonique" by the
miserable Liszt. They set my teeth on edge. . . .

May 6, MONDAY. College trustees this afternoon. Drisler tells me
poor old Anthon is ill again since last Monday. He can certainly do no
more work this term and is unlikely ever to do any more. Symptoms are
failure of digestion, great weakness, oppression on going upstairs, and

insomnia. Also, the very grave symptom of seventy-nine years. Indigestion is easily accounted for by the way he has overworked his stomach this long while. Probably there may be also disease of the heart, either organic or functional, and connected with dyspepsia. . . .

May 9. . . . Long talk with Fish the other day in Wall Street about college affairs. He is, as usual, perturbed and dissatisfied about everything except perhaps the School of Mines, which is, as he seems to admit, doing even more than we could have hoped for. There is the question about Anthon's chair, now practically vacant. How shall it be filled? Charles D. Morris, he thinks, won't do, for sundry reasons that are not without weight. The undergraduate course is inefficient (true), and the remedy is to move the College into the country (which I doubt). This criticism is founded on Fish's observation of his own sons, now in college, who don't like study and are not coerced into study by domestic influence. The Law School is only Professor Dwight's school, and would instantly collapse if Dwight should leave it. (Which is very true indeed.) And so on. . . .

Rumors of imminent riot; Celts and Teutons stirred up to insurrection by the excise law and the police. I confess that the ordinances that close all grog-shops and lager-bier saloons on Sunday seem to me a severe strain on the endurance of the *hoi polloi*, and not the less so because they are ancient laws now enforced for the first time.

May 10, FRIDAY. . . . Our proposed "Whiskey Insurrection" is now set down for next Sunday. Insurrections with notice are apt to fail. Kennedy and his myrmidons are vigilant. Governor Fenton is a "Republican" governor, thank Heaven, and will not shape his course by the precedent set by Governor Seymour in 1863. And our Seventh and other militia regiments are not miles away, on the Potomac, this time. I think there will be no riot, but if there be any, it may prove disastrous. Target companies and Irish regiments with a fellow feeling for rioters might make the contest of law with lawlessness not so very unequal.

May 11. Nothing new, except that Jeff Davis is to be habeas-corpussed out of Monroe and into Richmond before a United States Court where he will probably be discharged, and if tried, certainly never convicted. . . .

May 15. . . . Law School commencement tonight at French Theatre, West Fourteenth Street. Drisler presided. House quite full. I was on the stage with the other nobs. Professor Dwight, the Warden, made, as usual, a graceful and effective introductory address. Then Mr. H. Everett

Russell delivered the "alumni address." His manner and delivery were exceeding good, but he propounded the most ultra-radical theories, among them, that women ought to vote and possess a natural, inherent right to the elective franchise. This produced an interesting little contest between hisses and applause. I think the former predominated. Benjamin D. Silliman followed. . . .

Drisler tells me that Professor Bull Anthon gains no strength. He is barely able to drive to the college now and then, for the sake of sitting ten or fifteen minutes in his empty lecture room, and then to drive home again. Even this is thought rather too much for him, but it is his only comfort. All who have seen Bull's intense, life-long devotion to his lecture-room work will feel that this fits in with all his past career. One might write a poem about it, if one had the faculty.

Jeff Davis, liberated on bail, will be in town tomorrow on his way to Canada, to see his children at school there. Why doesn't the Common Council offer him the governor's room in the City Hall to receive his friends in?

May 18. Walked uptown with George Anthon. He was sitting with his uncle, Professor Bull Anthon, last Thursday evening, when the Professor experienced a slight stroke of apoplexy. His face became distorted, "one side of it seemed to fall down in a single instant," says George, and he lost consciousness for a brief space. But he soon rallied and shewed his usual pluck. He walked upstairs to bed, in spite of Dr. Hinton's remonstrances, though he was obliged to pause awhile and pant for breath when half-way up. . . .

May 21. . . . Professor Van Amringe called last evening to discuss college affairs. It is generally conceded that Bull Anthon's chair is now practically vacant. Drisler wants to become Professor of Greek, and Van Amringe would like to take Drisler's place as Professor of Latin. I did not at first like the suggestion. But Van Amringe taught Greek and Latin before he was connected with the College, and says that while serving as tutor and as adjunct professor of mathematics, he has always kept up his classical reading. He evidently understands himself very well, and Drisler endorses him. First-rate classical scholars are rare in this community. . . . I know of no other available candidate. The white cravats of the board will doubtless produce some decayed, insolvent parson, and will work hard to elect him. Jesse Spencer will, of course, send in his "testimonials" just as soon as he has smelt out the vacant professorship.

The pencil memoranda found in J. Wilkes Booth's pocket diary,

written down during his dismal flight from the scene of his great crime
and now first published, are most interesting. It seems clear that when the
poor wretch commenced his flight, he was fully and serenely satisfied
that his fearful crime was an act of Roman heroism, patriotism, and virtue,
but that a dismal change of feeling was soon brought on him by the
abhorrence with which he was regarded even by the unrepentant rebels
of Virginia, whose sympathy and shelter were his sole reliance. Even
poor Dr. Mudd's professional aid seems to have been given with ill-
concealed aversion and unwillingness. All this seems to have opened the
eyes of the murderer. Instead of comparing himself with Brutus and Tell,
as he does in his first memorandum (and to his own advantage), he prays,
in the second, that God may "try and forgive" him, for, as he infers
from the demeanor of the men he has discoursed during his flight, his
crime must be, or at least may be, outside the range of God's mercy.
The assassin fairly avows at last that he felt the curse of Cain upon him,
and saw no prospect but that of speedy death as a criminal. He thought of
riding back into Washington and surrendering himself to the Provost-
Marshal. What a ride Booth must have had through the dismal woods
of Virginia, after the murder! He was tortured by a broken limb, "tearing
the flesh at every jump" of his horse, tortured still worse by discovering
that nobody thought his grand, heroic Roman pistol shot anything better
than a pitiful, cowardly assassination, and looking forward to speedy
capture and certain death. This fugitive horseman, with a wicked, unprovoked murder ten days old behind him, a broken limb tormenting his
body, and misgivings about the past tormenting his soul, riding on under
all manner of torture—bodily and mental—hoping only to escape the
gallows and to die in conflict with his pursuers (as he did), this wretched
outcast is a subject for some "sensational" painter. Gustave Doré could
do justice to it. I can conceive how Gustave Doré would treat the subject:
the jaded horse, the wearied rider, the ghastly pine trees, and through
their branches, perhaps, a glimpse of setting sunlight resting on a distant
clearing, over which blue-coated cavalrymen ride in pursuit.

May 26, SUNDAY. . . . At Trinity Church Morgan Dix preached at
some length, but his sermons are always full of deep thought and refined
poetical feeling.

May 29. . . . Maximilian of Mexico has surrendered at discretion. It
is reported that he and his generals are to be shot. This latter statement
is not so well authenticated as the former, but is altogether probable.
Poor Maximilianus Augustus must have known, however, that when he

stirred up that nest of cut-throats, he was taking his life in his hands. This ending of the Mexican crusade won't add to Louis Napoleon's prestige and strengthen his dynasty.

Beyond references to the release of Jefferson Davis on bail, and to the dismissal by the Supreme Court of a bill of complaint brought in the name of Georgia to prevent the Military Reconstruction Act from being carried out, Strong takes but little notice in his diary of the great drama being enacted at the South. This Act had been passed over Johnson's veto. It divided the ten unreconstructed states into five military districts, each under the rule of a commander appointed by the President. State constitutional conventions were to be elected on a Negro suffrage basis, and constitutions were to be drawn up which gave the Negro the ballot. When this had been done, and when the legislature had ratified the Fourteenth amendment, safeguarding the civil rights of Negroes, the state might be readmitted to the Union. From the brief allusions he makes to the subject, it is evident that Strong approved of this plan of reconstruction. The scheme was duly put into effect in March; Generals Sheridan, Schofield, Ord, Pope, and Sickles took charge of the five districts; and the work of forming the "black and tan" conventions began. Meanwhile, the talk of impeaching Johnson continued, and the Nation *and other organs were definitely supporting such action. The President, accompanied by Secretary Seward, made a trip to Boston in June and delivered a few harmless speeches on the journey. It is clear from the diary that Strong now regarded him with fixed disfavor.*

As Strong's entries show, the adventures of Maximilian in Mexico were approaching their tragic finale. The last French troops had left the country in February of this year. If he had acted promptly, Maximilian might have abdicated and escaped with them. But he bravely decided to remain in order to try to obtain better terms for his supporters, who had been denied clemency by Juarez. His attempts to bring his opponents to a conciliatory frame of mind failed. Captured at Queretaro, this most attractive of the Hapsburgs faced the fate of other filibusters.

May 30. At College this morning, before going downtown. Drisler tells me Professor Anthon has had a second slight touch of apoplexy, and that he thinks the professor hopelessly disabled. This looks like active, progressive cerebral disease.

In School of Mines the geological cases are finished, all but glazing. There are considerable additions to the mineralogical cabinet, especially from one of the young Primes, now a student at Freiburg, who sends us some sixty or seventy very interesting and splendid specimens.

June 3, MONDAY.   Very muggy weather. Session of College trustees this afternoon livelier than usual. The annual report of the acting-president brought up the question of relief to our short-handed faculty, and Haight moved to make Drisler adjunct professor of Greek and Van Amringe the same of Latin, and to empower the president to provide for additional instruction in the mathematical department rendered necessary by Van Amringe's transfer. O[gden] opposed this very earnestly, and there was a rather sharp debate. It was urged that if we made any arrangement in Barnard's absence, it was ten to one we should make some serious mistake. This gave F[ish] an opportunity to say, quite effectively, that if we were incompetent to act without Barnard, we had better resign our seats in favor of a more intelligent board. Something was said about H[aight]'s "object," and he "repelled the insinuation with scorn." In short, it was quite like old times. Result, a special committee of five to consider and report to a special meeting of the board a fortnight hence. I'm on the committee. There will probably be a squabble before the matter is disposed of.

Murray Hoffman dined here and we went with Ellie to hear *The Messiah* at Steinway Hall. This is the first of a series of performances, oratorio and concert, that are to continue for the next seven or eight evenings—a "Grand Musical Festival," so-called. Tonight there was a crowded house of appreciative people, and Handel's noble music was rendered with fidelity and spirit by a very massive chorus and orchestra. Mme. Parepa Rosa, Mrs. Seguin, and others were excellent in their solo parts. I never enjoyed this great work so keenly. It has taken me twenty-five years to begin to see what it is, and I feel that I am still merely feeling its surface and far from sounding all its depths. . . .

June 6. . . . Tonight with Ellie and Temple to Steinway Hall for the fourth evening of this "Musical Festival." Tonight was a "miscellaneous concert," beginning with the *Eroica*. We perspired until the last chord of its matchless peroration had been sounded, and then came home (still perspiring, by the by) for there was much bosh in the rest of the programme. Tuesday night's performance I did not attend. . . .

Last evening was the *Creation*, which supremely beautiful work I have not heard for years. It was excellently well brought out. I saw the power and beauty and healthiness of it all, even of Adam and Eve's colloquies, which I used to think spoony and weak. . . .

Rev. Vinton has got into a scrape. His accounts as executor and testamentary guardian of some young woman or other are under investigation before the Surrogate of King's County, and contain the most damaging entries. Besides commissions calculated at some extravagant rate, there are $— retained as compensation "for one day's service collecting interest on —'s mortgage"; $— for "ten days employed in investing money in the—"; "$— expended in gas consumed while writing up accounts," and so on. It has an ugly rapacious look, but there may be another side to the case. . . .

June 10. . . . This evening to Governor Fish's. Meeting of our special committee: Fish, Edward Jones, Dr. Torrey, Astor, and myself. Long discussion. Decided to recommend Van Amringe's transfer from the adjunct professorship of mathematics to that of Greek and Latin; Drisler and he to divide the duties of Anthon's chair. I believe him fully qualified for this, but we have hardly any other course. We cannot open the next term with a disorganized faculty. Accomplished Grecians and Latinists are scarce in this country—they "do not come" now. There is no time to hunt one up between this and October, and perhaps the search would be a failure. . . .

June 17. Uptown early for College meeting at Law School. Special order was the report of our committee on the weakness of the faculty caused by Professor Anthon's illness. Committee recommended Van Amringe's transfer from his present chair to that of "adjunct professor of the Greek and Latin languages." Ogden opposed this, at great length, but with some force. Rutherfurd took the same side. So did Anderson, but with so many qualifications and provisoes and circumlocutions that I was not quite sure whether he was for or against the report until his vote furnished a commentary on his speech. Edward Jones, as chairman of the committee, defended the report. It was very hot; we were all very languid and inert, and the question being taken, the recommendations of the committee were rejected five to six, one or two not voting. Then it was referred to a committee of three, including Drisler, to make temporary provision during the next term. F⌈ish⌉ seemed disgusted. . . .

Mr. Ruggles, by the by, is in high feather, attending all that is most swell of Paris fêtes, balls, and pow-wows. Has had an august audience of Imperial Majesty itself. Subject of the audience was Mr. Ruggles's hobby, uniformity of weights, measures, and currency. He said Europe had never enjoyed the blessing of a uniform currency since the Roman emperors. I can conceive his Majesty to have inwardly purred at this delicately suggested analogy. The metric system is clear and simple, but just imagine a Connecticut farmer saying that he doesn't live more than a centimetre from the meetin' house, or selling his crop of onions in decimal terms of quantity!

June 22, SATURDAY.   The illustrious Andrew Johnson arrived here last evening. He was received with the honors due his great place. A July session of Congress seems inevitable. Monied men talk of trouble to be caused by this session. I suppose there is no doubt that a financial panic and crash will come before long, and that repudiation of the national debt is not unlike to come next.

June 30. . . . A. Johnson the Pig-headed is just closing another stumping tour. His utterances as itinerant evangelist of "My Policy" have been copious and characteristic. But he has kept himself tolerably sober this time. May a quorum of both houses appear at Washington July 3rd, for Johnson is doing South and North immense mischief every day, and needs a little more Congressional snubbing.

July 1. . . . It is all but certain that Maximilian—*soi-disant* Emperor of Mexico, Archduke of Austria—was shot at Queretaro 19th June, by order of Juarez, chief of the Mexican "Liberals," or by sentence of some half-breed (and more than half-savage) court-martial of his. The "Liberal party" had its provocations, and could hardly be expected to depart from the settled practice of all Mexican administrations in their hour of victory. Austria and France will be furious, but what can either do about it? If it *should* turn out that Mr. Seward has been getting our diplomatic relations with Mexico into a muddle, and preventing our minister "near" that government (only as "near" as New Orleans) from doing anything to save poor Max, the Secretary of State will find himself in hot—yea, in boiling—water.[5] No power could have intervened and remonstrated so effectively, and this unfortunate prince is spoken well of by all men as amiable, honest, accomplished, and valiant.

July 6, SATURDAY. . . . It was a very quiet Fourth, the ordinance against amateur firearms in the streets being enforced for the first time within or without the memory of the oldest inhabitant. Dined here Blake, Hoffman, Graham, Colden Murray, Jem Ruggles, and Townsend. . . .

[5] Secretary of State Seward had indeed tried to persuade Juarez to extend clemency to Maximilian, but the demands of the Mexican Army were inexorable.

July 8. Downtown awhile today. Vestry meeting tonight. Much work done without much waste of time. The "nave" organ of Trinity Church is to be enlarged $3,000 worth. Erben says that will make it the finest instrument in the country, but no whale ever swam that can match Erben in "blowing." . . .

"Ex-Governor" John A. King died yesterday of paralysis—at Jamaica. He was visited by this disease last Thursday. When I last saw him, at his nephew's funeral (James G. King's), he looked vigorous. I am surprised to learn he was in his eightieth year. . . .

July 15, MONDAY. Ellie and the boys went to Brattleboro this morning. I lay in bed, nauseated and wretched, as I have been these last three days.

I am *living beyond my income*, pauperizing Johnny and his little brothers. That is what's slowly killing me, and killing me by slow torture. Ellie is quite ready to give up every social enjoyment of her own. She would give them up most cheerfully. Of course, her little parties and socialities are my ruin, but I would rather die than ask her to give them up and subside into a dull, humdrum existence. These things are her life, after the interests of her children and her husband. If I cannot afford her these social enjoyments, the sooner I die the better, and I fear I can afford them no longer. So I am the less unhappy about these daily recurring pains and aches. My incapacity for work and duty grows worse every day. I confess myself "played out," and "used up." My only hope is in the fact that our Lord raised men from the dead. I am in living death. Without His Almighty saving help, I have no hope at all.

July 16. . . . All Europe in great wrath over the murder of the poor Hapsburg Archduke Maximilian, who died with the words "poor Carlotta" on his lips. It's very sad, but what can anybody do about it? When the "archduke" interfered in Mexican affairs, he must have known the penalty of failure.

July 19. . . . Oh, the fearful, deathly depression of today! Found my bank account run down to $200, and had to appropriate another $1,000 of capital to current expenses.

"We," the standing committee of the diocese, are the ecclesiastical authority of the diocese just now, *vice* Right Rev. Bishop Potter, gone to Lambeth for the "Pan-Anglican" Councils. In that capacity we held a tedious session at Trinity Church yesterday over questions connected with the next diocesan convention and its proposed adjournment to November. . . .

July 22, MONDAY. . . . Professor Charles Anthon will not survive many days longer. . . . That excellent little Rev. Houghton (who married his niece, J. Anthon's daughter) has been trying for an interview with him for sometime. One night last week he made his way into the sick-room, knelt by the bedside, and prayed. The professor lay as unconscious. Next morning the professor said to George Anthon: "That little fellow Houghton got in here last night somehow, and flopped down on his knees by my bed, and said some prayers, sir. Did you ever hear of such a piece of impertinence, sir?" Poor "Bull"! He can no longer keep up a consistent train of thought for five minutes, nor for two. *Quantum mutatus ab illo tauro* of 1834–38; my terrible tyrant in those days. His decision that "You are *falling off*, sir," was a tremendous judgment, crushing and without appeal, when I was in the grammar school, and in the Freshman class of Columbia College. . . .

July 25. . . . I have seen nothing of George Anthon since Monday, and heard nothing more of the old professor. I have not ventured to enquire at the house in Thirty-seventh Street, for George told me that a ring at the front doorbell always aroused him to a state of twittering nervousness. "What's that? Who can that be? Go and see what it means." He has long led the life of a recluse. It must be thirty years since he has left the city limits. And when the old college buildings were demolished and he moved uptown (some eleven years ago) he was astounded by the high ceilings and the modern improvements "of his new domicile." His notions of a house (anywhere but in Rome or Athens or Pompeii) were drawn from his observations of New York houses in 1820 or in 1830, at the latest.

Forgot to mention that in the procession at Trinity Church this morning, that jackanape J. H. Hopkins, Jr., deacon, carried a polychromatic crozier before his Rt. Rev. Papa, Presiding Bishop and apologist of the *ci-devant* slaveholders and woman-floggers.[6] I do not at all object to the crozier, but the deacon should not be permitted to carry even a broom in Trinity Church till he has asked pardon for the sins of scurrility, slander, and all uncharitableness by him perpetrated against her for the

[6] The elder John Henry Hopkins (1792–1868), first Protestant Episcopal bishop of Vermont, had become presiding bishop of the Church in 1865. His brochure entitled *Slavery: Its Religious Sanction* . . . (1851), his other apologies for slavery, and his pacific attitude toward the South during the Civil War, were bitterly remembered by a multitude of Northerners. His son, J. H. Hopkins, Jr., who held high-church doctrines and expounded them in the *Church Journal*, published a life of the father in 1873.

last ten years. This deacon tried to perform the office of crozier-bearer some years ago, when assisting at the consecration of a church up the river by Bishop Potter. But Bishop Potter took him aside while the service was going on and told him that unless he removed that implement from the chancel, the service should go no further. Potter is timid, and dreads any departure from *les convenances* as now established. But I always rejoice (though perhaps it's wrong) when I hear of this impertinent, self-sufficient, intrusive, low-minded little busybody of an ecclesiastic as snubbed and suppressed by anybody. As editor of the *Church Journal*, he has done his best to rival Bennett of the *Herald*. He has lowered the tone of "religious" newspapers (so-called) as Bennett has lowered that of the secular press, and by the same weapons, smartness, flippancy, plausibility, sophistry, and utter unscrupulousness.

July 29, MONDAY. Tonight's *Post* announces the professor's (Anthon's) death. I did not expect him to last so long. . . .

I feel really much cut up by this news of poor old Bull Anthon's death. He did so tyrannize over all my boyhood from thirteen to nineteen! But it was not without intervals of kindliness. This kindliness, however, was uncertain. The professor was somewhat like an old cat. While one stroked his fur the right way, he would purr most genially and make himself the most sympathetic, patronizing, complimentary, and delightful of companions to any boy whom he liked for the time. But if you happened to stroke the fur the wrong way, he would turn and claw you—or rend you —with fearful effect.

How well I remember his style of work in the horrible old grammar school! *Scene:* twenty boys in a lecture room, no teacher yet in his place. Time, nine o'clock in the morning. Some little subdued talking and skylarking in progress. A wretched creature called "a monitor" in nominal charge, vainly beseeching his classmates to be quiet. The professor comes swiftly upstairs, full of business, with a big watch in his hand and twirling the big seal and the ribbon round his forefinger, and *loquitur*: "Too much noise here! Any names, monitor?" Monitor replies (distracted between his dread of discipline and his dread of lynching by his classmates), "No, sir. I didn't think—" Professor rejoins, Napoleonically, "I don't want to know what you think, sir. Take *this* down to Mr. Shea." "*This*" was a scrap of paper inscribed with the words "six blows" or "twelve blows," as the case might be. They were delivered by the rattan on the hand. Shea was lictor of the infernal old school and rattan-bearer. I do not think poor old James Shea liked his office much. So it was when we were in the "first Latin class" of the school. An imperfect recitation was punished by the order "Take *this* down to Mr. Shea." So was a bad weekly report. Shea was muscular, six-foot high, and I think kindhearted, though he did use to say, with the utmost aggravation of manner, as he flourished his rattan, "Now hold your hand straight, my sonny, or I may hurt your knuckles."

July 31.   To St. Mark's Church at 10:30 A.M. for poor old Professor Bull (or Charles) Anthon's funeral. I was invited to attend as *pallbearer*, everybody being out of town. . . . Before the coffin was taken out of the church it was opened and everybody looked at the professor's still, stern face. It was natural—not at all unlike his lecture-room face, only *whiter*. While I looked on it, there came on me the thought, "Suppose that figure should rise and say, 'Strong! You will now translate *Oedipus Tyrannus*, lines 213–227!' What answer should I give him?". . .

One of the professor's pallbearers was old James J. Roosevelt, his only surviving classmate, and a most pernicious old Copperhead. During the last thirty-six hours, the professor fought hard for his life, against suffocation from dropsy or from an hypertrophied heart, or both, and seemed to struggle and suffer terribly. But I hope his symptoms of distress were mostly automatic. He retained his consciousness till very near the end and expressed a wish for an autopsy, which Dr. Hinton thought unnecessary. George Anthon says the professor was indignant at the suggestion that there could be anything wrong with his brain, and wanted to have himself set right by a post-mortem. His truculence and power of command were left with him till almost the last half hour. He would not be interfered with, and repelled offers of help and comfort.

Thus has died the last of our Grecians. "Classical" studies have long been losing ground, and there is no one to take the professor's place. Not that he was a Heyne or Porson. But as a drillmaster in the ancient languages, he was unrivaled.

Anthon's death removed one of the most widely known of American scholars; a man who, as professor at Columbia and editor of a tremendous array of textbooks and reference works, had done much to fix the scholarly standards of the time. Of his ability as a teacher there had never been any question. The Nation *spoke truly when it remarked: "His ready and extensive information, enthusiasm, and tact, and knowledge of men—qualities most serviceable to a teacher—*

gave him an unusual degree of success in dealing with his classes. His students became warmly attached to him, and we are inclined to think carried away a heartier love of the classics, and a readier familiarity with them, than are acquired from many professors vastly superior to him in genuine scholarship." Upon his literary work there was more division of opinion. He had edited, enlarged, and revised a number of important European reference works and grammars, *converting* Lemprière's Classical Dictionary *into* Anthon's Classical Dictionary, *for example.* He had brought out the first critical and exegetical edition of a classical author, with full notes and commentary, to be issued by an American; his Horatii Poemata *of 1830, a duodecimo volume, filled more than a thousand pages. He had edited for academic use the works of* Homer, Xenophon, Caesar, Cicero, Horace, Juvenal, Sallust, Virgil, *and* Tacitus. *Nobody had done so much to stimulate classical studies. But he had tried to do too much. In fact, he had tried to deal with the whole corpus of classical literature, when it was obviously necessary to divide the work among a number of expert hands. His editions, moreover, were criticized because they contained altogether too much explanatory matter and too many translated passages. He asserted that this was necessary because of the dearth of competent instructors in America. It was generally felt, however, that he had gone too far, and his copious aids injured rather than assisted the pupils.*

Reconstruction was making progress, but plainly against the will of Southerners who did not relish Negro domination. The Ku-Klux Klan was soon to be heard of. The sympathies of the diarist were more and more strongly with the Radical Republican leaders. He had written on June 27 of a friend who, once violently anti-radical, had experienced a change of heart after revisiting his old Kentucky community. "He says that his people and friends and all well-born Kentuckians are rebels at heart, and truculent, minatory, forceful rebels, lawless and murderous just as far as they dare venture—that they all look up to A. Johnson as their patron and ever-present help in time of trouble—that every mother's son of them should be disfranchised—that we made a fatal mistake in not hanging poor Jeff Davis the night we caught him, and in not hanging a dozen prominent rebels every day from that time to this." Strong thought such talk "injudicious"! But he added: "I think Johnson's policy, and his discord with Congress, is doing the Southern people immense mischief. It keeps alive and smouldering the old fires that were all but quenched two years ago." He did not blame Congress for keeping the old fires smouldering!

August 1. . . . Mr. Ruggles returned this morning in the *St. Laurent*. Long talk with him at No. 24, about emperors, kings, princes, archdukes, and such like cattle.

Mr. "Zbrowski" was married the other day, at Paris, to the widow of some Southern man. He told Mr. Ruggles that he proposed investigating Sclavonia thoroughly, and begged he would get him, from Seward, a special safe-conduct that would protect him against Russian emissaries who might endanger his life. What an ass he is!

August 5. . . . The political event of the last week is the Tennessee election, wherein "Conservatism" was smitten hip and thigh by the so-called Radicals, led by the refined and amiable Brownlow. A large class of white Tennesseans were disfranchised, and the freedmen voted the "Radical" ticket. Hence, we infer the triumph of a Republican ticket in every Southern State, even in South Carolina itself. The nigger vote seems likely to carry every state of them. What a bitter dose for their arrogant aristocracy of only seven years ago! Was there ever a more tremendous and searching social revolution? I know of none since the *noblesse* of France were crushed by the *canaille* of Paris. What would the Rhetts and Keitts and Trenholms and Hamptons of Buchanan's time have said to any one who told them that within ten years they would be respectfully soliciting their own and other peoples' niggers for seats in Congress and in their own state legislature—candidly submitting to Sambo's enlightened judgment their claims to his vote—recognizing their slaves as their masters?

It is terrible to think of the sum total of arrogance, insolence, arbitrary power thus unhorsed and paralyzed, at least for the present, and of the humiliation of the *ci-devant* aristocrats and floggers of women. Floggers of women and vendors of babies, those were the functions on which the welfare of their social system depended. Of course, there were excellent and exceptional households whose slaves suffered nothing of the kind, unless when the sheriff intervened in the interest of a creditor, and put up nigger poppa, and nigger mamma, and nigger baby as three several lots. But the social system of "the South" has been founded on crime and oppression for years and years. The South is suffering and will long suffer for that great crime. We are suffering for our acquiescence in it. Hence my taxes and impoverishment.

August 6. Charley Strong arrived at noon. Thank God! He has much to say about Oxford, York Cathedral, and so on, and about the Queen of England, who seems by his report, most unpopular with Englishmen.[7] I am surprised to learn how deep and how general her unpopularity has become. The Guelph blood is bad. From George I to William IV, every sovereign of them all has been either vicious or stupid or more or less cracked; and now her present Majesty seems in a queer mental condition—a sadly morbid condition from all accounts. But the old traditions of English loyalty (to say nothing of decency) must be well worn out when Englishmen of repute and position can talk as they do about this poor lady. They hold her answerable for the little extravagances of the Prince of Wales, and his Royal Highness *does* seem disposed to walk in the ways of his illustrious predecessor, *Georgius IV*.

August 8.   Mr. Ruggles is very sore about his red ribbon of the Legion of Honor, which he has never worn and won't wear, here or abroad. He begged General Dix to intercede for him that he might be spared the infliction, but if the General did so, his prayer was unavailing. I had intended to accost Mr. Ruggles in a jocose manner as *M. le Chevalier*, but I do not dare to. I think my venerated father-in-law would brain me if I tried the experiment.

Washington affairs look squally. A. Johnson writes Stanton that important public considerations would induce him to accept the resignation of the Secretary of War should it be tendered. Stanton replies, with equal urbanity, that important public considerations induce him to hold on to his secretaryship till Congress meets. The correspondence, as printed in this morning's papers, is remarkable for its brevity and condensation, or concentration. That is a rare virtue with our public men. They seldom economize on words. These two letters are models. War to the knife has seldom been declared with such distinctness and such brevity. Whether the President can decapitate the Secretary under the "Tenure of Office" Act seems uncertain. I should say he could. If he can do it, he will, for his pigheadedness is infinite. . . .

There is a break in the diary here; Strong took his first vacation in a number of years, spending it in Brattleboro with his family. Back in New York on August 29, he wrote of having walked in the woods with real enjoyment for the first time since the summer of 1860 in Great Barrington, and said that he felt "at least 500 per cent better for this experiment."

[7] The death of Prince Albert in 1861 had left Queen Victoria inconsolable; she declined to resume residence in London, and almost ceased to perform the public duties of a sovereign. Suggestions were now being made that she abdicate in favor of the Prince of Wales, while various leaders, including Sir Charles Dilke and Joseph Chamberlain, were shortly thought to lean toward republican ideas.

August 30.   Paid a visit to School of Mines this afternoon, and spent an hour with Dr. Chandler and his assistant in the assay-rooms, Mr. Day. School seems prosperous. There is promise of many applicants for admission next fall. Geological cases are all finished and begin to be occupied by Percy R. Pyne's donation, by that of the Delaware & Hudson Canal Co., and by Newberry's private collection, which the college ought to buy. Thereafter to Grunow's on Thirtieth Street and home. Mr. Ruggles here this evening, very blue about the Constitutional Convention.[8] He thinks we are to be taxed to death and is probably right.

September 3. . . . Affairs at Washington do not improve. A. Johnson grows more pigheaded every day, and more sympathetic with the *cidevant* aristocracy of the South. I fear the instincts of the village tailor— the "poor white"—survive in the acting President of the United States. Thank God, Grant seems sound, as witness his letter on Sheridan's removal.[9] Were he unsound, no one can guess what wild revolutionary scheme A. Johnson might contemplate. . . .

Candidates for poor Professor Charles Anthon's vacant chair begin to swarm. Letter from Mrs. Dr. Alexander B. Mott urging the claims of her brother-in-law, Charles E. Anderson (Miss Louisa's papa), who has long been conspicuous to denizens of Wall Street as an impecunious peripatetic of its sidewalks, looking for "something to turn up," like Dickens's Mr. Micawber. He is reputed an awful Copperhead, too, and came near getting his head broken for some inconsiderate speech; like to oblige Miss Louisa. Jesse A. Spencer presents himself, of course. . . .

September 10. . . . News in New York not much. The Rev. Thomas House Taylor, rector of Grace Church, died at his place up the River yesterday, after many months of incapacity. He was rector of Grace Church some thirty-five years. Never my ideal of a rector, or of a clergyman. Said to be rather unduly appreciative of pomps and vanities. Certainly most bitter and extravagant in his treatment of those with whom he differed; *vide* the record of the Trinity Church controversy in the legislature of 1857. His parish, the wealthiest of our city parishes, has never been in any but a mere nominal relation to the diocese. Dr. Taylor was practically bishop of Grace Church, recognizing no allegiance to any

[8] A constitutional convention, the first since 1846, was sitting for New York.
[9] Under the Military Reconstruction Act, Sheridan had been governor of the fifth district, Louisiana and Texas. His repressive policies made him much disliked, and President Johnson removed him—though Grant defended his acts.

ecclesiastical authority. I respect his memory, however, because he married me to Ellie, May 15, 1848.

September 13.　Died at Paris, Woodbury Langdon. He had no tangible disease, but has long been slowly failing. Ellie's young cousin, Mr. Rogers of Philadelphia, a West Point cadet, is engaged to Miss Sue Fish, Hamilton Fish's daughter. The young lady is a beautiful blonde, and he is said to be a fine fellow.

Andrew Johnson is certainly the best-hated man this side the Atlantic. Even the Democrats repudiate him, and he has no supporters outside his office-holding gang. The elections in Maine and California may indicate reaction against Congress, though I think they do not, but no one claims them as an endorsement of A. Johnson. Some talk there is about trouble when Congress meets. People say that Johnson's more intimate pals talk as if he contemplated a *coup d'état*—a purging of Congress after the manner of Cromwell. He is a public calamity, anyhow. One might be pardoned for hoping he would undertake some great crime and outrage, if one were sure he would be hanged for it.

September 17, TUESDAY. . . . Uneasiness about the state elections now at hand. The "Radicals" complain of general apathy, and the Democrats crow over an expected reaction. I confess misgivings about Negro suffrage (though it's hard to get on without conceding it), but I don't want A. Johnson to be encouraged in his execrable courses by anything he can construe into a popular endorsement. I fear he is among the worst men we have ever had in high place. Will he be impeached next November? Probably, and his impeachment will breed no end of agitation and mischief. Far better to let him go on eating dirt till his term ends, and then set up a tailor's shop in Tennessee, conducted on strictly constitutional principles.

September 24. . . . Signs of a reaction against the Republican Party, or against its more "Radical" wing, are vague but seem to multiply. I fear the Pennsylvania election will make them very definite.

September 25. . . . Dined here John Sherwood and went with Ellie to Wallack's. Dr. Barnard writes from Paris that he would like $2,000 (gold) to invest in apparatus for Columbia College.

Charles Halpine (alias "Miles O'Reilly") has spent two hours in irate conference with our politic A. Johnson at Washington, and holds that great man rather cheap. "He talked all the time, but didn't say much. I think it clear he means to lie on his oars till after the fall elections, and then, if Radical majorities turn up in New York and Pennsylvania," *then* (quoth Miles) "the country will go to *Hell, or* A. Johnson will go to the penitentiary, within thirty days. But, of course, you must not repeat this, because I'm a Democrat, and doing my best to carry this state for my party."

Even with the apocryphal "rebel militia of Maryland" to back him, A. Johnson can hardly be such a caitiff and such a fool as seriously to contemplate violence and an internecine war. But his folly is prodigious, no doubt. James II seems the only historical fool that can be compared with him.

September 29, SUNDAY. Death of Charles King, at Frascati, announced by cable. . . . I deeply regret Charles King, one of the jolliest of genial old gentlemen, though perhaps not the ideal of a college president.[10]

October 2. . . . The Pan-Anglican Council of Lambeth seems little more than an ecclesiastical palaver, like our "religious" anniversaries, except that its orators mount the pulpit instead of the platform or the stump. It is a Grand International Sermon Exposition. Potter, Whitehouse, and other American prelates have duly perorated or are to perorate. The Council is said (per cable) to have fulminated against Colenso and Mariolatry, but it will do well to leave all living questions within the church severely alone. It can safely censure, for example, Mormonism, condemn the tenets of the Beulah Particular Baptists, define its position on the Supralapsarian controversy, or declare that the church of the Abyssinians hath erred in doctrine. But if it undertake to legislate or to pronounce an opinion on the questions between High Church and Low, or to establish canons of ritualistic discipline, the bishops will soon be shying prayerbooks at each others' heads. . . .

October 5, SATURDAY. . . . State Democratic Convention, and that oily Copperhead, the Honorable Horatio Seymour, conspicuous as of old. I wonder he does not hide himself in the Antarctic continent from the sight of men, so base is his record for the last seven years.

Johnny makes a daily expedition to the Thirty-fourth Street ferry and returns with a pail of salt water for his aquarium, which is nearly full, at last, and ready to be stocked. The water seems pure and wholesome, though obtained so near the city.

Cable News. Row in Italy. The notable Garibaldi set off the other morning to take Rome, without the least regard for the Pontifical police.

---

[10] Old President King (1789–1867) had been living in Rome, where his son, General Rufus King, was the last United States minister to the Papal States. He had been president of the college 1849 to 1864.

Victor Emmanuel thereupon arrested Garibaldi and incarcerated him in the local "Tombs" without bail, upon which the Garibaldians began committing misdemeanors and breaches of the peace and getting up revolutions, at Acquapendente, Viterbo, and elsewhere. When last heard from, they were still at it, with what measure of success we do not know.[11] If they make too much disturbance, Louis Napoleon will send down a squad of Zouaves and squelch them, but it is quite possible that before the Zouaves come, His Holiness may find it prudent to decamp, disguised as an elderly lady, with his tiara in a bandbox, having previously sent off by express a few priceless and immoral antiques from the Vatican. All which (like most human transactions) "*may* lead to grave complications," as the newspapers say. The papacy is a most respectable institution, and I suppose Pio Nono to be an amiable old clergyman, though a goose; but to see Rome absorbed into the Kingdom of Italy, and duly digested and assimilated, would not afflict me.

October 9, WEDNESDAY. As I expected, yesterday's elections shew Democratic gains in Pennsylvania and Ohio, large enough for the New York *World* to crow over in a disgusting manner.[12] Sons of Belial have been firing salutes in the Park and elsewhere. They are making night hideous now (9:30 P.M.) with their artillery, in Tompkins Square, I suppose. There is joy among the *canaille* of Manhattan tonight. Its "Dutch" lager-bier saloons and Celtic whiskey-mills lift up their heads, for their Republican "Puritan" excise law and Sunday law enemies are smitten, at least for a season; and the chance of their discomfiture in New York next month is doubled. "Hurrah for ould Oireland, and down with thim d—— Yankees and Naygurs!" . . .

Last night with Charley to hear *La Grande Duchesse de Gerolstein* at the Fourteenth Street French Theatre. The opera is lively nonsense, admirably well brought out, with the most delightful caricatures of the manners and costumes of court and camp a hundred and fifty years ago. Offenbach's music suits this extravagant burlesque. It is very pretty and not at all profound, but considerably better than that of most "grand" operas of

[11] Garibaldi, eager to overthrow the temporal power of Pius IX and bring the papal states within a united Italy, had prepared to invade the domain of the Pope when, as Strong notes, he was arrested. Exiled to his island home of Caprera, he promptly escaped and made a second attempt; but this time his invasion was defeated by papal guards and French troops.

[12] Pennsylvania retained a Republican legislature, but the Democrats made heavy gains in Philadelphia. In Ohio the ordinary Republican majority was cut down to near the vanishing point, and Rutherford B. Hayes won the governorship by a very narrow margin over Allen G. Thurman.

the Verdi school. This *opéra bouffe* company draws great houses and is decidedly our most popular entertainment just now. Everybody knows "Voici le sabre de mon père" and

> Pif paf pouf, tara pan poum,
> Je suis moi, le Général Boum!

Was buried today old Peter Lorillard, tobacconist and millionaire. How many cubic miles of smoke and gallons of colored saliva are embodied in the immense fortune that was *his* last week! Stupendous thought! He doubled his profits by judicious investment and paid taxes on nobody knows how many city lots. Like King Cambuscan,

> A faire person he was, and fortunat,
> And kept always so well *Real Estat*
> That there n'as no wher swiche another man

except William B. Astor, and a few other of the *Dii Majores*. "How much has he left?" asked somebody in regard to a like case, and the answer was, "Well, he's left every dollar he had in the world, hasn't taken a single cent with him." But I think I have heard of some large benefactions by Lorillard to church objects; probably Low Church objects, but it doesn't matter. He had long been suffering from Bright's disease, or some other derangement of the kidneys, and died at Saratoga after much suffering, it's said.[13]

October 11. . . . Democrats continue to crow. Today's story is that the judicious Johnson means to spew Seward & Co. out of his mouth, as being neither hot nor cold, and to make up a new cabinet of really sound constitutional statesmen, like Vallandigham and G. H. Pendleton and Horatio Seymour. Perhaps Robert E. Lee will be Secretary of War and Admiral Semmes of the Navy; Honorable Henry A. Wise would make a pretty good Attorney-General for Johnson. And if Pennsylvania will only prevail on the venerable Buchanan, the sage of "Wheatlands," to aid the United States Senate with his counsel once more, things will begin to look a little like practical Reconstruction (on the Johnsonesque plan) at last. . . .

October 13, SUNDAY. The Rev. Mr. Vinton preached at Trinity Church one of those commonplace conventional sermons on which it's hopeless to try to fix one's attention. The words run off one as fast as they are

---

[13] Peter and George Lorillard had established a great business in smoking tobaccos and snuff, which Peter, Jr., continued to carry on. The Lorillards had a reputation for stinginess.

spoken, like water off a duck's back. Were it gently rubbed into the plumage, a very little of it might stick, but being vehemently *squirted*, it all hops off like hail. Even so does the truculent emphasis with which Vinton's truisms (or sophisms, as the case may be) are hurled at the sinner, cause them to rebound unfelt and ineffectual. All I remember of this "lengthy" discourse is Vinton's bold and unqualified statement that one of the parables (I forget which) was *not* "intended as a mere play of fancy to amuse an idle hour." (!!!)

October 16. Beautiful Indian summer. Poverty has its compensating advantages. Were I a millionaire, I might be weak enough to own a box at the Academy of Music and feel bound to appear in my place two nights out of three. How dreadful that would be! I feel it keenly, for [William] Travers very kindly sent us his nice proscenium box for tonight, and I went with Ellie and Miss Minnie Parker and her brother Harry, and also Charles Blake, who dined here. Opera was *Huguenots.* I sat but three acts of laborious feebleness, and then came off, with the sensations of a Norwegian who has been supping on bread made of sawdust, and no butter. The party in the box was pleasant, but Meyerbeer's music, with all its elaboration, seems to me utterly barren and vapid. . . .

October 17. . . . The Garibaldians are making headway, and are prevailing against the Pope's Zouaves. So say the cable despatches. But "telling a telegram" is a polite circumlocution for lying.

Our political prospects are unchanged. The Democrats seem safe to carry the state. But they carried the state in the black days of November, 1862, and we survived the calamity somehow. Though their probable victory next month will be a serious misfortune to the country, we must not forget that the world has been moving during the last seven years, and that even "Democrats" (a few inveterate old Copperheads excepted) have moved with it, in spite of themselves. They are no longer what they were. Their position is now in advance of that held by the Republican rank and file and by Republican leaders in January, 1861.

Of course, there is still danger from any Democratic triumph. They may renew their old alliance with "the South" when the Southern States are *sui juris* once more. They may then try to resume the business of that long-established firm of "Celt, Doughface, and Chivalry," now in the hands of a Republican receiver, and the devil is always on hand with a large capital which he will be glad to put in as a special partner. But I think the firm can never recover the monopoly it enjoyed in the good old constitutional days of Pierce and Buchanan. The North is stronger, the

South vastly weaker. Slavery is gone, and with it the power of that dark spell, the awful word "Abolitionist." Its utterance used to make Northern people hoot the wretch to whom it was applied. Its whisper inspired Southern gentlemen to hang him or at least to tar and feather him. But those palmy days of the republic are departed. A man who denies the absolute perfection of "Southern institutions" can no longer be safely treated like a mad dog. Any future league of Northern Democrat and Southern rebel is thus deprived of a weapon that was once most prevailing. Moreover, many Northern Democrats have lost all taste for the dirt they used to eat, and not a few of the most combustible rebel chiefs seem so thoroughly cured of chivalry that they actually talk and write and sound practical. Our next battle will be on the issue of *repudiation*, more or less disguised, and the infallible instincts of the Democratic party will certainly put it on the wrong side of that issue, as of every other.

One thing seems pretty clear (and I understand Dana thinks so, too) viz.: that the recent elections have killed off a score of aspirants for the next presidency—Chase among them—and that Grant is now sure to be nominated. If nominated, he will be elected, unless the more extreme Radicals (so-called) bolt and put up a candidate of their own. They might thereby throw the election on the House, in which their man would be likely to succeed.

October 19, SATURDAY.   To Coney Island today with Temple to look after marine zoology. The expedition was not brilliantly successful. The horsecars took two hours and a half to make their ten miles, and when we reached our destination, Temple was nearly famished. . . .

Had my first glimpse of the unfinished "Prospect Park" of Brooklyn, which will soon become a formidable rival of our "Central Park." It begins its career with well-grown trees, and I am told it commands a noble outlook over the two cities, the harbor and the sea.

October 22.   To Fifty-ninth Street this afternoon, traversing for the first time the newly opened section of Madison Avenue between Fortieth Street and the College, a rough and ragged track, as yet, and hardly a thoroughfare, rich in mudholes, goats, pigs, geese, and stramonium. Here and there Irish shanties "come out" (like smallpox pustules), each composed of a dozen rotten boards and a piece of stove-pipe for a chimney. Found Newberry in the School of Mines, spent a couple of hours in the geological room and walked down with him, stopping to admire the new cruciform synagogue on Fifth Avenue, now nearly roofed. He told me once more that he must resign unless his $3,000 salary be raised when Barnard returns. His wife and seven children are at Cleveland, because they cannot live here on this salary and his private income together. . . .

Looked through the geology collection with Newberry. Two-thirds of it are his own property brought on from Cleveland, and not yet fully displayed. He explained and commented on it, as my ignorance required, this being the first considerable shew of paleontology I ever saw. It was profoundly interesting. Compared with some of these antiquities, the everlasting hills are modern work and mankind a mushroom. The period that separates the pyramids from the last Fifth Avenue brownstone front dwindles to a point when we think of the ages that have passed since any one of Newberry's trilobites gave his last flop or wiggle and settled down into the fast stratifying mudflat on which rested the waters of his native estuary or lagoon. (That is a fine sentence.) I do not see how we can answer the geologists when they tell us of these vast periods, nor do I see why we should admit their statements reluctantly, when they are fairly borne out by evidence. Even if we think ourselves bound to search the Scriptures for physical science and that the Bible was meant to in- struct us therein, its teachings are *not* contradicted by geology, while its revelation of the infinity of Creative Power is thereby most awfully en- forced and illustrated. . . .

October 26, SATURDAY, or more properly Sunday morning. At "Fair of American Institute" this afternoon in West Fourteenth Street (where the "Metropolitan Fair" was had and solemnized in 1864). A curious and interesting *omnium gatherum*. Especially interesting was the multitude of plainly dressed men with hard, keen faces, mechanics, inventors, engineers, and the like, who were peering sagaciously into the mysterious engines and exchanging monosyllables about their respective points. There were microscopic photographs there taken with one of William Wales's one- eighth-inch objectives that made me gnaw my fingers with envy and hope- less desire. They were miles beyond the utmost my one-eighth or even my one-twelfth (Ross 1854) ever dreamed of. But my highest earthly aspiration now is sufficient bread—and perhaps a film of butter—for Ellie and the children.

Evening with Templetoniculus to Steinway Hall for Theodore Thomas's first concert (I beg his pardon, "Sinfonie Soirée").[14] The little man begged

[14] Steinway Hall on Fourteenth Street, built by the piano manufacturer Henry E. Steinway (1797–1871), was formally opened this year; the building combined ware- rooms, offices, and a concert hall. Theodore Thomas's symphony *soirées* had been begun in 1864.

the privilege of hearing the C Minor. Programme uncommonly good. Bach, suite No. 3 in D (three movements), was fuguey, but forcible; its third movement (a "gavotte") exceedingly vigorous and melodic. Mme. Parepa Rosa sang a very charming aria from Gluck's *Armide*. Then came a long orchestral movement from Cherubini's *Medea*, which was melodramatic and suggestive of infanticide and red fire behind the scenes. Then Mme. Parepa Rosa sang "Deh, vieni non tardar" from *Nozze di Figaro*—sang it exquisitely, too, and was encored. There followed two movements of an unfinished symphony by Schubert, quite brilliant in a sensational "scratch-cat" way, but abounding in gracefully contrasted passages of melody. These sounded a little like reminiscences, however. The second part was that blessed, radiant, glorious C Minor Symphony, the greatest of orchestral works. Compared with it, all others are nowhere. The matchless sunburst of the fourth movement out of the vague, weird passage that connects it with the third was nobly rendered. So was the whole movement, and it brought the audience up to a hurray! at its close. Had any one proposed "three cheers for Beethoven" they would have been heartily given. . . .

October 30. . . . Affairs in Italy look mixed. Victor Emmanuel put Garibaldi under arrest by order of Louis Napoleon. But Garibaldi would not stay arrested, and was, at last accounts (by cable), skrimmaging away quite near the Holy City. The Pope has retired to Castel Angelo, and probably locked himself up in the garret. Victor Emmanuel doesn't know what to do. His people are at boiling point and clamorous for Rome. Meanwhile, transports have quietly sailed from Toulon and are probably on the coast of Italy by this time.[15]

Elections have just been held in Virginia, Alabama, and Louisiana. The freedmen voted for a reconstruction convention in each state. The whites were against it (preferring continuance of military rule), and the freedmen have prevailed. In Alabama and Louisiana the whites were apathetic and kept away from the polls, but in Virginia they put forth all their strength. It was in vain, for very many ex-rebels are still disfranchised in spite of A. Johnson, and Cuffee outnumbers his late master in power of vote. So it looks as if the two races were to be henceforth hostile and antagonistic. This is not very surprising, all things considered. But the *ci-devant* slaveholders could have done much to avert the calamity by tact

[15] Garibaldi was temporarily checkmated by French power; but as soon as the Franco-Prussian War paralyzed Napoleon III, in 1870, Victor Emmanuel II was to do what Garibaldi failed to effect—make Rome the capital of united Italy.

and conciliation. Instead of this, they have, by all accounts, treated the freedmen as their natural enemies, and studiously displayed hatred and contempt toward them, which must have been nearly as galling as the tyranny of the old regime, and under the new state of affairs, wholly intolerable. Perhaps this is quite natural, too. Even now they are trying to make matters still worse, if possible. In Virginia, the hands employed in mines and factories and on farms are being discharged by wholesale "for voting the radical ticket." An inviting field for immigration! Unpromising enough two years ago, this development of irreconcilable social discord has made it the last region on earth in which a sane white mechanic or laborer would choose to live, or a Northern or European capitalist to invest a dollar. And for this, Southerners may thank their own blind, arrogant self-will, their inveterate obstinacy of pride and bad temper.

This antagonism will make the black race masters of the South, unless something unforeseen prevent it. Very bad for the ex-chivalry, and not very good for us at the North, or for the nation. It may keep us unsettled for an indefinite period. Should it develop its legitimate fruit, it may expel the white race from the South, bring about a Jacquerie, or fill the country with rows, bloody feuds, and murderous little bushwhacking campaigns from the Potomac to the Gulf. It is said that the result of this election has brought to Washington "several prominent gentlemen from Virginia," who represent to A. Johnson that a nigger uprising is already organized, that all the white people are to be massacred, and that there is need of stronger military force without a day's delay. I dare say the chivalry is scared. Dethroned tyrants are apt to be nervous and scare-y. I disbelieve in the contemplated Santo Domingo plot. But no one can tell to what crime and outrage these newly freed serfs may yet be tempted by petty persecutions, by treatment as pariahs viler than the slaves they were, and by systematic denial of work whereby to earn their bread.

October 31. . . . Governor Andrew died yesterday in less than twenty-four hours after an apoplectic stroke. No state governor did the country better service during the war, or was so well prepared for it when it came. He was not only honest and able and a successful politician, but a man of culture and refined, agreeable manner. . . .[16]

The late signs of political reaction (be the same more or less) have brought out a suspicion that the fine old rank-smelling Copperheadism of

[16] John A. Andrew, the great war governor of Massachusetts (1818–1867), had retired from office, quite worn out, near the end of 1866. He used his farewell message to advocate a kindly, conciliatory policy toward the South.

former days is not dead, but has been sleeping and begins to awake. Democratic papers now speak of Lincoln as the vilest of mankind and of Jeff Davis as the best and greatest. They aver that "Southern social institutions" promoted the noblest interests of humanity, whereas Northern society is founded on a "mongrelism miscalled freedom." Theories that are dead and buried should not be allowed to rise from their graves and parade themselves, stinking on the public streets. It is still more improper for them to get down from the gibbet on which they have been hung in chains as convicted of murder and treason on the most gigantic scale, and then to go about shrieking and gibbering the criminal nonsense they uttered when in life. On the whole, I believe the plantation philosophy of 1860 to be really defunct (at the North, that is; in Southern barrooms it doubtless survives), just as Jacobitism was dead in 1750 and American Toryism in 1790. Neither carcase was wholly decomposed for several years, or decades, after death. Either could have been galvanized into a display of local irritability for some time. Even so, fools will probably be found in New York and Philadelphia for the next ten years who are not ashamed to reproduce the obsolete gabble of the Charleston *Mercury* and *De Bow's Review*. But they will gradually die out.

Found Travers here when I got home. Full of fun as usual. He warned the Honorable John Morrissey, when about to take his seat in Congress, "to take care he didn't make a mistake and call the Speaker, Mr. Referee."[17] To whom Morrissey: "I don't know much about the Rules of the House, but I know something about the rules of the ring, and if I get into a difficulty with the Speaker or anybody else, I'll just ask him to step out into the redundy (query: rotunda?) with me, and settle it there."

November 1. Exec. Comm. of Sanitary Commission this evening at 21 West Twelfth Street; Newberry, Agnew, Gibbs, Blatchford, and I. Struggling to get our affairs closed—arduous work. There must be mismanagement somewhere. Everything lengthens itself and drags along, in spite of all we can do to pin it down. Warriner wants another six months (i.e., a year) to finish his book, and I believe he is working faithfully.

November 2. Indian summer. Just from Century Club, where Gibbs, Newberry, Agnew, and I conferred on Sanitary Commission affairs. Discoursed with divers people; General Barnard, General Vinton, Fithian,

[17] John Morrissey, the pugilist-politician, had been supported by some wealthy New York sportsmen, including William R. Travers, in building his racing track, "Horse Haven," at Saratoga. With the support of Boss Tweed, he had been elected to Congress in 1866 from the Fifth New York District.

the Reverend Vinton, and others. General Cullum in a nervous twitter about a nigger insurrection or social war in Virginia, which he considers probable, and thinks will be likely to increase our national debt. As that debt is likely to be repudiated by Western votes within five years, any increase of its nominal amount makes little difference. But I'm sorry for Southerners, whether black or white. . . .

November 4. Meeting of college trustees at Law School was long. Samuel Blatchford elected trustee in Charles King's place. The Committee on Resolutions, and so on, in view of the death of King and Anthon, was called together for the first time half an hour before the board met, so there was little time for consultation, but the affair took a satisfactory shape. Betts had prepared certain decorous resolutions, and we recommended $750 to be appropriated for a portrait, and also the establishment of an "Anthon Scholarship" with an exhibition of $300 to be held during the Senior year by the student who at the end of the Junior year shall stand the best examination on, for example, some Greek play not included in the undergraduate course. . . .

November 5. . . . To meeting of Life Insurance & Trust Company trustees. Much discourse about the "financial earthquake" that is expected. It will come in due time. The shameless New York *Herald* is preaching *repudiation* and enforcing its doctrines by appeals to the lowest and vilest motives. That is a question on which the West cannot be trusted, and its voice will be decisive. Ohio is said to be especially unsound. The chivalric South (when reconstructed) will, of course, take its habitual position as to the payment of debts due Yankee scum. And probably the cry of "no privileges to bondholders, no aristocracy of wealth, no more payments of the work-man in paper and the public creditor in gold," will enlist all the dishonesty, selfishness, and baseness of the whole country.

Evening—to Union League Club. Have not been there for many months past. It seems much changed. Very few of the old set were there, though the rooms were full of seekers for election returns. Everybody looked sober. There have been large Democratic gains everywhere, and the Democracy has doubtless carried the state. Other states voted today and have probably gone and done likewise. Rejoice, Oh A. Johnson!

The Republicans of New York and Massachusetts have a liquor law to carry that has alienated the Germans and stimulated the enmity of whiskey-millers and corner grocers (who have always been Democrats) to increased activity. Moreover, our party leaders have been going a little too fast for the masses. Many honest, patriotic people who exult over the downfall of slavery are startled at the prospect of Negro sovereignty south of the Potomac and Ohio, and are by no means sure they would like to see the Honorable Mr. Quashee Hampton or Sambo Davis claiming a seat in Congress as a representative or a senator from South Carolina or Mississippi. It is useless to say that this is all a prejudice against a black skin, and that if Quashee is not a gentleman and a statesman, it is because he is degraded by servitude that has lasted for generations. People hesitate about the Negro senator, not because of his dark cuticle, but because he belongs to a race the average intellect whereof is (in 1867 at least) of lower grade than ours; because we are familiar with the notion of a nigger servant, bootblack, barber, or field hand, and not familiar with that of a Negro legislator. We have had, to be sure, something of Soulouque and his court, the Duc de Marmalade, and so on, but generally with a disposition to grin, and we know little or nothing of the black barristers and assemblymen who hold their own in the British West Indies. To the Northern man of plain, ordinary, common understanding, a colored person helping to regulate our national finances and our foreign relations seems out of place and anomalous. Perhaps his unfitness for legislation (real or apparent) is caused by the tyrannous wrong to which he and his progenitors have been subjected. It is no doubt due, in very great measure, to that cause, and he is not to be blamed or despised for it. But his unfitness is believed in by most people as a fact, and they do not see that it is any the less a fact because it has been inflicted on him by the atrocious system of slavery.

The fall elections of 1867 were not particularly important in themselves, but attracted attention as throwing light on the prospects of the coming presidential campaign. Eleven states sent voters to the polls, some choosing a governor and legislature, some only local officers. In general, the result was adverse to the Republicans. New York went Democratic, as Strong says, by very nearly fifty thousand votes; New Jersey by sixteen thousand; Ohio elected a Republican governor by a majority of 2,983; and in Wisconsin, Minnesota, and Kansas the Republican majorities were very narrow. Prohibition played a rôle in some states; in Massachusetts, for example, the Republicans were identified with the Maine prohibitory law, and the Democrats with a proposal for saloons under license. But there could be no doubt that the elections registered a widespread dissatisfaction with the Reconstruction policy of the Radical Republicans. Although the Radicals were forcing Negro suffrage upon the South, Negro suffrage amendments to the state constitutions were defeated in New Jersey, Wisconsin, Minnesota, and Kansas. As Strong writes, the voters were not convinced that the Negro was yet qualified for a share in the government. "The Democratic Party," remarked the Nation *of November 7, "is evidently going to be strong enough next year to make it worth while beating them." Itself a Radical organ, the* Nation *admitted that "Negro suffrage is none too popular, whether existing North or South."*

Despite the elections, Congress met on November 21 in no chastened mood. Representative George S. Boutwell of Massachusetts presented a majority report in favor of the impeachment of President Johnson. It was a report that the country refused to take seriously, for most of the charges were farcical. Johnson was accused of vetoing bills that he should have approved, of having given advice to Southern legislatures that he should not have given, and of having pardoned deserters whom he should not have pardoned, his accusers forgetting that he had just as much right to use his own judgment with regard to the veto and the pardoning power as Congress had to use its own judgment with regard to bills. The impeachment scheme temporarily collapsed amid public ridicule—but only temporarily, for Thad Stevens and Ben Wade were determined to have their way. The House showed its implacable temper when it called on the President for full information about his pardon of rebels and perjurers, and for the correspondence between him and General Grant regarding the removal of Sheridan and Sickles as commanders in two of the military districts in the South, and the attempted removal of Secretary of War Stanton. But the day of reckoning between Johnson and the Radical leaders was not yet. As the year closed, the principal topics of public discussion were the Alabama *controversy with Great Britain, which had reached a deadlock; the mayoralty candidacy of Fernando Wood, who had announced that "if the old charges are brought up against my character, I will not attempt to refute them"; inflation, which, with great quantities of paper money in circulation and a general spirit of speculation rampant, was a very grim reality to people (like Strong) of static incomes; a quarrel between the touchy J. L. Motley, minister to Austria, and Secretary Seward; and the progress of the Negro-Carpetbagger regime in the South, where the new Negro-suffrage constitutions were about to come into effect. The nomination of Grant for the presidency was now generally expected by most Republicans. A happier note was struck by the arrival of Charles Dickens to give public readings from his novels.*

November 6.   A. W. Bradford died last night. He would be a greater loss to the College and to Trinity Church but for a certain weakness that made him always adverse to rigorous action against anybody, and in favor of giving everybody every indulgence and all the money they might ask. . . .

Miss Louisa Catlin dined here, with General Badeau[18] of Grant's staff, and we went to the French Theatre and heard Offenbach's *Grande Duchesse de Gerolstein.* Exceedingly fresh, pretty, and sparkling. No wonder it has taken the wind out of Maretzek's sails, and keeps its popularity so long. Badeau told me, of his own knowledge, and on the authority of his own eyes and ears, certain queer stories about Mrs. Lincoln. I always heard she was underbred, but I never supposed it possible she could be the "stuck-up" vulgar vixen he says she was. I listened with interest, because I signed a paper only this morning, and at the request of young Ingersoll, recommending or endorsing a proposed movement to raise $100,000 for her benefit.

The incidents Badeau mentions were in 1864 and 1865. He says he knows that Grant and Stanton with their respective wives were invited to be of the theatre party on the fatal night of April 14, and that the ladies demurred and declined because of Mrs. Lincoln's uncertain temper and manners, and kept their husbands away. But for this, the night might have been yet more disastrous. Badeau was then on Grant's staff.

November 7.   Leaden sky, and the air has seemed to be holding a snow storm in solution, ready to come down at any minute.

Democratic majorities in this state will foot up nearly 50,000! The Morganists regard this as a triumph over the Fentonites and Thurlow Weed rather than a Republican defeat. Many Radicals rejoice greatly, and George William Curtis among them. I hope their joy may not be turned to mourning by grave mischief at the South.

Sudden eruption of disagreeable stories about poor Bradford. Everybody seems to have known for months that he was drinking too much, morning, noon and night, in a secret way. I never suspected it. People say they have seen him at his office and in court quite incapacitated by drink! Amazing and hardly credible. But his father, a Reformed Dutch clergyman of Albany, his brother (a man of great promise), and two of his sons are said to have died of alcoholic poison, and the third son is reported to be

[18] Adam Badeau, who remained on Grant's staff until the general became President in March, 1869. He was now preparing the first volume of his *Military History of Ulysses S. Grant*, which appeared early in 1868 and was warmly received.

going the same way. So the deadly appetite was in his blood, and it may have grown uncontrollable when he was in grief and misery.

November 8, FRIDAY.   There was a great attendance at Trinity Chapel this morning (ten o'clock) for Bradford's funeral—bar, bench, and a host of clients and friends. Interment was to be at Albany. I fear the worst stories about him are true! He had long been going down, and sank at last to a depth below hope, and some say to delirium tremens and fits of violent mania. This seems to have been known to many, who wisely refrained from reporting it. His professional income probably exceeded that of any lawyer in the state, for he had a great practice and charged enormous fees ($50,000, for example, in the Rose Will case), but he spent money recklessly, and according to Nelson Chase (that universal intelligencer) his assets will not pay his undertaker's bill. How little we know of people we meet every day! . . .

Poor Bradford's last act as a trustee of Columbia College was characteristic. He sent to our October meeting, which he was too ill to attend, a letter with a resolution he wanted to have brought up, *raising all salaries.* . . .

Letter from Bellows at Berlin. Lamentable tidings of the philanthropic M. Henri Dunant, author of the *Souvenir de Solferino* and chief engineer of international conferences on battle-field relief.[19] He has made a "bust-up" and fled from Geneva to Paris, where his life is rather shady and obscure. It is said to be an ugly case of defalcation. So General Dufour tells the Reverend Bellows. Also, Bellows is disillusionated about Dr. Evans of Paris, who reports himself the originator and father of the Sanitary Commission, and says it all grew out of his (Evans's) counsels and exertions during the first year of the war—whereas, we never heard of his existence till long afterwards. This disgusts the Reverend Bellows.

Later (tomorrow morning in fact). Ellie came in with her little party from Niblo's (*Black Crook*) at eleven o'clock, and we had a small supper. There were Murray Hoffman, and Colden Murray, Jack Ehninger, Graham, Lee, Dr. Alexander Mott, and others; *ac etiam* M. le Marquis de Talleyrand-Périgord, and his seven or eight months' wife, who is some sort of cousin of Murray Hoffman's, a great-granddaughter of old Joseph D. Beers. M. le Marquis is an insignificant looking little man, what a Missourian would call an "ornary cuss"; but he has served as a private in Algeria, Italy, and Mexico. Moreover, he is to be M. le Duc some day—*teste* Murray Hoffman. The lady, née Curtis, is not pretty, but gracious,

[19] J. Henri Dunant (1828–1910), of Switzerland, founder of the International Red Cross.

"cunning," and captivating. Speaks her native tongue with a pretty little accent, sings French comic songs in a "ravishing" way, and seems altogether graceful and nice. . . .

November 11.   Uptown with William Schermerhorn at three o'clock for College Library Committee. Visited Newberry and spent three quarters of an hour very agreeably, wondering over his paleontological marvels, the new "dinichthys" included. It is a magnificent collection. Home by Sixth Avenue railroad, and then General Sheridan dined here; also his aide, Colonel Crosby, who's among the handsomest young men, or boys, I ever saw. Also, Charley Post, and Miss Minnie Vail and Miss Fanny Smythe, both very beautiful, charming, and gracious. The general is a stumpy, quadrangular little man, with a forehead of no promise and hair so short that it looks like a coat of black paint. But his eye and his mouth shew force, and of all our chieftains he alone has displayed the capacity of handling men in actual shock of battle, turning defeat into victory, rallying a broken fugitive mob and hurling them back upon the enemy. Grant, Sherman, Thomas, and others may be great strategists, but I am not aware that they ever did that thing. His talk is pleasant, and that, with the presence of the two beauties, and with Ellie's unfailing tact, made our symposium agreeable. I feared it would be a bore. They all went off to *Midsummer Night's Dream* at the Olympic, and I went at half-past eight to Trinity Church vestry.

At vestry meeting, S. P. Nash was elected vice James G. King, deceased, unanimously, though old Verplanck made some kind of muddled objection that nearly all the diocesan standing committee comes from Trinity Parish. Recommendations of Committee on Music were adopted; proposition to buy land adjoining Trinity Church cemetery, and another to buy land somewhere about Thirtieth Street for a "Mission Chapel" (under Act of 1867) duly referred; $500 voted to Ellie's Industrial School. . . .

November 12.   This afternoon with Agnew and Blatchford discussing Dr. Warriner's book, over which he has been pottering and drawing pay for two years, the final report of the "Special Relief" and "Supply" Service of the Sanitary Commission. It will never be finished. We ought to recognize the fact that Warriner is a failure, like Knapp, whose material Warriner was to incorporate in this report. We ought to give up the job as hopeless and spend no more money on it. But Agnew thinks otherwise, and wants us to pay Dr. Warriner another $1,000 on his pledge that the book will be ready for the press next May. I dissent from this view. We have been unlucky both in Knapp and in Warriner. Each seems the most dilatory of mankind. Knapp sent in his MS at last, under great pressure, but it is rubbish. Poor Knapp! He has given up philanthropy and is speculating in cranberries. He has got up a great cranberry company in New Jersey, and the more feeble-minded of his friends are taking stock therein.[20]

November 13. . . . N.B. "F'nandy Wood" is nominated for mayor once more, and will be elected. Such are the blessings of Free Institutions, and the enlightenment and moral sense of the sovereign people. A community that chooses F. Wood as its chief magistrate has no right to turn up its nose at nigger suffrage in South Carolina. . . .

November 16, SATURDAY. . . . Charles Blake dined here and went with Mrs. Ellie to the French theatre. I went with Temple to the Philharmonic Concert, at the Academy of Music, sat in one of the galleries, and came off at the end of Part I, not caring to hear an Overture to *Manfred* by Schumann, and strongly preferring not to hear at any price "Mazeppa," a "Poème Symphonique" by the galvanic Abbé Lizst, or Liszt, or whatever his name is. So we heard Beethoven's *Pastorale*, and a piano concerto (Op. 8) by Mozart. . . . The Mozart concerto is delightful, its second movement quite memorable for the exceeding beauty of its melodic subject, which is strongly flavored with the real original Mozart aroma, for which Mozart had an exclusive patent (*vide* the Jupiter Symphony, "Vedrai Carino," and the "Benedicites" of the *Twelfth Mass*) and which Handel, Beethoven, and Haydn never produced, great as they were. Hoffman marred two movements of this concerto by interpolating two elaborate inane "cadenzas" to shew off his fingering. He might just as well have done a little legerdemain, exhibited a conjuring trick with cards or a bottle, or turned three back sommersaults over his piano. Neither interpolation would have been more impertinent and unseasonable than was the introduction of these senseless phrases into Mozart's pure crystalline music. . . .

November 20. I am maddened by the cost of living. Things tend from bad to worse, and I keep running behindhand every year, and cannot bear to give Ellie a serious talk about retrenchment—fewer little dinners, less opera, and so on. But I believe my hesitation does the brave little woman injustice. Opera, by the way, has evaporated for the season. Gounod's *Romeo and Juliet* did not draw. The chorus revolted, demanding higher pay, and Max Maretzek collapsed.

[20] The Sanitary Commission was unfortunate in its historians. Charles J. Stillé's *History* or *General Report*, published in 1866, was a satisfactory general survey, to which Strong contributed an excellent chapter on "Financial History of the Commission"; but the supplementary works which had been planned came to nothing.

Death of Fitz-Greene Halleck at Guilford, Connecticut. I owe his memory a grudge for "Marco Bozzaris," which I had to spout, with inexpressible loathing, when I was a small boy, and I see nothing in anything he ever wrote higher than a certain clearness and smoothness. How I used to hate

> Strike till the last armed foe expires,
> Strike for your altars and your fires,
> Strike for the green graves of your sires!! etc., etc.

and the pump-handle movement that was expected to accompany each adjuration![21] . . .

November 22.   This afternoon to Law School; Drisler, Betts, Egleston, and I, representing two committees, viz.: on School of Mines and on the Anthon Scholarship. The School receives quite liberal gifts of government publications from France, Austria, and other countries. Walked uptown with Egleston. How much might be done for that School if one had $100,000 to spare!

Morning papers full of Congress, now sitting. Honorable James Brooks leads off in high howl over the dear ruined Constitution. That luminous statesman and judicious Celt, the Honorable Something Robinson,[22] moves that Adams, Minister at London, be ordered home by telegraph, and impeached, for that he did not somehow prevent a verdict against certain Fenian runagates now under sentence of death for treason and murder. These criminals are naturalized Americans, who recrossed the Atlantic and proceeded to set up a republic in Ireland by the Hibernian method of murdering a policeman in Manchester. (I think it was Manchester.) Their American citizenship is claimed to give them some sort of protection, but that shuts them out from pleading Irish patriotism as excusing or palliating murder.[23] If naturalization discharged them from their native alle-

[21] Fitz-Greene Halleck (1790–1867) had dwelt in semi-retirement in Guilford, Connecticut, his birthplace, since 1849; but had often revisited New York, where Strong saw him at the Century Club. Minor poet though he was, he had touched an American chord, and a decade after his death was given a statue in Central Park.

[22] This was the Irish-born William E. Robinson (1814–1892), who was in Congress 1867–1869, and 1881–1885.

[23] The Fenian movement had now invaded England itself. A number of Irish and Irish-Americans had formed secret associations in English cities, conspired to seize magazines and armories, attacked officers of the law, and finally in trying to rescue some prisoners had killed a Manchester policeman. Those responsible for the murder were brought to trial in Manchester and sentenced to death. One Warren, who called himself a naturalized citizen of the United States, attributed his sad fate to the negligence of the American minister in not somehow stopping the English trial. A number of the baser American politicians tried to make capital out of the affair.

giance to the Crown of Great Britain and Ireland, it released them also from any insurrectionary or homicidal duties in the cause of Ireland. Adams could not interfere, even if so disposed, and it is lamentable that folly like Mr. Robinson's should be tolerated by Congress, and his insane motion referred, or in any way treated as a serious proposition.

November 23. . . . Three Manchester Fenians duly hanged today, and very justly, I think. "Political crimes" used to be held the highest crimes of all, and deserving the sharpest punishment, as witness the savage laws enforced in England almost to our own day in cases of high treason. *Now* it is held by most people unworthy this enlightened century to punish any political crime with death, and many think so who have no scruple about hanging a murderer. But crimes of this class (to say nothing of government being a divine institution) generate more crime of every class, and more misery, than any other offense we can imagine. Look at the history of the Civil War, and the present state of the South!

November 24. . . . Rochefort touched Omaha, Atlanta, and Charleston during his flying excursion into the country.[24] Thinks Charleston has no future, is as dead as Palmyra or a red herring, has no money, no business, no energy, and no hope, and will soon be wiped out by mere taxation.

November 25. A majority report in favor of impeachment was presented to the House this afternoon at two-thirty. If the Republicans act on it they are lost. A. Johnson can beat them on that issue before the people, if not in the Senate, unless the evidence collected by the labors of the committee during the past months be very much stronger than I believe it to be. Smythe told Charley Strong that A. Johnson—his court and Cabinet—were in great buzz and ferment over the prospect of this report, and that our venerated Chief Magistrate intends "to raise H——."

November 26. . . . Report of "Impeachment Committee" seems two-penny stuff.

November 27. . . . Saw Mr. Ruggles this evening, just from Washington. He presented his Report on Weights, Measures, and so forth, to the enlightened A. Johnson (who "did not seem quite to understand the matter"), together with one of the six model twenty-five franc pieces struck by the French government, as patterns of the future currency of the world; a great prize for some coin collector hereafter.

The impeachment business is generally pooh-poohed. Even the *Tribune* turns it a cold shoulder. "Fenians" are holding meetings; there was a grand

[24] Henri Rochefort, pen name of Henri de Rochefort-Lucay, French publicist (1830–1913).

palaver at Cooper Institute last night to denounce Great Britain for hanging American citizens convicted of murder in England and for not giving the prisoners a mixed jury; that is, a jury *de medietate linguae*, which they construe to mean one-half American. Poor Ould Ireland is in low estate because the majority of Irishmen are jackasses, and not through the machinations of any "dasthardly opprissor"—Saxon, Norman, or Dane.

Pauper sum et miserrimus. Grave talk with Ellie after I got home from Wall Street. Her pluck and good sense are excellent. But *sursum corda*—or (as one would say to a frightened dog) *"sursum cauda!"* Things may not be as bad as they look, or I may be able to improve them. At worst, I could probably get the boys into free scholarships at Columbia College and gain my own bread with a hand organ and a monkey. I would make that neglected instrument an agency for elevating the standard of popular musical taste, and refine and exalt the souls of street children and of servant gals at area railings, with the most exquisite scherzos and adagios by Mozart and Beethoven.

November 28, THANKSGIVING DAY. . . . After dinner, I marched off Miss Mary Bostwick to hear Haydn's "Seasons" at Steinway Hall, where I had reserved seats. It was my first experience, for many a long year, of that much-loved composition, and the old memories came freshly back, reinforced by a multitude of beautiful points that seemed new. The work as a whole is unhappily an anticlimax in design, for the music of winter must be cold and dreary after that of summer and spring; and in execution, too, Haydn seems to have got a little tired of it as he neared its end. I think it is so with many of his works. But each of these four parts is admirable and delightful in its degree, and the first is almost absolutely perfect. The opening chorus ("Come gentle spring") and the finale of the second part (the summer evening chorus—"die Abendglocke") are matchless. The existence of so noble and beautiful a work one may well reckon among the blessings to be remembered on Thanksgiving Day, as a setoff against much that is bad, a comfort in trouble.

November 29. . . . Died at Saratoga, his residence, old *Walworth*, last of the chancellors.[25] He left the bench with an exalted reputation for learning, ability, and integrity, but his record since then has been less brilliant. He married a splurging Western widow (Mrs. J. J. Hardin) for his second wife. It's said that her fast, expensive ways demoralized the staid, straitlaced, rather puritanical old fogy; threw him off his bearings, and made him

---

[25] Reuben Hyde Walworth (1788–1867) followed James Kent as Chancellor, and made important contributions to equity jurisprudence in New York.

rapacious, if not corrupt. He was referee in several great cases, among them the very important patent case of Burden and Corning. In this case he is said to have bled the parties heroically, demanding a thousand or two on account of referee's fees whenever he found himself a little short, and to have pushed the process of depletion till the parties decided to abandon the suit. Such is the story, whispered about and disbelieved at first. . . .

In the last *Saturday Review* is a most caustic, clever, malignant article on Bishop Potter's address to his clergy at Trinity Chapel after he returned from the Pan-Anglican Council. The Bishop dwelt, perhaps with more emphasis than the occasion required, on the "blessed atmosphere" of Episcopal palaces and the pious works of church-loving peers. The reviewer distorts and exaggerates all this, and certainly succeeds in the laudable work of making Bishop Potter look ridiculous, and in producing something not unworthy of appearing as an appendix to the next edition of Thackeray's *Snob Papers*. I fear the Bishop was a little too exuberant on this branch of his subject, but the article is malicious and ungenerous. If American churchmen are so weak as to regard the prelacy of the Mother Church of England with a little too much of reverence and honor, if the historic names of Canterbury and Oxford, Exeter and Lincoln, have power to throw us a little off our balance for a moment, if we make ourselves sometimes a little absurd in expressing the gratification we have felt at finding ourselves in actual contact with those who now hold those venerable sees, it is shabby and snobbish in an English scholar to set about making this generous and honorable feeling ridiculous.

November 30. . . . The impeachment project drifts to leeward every day. Congressional projects of public fraud make headway!

December 1, SUNDAY. . . . Long talk with Egleston about church and college matters. I know of no one whom the much overworked adjective "earnest" describes more accurately. He is *ohne Rast* but perhaps not *ohne Hast*. How happy he must be with his energy and self-devotion! Mme. de Talleyrand here this afternoon. M. le Marquis is setting off for Florida to look after his wife's "estates." They are quite a principality. If their resources be judiciously developed, that nobleman will be able to supply the menageries of the old world with rattlesnakes and "to control" the alligator market. I rejoice to hear that Lewis Rutherfurd is a little better, and has walked out today without fatigue. Graham is enthusiastic about "The Seasons," heard by him Thursday night for the first time. He is not far from insight into the difference between that kind of music and the inane spasmodic stuff of modern opera on which he has been brought up. May his perceptions go on growing clearer. Blindness to the distinction between Haydn and Verdi is a calamity and grave deprivation to any man who is at all capable of feeling the power of music, but such blindness is epidemic among opera-goers, amazing and incredible as it seems. How any man—but no matter. The clock strikes one! George T. Strong will now proceed to wind up his watch and retire.

December 2. Sold out a couple of $1,000 railroad bonds. This process of depletion cannot be long kept up. It is mere gnawing misery just now. Perhaps I shall be less wretched when an acknowledged pauper.

Columbia College meeting at two o'clock. . . . The faculty had passed resolutions eulogistic of Bradford, and Drisler had suspended college exercises on his death and again on the day of his funeral. Mr. Ruggles and Fish severally found fault with this, and justly, I think, so far as relates to the mortuary holidays. But I see no reason why the faculty should not enjoy and exercise the inalienable right of all American citizens to pass resolutions about anybody or anything. . . .

December 3, TUESDAY. Dull day. City election. Three candidates for mayoralty, viz.: W. A. Darling, Republican; Hoffman (present incumbent), Democrat; and F. Wood, Democrat and Belial. Darling stands no chance, and a vote for him would practically aid the King of the Dead Rabbits, so I voted for Hoffman, not willingly. Hoffman is in league with the Ring, and, according to his enemies, robs and steals considerably; but if so, he robs and steals with comparative decency, whereas F. Wood stinks in the nostrils of mankind—the congenial *canaille* of New York excepted. Before and during the war he was as traitorous as he dared be, and his dealings with the city government have shewn him to be the consummate ideal of a clever demagogue and scoundrel. I never heard aught but bad of him in private or public life. I believe the city has been spared the disgrace of such a mayor. Tonight's extra reports Hoffman undoubtedly reëlected by a great majority. . . .[26]

December 5. . . . Yesterday Mrs. Albert Gallatin, Blake, and Jem Ruggles dined here, and went to the opera to hear *Trovatore*, poor souls!

There was a great meeting at Cooper Institute last night to nominate Grant and to formulate a Grant Party. The operators seem a mixed lot.

[26] The handsome, debonair John T. Hoffman, now chosen for his second term, was Grand Sachem of Tammany, and hand in glove with the Tweed Ring. This was the year that he appointed Peter B. Sweeny, one of the Ring chieftains, as Comptroller. He was destined to rise to the governorship, and with the destruction of the Ring, to fall to political ruin. While personally honest, he doubtless knew much about the thievery of his associates.

There were men like A. T. Stewart, William B. Astor, and Moses Taylor, who are seldom prominent in a political movement, and there were other names that retain some slight coppery smell. The morning papers inform me that I assisted as a vice-president, which I didn't. Grant's chance for the White House is worth tenfold that of any other man. This is due partly to the general faith in his honesty and capacity, and partly to his genius for silence. He is distrusted by Radicals and is disliked by extreme Reactionists, but I believe seven-eighths of the people (of the North) would vote for him tomorrow. So the new party machine can hardly fail, if it be run with ordinary skill. The great difficulty will be to make a platform with an outline sufficiently ill-defined. No one, by the by, even pretends to know that Grant would accept the presidency if it were offered to him. He is in the position of Fritz with the "Grande Duchesse" making love to him. Acceptance involves the sacrifice of "Wanda," that is, his office of general-in-chief for life. He will have to choose between marriage and a four-year liaison. But if he decline, he is no American citizen. I expect to vote for him next fall. We know next to nothing of his political notions, to be sure, so choosing him is a little like buying a pig in a poke, but then his integrity has never been questioned, and a man who can conduct great campaigns successfully and without being even accused of flagrant blunders must possess a talent for affairs that fits him for any administrative office. Therefore, hurrah for Grant!

December 7.   I believe our long-lost stray Irish fossil elk has turned up at last. I paid the freight this morning on certain boxes which are supposed to contain his venerable bones, and then put the very imperfect bill of lading (an incomprehensible document) into the hands of Edward Bibby, as custom-house broker. He (the elk) has been lying about in this port since last June, by reason of somebody's blunder as to the name of the consignee. The whole transaction has been singularly botched, and we may have much trouble before the remains of this extinct but interesting quadruped are duly mounted (or gibbeted in chains) in our 〔School of Mines〕 geological museum. . . .

Niggers seem helping to reconstruct the chivalric South with a degree of sense and moderation I did not expect. Reports of their doings in convention vary, of course, but the funny narratives furnished the *World* and its Democratic congeners, or very possibly manufactured to order in New York, are probably caricatures, easy to draw. A few scraps of nigger dialect ("suffiz" for *suffrage*, and so on), a few specimens of the ignorance

natural to the enfranchised field hand, a phrase or two about the honorable member from Congo, and the intelligent boot-black who represents
the county of Tackahoosho, and some stories of black voters putting
their ballots into the post office, are quite enough to make these pepper
and salt conventions ridiculous in the eyes of Copperheads. It is strange
that Our Own Correspondent at Richmond or Montgomery does not
make his letters yet funnier than they are.

December 10. . . . Barnard returned in the *Hecla* after a long rough
passage. Charles Dickens's first Reading last night at Steinway Hall is
said to have been admirable.[27] It doubtless was so, but I am in no fever
to hear him. I remember the *American Notes* and the American chapters
in *Martin Chuzzlewit*, which were his return for the extravagant honors
paid him on his first avatar twenty-five years ago. I also remember that
both books, especially the former, were filled with abuse and sarcasm
against the slaveholding republic, and that during our four years of
death-struggle with slavery, Mr. Dickens never uttered one word of
sympathy with us or our national cause, though one such word from the
most popular living writer of prose fiction would have been so welcome,
and though it would have come so fitly from a professional "humani-
tarian." I fear Mr. Dickens is a snob of genius, and that some considerable percentage of his fine feeling for the wrongs and the sorrows of
humanity is histrionic, but perhaps I do him injustice. Anyhow, I should
like to hear him read the *Christmas Carol*: Scrooge, and Marley's Ghost,
and Bob Cratchit.

December 12. . . . Another sale of Trinity School lots to pay assessments,
and a very good sale. Proceeds $42,800. Our bill against the school for
eight years' anxious and responsible services has been sent in. They have
resulted in a decision of the Court of Appeals that the title of the school
to its splendid endowment is good and marketable, and have saved that
endowment from being sacrificed wholly to assessments, which the school
could meet only by sales of a portion of it and for which, without this
decision, it could have found no purchaser. . . .

Thermometer in the hall downstairs is below 50°, and the wind
howls malignantly. It's said there are fifty thousand men and women,
young men and maidens, out of employment in this city at this time—

[27] Dickens had already given readings, with immense success, in Boston. When
tickets went on sale in New York, a long line of prospective buyers assembled the
evening before the day of sale, and more than five thousand buyers were waiting an
hour before the window opened. Everywhere in America he met a popular enthusiasm
that verged on idolatry.

unable, that is, to find work whereby to secure their daily bread, without butter. God help them, but that is a cheap aspiration. I ought to be sallying out to look for them and carry them material aid and comfort. But fine houses and "social position" use up all one's money, and more. God help *us* and deal mercifully with us, who leave that work undone, or, at best, play at doing it, by the mechanical process of subscriptions to societies, even though Christmas is at hand, when, if ever, one should think of poor women and of poor children. . . .

December 14. . . . Great excitement and wrath in London. A new gunpowder plot, and more effective than the old one. About one hundred feet of the outer wall of Clerkenwell Prison, where certain Fenians are in ward, blown up yesterday, neighbouring houses smashed, and sundry people killed, sundry others "kilt." So reports the cable. This goes to confirm what a clever writer in last *Saturday Review* maintains, viz.: that a "Reign of Anarchy" has begun in England, and that for the first time in English history "government is cowed." To prove anarchy he cites Fenianism, the bread-riots, the trade union atrocities, the illegal mob conventicles in the parks and other public places, the invasion of the Home Office (or some other sanctuary) by a gang of Liberals and sympathizers, who, on being refused an audience by the Great Man of the Place, organized an indignation meeting in an outer room, passed resolutions, and "sassed" ushers, janitors, and others, as hirelings, and menials, and many others.

December 16.   The antlers of the Fenian elk ("Brian Boroo" we must call him) displayed on the floor. Very gigantic for so small a head. They furnish a precedent and authority in nature for the preposterous "waterfalls" and capillary towers in which womankind delight.

Conference with Newberry and with Egleston, and then with Dr. Barnard (very jolly after his sojourn abroad) about the question of salaries. I want to begin by screwing up salaries in the School of Mines, whereas Barnard thinks it more judicious to begin at the other end, viz.: with the academic corps. All I fear is some delay that may lose us Newberry and perhaps Egleston. Barnard is a sagacious practitioner and knows how to manipulate the board. He holds the School of Mines to be superior to the schools at Paris and London and at every other scientific centre which he visited. We shall make a shew when the elk is set up, when Barnard's purchases arrive, and when we receive the collection of books and minerals given by the Emperor of Russia which Osten-Sacken reports worth 2,500 rubles (or $2,000) in gold at St. Petersburg. . . .

Southern affairs do not improve. There are wide districts there in which society seems dissolving; in which the white race seems not only insolvent, but prostrate, despondent, apathetic, and paralyzed, and short of food besides, while the blacks are idle, shiftless, and predatory, and in a fair way to become mere loafing, thieving banditti. So say "Democratic" correspondents. Their newspapers charge all this terrible mischief (and though it may be exaggerated, it is doubtless grave enough) to Congress and the Radicals. But the general revolutionary smash caused by the war and by the overthrow of slavery is sufficient to account for it. The ruling race was always improvident and lazy, and lived in dependence on Cuffee, just as the slaveholding ants depend on their hexapod nurses and breadwinners. Without his serfs the patrician insect perishes, and such, I fear, may be the lot of the *ci-devant* slaveholding biped of Alabama and the Carolinas.

December 18.   College trustees met this afternoon and sat long. Mr. Ruggles absent, at Washington. Judge Blatchford present, and seems inclined to be an active member.[28] Report to Regents of University was read—in part—and adopted. S. P. Nash nominated as trustee. I nominated Trowbridge—the "Billy Trowbridge" of West Point years ago, now vice-president of the Novelty Works. Barnard brought up the question of salaries in School of Mines and moved that its professors be put on the same footing with those of the undergraduate course, which had just been made five thousand dollars for another year. He made a very long speech, and the Bishop seconded him at some length, and with much warmth. He said the School had ceased to be an experiment; was established among the first of existing scientific institutions; that its unhoped-for success was due to the generous enthusiasm and energy of its faculty; and that they ought to be generously sustained. Good for the Bishop. His hearty avowal suppressed the demurrer to Vinton's claim which Torrey, Fish, and Ogden were rather inclined to interpose (not without shew of reason), and the resolution passed *nem. con.*, a result beyond my hope. Called at Egleston's (10 Fifth Avenue) to let him know, and left a note for Newberry at the Hoffman House. Egleston was delighted, not on his own account, but for Newberry's sake. He thinks Newberry will certainly not resign, now. I got it referred to the library committee to

[28] Samuel Blatchford (1820–1893), who had been graduated from Columbia College in 1837, and had become a prominent lawyer, had recently been appointed a federal district judge. President Arthur later raised him to the Supreme Court. He was learned, very hardworking, and in college matters progressive.

enquire about Professor Bull Anthon's library, what it can be got for, and on what terms, and whether its purchase be expedient. Ogden rather objected to any enquiry even, lest it should lead to an outlay inconsistent with our "policy." I don't expect anything to come of it; perhaps we can use our money better than in buying some $20,000 worth, more or less, of Greek and Latin. But the matter is worth looking into. . . .

December 19. . . . To Forty-ninth Street this afternoon. Saw Chandler and Newberry. Both joyous over the decision of the trustees, and both, as usual, giving me a larger share of the credit of bringing it about than I deserve. The gentlemen of that faculty seem under a strong delusion which leads them to hold me responsible for every good fortune that befalls the School. If a two-thousand pound aerolite tumbled down in front of their door tonight and was bagged for their cabinet, I believe they would remark in chorus, "Just observe the interest Mr. Strong takes in the School of Mines. We couldn't get on without him!" I cannot suppose that it's anything but a delusion, or that these gentlemen would condescend to humbug, even if it would do them any good to flatter me with dishonest compliments. Even Dr. Barnard in his letter to Chandler said the prompt action of the trustees yesterday was due to the "Bishop and Mr. Strong." It was due to the Bishop, who advocated it warmly and effectively, and to Barnard himself, but I did not say a word on the subject, except in whispers to one or two of the board. Never mind. It's pleasant to be thought of kindly by Egleston and Newberry and Chandler and Vinton. I am sure my intentions are good, and if they choose to think me not only well meaning but efficient and serviceable, I have no objection whatever. Only it seems a little like sailing under false colors.

Mrs. Ruggles had a "reception" this afternoon, which was very successful, Ellie says. After dinner to meeting of "American Church Union" at Trinity Chapel School house. Eighty or a hundred present, lay and cleric. I signed the constitution, stayed a little while, and came off. This is a nascent organization, of which I know little. It seems meant as an offset or counterpoise to the "Evangelical" or latitudinarian societies of the Low Church clique. They are mischievous, and it may be necessary to fight them on their own ground. But the church itself seems to me the appointed society for the suppression of heresies and schisms, big and little.

December 21. . . . . Talk with Professor Anderson, chairman of the College Library Committee. He hankers after the Anthon library—"if we can get it for twenty thousand dollars." I had not felt disposed to bid

quite so high. We discussed the several candidates for the Latin professorship, and I said that one of them (Rev. ——) would never secure
the respect of his classes, that he was always asking his friends for money
and writing mendicant letters and was repressible by no amount of
snubbing, and that he seemed to have no personal dignity whatever.
"Well," said H. J. Anderson, "perhaps his efforts to borrow money are
a self-imposed exercise in humility." The remark is deliciously characteristic of Professor Anderson. . . .

December 25, WEDNESDAY. . . . Among Christmas presents I note a
copy of the "Legende of St. Gwendoline," a folio, with photographs
from Jack Ehninger's crayon drawings. They seem the best work Jack
has ever done. Another folio, Tennyson's "Guinevere and Vivien,"
from *The Idylls of the King*, is illustrated by G. Doré, and the engravings
are favorable specimens of M. Doré's art. They shew his good points,
and his bad points do not appear. But he cannot draw the form or face of
a pretty or of a beautiful woman even when stimulated by the text of
Tennyson. This seems strange, but I think Doré represents the highest
(or lowest) type of Parisian art, which delights in sensuality and (by
some inscrutable law) loves carnage and torture as an inverted or per-
verted sensualism. It is certain that he—Doré—is brutalized by the
atmosphere he breathes, and so effectually that with all his talent and
fertility he cannot conceive a beautiful human form, male or female, or
record one on paper if he see it.

December 27. . . . George Anthon called—in one of his cranky fits—
because he thinks Jack Ehninger may possibly be chosen to paint Professor Anthon's portrait, also because Professor Drisler, who casually
looked through the Anthon library, said he thought it might be worth
twelve thousand dollars. George won't sell it for less than fifteen thousand dollars. "So I don't see that your committee need trouble themselves
any more about it," quoth George, acetically and Anthonically. "I shall
make some other disposition of the books." There are about 6,500
volumes, bound and unbound, big and little. I doubt whether they will
average much over $1.50 per volume here, for Greek and Latin classics
are a drug in this market. George thinks of shipping them to London,
where they may sell a little better. . . .

1868

*T*he great drama of Reconstruction was now reaching its climax, and the American public watched with eager interest the highhanded activities of the Radical leaders in Congress. They were intent on impeaching and trying President Johnson—a fact demonstrated when, immediately after the New Year, the Senate refused to concur in President Johnson's removal of Secretary of War Stanton, thus in effect challenging the Chief Executive to violate the Tenure of Office Act by a second removal. Many Radical leaders were equally intent on disciplining the Supreme Court, for it was believed that five of the nine judges regarded the Military Reconstruction Act as unconstitutional, and in the case of ex parte McCardle—a Vicksburg editor charged, in effect, with obstructing the reconstruction of Mississippi—a decision hostile to Radical policy was feared. The House in January hastily passed a bill forbidding fewer than two-thirds of the Supreme Court judges to pronounce any law unconstitutional. In the South, the first weeks of the year found "black and tan" or mixed Carpetbag, Scalawag, and Negro conventions sitting to complete constitutions which, embodying Negro suffrage provisions, would be submitted to the voters for adoption. That of Alabama went to the people early in February. Thad Stevens, Ben Wade, Charles Sumner, and others of the Radical Junta seemed temporarily in control of the destinies of the nation, trampling down all opposition. Yet it was by no means certain that they could long maintain their sway; it was not certain that the Republicans, even with the aid of the magical name of U. S. Grant, could carry the presidential election in the fall.

Of the lesser topics of the day, the most painfully interesting to Strong was

BROADWAY AND CITY HALL PARK
PHOTOGRAPHED SHORTLY BEFORE THE CIVIL WAR

THE BURNING OF BARNUM'S MUSEUM, 13 JULY 1865

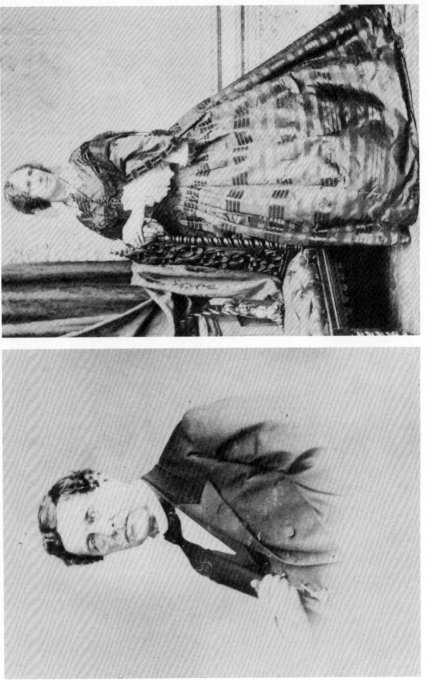

MR. AND MRS. SAMUEL BULKLEY RUGGLES

the high, the almost intolerably high, cost of living, which bore heavily on workingmen and the middle class alike. People were also discussing the Ala-bama question, which would have to be settled before good feeling could be restored between Britain and America; the speculation in gold; the activities of the Tweed Ring, the Erie Railroad Ring, and other nefarious combinations; and the activities of the Fenians on both sides of the Atlantic.

January 10, FRIDAY. . . . The Rt. Rev. [John Henry] Hopkins has died at Burlington, Vt.; presiding bishop or senior prelate, and volunteer champion of slave-breeding. He was smart, but had a latent crack some-where in his cranium. Being a virulent Copperhead, he was rather de-tested in his diocese. His talents and acquirements were respectable, but made of none effect by lack of common sense.[1]

January 13. . . . To College this afternoon. Saw Newberry, Egleston, and Chandler. "Irish Elk" not yet quite set up. Every room in the School fairly hums with industry and earnestness. . . .

Have looked carefully through Dr. [Austin] Flint's volume of Med-ical Reports (Sanitary Commission). So far as I can judge, it is exceed-ingly well edited. Many of the papers seem valuable, especially the report by Professor Jones of Nashville to the Rebel Medical Bureau on the condition of prisoners at Andersonville, an elaborate and able paper, barring some tendency to repetition. . . . I fear that, as a body, our rebels were a depraved set.

January 15. . . . Affairs at Washington look stormy. A disastrous explosion of some sort is very possible. The Senate finds (under the Tenure of Office Bill) that Stanton was removed without sufficient cause, so he has gone back to the War Office. Grant let him in without opposition or protest, thereby causing intense disgust in the great soul of A. John-son. A. Johnson is reported this evening to have given Grant a piece of his mind about it, and to have objurgated him *coram concilio*, that is to say, in presence of the Cabinet. Grant's course seems rather to indicate his final adhesion to the Congressional side. The President is said to have issued an order that no one connected with the executive depart-ments, or the army, recognize Stanton or any of his works. (The President didn't.)

[1] Bishop Hopkins, whose eccentric defenses of slavery on biblical grounds have previously been mentioned in the diary, had been so conciliatory in attitude toward the South during the war that just after it he was able to take a leading part in Episcopal reunion. Oxford had given him a D.C.L. in 1867.

Meanwhile, Congress is pushing on new and more stringent measures of Reconstruction, and for bridling the Supreme Court, all of which the Democrats denounce as unconstitutional and revolutionary. Honorable F'nandy Wood let off a good deal of foul language in the House this morning, and railed at this "infamous" Congress, refused to apologize, and was reprimanded by the Speaker, in pursuance of an order. The impudent demagogue will parade this Radical indignity with great effect before his enlightened constituency, the roughs, blackguards, and rum-sellers of New York.

All this makes up a threatening prospect. They are having a bad time in England, too, with their Fenians. It is unpleasant to believe (rightly or wrongly) that certain squads of semi-humanized gorillas, with the outward aspect of unwashed Celtic Christians, and with faculties so far developed that they can use phosphorus and gunpowder, are crawling about the streets at night, trying to blow things up. . . .

January 17. . . . Mr. Ruggles here, from Washington last evening, bringing an invitation to Ellie from Secretary McCulloch and his wife to sojourn with them awhile—very kind of them.[2] Mr. Ruggles's scheme of monetary unification, which is to reduce the coinage of Christendom, and perhaps of Heathendom, too, to one uniform standard, has met an unexpected check. This scheme involved the reduction of the dollar by two or three cents, so that the half-eagle should be the equivalent of, for example, the new twenty-five franc piece. Such reduction would be unobjectionable. But certain Congressmen, with an appetite for any-thing fraudulent, want to make the proposed new dollar a legal tender in payment of debts contracted when the dollar was worth 100 cents. And if that amendment be adopted, Mr. Ruggles will, of course, have nothing more to do with the measure, though he has given it so much labor and research. It is amazing and alarming that so atrocious a move-ment for the partial repudiation of all debt, public and private, should be even suggested among our lawmakers. But Congress is full of rascals.

I have "no confidence in either party," like Colonel Sibthorpe (*vide Punch*) nor in any member of either House. If the Radicals are right in their radicalism, I believe it is by accident. Mr. Ruggles reports a very savage and despiteful state of feeling between the two parties at Wash-ington—so grim as materially to affect social intercourse and check the current of the life-blood of "society" through the capillaries of tea-

[2] Hugh McCulloch was Secretary of the Treasury.

drinkings, receptions, dinners, and so on. But the "Diplomatic Set" still keeps up its independent circulation.

January 18. . . . Washington affairs are unchanged. "All quiet on the Potomac," as the newspaper despatches used to report in 1861 and 1862. Congress seems unterrified by the alleged popular reaction against "Radicalism." I think there *is* such reaction and that it will prove formidable. Meanwhile, A. Johnson seems to have suppressed himself for the present, and to be "laying low," in a passive condition, waiting for Congress to make a false move. That is his best policy. Almost every positive affirmative step of his for the last two years has done harm not only to the country, but to himself and to his party, if he have any party. "Andrew's Adventures in Blunderland" would be a good title for a political squib. But it would be hard to write anything with that title that would not suggest most disadvantageous comparisons with that wonderfully clever and original little *Kinder-märchen, Alice's Adventures in Wonderland.*

January 19. . .. . This evening Mr. Ruggles was here; General George Ruggles and his wife—she was a Miss L'Hommedieu of Cincinnati, and is a little beauty; Charley; "Dismal Jemmy" Lawrence; a clever Mr. Stanly from eastern parts; a M. Nagelmacher from Belgium—Liège—who is making the grand tour of this continent, and hopes to shoot many "boofalo" next spring.

Cable announces that that windbag, George Francis Train, and two of his fellow-passengers were arrested as suspected Fenians on their steamer's touching at her Irish port, and haled off to dungeons by the hired myrmidons of British tyranny.[3] O proud Bird of our Country, and O shades of Gineral Jackson, Mister Freeny, and Brian Boroimbe, shall such things be unavenged? Mr. George F. Train would not have missed this experience for $10,000 in gold. But a certain amount of folly, on either side of the Atlantic, may make the event produce great disaster. There will doubtless be several splurging star-spangled speeches about it in the House tomorrow, and probably some resolutions breathing battle, murder, and sudden death. As far as I'm concerned, the bloated aristocracy of Britain are heartily welcome to Mr. G. F. Train, and I would take it very kindly if they would relieve us of a few more of our braying, mischievous vagabonds. Of course, I assume that the British

---

[3] This irrepressible promoter and adventurer (1829–1904) had actually espoused the Fenian cause. He was arrested, briefly jailed, and then when the American minister insisted that he be either tried or discharged, was released.

government is not so absurd as to have arrested these men for any conspiracy or malfeasance, contemplated or committed in *this* country, and that they are secured because they are believed to design some breach of the peace on British soil. Their arrest and arraignment for a conspiracy in America would be a *casus belli*.

January 20. . . . Of course, the morning papers are in high cackle over George Francis Train and his brethren in bonds. An American army must go and overrun England at once, as England is dealing with Abyssinia, and get Train & Co. out of jail. Meanwhile, George F. Train is doubtless in the highest feather, eating his victuals with uncommon relish and appetite, writing the most stern and appalling protests, and hurling a haughty and disdainful defiance (on paper) at the Ministry and the Lord Lieutenant and the other mercenary, etc., etc., minions of an effete, etc., etc., despotism. But N.B. If the Irish or English authorities have made a false move in the premises, and if we *are* entitled to demand the liberation of these land-louping peddlers of sedition, let us adopt the precedent given us by our loving cousins and allies in the matter of Mason and Slidell, and help Britannia to a slice of humble pie. To *that* end I would make a row over the wrongful detention of an American bedbug, no matter how much the offensive conceit of the insect might be thereby stimulated. This little speck of possible trouble has sent gold up. Professor Tyndall's best thermo-electric pile is not more sensitive than that metal. Indeed, gold has the advantage, for its index rises at the mere contingency of future friction or collision.

January 21. . . . Read tonight volume one of Colonel Badeau's *Military History of General Grant*, a copy of which he has sent to Ellie. Very good —clear, compact and untainted by bunkum and fine writing. He is "down upon" General McClernand, justly, I think, and not particularly eulogistic of Halleck and Burnside. Rosecrans suffers somewhat. Sherman is the most prominent figure after Grant, and probably *ex debito justitiae*.

January 22. . . . Cable reports the great Train out of jail again and that he has "sued the British Government" (?!) for false imprisonment. Damages £100,000, which is £99,999, 19s. 11 $\frac{3}{4}$ d. more than the aggregate value of a whole ship load of Trains, at retail prices. . . .

January 23. . . . Miss Rosalie dined here and went with Ellie and me to Steinway Hall, for *The Creation*. Not very crowded. Chorus admirable, orchestra very good. Soli respectable, but a little deficient in strength and spirit. The tenor was perhaps an exception. "In Native Worth" was charmingly sung, as it well deserves to be, and was encored. We missed

Parepa's fire and power and brilliancy, especially where the soprano sings against the chorus, as in "The Marvelous Works." But her substitute, Mrs. or Miss Brainard, was of average merit, or above it. The audience seemed appreciative, and did not *talk*. . . .

January 29. . . . Dined at the bachelor quarters of Charley Strong, William Robinson, and John Cadwalader.[4] Present the triumvirate, and Tappan. It's a nice little house in East 26th Street. C., Tappan, and I went through the weather to see *The White Fawn* at Niblo's—a grand new show piece, manifestly got up at very great cost, and said to surpass *The Black Crook* itself, which drew crowded houses for a year and a half. Ballet, spectacle, machinery, and pink legs are its chief constituents. The dialogue is senseless, the plot undiscoverable, and the music common-place—plagiarism from the *Grande Duchesse* excepted. But the dresses, properties, decorations, and the like, are novel and lavish, except the costumes of the ballet girls, which are the reverse of lavish in quantity, though various and pretty in design and color. A grand procession of fishes, oysters, and lobsters is very grotesque and carefully equipped. The final tableau or "transformation scene" is particularly elaborate and pretty. A scene shifter would call it gorgeous. In a meretricious sort of way it is quite artistic, with its slowly shifting masses of color, chang-ing lights, and groups of good-looking young women (with very little on) nestling or hanging about everywhere. But the whole production depends for its success mainly on the well-formed lower extremities of female humanity. It is doubtless the most showy, and the least draped, specimen of what may be called the *Feminine-Femoral* School of Dramatic Art ever produced in New York. House packed—men mostly—and enthusiastic.

Curious "progress" has the drama made since the days of old Samuel Johnson, E. Burke, J. Reynolds, and Davy Garrick!

January 30. . . . The Republican majority at Washington evidently means to persevere in its Radical policy and "fight it out on this line,"

[4] This was John Lambert Cadwalader (1836–1914), a graduate of Princeton and of the Harvard Law School who was now practising law in New York. A brilliant and energetic man, he was Assistant Secretary of State under Hamilton Fish 1874–1877, making a distinguished record. Later, as a partner of Charles E. Strong, he maintained and enlarged the great reputation of the law firm established by John Wells and George W. Strong and long headed by the latter's son, the diarist. Charles Strong had joined the two men in bachelor quarters after selling his house on East 22nd Street in the spring of 1866; his wife and daughter went to live in Europe in the early summer of that year, where he periodically joined them.

undaunted by signs of popular reaction. It seems prepared to ride over President and Supreme Court both, unless they get out of its way. This looks like a courageous adherence to principle very rare among our politicians. Democrats maintain, of course, that it is merely a desperate effort to keep power in the hands of the so-called Radicals by consummating a lawless reconstruction of the Southern States under military rule, and with a view to nigger supremacy, before the next presidential election. Each of these theories may be more or less accurate. Meanwhile, the "Reconstructing" Conventions seem to work hopefully, and without sign of undue haste or of any vindictive temper. It is easy to write reports of the proceedings of "black and tan conventions"—"whitey-brown committees"—"Meade's Minstrels"—and the like. Specimens of the Negro dialect and pronunciation can be recorded or invented by any newspaper correspondent, and they seem quite funny when connected with the debates incident to the framing of a Constitution. But I guess the *patois* of the Poor White is ruder even than Cuffee's, and many of these black barbers and artizans shew better taste and temper than some of their chivalric colleagues, and quite as much good sense—or as little, whichever you please.

February 1. . . . General Vinton dined here and we went with Ellie to the Philharmonic concert. House most uncommonly full. Every standing place occupied. We went very early and experimented on the amphitheatre, or top gallery, which is apt to be almost empty. Being early, we got good front seats there, but its whole area was flooded with people a few minutes later. Our experiment was successful. It's the best place in the house. The music comes up from the orchestra through free space, clear and sharp, instead of being muffled and deadened by passing over bales of furs and velvets and broadcloth, as it has to do before reaching the balcony or the rear parquette seats. The difference is like that between looking at a landscape with one's near-sighted eyes and with an eyeglass. The crash of the orchestra is not so heavy in the amphitheatre, the object seems smaller, as it were, but it is better defined, and all its details can be followed. There is a little less noise and a great deal more music.

Only three pieces produced. Spohr's Overture, Schumann's piano concerto, op. 54, with Mills at the piano (excellently played, but inane and long-winded as it seemed to me), and the Ninth Symphony. The chorus did its ungrateful work fairly, but the quartette was clearly insufficient and broke down a little once or twice. There are great points in this symphony, especially its noble, saintly adagio, but as a whole it is unequal to the others. Its spasm and oddities foreshadow the degradation Beethoven's peculiarities have undergone at the hands of those who think themselves his scholars and successors.

February 2. . . . A rather good Anti-Fenian riddle, got up by some bloody and bloated British oligarch, is well received: viz.: "When my first makes my second, he calls himself my whole." Give it up? Ans.: *"Patriot."* N.B. Osten-Sacken says Barnard tells him that the valuable gift of Ye Tsar of Moscovia to ye School of Mines is in port. It is understood to consist of certain books of price, and a fine suite of Russian minerals. Long live the Czar! and may the batteries of his next Sebastopol prevail against its besiegers! If this Imperial contribution to our library and cabinet prove important, as I hope it will, we must convert it (by "correlation of forces") into an agent for getting the School fame and credit through the newspapers. "Another proof of Russia's cordiality toward America," and so forth *ad libitum.* After the uncommonly good sale the Czar has just made of the rocks and glaciers and icy bogs and lonely islands and foggy coasts of Walrussia, he is very likely to have felt jolly and generous, and to have sent us a brilliant "donation" if any. . . .

February 3. College trustees met this afternoon; not a great deal of business. On Barnard's motion, we ordered Newberry's private collection to be insured for $10,000, or about half its estimated value. This was clearly right, as we have its use for nothing, and it passed *nem. con.* Then we went into an election for trustee to fill Bradford's place. Dr. Beadle and I were tellers. . . . Fourth ballot: Nash 7, Emott 7; fifth: Nash 9, Emott 4, Denning Duer 1; so Nash was elected. I voted for him on the 1st, 4th, and 5th ballots, and for Pierrepont on the 2nd and 3rd. It's a good choice. . . .[5]

Alumni will growl at the election of Nash, who is not an alumnus. But what have alumni done for the College? They have founded some little prize for scholarship, and they keep alive a little alumni association. The most valuable "donation" ever made the College by a private person, viz.: the Herbarium and Botanical Library, we owe to Dr. Torrey, an outsider. When we were trying to raise funds from the public for the nucleus or germ of our School of Mines, very few alumni did anything.

[5] Stephen P. Nash proved a progressive trustee, who later contributed much to the establishment of a graduate School of Political Science; John W. Burgess speaks of him as a man of superior intelligence and organizing ability, "chafing to move forward."

I remember only Agnew, Travers, and myself. It was William E. Dodge, Talboys, Cotheal, John Caswell, George Cabot Ward, and other outside barbarians who gave us substantial aid. A dozen wealthy and distinguished alumni to whom I applied turned up their noses at me and pooh-poohed the College and all its doings. So our graduates have no right to grumble if we choose trustees from without their ranks. . . .

It is a question worth considering, what can have been the special weakness or error of its trustees, from the date of its reorganization after the Revolution down to the present time, that has kept it so low in public favor, compared with Harvard, Princeton, and Yale, and has almost wholly turned away from its Treasury the great current of private munificence—donations and bequests—that has sustained and enriched those institutions, and created scores of new ones, many of them worthless enough, to be sure. It must be confessed that Columbia College has been, at least till within the last ten years, a "one-horse concern," and that if it has risen of late to higher grade, its rise is due simply to the increased value of its endowment, to the increase of its income by reason of the progress of the city, and not to anything its trustees have done. . . .

February 4. . . . Gold is UP, and there are experts who say it will rise to 150. There is uneasiness about the *"Alabama* claims," and possible breach with England, and also about home affairs. People vaguely apprehend some grave mischief from the discord between Congress and the President. In the *Alabama* correspondence it is curious to observe that each party decorously abstains from all allusion to what each probably feels to be among the weightiest considerations connected with his case. Great Britain is painfully aware that if she refuse to admit her liability in damages for the "escape" of that petted pirate from her ports, it will be a terrible precedent against her the next time she finds herself involved in war, and that pirates equally maleficent will, in that case, "escape" in swarms from every "neutral" port and play Old Scratch with British commerce. Of course, Seward understands this with equal clearness, and never forgets, while he concocts his voluminous despatches, how extremely difficult it will be to keep privateers from dodging out of American harbors whenever an "Eastern difficulty" or any other difficulty shall give them a chance to go forth against British merchantmen, with the advantage (which the *Alabama* did not possess) of sailing under some recognized national flag and turning their prizes to substantial profit. But both diplomats are silent on this point. English reasoning against making the recognition of the South as a belligerent part of any case to be submitted to arbitration (*vide* letter of "Historicus" to London *Times*[6]) is founded on the doctrine of estoppel. It will be held cogent by special pleaders, if any of that race have survived "Law Reform," but I think a statesman would give it very little weight.

If A. Johnson be the selfish, ambitious, profligate partisan his adversaries think him, I do not see why he should not make the *Alabama* a *casus belli*. The right being clearly with us, and long negotiations having come to naught, he could plausibly justify himself in declining further negotiation and proceeding to levy our damages by reprisals or by an assault on the new Dominion of Canada. A war with England would unite the whole people, property holders and taxpayers excepted, in cordial support of his Administration. Many of that class would join in its support, with all their hearts, for the old reverential love of England that was so strong during the ten or fifteen years before 1861 is quite extinct now. All the Irishry of the land would lay itself, its votes, shillelaghs and dudeens, at the feet of the New Deliverer of the Isle of Saints. The Administration would become invincible. Congress would have to concur or perish. There would be a grand shindy and general ruination on this side the water, and some little tribulation, I think, on the other side thereof. But I guess that A. Johnson, with all his passions and prejudices, understands that national bankruptcy is a bad thing.

February 7. . . . The New York Republican Convention having endorsed Grant, he is almost sure of the nomination at Chicago. The New York *World* considers it certain and settled that he will be the Republican candidate, and opens fire on him accordingly with the filthy missiles its party loves. It says Grant is a "commonplace man. Has no military talent—a very dull fellow, indeed. He is hated by the army. He is generally drunk. He never goes to church," and so forth. . . .

February 8. . . . Walked uptown with George Anthon. Spent an hour at Society Library looking over a large collection of books, a thousand or two, given it by Robert Kennedy. These books were part of the stock of [the owner of] a circulating library at Newport for about fifty years, perhaps longer. He died, and Kennedy bought all his books that were printed before 1820. They are mostly American, and *such* rubbish! But they may—or some of them may—acquire a bibliomaniacal value hereafter, and these idiotic novels, plays, and poems possess a certain value

---

[6] "Historicus" was later disclosed to be William Vernon Harcourt; and British recognition of the belligerency of the Confederacy was in time admitted by all to have been proper and necessary.

even now, as being the current co-temporary literature our grandfathers bought and read. . . .

February 10, MONDAY.   To Forty-ninth Street at half-past three, for College Library Committee: Barnard, Schermerhorn, and I and our very meek librarian, Mr. Betts, who seems diligent and faithful in his little orbit of small duties. We "passed" certain lists of books to be bought, and then Barnard invited Schermerhorn and me into the President's room to talk of the vacant [Latin] professorship, and the coming election. Barnard is in a twitter of fidgets. He has written me about it, and I have responded that I could not see why he was so anxious, that the election of Morris would be no grave calamity. But it now appears that he fears feud and discord in the board, like the squabble about Wolcott Gibbs fourteen years ago. I see no signs of it. . . .

February 12.   Ellie is in Washington, dining with diplomats from the uttermost parts of the earth—Blaque Bey included[7]—with generals, heads of departments, and other swells. N.B. The New York *Herald* has swung around again, and upholds Grant for the presidency. Bad for Grant.

Sorry to find that disloyalty to President Barnard is whispered among College trustees. His action as to the salaries of professors has given offense. I think it was a mistake to raise the salaries of the college faculty, but Barnard did not press that measure unduly, and if any one trustee be responsible for the proceeding, it is the Bishop. When this extra allowance comes up for renewal, there will be a fight over it.

February 14.   In all my reading I have seen nothing worse than the spite and fury of the "Democratic" newspapers. The New York *World* seldom refers to *Abraham Lincoln,* except as "The late lamented," or "our Martyr." Rebel newspapers were hardly so bitter during the war.

February 17. . . . Political affairs look ill. Reconstruction makes no headway. The new Constitution of Alabama seems rejected and defeated, because a majority of Alabamians, black and white, stayed away from the polls. Such is the result under the last Reconstruction Act. But it is now proposed to recognize this Constitution, though repudiated according to the terms of the law under which this election was held, and to admit such Congressmen and such electors as shall be chosen under its provisions. This seems a strong measure, though I admit that no measure can be much too strong for the hating and hateful half-suppressed rebels and nigricides of the South. They are of a race "that cannot be domesticated," as Agnew said years ago.

[7] The Minister from Turkey.

February 18.   Went this afternoon with Miss Rosalie to Academy of Design, where are the pictures that went to the Paris Exposition. In another mood I should have enjoyed their inspiration, for I never saw so many covetable pictures together—Eastman Johnson's "Old Kentucky Home," Cole's "Triumph of the Cross" series, Church's "Niagara" and "Rain in the Tropics," Bierstadt's "Mount Hood," with many other fine things and few that are absolutely bad. Talking of the Exposition, Blatchford has received the first class gold medal awarded the Sanitary Commission. It is a "big thing," for it weighs 18 ounces and I had not seen so much bullion for years. But its design is inartistic and clumsy, and the two naked boys on the reverse look beefy and bloated.

February 19. . . . . Standing Committee of the diocese at Trinity Church two P.M. After a little routine business—helping make a bishop or so—we gossiped about the Tyng case, which Nash, for the Presenters, closed yesterday.

N.B. It seems to me far from unlikely that "Low Church" will secede from "High Church" within ten years. Ritualistic and (so-called) evangelical tendencies are developing at such a rate that I don't see how the adherents of these two antagonistic schools can dwell together in unity much longer. . . .

February 20, THURSDAY.   Daniel Lord is reported much worse, and unlikely to live long.

The elder Tyng preached a speech at St. George's Church last night about his son's trial.[8] As reported, it was an intemperate, waspish harangue, and perhaps a little indecent, for the case is still *sub judice*, and this philippic seems meant to bully the court and the Bishop by warnings of woes to both if Tyngulus be censured. Of course, the secular press is all on his side, and considers the whole proceeding illiberal and unworthy the nineteenth century. The result will be (I think) that the Bishop will remit any penalty the court may impose, on the ground that the construction of the canon has never before been judicially settled. Then little Tyng will go and do it again, and the penalty next time will have to be

---

     [8] Stephen Higginson Tyng, Jr., son of the rector of St. George's Church in New York, was being tried for an alleged infraction of canon law. He had come into conflict on matters of church practice with Bishop Horatio Potter. A convinced evangelical, greatly interested in missions for the poor, in Sunday schools, and in sermonizing, he abhorred the development of ritualism under the influence of the English tractarian movement. As Bishop Potter was a conservative with High Church leanings and Tyng was a progressive who refused to budge from a Low Church position, conflict between them was inevitable.

more than nominal. He will probably refuse to submit; he will find plenty of backers, and we may have a schism before we know it, and all because a wordy little pragmatical coxcomb lusts after notoriety and martyrdom. . . .

February 22. . . . Great news from Washington. It is vexatious that there are no evening papers, this being a public holiday, but if anything had happened at the Capitol, or the White House, or the War Office, we should have had two or three lively extras before this.

That uncomfortable person, A. Johnson, has thrown another cracker into our pile of shavings. He has for the second time dismissed Stanton, and has appointed, or nominated, or is to nominate, General [Lorenzo] Thomas, Secretary of War. This is not the fighting Thomas of Nashville, but the doubting Thomas, of whose loyalty people talked unpleasantly during an early period of the War. Many ventured to say they believed him to hold treasonable correspondence with Rebellion. In all human probability, he did no such thing. But such a rumor, even though unfounded, throws some light—more or less—on his political views. No one ever whispered such a thing against Grant or Sherman or Burnside or Rosecrans. But this is a digression. Our last advices, the morning papers to wit, inform us that Stanton declines to recognize the validity of his dismissal and is ensconced in the penetralia of the War Office, hushed in grim repose; that Thomas has acted on his appointment by issuing some order or other as Acting Secretary; that he has been or is to be arrested and held to bail under the provisions of the Tenure of Office Act; that both Houses are in highest wrath; and that the impeachment project is revived.

Moreover, A. Johnson has nominated Mr. G. B. McClellan for Adams's place at the Court of St. James, but that's of little importance.

This move of A. Johnson's against Stanton will do him no good, I think, though it may do the country much harm. It will probably send gold up many units next Monday. It looks to me like the act of an angry, headstrong man, willing to risk throwing us into utter confusion for the sake of his own piques and pugnacity—an unstatesmanlike act—gratuitous defiance like that of the conventional Irishman at Donnybrook Fair. We shall be lucky if it do no worse mischief than widening the breach between Congress and the President.

February 23, SUNDAY. It appears that General Thomas has made formal demand on Stanton for possession of the War Office. Stanton replied by ordering him back to his own subordinate bureau, and Thomas was, thereupon, arrested under the Tenure of Office Act and gave bail. The House was in a ferment yesterday. The Committee in charge of the subject reported in favor of impeachment, and a vote is to be taken at five P.M. tomorrow. Brooks opposed the adoption of the Report with characteristic swagger and fustian, but it will be adopted, for all the moderate or conservative Republicans are of one mind with the most radical. I think they are right. But for Heaven's sake, let them avoid the blunder of enacting the suspension of the President *pendente lite*. That would be unconstitutional and probably disastrous. Anyhow, it's a grave crisis.

> The times are out of joint, O cruel spite,
> That I see nary way to set them right!

February 24. . . . M. Hoffman and Charley Strong dined here—then with Miss Rosalie to the *Grande Duchesse*. A very spirited performance. The music grows on one. The melodies are saucy, piquant, and pretty, and some of them are rather more than that. All the parts are fairly well filled—and a more reckless, abandoned piece of extravagant fun and nonsense was surely never put on the stage. Some people call it *immoral*, but I don't. One cannot predicate morality or immorality of an extravaganza, like *Bombastes Furioso* or *Tom Thumb*. Vulgar it may be, in spots, but not in a way to hurt anybody.

The Washington row stirs the gold market less than I thought it would. Talk about it is copious, earnest, and rather bitter. Of the morning papers, the *World* treats the matter as a mere personal quarrel, and asks whether Stanton be really so necessary to the life of the country that everything must be turned upside down for his sake; the *Herald* sides with the President, but cautiously; the *Times* is feeble and indefinite as usual; and the *Tribune* heartily endorses the expected action of the House, though that paper has up to this time opposed impeachment. The *World's* leading article on the subject seems to me rather remarkable, as passing over the real questions (if there are any) involved in the dispute. It looks a little like a *pro forma* defense, confined to an immaterial point, and meant to leave that respectable organ at liberty to throw A. Johnson overboard on the merits, if it shall seem expedient hereafter. That would be ungrateful after the state dinner A. Johnson has just given Mr. August Belmont and the rest of the Democratic Central Committee. But the "Democrats" are a sagacious folk, and they know that a renegade-partisan seldom does his adopted party much good. . . .

February 25. . . . George Anthon tells me his uncle's library is appraised at $15,000, which puts an end to any expectation of its purchase by the College.

The Impeachment Resolution was carried yesterday (126 to 47, I think),[9] and a Committee of the House duly appeared at the bar of the Senate today, and announced the fact. Clamor of newsboys today recalled the most exciting period of the war. " 'Ere's the Extry *Telegram*—got the great excitement at Washington!"

February 26. . . . Sundry Copperheads, sans-culottes, bummers, and bounty-jumpers are enrolling themselves here (and I believe elsewhere) as a volunteer army to defend the President against a Radical and Revolutionary Congress. There are land-louping, beggarly Southern desperadoes about—"broken men"—who would hold it a labor of love to organize a ragged corps of Northern roughs for the purpose of making a muss at Washington, or anywhere else, and I think Democratic millionaires could be found on the Fifth Avenue who would contribute largely to the military chest of any expedition with that object, were there much hope of its doing serious mischief.

According to "kitchen-gossip" from the capital, Chase, C.J., and A. Johnson are in alliance on this impeachment question, wishing to defeat the supposed aspirations of their common enemy, Grant. But I respect Chase too much to believe this.

Johnson's friends foolishly maintain that he was not bound to obey the Tenure of Office Act till the Supreme Court should have affirmed its validity.[10] Surely the President is no less subject to the law of the land than any private person. He may disobey a statute in order to test its constitutionality, if he please, but he does so at his peril, and exposes himself to the penalties of disobedience if he prove to be mistaken. Otherwise, every man may treat any statute, state or national, as a nullity till its validity is affirmed by the highest court having jurisdiction in the premises.

But A. Johnson's course shews that his object was not to "make a case" for the courts, but to oust Stanton, and that he would have ousted

[9] The vote was 126 to 42; all Republicans but two voted aye.

[10] President Johnson himself sent a message to the Senate defending himself from any imputation of illegal conduct in appointing General Lorenzo Thomas to the Secretaryship of War. His sole object, he declared, was to bring the question of the constitutionality of the law before the courts. E. L. Godkin, in a judicious editorial in the *Nation*, agreed that the step was justified—and every historian of importance since then has so held. The law was certainly unconstitutional, as a subsequent decision of the Supreme Court showed; and there was no way to get it before the courts except to violate it.

him *vi et armis*, if he could have done it. I don't blame him for wishing to be rid of such a "hedge-pig" as Stanton unquestionably is, with all his great abilities, nor do I uphold the act in question as a sound or a politic piece of legislation. But if it be constitutional, A. Johnson was bound to obey it. Indeed, it can be very plausibly maintained that the President is bound to obey every Act of Congress, constitutional or not, till it is judicially overthrown. It makes no difference that cases may be supposed of legislation that is grossly, extravagantly, and palpably unconstitutional. This is not of that class, and I see no ground whatever for holding it other than perfectly valid. What an immense fact it is, and how thankful it should make us, that not one of our great captains—Grant, Sherman, Sheridan, Thomas, and others—seems inspired by selfish ambition! There is a great opening for a military chieftain just now, if he were willing to conspire with A. Johnson against the life of the country. . . .

February 27. . . . This is an *entr'acte* in the Washington Grand Opera. Nothing doing except behind the curtain. Doubts are whispered whether two-thirds of the Senate can be "depended on." The suspension project seems given up—most happily. A. Johnson and Stanton are severally reported serene and *"cam."*

Daniel Lord continues very low. People say his family make a kind of mystery of his illness, as if a worn-out brain were discreditable to a laborious lawyer of more than fifty years' active professional life. . . .

February 28. . . . Philharmonic Rehearsal two-thirty P.M. Mozart's lovely Symphony in G Minor, his finest, I think, after the *Jupiter*. The tenderness and delicacy of its trio are inexpressible. One might easily write much bosh over it. There seems to me an undercurrent of melancholy throughout the whole work, felt even in its brilliant opening and finale. Then Wagner's Introduction to *Lohengrin*, which is certainly effective, clever, and queer, without much inspiration, and then Mendelssohn's Italy Symphony, in A major. It impresses me as first-rate second-rate work. Vastly above the Wagners and Schumanns, but differing generically from the creations of Haydn, Mozart, and Beethoven. . . .

Finding of Tyng's court reported adverse to respondent. Punishment an admonition. Much he will mind it! . . .

We are to elect our Latin professor next Monday. There has been much active lobbying for Morris, and the vote will be close. . . .

There is talk of Dr. Pech's getting up some little musical meetings on these premises, Haydn's 2nd Mass to begin with. . . . Mr. Ruggles called this afternoon. He has abolished his grey moustache and looks ten years younger. I infer from what he said that he feels rather strongly about tomorrow's college election—thinks that Morris has been unduly preferred by Ogden and by outsiders. So he has been, perhaps, but the same kind of pressure was among the objections that the fogies of the board urged against Wolcott Gibbs during the long campaign of fourteen years ago. The objection has no weight. We are bound to vote for the best man, whether his merits have been "duly" or "unduly" brought within our knowledge. I expect to vote for Short. . . .

March 2. . . . Columbia College trustees met in Lafayette Place at two P.M. Twenty-two present! Absent, Dr. Jay in Europe, and the Reverend Spring. After sundry minor matters, we went into an election for Professor of Latin, without any skirmishing or discussion. Zbrowski and I were tellers. The result of the first ballot proved my faculty of prevision to be untrustworthy. It was thus: *Short* 12; *Morris* 4 (!); *Reverend Mytton Maury* 3; *Reverend Jesse Spencer* 3 (!) So Short is elected.[11] I understand that on a second ballot he would have had most of the votes that were cast for Maury and Spencer. . . . Our session was uncommonly short. After adjournment, I had a pleasant talk over things in general, with Lewis Rutherfurd, who seems fully convalescent, I am happy to say. So, he tells me, is Professor Rood, now at Munich with his wife's family. Barnard put through one or two little matters for benefit of the School of Mines, very quietly and cannily. He is an admirable executive officer, and leads the board admirably. Strange to say, his impenetrable deafness strengthens him in his leadership. We are a gentlemanlike board, and no one of us likes to oppose or object to any proposition of the President's, because it's rather difficult and painful to make the President hear or understand the objection. So we commonly acquiesce, unless the matter be grave. I sometimes think he has the faculty of not hearing what he don't want to hear. That was the late Professor Anthon's opinion. But the President's propositions are, fortunately, apt to be wise and judicious. He possesses a remarkable talent for quiet, imperceptible, *douce* management and manipulation of his colleagues. I think he has the precise measure of every trustee. Perhaps Short owes his success to the President's subtle influence, for Morris had a very good show and strong backers. . . .

[11] Charles Short (1821–1886), trained at Harvard and until 1867 the president of Kenyon College, was to remain professor of Latin at Columbia for the rest of his life. He was an able teacher and, according to Brander Matthews, a man of "many amusing peculiarities." Two of his students, Robert Arrowsmith '82 and Harry Thurston Peck '81, made a book of his classroom remarks and stories, *Short Commentaries on the Latin Language and Literature* (1905).

March 3. . . . My downtown omnibus this morning was turned off into a side street by fire engines and a cordon of stern policemen. Barnum was burned out again last night. His new show-shop was the old Coster house, a well-known granite front, 541 Broadway. It was gutted, but still smoking, its front a thick sheet of ice with a pendent fringe of long icicles from every projecting coign of vantage—the big lampposts before its entrance looking like great ice stalagmites. One of the "steamers" playing on the ruins was fairly embedded up to the hubs of its wheels in a flinty deposit of ice. The fire made sad havoc among the denizens of Barnum's very respectable menagerie. The tiger is reported to have fought his way through the smoke and the smother into the street, and to have been then brought to by a jet of cold water from a fireman's hose, and knocked over by the revolver of a circumambient policeman before he could recover his presence of mind and think about making fight. This was ungenerous and unchivalric. . . .[12]

March 5. . . . Daniel Lord died yesterday at 73, having been prominent at the bar, and as a good citizen, for more than thirty years. He was commonly held our strongest commercial lawyer. His drawbacks were a grandeur and magnificence of manner not unusual in men of small stature, and a certain waspishness when worried or fretted. But I never had reason to complain of this. In 1861, he got somehow wrong about public affairs, probably from the accident of a retainer for certain rebel privateersmen indicted as pirates, and he never got quite right again.[13] He was not to be classed with Copperheads, but rather with those who (like M.S.B.) have no confidence in any body, any party, or anything, and so he never, to my knowledge, shewed the least sympathy with the national cause by word or deed. Still he was no doubt a loyal man, though passively so. His honesty and ability were never questioned, and there are few who can fill his shoes.

[12] Most of Barnum's animals were burned to death in their cages. The loss was heavy, and he accepted this second great fire, on Greeley's advice, as notice "to quit and go a-fishin'." His famous American Museum disappeared from New York forever. But he shortly embarked on another great enterprise, a travelling three-ring circus, "The Greatest Show on Earth," which for ten years, 1871–1881, scored a tremendous success. Barnum then combined it with the circus of his principal rival under the firm of Barnum & Bailey, and it flourished long after the great showman's death in 1891.

[13] Lord had published in 1861 a pamphlet on "The Legal Effect of the Secession Troubles on the Commercial Relations of the Country." His death at the age of nearly seventy-three removed a pillar of the law, who had appeared in many famous will, tax, and prize cases.

Impeachment is marching on. The C.J. has taken his seat, and the Court is sworn. He disagrees with the Senate on certain questions of practice. There is an additional article charging Johnson's wild, tipsy, stump-speeches during his presidential progress as a disgrace to his office, and an insult to Congress, and thus a high crime and misdemeanor. This impeachment promises to help the Republicans but little in the long run. I fear it will cost them New Hampshire next week, and put some Democrat into the White House next year. Recovery of executive patronage will not compensate them for a popular outcry against "party persecution."

March 6. . . . The Court of Impeachment sat today, and the objection to Ben Wade, Vice-President of the Senate, as interested in the result, was withdrawn. Wade was sworn in. Such objections seem inadmissible in a court for the trial of an impeachment for political offenses, as in Parliament on a Bill of Attainder or of Pains and Penalties. However substantial in themselves, they cannot be listened to by a tribunal every member of which must, in the ordinary course of things, have committed himself on the merits of the case over and over again. Probably every Senator would be disqualified by the tests we apply to jurors.

March 7. . . . Bidwell attending Lord's funeral at the Brick Meeting House. Should have gone, too, but the funereal prayer-preachments of Presbyterian divines always make me ill.

With Temp'kins to Philharmonic Concert. Very good concert. Mozart's G Minor Symphony. Mendelssohn's in A Major. Wagner's queer but clever "Introduction to *Lohengrin*." The superb scene from *Oberon* ("Ocean du Ungeheuer") and "Deh, vieni" by Mme. Parepa. The lady, being vehemently called out, gave us "Batti, batti" also. So the material of the concert was nearly all of a very high order. The first and third movements of the Mendelssohn symphony are certainly specimens of most thorough and elegant work; only not *quite* first-rate. I think Weber's faculty of expressing passion in legitimate music—music, that is, which can *stand* alone, without depending for its effect on a vocalist's magnetic or histrionic power—is second only to Mozart's. I never hear the concluding intensities, joyous as they are, of this *Oberon* scene, or of Agatha's in the *Freischütz*, without "a great disposition to cry." The latter is unmatched, so far as I know, by anything ever written for the voice of woman. As to Wagner's "Introduction," it may be defined as two squeakinesses with a brassiness between them. It seems uncommon nonsense, but with an occasional gleam of smartness, like the talk of a clever man who is just losing his wits. I do not suppose, however, that Wagner is a half-crazed genius. I take him to be a composer of considerable ability and of plodding industry, and that he writes like a lunatic in order to attract the notice he could not secure by putting his conceptions, such as they are, into the forms of plain sense and artistic propriety.

March 10. . . . The story is that Johnson will first object to the court, because the Rebel States are not represented on the bench—he will then challenge Senators who have expressed an adverse opinion—then demur to the Articles of Impeachment, and then resign. Stories about the impeachment are discordant and contradictory, but this *fama* as to A. Johnson's probable course seems plausible enough. I suppose him "indifferent honest," but so mulish, piggish, and pugnacious, as to be unfit for high office, and that the sooner we are rid of him, the better.

March 11.   Aunt Olivia [Miss Olivia Templeton] died at about three this morning, quite conscious and composed to the last, and without suffering. . . .

After a hard fight the Democrats are beaten in New Hampshire! This is a cruel disappointment to the N. Y. *World* and will add impetus to Impeachment. The Democratic party has not yet learned that its old Copperheads, its Pierces, Touceys, Henry Clay Deanes, etc., are as a millstone round its neck. Thank God it is so. The stump oratory of these caitiffs damages the party they support. So does the N. Y. *World*, tho' conducted with so much smartness and venom and brutality. . . .

March 13, FRIDAY.   Overcast, but stars are out tonight. Poor Aunt Olivia's funeral was at Trinity Church this afternoon, after evening service. . . .

This evening at her house, with Binney and his wife, cousin Eliza. She had found certain papers throwing light on the history of my mother's family, and dating back to 1750 or thereabouts, which she kindly insisted I should keep. William Brownjohn's father's name was Massey. He lived at or near Liverpool, and seems, from his will, to have been quite a landholder there. Why the son (my great grandfather) changed his name, does not yet appear. There is a memorandum, purporting to have been extracted from the Heralds' Books, shewing that his ancestor, Hamon de Massey, "came over with William the Conqueror." Perhaps that will do to set off against my descent on the *Strong* side, from Earl Leofric of Coventry, and the *Lady Godiva*—for which interesting and most indisputable bit of genealogy, *vide* the history of the Winthrop family, printed at Boston ten or twelve years ago. There are the wills of Dr. William Brownjohn and of his father. Both seem to have been prolific. I cannot guess what has become of their descendants. Except the children and grandchildren of my mother and of Aunt Johnson, I *know* no one who can claim relationship by blood with Aunt Olivia. There are certain Bradfords, whom I never knew or saw. The Vanderveers and Motts of Brooklyn and Flatbush are reputed of the same stock. I don't know through what channel. I used to hear of certain Hursts of Philadelphia and of a Mrs. Stockholm of somewhere or other in Western New York as kinsfolk of my mother's, and we used thirty-five years ago to visit an ancient Mrs. Vernon, who was some kind of cousin of hers. She lived in William Street. This dying out of a family that gave every promise of increase and multiplication a hundred years ago is rather remarkable. There are also certain pencil drafts of coats of arms, which entitle me to "bear" certain *eaglets gules*, and certain *fleurs de lis argent*, and certain other phenomena besides. I have "nothing agin" bearing anything of the kind. There are also letters written by me to Mary Johnson in the summer of 1838, when she was at Schooley's Mountain and I at the Scotts', Whitestone. (N.B. George Anthon says that my hypothetical ancestor who "came over with the Conqueror" must have borne the title of "Lords' massey.")

March 14. Mild, dull weather. Went to Church of Transfiguration, Twenty-ninth Street, at twelve, being summoned by the Bishop, as one of his Cabinet, to attend the *Admonishing* of the Rev. S. H. Tyng, Jr. Congregation mostly feminine, and as I thought generally in sympathy with the victim. Certain collects were read, and then the Bishop, sitting in his chair and robed in his pontificals, proceeded to read the admonition —about half an hour long. The Martyr and the Martyr's papa sat in secular dress. The Martyr did not think it worth while to rise when officially addressed by his Bishop. The Admonition was an ably written paper, and more virile than was to have been expected. The Bishop mentioned arguments of counsel at the trial as having carried "freedom of speech to its utmost limits, and left no form of appeal to prejudice and passion untried." It was very strong and masculine, but temperate and dignified withal. Mr. Ruggles is most enthusiastic about it. Walking down Madison Avenue after the adjournment we encountered the Bishop and heartily congratulated him. He seemed to feel the transaction very deeply. When the Bishop got through, the Rev. Tyng the elder got on his legs and began in his sonorous voice to read, "Rt. Rev. Father in God, I, Stephen H. Tyng"—at which point Rev. Houghton resumed the prayers, all the clergy within the chancel kneeling. Tyng had the decency to hold his peace. But the moment the benediction was pronounced, he rose again. Whereupon the organist, probably forewarned, let off the full organ with the common chord of C Major, and played a lively voluntary with the trumpet stop drawn. So Tyng was silenced once more, as state criminals have been silenced on the scaffold by drum and trumpet. . . .

March 20. . . . Dined this evening at William Schermerhorn's, Twenty-third Street, with Dick Emmet, Charley Strong, William Astor, the Newport Ogden, Lydig Hoyt and Edward Jones. Mrs. W. C. Schermerhorn and her pretty-mannered little Miss Chattie (18 now!) honored us with their presence.

I have received from poor Aunt Olivia's ancient bureaus and boxes a further supply of sad old papers and letters, about Lt. Colonel Joseph Barton, who "fit into the Revolutionary War" (on the wrong side), emigrated to Halifax with his wife (my great-aunt), and died there in 1788. I dimly remember to have been told he was killed by the fall of a tree. But I may have dreamed it. Among these papers are his commission (on parchment) and his order book when at Staten Island, 1780.

There is also a profoundly interesting series of letters to my mother from Mr. Theodore V. W. Varick, a nephew, it would seem, of old Colonel Richard Varick. *They were engaged.* He emigrated to the "far West" of 1817, viz., Illinois, to make his fortune. His letters are most lover-like and charming. He must have been a highly cultivated, refined, genial person. But it's evident on the face of the papers that his habits were bad. He was constantly relapsing and repenting and reforming and relapsing, or else denying reports which I fear other letters (from his sister, and from his companion, a Mr. Henry S. Dodge) shew to have been true. Poor, poor fellow. It's the saddest story. He died in October, 1818. . . .

March 22, SUNDAY. Sunshine and thaw. The city is in soak. To church with Ellie and the boys. Anthem (Haydn's *Mass No. 1*) and the offertory (Mozart) were very good. Vinton's sermon was wordy and pompous. . . .

When the "collection plate" was handed into my pew this morning, by Meurer the sexton, and I looked at the Royal Arms engraved on it, and the inscription, shewing it had been used in the parish so long, I thought how many Brownjohns and Bartons, Templetons, Johnsons, and others had doubtless deposited their guineas, or shillings, their dollars or dimes, in that *identical depository.* Doubtless it had often received the communion alms of my mother and her sisters. . . . Three generations of my forbears, on the mother's side, have been regular attendants at Trinity or St. Paul's.

March 24. . . . President's Answer to Impeachment Articles. Substantially a demurrer to the allegations about Stanton, etc., and the general issue of the charge of disgracing his office by indecent stump orations. He seems likely to be convicted, but the vote will be close. . . .

March 30. . . . Apropos of the name of my great-grandmother's family, here is a righte merrie jeste that I heard when I was a child. Once upon a time, when George the Third was King, perhaps a hundred years ago, there dwelt in the village of New York a distinguished Person of Color, whose name I forget, and who was commonly known as *Black Sam.* He was the Delmonico of his day, a culinary artist and a purveyor of suppers and dinners, and a very high and mighty personage. It so fell out that one day a Mr. Bayard, or Ludlow, directed a servant to go to "Black Sam" and order of him something or other in the way of his profession. And the servant, being probably a Negro recently imported from the Guinea Coast, and ignorant of *les convenances* and of the ways of the town, did his master's bidding according to the letter, and instead of asking for Mister ——, enquired "Where is Black Sam?" Hearing which, the affronted artist kicked the enquirer, punched his head, and eliminated him from the premises.

And not long thereafter, his master bade the same menial go on an errand to Mr. Brownjohn. Whereupon the nigger shewed signs of alarm and replied in substance (I idealize his remarks as handed down by tradition): "O Lord, mas'r! Mas'r is foolin' dis child! *Black Sam* most knock dis nigger's dam head off! Had 'nuff o' dem sort o' folks. Dis nigger don't go a-lookin' after no *Brown John,* now I tell yer!" . . .

April 5. Tonight at supper, Hoffman, and Mr. Ruggles. Hoffman has just returned from Savannah and St. Augustine, after a three weeks' absence, with Mr. and Mrs. Colden Murray. Others called during the evening, but I told the butler we were at home only for two or three.

Hoffman has much to tell of Southern talk about the atrocities of "Mr. Sherman" and his horde, of orange groves and yellow jessamine, alligators and white cranes, of Bishop Young and the Marquis Talleyrand and his gay little wife, who are settling down in a little chateau they have bought on the St. John's river, and so on. Also, of Mrs. Theresa Yelverton (heroine of an Anglo-Irish scandal and *cause célèbre*), who was one of his fellow travelers, and who carries about in her trunk a coffin plate inscribed, "The Honorable Mrs. Yelverton. Born so and so," with a blank for the date of her death, so that in case of accident she may be provided with a post-mortem certificate or record of her matrimonial title, or of her claim thereto.

Talk with old [Gulian C.] Verplanck and with William C. Bryant at Century last night about Robert C. Sands, apropos of the New York *Talisman* for 1828, a copy of which I found among Aunt Olivia's most miscellaneous *reliquiae*. I had not seen the book since I was a boy. It's very clever. We have no one now who can write anything like the "Legend of the Devil's Pulpit," by Sands, to say nothing of Bryant's beautiful "Death of the Flowers."

Bryant says he and Verplanck composed the name "Melsingah," which I always took for genuine "Old Indian." I well remember my visit to that pretty little waterfall and its romantic ravine in 1830, with my mother and Mr. and Mrs. Johnson, and Mr. Johnson suggesting to me, facetiously, that I ought to write some Latin hexameters and pentameters in honor of the nymph of the brook, or the *genius loci*. *Eheu fugaces, etc., labuntur anni,* as old McVickar would say, were he asked to say anything on the subject.

April 6. College trustees this afternoon. Long sitting, but nothing very important came up. Barnard brought up a resolution looking to the purchase of Newberry's collection and Egleston's, and the subject went to a special committee. Walked up with Fish, who is, as usual, disgusted with everybody from the President down, and thinks the faculty not worth its salt.

Trinity Church vestry tonight, in the next room appended to Trinity Chapel. After adjournment there was an informal balloting for a name to be put on the Easter Tuesday ticket in Bradford's place. Allan Campbell got 13 votes, and Egleston 3; mine among them. We had a report from our engineers, that if the "Arcadian" railroad be built,[14] Trinity Church steeple will come down, and that it can't be shored up. Home. General Vinton, Jem Ruggles, and some nice mass music.

I fear the Irish Church establishment is doomed, and church rates in England, too. Hurrah for Mob and Snob, and Tag and Rag! "Reform" gains additional momentum year by year and *may* become Revolution. It seems certain that tinkers and tailors will rule Great Britain before long, but their accession to sovereign power will probably be peaceable and parliamentary.[15] There is no pluck or heart in Peerage or Gentry, and

[14] A proposed underground railway following Broadway.

[15] Although it was the Conservative Party which had carried through the Reform Act of 1867, the Liberals now (1868) came into power under Gladstone, pledged to a policy of economy, peace, and internal readjustment. Although Gladstone was a good Anglican, he stood for the disestablishment and disendowment of the Anglican Church in Ireland; and this measure became law in 1869. Strong comes close in this passage to a prophecy of Labor government in Britain.

they will surrender without firing a gun. Were any grain of their ancestral spirit left them, there would be a struggle and a crash. As it is they will succumb, give up their ancient rule, and try only to save their acres and their consols. There will be dry eyes on this side the Atlantic when they fall, for they have shewn little love toward us, but I cannot help a little sorrow for the approaching degradation of England.

April 7. . . . A Democratic governor elected in Connecticut. But the Republicans claim the legislature, and count on electing a Senator in Dixon's place.[16] Dixon was always weak-backed, and has of late Johnsonized his worst. The "braves" or "bravoes" of the "Ku-Klux Klan" seem busy in sundry portions of the South. The vocation of these chivalric creatures is to go about nocturnally in large parties, masked and disguised, shooting inconvenient niggers and uncomfortable Union men. Southern papers applaud and encourage them in a guarded semi-ironical way. Celts and Southerners have a monopoly of murder and assassination.

April 9. . . . Bench and bar settle deeper in the mud every year and every month. They must be near the bottom now. Witness the indecencies done and suffered by Dudley Field, Barnard, Brady, Haskin, etc., in General Term of Supreme Court, as reported in the newspapers. Their reports are emasculated, and many bits of specially pungent Billingsgate are suppressed as too filthy for print. This combat of night scavengers was an affair of outposts in the great Erie Railroad war, the controversy of Drew and Vanderbilt. The Supreme Court is our *Cloaca Maxima*, with lawyers for its rats. But my simile does that rodent injustice, for the rat is a remarkably clean animal. Johnny's pet is always cleaning himself. Its fur is always glossy. After eating, and after being touched (for the creature is half-tamed and lets itself be caressed), it invariably goes through with a course of ceremonial ablution, wetting its paws and washing or scratching itself all over. If touched during that process, it bites like a demon.

Haydn is very great. There are *three things* for which we should give Almighty God special thanks, as being extra, and (so to say) gratuitous, sources of happiness to men and quite unnecessary (so far as we can see) to the working of the material universe—mere gifts "without consideration" and without any object save that of giving us the purest enjoyment. They are the loveliness of Flowers, the splendors of Cloud Scenery, gorgeous sunsets, etc.; and above all, our capacity of receiving the unspeakable

16 In the heaviest total vote yet cast in Connecticut, the Democrats elected James E. English governor. But as Strong notes, the Republicans held the legislature and chose ex-Governor William A. Buckingham as Senator.

suggestions of beauty and of all that is good and true and noble and glorious from mere sounds, or noises, skillfully grouped and combined. The great masters of music—Haydn, Mozart, Beethoven—*enarrant Gloriam Dei* even more emphatically than the "spacious firmament on high." . . .

April 15. . . . I rather think No. 107 East 21st Street [Aunt Olivia Templeton's house] is sold to one Wesley, formerly of Wesley & Kowalski, for $32,500.

At the new Union League Club House this afternoon (Jerome's establishment, corner Madison Avenue and Twenty-sixth Street).[17] Very handsome. Ellie has just gone to the Assembly at Delmonico's to matronize pretty Miss Emily Fuller.

April 16. Grand reception of the Union League Club in their new building at Twenty-sixth Street and Madison Avenue. Many nice people; great crowd, and heat unbearable.

Another railroad accident (so-called) on the Erie Road. Scores of people smashed, burned to death, or maimed for life. We shall never travel safely till some pious, wealthy, and much beloved railroad director has been hanged for murder, with a "gentlemanly conductor" on each side of him. Drew or Vanderbilt would do to begin with. We talk of the judicial murders committed under the rule of the Stuarts and of our advance in civilization since the Popish Plot trials, and the Rye House plot trials. But have we made any real progress? A party of travelers cannot go from this town to Buffalo or Boston or Albany, without imminent danger of being killed by a certain railroad corporation under certain corporate franchises conferred by the state. It's a choice of evils, to be sure, but I should prefer execution under the sentence of Scroggs or Jeffrey. . . .

April 22. . . . Impeachment trial draws near its close. Result dubersome.

Miss Helen Gilson, one of our Sanitary Commission heroines all through the war, died at Newton, Massachusetts, the other day. She had married one Osgood. This young lady was bright, earnest, warm-hearted, self-denying, full of resources, sweet-mannered, efficient, and a lot of adjectives beside. A noble specimen of the New England girl *pur sang*, and modest and maidenly in all her rough hospital work. She worked with Ellie on our hospital transports at Yorktown, White House, etc., in 1862. . . .

[17] The club had leased for ten years the "elegant and commodious" mansion formerly occupied by Leonard Jerome, whose daughter married Lord Randolph Churchill. The fine old house overlooking Madison Square is now (1951) occupied by the Manhattan Club. The Union League Club moved to new quarters at Fifth Avenue and 39th Street in 1881.

April 25. . . . The New York *World* is quite smart in its wicked Copper-head venom. Alluding to some probably false story about General Butler's financiering with commissaries and the like for his own private profit during the war, it says: "Now this Butler was more Sutler than any other Beast in the field!" That little drop of concentrated virus is quite too pungent to have been distilled from the poison glands of a mere common-place North American Copperhead Snake. It is not unworthy of the most maleficent and malignant cobra that ever squirmed in the jungles of Bengal. . . .

April 27. . . . Johnny and Temple heard *Richard III* read by Mrs. [Fanny] Kemble this evening. They enjoyed and appreciated it, though Temple "does not see why Mrs. K. should holler so." . . .

April 29. Last night with Ellie to the theatre appurtenant to the Union League Clubhouse, whilom "Jerome's Theatre," and heard Mrs. Fanny Kemble read *Cymbeline*. It was an admirable reading, but perhaps a little stagey and overdone, here and there. I am specially fond of that play, for Imogen has always seemed to me the most lovable and the very noblest of all Shakespeare's portraits of noble and lovely women. And while Mrs. Kemble read, I was obliged to fix my thoughts, sometimes, as firmly as I could, on the fooleries and buffooneries of *La Belle Hélène*, to keep myself from snivelling. Her great talent and her careful study of the text make her reading an instructive commentary upon it. She brought out many points that were new to me; for example, Imogen's question in the last scene, "Why did you throw your wedded lady from you?"—so delightfully appropriate to her loving, generous, and loyal wifely nature. I have always understood this as a cry of passionate joy uttered as she throws herself into her husband's arms. But there is far more delicacy and truth in Mrs. Kemble's rendering. She gives it in a faint, broken whisper —as the instinctive utterance of one hardly yet half conscious and only just beginning to recover from the blow that has stricken her down— without the least trace of complaint or resentment and without any intensity of expression.

Pity Mrs. Kemble is such a Tartar. The ladies (Mrs. Cooper, Mrs. Barlow, and others) at whose request she read last night, for the benefit of some charity which they administer, addressed her a very civil note, proposing to send a carriage for her, and to meet her at the door, and introduce her into the house. Mr. Tighe tells me he saw her answer. "She would be happy to read for the benefit of the (whatever it was); she needed no introduction, and she could pay her own hack-hire. Yours resp'y."

In the same key was her reply to one of the Fields, at Stockbridge, who remarked by way of civility, "Madam, you ride that horse better than I can." The reply was, "Of course. You are afraid of the horse, and the horse is afraid of *me*."

Poor Pierce Butler! I fear his married life was stormy.

May 2. . . . Evarts has actually got through his oration in defense of the President. Strange so clear-headed a man should not have seen that the merit and weight of a forensic argument are apt to be inversely as its bulk. Witness Somers's speech in the Seven Bishops case, and Erskine's in the Greenwich Hospital case. Each was the foundation of a great name, a great fortune, and the highest rank a professional man can aspire to, and neither occupied much more than an hour, if so much. Evarts has talked through the sittings of four days. His argument might have been made powerful by compression into one-twentieth of its bulk, or by evaporation of its wordiness. In its diluted form, it seems inert, as an ounce of Epsom salts dissolved in ninety gallons of dishwater.

May 4, MONDAY.   Spring weather, flavored with a dash of east-wind-vinegar.

Trustees of Columbia College held a rather long session. Barnard was a little prolix about the Russian minerals, and how some of them were lost by perils of the sea, and how the Russian government promised to make the loss good, and how he rather thought it would, and why he thought so, and so on. Also, about the Senior class, how it's in a state of discord, and how the management of Commencement will have to be taken off its hands, and so forth. Report of Committee on Greek Prize Scholarships. My colleague and venerated father-in-law got himself into a heat because they were to be called "*Anthon* prize scholarships"—couldn't see why they should be so designated, "especially as there were to be two of them," and moved to strike out the prefix, which motion prevailed. "Why," quoth Mr. Ruggles, "is *everything* we may hereafter do to promote Greek scholarship necessarily to be called after the late Professor Anthon?" I must say that the query seemed to me worthy the Gouverneur Ogden of fourteen years ago. It was perfectly understood that these prizes were to be established in memory of the old professor, and it was eminently proper they should be established in his name. *Dis aliter visum*. I am vexed by the result, and especially vexed that the objection should have come from Mr. Ruggles. I contented myself with an expression of decided dissent, and the two anonymous scholarships were duly established. . . .

May 7. . . . Arguments of Counsel in the Impeachment Case are closed. Senators will probably emit gas among themselves for a fortnight at least before coming to a vote. Result of that vote cannot be confidently predicted. Johnsonists assert that sundry Republican Senators will vote to acquit, and that a two-thirds vote against the accused cannot be had. Maybe so. The violence of the New York *Tribune* and its denunciation of every Republican Senator so voting, as a traitor to his party, looks as if the Honorable Horace Greeley felt a little anxious about the issue. He forgets that Senators, sitting as judges, must decide *secundem allegata et probata*, and ignore everything else, even party obligations. He thinks the managers have made out their case, and so do I. And I believe Johnson's conviction and degradation desirable and expedient. His sentence would be *veri justum aequum et salutare*, according to my best judgment. But I'm not disposed to rail at everybody who thinks otherwise.

May 9. We closed the [Law School] examination at eleven last night. *Evöe!* That bore is finished. We privately examined two of the class, Goodhart and Hervey, who seemed shaky, and passed them both, but not without misgivings about the former.

When the public examination was finished, and we were drawing long breaths and rising to go, Mr. David Judson Newland, of the graduating class, got on his legs, and addressed Professor Dwight with a few remarks, evidently committed to memory. They were condensed and well worded. "He was deputed by the class to declare their respect and affection for the Professor. Most members of the class came to the school from first-class colleges. They could, therefore, testify from personal knowledge that such teachers as Professor Dwight were rare. And he begged to present on behalf of the class this slight testimonial of" etc., to wit, a handsome silver tea service. The Professor's surprise and deep feeling were clearly genuine. He replied in broken sentences, with eyes full of tears, and very briefly. "Ten years ago," said the Professor, among other things, "I lost an only son, and I think I shall never have another. The memory of this loss has made me love young men and love the work of training them." These words may seem unreal to any one who did not hear them spoken, but they evidently came from the depths of the speaker's heart, in unpremeditated simplicity. . . .

May 10. . . . The old "table-moving" fancy seems reviving. Miss Louisa brought here a new device called a "planchette," now in fashion.

It's a little board that moves freely on little rollers, with a pencil stuck through it. . . .

May 11. . . . Benjamin R. Winthrop told me not long ago that poor Theodore Winthrop of Big Bethel memory had converted his sister, Mrs. Laura and her husband, "to infidelity." I denied the allegation. But that brave, brilliant, and unfortunate young fellow used to avow his disbelief in the commonly received doctrines of Christianity with more frankness and freedom than good taste. I well remember his doing so, on these premises, and the avowal was quite gratuitous. He was clever and bright and energetic in talk, and exercised much influence over his associates. . . .[18]

May 12. . . . I notice more building this season than usual. Work is begun on the site of the Society Library (afterwards Appleton's), southeast corner of Broadway and Leonard Street. The southeast corner of Cedar and Broadway and several old buildings adjoining it are coming down, and a grand insurance building is to take its place. Thus is swept away Guerin's ancient lunching place, which we law students used to haunt. . . .

May 13. Stormy day, and at last a steady deluge of rain, like a summer shower indefinitely prolonged. Hence a scanty attendance at Law School Commencement at the Academy of Music. It was barely half full. Mr. Ruggles, Judge Blatchford, Edward Jones, Governor Fish, and I, of the trustees, looked as imposing as we could behind the footlights. Barnard presided, of course, and said *auctoritate mye hyc commissa*, and so on, as usual. But he was educated at Yale, "one of those *habebam* colleges in New England," as Bull Anthon used to call them. Blatchford brought old Judge Nelson of the Supreme Court, U.S.,[19] who sat with us and looked leonine and learned enough to represent Ellenborough and Kenyon and Mansfield and Marshall all in one. "Alumni address" by L. Bradford Prince had its good points, but was rather anserine. He complimented the Faculty of the School and particularly Dwight, "without whom," he said, "the School would resemble *Hamlet* with the part of the Prince of Denmark omitted"— a line of observation which probably did not gratify Lieber. It was none the pleasanter because it was true. . . .

[18] For Theodore Winthrop's death in battle, see the diary for 1861. The posthumous publication of *Cecil Dreeme* and two other novels, and of *The Canoe and the Saddle* and *Life in the Open Air*, had given him an enduring if minor niche in American literature.

[19] Judge Samuel Nelson, born in Washington's first Administration, had been one of the most conscientious and industrious members of the Supreme Court since 1845. He was a graduate of Middlebury College. Samuel Blatchford (1820–1893), a graduate of Columbia College in 1837 and a long-time friend of Strong's, had been appointed federal judge for the Southern District of New York by President Johnson in May, 1867.

Something must be done about this Law School, and our Committee is to meet this week and consider what should be done. It has become too strong and useful to remain, as it is, entirely dependent on Dwight's life and health. It is *his* School. Were he to die or resign tomorrow, it would evaporate and evanesce the next day. If it is to be permanent, he must have a staff of associates and coadjutors and they must be of high grade and well paid. He has Lieber as professor of constitutional law and political history. We pay Lieber $4,000 a year, and his last year's work consisted in dispensing scraps from his memory and his note books to *six* of the graduating class, who chose to attend his "optional" course. I don't believe he gave the School forty dollars' worth of work. We shall have to throw him over and make his salary useful. [Dr. John] Ordronaux is probably of little account, but then he comes comparatively cheap. [Charles Murray] Nairne with his "Ethics of Jurisprudence" costs the School nothing, so he and the School are probably square.

May 14, THURSDAY. Something like spring again. Met Evarts, just from Washington and cocksure of his illustrious client's acquittal. Mr. Derby writes from Washington that Sumner is much cast down, but still hopes for conviction by one or two votes. General Burnside, who is rather violently anti-Johnsonian, writes that he is disgusted by the requests addressed to him by prominent politicians from New England and the West to use his influence with Sprague and Anthony of Rhode Island in sundry illegitimate ways. . . .

May 15. Law School Committee sat from eight to eleven, this evening, at the School.

Poor Lieber! The Committee was hardly kept from recommending that he be suppressed altogether. Dwight saved him by insisting that his name carries weight and brings students to the School, though they mostly decline hearing his lectures after they have joined it. But he certainly doesn't earn half his pay. It will not be easy to get him into working relations with any readjustment of his duties and his salary. He has plenty of learning and ability, and a keen appreciation of the money value of any position in the College. But he has little common sense. He is such an *owl*, so wise and lazy, and so puffy with self-importance, that I fear we shall have to choose between leaving him as he is, and dropping him altogether.

May 16, SATURDAY. Another day of dull uncertain weather. Before two o'clock it was generally known that H.E. the President was acquitted, and the streets were full of newsboys, whose extras confirmed the report.

It was close work—19 to 35. I don't know why this result should "disintegrate the Republican Party" as the *World* and other malignant Copperhead organs joyously predict it will. It merely proves that many prominent Republicans are superior to party obligations and influences, whereas the Democrats have voted together on every interlocutory question and on the final decision, as a strictly partisan corps. Johnson's term will soon end, and this narrow escape warns him that he must be wary for the future. . . .

May 17. . . . I think with Mr. Ruggles that this acquittal is worth many thousand votes to the Republican Party, for it excludes A. Johnson from the prestige of martyrdom. But it was an error. As the *Tribune* suggests, the right claimed by the President to ignore any law he deems unconstitutional enables him to dispense with "any statute for about two years, or until a case can be made and carried up to the Supreme Court." For example, he may honestly hold a protective tariff unconstitutional, and prohibit collectors at every port from enforcing it. He can nullify all legislation for at least half his term of office, and excuse himself, at last, under the plea of *ignorantia legis.* It would seem that Senators were misled by the words "high crimes and misdemeanors," and that the Managers made little effort to set them right. Counsel and the Court seem to have taken it for granted that crimes and misdemeanors must be made out analogous at least to those of which Grand Juries and Courts of Oyer and Terminer take cognizance. I suppose the word "misdemeanor" to be used not in its technical sense, but as synonymous with misbehavior—official misconduct—grave departure from sound public policy. I suppose the functions of the Senate on an impeachment to be partly judicial but partly legislative, too. It is the grand inquest of the nation, assembled to see that the republic takes no detriment. . . .

Strong's view of the impeachment proceedings was that which the Radical leaders had taken. Senator Sumner had declared that "this proceeding is political in character—before a political body—and with a political object." Happily for the best interests of the republic, more than one-third of the Senators had taken a different view. William M. Evarts, who made the ablest speech in defense of the President, asked what high crimes he had committed. Had he betrayed a fortress, surrendered a fleet, or sold public offices? On the contrary, he had done nothing but attempt—unsuccessfully—to remove an insubordinate Cabinet member. Why the effort, inquired Evarts, to dispel the conception that the Senate was sitting as a court of justice? This was but a confession that if the Senate were a court, it could find no sufficient grounds for a judgment against the President; it was essentially an effort to get the Senate to enact a bill of attainder. And if the President were removed, Evarts warned, then all balance among the three departments of government would be lost. Congress would become omnipotent, with the executive and judiciary its mere tools.

The first vote in the Senate was taken May 16 on the eleventh or omnibus article of impeachment, which not only dealt with various charges connected with the removal of Stanton, but asserted that President Johnson had termed the Thirty-ninth Congress "a Congress of only part of the states," thereby implying that its legislation was invalid. This touched the pride of the Senate, and the article was thought to offer the best chance of obtaining a conviction. When the roll was called, thirty-five Senators voted "guilty" and nineteen "not guilty." Of the staunch nineteen, seven were Republicans—Fessenden, Fowler, Grimes, Henderson, Ross, Trumbull, and Van Winkle. The pressure brought to bear on Grimes of Iowa, Henderson of Missouri, and Ross of Kansas had been terrific. Lincoln's old friend Lyman Trumbull of Illinois, and Lincoln's one-time Secretary of the Treasury, Fessenden, also showed great courage. It was said later that had more votes been needed to save Johnson, one or two Republicans would have cast them. The verdict, sustained by later ballots, was a sore humiliation to Ben Wade, who had hoped (as president of the Senate) to succeed to the White House, to Thaddeus Stevens, vengeful and arbitrary, and to Sumner, who had actually called Johnson "the impersonation of the tyrannical Slave Power." It left men like Strong, who deemed Andrew Johnson too erratic, undignified, and blundering for his high office, dissatisfied. But it preserved the dignity and authority of the presidency, kept the power of the executive in balance with that of the legislative branch, and saved Johnson from a stigma which he in no wise merited.

Strong was now, in characteristically unselfish fashion, giving a great part of his time to Columbia, and striving earnestly to improve the Law School and School of Mines. On the day that news of the vote in the Senate came, he tried to convince S. B. Ruggles of the necessity for erecting a fire-proof building to house the library, the fine geological specimens accumulated by the School of Mines, and Dr. Torrey's Herbarium. Such a building would cost only $75,000, he thought, and Columbia would soon be repaid the cost by an increase in valuable donations. The diarist was worried about the precarious position of Francis

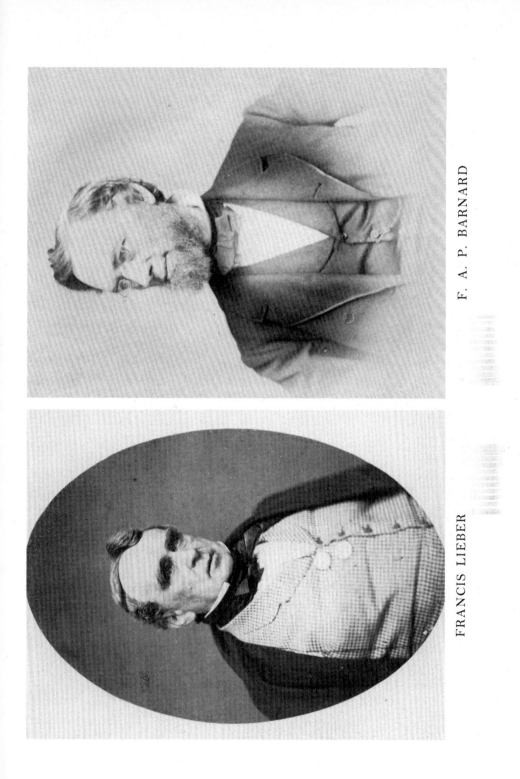

FRANCIS LIEBER

F. A. P. BARNARD

THE HONORABLE WILLIAM MARCY TWEED

Lieber, who since his transfer to the Law School remained a poor teacher if a great publicist. Nobody could foresee that in little more than four years Lieber would be dead.

May 18. . . . *The Messiah* tonight with Ellie, at Steinway Hall. That ineffable music was fairly rendered. Parepa did her part full justice. . . .

May 19. Law School Committee sat two hours and a half this afternoon. We agreed to recommend the appointment of an assistant professor with very narrow function (a small step the right way) and also that a change be made in Lieber's department, which he can rightly understand as a notice to quit at the year's end—to be enforced unless he can so modify his style of work meanwhile that students can be induced to attend his lectures.

Steinway Hall tonight. Second evening of the "Musical Festival." Bach's Suite No. 3 in D. Third movement very strong, like Beethoven in ruffles and a bag-wig. . . . Mendelssohn's *Reformation Symphony* produced here for the first time. Its second movement, a sort of scherzo, is delicious, but what it has to do with the "Reformation" I cannot guess. . . .

After this, I came home—for nobody offered me fifty dollars to stay and listen to Berlioz's "Dramatic Symphony," *Romeo and Juliet,* and I would not undergo that majestic work for a cent less.

They are beginning to pull down old St. George's in Beekman Street, a venerable landmark. All the west side of Broadway between Eighteenth and Nineteenth Streets is coming down—a row of twopenny little two-story shops. Cheever's Meetinghouse, west side of Union Square, is in course of rapid demolition. Tiffany & Co. are to build on its site. It will be an improvement—the change will. Real jewels will be sold there instead of bogus ones. Cheever's pew-holders paid high prices for their bogus acquisitions. Tiffany's customers will pay still larger sums, but they will secure a genuine article.

May 21. After Wall Street, I went to School of Mines. Saw Chandler, Newberry, and Egleston, severally full of work and of hope. Our collections begin to grow precious, and I shudder when I think of this old barn of a building, with white hot assay furnaces in its cellar and of the remediless mischief that may befall us at any moment. . . .

May 22. . . . Hurrah for Grant and Colfax, nominees of the Chicago Convention, for whom I hope to deposit a little vote next November, if I'm alive, and out of the State Prison. Colfax's character is decent, considering that he's a politician, and my faith in Grant's honesty and ability is very strong.[20]

Mrs. Secretary McCulloch here this afternoon; a nice jolly woman, full of talk about affairs at Washington, and especially about the impeachment case. She upholds A. Johnson, of course, and I said nothing to his disparagement.

I'm in discourse with the Schermerhorns (William and Edmund) about a partition, between themselves, John Jones Schermerhorn, and Mrs. Augustus Schermerhorn's family, of the great estate they now hold in common. It would be a serious undertaking. . . .

May 23.   I went to Steinway Hall for a "Miscellaneous" Concert, of the "Musical Festival" series. Cherubini's Introduction to 3rd Act of *Medea* was very good. Thereafter, I sat through a symphony in A by F. L. Ritter, conducted by that maestro in person. It was well enough, but who is F. L. Ritter that we should have to hear his commonplace compilations, while so many orchestral works of great composers are but half known to us or wholly unknown? . . .

General prophesying that Grant and Colfax will sweep the country. No ticket can be put up that has a chance against them. On this point Republicans are positive and unanimous. But I remember 1844, when "the Whigs took Clay and made a *bust* of it." Clay was nominated with enthusiasm and unanimity. Like Grant, he "would only have to walk over the course." But the Democrats dug up, out of his congenial dirt and darkness, one J. K. Polk, and somehow or other contrived to carry the day. Then there was the famous match between General Scott and the nonentity, Franklin Pierce. Grant's prospects are hopeful, but we must not be too sanguine. Every Yahoo of a Democratic editor will pelt him with dirt for the next six months, and some of it may stick. The influence of the Administration will be used against him with little reserve or scruple, and it is tenfold stronger than it was in old times before the war. The Democratic nomination may be a specially lucky hit. Grant's friends may over-eulogize him and thereby disgust the "masses." Many things may happen before next November. Grant is not elected till the electoral votes are counted and the result announced.

May 24, SUNDAY.   Rain. Rain. Rain. And headache. Fate seems against

[20] The Republican Convention, meeting in Chicago on May 21, adopted a brief platform endorsing the Radical reconstruction policy, and nominated Grant on the first ballot by unanimous vote of the 650 delegates present. Five ballots were required to nominate Schuyler Colfax of Indiana for Vice-President.

my going to church. This evening Mr. Ruggles here and Murray Hoffman, Wolcott Gibbs, Alexander (the ostracized Unionist of Baltimore), Rueful Jeames, Bramwell, Jem Ruggles, and one Ashworth, an English yachtsman. . . .

Gibbs had a story—positively authentic—of the Reverend [Samuel] Osgood, one of our Unitarian philosophers, traveling uptown in a crowded horse-car, and haranguing the crowd, *more suo*, under cover of conversation with a friend. When he gets out, some wild Western man who had been sitting opposite accosts his neighbor thus-wise: "Stranger, who is that man that's just *gitted*?" "That's the Reverend Dr. Osgood, etc." "Wal, stranger, I should say he was lookin' out for a vacancy in the Trinity." !!! Somewhat profane, but not infelicitous. Finite limits can hardly be assigned to Reverend Osgood's self-appreciation.

This Mr. Alexander, by the by, seems much more of a man than I have thought him. It seems that reports are multiplying that the Democracy will adopt Chief Justice Chase as its candidate. "Prominent Democrats" have confirmed these reports. They have been current some time, but I have held them incredible, and do so still. The Party would thereby repudiate its record, and its platforms of the last twenty years at least, and would throw overboard all its Vallandighams, Seymours, Touceys, *et id genus omne*. It would become a new party—"of like substance," at least, with the Republican, and far in advance of the Republicans of 1861. Thus purged of Copperheadism, reformed and penitent, supporting Chase, that "d——d Abolitionist" of a few years since, renouncing all its traditions, the Democratic Party might entitle itself to the confidence and respect of the country, after some little probation. But it will do no such thing, and I am surprised to find intelligent people talking as if they thought such a somerset possible. Would it were possible! What a blessed event for the country it would be if the old Copperheads and Peace Democrats were rejected by both parties and finally consigned to the Limbo of political insignificance, wherein are no offices! Their infamy should consign them to some still lower depth. Many of them were doubtless honest, but they were most sadly misguided—"sair left to themsell"—and the country can never safely trust one of them again. When I think of Toucey, and Horatio Seymour, and even of poor Washington Hunt, who was so sound and useful outside of politics, and so warm a friend of Mr. Ruggles, I tend to become vitriolic and vindictive, and think not unfavorably of guillotines and committees of *Salut Publique*.

The learned Lieber is in some excitement. But it's too late to go into that. Two-fifteen A.M.!

May 25. . . . The New York *World* is denouncing General Grant as without brains, and as especially wanting in capacity for military command. It proves to its own satisfaction that any dolt could have done as much as Grant did toward suppressing the Rebellion. The *Tribune* replies by reprinting the *World's* eulogies on Grant as the greatest of modern commanders, and the most single-minded, clear-headed and upright of men— which eulogies were published when the *World* thought Grant willing to play into the hands of A. Johnson. . . .

May 29. Sanitary Commission this evening at 13 East 16th Street, to which Blatchford has removed our headquarters. There were Newberry, Agnew, Gibbs, and Blatchford. Our cash balance is $28,000, besides the special Philadelphia fund of $20,000. We cut into it to the amount of some $4,000 for the benefit of Gould's Statistical Report, etc.

Our musical evening, Haydn Number Two, was last evening. It was "a success." Everybody was delighted and the performance was pronounced admirable, even by some who (like D'Oremieulx) would have rather liked to tell me that there was just one thing that might have been better. I am specially glad of this for Dr. Pech's sake, whose merits as a conductor and drill-master were thus made manifest to a number of nice people, and who made certain acquaintances that he may find useful. Our chorus, about whom I was uneasy, got on very comfortably and seemed to be pleased and gratified. Though the ladies are real ladies, and just as good as anybody, I feared they would not mix in with the audience, after the performance. But they did. As to the Orchestral Deutschers, I gave them a good drink all round when their work was finished, and then took them up to the library with a supply of cigars and left them there till I summoned them downstairs to supper. They were not in evening dress, and this seemed what suited them best. They would have been out of their element in the parlors. People in their position cost one some thought and anxiety on occasions like this. They ought to be and must be treated with cordiality and with rather special attention. They deserve it, as "artists"—or rather as interpreters of art. But you can't quite comfortably present a seedy Teutonic doublebasso to Miss — or Mrs. —.

Our audience was about 150. There were the habitués of the house. Also, sumptuous Mrs. Adelaide Bell, Reverend Morrill of St. Alban's, Reverend Dr. Frank Vinton, Dr. Barnard (who came in late, after Drisler's eulogy on the late Professor Anthon) and his round ball of a jolly wife,

General Waller and wife (nice people) from Governor's Island, and a dozen naval Spaniards from some Spanish frigate now in the harbor. They were brought by General Waller. . . .

June 1. . . . Death announced of Charles Edwards, connected many years to H.B.M. Consulate, and a rather hard, sharp, narrow practitioner. Also, of William McMurray, sometime rather conspicuous as a Democratic politician in a moderate way. He was found dead in his bed. Apoplexy, it's said. Also death of Honorable J. Buchanan, once President of these United States. He will long hold a more conspicuous place in our history than could have been attained by ten times his talent. He has gained this prominence partly by the accident of his coming to the presidency in critical times, and partly by his want of political honesty and courage. This moral weakness hurried on the Civil War, the preliminaries of which will make the last year of his official life memorable for its dishonor.

College trustees sat from two to five P.M., and did much work—mostly matter of routine. Dr. Barnard read a long report on College affairs for the last year, bringing up certain important matters; for example, the question whether we are to keep in view a probable removal of the College to a new site. This was referred to a special committee of seven, well selected. He produced a bushel of drawings by members of the School of Mines of blast furnaces and metallurgical and engineering works of all sorts, with carefully prepared MS descriptions of each and estimates of cost, etc. Our colleagues inspected these, and expressed much surprise and delight at the evidence they furnished of practical training and discipline. Their surprise was natural, for too many of them know nothing of the School by actual observation. As I seem to be held, for some unknown reason, a special friend and backer of the School (perhaps because I am somewhat intimate with Egleston and Newberry and Vinton), I was rather pleased by this convincing display of its efficiency. . . .

President Barnard reported about the "Greek Prizes." . . . He had invited George Anthon to be one of the alumni examiners of the prize papers and "regretted that he was obliged to read to the board the following note in reply." How much more did its writer's personal friends regret such a display of bad taste! . . . George "declined to assist in carrying out what the trustees proposed, but did not intend thereby any disrespect to Professor Drisler, whose eulogium of the late Professor was quite worthy of its subject." Of course, the inference is that he meant to declare himself disgusted with Barnard, or with the board, or with both. I have not talked with him about it for some months, but I hear that he considers his uncle's

. . . memory maltreated by our choosing Jack Ehninger to do his portrait, and also (strange as it seems) by our not designating his successor's chair "the Anthon Professorship of Greek." It is a cropping out of the petulance and angularity he inherits from the last generation of his family. . . . I don't mind it, for I well know George's compensating good traits. But it will be remembered against him by a dozen respectable men whose good opinion he would like to retain. . . .

June 11. Meeting at Mott Memorial Library, eight P.M. (58 Madison Avenue), to organize a National Academy or Institute to promote the study of all arts and sciences. There must have been some sixty present. W. C. Bryant was put in the chair, and Dr. William A. Hammond[21] made secretary. A constitution was adopted "provisionally" and a kind of Executive Committee on organization appointed—fifteen, including my artistic and scientific self. Mr. Ruggles made one or two telling little speeches. [Eben N.] Horsford of Cambridge and [Arnold H.] Guyot of Princeton, and one Plummer of Charleston, spoke very well. Ripley, Dr. Elliot, Reverend [Octavius B.] Frothingham (an ultra-Unitarian pulpit philosopher and a theist in some sense or other, I believe), and eminent Dr. [Josiah C.] Nott, late of Mobile, the enlightened George Opdyke, and others. The meeting was a strong one and looked well for the success of the undertaking. I know as its engineers only R. G. White and Dr. Alf Carroll. If their plan succeed, it will give them much kudos. But institutions seldom live and thrive that originate in so large and elaborate an organization on paper, with all their parts and functions defined in advance of their existence. Institutions must conform to a general law and consent to be born little, if they are to grow big. This meeting was very large (foul weather considered). It was hearty and harmonious. The movement is supported by strong men outside the city, as well as by New Yorkers. But the chances are 100 to 1 against its success on any large scale.

June 12. . . . Strange as it may seem, many Democratic leaders are clamoring for the nomination of Chase, who was abused as an Abolitionist before the war, and was one of Lincoln's Secretaries. I do not expect to see him nominated. It would be equivalent to a re-forming of parties—a renunciation by the "Democrats" of all their cherished platforms and principles, and a repudiation of the Copperhead element, including Vallandigham, Horatio Seymour, and all that gang. Many Republicans denounce Chase for allowing himself to be talked of as a possible Democratic nominee.

[21] See the many references to Dr. Hammond in the Civil War volume of this diary. The National Institute of Letters, Arts, and Sciences, as Strong feared, came to nothing.

I fear Chase has presidency on the brain—an unfortunate disease for a Chief Justice. But his nomination might prove a good thing for the country.

June 15.　At Dr. Hammond's tonight, 162 West 34th Street, for the committee that is to organize a "National Institute," if it can. There were the Doctor; R. G. White; Dr. Alf Carroll; Thomas Hicks, the artist; [W. C.] Church, the editor; Professor [Charles A.] Joy; Dr. Smith (Reverend I believe); Frederick Law Olmsted; William P. Trowbridge (just the *brick* he used to be); and perhaps one or two more. We incubated about two hours, and divided ourselves into sub-committees on the various "academies" that are to form the polypoid organization of the prospective "Institute." I believe I am responsible for the interests of "Political Economy and Law." Whether this plan succeed or fail, it is evident that the want of some central association of the kind is felt throughout the country. There are three or four hundred letters from men of some note in Philadelphia and Boston (!), Detroit, Chicago, Maine, South Carolina, and other places, all of whom give a cordial adhesion to the movement, and most of whom seem enthusiastic about it. I must humbly confess that I can't form a distinct achromatic image in my own mind of its immediate aim and end. But it may possibly become valuable as a nerve-filament of national unity, should it ever come into being at all.

The New York *World* comes out this morning decidedly against Chase as leader of the Democratic Party, and assigns unanswerable reasons for its position. This is equivalent to a pronunciamento by Belmont and Barlow and the other Sagamores of the Manhattan Club, and is a sore discouragement to any aspirations the Chief Justice may have been weak enough to cherish.

June 16. . . . The Athenaeum Club has "busted" and dissolved. Its assets—furniture, pictures, etc.—sold out yesterday. . . .

June 17, WEDNESDAY.　A misty, muggy day. Diligent in Wall Street. Slight dinner here in honor of Blacque, the Turkish Minister, Ellie's hospitable friend of last winter. I did not know but that I ought to provide His Excellency a lamb stuffed with pistachio nuts, and other viands specified in the Arabian Nights, but this Turk is an amiable, simple-mannered French gentleman of the Christian persuasion, and took his victuals and drink on Christian principles. . . . Blacque is very genial, intelligent, and nice. His wife is of Armenian parentage, I believe, but of French bringing up—a pretty brunette, with little English. . . .

June 19. . . . Everson has resigned his tutorship, and intends to open a private school next fall. I think seriously of transferring Temple and Louis to his tuition, so deeply am I disgusted by George Anthon's ill-bred and impertinent letter to the trustees. I should do so with great regret, but the letter was an unprovoked and studied affront to every one of us. I fear the transfer would amount to a final incurable rupture, for he has withdrawn himself wholly into his domestic shell and is seen of his old friends but seldom, so opportunities of making up will henceforth be infrequent—and may never occur. Breaking off an intimate friendship of thirty years is bad business. But I do not want boys of mine to be trained by a man who can excuse himself from the charge of utter boorishness only by the plea of insanity. His insanity cannot be justified or palliated as a spasm of excessive loyalty to the late Professor's memory, for it's but a few years since George Anthon went through certain weeks of black rage with me because I had not induced the trustees to suppress the Professor as head of the Grammar School, and during at least three-fourths of the time since George left College (prematurely, because Cornell and Arthur Carey ranked him), he has not been on speaking terms with his venerated uncle. There are those who maintain that poor Carey's persecution in 1843, and all the "Carey ordination" squabble, grew out of the Reverend Henry Anthon's distaste for the young man who took the college honors he counted on for his son. That statement is extravagant, but I dare say the Reverend H. Anthon's inquisition into Carey's orthodoxy was a little sharpened (doubtless unconsciously) by Carey's position *quoad* George Anthon a few years before. The Anthon brethren of that time—the lawyer, the clergyman and the professor—were a most peculiar and unaccountable people, and George certainly inherits his share of their crotchets.

June 22.   Much exercised by a kind letter from Hasket Derby begging me to join him next month in a sixty-day tour through Switzerland and to Vienna. A tempting offer, for Hasket is an expert in European travel. I should have a nice companion and be free from all bother about languages and currency. Moreover, it is just what Peters and others have been urging on me for two years as a move that would restore me a healthy mind and some little efficiency. I said at dinnertime that it would be delightful, but that I didn't feel like spending so much money on myself; whereupon the three boys broke out in chorus: "O Papa! Do go if you want to. You shall stop my weekly allowance" !!! I was rather moved by this. It seems tolerably clear to me that I ought to go, but it is a tremendous effort to get out of my deep ruts, which is just the essential part of the proposed expedition. . . .

June 23.   At office of *Army and Navy Journal* (39 Park Row) for a couple of hours this afternoon, with our "organizing" committee on "National Institute." There were R. G. White, Dr. Carroll, Dr. Dalton, Olmsted, [George] Ripley (of the *Tribune*), Dr. Hammond, Professor Joy, Thomas Hicks, etc. Sub-committees had worked, as their reports proved, and everybody seemed in earnest. Tonight to College Library for annual meeting of Alumni Association. Near 100 present, including sundry old acquaintances whom I seldom see, and several of the elder alumni whom I did not know, but who seemed to retain a lively interest in the College. Professor H. J. Anderson presided. Fred and James F. DePeyster were very busy, both alumni of near sixty years' standing.

June 24. . . . [At Columbia Commencement] Barnard, inspired by what he saw at Oxford and Cambridge last summer, has imported the loudest specimen of academic haberdashery I ever saw; viz.: a gorgeous scarlet robe, in which he looked like something between a cardinal bird and a "long-legged flamingo." He was also adorned as to his cap, with a gilt tassel "conspicuous from afar." Speeches better than usual—much less callow and crude. The valedictory, by Rives's eldest son, was very graceful and creditable. The Greek Salutatorian was in such trepidation that he forgot every word of his speech and could scarcely hear the vociferations of his anxious prompter—so the speech produced the effect of a hexameter collocution. . . . Twenty-seven A.B.'s, about as many A.M.'s, and sundry D.D.'s and LL.D.'s. They appeared on the stage in person to take their diplomas, with the same formality as the A.B.'s—a novelty, and I think an improvement. Fourteen men from the School of Mines took the degree of Mining Engineer in like manner. Egleston and Chandler rejoiced greatly thereat.

One of the graduating class, Mr. Horace Holden Thayer, came near being excluded from the public delivery of the degrees. Certain lines of his "poem" had been stricken out when it was inspected by the authorities, but the ambitious and audacious juvenile "spoke" them, nevertheless. So the President privily sent for him to come on the stage and told him not to present himself for his degree with the class. The poor young fellow begged and apologized and said he supposed himself only *advised*, and not *directed*, to cut out the passage, whatever it was—so Barnard let him off. . . .

One should thank God for the expansion and improvement of the College since 1838, when I took my degree. Or perhaps, I should rather say since 1853, when it merely cumbered the ground. For some years immediately preceding 1853, I suppose there was no life in any one of its departments, except what survived in the indomitable old Anthon's lecture room. The faculty enforced no discipline, the students displayed little sense of decency, and the institution seemed about to decompose and perish. The prodigious row about Wolcott Gibbs in 1854 acted on it as (I suppose) a moxa acts on an atrophied or diseased member, and the slow and interrupted progress of the College toward convalescence began in that year. It is still weakly, but it seems doing well. Were our trustees in any degree up to their work, the promise of its future would be splendid.

June 26. . . . With Mr. Ruggles this evening signing papers about a little joint operation in South Minnesota railroad bonds. I don't at all like endorsing notes, not even his, but he pressed this on me so earnestly as perfectly safe and certainly profitable that it would have seemed ungracious and ungrateful to decline "going in." It looks promising, but it is not in my line, and I shall feel unhappy till these notes with Trust Company and Bank of Commerce are taken up.

William Schermerhorn spent last evening with me, and our talk was of Monte Rosa, Interlachen, the Salzkammergut and the Tyrol. . . .

June 28, SUNDAY. . . . Saw Charles Blake who thinks the Democrats will nominate Chase on the 4th of July, and is confirmed in that opinion by Isaac Bell—a high authority! The general opinion is that the Chase movement has failed, though the *Herald* still pleads his cause, and that the West will insist on Pendleton, and triumph.

Murray Hoffman tells me that the Reference in Pete Strong's case is proceeding before Nicoll as Referee, unopposed, though McKeon attends to represent the defendant. Pete is "off fishing," and his counsel are doubtless thankful that he is out of the way. Dr. [James] Pech, who spent the evening here accompanying Dame Ellen at the piano, says that Barnard's "gold-tuft" was illegitimate, that appendage not being a badge of academic rank, but the peculiar adornment of the youthful nobility.

June 29. . . . Two curious results from my talk of spending sixty days on the "other side": *First,* a general chorus of adjunction to *go,* like that addressed to the "pensive Menelaus" in *La Belle Hélène*—"le Roi pensif qui s'avance," etc. . . . *Second,* the vehemence with which all my friends who have been abroad insist that I must go everywhere, see everything, and execute an infinite amount of work within a very limited time. . . .

July 1. . . . Charley Strong has had a conference with George Anthon. I regret to say that George is even more cantankerous, morbid, and wrong than I supposed him to be. He is delighted to hear that the college trustees, or some of them, were surprised and disgusted by his boorish letter of last month, for he meant to "affront" them. Henceforth he will do his best to send his pupils to some other college, and so on. What a child he is—and what an ill-bred child! All his pique and passion and impertinence (to men like Dr. Torrey, Anderson, Rutherfurd, Dix, Barnard, and to Astor, Schermerhorn, Fish, etc., whose hospitalities he has enjoyed scores of times) he thinks natural and right, because the trustees did *not* enact that their chair of Greek should be styled the "Anthon Professorship" . . . and because the trustees selected to paint the Professor's portrait the only artist in the city who was an alumnus of the college and who had ever seen the Professor. As to his letter of June 1st, it had not the dignity of an *affront*: it was a mere incivility. . . .

I have stood up for this old friend of mine and defended him against charges of brusquerie and bad manners for thirty years, and I mean to do so still, but I will not leave Temple and Louis to be trained by such a teacher. He is not to be blamed for these hereditary traits, which were so conspicuously manifested in the career of his reverend father. . . .

July 3. . . . The city is swarming with wild Southern and Western delegates to the Democratic Nominating Convention, which meets tomorrow in the new Tammany Hall on Fourteenth Street.[22] Pendleton seems ahead today, and Chase nowhere, but there are wise Sachems who say that Pendleton has no chance of a nomination, and that some unknown third person, some Pierce or Polk, will be adopted. The delegates are a rough lot—hirsute, porky creatures, in linen "dusters," with badges in their buttonholes. They sally forth from the Astor House, the St. Nicholas, and other hotels in squads of a dozen, and invade the already occupied omnibus. "Here's a seat, Governor." "Hello, Senator, is that you? You sit in my lap," "I reckon we'd better stop at the New York Hotel and licker up,"—and so on.

July 6. . . . Democratic Convention seems to have reacted itself into white heat. Pendleton's chance of nomination still seems the best. Horatio Seymour is understood to decline. Chase has faded out of view. General Hancock and Honorable Hendricks are possible nominees.

[22] The Democrats had plucked up heart since their defeat in 1864 and entertained real hope of victory in the fall elections, despite the fact that Virginia, Mississippi, and Texas could not vote (they had not been readmitted to representation in Congress), and the practical control of the rest of the South by the Republicans. The convention met on Saturday, July 4, and that day organized by selecting John M. Palmer of Illinois as temporary chairman. The battle lay between George H. Pendleton of Ohio, who believed in paying the government bonds in greenbacks instead of specie, and various Easterners who stood for "sound money."

July 7. . . . Democratic Convention is in lively session. Horatio Seymour and Wade Hampton are taking sweet counsel together, which is quite natural and not to be wondered at. They were allies five years ago. The Convention has adopted a "Repudiation" platform, and has balloted for a nominee, but as yet without result. Pendleton is ahead so far, but has not yet secured a two-thirds vote. A. Johnson gets a large vote. Sanford E. Church is voted for by the New York delegation— provisionally.

Late last night foxy old Peter Cagger of Albany and John E. Devlin undertook a drive through Central Park after a "reception" at the Manhattan Club. They were probably "tight." Something broke. They were thrown out of their drag. Cagger was killed dead, and Devlin desperately hurt. Another delegate came to grief Sunday night. He was walking down Grand Street in state of d[elirium] t[remens], believing himself pursued and persecuted by the monkeys, when he was arrested by a circumambient policeman and consigned to a cell in the Tombs, where he was found dead next morning. These Southern and Southwestern delegates infest our *omnibi,* and generally demean themselves like noisy, swaggering blackguards and swashbucklers.

Some say that Chase, who has not yet been named in the Convention, will be trotted out tomorrow by the New York delegation, which have thus far voted for the Hon. Sanford E. Church—a man of straw. Chase's friends expect New York to be seconded by Pennsylvania, and that would give Chase great strength. But I do not believe he will be brought forward at all.

July 9, THURSDAY.   Sultry. . . . At noon came news that the Democratic Convention had nominated that wretched caitiff and traitor, *Horatio Seymour,* for President, and an hour or two later that Frank Blair is their candidate for the Vice-Presidency. When I came uptown at four o'clock, there was great excitement and much crowd in East Fourteenth Street and around Union Square. They were firing a six-pounder, and driving about a wagon with transparencies and a bell, paid for by Belmont & Co., no doubt.

The nomination of Seymour fell like a thunder-stroke upon Democrats and Republicans alike. As it became evident that Pendleton, even with the support of the Northwest, could never gain two-thirds of the Convention, the selection of Salmon P. Chase had seemed overwhelmingly probable. He was a man of great abilities; he had played a great rôle in national affairs for more than twenty years; he would bring into alliance with the Democrats, it was hoped, a host of Republicans who disliked the policies of the Radicals and the military character of Grant. A majority of the New York delegation were for him, and Horatio Seymour himself expected to see the Chief Justice named. The balloting lasted for three days. First Pendleton was ahead, and then Winfield S. Hancock of Pennsylvania—but neither came within sight of the necessary two-thirds. Then, just as the situation was ripe for a general movement to Chase, on the twenty-second ballot a member created a furor by giving some votes to Seymour, the president of the convention. Before the leaders could deal with the sudden shift, a stampede had begun. Seymour hastily withdrew from the chair; amid clamor and enthusiasm, votes were hurriedly changed; and he was nominated by the unanimous voice of the 634 delegates.

For the Democratic Party it proved an unhappy nomination. Chase might have had some chance of carrying the election; Seymour, with his unsavory reputation for Copperhead policies during the Civil War, had none. Nor was the ticket strengthened by the hot-headed, impetuous Blair, who had just written an indiscreet letter and who was known to be a heavy drinker. Business and financial interests, fearful that the Democrats, if victorious, would adopt unsound monetary policies, rallied behind Grant. Strong entered in his diary: "I respect Grant and detest his opponent. My vote will be not so much for Grant as against Seymour, the base sympathizer with the Public Enemy, and with the brutal mob of 1863. I think the Convention wanted Chase, but was coerced by wire-pullers." This was unjust to Seymour, but multitudes agreed with the diarist.

July 10. A hot and busy day. The usual lunch of roast clams at Downing's. Discoursed with Randolph Robinson and Henry Nicoll. Both are indignant at the nomination of that chief of Copperheads, Seymour, and declare they will bolt. . . . Western Democrats are much disgusted by it, and think themselves out-manoeuvred and swindled by the Manhattan Club and by New Yorkers generally. "Democracy" will make a hard fight, however, and I am by no means confident of the result. As a manifestation of popular enthusiasm, the Democrats are driving up and down the streets a large vehicle, something between a hearse and an advertising van, decorated with a signboard portrait of H. Seymour's smug face, and equipped with a large bell, which clanks slowly with an eminently depressing and funereal effect.

It's a bad sign that the New York *Herald* comes out strong against Seymour. It is almost always on the losing side. . . .

July 13. I can scarcely believe—it seems like a dream—that within forty-eight hours I shall probably be steaming eastward toward the Old World—that within a fortnight I may set foot on the soil of England— that a month hence I may have actually seen a Cathedral and an Alp, the two chief wonders the Old World has to shew us. Well, may Heaven preserve Ellie and the boys while I am away! How seasick I shall prob- ably be before next week!—but that's a trifle more or less. How un- accountably kind it is of Hasket to insist on charging himself with this incumbrance, and on serving as my unpaid courier. He must be more thoroughly unselfish than I had supposed him. The prospect of seeing Cologne Cathedral (if we do see it, for I'm not distinctly informed of the details of Hasket's route, and I will not interfere with his plans), or of seeing Westminster Abbey, even, and of watching the evening sunlight linger on Mont Blanc or Mont Rosa or the Jungfrau, seems bliss beyond my hopes. God be thanked for the joy of its anticipation, whatever draw- backs may impair its fruition. . . .

As to Public Affairs, Seymour's nomination seems to sit uncomfort- ably on the Democratic stomach. His name awakes no *furore* in any quarter. I do not "belong to" the Republican Party, though I have voted the Republican ticket for the last eight years. That party has its own corruptions and profligacies, perhaps inevitable, perhaps the inherent vices of every political party. They are bad, and mischievous. But Demo- cratic newspapers like the New York *World* and the LaCrosse *Democrat* ("Brick Pomeroy's" paper) always spell "loyal" "loil," as I suppose the Devil would spell Christianity with a K. . . .

A big article in the New York *World* about Mr. *Wade Hampton*, a rebel delegate to the Democratic Convention, was suggestive. Mr. Wade Hampton was like Claverhouse, a sabreur, and a defender of an aristocracy against an uprising of plebeians. He was wealthy and notable and his "rose gardens" covered ten acres. The gallant fellow was suppressed by the overwhelming force of Grant and Sherman. And now, just think how nice it is that he is willing to confer with representatives of New York and Pennsylvania and Massachusetts about reconstruction.

And this eulogy appears in a newspaper that professes itself an organ of the "Democracy"!!!

After his return from Europe, Strong wrote the following account of his travels "from the little notes, or catch words, recorded from day to day in my little pocket log-book."

July 15, WEDNESDAY. Fearful heat. Leavetaking. Drive to Jersey City ferry, etc., with Hasket. Get our luggage settled on the Cunarder *China*, Captain Hockley. Then Ellie and Temple and Louis, Mr. Ruggles and Jem, Dr. Pech and others come down to see us off. The boys inspect the marvels of the steamer. All ashore, adieux, and we haul slowly out of our berth, 2:30 P.M. Hot and hazy. Four sunstrokes among the hands. The patients brought on deck and douched out of buckets. The low Long Island shore disappears before six o'clock. Only about fifty passengers. Anthony Trollope (dogmatic noisy John Bull whom I got to like afterwards), Botta and wife, Reverend Yardley of Connecticut, Newman who married Miss Ellen Rogers, Frank Marbury, Governor Dinsmoor of New Hampshire and family, Miss Allen (Horatio's daughter), very clever and very absurd about England, Mr. Constant-Carow (son of old Isaac Carow), Townsend, Senator Bayard of Delaware, urbane and deaf, Thayer. One Crocker, proprietor of St. James's Hall, London, a drunken dog with a wonderfully pretty young niece, who's on her way to Rome to study and become a prima donna. But the young lady is not sure whether *she shall go to Italy* or not. And so on. Heavy thundershower 11 P.M.

July 16. Alternate warm fog and chilly fog, ending in rain. Wind ahead.

July 20, MONDAY. Rain and fog, followed by a stiff stormy northeast breeze. General stampede to deck from breakfast table to see *an iceberg*. According to Captain Hockley, it was two miles off (north), 1,400 feet high, and all the officers said it was the finest they ever saw. A great peak (like the Matterhorn, according to travelled passengers) shot up from an amorphous mass, probably more than a mile long. This peak was the color of certain pale green crystals of fluor spar. The rest of the berg was seamed with ravines and gorges, full of beautiful lights and shadows, and of exquisite tints of grey and blue. The whole thing like a huge opal. Great boulders lay on its ledges, shewing that it had drifted down from its parent glacier on some Greenland fiord without turning over. Everybody said we ought to have seen it blazing and glittering in full sunshine, but I thought it more impressive drifting down through cold fog, like a picket guard or reconnoitering party from the stern Northern sea.

July 25. Clear and bright. East shore dimly visible 11 A.M. Holy-head abreast 12:30 P.M. Sails multiply. We approach Liverpool. Docks, ships, steamers; tug 7:15. Walk to Lime Street Station. Bother about baggage. Reverend Yardley joins us. Birkenhead Ferry 10 P.M. Railroad —Chester 11 P.M. To Grosvenor Inn. Odd, old-fashioned, substantial, and comfortable. Great, wide old staircase. Supper and cigars.

July 26, SUNDAY. Fine. Walk on "walls" of Chester and under their towers with Hasket and Reverend Yardley. Old houses, strange streets, covered passageways. New sensations. Views of peaceful land-scape. Cathedral for service. Sat in choir. Full congregation. Intoning and music very respectable. Anthem. Mendelssohn. Creed in ante-communion very good. Bishop of Chester on his throne. Left before sermon. Cloisters. Lady Chapel. Norman arches. Many signs of seven-teenth century iconoclasm. Railroad from Chester to Liverpool. Then Liverpool to London. Trollope and Bayard with us. Fast train, pleasant quiet English landscapes, much parched by drought. Euston Square 9:15 P.M. To Golden Cross Hotel, Charing Cross (*vide David Copper-field*). Supper and stroll with Hasket. Dim outlines of Whitehall! West-minster Abbey!! New Parliament Houses, and other buildings. West-minster Bridge. Made a bow to dirty Father Thames. Fire near the bridge in an optician's store. Great delay and bungling. Building gutted. We do better in New York. Tired. Sultry night. Am living a year a day.

July 27. Waked early by the chimes opposite my window. "Sicilian Mariners' Hymn" and other familiar old tunes. Hot day. Cabs, shops, bankers, 9 to 12. This is *London*!!! Fleet Street, Temple Bar, Cheapside, the Strand, Trafalgar Square (with Nelson *mastheaded*) etc. Vast smoky concentration of wealth. St. Paul's!!! Hideous with smoke-stains and pagan statuary. Call with letter on Mr. C. Rivers Wilson (Treasury), 6 Palace Court (Yard?), who was most gracious, wanted me to spend the night with him at his place out of town, and so on.

The Abbey. Interior noble, but spoiled by a congregation of mon-strous modern monumental statues. Looks like workshop of a weak-minded sculptor gone mad. Were I a Member of Parliament, I should propose their removal to some extra-mural "Chamber of Horrors." Henry VIIth Chapel, ancient tombs, gabble of an irrepressible cockney verger. Evening services well sung. Anthem poor. Westminster Hall. Courts up. Six P.M. Dine at "Blue Posts," recommended by Anthony Trollope. Evening to "Gallery of Illustration," a *quasi* theatre: *Inquire Within* and *A Public Dinner* not bad. John Parry excellent.

Evans's Cellar, Covent Garden, queer old place, beer and steaks, capital singing, men and boys only; no low comedy, but good honest music.

July 28. Hot and clear. Said to be a phenomenon. Busy morning. Stroll about a little and railroad for Folkestone 1:25. Pretty country. Folkestone at 3:35. Chalk cliffs and the inevitable *Martello*. Channel like a millpond. Steamer (*Albert Edward*) full and fast. Encounter General Dix, whose family is at Brighton or some other English watering place. Land French soil. Good dinner at railroad restaurant. Railroad landscapes more American than those of England. St. Valery; sandhills, and seaside country. Amiens, etc. Grand Hotel, Paris, midnight. Paris streets still brilliant, people at tables outside cafés.

Dine with General Dix—(*Anti-Seymour* most vigorously). Thence to Closerie des Lilas, a vast place packed full. Not a pretty face. Dancing nomadic and brutal. . . .

July 31, FRIDAY. Overcast. Luxembourg. Modern pictures—many well known from engravings: Müller's "Conciergerie," Couture's "Decadence," and so on. Louvre: walked for hours through gallery after gallery. . . . Two Raphaels, a Velasquez, a Van Dyck, and a few Murillos I recognized as "very rich things." Most of all I appreciated coloring of the "Marriage at Cana." Rubens seemed to me flashy and sensuous. Most of the Correggios and Carraccis and Salvator Rosas I wouldn't take as a gift unless with the privilege of selling them. Tried devoutly to appreciate the Pre-Raphaelite pictures but could not. So much for private judgment.

Evening, Gymnase. Perfection of acting. No trace of staginess. All elegant, truthful, and spirited. One piece with but two characters, women. Then to *Mabille*. Garden brilliant and attractive, with colored lights, etc. A good band. Women of higher grade than the nymphs of the Closerie, and a few were well-looking. Some of them assailed us. Replying in English or in German did no good, for they all know a little of both languages. At last Hasket addressed me with scraps of Swedish from *Frithiof's Saga*, and I responded with fragments of the *Iliad* and the *Antigone*. A little of this dialogue, uttered with proper indications of respectful embarrassment, beat off the syrens.

August 4. Nancy, 4:15 A.M. Glimpse of Strassburg Tower. "Hier sind Deutsch gesprochen." Breakfast at Kehl. . . . Karlsruhe 10:17. All railroad stations beautifully adorned with flowers and shrubs; a novelty. . . . Augsburg 5:50. Sick headache developing. Munich. Doze indefinitely; half awakened at Salzburg for a nominal inspection of our baggage.

August 5, WEDNESDAY. Wake and pick up my wits at or near Linz. Ride thence most lovely. Fine woody hills and fertile highly cultivated Danube Valley. Great monastery of Melk. Vienna depot 9:30 A.M.

Strong spent the better part of a week in Vienna. Then he traveled by way of Salzburg, Ischl, and Lindau to Switzerland; descended the Rhine to Cologne, where he found the cathedral "most glorious to see"; had a hasty glimpse of Brussels and Antwerp; revisited Paris; and then on September 15 was in London again. His travel notes are the briefest of jottings, and he records no meetings with people of consequence. On September 19, he left Liverpool in the Cuba, *with General George B. McClellan as a fellow passenger. On the 29th he was safely back in New York; "Ellie and the boys well and happy and glad to see me."*

October 2, FRIDAY. Last night with Charley Strong to new Theatre or "Museum" (Broadway and Thirtieth Street). *Ixion* well rendered by a corps of uncommonly handsome English women. . . .

Political campaign bitter. Grant's election thought certain, but this state dubious. With Ellie to Niblo's: *Barbe bleue.* Irma is nice, but not up to the delectable Geistinger.

October 16. . . . Pennsylvania and Ohio elections, and those of Indiana. Their results look ill for the "Democracy." It would seem that the managers of the New York *World*, and of other Copperhead organs, think of changing front, even in presence of the enemy. They talk of convening Democratic conventions and committees, and of getting Seymour and Blair to decline their nominations, and then of putting Chase or Hancock or somebody into their places. That plan will not work. "Swapping horses while crossing the river" did not suit A. Lincoln, 1862.

October 23. Though the returns from Western Virginia shew a little falling off in the Republican vote, Grant's prospect seems still the fairer. I wish he were elected and in his place, for the reign of Southern ruffianism and murder has lasted long enough. Should Seymour succeed (which Heaven forbid!) we should have a new rebellion on our hands within thirty days. He has taken the stump in person, and talks plausibly, but not effectively and not at all like a leader confident of victory.

October 25, SUNDAY. To Trinity Church with the boys. Rt. Reverend the Bishop of North Carolina preached, soliciting alms for insolvent clergymen. One can't refuse to hear these appeals. But if I were a Southern bishop or presbyter, one of the class that ministered to the blind fury of the people in 1860 and 1861, and did more than any other class except the politicians and the women to bring on the most causeless of civil wars, and thereby to oppress the loyal North with taxation and an inflated currency, I think I should not have the cheek to come begging of Philadelphia and New York. . . .

October 27. . . . Visit from Mr. Derby this morning on his way to Lloyd's Neck. Gave [George] Ripley of the *Tribune* certain financial lucubrations of Mr. Derby's, commenting on A. Johnson's recent letter. Very becoming in a President of the U.S. to issue an unofficial letter running down the national credit! This commentary may be valuable, but Heaven help the compositor who has to set it up. . . .

Grand Democratic meeting around Union Square this evening. Rockets, Roman candles, cannon, and calcium lights. Fourteenth Street a very pretty sight, hung with lines of colored lanterns. I saw no sign of enthusiasm, nine P.M.

No new political symptoms. We are hopeful about Grant, but much afraid that John T. Hoffman will carry this state and transfer the City Hall "Ring" to Albany.

Would that I possessed a little political weight for use against these flagitious pseudo-Democrats! With each new campaign that party falls farther and farther away from its ancient traditions, and embodies more and more of whatever is base and mean in our popular impulses. The party of the "Rights of Man" is fighting for a restricted suffrage "democratic" party, its newspapers and orators talk like the meanest flunkies about "Southern gentlemen" as distinguished from Northern commoners, and have not a word against the formal declarations of Southern landholders that they will coerce the laboring class and the poor into voting their way by refusing them employment unless they do so. The party of universal education and enlightenment, its "organs" speak of teachers as "school-marms."

October 28. . . . Dined here, Murray Hoffman, Professor Van Amringe, to whom Johnny has taken a great liking, and young Robert Hunt, a College Senior—son of late Honorable Washington Hunt, and a good fellow, I think, much devoted to church matters. This was Herr Johnny's dinner party. It may be a good thing for him if I can dine here now and then some one of the faculty and some undergraduate friend of his. His relations with the professors will be so far improved that he will be less likely ever to forget that they are gentlemen and to be treated accordingly.

I think the tone of the undergraduate corps would be greatly raised if the fathers of students would frequently do the same thing. Van Amringe made himself very agreeable.

October 30. . . . Old Professor McVickar died yesterday afternoon, at eighty-two. And I hear tonight that Dr. M. M. March, whilom of the United States Sanitary Commission, who did good service on Morris Island and elsewhere, died last week in Ohio, of injuries received from a fall from a wagon.

Theodore Weston . . . received a cable dispatch from Mrs. Laura Johnson at London, announcing that William Templeton Johnson died yesterday. . . .

Saw Bishop Coxe (Western New York) this morning. Delighted with tone and temper of General Convention. "Not a single party vote taken in the House of Bishops," he says, and Bishop Bedell says so, too.

This evening at the Rev. Dr. Bellows's. With him Agnew, Newberry, and Blatchford. I hope the Sanitary Commission is nearly wound up at last. Action about Mr. Warriner's book, our archives, and so on. Poor Alfred J. Bloor had a hearing at his own request about certain grievances of his, now four years old, mostly new to me, and most intangible. It is hard to distinguish his morbid sensitiveness and suspiciousness from insanity. . . .

Old McVickar's lecture-room 1835–1838 did more to influence me and mould my way of thinking than any other feature of my college life.

October 31. Some fears are expressed of riot and disturbance next Tuesday. Disputes about fraudulent naturalization papers may breed more or less row, but the Democrats have a strong inducement to keep the peace, for they count on an immense vote in the city, which would be diminished by any considerable disorder.

Binney writes me, *inter aliis*, of a rather smart legend he saw on a banner or transparency in some Republican procession at Camden. It was "Grant takes his cigar—Seymour takes the stump." I hear with amazement that [W.T.J.]'s "habits had been bad" for some years, and that friends of his, such as H.C.D. and W.R., speak of his having "drank himself to death," as of a notorious infelicity. I suppose it must be true. Living at Staten Island in a rather poky, secluded way, without much business to interest and excite him, he has slipped into habits of over-stimulation. He was quite free from them in old times. But the extent to which private drinking prevails is astounding. I hear almost daily of some new sufferer, cleric or lay. The practice grew enormously during the war, and is one

of the many evil results for which a rebellion without pretext is responsible. Its aggregate daily mischief must be beyond computation. My
practical conclusion is that I will keep no more whiskey or brandy in the
house to offer to our guests, however unusual and inhospitable the omission may seem. If any be asked for, I will state why none is forthcoming.

November 2. . . . Tomorrow will be an anxious day. I fear the state of
New York cannot be saved the humiliation of John T. Hoffman for
governor, but Grant's election seems probable. Hoffman has issued a
gratuitous and most flagitious "proclamation" about the efforts certain
honest people are making, through the legitimate agency of grand juries
and U.S. Commissioners, to check the wholesale manufacture of fraudulent votes by procuring indictments against the scoundrels engaged in
that business. He denounces this interference with their business as an
attempt to intimidate the voters of New York, and as a measure likely to
produce breaches of the peace. This impudent and insidious manifesto
will surely cost Mr. Hoffman a few votes in the rural districts. Meanwhile, what has the "Democracy" to say about the openly avowed and
systematic intimidation of Republican voters in Mississippi and Georgia,
by pledges to refuse them employment, custom, and social toleration?
What about the murder of scores and hundreds of voters of that persuasion
in every Southern State from Virginia to Texas?

November 3, TUESDAY. . . . At Union League Club tonight. Large
attendance. Few returns yet (ten P.M.) but those few look well. Were I
a "sporting" man, I should bet 2 to 1 on Grant's election; 3 to 2 he
carries this state; and (also) 2 to 1 that Hoffman is next governor of this
state.

Midnight, or later. Ellie returns (from a little farewell theatre party
for nice Miss Louisa Anderson, who goes to Newport tomorrow and
winters there) and I secure an *Extra News*. Extras are strangely infrequent
for the evening of an election day in this very Democratic city, controlled
by the purest of the Cork-asian race, and their paucity is a good sign. My
extra professes to give returns up to ten-forty-five P.M. In this city only
50,000 Seymour majority. Hoffman's majority said to be larger. Large
Republican gains in the interior; also, in Pennsylvania, Indiana, Ohio,
Maine, and Connecticut. Maryland Democratic, of course. All this looks
well, but we shall know more tomorrow. The *News* says Governor Fenton
says Griswold has beaten Hoffman by 10,000. I should like to believe it.

November 4. Fine day. Grant is certainly elected, but this state is
lost, thanks to the enormous crop of fraudulent voters in the culture of

which I believe Hoffman himself is none too good to have worked with
Barnard and McCunn and other ornaments of the Bench. There is talk of
contesting the returns, but it will come to naught, and the next session
at Albany will be a long Walpurgis night of all political filthiness and
corruption. . . . The new Tammany Hall, 14th Street, was on fire this
afternoon, I hear, but unfortunately not burned up. . . .

*Grant had won the presidency by a handsome margin. He had a popular vote
of 3,013,000 against Seymour's 2,703,000; an electoral vote of 214 against
Seymour's 80. All of the Southern States which voted, except Louisiana, went
into the Republican column, for they were controlled by the Carpetbag-Scala-
wag-Negro combination. Much fraud was alleged in various parts of the country,
but particularly in the city and state of New York. Going Democratic by
precisely ten thousand votes (a result said to have been arranged in order to
settle certain wagers), New York chose John T. Hoffman for governor. At
the same time William M. Tweed was elected state senator. With Tweed
managing the legislature, and the pliable Hoffman in the Executive Mansion,
New York was indeed fated to endure the Walpurgis night of corruption which
the diarist prophesied. The national House and Senate were both Republican.*

November 6.   Dined here this evening a small party, namely: Governor
Morgan, Mrs. John Sherwood of Philadelphia, Charles Blake, Mr.
Ruggles, Charles Barclay of Philadelphia, Mrs. Blake, Sherwood, Mrs.
S. B. Ruggles, and Mrs. Morgan. . . . Our talk at dinner was mostly of
our civic woes; of election frauds and of our disgraceful judiciary, and of
the probable Vigilance Committees of the future.

November 15. . . . This estrangement from George Anthon is a bore.
. . . As the case now stands, he is exasperated with me not only for my
share, as trustee, in giving the commission to paint Professor Anthon's
portrait to Jack Ehninger, but also, and most especially, for my with-
drawing Temple and Louis from his school. This step he attributes (of
course) to personal feeling against him, and supposes me enraged by his
very insolent letter read to the trustees last June. It would be in vain for
me to assure him that I am not enraged, and that I took the boys away
because I thought it due to my colleagues to take some formal notice of
his gross discourtesy to them. He is incapable of believing such a statement, and I am, therefore, indisposed to make it. . . .

November 20. . . . Died *William S. Mount,* aged sixty-two. Thirty
years ago he was among our most promising artists. His "Farmers

Bargaining for a Horse," painted for Luman Reed, was an uncommonly clever picture. Later, were his bad portrait of my father (next door) and two quite respectable pictures embodying scenes from my father's boyish days "on the farm." One of these is at Mary's, next door, and the other with Eloise at Boston. His few productions during the last twenty years have been extremely bad. He has been living at Smithtown all that time, or elsewhere in eastern Long Island, that paradise of loafers, and amusing himself and his friends with his fiddle and his pencil sketches.

November 24. . . . Lively time in and around the City Hall. *Mugit litibus insanum forum.* Indictment against Fullerton, etc., growing out of his controversy with Mr. [U.S.] District Attorney Courtney, etc. Each party accuses the other of confederacy with the "Whiskey Ring" and of trying to defraud government. Mr. Justice Barnard and Mr. Justice Sutherland "collide" in the course of the new Erie Railroad war that has just broken out. One or both ought to be impeached and degraded *instanter*. The audacious Barnard harangues the Grand Jury about his virtuous poverty and his judicial purity, and invites them to indict all the newspapers that have called him names. And so forth. This is a thoroughly rotten community, and something must give way soon.

November 25.   Charley Strong shewed me this morning, rather ruefully, a letter just received from Madame at Paris, announcing her "reconciliation" to the Roman Catholic Church. Just what has long been predicted. The lady is a strange compound of cleverness and foolishness; she is jaded with French novels; she wants a new sensation, and she has been talked over by experts in the art of conversion, French and English priests, flattered and caressed and wound round their fingers. Her letter is well written, however, and she declares she will scrupulously abstain from influencing dear little Pussy. I don't expect she will take much trouble to do so, of her own volition. But her Spiritual Directors will enjoin it on her as a duty, and Pussy will be somehow manoeuvred into Popedom before she knows it. Much as I like the mamma, and fully as I recognize her brightness and her many good points, I cannot help seeing that in this transaction, as in many other grave transactions of her married life, she has behaved like a goose. . . .

I am more and more satisfied that what we call "ritualism" is not merely the effect of an instinctive craving felt by American and English churchmen of our own time. It is what the American Catholic Church needs to enable it to compete on equal terms with its modern Romish adversary. All "Protestantism" needs the same thing. Protestantism and

Romanism agree in resting their respective claims on the human intellect and the human heart. But Romanism appeals, moreover, to the human senses, and to man's love of the beauty that can be embodied in art and expressed by symbolism. With this advantage, Romanism holds a winning game. The odds are obviously in its favor. Mere Protestantism cannot, from the law of its tradition, attempt to fight Romanism on equal grounds, but the American Catholic Church *can*, and I don't see why it shouldn't. . . .

November 27. . . . Charley is a good deal cut up by his wife's "reconciliation" with the Papal See. I tell him that dear little Pussy, my godchild, will inevitably gravitate the same way within six months, unless he do something decisive about it. The dear child's affectionate loyalty to her mother, her docility and goodness, will carry her along in her mother's footsteps, were no influences from without brought to bear upon her. But Charley "don't see how he can do anything," but write her a letter.

November 29, SUNDAY. To church with Johnny and Louis (Temple has ritualistic tendencies and went to St. Alban's). *Te Deum* new to me and rather spasmodic. Before going into the pulpit, the Rev. Dr. Vinton announced that many people had been in the habit of leaving church during sermon (small blame to them) and that therefore the doors would henceforth be closed during that solemnity, and until the end of the prayer for the Church Militant. There he had us, and the incarcerated congregation underwent forty minutes of sesquipedalian rigmarole, etymologies, pious quibbles, and devout conundrums about the Book of Revelation and Donnegan's *Greek Lexicon*. The offertory, "Sleepers, wake!" (from Mendelssohn) was felicitously chosen. Sermon and anthem, an inane production of Cutler's, were both insults to an assemblage presumed to possess common sense and able to distinguish real music from sham.

The Rev. Dr. Vinton, with his $10,000 salary and allowance, is a positive deadweight upon the parish. His sermons are enough to make one turn "Positivist" or Swedenborgian or anything else, and I do not know of his doing parochial work of any value, but perhaps he does.

As to our *Kapellmeister*, Mr. Messiter, I shall tell him that I mean to oppose any further appropriations of money to the musical expenses of Trinity, until he stops nauseating people with "Anthems by Cutler" and vapidities of the same low grade! It's no use spending money to improve the performance of worthless music. Rendered by the choir of the Sistine Chapel, it would be worthless just the same.

December 1. . . . Dear little Miss Pussy writes the prettiest and nicest of letters from Paris to her papa, who is much consoled and comforted thereby. She deplores this recent prank of her mamma's, and declares she will never do likewise, but without a word that's unbecoming. "You and I will always go to church *together*, Papa," says the dear little soul.

December 5. A lying rumor of Louis Napoleon's sudden death sent gold up this morning, for which end the rumor was doubtless invented. . . .

Meeting of Law School Committee. Mr. Ruggles, Dwight, Fish, Ogden, Nash. Questions as to our locale should A. T. Stewart turn us out of 37 Lafayette Place next May, as he probably will; as to Lieber; and as to an assistant professor of Municipal Law. Such assistant is most desirable. It's *Professor Dwight's School*. Failure of his health would destroy it. The snub we gave Lieber last May has done good. Somehow or other, there is much larger attendance on his lectures. So we recommend the continuance of the $200 prize in his department for another year. He is very lazy, and is devoured with such hyperbolical vanity and egotism that he occasionally makes himself ridiculous and repels his students. But he is a sound thinker and a useful teacher. If he would condescend to be systematic, he would be very useful.

December 10. Clear and cold. Long session of Standing Committee of Trinity Church, the rector with us. Several applications from anemic little city parishes—Mullen, Stewart, etc. The real difficulty of the Church is the want of live men. Our clergy are generally a feeble folk. I don't think any one of the first-grade assistant ministers of Trinity Parish earns a quarter of his salary. From every convention, general and diocesan, there rises a prolonged howl or wail over the low rate of clerical compensation. There's the Reverend Henry Y. Squabb, Rector of St. Peter's, Skunkville Centre, St. Lawrence County, wife and six children, and only $— per annum. What a shame and disgrace to the church and to the country! What a so forth and so on! How can we and so on? There is some force in all this. But there are certain pertinent queries that the Devil's Advocate is fairly entitled to ask before the case goes to the jury. For example: How much do the village lawyer and doctor of Skunkville receive as their annual professional income? How much would the Reverend Rector probably have made in any secular profession? What would he make out of a good lease of a good farm, or by keeping a country store? . . .

That incorrigible malefactor, A. Johnson, has disgraced the country and disgusted all decent men by his very nefarious message, which both

Houses rightly resented as an insult. In this flagitious document, he recommends repudiation of the public debt, without circumlocution or apology. This, coming from a President of the United States, even though he represents no party (except his postmasters and internal revenue collectors) may injure our credit abroad most disastrously. But we deserve to suffer for putting so base a demagogue into high office and giving him the power to do mischief. He berates Congress for unconstitutional and partisan legislation as if he were lecturing a lot of sinful schoolboys, but that is a small matter compared with the impudence and the atrocity of his financial suggestions. Cisco tells me tonight, however, that he thinks all this will make very little impression in Europe, and his opinion is entitled to weight. . . .

December 18. . . . After dinner to anniversary (66th) of the old Philolexian Society at Academy of Music. Crowd. Large percentage of fresh young girls, as pretty as possible, and all in high giggle. Stayed out two or three "orations." I thought them creditable—healthy and manly in tone, or at least far less crude and sophomorical than I expected, and clothed in very fair English. A horrible doubt occurred to me whether they were not perhaps privily and fraudulently polished up for public display by outside experts????!

December 19. . . . Death of Judge Anthony Robertson at sixty, of pneumonia. One of our most respectable judges, so far down have we gone. He was quite a luminary beside our McCunns and Cardozos and Barnards, but we held him no ornament to the bench a few years ago. Thus do we sink, bench and bar together. Any reaction must come soon, or we shall reach a stage of social gangrene and putrescence past help from galvanism or from anything else. The body politic of this city and country, judges, aldermen, councilmen, supervisors, and so on, our whole local government, is so diseased and so corrupt and so far gone that we can no longer count on any recuperative, restorative action of its vital forces. People talk of the pride a New Yorker must feel in his great city! To be a citizen of New York is a disgrace. A domicile on Manhattan Island is a thing to be confessed with apologies and humiliation. The New Yorker belongs to a community worse governed by lower and baser blackguard scum than any city in Western Christendom, or in the world, so far as I know. Our rulers are partly American scoundrels and partly Celtic scoundrels. The Celts are predominant, however, and we submit to the rod and the sceptre of Maguires and O'Tooles and O'Shanes, as Cedric the Saxon knocked under to Brian de Bois Guilbert and the Templar.

December 24. . . . Fithian appointed by Fenton, the governor, to fill Robertson's place on bench of Supreme Court. Good appointment, as things go—but Fithian's grammar is sometimes a little wild. Still, a new judge not generally believed corrupt is an acquisition.

December 25.   Xmas, and a happy Christmas it has been, *Dei gratia.* Morning clear and bright; afternoon and evening cloudy and blusterous, with a heavy snowstorm seemingly just at hand. But the clouds broke away—"the stars shone bright and the moon gave a light, a little before the day," or at least a little after midnight. With Ellie and the three brats to Trinity Church. Crowd. Offertory was "For unto us a child is born" (excellently done). The rest of the music was vapid Anglican commonplace. . . . Vinton's sermon was as long, windy, and worthless as usual.

With Ellie and Miss Mary Bostwick to Fourteenth Street Delmonico's, where we lunched. This evening a small symposium. Parties, Mr. & Mrs. Ruggles, Jem, Jack Ehninger, Jem's friend and partner Edwin Taft, who came so near perishing by collision of steamboats and by a burning deck-load of petroleum a week or two since on the Ohio, Colden Murray and wife and her retainer Miss Brett, John Sherwood and wife. . . . Johnny found his duty of accompanying mamma on his 'cello before a few people less formidable than he expected.

December 29.   Dined with Ellie at John Astor's. Convives, Mr. and Mrs. Dick Hunt, Denning Duers, Hayward Cuttings, G. G. Howlands, Nelson Potters (the lady is just married and was Miss Edward Jones), young Willy Astor, the son of the house. . . . Willy Astor is near 21, and not handsome, but well-bred, modest, self-possessed, and agreeable. He inherits something of his mamma's refined, courteous manner. Mrs. Hayward Cutting looked even lovelier than she did when Miss Lily Mason. She's a supreme beauty. . . .

1869

With Ulysses S. Grant about to come in as President, everybody in the North was discussing his probable Cabinet and policies—the South having more immediate problems to worry about; but on neither his Cabinet selections nor his measures did Grant himself throw a ray of light. Not one of the great questions bequeathed to the country by the war had yet been settled. The reconstruction of the South was far from completed, or from a satisfactory approach to completion. No adequate system of assistance to the freedmen had been instituted. The heavy national debt had not yet been reorganized and refunded, and the wartime system of taxation had not received the radical overhauling that it needed. No civil service system had been applied to the great body of Federal officeholders called into existence by the conflict. The nation displayed a touching faith, however, that Grant, the strong silent leader whom everybody admired, would rescue it from all its difficulties. Meanwhile, the Johnson Administration attempted nothing, and the Fortieth Congress completed its career without any new legislation of much importance. The one event that attracted attention and aroused controversy was Secretary of State Seward's submission to the Senate of the Johnson-Clarendon Convention for the settlement of our heavy postwar claims—based on the depredations of the Alabama and other cruisers—against Great Britain. When the text of the convention was published, it turned out to be so favorable to the British government that its rejection became a foregone conclusion.

But in general the New Year opened auspiciously. The country was prosperous, and was just finishing one of its greatest works of internal improvement,

the Union Pacific-Central Pacific transcontinental railroad. The whole world,
barring some small Russo-Turkish difficulties, was at peace. Strong was busy
as usual with the affairs of Trinity Church, the Philharmonic Society, and
Columbia—for example, he and other trustees were discussing the grave question
of an assistant to Theodore W. Dwight at the Law School.

January 2, SATURDAY.   The New Year opened with cold rain that froze
and covered all out of doors with a slippery veneering of ice. On top of
this, a layer of sleet or minute hail, or spheroidal snow particles, was
depositing itself copiously all day long. So the sidewalks and people's
front doorsteps were perilous. Called for Charley [Strong] at 125 East
Twenty-sixth Street a little after eleven, and after a little talk with John
Cadwalader[1] and William Robinson, set forth on our formidable undertaking. I had prepared an elaborate "list," but before we got very far, it
became evident that my designs could not be fully executed. One's feet
were soaked and chilled in merely going from the carriage to the first
half-dozen doors. I won't walk in overshoes into a lady's drawing room
(though I saw some swells who thought it right to do so), and taking off
one's overshoes in entries is a piece of work; and then I nearly broke my
neck in ascending and descending door steps on more than one occasion.
We went to Morgan Dix's in Varick Street. Sorry the Rector don't
approve the proposed "Carillon" machine. Bidwell's (slow as usual).
Mrs. Augustus Schermerhorn's, 71 University Place, very kindly and
pleasant. Mr. Ruggles's, No. 24. Mrs. Lewis Jones's (12 West Thirty-
second) very nice. They are just at home again after long expatriation
in Europe. So is Mrs. Colford Jones (Madison Avenue), who is about
building on or near Central Park. Bishop Potter. Mrs. Dix and Mrs.
Blake, with her two pretty fair-haired children. Mrs. William Schermerhorn, kindly as ever. Miss Chat looked remarkably fresh and pretty.
Miss Fanny, the bride-elect, did not shew. Mrs. John Sherwood, with
Miss Fanny North in fullest tide of chatter. Mrs. John Astor and Mrs.
William Astor, both nice, as they always are. . . .
January 10, SUNDAY.   A genial spring day. Music at Trinity Church
included "He Shall Feed His Flock" and "The Glory of the Lord Shall
Be Revealed," from *The Messiah*, so it was decidedly above par. Not so

---

[1] Inasmuch as John L. Cadwalader was living with Charles Strong in their bachelor
quarters, the diarist naturally saw a good deal of this brilliant young attorney, who
at this time was practicing law in partnership with Dorman B. Eaton and Henry
Austin Tailer.

Vinton's long sermon, which was so remarkably bad that I could not keep myself from listening to it, though I tried hard. It was bombastic, hyperbolical, kompomatous, verbose, pleonastic, periphrastic, and preposterous. He talked of "the poor of this great metropolis, languishing in their lonely cots," thereby meaning their crowded tenement houses. He defined words as "the airy nuncios that carry intellectual conceptions into the mysterious presence-chamber of the human mind." He drew a vivid picture of a fashionable gathering—a "soirée." Kettledrum, or what not—"flushed faces"—"costly dresses"—"ardent looks" (bored looks more common)—"voluptuous swell of music"—and (horror of horrors) "people talking in *promiscuous groups*!" How the *Dragon* would he have them talk? After church, John Astor quoted the remark of some theological critic of the West, who said that "if a preacher couldn't strike ile in *twenty minutes*, it must be because he hadn't got no gimlet or because he didn't know how to use it." Vinton averages three-quarters of an hour.

February 1. Columbia College Trustees two P.M. Long session. Nothing *very* special came up. One or two of Dr. Barnard's motions were quietly negatived, without debate. Some of the trustees think him disposed to spend money too freely. Perhaps they think right, but Barnard is a very valuable man, nevertheless. Barnard asked for a committee on a question of discipline—of "marks," and the like—as to one branch of which I had drafted a resolution of inquiry, prompted by Schuyler Hamilton. Committee was appointed. Barnard and myself are on it, and William Schermerhorn and Judge Blatchford, I think. It's a most important committee. Its conclusions will exert material influence on all the life of a lot of nice boys, undergraduates of Columbia College for the next $(x+y)$ years. . . .

February 3. . . . Ellie is enthusiastic and wild over a novel of Miss Charlotte Yonge's, which I insisted on her reading: *The Dove in the Eagle's Nest.* No wonder. It's a nice romantic story that keeps its reader in an atmosphere of purity and piety. So do all Miss Yonge's books. But this is, moreover, a carefully studied picture of social life in Germany at the time when mediaeval usages and robber-baronies were going out and modern civilization coming in. This little novel embodies much thought and reading about burgher-life as contrasted with that of the nobles, and so on.

February 4. . . . Special Committee of College Trustees on "Discipline," and the like, met at St. Paul's clergy office this afternoon:

Barnard, Reverend Haight, Edward Jones, Judge Blatchford, and I. We are of one mind—viz., to abolish all our petty regulations about "crimes," misdemeanors, admonitions, and warnings; to substitute for them a general statute that the faculty may dismiss any undergraduate who misbehaves himself; to require no more "excuses for absence," but to send each boy's father a monthly statement of the days on which the boy has made default; and to have no more "marks" for the value of daily recitations, but to determine relative standing in class by the results of examination on written papers. We did not act finally on these proposi- . tions. . . . Barnard holds that the proposed change will raise the moral tone of the undergraduate corps, that the boys, finding themselves treated like gentlemen, and put on the same level with students of the Law School and the School of Mines, will be more likely to behave like gentle- men—and from talk with Johnny about the views and feelings of himself and his classmates, I think Barnard may probably be right. . . .

February 12. . . . Crimes of violence—burglaries, highway robberies, and murders—have been of late many and audacious beyond example. There has been much common talk, not more than half serious (but *not much less than half*) about a *Vigilance Committee* as the only remedy left us while the Judiciary continues *elective*, worthless, and corrupt. I have thought this talk premature, though well aware that we shall probably be driven to that dangerous remedy before many years. But tonight's *Post* speaks of "secret meetings of respectable citizens" and of Vigilance Committees already organized and ready for action in *this* ward and in another. We want a *Vehmgericht* badly, but even in the best hands it would be a fearful experiment, and then it might so easily fall into the worst hands. . . .

February 13. With Ellie tonight (and with Johnny) to Booth's new theatre, Twenty-third Street and Sixth Avenue. Very handsome build- ing, within and without, and well filled.[2] I'm glad of this and hope it may last, for if this theatre go on as it has begun, it will be a humanizing and educating influence. *Romeo and Juliet.* Magnificently put on the stage. Costumes unconventional and studied from mediaeval precedent. Scenery likewise copied from North Italian street architecture and interiors. Certain scenes were hardly to be improved on; for example, the ballroom,

[2] Edwin Booth had played at the Winter Garden in New York until it burned on March 23, 1867, with his scenery, costumes, and library. He resolved to build the most beautiful playhouse in the country, and Booth's Theatre on Sixth Avenue was opened February 3, 1869, with *Romeo and Juliet.*

the graveyard, and especially the balcony. Columns and monuments and projections of buildings were *real* (that is, pasteboard or canvas) and not painted. Romeo (Booth) was excellent. Readings always admirable. If one must be critical, he looks a little too grave, thoughtful, and earnest for a passionate boy. Miss McVicker (Juliet) graceful, ladylike, rather pretty, and manifesting the most intelligent study of her part, but not quite up to my ideal. Was anybody ever even halfway up to one's ideal of that part, or indeed of any of Shakespeare's greater conceptions? . . .

February 18. To College at 9:30. Ogden, Dr. Torrey, and the Reverend Mr. Haight were there and we went into chapel with Barnard and the faculty. After the usual chapel service, Barnard announced the new provisional or experimental scheme of discipline, which puts the boys in great measure on their honor and on the same level with students of the Law School and School of Mines. What he said was judicious and good, but as usual a little prolix and prosy. . . . Afterwards, the applause was long and loud, and when outside the chapel, our boys cheered exuberantly and joyously.

March 1. Special Committee on College site. Reverend Mr. Haight, chairman. After some little discussion we agreed that any action looking to a change of site was inexpedient for the present. Also, we recommended that the board refer it back to us to consider the question of a *fireproof building for our books and collections.* I had the honor of moving this recommendation, which the board adopted without debate. The wedge is inserted, *Laus Deo.* . . .

March 3. . . . Last day of A. Johnson's mal-Administration. There will be dry eyes at his exodus from the White House. Nobody knows yet anything about Ulysses the Silent's Cabinet, that is to be. Everybody has been guessing for a month past—many have tried to pump—many have "suggested names"—but all in vain. Odysseus knows how to keep his own counsel, and shuts up, close as an oyster. A good sign. I have "singular hopes" of Grant, and believe that his honesty will stand the ordeal it is to undergo for four years from tomorrow. No doubt extreme Republicans and men of one idea will be denouncing him within a month. But a certain pachydermatism seems to be among his virtues, and he can stand a good deal of newspaper fire. . . .

March 8, MONDAY. Clear and less frosty. Most people disapprove any repeal or suspension of the Act under which A. T. Stewart is ineligible,[3]

[3] He was ineligible under a law of 1789 disqualifying for the Secretaryship of the Treasury any merchant in the importing trade.

because it would make a bad precedent. They are probably right. But Stewart's reputation and exalted mercantile credit throughout every dry goods-selling part of Europe would have done much to strengthen our public securities abroad. Pity Grant should have begun his Administration with so conspicuous an oversight, giving Belial occasion to be blatant.

Today's "slate" is Boutwell for the Treasury, Hoar of Massachusetts to resign and Edwards Pierrepont for Attorney-General. We shall see. Sounder men than Edwards Pierrepont could be hunted up without over-exertion or fatigue. So I think, at least, and I know that gentleman of old.

This afternoon at Law School for meeting of Committee on School of Mines. Betts, Fish, Barnard, Edward Jones, and I—of the Committee—with two or three of our "associates," and most of the faculty. Barnard made a rather protracted oration about the wants of the College—its reputed wealth—the insufficiency of its income—Newberry's Collection —$12,000—a subscription, and so forth, and then I moved in all simplicity of heart that the subscription paper read by Barnard be printed and copies of it sent to all the gentlemen present, with the recommendation that they try to raise the needed $12,000. To my amazement, Fish got up and objected that "the board ought to be first consulted," and its permission and authority obtained in due form. He was our special *Remora* or sucking fish, and seemed likely to retard our progress effectually. I wanted to say several things, but a debate would have been unseemly before outsiders. So I withdrew my resolution, and then there was a long pause. Fish felt he had made a false step (or wiggle, more properly) and devised another resolution, amounting to nearly the same thing, which I declined to move, feeling bewildered by what he had said, and uncertain whether any motion whatever might not subject me to a vote of censure from the board. Barnard was asked if he would move it, and seemed to assent with more or less understanding of the question. The resolution passed, *sub silentio*, and we adjourned. . . .

Barnard's long speech was a *Jeremiad* over the sad neglect this college has experienced from rich and public-spirited men, as compared with Yale, Harvard, the "Cornell University," and scores of one-horse seats of learning all over the country. Fish's demur and objection came in as the most admirable explanatory note to Barnard's lamentations, and shewed *why* the College is overlooked. He expressed the traditionary feeling of the board—viz., that it is irregular for any of its members or committees or for anybody else to take the liberty of asking anybody to buy a valuable collection and give it to the College, without first obtaining leave of the trustees. How the governors of every other college in the country would grin at the suggestion of such a rule! . . .

March 11. Washburne resigns from the State Department and Hamilton Fish succeeds him. Excellently qualified for routine business by deportment, respectability, and formalism, but utterly unfit for grave responsibilities and complications. There is a peculiar defect in his mental vision. He sees everything, great and small, essential and non-essential, *of the same size,* and as Secretary of State, would put a despatch sealed with wafer of wax in the same category with the *Alabama* piracies.

April 7. . . . Cunard died last night at his Fifth Avenue house. Disease of the heart, they say, of which the very first symptoms appeared on Monday. A nice person was Sir Edward and much liked. . . .[4]

April 10. . . . At Astor Library this afternoon, in our [Sanitary Commission] "Archive Room" with Bellows, Gibbs, and Blatchford. Dr. Gould's big Report on Statistics is out at last, and pronounced by Gibbs, Dr. Hammond, and others, the finest and most exhaustive work of its class extant. But for general reading, I prefer Walter Scott. . . .

April 12, MONDAY. . . . John Jay, my *doppel-gänger,* is probably Minister to Austria. Enviable post. Such a nice city to live in, and nothing to do. Karlsbad and Salzburg within comfortable striking distance for summer. John Jay wanted to be sent to London instead (!), and to assume grave responsibilities, to which he's quite unequal, though he thinks otherwise.[5]

April 16. . . . "Settlement" of the ancient suit of Nicaragua Transit Co. stockholders against that nefarious old Cornelius Vanderbilt, much talked of by John Griswold and others. Vanderbilt compromises by paying $450,000, of which sum Henry Cram and John Sherwood (counsel) and Colden Murray (receiver) absorb one-half, and the creditors (i.e., Foster and Thomson, who have been collusively buying up judgments against the company at about one cent on the dollar), appropriate the other half. It is not a well-flavored transaction.

Sumner's speech on the proposed *Alabama* Treaty—the best thing he ever did—generally applauded, puts him in a new light. Treaty rejected in Senate all but unanimously. A single benighted Senator, a Kentuckian,

[4] Son of Sir Samuel Cunard, founder of the great steamship line.

[5] Jay went to Vienna, and did good service there, although Bancroft Davis reported to Secretary Fish in 1872 that he was "weak as dishwater—needs a strong plaster put to his back every other day."

voted to confirm it. Unpleasant for Reverdy Johnson, that Chief of Diplomatic Toadies. Sumner makes our case against John Pecksniff Bull even stronger than I thought it.

May 4. . . . Columbia College Trustees met yesterday. Robert Ray in the chair. Long session. Discussion mostly as to enlarging course of School of Mines by instruction in Civil Engineering and in Modern Languages. The proposition was referred back to the committee for further report as to details. Sorry to say that Mr. Ruggles and Edward Jones objected, with the commonplaces of stolidity (as I thought). But for them, the measure could have been carried.

Opening of Church Street from Fulton to Greenwich begun, and makes havoc with the old familiar places.

May 10, MONDAY. Fine weather. The Pacific Railroad was (or was to have been) formally completed today by the laying of its last rail. So there was a *Te Deum* at Trinity Church at twelve, by request of Chamber of Commerce. Church very full, considering the little notice given. . . . Vinton's address or sermonicule was really good. He took for his text the congratulatory telegram (written by Mr. Ruggles) from our Chamber of Commerce to that of San Francisco. This seems to have been the only public notice in New York of a most important event—national and international. . . .

May 20. . . . Last night, Law School Commencement, Academy of Music. Good house in spite of foul weather. Address by Professor Dwight, excellent, of course. Alumni Oration by Henry E. Tremain surprised everybody by its vigor. Address by Harry Nicoll long, diffuse, commonplace, and monotonous. But a large portion of it was inaudible on the stage and may have shewn the highest genius, for aught I know. Valedictory by George Chandler Holt not bad, though badly delivered. It is notable that these four speeches, prepared without concert, should each have been mainly an expression of the same thought, viz., that corruption in our legislative bodies, our great corporations, and now even in the state judiciary, and in the sheriff's office, has at last reached a stage that must produce revolutionary action if no legal remedy can be found. Such things are "in the air." The strongest expressions to this effect received the loudest applause, and every condemnation of our accursed elective judiciary system brought down the house. I verily believe we are nearly ripe for a Vigilance Committee. No help from Albany can be hoped for. Railroad kings (Fisks, Vanderbilts, and the like) and scoundrelly "Rings" control our state legislation. The dishonesty of every man in public office is a violent presumption, and universally recognized as such. No decent man can take public office without imminent danger of losing caste, unless he compel the respect of a defrauded but corrupt community by the accumulation of at least one or two millions of fraudulent profit. This state of things cannot last much longer without an explosion.

May 26. . . . Otis Swan, who has taken the late Washington Irving's place for the summer, tells me of the vexations to which he and his wife are subjected by intrusive and pertinacious tourists. "I have come all the way from St. Louis, sir, and I cannot go back without looking through the immortal Irving's house and grounds." So they force themselves in, roam about, poke their noses into everything, and make audible comparisons between Irving and the present tenant of his classical country seat, to the disadvantage of the latter. They have carried off nearly all his ivy, as relics, like so many leaf-bearing ants, and I told him they would soon begin appropriating chips and slivers from his piazza railings and stair balustrades with the same pious intent.

June 1, TUESDAY. . . . To Point Judith with Temple (how we miss him!), Thursday, 12:15. Comfortable ride. Anthony's vehicle awaited us at Kingston depot and we reached his hospitable farmhouse a little after dark, tired and very hungry. Hunger and fatigue soon appeased. Came off yesterday at eleven A.M., and was at home by seven-thirty. . . .

June 7. Columbia College Trustees met this P.M. Nothing important done. Barnard read his annual report. It was ordered printed. An excellent paper, but it would bear condensation. Barnard reads its argumentative passages with vehemence and emphasis, as if smiting some nonexistent adversary—just as Anthony's hot-blooded little dog Ginger will bark and scratch around a woodchuck's hole, though he knows perfectly well that there is no woodchuck in it.

June 9. Sent out notes and printed circulars about our proposed "Sacred Music Association." As $5,000 are required to hatch this egg, it will probably come to naught, and therefore I record what manner of chicken would come to light under favorable conditions. Three concerts next winter, with four rehearsals each, open to subscribers and the invited friends of subscribers. No tickets sold and no reporters admitted. Music to be Haydn and Mozart . . . with full orchestra, paid chorus of fifty as a nucleus, reinforced by amateur talent, and the soli to be taken from our cultivated young amateurs. . . . If this plan could be carried out, it would have a civilizing effect and elevate the standard of church music. . . .

June 15. To Point Judith Thursday with Louis by 12:15 train.

Reached Anthony's in due season, and found Temple ragged, dirty, and joyous. He has gained health and vigor since he left town, but it still pains him to read. Came away in the rain yesterday at eleven and was at home by seven-thirty. Ellie was on the lookout at the front door. Incidents of our sojourn were few. We collected bugs for Johnny—two or three fine beetles among them, new to me. Spent much of our time on the rocks and on the beach, tossing driftwood into the surf, and watching the *Merrimac* and the *Monitor* and the *Great Eastern* come ashore. This was bliss in solid chunks. Surf yesterday morning was quite grandiose. Now and then came in a big roller that reminded me of Thomas Hood's picture:

> —it was a dreary mount,
> Its base as black as night,
> Its top of pale and livid green,
> Its crest of awful white
> *Like Neptune with a Leprosy,*
> And so it reared upright. . . .

June 18, FRIDAY. Sultry. Henry J. Raymond died of apoplexy last night. He was a favorable specimen of our politicians, for he had some culture and good manners. But he was always a little afraid of his own principles. He liked to dwell on the good points of the enemy's platform. Hence he got the reputation of a vacillating, time-serving man and editor, which I think he did not deserve.[6]

June 21. . . . The Lords protest against the Irish Church Bill as wrong in principle and policy, but pass it submissively, because they have no right to disagree with the Commons. Hence the query is suggested to the thoughtful and impartial observer of events: Wherefore does the Upper House come together at all? Why do they bother themselves with debates and deliberations? What is their precise function in the great Constitutional Organism of Britannia? . . .

June 28, MONDAY. A most sultry night. Fared to Point Judith by railroad last Thursday at 12:15 P.M. with Louis. . . . A month at Point Judith or Nahant would drive me melancholy mad, I fear. . . .

Queries during this sojourn. "Papa, is it true that every cat has nine *wives*?"—"Why is Jealousy called a green-eyed lobster?"—"What is a

[6] Henry J. Raymond (born January 24, 1820) had joined with George Jones to found the New York *Times* on September 18, 1851. His moderation and tendency to temporize crippled him as a politician, though he helped to found and lead the Republican Party. As an editor, however, his enterprise, balance, fairness, and moral earnestness gave him a place of the highest distinction. During the war he had been a staunch supporter of the Union and the Lincoln Administration.

Ho-ax?" (pronounce Hoe-Axe). How the boys enjoyed sailing muscle shells in sheltered nooks among the rocks! And how the muscle shells *would* founder whenever a big roller came in! . . .

July 3. . . . Queer proceeding by that corrupt caitiff Judge Barnard. Morris Ketchum got out a habeas corpus for his son, Edward Ketchum, now in Sing Sing, under conviction, by his own confession, of forgery on a great scale in 1864. On the return of the writ, Barnard remarked that he had looked into the matter, and had pretty much made up his mind!!! Still he was willing to hear the District Attorney (Garvin). Garvin was heard, and then it became evident to the judicial mind of Barnard that his intended violation of law was a little too flagrant. So Ketchum, Jr., was wheedled or bullied into stating (through his counsel) that this motion had been made without his consent, that he felt it due to society that he should serve out his full term, that he was unwilling to escape the full measure of his deserved punishment because of an alleged flaw in his indictment, with other gammon to the same effect. Thereupon Barnard got out of his scrape by announcing that this statement left him no alternative but to remand the prisoner.

July 8. . . . Died old Jacob Cram at eighty-seven, a remarkable old codger who would have made an admirable study for a Silenus. A notable distiller in his day. He was for many years at the head of that profession, and acquired therein a large amount of the circulating medium, and he doubtless leaves a million or so at least. So H. A. Cram, who comes in for a quarter, will doubtless give up legal practice altogether. He's already very rich, but I regret to say that prosperity has developed his bad traits and made him insufferably purse-proud, arrogant, and dictatorial, and lavish in evil speaking beyond all example. He describes every man he don't like, and he likes but few, as being simply an unmitigated brute, scoundrel, thief, and pirate, and generally *knows*, sir, yes *knows*, what he's telling you to be true—that he ought to be in the State Prison for fraud or rape or perjury. These views he likes to set forth in rather impassioned dinner-table harangues, as if he were practising for his next jury, and he does this kind of thing so freely that I am surprised he has never appeared as plaintiff in an assault and battery case.

July 10, SATURDAY. Dined here Mr. and Mrs. Ruggles, who sail Tuesday in the *Silesia* for a summer in Europe. Also Jem. Mr. Ruggles goes as Commissioner to an "International Statistical Conference," or Congress, at The Hague, to represent our Government.

July 12. Vestry meeting more animated than usual. First there was

debate as to whether we should apply for our *pro rata* share of the money
appropriated by the legislature for the free schools of the city other than
the public schools (an iniquitous measure for the benefit of Roman Catholics). Cisco, Nash, and I were for doing so. Dunscomb, Ogden, Davis and
Sackett, contra. The Rector expressed the same adverse opinion, but it
was carried 8 to 6. Our declining to apply would simply have thrown a
little more money into Papistical hands, but for sundry reasons it was a
question about which there was room for two opinions.

Another debate was about a curious matter. The New York *World*
lately published certain ferocious articles against General D. E. Sickles,
making certain charges that are true, others that may be true, and one
(at least) that is utterly false, and probably invented on the spur of the
moment by a malignant writer of smart editorials, viz., that Trinity
Church paid Sickles ten thousand dollars for his speech in the State Senate
against the Act of 1857, confiscating the church endowment. Sickles is now
Minister to Spain and fears for his confirmation by the U.S. Senate. He
had conferred with Ogden, who introduced a resolution of thanks to
Sickles for his gratuitous services—or "disinterested" services, rather—
to the church in 1857. This was to be used before the Senate committee
on the question of confirmation. I suggested that this was a very delicate
proceeding—that every word of such a resolution ought to be weighed
and tested and examined under the microscope, and that it ought to lie
over for another meeting, especially as there could be no action on Sickles's
confirmation till next December at the very earliest. . . . Cisco came down
upon the General like a wagon-load of wild cats. So it was withdrawn,
and referred to a Select Committee of three, viz., Ogden, Cisco, and Nash,
to report upon. It's a hostile committee. . . .

July 13.   Attended this morning to those ——(fill up the blank . . .
with the strongest adjectives you can find) income tax payments, of which
I have to make three, as Trustee and so on. How each of these annual
transactions exasperates one against the secessionist politicians of 1860!
Confounded be the memory of the great-grandmothers of the *accoucheurs*
who presided over the births of each and all of them. . . .

July 30. . . . After dinner, Ellie, Miss Maggy Taylor, Talmage, Van
Rensselaer, and I took a starlight drive in the Park and spent some time
at Theodore Thomas's Concert Hall or Musical Lager-bier Garden.
Crowded. Orchestra good. Programme generally rather mediocre; much
of it flashy, but better than any mere popular concert-music we have had.
Of course, it will not do to be wholly "classical" till people are educated

up to that standard. This seems a civilizing institution. It is in operation every night and is cheap and innocent. There are no signs of rowdyism—people seemed mostly drinking nothing heavier than lager, and I dare say Theodore Thomas has kept a good many young clerks and others out of mischief. . . .

August 1. This evening were here Miss Rosalie, on her way from Richfield Springs to Narragansett Pier; Murray Hoffman; Morgan, of Dixie, and his friend, Cary; James Geddes Day, etc. I wish James Geddes Day talked less of the "foring Nobs" with whom he is intimate. Cary is an intelligent young ex-rebel of twenty-four, bankrupted by the Southern revolution, out of health, and proposing to administer to himself a voyage to China before the mast by way of tonic. It seems harsh treatment for a case of cardiac derangement. On the mother's side, he is of the high and mighty F.F.V. Fairfaxes, but his manners are, nevertheless, quiet, refined, and gentlemanlike!

Morgan says he don't know a single Southerner, except himself, who was not "worth more than two millions before the war." Doubtless that will be the most familiar formula of Southern brag for many generations, corresponding to the prevalent Irish boast of descent from Brian Boroo and other mythical potentates.

August 7, SATURDAY. Quite an October day. It has been cool of late, and a sagacious man remarked to me this morning that he "hoped we should have a little seasonable weather when this confounded eclipse was over." People were peddling bits of colored glass about the streets, and seemed doing a brisk business. At five, Murray Hoffman and I took our stations on the roof and stayed there an hour and a half, or until the sun was decidedly convalescent. Clouds drifting down from the northwest interfered with the performance a little, but the afternoon was more favorable than I expected, and the greatest obscuration occurred in a patch of clear sky. The eclipse was all but total; only the most delicate crescent could be seen. From six to six-fifteen, the light was wan and strange, like that of the afternoon of a stormy December day when the sun looks out for a moment through a rift in the clouds. But this was combined with a sky which was but partially occupied by light clouds, and which shewed, wherever it was clear, most unusual and beautiful tints of greyish greens and blues.

August 10. To Central Park this afternoon to inspect the live critters assembled in and around the old Arsenal building—the nucleus of our future Zoological Garden. The collection is not large, and consists of donations sent in and received without any system: sundry bears, black bears and a grizzly bear, prairie dogs, foxes, beautiful ocelots, owls, eagles, two meek camels, pheasants, monkeys, macaws, etc. It amounts to little. But the critters look healthy and receive much attention from visitors. Long walk tonight.

Yesterday they broke ground for the new Post Office at the south end of the City Hall Park, and today a great wooden enclosure is going up around its site. This will destroy the best-known and most characteristic street view in New York, viz., looking up from Fulton Street and Broadway across the Park to the South front of the old City Hall. "The Park" will be destroyed, but it has long survived its usefulness, except as a place for blackguard boys to pitch coppers in all day, and for thieves and ruffians to meander through all night. No reference to the Common Council.

August 17, TUESDAY.   Murky, muggy, wet day. At noon, Mr. John R. Strong, alias *Don Giovannuccio*, appeared to me in Wall Street, looking well, jolly, and nut brown. He had come to town for one of his college books, which he wanted to look over before next session, and gave a very good account of himself, and of Louis and Temple. He has three wasp's nests in his sleeping apartment, which add much to his comfort, and he is entomologizing diligently. Temple is "building a house" in "the Glen." He observed a big wasp's nest on a currant bush branch, took it for some remarkable fruit, tried to pull it off, and got his fingers stung. Little Louis had his arm badly banged by the handle of a well-pull revolving as the bucket went down. Lucky the arm was not broken. It was badly bruised. But Louis never even whimpered, and Johnny "was so proud of him." Good. This is the kind of feeling I feared wanting in Master John. He went back to Cornwall by the *Mary Powell* at half-past three, after dining with me at Hampe's on Aal-suppe, Spanish mackerel, filet and so on, which he seemed to appreciate, having breakfasted before seven A.M.

Lonely, forlorn stroll tonight. Society Library—magazines and the like. Rubbish. Letter from Ellie as usual. She has a good time with the fair Miss Margaret. I have had a *tendresse* for all "fair Margarets," ever since I fell in love—at the early age of eight—with Sir Walter Scott's Fair Margaret in the *Lay of the Last Minstrel*. Names are substantial things. I could never have fallen in love with a Deborah or a Sally.

August 21. . . . An article in *Atlantic Monthly*, attributed to Mrs. H. B. Stowe, causes a certain amount of discussion, and will cause more when it's read in England. Mrs. Stowe professes to settle the vexed question of the separation of Lord and Lady Byron, on the authority of Lady Byron herself, who communicated the facts to Mrs. Stowe and died in 1860.[7] We are now informed that Lord Byron lived during his marriage in incestuous intercourse with a "very near blood relation" (his sister Mrs. Leigh, named in his will), and that instead of Lady Byron's dropping her husband without vouchsafing him a reason, she was turned adrift by him, because she would not connive at this fearful connexion, and was to him an "incarnation of his own conscience." The article is not so written as to persuade one to believe its statements. It is vague and not issuable as to particulars of time and place of the crime and of its discovery, and so forth. As to so important a matter as the period during which Lord and Lady Byron lived together, it is grossly wrong. Mrs. Stowe makes the period *two* years, whereas it was notoriously very little more than *one*. Other statements seem to contradict those of Moore and of others, but may be true, nevertheless.

Assuming the whole story true, however, I should not have liked to be its publishers. *Nil de mortuis nisi bonum* is a most questionable maxim, for only the living are injured by evil report, and this article claims to be a vindication of *Lady* Byron rather than an attack on her husband. But is one justified in raking up and bringing to light a filthy charge that has been buried for half a century, merely to prove that this excellent lady was not a mere heartless model of propriety, and did not separate herself from her husband merely because he was "a little wild"? For sundry reasons (among them a passage in "Cain") the charge is not absolutely incredible. But Mrs. Stowe has damaged herself by bringing it forward. N.B. I have no love for Byron and hold his poetry cheap and himself (as represented in his published letters) a clever, aristocratic snob. I never went through a period of "Byronism." Coleridge and Scott were the divinities of *my* gosling age.

August 23.   Society Library tonight. A score or two of English maga-

[7] Mrs. Stowe and Lady Byron, both enlisted in the antislavery cause, had become intimate friends. On Mrs. Stowe's second visit to England (1856) Lady Byron entrusted her with a secret story of Byron's guilty love for his half-sister, Augusta Leigh. The general belief at this time was that when the poet and his wife separated in 1816, Lady Byron had acted with unjustifiable severity toward a wayward but not wholly vicious spouse. With both Mrs. Leigh and Lady Byron dead, Mrs. Stowe felt it proper to vindicate her friend's memory by publishing in the *Atlantic* in September, 1869, an article entitled "The True Story of Lady Byron's Life." Few contributions to the periodical press have made so great a sensation. England and America rang with the ensuing controversy, and when the *Quarterly Review* published material injurious to Lady Byron's case, Mrs. Stowe came out in 1870 with her more elaborate polemic, *Lady Byron Vindicated.*

zines, and each mainly occupied by two or three chapters of some half-dozen "serials"! So it is with our periodicals, down to the Sunday newspapers, and so it seems to be with the periodicals of France and Germany, and probably with those of Hong-Kong, Hakodadi, Australia, Tunis, and the Galapagos Islands. What a portentous phenomenon! Never before in the history of mankind have so many brains—generally of small calibre —been employed in spinning moonshine, and setting up certain unsubstantial phantasms (most unlike human creatures) devising orbits for them, and "plots" and "striking situations." . . .

August 29. The Reverend Mr. Cooke called this afternoon on the subject which most frequently induces clerics to visit vestrymen, the temporalities of his office. He wants more salary. Junior assistants have $4,000, senior assistants $10,000. The latter salary is certainly too large; the former probably too small. Troublesome question. How enormously is the Romanist Church strengthened by the price at which it secures working, self-denying presbyters! For what we pay one absolutely valueless servitor she gets *ten* efficient agents. . . .

Death announced of Mrs. Reverend Dr. Bellows, whom I always found a kindly, simple-minded woman. But I believe she bothered her husband and her more intimate friends by a certain hyperaesthesia of conscientiousness, and commonly hesitated about going out of her house till she had made up her mind whether duty required her to walk on the right hand or the left hand side of the street. So they say. Reverend Bellows is the most social, mercurial, and enterprising of men and Unitarians, ever ready to undertake some new philanthropic work. This lady rather bewailed and discouraged his erratic tendencies, and wanted him to keep himself down to his strictly legitimate duties of weekly lecturer to certain people who pay him for his lectures, and make believe that he is a clergyman and that they in some sense are a church.

September 2. . . . Long walk tonight. I am systematically exploring the West Side Avenues, which have grown up quite out of my knowledge. The Eighth, for instance, is now a brilliant shopping street—far more brilliant than the Sixth. The Seventh seems all compact of the lowest tenement houses and whiskey mills, an elongated Five Points. This evening I lost my way completely in that enchanted region of irregular by-ways—Hammond Street, Jane Street, Greenwich Avenue, and so on—as I do whenever I visit it. Got myself utterly dis-oriented, and found myself at Greenwich Street, making straight for the North River, when I thought myself marching eastward and near Sixth Avenue.

September 15.   Death of General John A. Rawlins, Secretary of War, a valuable man. . . .

Meredith Howland engaged to Miss Torrance, a granddaughter of old Vanderbilt, whose recent marriage to some young woman or other gives rise to a large number of questions in which the arithmetical relations of seventy-five to thirty are made to bear an indelicate aspect.[8]

September 22.   The Byron-Stowe controversy is becoming a bore. Every newspaper and every magazine has something to say about it every day and every week. All denounce Mrs. Stowe, though a very few (as the *Saturday Review*) believe the story, while they clapperclaw its author. Even poor Peter R. Strong of Flushing Bay has done his little versified evacuation upon her. One would have thought that a forbidden subject in his house —at least in his presence—like talk of halters in a household a member whereof has been lately hanged; but Peter R. Strong seems to think his late nuptial troubles give him a kind of triumphal privilege of distinguished notoriety, and rather likes to trot them out.

Apropos of the Park, I hear that many of our Teutonic fellow citizens who crowded to witness the "unveiling" or "dedication" of the bust of Humboldt near the Fifth Avenue gate supposed they were doing honor to Helmbold, the sporting druggist, who has a flashy shop on Broadway and who is said to have acquired a vast fortune by pictorial advertisements of "Humbold's Bucher" all over the city, if not the universe. The bust, by the by, is quite good, unobtrusive, and inoffensive.

September 26, SUNDAY. . . . Terrific battle of the Bulls and Bears in the Gold Room Friday. A Bedlam, it's said. Gold actually fluctuated during two or three hours of the wildest frenzy between 135 and 170. At last the Secretary of the Treasury appeared with heavy artillery ($4,000,000) on the flank of the Bulls, and the Ring broke and collapsed and ran (as we did at Bull Run). Gold closed at about 135. We do not yet know the killed and wounded, because the combatants were *too much prostrated* yesterday to write up their accounts, and there was an armistice by mutual consent. Their clearing house, moreover, could not get through the work Friday imposed upon it. . . .

The disgraceful episode since famous as "Black Friday" had convulsed the financial machinery of the country. Three men—Jay Gould, James Fisk, Jr., and

---

[8] Cornelius Vanderbilt, the old "Commodore," whose first wife had died in 1868, married Frank Armstrong Crawford of Mobile, a tall, handsome young woman of about thirty; the union had no issue.

Abel Rathbone Corbin (who had married President Grant's sister)—had laid a plot in the summer of 1869 to corner the limited gold supply of the country. At this time the United States was not on a specie basis, and a special gold exchange did business in the metal in New York. The trio succeeded in drawing the recently appointed head of the New York sub-treasury, General Daniel Butterfield, into the scheme. For various reasons a corner in gold seemed feasible. The New York banks at this time had only about $14,000,000 of it; not more than $1,000,000 more was kept in safes and tills, and it would take time to import more from Europe. Butterfield was expected to help keep the United States Treasury from selling any of its gold stocks. The three conspirators systematically bought gold for future delivery, until they had contracted for far more than the available supply. By Thursday, September 23, the price of gold had been forced to such a high level that a grave financial crisis impended. Bankers' paper was unsalable except at a high premium, and merchants' paper could hardly be sold at any price, with the result that both foreign and domestic trade were heavily deranged. On Friday morning, the 24th, the panic in New York mounted to a frenzied climax. The gold exchange was a scene of mad excitement; brokers were driven crazy; business all over the nation was completely suspended. At last came news that the Treasury had intervened, and that Secretary Boutwell had ordered the sale of $4,000,000 in gold. Within a minute the price of the metal crashed. But evidence was later produced that Butterfield gave Jay Gould secret foreknowledge of the government sales, and that Gould used the twenty-five minutes' leeway he thus gained to unload much of the trio's gold at high prices. Although the remainder was sold at lower figures, they escaped any real loss by the simple process of letting Jim Fisk's responsible partner, Belden, repudiate his debts!

Many were ruined by "Black Friday." Great numbers of innocent men all over the country suffered losses. But Gould, Fisk, Corbin, and Butterfield escaped any penalty except loss of reputation—and the first three had none of that anyhow. To many observers the saddest aspect of the affair was the shadow it threw on Grant, who had consorted with Gould and Fisk during the summer and had appointed Butterfield without inquiring into his qualifications.

September 30. Johnny returned from Cornwall "for good," so the dinner table looks natural once more. Have been in Wall Street as usual. . . .

Wall Street still panting and exanimate after last week's spasm, like a man convalescing from tetanus, or delirium tremens. But some say we are not convalescing at all, and that this was only the first stage of the attack. They prophesy general revulsion and crash, of which they say the crash yesterday of Lockwood & Co. and of other respectable stock-dealing houses was the small beginning. So growl the Bears. James Fisk, Jr., keeps in some shady place, and is commonly said to have become a *non-est* man at last. He could not shew his ugly face in Wall Street without bodily peril. Old Vanderbilt is no less dearly hated. These great operators and Railroad Kings (or other Vikings of the stock market) will discover some day that ruining their weaker neighbors by a piratical combination of capital, though good for the assets, is bad for the bones, perhaps even for the vertebrae of the neck. . . .

October 2. . . . Died at Chicago, Wednesday, my old friend and class-mate, Isaac V. Fowler, sometime postmaster of New York, who fled as a defaulter to government in 1860, but with as little moral guilt as can attach to a defalcation. His official superiors, in the wretched days of old Buchanan, connived at his use of public funds for *party* purposes (not for his private gain) till the deficit grew uncomfortably large, and then they threw him over. He had many good points and much ability, which was all wasted on the petty intrigues of Tammany. . . .

October 9. . . . Application from three infatuated young women for admission to Law School. No woman shall degrade herself by practising law, in New York especially, if I can save her. Our committee will prob-ably have to pass on the application, *pro forma*, but I think the clack of these possible Portias will never be heard at Dwight's moot courts. "Women's-Rights Women" are uncommonly loud and offensive of late. I loathe the lot. The first effect of their success would be the introduction into society of a third sex, without the grace of woman or the vigor of man; and then woman, being physically the weaker vessel and having thrown away the protection of her present honors and immunities, would become what the squaw is to the male of her species—a drudge and domestic animal. . . .

October 10, SUNDAY. At Trinity Church a missioneering presbyter from North Carolina preached. Sermon was bosh, but then it was a new style of bosh, unlike Reverend Vinton's bosh, so flat and stale to us after many years' experience. So it seemed quite good and rather original. The itinerant system of Methodism has its advantages. . . .

Music at Trinity Church this morning was beneath contempt. But it was well executed. The reorganized choir is strong, and seems well drilled. . . .

October 12. . . . Two important state elections today, Pennsylvania and Ohio. Result doubtful. I fear Grant does not stand quite as well with the swinish multitude as he did a year ago. So much dirt has been thrown at him that some of it must stick. Democratic victory in these two states would impair public credit and inflame Southern malignancy, of which there is plenty still smouldering.

October 17. . . . Pennsylvania and Ohio have elected the full Republican ticket. Majorities reduced, of course, for this is an "off year," of comparative apathy, and in both states the party was much weakened by the concurrence of manifold mistakes on the part of the Administration. But the defeat of Pendleton, the Apostle of Repudiation, is a great gain.[9] Nearly half the West is lusting after a breach of public faith. It will be soon reinforced by the reconstructed South, wealthier and stronger than ever, and unanimous against paying a national debt incurred for its own subjugation. Ohio's adhesion to this swindling policy would have been a blow to public credit.

Hours grow later and later. Our friends did not disperse tonight until near one A.M. Jemmy is furious against Dr. R. Ogden Doremus for mismanagement of the Philharmonic Society, whereof the doctor is president. According to Jem, he issues tickets far beyond the capacity of the Academy of Music, and lets his friends in by some back-stairs, so as to half fill the house before its doors are opened to the common herd of subscribers. The doctor has publicly denied the latter charge. But, on the whole, I shall not subscribe this year. If the Society play anything better than Liszt and Wagner, I can buy a ticket. I was a faithful subscriber from the very first concert (1842) to 1849, and then with an interval of a year or two, until the last season.

But under Doremus's administration, the concerts are most unlike what they were ten years ago. *Then*, there was an audience fit though few. Now you must struggle for room to sit or stand, with people gabbling all round you. *Then*, the Society delighted in Beethoven, Weber, Mozart. Now it gives us "Readings from Manfred" by the very estimable Mr. Edwin Booth, and similar clap-trap. I mean no disrespect to Mr. Booth, but a performance of the Overture to *Der Freischütz* with blue lights introduced to illustrate the more demoniacal passages would not be more alien from the true purpose of that society than these readings. Doremus

---

[9] George H. Pendleton, sometimes called "Gentleman George," had urged that government bonds issued during the war be paid in greenbacks instead of coin. He was defeated for the governorship of Ohio by Rutherford B. Hayes.

wants to make the Philharmonic concerts "draw," and he has succeeded. He has made them pay better than ever before. That is to say, he has increased the annual dividend to each member of the orchestra by perhaps as much as five dollars, but he has made the Society and its concerts worthless.

October 18. Came home early and improved the afternoon by a car ride with Ellie to Fifty-ninth Street, and a long walk thereafter in the park, a diversion to which she is partial of late. Very pleasant. The park foot-paths are lovely. The place reveals its full beauty to pedestrians only. Everything in it seems complete, well appointed, and well regulated. It's a boon to the city, and must exert much influence for good. . . .

October 26. To School of Mines this afternoon. Egleston has brought home from Europe books, apparatus, and the most magnificent minerals, and what is more, has raised the money to pay for the latter from G. Kemble, Parrott, and others, having overrun the sum put at his disposal by the trustees. Egleston is always glowing in the heights of prosperity and hope, or else wailing in the depths of despair. He was in this latter mood today, and refused to be comforted. . . .

Paris seems uncommonly uneasy, and many think an *émeute* (*Anglice* "muss") certain to come off within a day or two. Louis Napoleon is not Louis XVI, nor Charles X, nor Louis Philippe, and any gentleman who may contribute his talents to a Parisian outbreak in 1869 will probably experience considerable discomfort. But there will be no row. The New York *World* prints a nasty little paragraph denouncing the "exclusiveness of the proposed Church Music Association concerts." It emanates from some penny-a-liner, whose bile is stirred up by rumors of concerts to which the Reporting Fraternity is not to be humbly invited, and is not to be cuddled or bribed for a favorable report in tomorrow's papers. If we succeed at all, we shall be wholly independent of these *condottieri*, for we want to sell no tickets. The more they abuse our "exclusiveness," the more strongly will people more or less tainted by snobbishness be tempted to ask admission as subscribers. We have now $5,400 subscribed. . . .

October 31. . . . Morgan Dix tells me he has many applications for tickets to the Church Music Association concerts of the future, and they begin to be talked of quite generally. O, for one or two good tenors and soprani to secure their success! I have letters and visits from lots of people who want to sing, but I refer them all to Pech. It is essential that he have absolute control of orchestra, chorus, and solo singers. He must be dictator in that department, and allow the committee to be supreme on all questions of money.

November 1. . . . If the Democrats carry the legislature tomorrow, our city "Commissions" will be swept away, and the most profligate city government in Christendom will lay its claws on the Central Park, the Police Department, and whatever else is as yet managed with any degree of decency. They (the Democrats) are confident; Republicans, apathetic. Some think that German New York is prepared to renounce its Democratic allegiance and "antagonize" the Irishry. Sigel was nominated to allure the Teutons that way. But they know the Republican party only as an anti-lager-bier party, and loathe its stupid "Sunday Laws," which deprive them of enjoyments they consider innocent. I fear they will not "fight mit Sigel" when that donkey, H. Greeley, presents himself at Sigel's side and on the same ticket.

N.B. The Columbia Trustees exorcised that deaf and dumb spirit, Zabriskie, alias Zbrowski, by accepting his resignation.

November 3. Dull. The Democrats claim a victory and have doubtless elected their state officers, but there is hope that they have not secured a working majority in both Houses. . . .

November 11. The grand *Vanderbilt* Bronze on the Hudson River Railroad Depot "unveiled" yesterday with much solemnity. There was a prayer and there were speeches.[10] Vanderbilt began life penniless. He acquired a competence—honestly, I assume—by energy, economy, and business tact, and then increased his store to a colossal fortune of sixty millions (as they say) by questionable operations in railroad stocks. Anyhow he is a millionaire of millionaires. And, therefore, we bow down before him, and worship him, with a hideous group of molten images, with himself for a central figure, at a cost of $800,000. These be thy Gods, O Israel! *Vide* Carlyle's Latter Day Tract entitled "Hudson's Statue." But it is not clear, after all, that this act of Idolatry and Mammon Worship—

[10] Commodore Vanderbilt had himself supervised the building of the great three-story freight station, buying St. John's Park from Trinity Church for the site. One of his friends proposed erecting a bronze pediment as a monument to him and to the development of American transportation. The design of this colossal pediment, more than one hundred and fifty feet long and thirty feet high, was by Ernest Plassman. A central niche revealed the Commodore standing in a fur-lined overcoat. Neither the statue nor the bas-relief was a creditable work of art. Mayor Oakey Hall presided over the unveiling. The overcoated Commodore now stands before the Grand Central Station at the top of the ramp by which Park Avenue traffic reaches the elevated roadway around the building.

the honor thus paid to a successful money-maker as a Hero—is to be charged against the community of New York, though that community is rotten and snobbish enough for almost any conceivable baseness. The money may have been raised among Vanderbilt's jackals and subordinates. Perhaps he was himself the largest subscriber. Moreover, it is to be remembered that Vanderbilt did a grand thing or two during the war. . . .

November 15. Weather atrabilious and grey. Committee of Church Music Association met at my office three P.M.. and sat long. Settled about securing orchestral and vocal parts, and so on, and agreed that Haydn's 15th Mass and Beethoven's in C should be produced at the second and third concerts. We are trying hard to keep within our estimates. They may be exceeded on the items of "paid chorus" and of printing programmes and the like, but on other items we seem likely to have a margin. Pech dined here. Ellie and Dominus Johannes have gone to the Opera (*Norma*, I think) with Miss Fanny Reed.

Have inspected the grand $800,000 Vanderbilt Bronze. It's a "mixellaneous biling" of cogwheels, steamships, primeval forests, anchors, locomotives, periaguas ("petty augers" we called them when I was a boy), railroad trains, wild ducks (or possibly seagulls), and squatter shanties, with a colossal Cornelius Vanderbilt looming up in the midst of the chaos, and beaming benignantly down on Hudson Street, like a *Pater Patriae*— draped in a dressing gown or overcoat, the folds whereof are most wooden. As a work of art, it is bestial. . . .

November 23. Chilly and wet. Busy day. Committee on School of Mines at Betts's office. Betts, Edward Jones, Barnard, and I. Barnard's prolixity terrible. Were he not an able man or an admirable president, we should flee his presence. The trustees of the Cooper Institute are not disinclined to transfer their whole establishment to us, thereby giving us a fireproof building for our cabinets and bringing us in contact with the people. What an opportunity for a live board! But I prophesy that it will be neglected. We have not even ambition enough to look at it favorably. To do the committee justice, however, it heard this afternoon that W. H. Aspinwall, M. K. Jesup, and Parrott of Cold Spring had given Egleston money (toward paying for minerals bought in Europe) without resenting their intrusion, and decided to admit that a word of thanks to them might not be out of place.

November 24. First rehearsal tonight for Church Music Association to which I had looked forward uneasily. Ellie and I drove far uptown to pick up Mrs. Henry Howland . . . and then proceeded to Trinity Chapel

Schoolhouse. C.M.A. made a much better beginning than I expected. About fifty amateurs appeared. . . .

It will be cause for hearty gratitude if this undertaking succeed. Its success will teach New York fashionables something about true religious music, as distinguished from the flashiness of adaptations from modern Italian operas and the dullness and deadness of Anglican "services." The prospect looks well just now. If it succeed, Ellie will be entitled to most of the credit of its success. When I "set the ball in motion" last May, I never dreamed that any work would be devolved on her. But she saw, with her feminine eyes, that the active aid of some rather prominent and popular "woman of society" was essential to the success of the undertaking. So she took hold and has for the last month been working like a horse, or rather a pony, writing notes to people, calling on people, inciting people to call on other people, and so on, and has thus enlisted in the cause a certain large and influential element of the "fashionable world.". . .

November 25. . . . There are some who foresee a war with Spain, and an Invincible Armada descending on our coasts—all to come of our stoppage or seizure of the Spanish gunboats, and our not improbable recognition of the Cuban guerrillas as a belligerent power.[11] But gold does not rise.

Erie Railroad War breaks out in a new spot. Formidable onslaught upon Fisk and Gould and their pals, engineered by Eaton. May he prevail against that gang of rampant scoundrels—amen. I don't believe he will. But the Devil's turn to deal with each of them will come at last, and he will not recognize injunctions issued by Judge Barnard or by any of the Judges who are kept by the Erie Ring. We heard this morning that Judge Murray of Delaware County had issued an injunction, and a rather remarkably sweeping one, against these magnificent sharpers. Tonight's *Post* announces that Judge Balcom, acting for Fisk & Co., has issued injunction No. 2, and so on indefinitely. This is a specimen of the disgrace brought upon the judiciary and the mischief brought upon the people by the elective judiciary and the New Code, for which we may thank David Dudley Field, Esq. May Pirates and Pettifoggers defile their graves! . . .

December 3, FRIDAY. Clear and cold. At 5:30 with Ellie, Trenholm, and Murray Hoffman to "Sunset Service" at the grand new Synagogue of the Reformed—Porkophagous, or porcivorous—Jews, on Fifth Avenue.

---

[11] John A. Rawlins, Secretary of War in Grant's Cabinet, had headed a party which demanded recognition of the insurgent Cubans; Hamilton Fish, Secretary of State, led the opposition and was ultimately triumphant.

Interior glowing and gorgeous with gold and color, arabesque wood carvings, and columns of polished syenite. Congregation thin. Service polyglot—Hebrew, German, and English alternately, and mostly choral. Fine choir, with sundry good soli. All the music respectable. As a finale, we were astounded by the splendid "Gloria" of Haydn's No. 2, followed by the "Qui Tollis," and all the rest, adapted to German words (not a translation, of course), and effectively rendered. Trenholm and Murray Hoffman dined here, and Trenholm had much to tell about Southern life in war times.

December 4. . . . The Reverend Henry Ward Beecher's indiscretion in marrying Albert D. Richardson, on his death bed, to the wife of his murderer—for she was his wife, barring a worthless Western divorce—is pretty generally denounced. It tends to turn the tide of feeling that was running very strongly against McFarland, the murderer, and may save his neck by no very logical process.[12] I fear there is a good deal of rather lewd practice among women of the upper middle strata. A newspaper correspondent, this morning, thinks so and takes high moral ground about it, and also complains that it diminishes the legitimate profits of the poor girls who make their living that way! The New York *World* attacks Beecher with great bitterness. That's no new thing, of course, but this attack is really damaging. Strange that everyone assails *him*, and passes over Reverend Unitarian or Parker-ite Frothingham, who helped officiate at this sacrilegious mockery of marriage rites and consecration of bigamy. Probably people are prepared for anything from one of his tribe. It seems a rule that these popular sensational "free-thinkers" of the pulpit and the platform, such as Beecher, Frothingham, Bellows, and others, have a screw loose somewhere. They are brilliant, clever, astute talkers, efficient in business—"men of the world" and of affairs, far more than ordinary clerics; yet every now and then their common sense gives way and lets them down, with a grievous fall, into some flagrant disastrous blunder, like this one. . . .

December 6. College Trustees two P.M. . . .

A special committee of five was appointed to negotiate with the Cooper

[12] The tragic attack upon the distinguished journalist Albert D. Richardson by Daniel McFarland, whose estranged wife Richardson had courted, took place November 25, and aroused a tremendous sensation. Before Richardson died a week later, Beecher married him to Mrs. McFarland. Various views were taken of the matter. The *Nation* took one which Strong evidently shared; namely, that it was not proper "for a married woman to transfer her affections to another man than her husband, and go with her lover to another house, and there occupy what was to all intents and purposes the same room with him, and for the man to announce in print that as soon as she got a divorce he was going to marry her."

Union people, and nobody objected. *Evohe!!!* John Astor resigned, I'm sorry to say. His duties at the office require all his time. The poor fellow might as well be a bank clerk on a salary. Two vacancies, therefore, to be filled, and a batch of nominations—A. S. Hewitt, Charles Swords (Ogden), Delafield (Schermerhorn), W. H. Aspinwall (myself), and several names proposed by Blatchford—outsiders of the "wealthy and prominent" caste. E. D. Morgan and R. A. Witthaus among them. . . .

December 8. . . . A most sad piece of news. Edward Jones died very suddenly this morning, without a moment's warning. Disease of the heart, it is said. We shall miss him in our Columbia College board. Though a little over-cautious, he was among the very best of our trustees. . . .

December 11. . . . Talk with Drisler, Barnard, and Mr. Ruggles, about the Cooper Union negotiation. It seems in a hopeful way, but sundry petty questions of detail give trouble. One of them is what *name* the building should henceforth bear. Nothing would be more characteristic of our board than to decline this God-send on some contemptible point of etiquette. I suggested *"Cooper Hall,"* which Mr. Ruggles thought would solve this weighty problem. . . .[13]

December 13. . . . Much talk with Fitzhugh this evening about experiences in the field as a hungry rebel. Memminger of South Carolina was a foundling—a *filius nullius*—picked up as a baby from the wreck of a German ship, the *Memminger*, whence his name. His parents had perished in the wreck. He was adopted or at least educated by some rich Charlestonian, was clever, and married into some blue-blooded house.[14]

The judiciary of New York, which for years had been a scandal and offense, was now becoming intolerably corrupt. George G. Barnard, Albert Cardozo, and John H. McCunn were all identified with the Tweed Ring and all shameless in their prostitution of justice. Barnard, who had been elected city recorder in 1857 and advanced to the state supreme court in 1860, was an insolent, overbearing man of handsome face and figure who had for a time hypocritically posed as a reformer. Cardozo was learned, industrious, and gentlemanly, with qualities that might have made him a great judge; but he

[13] This hopeful plan for uniting Cooper Union and the College, warmly promoted by Peter Cooper's brilliant son-in-law Abram S. Hewitt, foundered (as Strong predicted) on the conservatism of the Columbia trustees.

[14] Fitzhugh was inaccurate. Memminger was the son of Christopher Godfrey Memminger of Württemberg; his widowed mother brought him to Charleston, and after her death the boy was rescued from the orphanage there by Thomas Bennett, later governor of South Carolina.

sold justice "as a grocer might have sold sugar." He had been a judge of the court of common pleas in the City of New York before his advancement to the state supreme court. As for McCunn, he was vulgar and ignorant as well as dishonest. These three judges had shocked the country by their naturalization frauds in 1868, when the supreme and superior courts of the state made nearly 38,000 aliens into voters. They were now assisting the Tammany Ring in a carnival of plunder and corruption, and we shall hear much more of them in this diary. The time was to come when Cardozo's son, the illustrious Benjamin Nathan Cardozo, would more than redeem the honor of the family name.

December 18. . . . N.B. Barnard and Cardozo (*arcades ambo*) seem to have fallen out a little. The stink of our state judiciary is growing too strongly ammoniac and hippuric for endurance. Like Trinculo, we "do smell all h—p—" whenever we read or hear of the sayings or doings of the average New York judge. He is as bad as the New York alderman, if not worse, because his office is more sacred. People begin to tire of holding their noses, and are looking about in a helpless way for some remedy. The nuisance must be abated somehow and that soon, but I see no hope of its abatement, except by a most perilous process, justified only by the extremest necessity, and after all constitutional remedies are exhausted. Some change is certainly needed most urgently. Law protects life no longer. Any scoundrel who is backed by a little political influence in the corner groceries of his ward can commit murder with almost absolute impunity. The sheriff's office is a den of Celtic thieves, roughs, and *Sicarii*. Law does not protect property. The abused machinery of Law is a terror to property owners. No banker or merchant is sure that some person, calling himself a "receiver," appointed *ex parte* as the first step in some frivilous suit he never heard of, may not march into his counting room at any moment, demand possession of all his assets and the ruinous suspension of his whole business, and when the order for a receiver is vacated a week afterwards, claim $100,000 or so as "an allowance" for his services, by virtue of another order, to be enforced by attachment. No city can long continue rich and prosperous that tolerates abuses like these. Capital will flee to safer quarters.

I think it was Edmund Burke who said that the one end and aim for which King, Lords, and Commons exist was to "get twelve honest men into a jury box." Perhaps it was Erskine, for it's much after his manner. But anyhow, it is true. President and Congress, Governor and Legislature, were established and are upheld for the sake of enforcing justice between man and man, and between the community and individuals. That is their first and paramount office, compared with which all duties as to our foreign relations are insignificant. For this cause, taxes are imposed, tariffs established, import charges collected, elections held. With us, in this state, this supreme object of civil government is so far from attainment that a judge of our Supreme Court is *prima facie* disreputable. His office is something against him, to be apologized for and explained away before one can recognize him as honest and a gentleman. I verily believe that by pulling one or two strings, I could obtain "an allowance" of $150,000 in the Schermerhorn partition suits now in my office, and that allowance would be a lien on all the real estate covered by those suits. It might be good fun to get such an award, just to see how shocked and confounded Edmund and William would be when they heard of it. But the joke would be indecent—a profane trifling over the corpse of a profession that was once most honored and noble. . . .

December 20. To Columbia College board. Barnard proposed to revive the "Visiting Committee" plan. This led to a prolonged palaver. . . .

Among people here last night were Mr. and Mrs. Burton Harrison, some time of Virginia. He was Chief of Staff, Private Secretary, or some such thing, to Jeff Davis, that pagan full of pride, before his overthrow. The lady is a nice looking blonde, cultivated, pleasant mannered, and with the most honest, earnest feeling for the best music.[15] A woman who tells me that she spurns Verdi, and who takes a copy of *The Creation* into the country for a summer companion, enslaves me at once. This lady is a sister of our nice young friend Clarence Cary, sings in our C.M.A. chorus, and attends its rehearsals with laudable punctuality. . . .

December 21, TUESDAY. Another dull December day, with an ash-colored sky, and with gaseous extract of damp streets by way of atmosphere. More Cardozo, and no progress. I think Nature meant Cardozo to sweep the court room, not to preside in it, and that he would look more natural in the dock of the Sessions than on the Bench of the Supreme Court.

Stanton, by the by, is made a justice of the Supreme Court at Washington. People differ about the merits of the appointment. A great war minister is not necessarily able to become even a second-rate judge. Stanton has been a successful advocate, and has industry, pluck, and backbone enough

[15] Mrs. Burton Harrison's father was a nephew of Thomas Jefferson; her mother a descendant of Washington's friend Lord Fairfax. Among her many books one is assured of a long life, her *Recollections Grave and Gay*.

for ten. But neither his mind nor his temper seem in the least judicial. I approve the appointment, however. With all his faults, he has done the country good service. . . .

December 23. Walked uptown this afternoon Christmassing. Broadway thronged with folk on the same errand. Was weak enough to stop at Tiffany's, resolving to be parsimonious this year and spend not more than $20 on a present for Ellie. But I was inflamed by a pretty cameo brooch, and involved myself to the extent of near $200, which was sensible of me, especially as I had been obliged to subtract a little *more* capital from the Trust Co. this morning to pay current bills. Never mind. I won't do so again, and I think Ellie will be much pleased with this bit of wampum, and then she has earned a nice Christmas present by her exertions in the cause of C.M.A. She had already got herself certain gimcrackeries which she insisted should be her Christmas present, but I could not let Christmas Eve go by without producing something new. I should not have felt right all through next year. . . .

December 24. . . . Flags at half-mast this morning. Edwin M. Stanton died at Washington three A.M. rather unexpectedly, though he had been quite ill for several days. He was broken down by the wear and tear of the work during the war. Six years ago, this would have been a great public calamity. Happening at this time, it is perhaps the best thing for Stanton's fame and repute. He *might* have made an uncommonly bad Associate Justice of the Supreme Court. The chances are that he would not have increased his reputation by his performance of judicial duties, and his reputation of honor as Lincoln's right-hand man during nearly the whole period of the war entitles him to an exalted place in our history, whatever the New York *World* may say. These three, Lincoln, Stanton, and Grant, did more than any other three men to save the country. Good and evil were strangely blended in the character of this great War Minister. He was honest, patriotic, able, indefatigable, warm-hearted, unselfish, incorruptible, arbitrary, capricious, tyrannical, vindictive, hateful, and cruel. Robespierre had certain traits in common with Stanton. I mean no disrespect to Stanton, who was infinitely bigger and better than that miserable Frenchman—but their several failings were not unlike.

December 27. . . . Church Music Association tickets are in demand. Speculators offer $10 a ticket for any quantity of them. If they could be bought at the music store, they would be a drug at $1.50. But this affair is "exclusive" and *therefore*, etc. In all matters of art, this community is Bœotian. It cares nothing for Mozart's and Weber's music, but is deeply interested in any "kid-glove" performance, on the programme of which stand the names of Mrs. Astor, Mrs. William Schermerhorn, and the like, as a "Ladies' Committee," and to which people are admitted only by favor. . . .

December 28. . . . Four P.M. Steinway Hall. Church Music Association rehearsal. Choruses from *Oberon.* Credo, fugue sanctus, etc., from Mozart, No. 12. Enjoyed it heartily. Attendance larger than it was last Tuesday. Among very many acquaintances were Henry Anthon, and Mrs. G. C. Anthon, who recognized me cordially. . . .

1870

SUCCESS OF THE CHURCH MUSIC ASSOCIATION · THE
FRANCO-PRUSSIAN WAR · SEDAN · THE SIEGE OF PARIS ·
UNIFICATION OF ITALY · MR. BRET HARTE

———————————◦❦◦———————————

*A momentous year was opening—the year of the Franco-Prussian War, the
overthrow of Napoleon III, and the siege of Paris; the year in which the
great causes of German and Italian unification received a tremendous new
impetus; the year which gave Europe an entirely new aspect. It was also the
year in which Secretary of State Hamilton Fish, conversing with the British
Minister, Sir Edward Thornton, laid a foundation for the Treaty of Washington and the great arbitration of the* Alabama *claims. In the history of the
Grant Administration it was the year of the President's battle to bring about
the annexation of Santo Domingo, and of the defeat of this project in the
Senate; an episode which, with other events, divided the Republican Party into
two hostile wings. In New York the year witnessed an intensification of the
struggle against the Tweed Ring. Led at first by* Harper's Weekly, *with
Thomas Nast as its cartoonist, this struggle finally brought forward the New
York* Times *under George Jones, which courageously published irrefutable
proofs of the Ring's corruption.*

*Strong, busy as always in his Wall Street office, was dividing his spare
time between Columbia College and his new enthusiasm, the Church Music
Association which he had done more than anyone else to found. "We are approaching a critical period in our development," wrote Strong on January 3.
"The orchestra and chorus come together for the first time tomorrow afternoon."
But with Dr. Pech for conductor, and with harmonious agreement on a
splendid selection of religious music to be rendered, he was full of hope. A little
rehearsal on January 6 in the Trinity Chapel School building, and a larger*

[268]

one on the 11th gave him great satisfaction, particularly as Mozart's 12th Mass, one of his favorite pieces, was the chief item of the concert. "I feel tonight," he wrote on the 11th, "as in the days of old, just after some of the Philharmonic concerts of twenty-five years ago when the highest music was still a novelty. First, intensely fatigued with long and close attention, mixed in this instance with a good deal of anxiety as to how the thing was going to go; and second, excited and wide-awake, and almost starting now and then as some jewel from the orchestral work flashes across my memory." He was so much consumed by his new enterprise that he had time to mention little else in his diary. He did pause, however, to write an acrid note on Harriet Beecher Stowe's new book, the Vindication of Lady Byron, *which he regarded as true but none the less offensive. All that she had done was to confirm her original* Atlantic Monthly *article and "to prove that the stink she has set free is a genuine, original, authentic stink, and none of her compounding. Cui bono?"*

Then came the great evening of the first Church Music Association concert.

January 13, THURSDAY.   Yesterday was springlike, clouding up toward evening. I spent the afternoon at Steinway with Edmund, the Rev. Mr. Cooke, and Dick Tucker, giving the final touches to our arrangements for the evening. Horace Binney and his daughter, Miss Maria, came from Philadelphia for the concert. . . .

We were at Steinway by twenty minutes to eight (concert at eight-thirty); but there was a line of carriages up Fourteenth Street and as far as Union Square. The room was three-quarters full; however, we secured good seats. Jack Ehninger, Bradley, a Mr. Vail, Morgan from the Trinity Church vestry office, and two or three more were on duty as ushers. The crowd soon became dense, but there were seats for all. A newspaper snob would have called the assemblage brilliant. I do not believe so many people of culture and refinement were ever before gathered under the ceiling of a New York concert room. . . .

I passed the word for a little applause when Pech should take his conductor's place, and it was given quite heartily. The precaution was necessary because Pech is still a stranger to a New York audience. The Berthold overture was well executed, and its choral finale ("Rise, Crowned with Light") came out effectively. The "attack" of the chorus on the first note—a difficult point to secure—was perfect. They came down upon it like a thousand bricks. Johnny, who is not given to enthusiasm, said it was the most splendid thing he ever heard and that it sent a thrill through the audience. As to the choral and orchestral work of the *Mass*, no words can do justice to it. Watson (*Art Journal*), a severe critic, "had heard nothing like it in America"—nor had I. *Oberon* went brilliantly, its music a fine contrast to that of Mozart.

I was overwhelmed with congratulations from scores of nice people on the success of the concert—congratulations which were due to Pech, and so I told them. It was, in fact, among the finest performances of music of its kind—and that a very exalted kind—ever heard in New York. But there were defects we must try to avoid next time. The concert was too long—from eight-thirty to eleven-fifteen—and with very brief intervals or entr'actes. The soli, except Miss Fanny and Centemeri, were not strong enough for the orchestra and chorus. . . .

January 17. . . . Commendation of Wednesday's concert is strong and hot and plenty of it, diluted only by the two very reasonable criticisms before mentioned. Doremus talks to Pech's friend, Todd, as if he were jealous of the Church Music Association as a possible rival of the Philharmonic. . . .

Died yesterday, Mrs. John R. Suydam (with whom I was near falling in love when she was Miss Annie Lawrence of Fourteenth Street), John L. Lawrence's daughter. That was almost a quarter of a century ago! I remember her well as very sweet looking, quiet, gentle, and "sonsie."

Fitz-John Porter sends me a pamphlet setting forth the grounds on which he seeks a rehearing of his case.[1]

January 19.   Temple, by the by, has a quite remarkable facility in music. He has caught certain difficult phrases from *Oberon* by ear and produces them on the piano for his own delectation very clearly and accurately, getting the unusual chords and harmonies exactly. I couldn't have done it at his age, and I was held quite a prodigy of musical talents forty years ago.

Last night our Church Music Association Committee was here till eleven-thirty. We decided to keep *Lobgesang*, or part of it, on our next programme. I think it's a heavy work; but others value it, and I didn't want to press my own opinion too strongly. Also, we decided to let in new subscribers, and I think we shall get them without much effort.

January 22.   Mr. Ruggles is confined at No. 24 by a novel visitor—gout. An unsafe visitor it is, *teste* 1855. I deeply regret to write that Mr.

---

[1] That is, a reversal of the verdict of a court-martial which had held Porter guilty of disobedience, disloyalty, and insubordination in face of the enemy during Second Manassas. The controversy was revived this year by Porter's pamphlet and by Lewis E. Mills's pamphlet on "General Pope's Virginia Campaign of 1862," which sternly indicted Porter.

Ruggles has seemed to me, since his return from The Hague last fall, to show signs of age. His vivacity and his quickness of perception are certainly less keen than of old. His years are those of this century, three score and ten; so this tendency toward failure cannot surprise me. But it is painful to see his extraordinary brilliancy beginning to be dimmed in the smallest degree. . . .

I am anxious about the finances of the Church Music Association. New subscriptions do not come in as a flood but rather as a small dribble. . . .

Thursday night I went to Mrs. Anna Payn's concert at the hall of the Young Men's Christian Association. They are pharisaical young men, judging by their name; but they have a handsome concert room. The music was "common doings." It's an evangelical clubhouse and will do a certain amount of good among young clerks from the country and "sitch." If it would condescend to open a smoking room and introduce a few barrels of ale and lager, it would do twice as much good.

January 24. . . . The Trinity Church Standing Committee met tonight with the Rector. It was summoned to consider the expediency of buying on a referee's sale . . . certain lots on Hester Street, Elizabeth Street, and on the Bowery, excellently fitted for the site of a new free chapel. We had no authority to act, but Cisco[2] said grandly that he would buy for us at any sum we might fix and take the risk of the vestry's ratifying the purchase. I wish it were in my power to say such things. I moved to authorize $100,000, but the committee decided on $80,000. The difference is unimportant, for the land will probably bring $120,000.

January 25, TUESDAY. At half-past ten last evening, Delano, wending his way home from a dinner at John Astor's, was set upon and robbed by three men on the corner of Fifth Avenue and Eleventh Street. Of course there was no arrest. Crime was never so bold, so frequent, and so safe as it is this winter. We breathe an atmosphere of highway robbery, burglary, and murder. Few criminals are caught, and fewer punished. Municipal law is a failure in New York, and we must soon fall back on the law of self-preservation. Among the most prominent candidates for informal execution are sundry ministers of justice—or rather of injustice—the most notorious scoundrels out of jail and far more nefarious than most who are in it. Secret, irresponsible tribunals are ugly and dangerous, as witness the English trades-unions, but they may become a necessity. . . .

[2] John J. Cisco, who, as assistant treasurer of the United States in New York, had done much during the war to sustain the faith of metropolitan bankers and businessmen in the government.

Old [James W.] Gerard and Dr. Barnard have been writing to the Rev. Cooke that it's a great shame my respectable name does not appear on our programmes as "president"; so the committee agreed to send me to the front. I don't care much about it, but I should prefer to be less conspicuous. My qualifications for the position will doubtless be the subject of newspaper criticism, such as has so exasperated Dr. Pech. For example: "The president of this association is a Wall Street lawyer named Strong, who knows as much about music as a cow does of conic sections." . . .

January 26. . . . Fifty years ago this day, January 26, 1820, was born at No. 50 Franklin Street, in the city of New York, a squalling brat, whose babyhood—being both croupy and colicky—required special vigilance and occasional anxiety and care worthy a better cause. The amount expended on him in doctor bills, druggist bills, and catnip tea might probably have been better invested. At compound interest it would have swollen into a small fortune by this time. This blessed baby has now drifted through nearly his whole life without praiseworthy service to church or state or appreciable benefit to anybody. He has manufactured good resolutions by the cartload, but they have proved an inferior article. He will probably continue to the end a more or less "respectable" and decorous dunce and drone. Perhaps he may think himself lucky if he get through without falling below even that standard. The almshouse is always visible in the "middle distance."

January 30, SUNDAY. . . . To Trinity Church with Ellie and the boys. There was a crowd at the door and a squad of police, and I learned that "the Prince"—namely, His Royal Highness Arthur of England—was expected.[3] The evening papers had announced his intention to be there. Meurer, the sexton, said that since I was the only vestryman on hand, I must "receive" His Royal Highness. To this I demurred as a piece of flunkeyism. But on consulting the Rector in the robing room, I found he rather wished it done; so I marched to the front door, where, by good fortune, I was joined by General Dix. The Prince and his train arrived nearly on time, and Archibald (the consul) presented Dix and myself. His Royal Highness's manner was well bred and simple. Besides Archibald, there were Thornton the Minister, and three swells—His Royal Highness's "tail"—who were not, I thought, distinguished in appearance. We escorted the party to the pews reserved for them to the tune of "God Save the Queen" from the nave organ, which was the only special notice taken of our visitors. The music was rather better than usual, and Morgan Dix's sermon

[3] Prince Arthur, born in 1850, was the seventh of Queen Victoria's nine children.

(on the Parable of the Talents) was among the best sermons I ever heard. The Prince is not so pleasant-looking as his brother Wales is—or was ten years ago. His face is vacuous and George Thirdish. There is nothing else notable about him, except that he was rather remarkably well bred and attentive to his prayer book all through the service and seemed to listen with interest both to the music and the sermon. The church was densely crowded; and after the service, the outside mob chased the princely chariots up Broadway till the mob got out of breath. . . .

February 2. Nothing very notable today, except lots of funny gossip about the toadyism and snobbery of our prince-hunters. It's evidently proper that people with fine houses and great wealth, like Belmont, Duncan, and others, should receive and entertain a "distinguished" stranger. I am glad that there are men in the city who can do it so well. But the amount of envy, hatred, malice, envyings, and jealousies which these entertainments generate among those who are invited and those who are not, is appalling. Ellie has just received an invitation from General McDowell to join an excursion party for His Royal Highness to visit the lower harbor on a government boat tomorrow morning. That would be pleasant, but she has a reception tomorrow afternoon. I also declined, for I do not believe that I am wanted without her. . . .

Last night's meeting (Twenty-sixth Street and Fifth Avenue, at George C. Anthon's school building) was successful. It sought to create a "bar association" and appointed committees for that purpose. The decent part of the profession was well represented. Nearly two hundred were present, and among them was the virtuous D. D. Field. Van Winkle was in the chair. Speeches by Judge Emott, Henry Nicoll, Evarts, John McKeon (!), D. B. Eaton, S. J. Tilden, and others were generally rather good, though too subdued in tone to suit my taste. But Choate and others told me that they thought moderation is best at first. I have not much hope of good from this movement, but it may possibly accomplish something.

Here is a specimen—a very mild specimen—of the way in which the Supreme Court of the state of New York does business. In these Schermerhorn partition suits, the parties—all *sui juris* and all represented— agreed on three commissioners, all well known as experts in real estate and as beyond exception. When the interlocutory decree appointing them is moved for, Mr. Justice Cardozo says that Mr. Gratz Nathan, another little Jew and a nephew of the judge's, must be a commissioner and that we may choose which of the three we will strike out to make room for him! Nathan would do no service and would charge $10,000 for doing it. Cardozo would confirm the charge and probably pocket half the money. . . .

February 4. Ellie joined the McDowell excursion after all. They inspected forts, reviewed troops, and enjoyed it all immensely. Miss Rosalie and Miss Emily "received" for her.

Late last night came a telegram from William Binney, announcing that his father had died that evening.[4] This is a great loss. There never was a better, purer, and more public-spirited man. For some reason or other, he always shewed a marked regard for me. During the last ten years, our intercourse and correspondence had been intimate. I can safely say that I never heard a word from him or saw a look that suggested selfishness or uncharitable feeling, and that I never knew anyone who came nearer to the ideal of a churchman and a gentleman. There was but one particular in which I thought him possibly a little—what shall I say?—injudicious or mistaken. He was brought up where an atmosphere of Puritan ethics pervaded the church itself, and his sense of religious obligation in every detail of daily life was uncommonly strong. So he made his Sundays a little Sabbathy and looked with disfavor on the theatre and the opera. I have heard it said by Philadelphians that this had a bad effect on his fine family of children; that they found home dull and stupid and got away from it as soon and as much as they could. His eldest son Horace seems to have recalcitrated against all this strictness, and there has been, I hear, something like open rupture between them for several years.

His great ability, strong sense, and practical skill in handling men and affairs were of vast value to the national cause all through the war. But he would never tolerate even a suggestion that he was more than an unprofitable servant. He got up the Union League Club in Philadelphia, and it was a real good talk with him, Agnew, Bellows, and Gibbs that led to our Union League Club. Both rendered good service to the country. I believe that he, more than any other man, kept [Charles J.] Stillé steady; and Stillé's pamphlet, "How a Free People Conduct a Long War," had great influence for good at a time when everyone was desponding. He was so simple, modest, and retiring that few recognized the value of his quiet hard work for the country. But that work was priceless. His high personal character and social position did much to keep Philadelphia

---

[4] Horace Binney, Jr., born 1809, died five years before his father, the renowned Philadelphia attorney (1780–1875). His wife was Strong's cousin, Eliza Johnson. In spite of the eleven years' difference in their ages, Strong and Binney had been drawn close by their association in the Sanitary Commission and other war-time activities. Horace Binney III had made a notable record in the army during the war.

in the right place. No use writing about it; he was among our very best men and among my oldest and most valued friends.

February 8. . . . In the Schermerhorn business, Judge Cardozo backs down, having been notified that we should simply abandon the suits and make a voluntary partition in case he persisted.

An important decision was made by the U.S. Supreme Court on the construction of the Legal Tender Act. Had it been pronounced eight years ago, I should now be less poor by some thousands. . . .[5]

February 12. . . . Opinions vary as to the construction that will be given this decision on the Legal Tender Act. The Bleecker Street Bank for Savings (Wednesday afternoon) postponed the question; so did the Standing Committee of Trinity Church on Thursday night. The Life and Trust Company will demand gold on mortgages which it holds as guardian or trustee; as to other mortgages, it will wait to see what other monied corporations do. This decision was given by a close vote, and many think the two vacancies in the Supreme Court will be filled by men who can be depended on to reconsider and reverse it. . . .

February 16. . . . People talk darkly about James Fisk, Jr., Judge Barnard, and the "Erie Railroad Ring.". . .[6]

February 19. I hear that Binney's will cuts off his eldest son Horace absolutely. A codicil gives him $5,000! The grounds for this must have been grave. Though strict on all questions of right and wrong, the testator was a charitable and placable man and a most affectionate father. . . .

We went to Niblo's to see Fechter's *Hamlet*.[7] . . . The performance was of unusually high grade: all the subordinate parts were respectable, and the King and Queen something more. There was an entirely new style of Ghost, with good effects of blue lights. Whether Booth's or

[5] In the case *Hepburn* v. *Griswold* the court, four to three, handed down the astonishing decision that Congress was without constitutional warrant for making the greenbacks legal tender. It was a decision that could hardly be allowed to stand—and in 1871 it was reversed.

[6] James Fisk and Jay Gould shared in control of the plundered Erie Railroad. Their abortive attempt to corner the gold market the previous September, culminating in Black Friday, was fresh in men's minds. Gould, Fisk, and Daniel Drew temporarily controlled the state legislature, manipulated the city government, and through Mr. Justice Barnard gained what they wanted from the courts. This year Fisk, who swaggered as "admiral" of the Fall River line of steamboats, bought the colonelcy of the Ninth Regiment of New York militia.

[7] Charles Albert Fechter, realistic actor and close friend of Dickens, had made his first American appearance at Niblo's Garden in New York on January 10 of this year.

Fechter's Hamlet be the better article is a question much discussed at present. Booth is elegant and artistic. Fechter is more real, spontaneous, and forcible. His accent is a little unpleasant at first; his readings are excellent, and his power and genius underlie all he does. One doesn't notice power or genius during the play: perception of it dawns on one twenty-four hours afterwards. At Niblo's it is rather Hamlet than Herr Fechter that one thinks of, while Booth's accomplishments and talent and faithful study of his part are so conspicuous as to draw one's attention away from Shakespeare's creation and fix it on the actor's professional ability.

February 21. . . . In this morning's *Sun* appears a column and more of personality and scurrility about the vestry, Dr. Pech, myself, and the Church Music Association. Its writer submitted it to Cisco in type yesterday and said that he is a Bohemian and was willing to be bought off. "Our great object," said this leader of Public Opinion, "in fact, our only object, is to make the *Sun* sell." In fact, it has become the lowest sensational newspaper in the city. Dana knows better, is capable of better things, and ought to be ashamed of himself. . . .

March 3, THURSDAY. Our second Church Music Association concert on Tuesday night was brilliant and successful. . . . The stage—with Ellie, Miss Catlin, Miss Emily Fuller, and a crowd of other pretty women grouped together in evening toilettes—looked like a flower bed. Such a chorus has never been seen in New York before, that is certain, and I think its equal has never been heard. Everything went smoothly. The chorus had improved in steadiness, confidence, and "attack" since January 12; so says the great Richard Grant White, who *knows*. The quartette was strong and true. I succeeded in enjoying even the *Lobgesang*. Haydn's Mass was much commended, but I think most people rather prefer Mozart's twelfth. Mozart's has become almost hackneyed; Haydn's is comparatively unknown. The former appeals more strongly to popular taste and feeling. But Haydn's is a delicious work; its rather confused and expressionless Credo is its one weak point. The two should not be compared any more than a bouquet of camellias and heliotrope should be compared with a bunch of wild roses and violets. Each is perfect in its own way. Haydn's Benedictus, for instance, is less refined and elegant than Mozart's, but what a sweet, simple, natural flavor there is about it! It suggests youthful mornings spent strolling about in woody lanes, gathering "clithora and cardinal flowers." I was much impressed by the splendor of the "trumpet calls" that occur throughout the Dona and by the beautiful lace work of accompaniment by the violins that hangs over the voice parts. After the concert, with Ellie, Miss Louise, and Murray Hoffman to supper at Delmonico's (Fourteenth Street). . . .

A meeting of the committee (Columbia College) on the "new system" was held. I fear it doesn't work. Our undergraduate corps is of lower moral tone than we supposed. It "cheats" at examinations, and the honest students who won't condescend to cheat are not strong enough to send their fraudulent classmates to Coventry. This is very bad.

March 5. Gold has touched 112 and closed today at about 113. Certain shops and restaurants begin to pay out silver change by way of an advertisement, and it is found a successful dodge. But there can be no general resumption till our flood of greenbacks subsides. Congress ought to apply surplus revenue to calling them in and burning so many millions of them per month, instead of using it to extinguish the funded debt that has years to run. . . .

March 7. The College trustees wasted a good deal of time this afternoon in accomplishing nothing, as they usually do on the first Monday of every month. One good thing, however, they succeeded in doing: they abolished the "new system." The merit of daily recitations will henceforth be recorded, and class grades will be determined by the results of the session and the closing examinations together. . . . Gowns (having large and convenient sleeves) are not to be worn at examinations. Our experiment has failed, as I thought it would, because our undergraduates are boys rather than young gentlemen. . . .

March 11. Long session with Cemetery Committee this morning over work on the Trinity Church cemetery made necessary by the opening of the new avenue. This will cost us no one can foresee how much. . . .

Our excellent friend, Dr. Pech, tries one's temper by his want of accuracy in money matters. Herr Fritsch (who sang the tenor part in Mozart's No. 12 so badly) writes me that Dr. Pech promised him $50 for that evening's work and has been putting him off with assurances of speedy payment. We supposed he sang as an amateur, and Dr. Pech had no authority to promise him one cent. Most professional musicians have to live some part of their lives from hand to mouth and nearly all their lives in a Bohemian atmosphere. Hence, they are apt to acquire loose notions about money dealings and to be always ready with a promise to pay anybody anything. But however this may be, Pech must amend his ways if a second season of the Church Music Association is to be attempted. Of course Fritsch must be paid, if pay were promised him.

March 15. Dined yesterday at John Astor's. Present: Astor *père* and William Astor; [Edwards] Pierrepont, the U.S. District Attorney, and Stoughton, his chief antagonist in the unfinished Fullerton case; Romeyn Brodhead, William Hoppin, General Dix, Judge Daly, Sidney Brooks, Carson Brevoort, Southmayd, General McDowell, Dr. Markoe, *cum aliis*. There were one or two more, whom I've forgotten. The dinner was sumptuous, of course.

I discoursed with Brevoort on fish (not from a gastronomic standpoint) and natural history in general. To be more accurate, I turned on the ichthyological faucet and allowed him to irrigate me with information. He is our best authority in that department after Agassiz (who is said to have had a touch of paralysis and to be closing his career); and in addition to what is gained from books, he has stores of knowledge gained by dredging in creeks and bays and deep water and by exploring on "shelving beaches and shallow sands beyond." Talked music with Markoe and Bull Run with McDowell, a subject to which he is very partial. . . .

March 17. We remonstrate with the house, or den of thieves, at Albany against the Broadway "Arcade Railroad" because it would undermine and bring down the Trinity Church steeple. . . .

One Revels, an Ethiop from Mississippi (or perhaps only a mulatto or octoroon), has been making a speech in his place as U.S. Senator. Ten years ago we should have thought a Feejee president not more absurdly improbable. The world does move, and the arrogant folly of Southern swashbucklers and fanatics in 1860 and 1861 gave it a shove such as it had not felt for centuries. The French Revolution took more time, and its causes had been longer at work. O Jeff Davis, ain't this a go? What do you think of the "genman" who sits in your seat and represents your own—your be-yutious, your chivalr-r-r-ric—state? To this have all your intriguings and blusterings and proclamations and conscriptions come at last! . . .

March 18. At the Trust Company I heard of G. C. Verplanck's death, at nine-fifteen this morning, at the Everett House. So said a letter from his grandson to David Thompson. He was eighty-four, according to this evening's *Post*; I had thought him older. He was taken off by a brief attack of diarrhea. The news surprises no one, for he has seemed of late somewhat failing. I met him last with the Life and Trust Company on March 1, and we had some little talk. He did not appear more infirm than he has at any time these two years. Verplanck will be missed, especially in art circles. He was the founder of the Century Club. In the Trinity Church vestry, his good sense and great experience made him useful. Yet it not infrequently happened that his judgment and sagacity would suddenly fail him all at once, and he would bring forward some utterly unpractical and absurd measure, which he would advocate temperately and candidly, and which would, out of respect for him, be sent to some committee and never heard of any more. His range of scholarship was wide and included many odd corners and byways of literature. He liked to expatiate on such forgotten books as *Alexander ab Alexandro,* the *Satyre Ménippée,* and so on, and did so without appearing pedantic. He always treated me with a degree of consideration that I thought flattering, and I have heard of his saying sundry very civil things about me. . . .

March 20.   Verplanck's diarrhea attacked him about ten days before his death but did not keep him within doors. The Rev. Cooke met him at Pott & Amery's bookstore last Wednesday. The *World*'s eulogistic obituary says: "It will hardly be credited that he was turned out of the presidency of the Century Club during the war for his political opinions." Such was the bitterness and fanaticism of those days. . . . I, for one, voted (with great regret) to turn him out; and I remember my vote, even at this time, with no shade of remorse. He was a Copperhead of the worst type— hotel-burners, draft-rioters, and consignors of small-pox clothing and bedding excepted. All his social influence and weight of character were thrown into the scale of rebellion. He did all he could to discourage and depreciate our endeavor to suppress it. The Century Club represents more fully than any other organization the intelligence and culture of the city and did right in deposing Mr. Verplanck from its chieftainship. *Vere dignum et justum erat, aequum et salutare.* But those times are forgotten now, except when some organ of moribund Copperheadism tries to recall them; and the memory of old Gulian C. Verplanck will be pleasant to me all the rest of my life.

March 21, MONDAY.   Verplanck had a great funeral at Trinity Church at one o'clock. The church was filled full, and there was a most unusual turnout of the old respectability of New York. Bishop Potter and some twenty presbyters officiated. The vestry attended in a body, walking in the aisle after the clergy and immediately before the coffin. Morgan Dix made a brief address from the pulpit, simple but excellent in manner and substance. The service was choral, and that part of it was omitted which is appointed to be said at the grave. The interment was to be at Fishkill. The lid of the coffin (or "casket," as it's now commonly called) was opened on the church porch. Its occupant looked much younger than for

ten years past and quite free from any painful or repelling expression. . . .
He is a great loss to our vestry and to sundry other boards and trusts and
to what literate society we have in New York. Had he only lived in
Boston, he would have been famous.

The vestry meets specially tomorrow to fill the vacant wardenship.
Some propose to elect me as senior on the list of vestrymen. I care noth-
ing at all about it; and, if anyone else is nominated or wants to be elected,
I shall be happy to withdraw in his favor. . . .

March 22. The Trinity Church vestry met at four, after a brief
session of the Cemetery Committee, and went into an election for warden.
No nominations were made, and there seemed to have been little consultation. Result of the ballot: George T. Strong, 12; General Dix, 2;
Skidmore, 1. I thanked the Parochial Conscript Fathers most briefly for
the honor they had conferred on me and for the personal kindness that
had prompted their choice. They were all very amiable and pleasant
about it after adjournment. It *is* an honor to be a warden of Trinity parish
and to succeed Verplanck. I care little about that; but I might have felt
a shade of mortification, being senior on the list, had anyone been chosen
over my head, unless it had been Cisco or General Dix, whose great
public services give them priority over the rest of us. I wanted General
Dix to serve, and he would have been elected, of course, had he been
willing. . . .

March 28. Something amazing has happened. Ten years ago, while
that accomplished and most impecunious J. W. Mould was building
Trinity Chapel School house, I lent him a couple of hundred dollars till
"day after tomorrow," or "early next week." Of course, he didn't pay,
and, of course, I didn't suppose he ever would, and I troubled myself
little about the matter. Then some rather disreputable proceedings of his
came to light, and as I wished him to avoid this house for the future, I
proceeded to cut him, mildly but firmly. I had nearly forgotten that the
tender tie of debtor and creditor bound us to each other, when a certain
lawyer appeared at my office . . . last Saturday with a check for $340,
being for my loan of $200 with ten years' interest at seven per cent!!!! I
took the principal, but returned the interest. Very glad to get back the
money, but such things are not altogether pleasant. They unsettle one's
convictions—tempt one to doubt first principles and to distrust the
plainest lessons of experience. . . .

March 29. The plug-muss between the two wings or rings of the
city democracy that was looked for last evening didn't come off. Tammany

closed her doors against both and girded herself with a cincture of police-men, several hundred strong. Both sides claim this as a substantial victory. The Tweed gang has refused battle and lost a little prestige. But the other ruffians, gamblers, and dog-fighters, calling themselves the Young Democracy, have lost time and will probably be bought up in detail. . . .

With Ellie and the youngsters to Academy of Music. *Oberon* rendered here for the first time in my day. Parepa-Rosa troupe. English text. Mme. Parepa-Rosa as Regia, and pretty little Mrs. Seguin as Fatima. They were both good; the former was superb. "Ocean, thou mighty monster" was gloriously rendered. None of the principals was below par. The orchestra was much too weak, and the chorus had only thirty. They did their work fairly well, however. I was, of course, comparing this with the execution of the same work by the Church Music Association last January. Our chorus and orchestra beat the opera troupe out of sight, but their quartette leaves ours nowhere. The quartette, "Over the dark blue waters," was rendered with amazing force and neatness. It's worth care-ful rendering, for there are few finer things of the kind extant. The "mounting" of the opera, which ought to be most elaborate and costly, was contemptible. The "transformation scenes" and fairy work in which it abounds were produced in the crudest way. But the opera, heard by us all for the first time as a whole, is most brilliant and full of deep expres-sion. Almost every "number" is a gem. Even the comic work of Scher-asmee and Fatima is unaffected and good—far beyond that of Papageno and Papagena in the *Zauberflöte*, if one may venture to think so. Weber died too soon, before his creative power was exhausted. In certain points, *Oberon* transcends *Der Freischütz*, though it contains but one movement, "Spirits of Earth and Air and Sea," that can be accurately weighed against the weird music of that opera. . . .

Died at San Francisco of apoplexy, General [George H.] Thomas, one of Grant's greatest lieutenants, ranking near Sheridan and Sherman. At West Point years ago, he seemed a grave, heavy kind of man, not at all interesting. But at Chickamauga, Franklin, and Nashville he made himself very interesting, indeed.

March 31. The New York Club has decided to dissolve. It has lost caste of late, and many members have resigned. Of the residuum of habitués, the great majority were sporting men and fast, young stock-gamblers. Its splendid drawing-rooms and conservatory were as perilous for a well-mannered young man as any drinking saloon or gambling house in the city. The administration of the presidency of my old classmate Harry Ward is blamed for this. Gross cases of rowdyism and drunken brutality have occurred within the club, and he is charged with endeavoring successfully to shield all offenders of that kind from discipline. So things have gone from bad to worse. The dissolution of the club will be a blow to him, for in it he has lived and moved and had his being for nearly twenty years, I think.

April 9. . . . McFarland's trial for murder of Richardson last fall is in progress.[8] The impudence of his leading counsel, John Graham, seems even more flagrant and bolder than it was on the trial of Pete Strong's case five years ago. Were I called as a juror in a case in which that beast was concerned, I should plead, as an excuse for serving, that I could not possibly render his client impartial justice—so repulsive to me is his unscrupulous audacity of assertion and of foul speech. He has reached the lowest depth attained by any advocate of our time, and is *anti*-professional rather than merely *un*-professional. But McFarland will be triumphantly acquitted of this seemingly deliberate homicide because of "provocation" (of remote date) and consequent "insanity," and also because of the change effected in peoples' feelings by the performance of Beecher and Frothingham.

April 11. This is Mr. Ruggles's seventieth birthday. He dined here with Miss Julia and Miss Rosalie Ruggles, old Mrs. Bostwick, Mr. and Mrs. D. C. Murray, John Sherwood, Murray Hoffman, Jr., and Jack Ehninger. I was obliged to quit the dinner table at an early stage and hasten to a vestry meeting. . . .

April 13. . . . Died, Mrs. William H. McVickar, daughter of old Thaddeus Phelps deceased, and mother of our lively little friend, Miss Kitty. She died at a little country house near Stamford, whither McVickar had retreated after the collapse of his fortunes and slowly starved to death by some enteric disease that made nutrition impossible. . . .

April 15. . . . There are discords at Rome, and the existence of a semi-mutinous minority is notorious, though the Roman press is gagged and

[8] This was the trial of Daniel McFarland, a partially-demented drunkard, for the killing of Albert D. Richardson, noted journalist and chief correspondent of the New York *Tribune* during the Civil War, over the former's divorced wife, Abby Sage McFarland. (See the diary for December 4, 1869.) The shooting occurred in the *Tribune* office. Strong's disgust was founded chiefly on the then common prejudice against divorce. There was widespread condemnation of Henry Ward Beecher and Octavius Brooks Frothingham for having married Mrs. McFarland to the dying Richardson. As a Fenian and a Tammany supporter, McFarland was fairly certain to be acquitted.

the Roman post-office is untrustworthy.[9] The congregated Fathers are
allowed to meet only under oaths of secrecy, which is more appropriate
to a lodge of Freemasons or a Carlist club than to a *soi-disant* general
council of the Church Catholic. But the *infallibilisti* and the *Gesuitanti*—
the "ring" of Rome—will prevail in spite of a few independent thinkers. . . .

April 17, EASTER SUNDAY. . . . Braem seems much gratified by his
election—or rather, by his nomination—to Trinity Church vestry. Vinton
was anxious that one Spencer, a justice of the Superior Court and a
regular attendant at Trinity, should be put on the ticket. What we hear
of his personal character seems in his favor. But when his name was
brought up at our little conference on Thursday week, his position on
the bench was held a fatal objection to him. He must have been put there
with the approval of the Ring and is, therefore, open to violent suspicion
of being everything a vestryman of Trinity Church should not be. The
objection is unanswerable, but what an illustration it is of the degradation
of this city! A seat on the bench of the Superior Court, where Duer and
Oakley sat twenty years ago, is now *prima facie* evidence of dishonesty
and has become a disqualification for any office connected with the administration of an important religious trust.

April 19. . . . Died, Philip Hone, my classmate at school and college.
. . . Poor Phil Hone, as I remember him in 1833 or thereabouts, must
have been among the handsomest or prettiest boys that ever lived. He
used to "speak pieces" very nicely at school, but that was all he could do.
He, Fred Anthon, and Jack Duer were great cronies. Tom Cooper, who
had ability which he wasted, used to consort with them in a patronizing
way. All four are gone. Tom fell in The Wilderness, doubtless fighting
hard, for he had plenty of pluck.

April 27. . . . The Albany banditti have dispersed, but not without
passing the Arcade Railroad bill. Will Hoffman, the captain of the gang,
have the courage to sign it? Can the corporators comply with the terms
of their charter? Can they get the money, to begin with? Will Trinity
steeple tumble down? . . .

May 2. [Mrs. Strong had been ill since May 1 with stomach cramp.]
It is twelve-ten. Ellie is easy, but I fear it is only because she is satu-
rated with morphine. I shall not undress tonight. The vigilant Lizzie

[9] Pope Pius IX had in 1869 convened at the Vatican the first general council of his
church since the Council of Trent. Nearly 800 churchmen attended, and out of their
discussions was born (July, 1870) the dogma of papal infallibility. A minority of prelates protested in heated terms, and part of the church rejected the dogma.

mounts guard and will rouse me if I be needed. God preserve us from all perils and dangers of this night!

May 3. . . . Peters tells me that F. B. Cutting is probably dying from disease of the heart. There are those who will express surprise at hearing that he had any heart, for he is held to have been a hard, cold, cruel man in all his business relations, grasping and oppressive beyond the dreams of common selfishness.

May 5. It is five in the afternoon. Peters says Ellie is "doing nicely" —would to Heaven I saw it. She has just been obliged to take more morphine and more chloroform by return of pain. I am profoundly unhappy. . . .

May 6. These are most wretched days. I have never known Ellie to suffer so terribly, and I am anxious and frightened from minute to minute, notwithstanding Dr. Peters's favorable prognosis. He says her suffering is mainly "nervous," but that does not mitigate its intensity. . . .

May 10. . . . I think there can be no doubt that Ellie is much better tonight, thank God. Her nerves are quieted. She is like herself again, asks about her friends, likes a quiet little talk, enjoys her infinitesimal rations of beef tea and milk toast, and suffers from weakness only. She has been remarkably free from feverishness all the time. . . .

May 11. . . . The homicidal McFarland is acquitted, of course. The trial disgraces everyone concerned in it. The counsel and court stink harmonious in the nostrils of mankind, but I fear they are good enough for this community. There was a long narrative in this morning's *Tribune* from Mrs. McFarland—well written, temperate, and seemingly candid. It reads like a fair statement, and puts the case in a new light. The Illinois divorce was wrong and bad, of course, but this poor woman was, according to her own story (which fits in with the evidence), so tormented, bullied, badgered, insulted, beaten, and generally outraged by her drunken, half-crazy husband that she may be pardoned, or at least but gently censured for any proceeding by which she could be freed from him under color of the law.

May 13. A wretchedly anxious day. Ellie was very miserable this morning after a restless night. Peters talked of asking Flint or Van Buren "to see her just once," as they might suggest something to make her recovery more rapid. "No other reason whatever." This was not pleasant. Then he prescribed pills containing a little mercury, which have made her unhappy all day. I thought he would have to come to that at last. The obstinate dull pain and soreness on the right side indicate trouble in her liver. Peters calls it "engorgement." The pulse does not point to acute inflammation. Tonight she is easier, but it's under morphine. God help us.

We have just closed the Law School examination. Our charitable committee decided to pass all the candidates—seventy-two—except the unfortunate Hessberg, who doesn't know what a bill of exchange is, a note, a bailment, a mortgage, a reversion, or anything else that we can discover. He has passed the Supreme Court examination and is understood to be a rising practitioner in justice courts downtown. . . .

Poor Ellie, how I wish I could take her place so that she could endure all this suffering by proxy! It would be a most desirable change if only because she feels disease so much more keenly than I do. Peters has left a scribbled note for me, saying that there is "no danger," which is kind of him, but I am frightened and anxious. . . .

May 14. . . . I believe that our execrable organ grinders watch for houses where doctors' gigs stop and tune up their screeching, braying, scrannel pipes under the windows so that they may be bought off. They infest our sidewalk. I have come near a single combat with two or three of the wretches. "Ten cent, sare—I go away." With three classes of men I confess myself not in Christian charity: (1) Northern Copperheads of 1861–1865; (2) gentlemen elected to office by the people of this city; (3) organ grinders.

May 15, SUNDAY. . . . I looked through the Hon. Benjamin Disraeli's novel, *Lothair,* which was anxiously expected and doubtless more extensively read than any new novel ever has been, unless possibly some of Dickens's. My judgment is that the book is bosh embodied in slip-slop English. But it introduces one to genteel society—for example, dukes with country seats on the scale of Versailles and princes of the Levant descended from Byzantine emperors. Its object seems to be anti-Romanism. There is a good deal of twaddle about the Aryan race, Semitism, and the "Madre Natura" (a secret society at least eighteen hundred years old), and some hints of the "Asian Mystery" of *Tancred* and *Coningsby.* The illustrious British swells with whom the hero consorts talk about their "mutual ancestry," and are "very pleased" with themselves and with each other. The writer's worship of rank, family, and landed wealth is painfully conspicuous and suggests a social culture characteristic of a parvenu or—may one venture to say it?—a snob.

May 16. . . . Hoffman vetoes the Arcade Railroad Bill. Good for him. Were he not allied with so much pure scoundrelism, he would probably shew himself a remarkably decent man for a politician. . . .

May 17. . . . Voted this morning, *pro forma*, being well aware that any number of repeaters would be produced to neutralize my vote should it seem likely to affect the result and endanger the scoundrel rule of Tammany. Both the Court of Appeals tickets are respectable, by the by; there is not much choice between them. . . .

The Greenwich Street elevated railroad tumbled down yesterday on being tested by a trial car. . . .

May 18. Ellie continues to improve, not very fast, but fast enough to justify us in thinking her on the road to convalescence. She was well enough this evening to send messages by me to certain of her friends whom I was to see at the [Church Music Association] concert.

The concert terminated at ten minutes before eleven and was what General Vinton called it, a "pyramidal success." The house was very full and of the "best" sort of people. The temperature was judiciously mitigated. Few went away before the last note of the finale. Expressions of approval were very strong; the audience was far more applausive than at the first two concerts. It would have encored Leggett's "Ruler of This Awful Hour" had the conductor permitted. Pity Leggett is such a Yahoo. After nice little Mrs. Brown's grand scene, the plaudits were long and irrepressible. Indeed, she sang it magnificently, with perfect aplomb, expression, and truth; and her beautiful, fresh quality of voice is quite beyond Parepa's. . . . Pech will go to sleep tonight in a nightcap of glory. The great Watson of the *Art Journal* had never heard such a chorus in America last March. Now he has never heard its equal anywhere. . . .

There was a Democratic victory yesterday, of course. The Republicans are apathetic. In this city it is said to have been the most fraudful election on record. Gangs of repeaters paraded the streets, working openly and unchallenged. The echoes of Albany and Tammany "roll from poll to poll and cheat for ever and for ever." Very free institutions are ours!

May 19. . . . Had a long talk with the Reverend Barnard and the Reverend Haight this afternoon over College affairs. The Cooper Union project lingers along, like a spider half-stung by a wasp for deposit in her nest—alive, and that's all. Our treasurer is the wasp. He considers it his official duty to devise objections and difficulties wherewith "not to do" anything that promises to develop and strengthen us if it involve expenditure of money, even though it bring us back, as this arrangement surely would, tenfold our outlay. He means right, but his influence is for evil, and his official position makes his influence potent. . . .

May 21. . . . The Church Music Association subscription papers (for a projected second season) have been issued, and more will go forth next week. . . .

May 22, SUNDAY. . . . The Hon. Clarkson Potter called this morning; he is on leave from Washington.[10] He says that the odious inquisitorial, demoralizing, unequal, unconstitutional income tax will *not* be repealed or essentially modified. Only about 287,000 taxable incomes are returned in all from the whole country! Of course, all who evade the tax like to see it continued. The Hon. Clarkson Potter is exercised about "centralizing tendencies," and thinks the dominant party means to commit Congress to a general incorporating policy—the granting of charters to railroads, banks, manufacturing companies, and so on. This, he predicts, will bring to Washington the greatest lobby ever heard of and make that city even as Harrisburg and Albany; and so the government of the whole country will be upon the shoulders of a few monster corporations—perhaps. I don't see why an average railroad president should be much worse than Mr. Jem Brooks or the Hon. Mr. Morrissey.

May 24. . . . Wonders have not ceased. Had a visit this afternoon from Bergner, Boehm, and another gentleman of the Philharmonic Orchestra and board of management. They want me to take the presidency of their Society, which it seems Doremus has resigned on account of some miff or tiff. I told them I knew absolutely nothing about the technicalities of music and had no qualifications whatever for the place. But they were urgent, and I agreed to think of it. I called on Edmund Schermerhorn after dinner to confer on the subject. He thinks it could do no possible harm to the Church Music Association—it might do good. . . .

May 25. . . . There was a meeting of the trustees of Leake and Watts at ten o'clock at the fluent and venerable Fred DePeyster's house, 76 University Place. . . . I was interested to see on the walls of DePeyster's drawing rooms a colored crayon sketch of Miss Emily Hone, now Mrs. Frederick Foster. When I was a Sophomore and used to go to her brother John Hone's house in Bond Street, I occasionally saw this young personage, then, I suppose, a young lady of eighteen or twenty. I never spoke to her in my life, but I was during several months horribly in love with

[10] Clarkson N. Potter, New York attorney, was in Congress 1869–1875 and 1877–1879, on the Democratic side.

her. The portrait is that of a very pretty girl. Is there any emotion in life exactly like that with which a young pup of fifteen regards a graceful, attractive girl who is his elder by two or three years? . . .

The newspapers say the Fenians have broken out again and are concentrating on the frontier for an invasion of Canada. . . .

May 26, THURSDAY. Our experimental Ascension Day orchestra at Trinity succeeded beyond my hopes. The service was communion and began at eleven. There were twenty-eight in the orchestra, of which sixteen played stringed instruments, and the whole orchestra was judiciously reinforced by bass diapasons of the nave organ. Of course the brass was too strong; the trumpet and trombone glared through the violin work as does a conflagration through lace window curtains. The choir and orchestra kept together wonderfully well, considering their remoteness from each other. The former seemed to me a little timid— awed by the new color and richness of sound against which they had to sing. . . . Everyone seemed pleased. Murray Hoffman . . . was delighted and so were . . . certain ladies from the Low Church parishes who happened to attend. Few of the congregation expected this novelty. It was the first time anything like an orchestra has accompanied an Anglican church service in New York. May it not be the last. I'm told something of the kind was done in Baltimore. . . .

Astonishing how much more effective church music is when it is rendered as part of a service than when it is better performed and on a larger scale in a concert room. This innovation will probably be denounced, but it is easy to defend. Within our own day, the village choir of many a New England Congregational meetinghouse has been supported by a 'cello and a flute instead of a papistical "chest full of whistles." . . .

Accounts of the movements of the bold Fenians are a little obscure, but it seems certain that a column marching from Vermont crossed the Canadian line and found itself in the presence of a strongly posted corps of British minions. It gave the sunburst of Erin to the gale. Its general (John O'Neill) harangued his undaunted band of patriots. The subordinate in command of his "skirmish line" responded in a few remarks of the flowering species. The patriots "preceded their chief to glory," whereupon the U.S. marshal and his police bagged the chief. He remonstrated and called attention to the fact that he had an army at hand, but was told that his captors were armed; whereupon he submitted, was bundled into a Rockaway wagon, driven rapidly off the red field of fight, and incarcerated at Burlington to await the action of the grand jury. Then there was firing "for an hour." Three, or else two, martyrs were promoted to positions in the calendar of Celtic patriotism. The rest ran away and, at last accounts, had recrossed the lines much demoralized and wanted to go home—if they only had money to pay their railroad fares. Very bad for the hen roosts of northern Vermont. . . .

The Church Music Association subscription amounts to $2,550, with an unfruitful prospect. I despond of a second season but shall do my little best to secure it. . . .

On May 31, Strong received formal notification of his unanimous election as president of the Philharmonic Society. Though gratified at the honor, especially as it had pleased Mrs. Strong, he accepted the new duties without enthusiasm. Anxiety over his wife's illness made him "far too blue to go heartily into any new work."

June 2. Ellie is certainly not quite so well this morning. Nausea threatened to return but was checked by a teaspoonful of brandy and no morphine. Then she slept soundly for nearly three hours and woke languid and heavy. Peters will bring Van Buren at three this afternoon. . . . The weather is gloomy and oppressive. These are miserable times. Heaven help us. . . .

My good friend, Van Buren, with Peters, made a thorough inspection this afternoon. He agrees with Peters that she is doing well and that the treatment is all right, but he tells me that she must have been in considerable danger. He thinks the point of suppuration is passed. I have had a feeling all day, perhaps improper in a layman, that this attack was more formidable and serious than Peters considered it. . . . Dear old Van Buren, how good and genial he was this afternoon—kindly and vivacious. One leans against Van Buren as against a rock. It's not only because he is wise in therapeutics, but because he is so thoroughbred a gentleman. One feels that every word he says is the word of an expert who would disdain to disguise any doubt in the language of quackery, who tells you what he knows of the case, and pretends to do no more. . . .

June 3. . . . At three this afternoon, the seven Philharmonic and Teutonic directors (members of the board of directors) met in the library and sat an hour and a half. There were Bergner, Matzka, Mosenthal, Herwig, Bergmann, Boehm, and another whose name I could not make out. I presided with dignity. Certain routine business was despatched, and we talked over the question of "reserved seats" without coming to a decision. Funny to see the deference with which these gentlemen treat me as "president"—each one of them having more capacity and knowledge pertinent to our purposes in his little fingernail than I have in my whole body, brains, and boots. . . .

June 9. . . . Received, with surprise, a formal note from George Anthon enclosing one of condolence and kind wishes addressed to Ellie. . . . It's my first communication from him, oral or written, for two years; and never was an intimacy so long as ours smashed on grounds so trivial or by perversity more babyish. Of course, I returned a civil answer. Charley Strong says that George, my *ci-devant* Pylades, avers that he has "made advances to me which were not met." I do not know what he means; I never heard of any advances. But when he is put out with any-body—with or without reason—his mind, memory, and understanding (and his memory, in particular) fail him for all purposes connected with the disagreement. I have often noticed the phenomenon; it's a feature of the strongly-marked Anthon constitution. . . .

This evening's *Post* gives me a superior puff as president of the Phil-harmonic and refers to the "wide art influence" I "wield." Heaven help art. . . .

June 10. . . . My usual omnibus companion, the *Evening Post,* an-nounced the news by telegram that Charles Dickens died yesterday at Gadshill soon after a shock of paralysis—an event in literary history. Since 1837 he has reigned by popular vote as monarch of prose fiction. His genius was unquestionable; his art and method were often worthy the lowest writer of serials for Sunday papers—as witness "Monks," Rose Dartle, Mrs. Dombey, the Sagacious Dustman in *Our Mutual Friend* (name forgotten), old Martin Chuzzlewit, the preposterous brothers Cheeryble, and others. Few men since Shakespeare have en-riched the language with so many phrases that are in everyone's mouth. His *Edwin Drood,* now appearing in numbers (said to be complete in MS), promises better than anything he has produced for many years. But he could never have written anything hereafter possessing the fresh-ness and vigor of *Pickwick, Oliver Twist, Nicholas Nickleby,* and the *Christmas Carol.* I think Dickens's name will live long, but one cannot tell. When I was a small boy, I used to hear a great deal said about "Doctor Syntax," but what mortal can now find a gleam of fun in its vapid doggerel and vulgar prints? So with "Tom and Jerry," now un-endurable. Perhaps Sam Weller, the Artful Dodger, Little Nell, Paul

Dombey, Mr. Pecksniff, and Mr. Bumble will share their fate, but they are likely to survive for a century or so. It would be well for Dickens's chance of "immortality" if a few stupid, wooden puppets, such as Lady Dedlock and Mr. Tulkinghorn, could be eliminated from his works and put into the fire. . . . I feel Charles Dickens's death as that of a personal friend, though I never even saw him and though there was so much coarseness and flabbiness in his style of work.

June 13. Ellie improves, but her strength returns by very slow degrees. She has made no progress today and has been in a rather depressed, despairing way, without much reason. . . .

At Trinity Church vestry tonight; full house. Debate on the question whether we should receive this year our share of the money voted (most importantly) by the legislature to churches maintaining free schools. The same ground was gone over last year. General Dix, Nash, and I spoke in favor of receiving it; Ogden contra, and Dunscomb made a muddled speech on the same side. But the proposition was carried. . . .

We put a stop to one of the Rev. Vinton's arrogant freaks. People have long been in the habit of getting up and marching quietly out of church after service and when he was about to invade the pulpit. They did not want their bellies filled by the eastwind of his flatulent, pompous, bad rhetoric. So he recently ordered his regulation closing the church doors before and during service strictly enforced, thereby subjecting the estimable sexton Augustus and his myrmidons to actions for false imprisonment. People could not come into church and could not escape from it; his fiat. We set it aside tonight by an informal but unanimous vote, which will not appear on the minutes.

June 21. Returning from Catskill at half-past seven last evening, there appeared unto me Mrs. George T. Strong promoted to a dressing gown and the second story Blue Room, and much stronger and better than when I left town. *Laus Deo.* . . . At four I found Ellie bent on a little experimental drive, which Dr. Peters had authorized, though perhaps not very explicitly. I dubitated but acquiesced; so she was wrapped in an opera cloak and her head swathed in a "nuby," and we drove up Fifth Avenue and about a mile into the Park and back again. The watchful and true Lizzie was with us. Then Ellie sat with us and with Miss Rosalie at dinner and received Miss Louise Catlin and Jack Ehninger in the Blue Room; also with Miss Rosalie till near ten. If there be no backsliding tomorrow from this exertion and fatigue, I shall feel as if her convalescence were fully established.

On Thursday, June 16, at nine in the morning, we left the foot of Thirty-fourth Street on the *Chauncey Vibbard.* Nice boat; well appointed, civil attendance, feeding arrangements, A-1. Hot day, but Temple and I sat mostly in the bow, with a strong tonic breeze in our faces, and enjoyed our voyage. . . .

Saturday, a northwest wind, but clear, intense heat. Walked with Temple to the falls by the road. He was much impressed by the ravine and by the upward view from the foot of the lower fall—a most dearly beloved locality. An inscription carved on the rock "In Memory of Vite, the Bayard of Dogs," who was killed in 1868 by leaping from the platform above the upper fall at his master's thoughtless signal to "jump," and fell 180 feet. Why "Bayard"? and why not, rather, the Marcus Curtius or Sam Patch of Dogs? I never heard of Bayard's executing any remarkable jump. "Vite's" owner was doubtless a man of "sensibility" and sentiment, but the Catskill stonecutter's bill of $200 remains unpaid to this day. . . .

Down the mountain Monday, at eight in the morning, in a carriage with Templein, Mrs. Nicoll, her son, and her son-in-law—nice kindly folk. On the steamer *Chauncey Vibbard* at eleven-thirty. Had a pleasant run down the river with Mr. and Mrs. George Schuyler. . . .

June 22. . . . Pech tells me the grand monster Beethoven Festival had proved a financial failure. The Festival owes him several hundred dollars for services as conductor, as per contract, which he considers a bad debt. . . .

June 25, SATURDAY. . . . Had to go up to Forty-ninth Street (College) at three. A long car or omnibus ride of heat and discomfort seemed to me actually perilous; so I was lavish and took a carriage. Even that was a severe experience of caloric. A little business in the library, and then inspected the president's house, as one of a special Committee on Repairs (the other members whereof made default, and small blame to them in weather like this). Subjected to a heavy fire of talk by Marm Barnard. . . .

Senate rejects, by vote of three to two, the clause in the House bill which renews the execrable income tax. May the majority have grace to stand firm, for that unequal, demoralizing, inquisitorial, unconstitutional tax would almost justify insurrection. But it passed the House, three to one; so we are not yet quite safe. The *Tribune, World,* and *Post,* which seldom agree about anything, concur in lauding the Senate.

June 27. . . . Trinity Church Music Committee at vestry office this afternoon. Agreed with the Odells for a new organ for St. Paul's; $6,000.

The ugly but ancient case is to be retained. . . . My resolution of reference as to "increased effectiveness of musical services" on high festivals was considered; and we agreed, without the least hesitation, to recommend an orchestra at the church on Christmas, Easter, Ascension Day, and Trinity Sunday. . . .

Died yesterday, Francis B. Cutting, aged sixty-five; a hard man but a good lawyer. He was a favorite student of my father's. . . .

June 28. This weather keeps poor Ellie sadly down. She has been weaker today and quite forlorn. Jem arrived today on the *Russia* and had a long talk with her in the bedroom, which rather set her up and cheered her. So did certain Paris bonnets and muliebral gimcracks, kindly given her by Jem and by her mamma. . . .

They say there was a small earthquake on Saturday at seven in the evening, "confined to the East side of the city below Fourteenth Street" —a most discreet earthquake. . . .

July 1. . . . Took a carriage at two, with Sackett of the Cemetery Committee and Duncan, our chief clerk, and drove to Trinity Cemetery at 155th Street, in spite of threatening weather. How that region has changed since the days when I knew every foot of the beautiful old Bloomingdale Road! It is now to give place to the new and ambitious "Boulevard." Inspected the cemetery grounds—well kept—and especially the "Boulevard" gulf over which we may decide to throw a bridge. Home by the Third Avenue. Growth and expansion of the East Side of the town is marvellous. . . .

Johnny went to Cornwall this afternoon with 'cello, insect net, and all. He is full of the Greek Prize of next year (*Seven Against Thebes*); and I have ordered through Scribner a long list of editions of Aeschylus— treatises on Greek metres, and so on—recommended by Professor Drisler. I don't expect him to succeed, but I rejoice at the interest he shews in the undertaking. Were there a prize for proficiency cn the 'cello or the piano or for clear appreciation of the aesthetics of music, I would bet high on Signor Giovannuccio. Bergner says he promises to make an excellent amateur violoncellist. He reads difficult piano music fairly well, and I listen to his criticism on any performance—orchestral or choral— with great respect and deference. His preference for the best music— and for Beethoven's and Mozart's above all—is strong and genuine. "Tolerable" music he will not tolerate. As for the Italians, he utterly renounces, defies, and abhors them and all their works.

July 2. . . . The Senate has backslidden on the income tax question, and there is a prospect of its reinfliction for two years; in which event, the Republican party will lose *one* vote. I only wish I were 50,000 voters judiciously distributed through several states. Much clamor among Republicans just now because of certain changes in the city appointments. Moses H. Grinnell goes out of the customhouse and one Murphy goes in,[11] and so forth. The *Times* and *Post* open heavy fire on Grant. He is "obstinate, wholly without judgment, gradually losing public confidence," and so on. But during the two years before April, 1865, we heard many such criticisms of Grant. . . .

July 4. An uncommonly pleasant Fourth. Ellie seems almost herself again and was singing at the piano this evening trying over old songs. Weather has been perfect, and there has been nothing like the din one expects on this day of pyrotechny and pistol-firing. It certainly seems as though the traditional usage of making this anniversary hateful with noise were dying out. May posterity be thankful for the improvement.

Temple and Louis and their well-mannered little playmate, Franky Conlon (a brother of Lizzy and Mary), had a good time in the yard between the two houses with their little crackers, among which were no "columbiads" (they were not asked for); and in the evening, we burned a few Roman candles and pinwheels and spent the day in the dining room balcony, overlooking their performances. . . .

July 10, SUNDAY. Ellie has vastly improved. Drives daily in the Park, and received two or three of our friends—Colden Murray, Murray Hoffman, Jr., and Lawrence—downstairs this evening. Sound of voices and laughter from the parlor was like the restoration of some pleasant usage of very old times now nearly forgotten. Dr. Keyes spent part of the evening with me. . . .

July 11. . . . Trinity Church vestry met here at two o'clock; about a dozen with the Rector. . . . Our Music Committee recommendations, including that for orchestral services on four of the high festivals, passed *nem. con.*!!! . . .

A war cloud has arisen in Europe, which has knocked down all securities in the markets of Paris and elsewhere, and has knocked up gold here. Spain chooses a Hohenzollern prince to fill its vacant and uncomfortable throne. Louis Napoleon warns Bismarck that France will not tolerate a

---

[11] Roscoe Conkling, now influential with President Grant, was responsible for putting Thomas Murphy—a very "gamey" politician—in charge of the Custom House; and Murphy soon filled it with Conkling henchmen and an odor of corruption.

Prussian kingdom on her southern frontier. Bismarck replies: "What is the matter? *We* have nothing to do with this business. Settle it with Spain. We haven't got anything to do with any Hohenzollern princes. Go away and let us alone." This answer seems to have been thought unsatisfactory, for France is arming in hot haste.

July 13. . . . Death of Admiral Dahlgren.[12]

The Hispano-Gallico-Prussia embroilment seems likely to be settled without venesection. Yesterday there was a beastly riot uptown. A procession of Orangemen held a picnic . . . with their wives and children. They were set upon by a swarm of base and brutal Celts, such as those who burned orphan asylums and got up a Negro massacre in July, 1863. The police intervened with good effect. Many Celts were knocked on the head; but many men, women, and children of the assaulted party were killed or cruelly mauled and maimed. Pity there was no grapeshot for the assailants. Execrable Celtic *canaille*! The gorilla is their superior in muscle and hardly their inferior in moral sense.

July 14. Very hot. Busy day downtown. Don Giovannuccio appeared unexpectedly at dinnertime. . . . Cable reports the dogma of infallibility carried 450 to 88. Amen. Its promulgation will not help the papacy. The war cloud across the ocean is rising and blackening; a severe storm seems imminent. Denmark, Holland, Belgium, Austria, and Spain may be caught in it. If there be war, I think it will be chargeable to the ruffianism that's so characteristic of Napoleonic France. On the demand of France, the Prussian candidate for the very uncomfortable crown of Spain withdraws his pretensions. Whereupon, France calls on Prussia to promise that no other Prussian princeling shall ever think of accepting a like offer —and to promise forthwith or fight.

July 15. . . . *France declared war today*, and Prussia seems eager to pick up the gage of battle.[13] Louis Napoleoniculus drags half of Europe into a whirlpool of carnage in the hope that some splendid success may drive his Mexican failure out of the memories of Frenchmen and so

[12] John A. B. Dahlgren (1809–1870), inventor of the Dahlgren gun, who had cooperated with Sherman in the capture of Savannah.

[13] Precise dates may be noted. On July 12, Madrid announced that Prince Leopold had voluntarily revoked his acceptance of the Spanish throne, and peace seemed safe. On the 13th, the French government arrogantly demanded a formal promise from the King of Prussia that he would never permit a Hohenzollern to ask for the throne of Spain; Bismarck edited the Ems telegram dealing with the affair; news of an apparent rebuff to the French minister reached Paris on July 14; and such a warlike frenzy at once arose that Napoleon III and his council decided on war, which the French parliament declared on the 15th with only ten negative votes.

strengthen his "dynasty." It is for the sake of the poor little Prince Imperial—just about Temple's age and doubtless a nice, innocent child—that so many tons of shells are about to be fired, so many volleys of grape delivered, so many peaceful country houses harried, and so many brave men slain.

England will keep out of the mess, if possible, for fighting costs money. But should she be compelled to take sides, she will make her choice as the interests of her trade may direct. Sordid old England has no principles now, save those that can be defined by examination of the ledger. Spain seems to have no interest in the matter. Were she to count herself in, France would merely be obliged to keep a corps of observations near the Pyrenees and give her strong ironclad navy a little easy work blockading Spanish ports. Austria will, I fear, be inclined to ally herself with France against north Germany.

July 16. France and Prussia seem to be straining every nerve in order to gain the initiative. Frenchmen and Teutons are individually full of wrath and of mutually homicidal impulses. Strange that François, the Paris *ouvrier*, should be suddenly inspired with such hate for Fritz, the Berlin street sweeper, that he would like to go and shoot Fritz at the risk of getting shot himself. There is no such question between them as that which stirred up the New Yorker against the Charlestonian ten years ago.

A probable but not fully authenticated report that Louis Napoleon has withdrawn his corps of occupation from Rome and that the city is in revolutionary ferment. The expulsion of Pius IX from the Vatican would have no logical bearing on the dogma of infallibility. It would merely prove that infallibility and omnipotence do not go together, as one would think they should.

July 17, SUNDAY. Heat most baleful. Did nothing all day but sit still and sweat. . . . I feed our dear little Gramercy Park sparrows every afternoon now from the library windows. A handful of cracked corn thrown into the street brings them together like so many chickens. They are pleasant neighbours. At daylight every morning, their earnest twittering begins—so earnest that it seems like squabbling. Poor Ellie used to take great comfort, even while severely ill, in hearing their clamor during weary wakeful morning watches.

July 19. . . . Gold is 121 plus. Report that old Judge Vanderpoel died this afternoon. . . . Paris is furious because London newspapers side with Prussia. We are not the only thin-skinned people extant.

July 21.   France and Prussia are dilatory in coming to blows. People here are impatient for exciting news of carnage and begin to say in school-boy phrase that "one's afraid and t'other darsen't." I guess that free hemorrhage will set in soon enough, and copiously. Yesterday, about one in the morning, the new French Minister M. Prévost-Paradol, shot himself in Washington, with premeditation it would seem. Cause— worry, anxiety, overwork, caloric, and disappointment at the new aspect of affairs in France. I cannot wonder that any Parisian banished to Washington for an indefinite period should feel promptings to suicide after a week there, especially a week of high-pressure July. A single walk on Pennsylvania Avenue from the White House with the thermometer at 100° would demonstrate the worthlessness and the misery of existence in that region. Mr. Ruggles saw much of M. Prévost-Paradol in Paris, liked him, and gave him a letter to me, which he was to have presented next fall.

The thunderbolt of war had fallen upon Europe suddenly and unexpectedly. The previous winter and spring there had been talk in Paris and Berlin of disarmament pari passu, *and the British ambassador to Prussia, supported by Lord Clarendon in the Foreign Office, had hoped for an exchange of pledges and guarantees. Then Clarendon had died. Bismarck showed a chilly attitude toward arms reduction, and Napoleon III was openly laboring to effect an alliance of France and Austria. Nevertheless, Europe in June, 1870, seemed enjoying a halcyon lull, when one Sunday the French government received word from Madrid that General Prim, who was directing Spanish affairs, proposed to put Prince Leopold of the House of Hohenzollern upon the Spanish throne. Already a Hohenzollern had become monarch in Rumania, or at least a sort of monarch. Every informed man knew that Napoleon III would not permit a Prussian prince to take charge of Spain, and that if Madrid and Berlin insisted on the project, war would result. The French ambassador was hurried to Ems, where the King of Prussia was taking the waters. He saw the king twice, and although William refused to insist that Leopold withdraw, the situation was soon given a peaceful turn by the young man's voluntary withdrawal of his candidacy. All seemed well. But then the French government made a blunder which played into Bismarck's hands. It sent a new demand to the King of Prussia—he must guarantee that the Hohenzollerns would not resume their aspirations for the Spanish throne. This was too much for Prussian pride, and King William refused to see the French ambassador. When Bismarck edited a news telegram from Ems to make it appear that the rebuff had been considerably sharper than it really was, France turned toward war. With crowds in Paris roaring "To Berlin!" the Chamber of Deputies voted for hostilities.*

As Strong indicates, the French armies paused before they began the advance from Alsace and Lorraine which Napoleon III expected to lead far across the Rhine. The first important engagement took place at Saarbrücken on August 2. Four days later a smart Prussian victory at Worth, and another at Weissenbourg, showed that Moltke's fast-gathering armies had seized the initiative. The French minister in Washington, Lucien A. Prévost-Paradol, an opponent of Bonapartism and a believer in parliamentary democracy, unstrung by the sudden outbreak of the war, had committed suicide within a fortnight of his arrival.

July 22. This summer will be infamous for heat, at least, if nothing else befall. . . . These are great times for bogus extras. Mendacious newsboys howl up and down Wall Street all day long and with new appeals to curiosity. Their cry this morning was "Great riot in France!" Yesterday it was "Great battle on the Rhine," and "Death o' Louis Napoleon."

There seems to have been a little affair of outposts near Saarbrücken somewhere in the Moselle country in which Prussia did not come off second best. Unless France conquer by a *coup de main*, as she did at Solferino and as Prussia did at Sadowa, I bet on the Teutons.

Certain newspaper philosophers incline to consider this a war of religions. There may be a little something in that view.

New York Fenians are swaggering on the side of France. The Celts of Dublin have held a grand demonstration, 100,000 strong, on the same side. Natural enough. France is the hereditary antagonist of England, and there is much in the history of the last 180 years to incline a Hibernian to that way: James II, Sarsfield, the "Irish Brigades" of France, General Hoche, and so on. But Fenianism, if too conspicuous in its French proclivities, may drive the whole German vote away from the Democratic party. In that way, perhaps, and in no other, is the opening war likely to do this country anything but mischief.

July 23. The cruel protracted heat of this summer begins to pass endurance. I have felt today absolutely worn out and wilted down by it. Thank God, there is a breath of sea breeze tonight.

July 25. . . . There seems to have been a Prusso-Gallic *velitatio*, or skirmish of moderate severity, at or near Saarbrücken on Saturday, and about a dozen were knocked over. Very probably no such thing happened. We know nothing trustworthy about the manoeuvres of either side. Each army marches (to speak Hibernically) with closed doors. Reporters are rigorously excluded.

July 26. A feeble dribble of rain at eventide, moistening patches of pavement here and there. No other sign of improvement. It has been "cruel hot." Even tonight's sea breeze is calorific, or caloriferous. Thank Heaven for Croton water and for the bathing tub wherein I hope to console myself before many minutes be past. I wonder poor Ellie in her weakness does not suffer even more from this terrible period of heat.

August 8. Good news from Europe. I have felt "fine" all day. Deutschland forever and *worse* luck to Napoleoniculus! The two battles of the fifth and sixth resulted in heavy discomfiture to that scoundrel. We have his own *cognovit*; so this defeat is beyond question. More properly there were two defeats, one at Saarbrücken and the other at or about Weissenbourg, Hagenau, Kirchhoffen, Niederbronn, or elsewhere. There or thereabouts was the redoubtable MacMahon badly beaten and forced, it would seem, into an eccentric line of retreat. The whole French line is driven back. Even Louis Napoleon himself is entitled to be believed when he tells this story.

The Prussians say they have taken thirty guns, two eagles, and several thousand prisoners. All this indicates that Louis Napoleon has been beaten in the first important conflict of the campaign, that he has suffered damaging loss of prestige, that Prussians fight better than the Austrians of Magenta and Solferino. It does not indicate a crushing defeat—a Waterloo or a Jena. But there must be more behind of which we know not yet to account for events at Paris. The city is declared "in a state of siege." Its ring of fortresses is to be armed and put into fighting order with all speed. The Empress Regent (poor Eugénie) puts forth a proclamation that recalls the time when the emigrés and the Duke of Brunswick were entering France. The lady has sent off a special train to bring her little Prince Imperial home, a sign that she doesn't think him quite out of harm's way even at headquarters. So the old soldiers of the Imperial Guard will have no further opportunities of shedding tears at "Louis' coolness under his baptism of fire"; *vide* the report of his veracious papa. The despatches of that great person speak of this defeat as a disaster "that can be repaired."

The statement may be quite true, but it lacks the ring of a Napoleonic bulletin.

Moreover, Paris is reported to be in agitation—an outbreak threatened. Query: a Republican rising? And Louis Napoleon is reported sick at Châlons, Dr. Nélaton being sent off from Paris to prescribe for him. Sick! I should think he would be sick. What would he give to have the last month to live over again! This last act of unprincipled aggression has not yet done much to strengthen his "dynasty"—not much. He counted on one grand melodramatic victory that should begin and end the war and cover him with a blaze of glory, dazzling and blinding to all Frenchmen. But he got instead what is at the very least a severe defeat on a pretty large scale, and sees all the blaze of glory (be the same more or less) blazing on the wrong side of the Rhine. Very annoying to an elderly emperor with an impaired constitution and all France looking on. There is a paragraph from London to the effect that the war will be closed in a week. But that is hardly possible. Louis Napoleon cannot possibly afford to make peace now. He has the Devil's own luck and great perseverance in adversity. He may fight through even yet. I believe the withdrawal of the French troops from Rome is a "fact accomplished." His Infallibility and Holiness is said to be much scared.

August 20, SATURDAY.   Left Brattleboro [whither Mrs. Strong had gone on August 4] at nine this morning, and at half-past five in the afternoon was restored to my native gutters. It was a hot ride and a dusty one. . . . Brattleboro looks as it did except for the effects of its grand conflagration of last October. That has left a great ugly scar on the corner of Main and Elliot streets in the very heart and vital centre of the little town. They are but just beginning to rebuild. . . .

Sundry deaths during the last ten days. Our great Sea King, the brave and good Farragut, died at Portsmouth, New Hampshire; also, William A. Bayley, and old Joe Hoxie at seventy-five, at Westerly, Rhode Island. . . .

The great case now on trial, Frank *vs.* Teuton, was our chief subject of discourse at Brattleboro. We got the Springfield newspaper every day at seven and the New York morning papers at about six in the evening. Each day of the last week seems to have been made memorable by its own battle and by its own slaughter and carnage on the largest scale. "Needle gun" and "chassepot" and "mitrailleuse" have slain their thousands daily. Why they have done it I don't clearly know, unless it is because Louis Napoleon thought a little war would endear "me and Louis" to the volatile population of Paris. (Poor little Louis—only a month or two older than my little Temple.) The experiment seems to have failed so far. All our reports are a muddle, and we are quite sure of very few things in the history of this campaign. But it seems certain that the French are being driven back on Châlons and that it is uncertain whether their retreating columns can reach that point before the Prussians. . . .

French armies are certainly demoralized—more or less. French commissariat (and quartermastering generally) seems to have broken down most disastrously. Strange; I supposed the one great faculty of the French government and people to be that of organization of everything, from the queue at an opera ticket office to the wagon trains and railroad transportation required to supply an army with food and firing.

August 21.   The news this morning of an alleged Prussian victory at Rezonville, or some such place, was announced; victory on a large scale and with great results. But *mebby* it ain't so. Paris said to be in agitation, and very near a revolutionary outbreak. I shouldn't wonder. But none of our war news is to be trusted till it has stood a few days uncontradicted. Prussian losses are doubtless immense. I suppose this series of daily battles since the 14th to be without precedent in military history. His Prussian Majesty, by the by, blundered when he said (if he did say so) that the elimination of Louis Napoleon from his ill-gotten throne would be one of the conditions of peace with France. The declaration must incline every Orleanist and Legitimist who possesses the spirit of a louse to support the Emperor against foreign dictation. And if Frenchmen prefer Belial or Robert Macaire as their anointed sovereign, it is none of Prussia's business. Louis Napoleon is a scamp beyond question, but he is good enough for the people he rules, and Germany has no right to interfere with their choice.

Will the mob of Paris by whose permission—not altogether divine— French sovereigns reign arise and kick him out, as an unsuccessful scamp? It looks not unlikely. But he has seen darker days than these. His resources of craft and audacity have seemed inexhaustible; his tenacity of purpose under hopeless discouragement has been unexampled. But his faculties may well be weakened now by advancing age and chronic disease; and, on the whole, unless his Bazaines and Trochus and palatinates can get up a showy victory or two, carry the war across the Rhine, or exhibit to the Parisians a Prince Karl or Fritz as prisoner of war, Louis Napoleon's prospects are gloomy. And there will be dry eyes at his downfall.

This astute and heartless adventurer won his imperial crown by perjury and set it more firmly on his head by the massacre of hundreds of thousands (no one will ever know the exact number) of unoffending peaceable citizens of his own capital. Ever since that day, he has been the great mischief maker of Europe. His maleficence has borne fruit on this continent, too; witness poor Prince Max of Mexico. And no American will forget his persistent efforts to induce England to join him in recognizing the Rebel Confederacy and destroying our national life.

August 22. . . . Sundry blocks of granite are deposited on the southwest side of Union Square destined for the pedestal of the Lincoln monument at last.

War news all one way, but hopelessly muddled as to details. The battle of Gravelotte . . . decidedly disastrous to France, after some nine hours of hard fighting. Bazaine is "bottled up in very bad spirits," at Metz; or else, he isn't, but retreating westward, much demoralized. Lines at Châlons said to be abandoned. The Paris *Siècle* says "we must make up our minds to a siege"!!! O Gallia, Grand Nation, Eagles Indomitable, has it come to this, after a fortnight's fighting? Barbarossa must have emerged from his long slumber in the Untersberg at last and be with the hosts of Deutschland disguised as a Prussian Feldzeugmeister von Pulverblitz, or some such thing. *Vorwärts, ihr Deutschen*, and remember the days of Jena!

People write and telegraph little about Louis Napoleon now. If we are to believe the reports about his physical health received during the last month, he must be "kind o' ailin'." He has gout; he has piles; he has "enlargement of the prostate"; he suffers from rheumatism; also from "fungus in the bladder," which is complicated with "febrile monomania" (whatever that means), and aggravated by stranguries and other bedevilments too numerous to catalogue. All which maladies, be the same more or less, are doubtless intensified by his Imperial Majesty's keen perception of the fact that he has raised the Devil and can't lay him; that he has got up a prodigious muss and cannot readily "count himself out" of it, though he is getting such a black eye and bloody nose as no French monarch has exhibited for centuries. "My Uncle" saw hostile standards threaten Paris, but that was after years of exhausting war, and they were the standards of all Europe. . . .

August 23. . . . Bazaine reported to have got away from Metz, moving northwest to join MacMahon. Louis Napoleon at Rheims—a cypher wherever he is. General Trochu[14] and a legislative committee rule *de facto*. Correspondent telegraphs to *Courrier des Etats-Unis* that Paris is "vir-

[14] Louis Jules Trochu (1815–1896), French general.

tually besieged," but I don't see it. The Bois de Boulogne is falling! Private letters from Paris (Fred Sheldon and others) report the agitation and excitement. . . .

August 24. Copious despatches from France and London severally important but contradicting and neutralizing each other. They leave it uncertain whether Bazaine and MacMahon have or have not effected a junction of their forces and whether a Prussian column is still marching on Paris. Louis Napoleon's grasp of his capital is weakened. A Paris paper (*Le Temps*) dares to say that things will not go well till His Majesty the Emperor ceases to interfere with the army and that Son Altesse, the poor little Prince Imperial, is doing great mischief by chattering about military movements and disclosing what should be military secrets.

August 25. . . . Cable news even more than usually incoherent. But Prussia seems at Seganne, sixty-five miles from Paris (N.B., the names of places mentioned in our daily despatches wake up recollections of one's readings about 1792 and 1814). The "Committee of Defense" (not the Emperor, you perceive) orders destruction of all crops and food in the districts threatened by the German advance.

A Paris newspaper (*Le Siècle*) thus irreverently comments on some statement about the "Imperial headquarters": "The Imperial headquarters are a mere 'superfectation,' a superfluity, a pretext for disaster. The only real headquarters are MacMahon's." The more probable opinion is that the French army is still dislocated. Rheims, not Châlons, seems the position it has chosen for its battle in front of Paris.

I don't expect any revolutionary outbreak in Paris just now, though Prussia is said to count on it. Only the smallest minority of factious, irreconcilable, impracticable fanatics will feel like rising against even Louis Napoleon while France is invaded. Louis XVI would not have been dethroned but for his sympathy with the invaders of France. The mob-insurrection here in July, 1863, was the work of vermin in alliance with the public enemy, and of such vermin (to give the Devil his due) there are very few among the Frenchmen of 1870. Bad luck to them, all the same!

August 26. . . . Great batch of papers and letters from abroad, with a letter from the Rev. Bellows sent me by Agnew. Sundry philanthropists at Paris and Geneva want us to resuscitate the Sanitary Commission as a neutral power aiding both belligerents. The Rev. Bellows inclines to try it. I do not. . . . This work would be an appendage, alien to the blood and life of that institution. Let some new organization take it up.

Pech called to talk of the proposition to merge the Harmonic Society and the Mendelssohn Society in the Church Music Association. . . .

War news of today is foggy. It seems certain, however, that Paris fully expects the Prussians to hurl a spear against her gates, even if they do no more, and that she is making active preparations for siege. There are domiciliary visits and "twelve hundred arrests" of persons "suspect," as possibly mischievous, or as certainly useless, being mere consumers of food. These are to be extruded from the city. There are inspections of all bakeries to ascertain whether they have on hand a stock of flour sufficient for the coming distress. French engineers are preparing to mine and blow up bridges on the Marne. N.B. I do not remember that today's despatches mention the Emperor at all.

September 6, TUESDAY. . . . The fighting of the last thirty days has been on a larger scale and more sanguinary than any Europe has ever known. Our chaotic telegrams seemed to indicate last week that France was beginning to recover from the shock of invasion and defeat and turning back the tide of war. But Saturday afternoon, Mme. Schnabel received from her husband two telegrams announcing the momentous news—the most momentous event in European history for fifty-five years, at least. I did not believe it till it was confirmed by the Springfield *Republican* on Monday morning.

Thus it stands this evening. The battle of Sedan. MacMahon's corps surrenders (that marshal badly wounded and probably dead). The "Emperor lays his sword at the feet of King William." The Empress-Regent has fled (poor Eugénie); the little Prince was in Belgium and is probably in London. On hearing of this reverse and of Louis Napoleon's captivity, the mob of Paris and the legislative authorities instantly decreed his dethronement, constituted a Provisional Government, and proclaimed the Republic. Only in France could action so grave be taken with levity so reckless and with so little deliberation about rights under existing law. But what can one expect from Frenchmen or from Irishmen (Celtic both) when their slave-driver is suddenly incapacitated for duty?

What will happen next? There will probably be a decree for a levy *en masse* throughout France, and France will respond to the call. But the new levies will be badly armed, and (unless a great general turn up) will be badly led. They will not be inspired by watchwords like those of three-quarters of a century ago. "Liberty, Equality, and Fraternity" are no longer words to conjure with. The Prussian legions will probably sweep away these new levies. Within the week, Prussia will be invading Paris, and we shall see how much patriotic desperation can accomplish against science and discipline.

Strassburg is suffering from bombardment; the cathedral is damaged; the library is said to be burned. Why could I not have been there to secure and carry off a few of its precious codices and early printed books? Dear, lovely books—for example, the Mazarin Bible, the Mainz Psalter, the Complutensian Polyglot, a score of Aldines *in membranis*, . . . priceless MSS, delicious things in uncial letters, exquisitely illustrated Froissarts and romances, artistic volumes of Hours. It sickens me to think of these priceless books perishing because Louis Napoleon wanted to strengthen himself on his ill-gotten throne. His precipitate surrender presents no element of tragedy. Hooted and execrated by his own soldiers, he probably felt safer and breathed more freely when under a Prussian guard. All we hear of poor Eugénie's abdication is that when she was urged to assert her rights as Regent against the sudden phantom of a Provisional Government and against the rabble of Paris, she replied that she "would rather be pitied than hated," and she abandoned throne and capital forever. The sentiment is worthy an imperial lady.

American sympathies in this European struggle, as Strong indicates, were overwhelmingly on the side of the Germans. Napoleon III and his despotic regime had always been detested in America; the war seemed the result of French aggression; Protestant feeling was against Eugénie's Catholic advisers; and the huge German immigration into the United States had made countless friends for German ways and ideas. Most Americans therefore looked on complacently as one French defeat followed another. The first French reverses compelled the evacuation of the greater part of Alsace. Then on August 18 Moltke defeated Marshal Bazaine in the bloody battle of Gravelotte in Lorraine, and forced him to retreat to the shelter of the fortress of Metz. It would have been wise policy for the French at this moment, as Marshal MacMahon saw, to concentrate all their forces immediately in front of Paris for a final determined resistance. But Eugénie and others informed Napoleon III that such a general retreat was politically impossible; that if it began, Paris would rise and over-throw the Empire. Napoleon and MacMahon therefore undertook a hopeless offensive movement in an effort to relieve the pressure on Metz. This culminated in the two-day battle of Sedan on September 1 and 2, where after heavy losses the Emperor surrendered his army of more than 80,000 men. The Second Empire had come to an end. On September 4 a Provisional Government organized in Paris under Léon Gambetta and others proclaimed the Third French Republic.

The war, however, still went on. Bismarck had already made it known that he would not make peace without the acquisition of Alsace and Lorraine; the French were determined, as Gambetta avowed, not to cede a foot of their sacred soil. The Germans, with an overwhelming preponderance of strength (for Prussia had received the hearty assistance of the North German Confederation and of South Germany), pressed the siege of Metz and Strasbourg while throwing great forces forward against Paris. Gambetta, escaping from the beleaguered capital in a balloon, proclaimed a mass levy of all men from twenty-one to forty. The French resistance was determined and heroic, but the early victory of the Germans was never in doubt.

September 7. . . . Mr. and Mrs. Ruggles and Miss Mary Bostwick arrived on the *Lafayette* this afternoon, safe and well. . . . Mr. Ruggles has very much to say, of course, about the things and the people he has seen and about this murderous war. He thinks it will lead to a general congress and an international prohibition of gigantic armaments like that of Prussia. . . . Riot, disorganization, and slaughter at Sedan seem to have been horrible. Florence said to be in republican insurrection, and Spain is uneasy.

September 8. Prussia at St. Ligier, Laon, Soissons, Rheims, and her columns are converging on Paris. . . . Paris blusters and brags, but its defensive capacity may be doubted. The whole military system of this Second Empire was evidently rotten, and it takes time to build a new one. I doubt if a smart paragraphist like Rochefort can build anything. Talk of barricades and street fighting indicates little faith in forts and outworks. To make Paris a larger Saragossa would simply destroy the city—a calamity the human race would probably survive, though Parisians think otherwise—but no such folly will be attempted. Paris is in greater danger from anarchy than from war.

Louis Napoleon is in courteous durance at Wilhelmshöhe near Cassel. "Morbleu, parbleu; what a pleasant excursion to Berlin."

September 9. An informal conference here from eight to half-past ten anent the proposed triple alliance of the Church Music Association, the Mendelssohn Union, and the Harmonic Society. There were Charles C. Dodge (General Dodge), a brother of William E. Dodge, Jr., and a strongly marked case of the suave, pleasant manner of his family; Todd,

Pond, and Brinckerhoff of the Mendelssohn Union; Burns and Spencer W. Coe of the Harmonic Society. Palaver protracted and certain propositions adopted that are to be submitted to the two societies and to our executive committee. I am not quite sure that I fully approve them all.

Mrs. Cottenet is dead—"suddenly," say the newspapers. She was the daughter of good old General Laight and mother of Mrs. Annie Schermerhorn. . . .

September 10.   Prussian cavalry "within ten miles of Paris," and the main army expected to beleaguer the city "next Wednesday" or thereabouts. How preposterous a prophecy of all this would have seemed only two months ago! The devastation of half of England by a hostile army would be less astounding; for against a host such as Prussia can master, once landed on English soil, England would be utterly powerless. Even the *Saturday Review* and the *Times* confess and deplore the fact. "Neutral" old England's turn may come next, and "Mein Gott, what a plunder," as old Blücher justly observed.

If siege guns can be silenced by tall talking, after the Chinese method, Paris may fairly be pronounced impregnable. *Vide inter alia* that ass Victor Hugo's proclamation or manifesto, issued in his capacity of Sovereign Ass, about barricades, mined streets, and so on. Parisian editors howl and shriek at the audacity and profanity of a siege, as I suppose the zealots and the Pharisees raved when they heard that Titus was coming for Jerusalem. To besiege Paris!!! It is to assail civilization—it *ees* to make war on humanity! As if Paris were exempt by special grace of God from such humiliation as it has inflicted within the century on Berlin, Vienna, and Rome—on nearly every European capital.

But the Provisional Government probably takes a more businesslike view of the situation. It seems to be urgent for mediation. If it be true that the French authorities will agree to pay the costs and disarm and that the Powers will not permit Prussia to annex Alsace and Lorraine, peace may be at hand. But the Hôtel de Ville will have an uneasy time after such peace is concluded.

Newspapers estimate 400,000 casualties on both sides since August 1! A strange phenomenon for the humane, highly civilized, enlightened nineteenth century, considering the ground of quarrel. In spite of enlightenment and electric telegraphs and the press and so on, human nature will be human nature still.

September 12 . . . . Today's war news is foggy. There seems to be an armistice in the air, but everything that reaches us today comes through the refracting, distorting lens of Paris, remarkable for its chromatic aberrations.

Prussia is said still to decline treating with any Provisional Government and to recognize only Louis Napoleon as authorized to speak for France. It would not much surprise me if that wily old practitioner were flourishing in the Tuileries again before November. He has seen darker days than these; he is incapable of discouragement by adverse fortune, and nobody can guess what a Parisian day may bring forth. He has twice the chances his uncle had at Elba, but his restoration would hardly last a hundred hours.

September 14. . . . The phantom armistice has dissolved into air. France will not condescend to ask it and cannot prevail on England to come forward as mediator. In this war, as in our rebellion, England's neutrality, so called, has simply caused her to be cordially detested by both parties. Her policy seems always inspired by the selfish instincts of a trader.

Prussian Uhlans are undoubtedly close upon the outworks of Paris, infantry and artillery only a march or two behind them. But we hear little, if anything, directly from Paris. Telegraph wires are cut and postal service suspended. Paris has "encysted" herself like a vorticella, or rather rolled herself up tight, hedgehog fashion, presenting a prickly exterior. Ingress and egress are forbidden, except to people on duty. Strangers who have elected to remain at the Grand Hôtel must now take their chance of what may be coming, projectiles included, and must, above all things, take care not to compromise themselves in the opinion of a Paris mob, which sees a Prussian spy in every foreigner.

The Kingdom of Italy seems to be gobbling up the territories of His Infallible Holiness. The "Papal Zouaves" generally retire quietly, but they made a stand at Civita Castellana and succeeded in negotiating a surrender without much loss of life.[15] It seems to me that the Pope will exert far greater power over the minds of men when he ceases to be tem-

[15] When the desperate Napoleon III withdrew the French troops from Rome, the Pope mustered a few foreign volunteers alongside his guards to defend the city. But the surrender of the French army at Sedan made it clear that the French garrison would not come back. Thereupon King Victor Emmanuel II, with the approval of Bismarck, set an army of sixty thousand in motion to occupy the Papal States. The Pope was helpless. After some vigorous protests and a mere show of resistance, he capitulated. The forces of the Italian Kingdom entered the Eternal City, and Papal Rome became Italian Rome. The temporal sovereignty of the pontiff, who retired within Vatican walls, came to an end.

poral sovereign of the worst-governed people in Christendom. The usual answer to this, namely, that the head of "The" Church cannot exercise his functions if he be subject to the civil authorities of any secular prince or power, seems to me a mere formula of articulate nonsense. It is intelligible only if we suppose that His Holiness and the Curia and the Jesuits really mean to carry out the propositions of the syllabus whenever they can and drag Christendom back to the days of the *Malleus Maleficarum* and the Holy Office and the Obscurantists of Cologne just as fast as they find it feasible.

September 16. . . . Italy is moving on Rome with little resistance, and is apparently pretty near a state of active republican ebullition. Trochu is making havoc of hamlets, forests, parks, and bridges for miles around Paris.

A "grand democratic manifestation" is to come off at London next Monday; that is, a perambulating mob of roughs, costermongers, thieves, mudlarks, tramps, and miscellaneous blackguardism, congregated for the purpose of "demanding recognition of the French Republic," which Republic is not born yet, and very possibly never will be. . . .

Last evening the new and illustrious prima donna, Miss Nilsson, was serenaded in state at Doremus's by her Scandinavian compatriots.[16] I was invited and spent two hours on the premises, perspiring as in a steam bath. Some sixty or seventy were present, mostly unknown to me. Was presented to the fair Christine, a very lovely, blond young lady, with an earnest, kindly, intelligent expression and a pleasant manner. At eleven, the serenaders became audible in the distance. Morris Miller and I perceived with alarm that, when they were once in position in the Doremus's courtyard, our escape would be cut off indefinitely. So we effected a timely and masterly retreat through the crowd that choked Fourth Avenue, came here, and I smoked a cigar. Doremus is too much elated with his Lioness and makes himself too conspicuous as showman.

Hope to be off to Brattleboro tomorrow morning. May I find Ellie and our trio prospering!

September 27, TUESDAY. . . . There was a tendency to sultriness even at Brattleboro, though the temperature was vastly better than this. We had two brilliant auroral manifestations there—last night and Saturday night. My ride of the 17th was through steady rain, the first completely

---

[16] Christine Nilsson (1843–1921), famous Swedish soprano with operatic successes in Paris and London to her credit, sang in the United States under the management of Strakosch in 1870–1872; she came again in 1873–1874.

wet day I have seen for months. . . . We want rain sadly in Vermont. The
Connecticut River is lank and lean; many streams are extinct. . . .

I left Ellie pretty well. . . . As usual, I spent much time with Temple
and Louis. John the Buster came home tired of Vermont a few days ago.
Temple and Louis are as amiable and as enterprising as ever. Louis rides
remarkably well for so young a Ritter. . . .

News from the other side: Italy has taken Rome. His Infallibility's
political status is not yet exactly defined. Russia seems getting ready for
a dash at the Dardanelles. France cannot interfere as she did seventeen
years ago, and sordid old England will not undertake an expensive war
without an ally. Much fighting around Paris. Results are diversely reported. But it seems clear that in a heavy engagement about a week ago . . .
General Vinoy was badly beaten. His Zouaves ran like sheep. Some of them
were shot by sentence of court martial, *pour encourager les autres*. The
Mobiles or "Moblos" seem to have behaved better. The "Capital of
Mankind," or "Metropolis of Humanity," is insulated and communicates
with the rest of creation only by balloons and carrier pigeons. Whether
there has or has not been an uprising of the Reds, plundering of abandoned
houses, fighting in the streets, is uncertain. If the siege last a month, that
symptom will appear without fail. Gallic brag and bluster remind one of
Southern editorials in 1864. We have Victor Hugo's manifesto addressed
to the German people in full now. It is worthy the author of *Les Misérables*.
Only a clever Frenchman could have written such foolishness.

September 28.   Strassburg has surrendered!!!! Strassburg the *héro-
ïque*, the indomitable, the martyrological. Probably the sublime people of
Paris will cease to decorate the colorful statue of Strassburg with wreaths.
This symbolical statue of Strassburg stands, with statues of other French
cities, not far from the place where the guillotine worked eighty years
ago.

Paris has been for a century or two an "eruptive cone" through which
the fires of hell have burst forth more vividly and more mischievously
than in any other city of Europe. It is memorable chiefly for atrocities
and for baleful influences upon England, Germany, and America. It is
beleaguered now, but I guess Prussia will push forward her siege works
slowly and cautiously and devote her energies rather to raiding through
defenseless France with flying columns of cavalry and field artillery. It is
said that order reigns in Paris; perhaps so. Outside pressure restrains the
effervescence of a champagne bottle. But whenever Paris is relieved from
Prussian pressure, the Reds of Paris will effervesce energetically.

September 29.   This afternoon was for three hours at the Aschenbrodel —the German musicians' club house on East Fourth Street—presiding over my faithful Philharmonics. They, or some of them, are rather diffuse and sometimes talk themselves leagues away from the subject under discussion. But they are not at all a bad lot to be associated with. They decided to advertise in six daily papers instead of the twenty or thirty they patronized last year. This change of policy will be attributed to the new administration; so the new president will probably be much denounced and derided during this season.

Remarkable piece of telegraphic news in one of our enterprising evening journals—namely: "The King will make his triumphal entry into Rome on the —— inst. and will alight at the Urinal." This must mean the Quirinal.

Inspected statue of Abraham Lincoln in Union Square. A grim, unearthly, weird, monstrous "sooterkin," suggesting a Caliban run to seed, or bogey, or Moloch. Its legs are as two steamboat smokestacks. Shameful so to libel a chief who, though neither handsome nor elegant, was great and good.[17]

There are reports that Russia is arming to maintain the equilibrium of Europe and not for a grab at the Dardanelles; doubtful.

Teutonia seems to be actually overrunning Gallia Infelix. Poor Gallia has had nearly spanking enough now, and I for one am willing to see her "let up" after, say, just *one* shell dropped on the Place Vendôme. But Prussia cannot let her up till she has a French government to treat with, and no new government organized while France is under duress and a great slice of her territory held by invaders can make a treaty that Frenchmen will respect an hour after the Uhlans have recrossed the Rhine. It seems a deadlock, and there is no praefector to proclaim: "In the Queen's name, let drop your swords and daggers." Who knows but König Wilhelm may march Louis Napoleon back to the Tuileries and treat with him there? Stranger things have happened. The future of France looks just now like anarchy partially mitigated by subjugation, and anarchy in France is apt to be of a remarkably virulent type and catching. Perhaps it can be averted or postponed only by a Bonaparte or an Orléans sovereign. But such a sovereign would be a mere Prussian viceroy and would not have a nice time at all after Prussia had gone away and left him alone with his subjects.

September 30.   A good hard storm of pelting rain and wind; a rainy day. We have not had one for months. . . . Steam whistles of the East River

[17] This statue, like that of Washington near by, was executed by Henry Kirke Brown.

ferryboats, signalling each other, are faintly audible, like the cries of night birds; and now the rain comes down again in earnest. As this storm was so sorely needed, we must pardon it for taking all the starch out of good old Admiral Farragut's grand funeral. Our civic braves—horse, foot, and artillery—were taking their positions as I omnibussed downtown. The gold-laced and high-plumed cavaliers looked like so many roosters just extricated from the shell—bruised, wet, woebegone, crestfallen, limp, and draggletailed.

The city is said to be full of severe typhoid and malaria, due, I suppose, to this unprecedented summer.

October 1. Inspected churchyards of Trinity and St. Paul's today. They are still very blossomy and thriving. Our example has led the city authorities to clean up the City Hall park (what is left of it), the Bowling Green, and even the poor, dear old Battery, long a desolation; and they have planted them with ornamental shrubs and restored the grass plots that have long degenerated into plateaus of dust and ashes. . . .

War rather languid for a day or two. The *World* and *Herald* report a grand French victory near Paris. Evening papers do not confirm this, but the tide may have turned at last. Strassburg has been badly cracked and chipped by Prussian shells. Myriads of martyred geese are avenged at last. But the cathedral is not seriously damaged, and the more precious books and MSS were removed from the library before it was burned. Private papers of Louis Napoleon, overhauled by his provisional successors, disclose grievous scandals and offenses—personal and political Parisian balloons bring reports that all is serene in Paris.

At Century tonight a Mr. Mundella, a Radical English M.P. and a civil-spoken person.[18]

Yellow fever said to be in possession of Governor's Island—a besieger more formidable than a Prussian army.

October 3. After [I had] waited at Twenty-seventh Street, strolling up and down between depot and tunnel (with Tom Lawrence—Dismal Jemmy) for an hour and a half, Ellie appeared with Temple and Louis forty minutes behind time. She was tired, after nine hours of railroad, and in decided sick headache. So she had to go straight to bed, poor little woman, and is now, at nine tonight, very forlorn, indeed. This makes me blue.

Mr. Ruggles has just been here awhile.

Charley Strong received a letter Saturday from Puss at Schaffhausen,

[18] A. J. Mundella (1825–1897), English educator and reform leader.

dated September 13. Her mother was ill. Bronchial trouble with great nervous prostration and irritability, making her difficult to nurse. Puss evidently alarmed. . . . Charley is clearly bound to go to his wife. She has been ailing all summer. . . .

October 5. Charley received this morning another and an urgent telegram from Geneva, and also a letter from Miss Puss dated at the same place September 18. Mrs. Eleanor's case looks rather more grave. She had borne the journey from Schaffhausen to Geneva pretty well. After her arrival, the hemorrhages from the bowels recurred and caused great prostration. Her physician would give no opinion as to the prospect. But on the eighteenth she was decidedly better, and Puss did not think it worth while to urge her father to come to them, as she had done on the thirteenth. So there must have been a serious relapse or change of some kind for the worse which prompted these cable despatches. Charley sailed at one this afternoon in the *Scotia*, Captain Judkins, and I must expect to be anxious for some time to come. . . .

Not much war news. What there is looks well to those who love France less and Prussia more. Were I King Wilhelm, I should strain my wits to devise some way of ending the struggle *now*. I do not see how he can end it. There is no responsible person with whom he can treat. But an experienced gambler always withdraws from the game while he is winning, and Uncle Wilhelm and his trusty counsellor, Bismarck, should beware of crowding France too hard. She has been fearfully beaten in battle after battle, but a hunted cat driven into a corner becomes a small tiger. Prussia should do her best to find or create some political organism with which she can make peace. She has already more than her share of triumph. For sixty days she has been winning victories, which in their aggregate and in their results seem to contradict history and all laws deducible therefrom, and to exalt her to military supremacy over the Old World. Let her pause now, if she can, and tempt Destiny no further.

October 6. . . . Paris is still "cooking in her own juice" (to quote the stern Bismarck). Franc-tireurs, both military and guerrillitary, seem to swarm around the Prussian lines like mosquitoes and to bite sharply. There was a roaring extra tonight; news not important. Prussia is getting her siege guns into position around the grand Metropolis of Humanity and will probably open on it before long with a blasphemy of projectiles. . . .

October 7. Sunshine and clouds. Ellie went to Narragansett with Lizzie to spy out the land with a view to future summer quarters. Busy in Wall Street and desperately blue. The old story—impecuniosity. . . .

The matrimonial discords of General and Mrs. Viele have got into the courts and the papers.[19] Bill and cross bill for divorce *a vinculo*, and every symptom of an uncommonly nasty public controversy. The allegations against him are generally believed. As to the lady, there are diverse opinions. *He* is said to have seduced a Miss D— on Fourteenth Street. *She* is accused of criminality with General Averill. The General's tastes must be abnormal.

October 8. . . . War news amounts to little. I suppose Prussia to be quietly nestling up closer to Paris and preparing to rain inflammatory kisses upon her in the shape of shell. Balloons are now first made useful for purposes other than those of observation. When favored by the breezes, they carry the Paris mail to some region as yet free from invasion, and it's reported that a balloon line is to be established for the benefit of those who desire to leave the city. Passage money (I think), two thousand francs. Getting out of Paris by balloon is not difficult, but getting in again by that mode of conveyance is nearly impossible. The attempt would probably fail ninety-nine times out of a hundred. So the Parisian supply of aeronautic experts must soon be exhausted. But I suppose no great skill or experience is required by the skipper of a balloon. Hydrogen carries him up, the wind carries him this way or that, and he has only to pull a valve string and let off his gas whenever he finds himself over a region that seems comfortable to come down upon. This period of isolation from all commerce with mankind, save by exceptional and irregular methods, is a memorable humiliation for the Metropolis of the Human Race. She has long lived and flourished on gas, and she is now forced to depend on gas for the transmission of a letter to Lyons or Cherbourg.

I am thankful that Ellie returned from her two days of railroad traveling without headache or unpleasant fatigue. In all my gloomy outlook, she and the three boys are points of light. But on the other hand, what a sorrow and shame is it that I can't do more for them!

October 10. . . . Motion by me [in Trinity Church vestry meeting] for a tablet in Trinity Church in *memoriam perpetuam* of the fidelity and the pluck of the young Rev. Davidson, who, being on leave of absence because of ill health, heard that yellow fever had broken out among the soldiers on Governor's Island, returned instantly to his post, was diligent in attending

[19] General Egbert L. Viele (1825–1902), who had been engineer of Central Park before the war, military governor of Norfolk in 1862, and proponent of the Arcade underground railroad after the conflict, was divorced in 1872, soon afterwards marrying Juliette H. Dana.

the sick and dying, caught the disease, and died of it. I asked for a committee to consider and report, which was carried; but Skidmore surprised me by demurring to the proposition. He thought an old parish should set up tablets in memory of no one who had not been long in her service—as if service like this (almost ranking with martyrdom) did not exceed in dignity thirty years of respectable routine duty! It was also suggested that the tablet or monument should be set up in the one "Chapel of St. Cornelius" on Governor's Island, rather than in the church. Some force in that. But I want it put where most people will see it, and I want "old Trinity" to be enriched with memorials of the good deeds of good churchmen who have been faithful unto death, because that church has a historical position of its own and is the most fitting place for such memorials.

October 11. . . . Here is a bore: Bellows writes me about our former Sanitary Commission clerk, Assistant Secretary A. J. Bloor. He was a useful officer, but in September, 1864, we had to dismiss him for gratuitous insolence embodied in a foolish letter. He was duly paid up in full. Then he put in a preposterous claim for services alleged to have been rendered, and traveling expenses incurred *after* his dismissal. Its amount was trifling. He was heard in person with the utmost courtesy and attention, and he wrote the most voluminous letters in maintenance of his claim. But though we were most desirous to pay him and so get rid of his teasing, and tried to find some grounds on which we could decently give him a hundred dollars or so out of our trust funds, we could not find any. Then he began writing us threatening letters, telling us that he would do something fearfully damaging to the good name of members of the Commission and send his statements throughout America and Europe unless he were paid. It seems he now proposes to print a letter to Dr. Bellows, of which he has had the kindness to send me a proof, making the dirtiest insinuations against us jointly and severally. I am, no doubt, thin-skinned; I know that any public attack on my honesty—in a trust of this nature, especially—would be a terrible wound, even though it come from this man Bloor, who has no weight or standing, and can be shewn to be at least half cracked. . . .

October 12. . . . From Tours we have a report of an important and successful sortie from Paris, near Fort St. Valérien. But French victories reported from Tours are often mythical. Bismarck has suggested a fearful complication that will arise in case Paris hold out till compelled to surrender by want of food. Where could Prussia find rations for the two million hungry men, women, and children who would in that event be thrown on her hands? How could she feed them for a single day? To supply her own

500,000 rank and file is a strain on her commissariat, and the country for many miles around the city is barely able to feed what is left of its own population. This siege may end with tragedy unprecedented in modern times, and horrible even to think of. But there were Marie Antoinette and the poor little Dauphin, Malesherbes, Lavoisier, Louis XVI, the Princesse Lamballe, and thousands of victims equally innocent. Later, there was Affre the Archbishop. Paris has a rather large amount of blood-guiltiness to expiate. . . .

October 13. Died at Lexington, Virginia, the ex-Rebel General, Robert E. Lee, whom it is the fashion to laud and magnify as one of the greatest and best of men. But a chief of staff who resigns his commission and instantly transfers himself to an enemy's service, taking with him all the military secrets of his commander and all the information he had acquired in his place of high trust, is not a man whom I delight to honor. A counsel who should throw up his brief for the plaintiff the day before the case was set down for trial and take a retainer on the other side would be hooted by his brethren and silenced by the court. I refer to a decent bench and a respectable bar, not to our New York institutions. But such a proceeding would hardly be tolerated, even here. How does it differ in principle from Lee's course in April, 1861?

Fighting on the Loire. France, as represented by her regiments of the line, behaved badly, it's said, and broke at the first fire. So Orléans fell and Tours is imperilled. M. Jules Favre's report of his conference with the ogre Bismarck is a pitiful story. M. Jules ate freely of humble pie but could not mitigate the monster's ferocity. Poor M. Jules! Poor France! Were she to sweep every Teuton across the Rhine tomorrow, it would take her years to mend the breakage of the last sixty days.

Saw Jack Ehninger this afternoon. Funny report of an interview with Mrs. Viele, at the M——s' ("People who are so d——d respectable that they can afford to live east of Second Avenue"). Mrs. Viele, dressed after the manner of the Queen of the Gypsies, *loquitur:* "What a shame it is that when I'm making charges against the General, and he is making the same charges against me, and while we are on even terms so far, the law should give *him* the custody of the children. Why, it is absurd. It's certain they are *my* children, but he has only my word for it that they are his."

Jack Ehninger: "Well, madam, you might take advantage of this doubt in the trial" (!).

Mrs. Viele: "Perhaps I will, for I care more about the children than I do for my reputation." N.B. This is not a specimen of our usual style of

drawing-room talk in New York, A.D. 1870. Jack is indignant with this
lady for writing him a letter about her troubles in which she says *"you
know* I am incapable of doing what I am charged with," and emphatically
underlines the "you know." This Jack considers to imply that he has
special reasons for knowing that the lady's virtue is of the ironclad class—
that he has ascertained the fact by experiment and failure. If this case go to
a public trial, it will tend to make adultery ridiculous—a wild, unlawful
passion for either party seems so preposterous and funny. One might as
well try to look seriously on the trial of Jack Sprat and his wife, or of
"the old woman who lived in a shoe," for some grave malfeasance.

October 15.   Busy with affairs of Wall Street and the Philharmonic.
All seats in the Academy, except a few cavern-like positions far back
in the balcony, were sold before this morning; this is exclusive of boxes,
which are to be sold at auction. I have been bombarded all day by notes
and calls from people who could not get good seats or any seats and are
sure there has been foul play somewhere. I expect a concentric fire of newspaper squibs. . . .

October 17. . . . Church Music Association subscription $6,025. Shall
we be able to go on with a Second Season? . . .

October 18.   France and Prussia in *statu quo.* . . . Went through the
farce of registering my name as a voter merely from a sense of duty. But the
new act of Congress for prevention and punishment of fraudulent voting
may do a little toward restoring the elective franchise to decent people.
Nothing the New York *World* has done for the last ten years exceeds in
infamy its persistent endeavor to stimulate "repeaters" and Celtic brutes
to resist the execution of this just and most necessary law by force of mob
violence. As the late Charles G. Halpine justly observed, "New York is
governed not by a party, but by a conspiracy." If misrule could ever justify
assassination of the ruler, ours would justify it; for in such *canaille* as
Bill Tweed and Barnard and Cardozo we have not only tyrants, but
tyrants beneath contempt—vulgar swindlers who ought to be in the penitentiary. . . .

October 19. . . . No material war news that looks trustworthy. The
torrent of Prussian victory is suffering from drought and runs lower than
it did. France gains (or says she gains) little advantages here and there,
which may restore some little confidence and pluck to her demoralized
braves and enable them, in their vast proponderance of number, to do something worth recording. Meanwhile, France is in anarchy. There is a
government in Paris, another (packing up its things) at Tours, another

(Bazaine) at Metz, and probably a fourth at Lyons. No great leader has yet been developed and called to the front by this great emergency. Under fire, the regulars are apt to break and run. The Mobiles and Nationals are a little firmer, but not much. They have little in common with the new levies raised by the first French Republic. As to the exploits of the franc-tireurs, or guerrillas, I take those gentry to be mostly peasants, turned out of house and home by the ordinary devastation of war, who, having nothing else to do, no work, and no dinner, naturally seek to harass the invaders by killing pickets, tearing up rails, cutting telegraph wires, and the like. . . .

October 20.   We had an earthquake in the city a little before noon!!! So the *Evening Post* informs me. I did not perceive it, and its effects on this island were confined to the east side of the city—the Sixth Ward, that is, and the East Broadway region. In that district, the terrified people swarmed out of tenement houses, children evacuated the public schools, and there was a panic, but no harm done. It was much more energetic elsewhere—at Cleveland, Montreal, Boston, Portland, and other cities; and at certain of these points, did some slight damage. Thank God, it visited us so lightly. A very moderate shock would convert half Broadway, with its tall, ill-constructed buildings, into two long rubbish heaps.

This evening, Osten-Sacken here, Jack Ehninger, and my charming nephew Henry Derby, alias "Dick," who just came from Boston with his mother. He has decided to set up his ophthalmological shingle here, instead of at San Francisco; and he is nearly certain to succeed, for he is thoroughly drilled in his specialty (under Grasse, whom he served as assistant), has genial manners, a fine person, and plenty of tact and talent.

Despatch from Charley Strong at Geneva: "Immediate danger over. Incurable tumors." . . . Poor Mrs. Eleanor! She had fine traits that might have made her a splendid woman.

Mr. A. J. Bloor has printed his wordy little malignant letter to Dr. Bellows and sends me a copy. We shall take no notice of it, at least for the present. I suppose he will give it all the circulation he can. He honors me with a special little stab, speaking of "the sums which it is understood the treasurer honorably paid out of his own pocket to make his somewhat dis-ordered accounts square." Now my accounts as treasurer of the Sanitary Commission were never "disordered" for a day, thanks to the accuracy of my two assistants, Collins and Lathrop, experts in bookkeeping, who did their work and mine so thoroughly and exactly that no error or omission was ever detected in it by our periodical auditing committees (which included such men as Binney of Philadelphia and Huntington Wolcott of Boston); or even by the outside accountant selected by Jonathan Sturges, A. A. Low, and John Astor, at our request, to overhaul our books and vouchers and make report upon them. What Mr. Bloor refers to in this dirty insinuation must be the fact that when a certain sum of between $50 and $100 was lost or stolen by someone in Mr. Bloor's Washington office, I thought it best (*propter evitandum scandalum*) to put that amount into the treasury out of my own pocket, so that there should be no evidence on our books of the fraud or the negligence of one of our employees, though I was in no way connected with the transaction. Agnew and the rest insisted on refunding to me their pro rata shares of the little sum, whatever it was.

Eleven or twelve years ago, Bloor introduced himself to Dr. Bellows because he could find no work and was starving. Bellows gave him money and obtained him a place on the Central Park and all the employment and position he has ever enjoyed or attained. So the printing of this letter would do the little cur remarkable and signal discredit, but for the fact that his mind is probably somewhat diseased. Brooding . . . has produced something very like madness.

October 21. . . . That "Republican France" should be invaded and ravaged by a brutal Prussian tyrant is more than the susceptible Radicals or Liberals of London can endure in silence. So the raff of that city, led by certain scurvy demagogues (Odger and the like) have just been treating themselves to a grand "demonstration" in Palace Yard, groaning at the mention of the Queen, listening to revolutionary harangues, and demanding in the name of The People that government recognize the "French Republic" instanter. The bestial fools, to suppose that this minority of a *corps législatif*, boosted into a dictatorship by the sudden caprice of a frivolous Paris mob, has anything in common with any republic, ancient or modern! . . . Such "demonstrations" as this have been allowed howling room in the parks and public places of London for a year or two, with a liberality that seems to indicate a timid government. And I fear the English government is, in truth, what Carlyle has been describing it for the last twenty-five years, *unkingly.* These fooleries of London tailors, costermongers, and oratorical guides toward chaos, will probably achieve no great mischief in my time, but they will bear their own fruit before very long. . . .

October 24. Much work in Wall Street. That objectionable blockhead, poor little Bloor (a case of possession, I think, by seven Devils of very low grade) turns up again. It seems he had sent a copy of his poor little libel to the New York *Times*, and that paper, before printing it, sent some one to the Rev. Bellows to find out what all this meant. The Rev. Bellows, thus "interviewed," said it was a case of attempted blackmailing. So poor Bloor sends me a second copy of the document, with an autograph MS note appended thereto, affirming that the Rev. Bellows's statement that he, Bloor, had been trying to blackmail the U.S. Sanitary Commission, is "an utterly groundless and exceedingly silly and impudent lie, spoken in the interest of incompetency, vanity, dishonesty, and revenge"!!! A very good shovelful and quite compact and condensed for Mr. Bloor. But if writing letters demanding monies to which the demandant has no legal or moral claim and threatening that if the demand be not promptly complied with the demandant will publish something damaging be not a call for blackmail, then do I not understand the meaning of the word. That Bloor has been doing this for years, in a sullen, morbid way, there is ample proof in Agnew's desk and in mine. . . .

October 25. . . . Disgusting and disgraceful scene yesterday on opening the trial of some political pot-house bravo for murder before the recorder (Hackett) and city Judge (Bedford). Counsel for defendant, the loathsome John Graham, read an affidavit of his client setting forth that the Mayor, Oakey Hall, was hostile to him and that the recorder was intimate with the Mayor, and that the defendant could not, therefore, have an impartial trial. On this affidavit, Graham moved that the recorder leave the bench and be examined by him, like a challenged juror. Hackett should have committed him for contempt instanter. Graham is the most impudent, shameless creature I ever knew, but that counsel should dare make this motion in open court shews to what depths we have sunk. The worst is that I daresay this dog of a counsellor may have good reason to doubt the impartiality of the judge. Involved in this case is a controversy between Tammany and the so-called "Young Democracy," two factions of our 30,000 tyrants.

October 26. . . . People talk a great deal of slop and mush about Prussia's want of "magnanimity" in her hour of triumph. No wonder, for human speech has expressed a thousandfold more nonsense than sense, from the time of Adam's first articulate observation till now. France was never magnanimous to a beaten enemy. The ex-Emperor began this war without provocation, and the French people exulted and applauded. They would do so again tomorrow if they thought themselves strong enough and grind Prussia to powder if they prevailed against her. Prussia's cause was just, and she has vindicated it. . . .

October 27.   A wet, windy, acrid day, but the weather held up a little toward evening; and the *canaille* had their grand "Democratic" mass-meeting around Union Square and Tammany Hall. They are still (ten-thirty in the evening) cannonading and racketing, and (to give the devils their due) letting off a profusion of some new and beautiful species of rocket. Each, as it explodes, sets free a large and most resplendent fire-ball—blue or red—that lasts a couple of minutes and floats like a balloon. They are so lustrous and intense that magnesium filings must enter into their composition.

The seditious *World* is still doing its villainous best to incite repeaters to disregard the new election law and to resist any interference with their performance of their professional duties. Expected riots seldom come off, but squally weather on the eighth of November looks not un-likely. An outbreak on a large scale, thoroughly repressed and followed by a month of martial law judiciously administered, might do New York much good.

Standing Committee tonight at Trinity chapel; a long calendar of agenda. We have at last a prospect of securing property on the south-west corner of "New Church Street," or Trinity Place (*ci-devant* Lumber or Lombard Street) and Thames Street for our parochial and Sunday schools. Morgan Dix much exercised by the proposal, which is likely to be carried into effect, to move the Theological Seminary out to a malarious, sequestered bog with a defective title in Westchester County. . . .

Garibaldi is reported (by Tours) as winning successes against a Deutsch column that is supposed to be moving toward Lyons. It may be so, but I don't believe it. That grand, gorgeous, patriotic creature's proper place seems to me to be behind the footlights. I doubt his abilities to do substantial work. And what is he doing in *this* boat? Why should *he* volunteer to fight for a knot of self-appointed dictators?

October 28. . . . Bazaine and Metz surrender!!! 170,000 men lost to France, and about 250,000 Germans disengaged for operations against Paris or for a tour through the southern and western departments. This will be known in history as the War of the Great Surrenders. Such events as Sedan and Metz are unprecedented. Ulm was a prodigy, Vicksburg exceeded it, but the capitulations of 1870 leave Ulm and Vicksburg no-where. Extraordinary that so great an army as Bazaine's could be bottled up and kept tightly corked for two months by any force less than half a million men. (But it is said that, being a strong imperialist, he is playing into the hands of the ex-Emperor.) France has now no regular army left, except such chips and splinters of MacMahon's corps as are in Paris. Nothing, it would seem, can save her from being penetrated and subjugated from low-water mark on her coasts to the very roots of the Pyrenees but some great general, as yet latent and undiscovered. . . .

What effect will this crowning disaster have upon the garrison of Paris and on the French people? Probably not much. They are weak, frivolous, and passionate; their hearts will be hardened; they will refuse to be awakened to a "sense of their situation." Victor Hugo will be hysterical for an hour and print his emotions during that period as a missive or brief "to humanity." Paris will crown somebody's statue with flowers and veil somebody else's statue with crape. If there be a Rue de Metz or de Bazaine in Paris, its name will be solemnly changed by a decree. Suspicions of treachery will spread and grow stronger. The power of the authorities, civil and military, will be weakened. Red republicanism will lift up its head. The siege of Paris will go on in a scientific way, and shells will begin to drop into the boulevards occasionally. And then?

October 29. . . . No material war news. The alleged grand uprising of the French people is manifested thus far only by swarms of franc-tireurs, the survivors of whom will mostly go into business as banditti when the war stops. Spontaneous social decomposition throughout all France seems not unlikely the moment the present pressure of foreign war is taken off (like the furious effervescence of a highly-charged solution of carbonic acid on experiencing like relief). Prussia may have to set up an armed protectorate alone or in concert with the other Powers to save the *Grand Peuple* from effervescing their way through anarchy to barbarism.

October 31. Did a good stroke of work in Wall Street and walked uptown inspecting the improvement of Laurens Street (whilom Rotten Row), which carries that fragrant thoroughfare across Washington Parade Ground, widens it, and connects it with Fifth Avenue at the north and College Place at the south. It will be a great highway.

The Provisional Government issues a hysterical proclamation apropos of Metz; informs the people of France that the time has now come for them to "reassert themselves," speaks of the ex-Emperor with lofty disdain as "the Man of Sedan" (whose boots every provisional governor of them all was ready to lick till the tide turned against him), and denounces Bazaine as a tr-r-raitor. Maybe he is so. But I don't believe these statesmen at Tours know it, or possess any prima facie evidence of his alleged treason. It seems to me that after being long paralyzed by the insubordination of his men, he was forced to surrender at last because they were beginning to starve. From Paris we hear of a sortie on the north side repulsed with heavy loss, and also of diminishing rations. Dijon has fallen. A Prussian despatch speaks of a "short winter campaign" as quite sufficient for "the conquest of France." . . . Was ever such a collapse, such a sudden fatal paralysis of a people reputed the most warlike and aggressive of all peoples? Everyone accounts for the catastrophe by the demoralizing effects of these twenty years of the Second Empire.

Strong believed that the roots of the French debacle lay deeper than the Second Empire, deeper even than the First. That it was a total debacle was now clear. Strasbourg had surrendered to the Germans late in September; and the next month Bazaine stunned the French people by giving up the powerful fortress of Metz and an army of about 150,000 men—the greatest capitulation of modern times. He was accused of treachery. The fact was that he was a man of very low moral and intellectual equipment, and was so ill trained in military affairs that he was totally incompetent to command a large army. He allowed himself, when shut up at Metz, to be drawn into political negotiations of doubtful propriety with Bismarck, which the German leader astutely prolonged week after week until the French food supply ran low and unconditional surrender was the only alternative left. The morale of France now sank to the lowest ebb. The siege of Paris had meanwhile commenced, the Germans completing their investment of the capital on September 19. Here the garrison, composed largely of ill-trained men of the garde mobile and garde nationale, was commanded by Trochu, another incompetent general. The Prussians were soon bombarding the city with long-range guns. Discontent, chagrin, and exasperation possessed the people, and it became plain that France was face to face with grave internal difficulties. On October 31 an uprising of insurgent groups in Paris, shouting for the Commune, was with difficulty brought to a peaceful end.

All these events shook Europe. As noted elsewhere, the army of Victor Emmanuel II occupied Rome and put an end to papal government of the city less than three weeks after Sedan. And in October the Czar denounced the old Treaty of 1856 which limited the Russian naval forces in the Black Sea. The balance of power in Europe had changed.

November 1. . . . Garibaldi is not doing well. French officers are jealous of him, and French *curés* loathe him. He is blamed for the fall of

Dijon, and he would do well to go home before he is clawed by some brute mob of infuriated patriots. The future of the French people looks darker and darker every day. The hearts of that evil and adulterous generation are hardened. They will not accept terms which the result of the war they declared, or endorsed, without provocation has made equitable and moderate; and their stupid arrogance prevents their seeing that every day of prolonged hostilities justifies Prussia in raising her terms and lessens their power of resistance. Jules Favre, Gambetta and Company probably know better, but they stand in awe of their Master and Sovereign, the Mob, whose ministers they are, and they dare not put their own necks in imminent jeopardy by making peace.

November 4. . . . Private Philharmonic rehearsal at two-thirty this afternoon, at Steinway. Beethoven's Eighth Symphony—much impressed by the glow and loveliness of the first and third movements; the queer, quaint, serio-comic allegretto is always delicious. The *Unfinished Symphony*, by Schubert, may gain on further acquaintance. The *Tannhäuser* Overture was grandly executed. The orchestral part of a concerto by Liszt (or Lizst; which is it?), very vile—a catarrhal or sternutatory concerto. One frequently recurring phrase is a graphic instrumentation of a fortissimo sneeze, and a long passage is evidently meant to suggest a protracted, agonized bravura on the pocket handkerchief. There were also coughs, snorts, and periods of choking. It's a great work. . . .

November 5. Clear and warm after a drizzly morning. Am just from a crowded monthly Witenagemot at the Century. Somebody leaves us $2,000 as a permanent fund for periodicals, and Mr. Charles Dix presents us with one of his clever marine pictures. Joy, Drisler, and Rood speak pleasant things to me about Johnny the Pythagorean—that he is solid and earnest and free from frivolity in the lecture room. . . .

Much talk at the Century tonight of next Tuesday's election. We cannot hope to dethrone the Ring, but there seems a bare possibility that under the new act for preventing frauds at election, there may be an honest minority large enough to frighten Tweed & Co. into moderation in fraud and plunder. I fear, however, that it will take a very strong minority to do that. . . .

November 7. . . . Amazing news from France. The Paris "government," so called, has broken off negotiations with Prussia for an armistice and the war goes on. It must be mad—or rather, since it acts under terror of the populace of Paris and Tours, it's the populace that is mad. Members of the "government" may see the situation clearly enough but value their own skins too highly to act on their own convictions. Of course, France may possibly be saved from utter ruin even yet by something like a miracle; but Jules Favre and Company have no right to count on miraculous interventions in their favor. . . .

November 8, TUESDAY.   Election seems to have gone off peacefully, thanks to the federal bayonets that have been snuggly stowed away out of sight at various points in and around the city. Walked up through the Bowery and sundry east-side streets this afternoon and saw nothing but good order. No news yet of the result. I hope the majority of the Tammany Ring is diminished.

Just from first Church Music Association rehearsal with Ellie. Surprised and delighted to find Trinity Chapel school room crowded. Nearly two hundred in the chorus; many of our old army and many recruits. Ellie was received with enthusiasm by her friends of last season. Dr. Pech made an allocution, in the course of which he took the occasion to pay me sundry compliments and to cover me with "goose flesh." The chorus applauded very good-naturedly. The Mass was Haydn's No. 3— roughly done, of course. But if we can secure good principals, it will be most effective.

Two letters from Charley Strong today: Geneva, October 20 and 24. Gloomy report of poor Eleanor. . . . General Burnside is at Geneva. His sympathies are with France, but he thinks the French generals and statesmen imbecile. The Prussians around Paris are in sound health and well housed. Terms offered by Prussia are generous, but the Paris *canaille* will not allow them to be accepted. "A shell or two dropped into Paris will settle the business," thus saith Burnside, according to Charley; and Burnside's opinion is worth a good deal.

Died, Edward Post of Whitestone, at sixty-three, last survivor of the family at whose little farmhouse on the East River was spent the most blissful of my childish days. His mother, the kindest and most motherly of old Quakeresses, died in extreme age a few years ago. Edward married late in life. If he have no issue, I suppose that dear old homestead goes to his sister, a Mrs. Valentine of Glen Cove, or to her representatives. I would rather own those fifty acres than fifty Fifth Avenue lots. Yet it would be a sad place to revisit, all about it is so changed, and almost everyone gone with whom its delightful memories are associated. I could write pages about my early history as connected with the little front porch and the back piazza, "the lane," and the brook ("the beer stream") at the head of the lane, the orchard, the garden with its currant bushes and its sage and thyme and wormwood, the cherry trees, the stile, the bank, and above all, the shore, and the "white rock."

November 9. . . . Hoffman and Tammany triumphed yesterday, of course, but by a reduced majority. Some twenty-six thousand votes seem to have been kept from the polls by the terror of U.S. marshals, federal bayonets, and courts that "Tammany does not own," and which are, therefore, prepared to punish fraudulent voters. Oakey Hall runs far behind his ticket, "which do please me mightily"—to quote Pepys.

Verdun has surrendered. Paris swaggers. Perpignan and Grenoble are in sanguinary ebullition. All France, outside the range of Prussian guns, is in anarchy. What semblance of government remains exists by toleration of the mob. Paris, fertile in resources, employs a flock of carrier pigeons as bearers of despatches to Tours and elsewhere. The Prussians (ingenious "creturs") thereupon organize a corps of hawks to chase the pigeons; so it's reported. Falconry is revived for new purposes. Paris ought to galvanize the eagles of France and set them flying after the hawks, but the imperial birds seem paralyzed beyond help from galvanism. M. Thiers is said to have got out of Paris in a balloon, which seems a rather ridiculous conveyance for a statesman—though perhaps it isn't.

The Church Music Association subscription list is $6,671.

November 10. Looked through the pamphlet distributed by the Rev. Vinton about his rather discreditable controversy with a Miss Wynns, a ward *cestui que* trust of his, which made some talk a couple of years ago. He made up a charge of some seven thousand dollars against an estate of sixty thousand dollars, including "services at five dollars a day": "Going to New York to collect interest on U.S. bonds, ten dollars" (that is, stopping at the Treasury on his way from Wall Street ferry to Trinity Church); "lights and fire while making up accounts," so much; "making up accounts," so much more; and so on. He considers himself "triumphantly vindicated"; the fact being that, inasmuch as these queer accounts had once been passed (by default and without examination), it was thought best for the ward to submit to them on condition that Vinton resign his trust—which he did.

The "Ballad of the Heathen Chinee," by some Californian [Bret Harte], is in everybody's mouth, and very funny.

Tiffany is moving into his hideous new iron store[20] that occupies the site of Cheever's hideous meetinghouse at Fifteenth Street and Broadway.

[20] Now (1952) occupied by the Amalgamated Bank.

There is a bare possibility that the Assembly may be Republican—or tied.

The College trustees agreed last Monday to buy Newberry's collection for $15,000 if he will take it. It is worth much more. . . .

November 11. Philharmonic rehearsal well attended. Remarkable change, noticed by several—the audience was perfectly silent and attentive. . . . The new system of reserved seats seems to give satisfaction to everyone. . . . Temple and Louis have just returned radiant from *Rip Van Winkle*, at Booth's Theatre. Bristow, by the by, the composer of the other *Rip Van Winkle*, that is, the opera which the English company is giving at Niblo's, met me after this afternoon's rehearsal and addressed me: "Mr. Strong, I believe? I'm Mr. Bristow. Strong, Bristow; Bristow, Strong. Know one another." And he thereupon vanished abruptly.

November 12. . . . The New York *Herald* is making war on the Philharmonic in an underhand, cowardly way. "Months of this season allowed to pass without a performance" (just as during every season of the last twenty); "programmes without novelty"; "management *formerly* efficient"; and the like. The milk in this particular cocoanut is accounted for by our having ruthlessly trimmed and pruned the "privileges conceded to the press." . . .

November 14. . . . To Trinity Church vestry tonight; full attendance, including old Dunscomb. Much business smoothly done. Purchase of the New Church Street property authorized; price not to exceed $70,000, and the title to be in the names of some of us as joint tenants until a general act be passed under which the church can hold the property. The Cemetery Committee was authorized to go on with the suspension bridge over the new boulevard, at a cost of $43,000, which will be increased 25 per cent, at least, when exact estimates come in. As we cannot build on the school property for a cent less than $50,000, we committed ourselves this evening to an outlay of $170,000, and probably a good deal more. But the expenditure is wholly legitimate. . . .

General Dix thinks Paris is beginning to feel some inconvenience from short commons. Trochu will hold out till they grow too short for endurance, working hard, meanwhile, to convert his mob of four hundred thousand, more or less, into something like an army, and then make a desperate rush at the weakest point of the Prussian lines, hoping to cut his way through and leaving behind him a garrison to hold the forts and the *enceinte*[21] a little longer. . . .

[21] That is, the ring of forts defending the city.

Bradley Lee (very recently from Paris), who was here this evening, tells me the number of vicomtes and ducs and other French swells who are dancing and dangling after women at Brighton and London and other places suggests the emigration of eighty years ago. Now and then they receive a strong hint from their lady friends in England that they might be better employed at home repelling invasion. Mrs. Joel Post gave one of them a pungent suggestion that way. But they always answer in substance that they are passionately longing to lay down their lives for *la belle France*, but to fight for this "vot you call *République*, this *canaille*, *c'est toute autre chose*. Bah!!! Thees polka, it ees *séduisant*. Mademoiselle will do me the *honneur*?" . . .

November 15. Just from C. M. A. Rehearsal No. 2. . . .

Old Thurlow Weed writes to the *Times* about facts within his knowledge as to the mysterious disappearance of Chancellor Lansing more than forty years ago: that he was murdered by certain persons of high social position; that the whole story was communicated to him under a pledge of secrecy during the life of the murderers; that they are dead; and that he thinks it best, on the whole, not to disclose the secret out of regard for their families.[22] A singularly superfluous publication on Mr. Weed's own shewing and supposing his statements true, which I have reason to think they are not. During a long, active, varied, and rather dishonorable career, Mr. Weed has walked through many dark and dirty byways and with very queer people and has doubtless picked up, as he went along, many choice scraps of iniquity not generally known. But this particular specimen is probably bogus. I have heard in a very direct way that the ex-chancellor died suddenly in a New York house of ill fame, that his family had him very secretly interred in Stephen Van Rensselaer's vault at Albany, and gave out (*propter evitandum scandalum*) that he left his house in the evening for the purpose of putting a letter on board a North River boat and must have slipped off the dock. . . .

November 17. . . . Russia claims the right to set aside the Treaty of 1856, so far as it limits her naval force in the Black Sea. Europe in general and England in particular are much moved by this proposition, and there are prophesyings of an Anglo-Russian war. But England is too fat to

[22] John Lansing, who was born in Albany in 1754, and who was one of the two New York delegates who withdrew from the Federal Convention in 1787, served as chancellor of the state 1801–1814. Retired at the constitutional age limit of sixty, he resumed his lucrative private law practice. On December 12, 1829, the aged jurist left his hotel in New York to post some letters, and was never again seen. His disappearance created an immense sensation. Weed's explanation has been generally accepted.

fight alone; and where will she find a stout ally now? Neither Austria nor Italy can afford expensive luxuries, and Prussia doubtless has an understanding with the Czar—besides having her own house full at present. In France *vs.* Prussia, the former seems recovering some small degree of pluck and vigor and tells us that the besiegers of Paris will soon be themselves besieged and between two fires. Time will tell. . . .

November 19, SATURDAY. . . . Philharmonic rehearsal number two yesterday afternoon. . . . The Eighth Symphony was clear, refulgent, and gorgeous. Schubert was well enough; pretty melody for the 'celli. Mills played the Liszt concerto with brilliant fingering, but that laborious composition is filthy and vile. It suggests Chinese orchestral performances as described by enterprising and self-sacrificing travelers. This may be a specimen of the School of the Future for aught I know. If it is, the future will throw the works of Haydn, Mozart, and Beethoven into the rubbish bin. Long meeting of directors after rehearsal. I suggested my plan of a circular to subscribers to be issued toward the close of this season, asking them what works they would like to hear during the next season. Suggestion favorably received. Answers to such a circular (if numerous enough) would throw much light on the aesthetic culture of the community; and the enquiry would flatter our subscribers, stimulate them to think a little about the relative merits of Liszt and Mozart, and increase their interest in the Society by making them feel as if they had some share in making up its programmes. . . .

Then the evening was devoted to the Church Music Association— Pech, Cooke, and Edmund Schermerhorn; sundry details settled. . . . Subscription gets on—$6,914. For second concert we propose the Beethoven Mass, repeated "by general request," and the first part of Haydn's *Seasons*, dearly loved by me for years.

November 22. . . . Our Sanitary Commission accounts and vouchers are now all ready for final examination by our Auxiliary Finance Committee—John Astor, Low, and Jonathan Sturges, who examined them through an expert whom they employed some five years ago. But there is a difficulty in the way of our calling on them again. Just before our last election, Astor, Moses Taylor, and others certified to the accuracy and honesty of the city comptroller's books (he having omitted to report as required by law), and no end of abuse has been showered on them all, especially on Astor, by the *Times* and other papers. It was, in fact, a strange proceeding for so sensible and so cautious a man. His investigation could not have been exhaustive—no expert was employed; it was

uncalled for, and he must have foreseen that he would be charged with
having sold himself to the Ring. . . .

November 23. . . . As I came uptown about four-thirty this afternoon,
the air was clear and cold, and the sky was covered with the blackest,
blue-black clouds, fraught with the northwest ventosities that came forth
an hour later. All at once the sun broke through some unseen rift in this
canopy of darkness near the horizon, and the upper stories of the long
line of white marble and whitened iron fronts on the east side of Broadway, lit up by this sudden effulgence, stood out most brilliantly against
the cold wintry sky. This unusually striking effect seemed to attract
everyone's attention. Even the steeple of Grace Church looked like a
pinnacle of alabaster, or a great crystal of rose quartz. . . .

November 26. Philharmonic concert tonight. . . . Concert brilliant.
It was crowded. . . . So the experiment of reserved seats seemed to succeed.
Close attention of the audience and the absence of clack are most blessed
novelties. Possibly the notices put into the hands of each person at the
Church Music Association concerts last year are bearing their fruit now.
People would come in and take their seats during the first movement of
the symphony, however. We must enforce our regulation against that
abuse more strictly. The Society and directors are much gratified, and
are very amiable to me.

November 27. . . . I look forward with anxiety to the extra Philharmonic
concert on December 17, fearing it will not pay expenses. I am not
responsible for the undertaking, for it had been resolved on before I was
connected with the management, though the formal resolution came afterwards. The *Herald* and *World* are rather down on last night's concert
and on the Philharmonic Society. The accuracy and the animus of their
criticism appear in their statement that the Academy was "not so full as
usual"!

European news stagnates. We seem impatient for more carnage, or
something, weary of news that all is quiet in Paris and in its beleaguering
camps. Though reports on the subject disagree, it seems probable that
Paris begins to feel serious distress from want of food. Wealthy Parisians
are probably restricted only in luxuries, as yet, but the *canaille* is on
short rations. They will grow shorter, and then there will be an *émeute*.

November 28. . . . Ellie has just returned with Jem from the wedding
of that splendid brunette, Miss Angela Terry, to Roberts, the Spanish
Minister, at the Roman Catholic St. Stephen's. . . .

November 30. . . . Paris "went for" Prussia yesterday in force, and at several points supported by gunboats on the Seine, but the sortie was repulsed with costs. On Monday the army of the Loire, or some considerable portion thereof, marched on Fontainebleau but ran against a German army corps at Beaune and marched back again, rather seriously damaged by the collision; so say despatches from Versailles to Berlin, and they are apt to be trustworthy. It's said that Prussia is collecting great magazines of provender for the relief of esurient Paris when she surrenders. That event seems not distant. The sooner it comes the better for all parties. But what will happen then? The demoralized, disorganized French people has not coherence or vitality enough to be treated with. "Virtue" left it long ago; and now its *virtus*—or manliness or virility— seems gone, too. . . .

December 1. . . . I am in closer contact with fine and great music this fall than ever before—I have been hearing it twice a week. It's a blessing to be devoutly thankful for. But I find myself haunted, in season and out of season, by scraps of Haydn, Beethoven, Schubert, and Wagner. Phrases from the Third Mass and the Eighth Symphony stick to me like burrs, especially the winding up of the first movement of the symphony. That gorgeous, glowing movement has culminated, and is just going off the stage with elegance and dignity, when it suddenly kicks up its heels, as it were, cuts a caper, wiggles its tail, and vanishes behind the scenes. The memory of that final phrase teases and worries me, night and day.

December 3. . . . Caisson of the East River bridge was severely damaged by fire yesterday. I don't believe any man now living will cross that bridge. This was the caisson on the Brooklyn side.

A clever and abusive letter from Carlyle to the London *Times* on the Franco-Teutonic controversy. But the objection that the Alsatians and Lorrainers of 1870 would rather belong to France than to Germany is not fully met by proof that their territory was German two hundred years ago and was wrested from Germany by a bullying, unscrupulous Grand Monarque. . . .

December 4, SUNDAY. To Trinity Church this morning with Temple (Ellie at St. Alban's; John at Calvary). Sermon from the Rev. Morgan Dix; not bad. Walked thereafter on the Battery with Temple, his first visit to that classical locality. It is a desolate tract now, conspicuous for nothing but excavations and rubbish heaps, brickbats, potsherds, and oyster shells. It will soon be swept and garnished, I hope, and will remind one of the Battery of forty years ago. But the bay under sunshine is always lovely, and the smell of salt water is refreshing. . . .

December 6. . . . The Rev. Vinton came to see me and to say that on examination it appears that poor Mrs. Vinton, who has been suffering from a cough and "cold" since last summer, has serious mischief at work in her right lung and is ordered by her physicians to Nassau for the winter. He wanted me to move for leave of absence by the vestry at our next meeting, which I assured him I would do with pleasure. I am happy to oblige him; and, moreover, while at Nassau, he will be inaudible in Trinity Church. . . .

December 10. Tonight with Ellie, Miss Nelly Smythe, and Diccon to the Mendelssohn Glee Club concert at Irving Hall. . . . The Club is a chorus of thirty or forty bassi and tenori, with Mosenthal as leader. Jem is much interested in it. They do songs—"choral scenes" and the like—by Abt, Masschner, Schumann, Wagner, and others, and do them most effectively, with evidence of careful study, good taste, and good drilling. . . . The audience was large and "select," the Club being sustained by subscription. . . .

Cisco came to see me this morning, and we had a long talk about Trinity Church affairs, especially the comptrollership. Dunscomb's resignation will be sent in Monday night; General Dix is acting comptroller, and I advise that he be elected to fill the vacancy. He is abundantly qualified for the place. The objection that his son is rector has no force. I have been talked of, but I would not take the position just now while Charley Strong is absent. We have secured the Trinity Place property for a schoolhouse, and Ogden is examining the title.

December 13. . . . A private Philharmonic rehearsal for the Saturday evening concert at two-thirty. . . . From the Academy at five to the Church Music Association rehearsal at Steinway Hall. Chorus present in great force, and Fourteenth Street was occupied by carriages in long lines. They were just finishing the *Et Vitam.* Splendid chorus, and our quartette is far better than it ever has been. Mme. Bishop's execution calmed Ellie's fears. Everybody seemed delighted, and everything looks encouraging just now; may it continue to look so! . . .

I've seldom heard so much great music in the course of one day, and I look forward to Saturday's morning rehearsal and evening concert. May Ellie be well and able to attend them! As long as we have enough to live on and opportunities of hearing great music so often, we should not grumble at our taxed, swindled, and impoverished lot. It's pleasant to think how much better off in this respect the three boys are than I was as a child, or even as a youth of Johnny's altitude, and how fully they appreciate their privileges.

December 15. . . . Died, A. Dumas, *père*, who has written a larger stack of lively, readable, preposterous novels than any man that ever lived.

France seems moribund. In Paris, the Lord letteth the Runagates continue in scarceness. . . . They have devoured all zoology as represented in the *Jardin des Plantes,* and are buying sewer rats at fancy prices. The military force within the walls is said to be discordant and insubordinate. It is now asserted that the often postponed bombardment is positively to open on Monday the 19th. Also, that the cannon of Teutonia can reach the very centre of Paris, which I do not believe; but if it be true, may shot and shell be guided away from Notre Dame and the lovely Sainte Chapelle.

December 17, SATURDAY.   I was at the Philharmonic private rehearsal (Academy) at ten this morning, introducing Ellie, Mrs. De Neufville, and Jem. Only the orchestral work was done, but that included the Seventh Symphony. Concert tonight was fuller than I expected, but we had been during the last twenty-four hours profuse of complimentary tickets. It was a very respectable house, but possibly unprofitable. . . . Our little box full of people seemed pleased with their evening. Morgan Dix was enthusiastic about the symphony and the *Egmont* music, both new to him. There was no second-class work on the programme. I do not think I ever before attended a Philharmonic concert consisting exclusively of first-class music and lasting nearly three hours. I am fuddled by the unwonted stimulus. Scraps of the symphony and of the *Egmont* Overture and of "Die Trommel Gernheit," and of the orchestral work of the concerto are all mixed up in my head, and I cannot write coherently about the evening's sensations. The symphony was never better done. Its weird allegretto came out in all its mysterious beauty. So did the magic light and shadows of the first and third movements. It occurred to me that the fourth, though most vigorous, is perhaps (dare one suggest it?) coarse and low. "Die Trommel Gernheit" is a blood-red diamond of purest water and beyond all price. What a pity I have lived so long without knowing it, and basely and brutally ignorant of all the *Egmont* music save the overture! The force and clearness of the concerto, and especially of its finale, are amazing.

December 18. . . . The siege of Paris is becoming a bore. Bombardment postponed again, and "supply of provisions sufficient to last till February." A month ago it was insufficient to last three weeks. Then the bombardment was certainly to come off in a day or two, on the nineteenth at the latest. I do not believe the besieging force has a gun in position that can reach the city. Mankind grows impatient of the delay. This entr'acte is too long. König Wilhelm, M. Gambetta, and General Trochu will please begin to do something decisive, or at least interesting, without further waste of our time.

December 21. . . . The Philharmonic Beethoven concert of the seventeenth does not result in loss but in a net profit of $28!!

December 22. Generals Burnside and Hazen, who returned in the *Russia* and have been studying and inspecting the war, think that France has "gone up." Stories about Prussian plunderings and wanton devastations they designate as bosh. As a rule, no private property is taken without just payments. The Prussian columns keep to the highway while on the march. The labors of the husbandman go on without interference. The army around Paris is kept up to its original strength by a steady stream of men and of material under a routine that they describe as wonderful. They think the cavalry on both sides inferior to ours in enterprise. There are no brilliant raids on the enemy's line of communication. French generals make the strange blunder of locking up their cavalry command in beleaguered places along with their infantry and artillery, as at Metz and at Paris, instead of turning them out on the rampage and letting them "hear the lark sing rather than the mouse squeak."

Second concert of the Euterpe tonight at Association Hall; a new choral society got up by John P. Morgan of Trinity and Cornell of St. Paul's. Its aims are high; its chorus is made up of a few picked voices. Music generally rather hard and dry. In a difficult, uninteresting motet by Mendelssohn the chorus got into a snarl, and Morgan thereupon stopped them, left the conductor's desk, gave them the note on the piano, and began over again. Mortifying and disagreeable to all parties, the audience included.

December 24. Christmas eve; clear and wintry. Delatour's thermometer 24° at noon. Tonight seems colder and is windy. Rampaged after Christmas presents on my way downtown. It is at this season that a lean bank account is most afflictive. But we ought not to grumble. This is a very black Christmas to thousands in France, and in Deutschland, too. . . .

December 25, SUNDAY. Christmas. A charming day; cloudless and not too cold—altogether satisfactory to remember. Railed by Fourth

Avenue cars to church. Morning service commenced at half-past nine
with a large congregation. Ellie came in afterwards (thank Heaven she
has been well and bright today) with Miss Rosalie. . . . Litany and communion service began at eleven. . . . The Rev. Vinton's sermon was
mercifully brief, but it would have been improved by the omission of a
bit of theatricalism—namely, "And on this great day, my brethren, let
all the myriad voices of Christendom ring out their loudest and most
joyous peals." Pause by the orator. Some signal given. Chimes in the
steeple ring triple bob majors for about three minutes, and on their conclusion the preacher resumes the thread of his discourse.

The crowd was dense. The music was far better executed than one
could have expected after hearing last Friday's rehearsal. Chorus in
chancel and orchestra in organ loft, though so far asunder, kept together
marvellously close, even in the two fugues ("Cum sancto spiritu" and
"Et vitam"). Messiter's adaptation of the English words to Haydn's
music was good, though it might have been improved in a few details.
This Mass has always seemed to me characteristic of its composer's
genius beyond all the other fifteen, most Christmas-like in sentiment of
them all, and surpassing all but number six in religious feeling. There is
an honest, hearty, downright Deutsch piety and gladness in the phrases
of the first Mass which can be found nowhere else. " 'Twas worth a year
of common life" to hear that first allegro phrase of the Kyrie, which I
have so loved for thirty years, rendered in Trinity Church; then the
grand sweeping phrase on which the Credo is built; the exquisite pathetic
melody of the "Et Incarnatus," and the varied, beautiful expression given
to the rest of the Creed, the splendor of the Gloria and the Sanctus. I
confess that as the orchestra rang out its magnificent accompaniment and
the fresh boy-voices soared above it, I found myself trembling and the
corners of my mouth twitching, and my eyes filling. This service brought
together two great things wildly separated till last Ascension Day: the
Anglo-Catholic Liturgy and an orchestra and chorus executing music of
the first order. Thank God I have had a little something to do with producing their combination. This example will be followed and cannot fail
of good effect. How fortunate it is that we have a rector like Morgan Dix,
of fine fibre and able to appreciate live music at something like its value!
Thirty years ago I used to enjoy such a service as this in waking dreams.
I never hoped to hear anything like it in this world. . . .

December 26. *The Messiah* tonight at Steinway; with Ellie. Mr. and
Mrs. Ruggles and Johannes sat with us. The Harmonic Society had very

civilly given me my choice of reserved seats. House was not so full as I hoped to see it. Orchestra was too weak for the large and excellent chorus. Miss Brainerd (soprano) and Mr. George Simpson (tenor) were excellent. Miss Hutchings (alto) also excellent but for the feline quality of her voice. Jewett (bass), fair but unequal to the florid portions of his work. All my enjoyment of the music was destroyed by whisperings near me. But in spite of the nervous irritation thus induced, which is as fatal to my enjoyment of music as having my teeth filed would be, I could see the immense grandeur of Handel's work and regret that I was prevented from appreciating it more keenly. . . .

Bret Harte's poems are just published, including "The Heathen Chinee," which is now in everyone's mouth; "Cicely," "The Society Upon the Stanislaus," "Chiquita," and "Dow's and Dat" are clever specimens of the California dialect. Tennyson's "Northern Farmer" probably suggested them. "Her Letter" is an echo of Praed, as "The Pliocene Skull" is of O. W. Holmes's "De Santy." But it is merely the form that is borrowed; the substance is original and racy. His recent volume of little prose stories ("The Luck of Roaring Camp," "Miggles," "The Outcasts of Poker Flat," and so on) is vigorous, and his "condensed novels," published some three years ago, may be mentioned on the same day with Thackeray's *Prize Novelists*.

December 27. . . . Church Music Association rehearsal from four to six this afternoon; orchestra, seventy-four. Overture to *Lurline*, by Wallace. . . . House quite full. . . . Wallace's overture is far better than I expected; a piece of first-rate work for a fourth-rate man. It is clear, sparkling, melodic, not in the least frivolous or commonplace, and suggests Weber. The Mass, with orchestra, was gorgeous. Every movement was enriched with color and new form. The performance was like seeing for the first time a great picture, engravings of which one has long loved. But the comparison is not quite accurate, because the orchestral work includes so much that the piano score omits altogether, or condenses into a mere hint of Haydn's conception. Mrs. Kempton sang her solo from *Preciosa* admirably well and with great approval. . . .

December 28. The evil snow is upon us at last. Its visitation began at nine, and by one o'clock had become serious. It became mush as it touched the pavements. At six o'clock it held up awhile, and the blessed moon glowed at us through the frost fogs overhead with a groggy, expressionless smile, and now, at ten this evening, the snow is coming down again in earnest. A century hence cities will be put under glass and

New York will be enclosed in a huge crystal palace, from the Battery to
Spuyten Duyvil. It will be thrown open in fine weather and closed on
days like this, and we shall be sheltered in the dog days by sliding panes
of some glass that is nearly opaque to the calorific rays. Any objections
from sanitarians will be met by the establishment of gashouses, constantly evolving a quantum sufficient of ozone.

Long visit from Benjamin W. Dwight of Clinton, Oneida County,
with whom I have corresponded about his forthcoming history of the
Strong family. He has worked at it for four years, ten hours a day, and
all for love and nothing for reward, holding reverence for the memory of
one's ancestors among the first duties of man. He expects his big octavo
twins to be born in March. . . .

Prussia is said to be about to convert the blockade of Paris into a
siege at last by pressure on the outlying forts east of the wall.

December 29.   At the Rev. Bellows's tonight; Executive Committee
of Sanitary Commission. With us were Wolcott Gibbs, Agnew, Blatchford, and Charles J. Stillé of Philadelphia. Pleasant little supper and
much good talk about the war, *inter alia.* We were all anti-Gallican. The
four or five hundred copies of our documents, reports, and so on which
were sent to European libraries and to notable persons in England,
France, Germany, and other places four years ago have probably done
good service in teaching people how to begin the work of voluntary aid
and relief to military hospitals and on the field. I brought forward a plan,
which was approved, for getting an authoritative examination of our
accounts—namely, to apply to Judge Blatchford or Woodruff by petition
for the quasi-judicial appointment of a referee. . . .

December 31. . . . We admit Drake as a partner, to his great gratification. He's a very worthy fellow—worth six of me. . . .[23]

Eighteen-seventy is nearly gone. Heaven carry us safe through 1871!
The financial prospect is not brilliant, but I hope to keep out of the alms-
house till January 1872. I should much like to know where France and
Germany will stand this time next year.

[23] Elias Guion Drake, Jr., Columbia 1854, resigned his partnership two years
later. Strong wrote then: "He has been my right-hand man for seventeen years."

1871

*Momentous events in Europe ushered in the year 1871. By a solemn cere-
mony at Versailles, the German Empire was inaugurated on January
18, just 170 years after the Hohenzollerns had assumed the title of King of
Prussia. Ten days later the city of Paris, whose people were freezing and
starving, capitulated. Under Gambetta, war minister of the new French republic, resistance to the Germans continued until the end of the month; then an
armistice was signed so that a national assembly could be elected with power to
make peace. It was high time that the conflict was ended; for its material and
moral effects on not merely France and Germany but other nations were becoming serious. The predominant American sympathy with the Germans was now
somewhat qualified by a friendly interest in the prospects of republicanism in
France. In Italy, Victor Emmanuel was settling his authority comfortably in
Rome, and by spring the Italian Parliament was discussing legislation to fix
the papal guarantees and the relations between church and state.*

*In the United States the situation of the South was deplorable. As military
government there came to an end, and as some of the new Carpetbag and Negro
régimes showed shocking incompetence and corruption, a spasmodic revolt by
certain elements of the white population produced sporadic violence. In South
Carolina, Georgia, Alabama, Tennessee, Arkansas and other states, public
order and security were painfully insecure. The Ku-Klux Klan and similar
organizations were responsible for outrages which demanded—and soon received
—curative federal legislation. Santo Domingo remained a contentious issue, the
President sending down a commission on the ship* Tennessee *to make a report*

on annexation, and Senator Sumner continuing to denounce the project. In March the country was astonished to learn that Administration Senators, by a large majority, had removed Sumner from his chairmanship of the Foreign Affairs Committee. Plainly, the Republican Party was heading toward a schism. Meanwhile, Americans continued to talk about the Tweed Ring, the revolt against which was reaching a climax; the impudent activities of Jim Fisk, Jay Gould, and other nefarious speculators; the demand of Victoria C. Woodhull that Congress affirm the right of women to vote under the Fourteenth Amendment; and the work of the High Commission which, thanks to Secretary Hamilton Fish's astute management, was sitting in Washington to deal with the Alabama *claims and other Anglo-American difficulties.*

Strong was pleased when his oldest and once-closest friend George C. Anthon made a friendly call on Mrs. Strong. He was proud of his Church Music Association, which gave its first concert of this season on January 4 with an admirable program brilliantly executed. Other entries show the diarist in good health and spirits.

January 3, TUESDAY. I . . . had a pleasant day. Called on Mrs. Burton Harrison and Mrs. Bowden (née Miss Alexa Stevens) at their respective "suites" of apartments at Rutherfurd Stuyvesant's new establishment on East Eighteenth Street. This substitute for householding seems to work well, and Rutherfurd is a public benefactor, especially to young people who want to marry on moderate means. Nothing could be brighter, more comfortable, or more refined-looking than these tiny, cosy drawing rooms. . . .

January 5. Standing Committee of Trinity Church vestry tonight. We have got title to the Thames Street and Trinity Place corner at last; or to be more accurate, the fee is vested in Cisco, Skidmore, and Astor, subject to a mortgage to the church for the purchase money ($67,000) until an act can be got through the legislature enabling us to hold the property. . . . Papers, especially, the *World, Herald,* and *Evening Post,* most exuberant in praise of last night's concert.

France seems to hold her own in the provinces and perhaps to be gaining a little ground. Prussia is pegging away at the forts east of Paris. That siege and the war itself have become extremely tiresome. After our allowance for French mendacity, it begins to look as if the Kaiser might have to make peace elsewhere than in the Tuileries. . . .

January 7. Mrs. Eleanor Strong herself writes from Torquay in good spirits, though not quite so well for the last day or two, and suffers somewhat. . . . Torquay is crowded; thirty-five American families winter there.

Philharmonic concert tonight; full house. Some good done by my rather strong printed notice as to the ill-breeding of entering the house while music is in progress and thereby disturbing those who have taken their seats in good season. Several snobs marched in during the first movement of the symphony; but quite a throng streamed in at its conclusion, having courteously waited in the lobby for a pause. . . .

January 9. . . . Call from old U. C. Hill about a "benefit concert" at the Academy next month, to which I very willingly subscribed. He is to give Beethoven's *Pastoral Symphony* and told me he proposed to illustrate the "storm" in the third movement by flashes of electric light and an improved thunder machine of sheet iron. I suggested to him that it might be well to consider the expediency of this somewhat maturely. Messiter came to talk of arrangements for the orchestra at Trinity Church next Easter, and General Dix came to talk of his position as "acting" comptroller, which he does not altogether like. . . .

Discourse today with my old friend Dr. Henry J. Anderson,[1] recently returned from Rome. He is much exercised about poor Pio Nono and the Temporal Power, and upholds papal right with his usual subtlety and plausibility. . . .

January 10. . . . First Church Music Association rehearsal for second concert at Trinity Chapel Schoolhouse tonight, with Ellie. . . . Beethoven's Mass to end of the Hosanna, and "Come, Gentle Spring" from *The Seasons.* Attendance large. . . .

Jim Fisk's last recorded antic was on New Year's Day. He made calls in a gorgeous chariot drawn by four high-stepping horses, with four smart footmen in flamboyant liveries. When he stopped before any favored house, his mamelukes descended, unrolled a carpet, laid it from the carriage steps to the door, and stood on either side in attitude of military salute, while their august master passed by. It is a queer world, and this is a "devilish lively" community.

January 11. Prussia makes no perceptible progress, and I begin to doubt whether Paris be destined to fall this year. A story that "shells have fallen in the gardens of the Luxembourg" seems incredible. Ernest

[1] One-time professor of mathematics in Columbia College, and now trustee, Anderson (frequently mentioned heretofore) spent much time in travel; he had been converted many years earlier to Catholicism.

Feydeau, author of immoral novels, issues a furious anti-Teutonic manifesto and avers, *inter alia*, in substance, that "when Paris is eclipsed, the
civilized world is in darkness." *Anything* to take the conceit out of Frenchmen! That is why I am willing to see Paris stormed and France overrun.
An almost unbroken series of defeats for nearly five months has failed to
humble them. They account for each disaster in some way that saves
their vanity: it was the imperial system; it was the commanding general's
treachery; panic among the Moblots; defective organization of regiments
of the line; or it was something else. They are still unable to admit, or
even to believe, that Frenchmen can be fairly beaten on a fair field.

January 12.   Clear as crystal and mild as May (49° at two P.M.).
Tonight to meeting at Academy of Music to celebrate "Italian unity."
I signed the call because I approved it and, more especially, because so
many of our prominent men refused to do so on some pretext or other;
but, in fact, because they dread to offend our Connaught Kakistocracy.
The house was full by half-past seven, and at eight there was no standing
room even in the passages; and I'm told a meeting several thousand
strong was organized outside. General Dix presided. I believe I was one
of a brigade of vice-presidents; anyhow, I had a card for the stage and
sat there with F. S. Winston, [Vincenzo] Botta, William E. Dodge, Jr.,
James Brown, and others. The stage was jammed. General Dix's introductory speech and the Rev. Thompson's (who presented the resolutions)
were good. Parke Godwin was long and heavy, but he warmed up at his
peroration and brought down the house. Brother Beecher followed him
at some length. His address was perfect in its way—full of points—
sometimes colloquial, sometimes in an exalted strain of expression and
thought, and pungent and fresh throughout. It was free from unbecoming
levities, but one could not help seeing that a capital low comedian was
lost to mankind when he "professed religion." Judge [Robert] Emmet
followed on the same side, but a great way behind, for he was painfully
sluggish, long, and dull. Horace Greeley made a brief and rather telling
little speech (first time I remember to have heard him in public). Dr.
[Henry W.] Bellows spoke for ten minutes with effect. He said it was so
late that he should print the speech he had intended to make. His strong
point was this: that it might be questionable whether New York was so
free and well-governed a community as to be entitled to pat Italy on the
back and compliment her as a good little constitutional monarchy at last.
William C. Bryant closed the session with a good speech, but I fear he
was not audible throughout the house.

Except in times of great political excitement, I think I was never present at so large and so *live* a meeting as this. It was made up mostly of "respectable" people admitted by ticket, and every point the speakers made was promptly recognized and clamorously applauded with waving of hats and handkerchiefs, especially after every allusion to the government of New York by a race not remarkable for love of other people's liberties—civil or religious. I am satisfied that, if the honest citizens of New York had a leader they could trust, they would soon organize themselves and dethrone their blackguard Celtic tyrants. . . . This meeting was important because ecclesiastics have been getting up meetings of Romanists in every city of America protesting against the outrage committed by Victor Emmanuel and his sacrilegious invasion of the papal dominions. It was desirable that some expression should be made of the view non-papal Americans take of the situation, and I guess that feeling will be expressed in other American cities.

January 15, SUNDAY.   This evening Egleston called, and as usual, to talk of a trouble and a grievance. I never knew a man who accomplishes so much and yet takes life so hard. Also here was Gissner of the Philharmonic to discuss the feasibility of raising half a million or so to build a grand Philharmonic music hall. Also came Murray Hoffman, Colden Murray, Miss Rosalie, Lombard, Talmadge, Van Rensselaer, General Vinton, Jem, Pech, Tom Lawrence (Dismal Jem), the vivacious Carroll, two little Faleses, Dickon, John Hay, and others. Also here were Mme. and Mlle. Hallier (friends of the Van Rensselaers), fugitives from France, wealthy, prosperous landholders six months ago, now penniless and anxious to get bread by the young lady's musical talents. She is a giant-like brunette and looks like a daughter of the Titans rather than a French girl. Her voice is fine and large but perhaps not quite broken to harness. She sang for us—and *inter alia,* the arduous *Freischütz* scene. The papa is eating salmi of rat in Paris, and the young lady's betrothed was last heard from when Bazaine's army was about to bury itself alive in Metz. . . .

January 21.   My little tentative reconnaissance of George Anthon's position ascertained nothing but gall and bitterness, grimly intrenched, and resolved to hold out. "His New Year's visit was meant for Mrs. Strong, and had no reference whatever to me"; so he tells Jack Ehninger. With all his good points, he is, when once put out, the most cantankerous and churlish of mankind. . . .

Thomas the waiter resigned Wednesday, the place being "too much for him." "Sorry to go, sir, on account of the byes; I never see three such nice byes." I must say I think this remark proved Thomas a good judge of character. His successor George is Teutonic, was in the Grand Hôtel, was extruded from Paris by the anti-Teutonic *civium ardor*, and is sent us by Delmonico. His English is in its infancy, but he gets on, seems anxious to give satisfaction, and has good manners. The observation and study of other than Celtic faults will be agreeable by way of change.

January 22. . . . A despatch in this morning's *World* announces that but *one* shell has yet fallen within the *enceinte* of Paris—the modern Troy. This conflicts with scores of recent telegrams about sporadic projectiles and their destructive effects. But this same Gallophile paper prints another despatch about the prevalence of typhus and smallpox and the increasing cost of food, and these are more disheartening than a shower of "196-pound" bombs. This despatch states, moreover, that the Paris government is now supporting about 800,000 Parisians. What will they do when peace is declared and they are thrown once more on their own resources? France looks like a decomposing nation.

January 24. . . . Trochu resigned, probably in hopeless disgust after the failure of his last sortie, which seems to have failed very badly, indeed. A military triumvirate was appointed by somebody or other to take his place. But for some reason or other, this appointment was reconsidered, and Trochu resumed his baton. . . .

January 26. . . . Paris seems to have pronounced the word "surrender," at last, per M. Jules Favre.[2] But Herr Von Moltke considers her terms too high. Like Grant at Fort Donelson, he thinks "chivalry" has nothing to do with business, and he will probably accept nothing short of an unconditional surrender. Tonight's *Post* reports diverse rumors about capitulation current at London but no definite facts.

January 27. . . . The clangorous brood of newsboys howled "surrender of Paris" (for which the more scholarly of them substituted "capulation of Paris") all day long, but there is no further intelligence there anent. Even the New York *World* now concedes that surrender cannot be postponed much longer. There are indications that the Kaiser, being unable to find a responsible government anywhere in France, means to bring Louis Napoleon back to the Tuileries and treat with him there. Prussia's terms, as reported, are these: Alsace and Lorraine to become Elsass and

[2] C. G. Jules Favre (1809–1880), veteran French statesman and a conspicuous republican, shared with Léon Gambetta the leadership of the provisional government of France.

Lothringen once more; Prussia to recover against France her costs of war and to hold Champagne and the Paris forts as security for their payment. With the approval and aid of the 300,000 Praetorians now prisoners in Germany, Louis Napoleon may be set up again, or the Empress may be made Regent; but in either case, a civil war seems likely. On point of right and law (of little weight in dealing with France, of course) Louis Napoleon is entitled to represent that bedeviled country. It recognized him by its plebiscite of last spring and has not yet recognized any other ruler. The "Provisional" military dictators that call themselves a government derive their authority from a Parisian *émeute*. They dare not convoke a constituent assembly, and it is by no means clear that such an assembly, fairly elected, would pronounce against the charlatan Emperor or in favor of a Republic. . . .

January 30. Paris the Invincible has surrendered. Prussia occupies her corona of impregnable forts and is turning their armament of heavy guns inside out; that is, directing their muzzles toward the city, so that they may help keep the boulevards quiet, if need be, and do police duty on occasion. There is an armistice for thirty days. A "Constituent Assembly" is to be convened at Bordeaux on February 19 to settle terms of peace and make a government for France. I doubt whether any Witenagemot of Frenchmen can be got together in 1871 by general suffrage, or otherwise, quite equal to the job this constituent convention will have before it—namely, to establish a kosmos in place of a chaos by a series of resolutions or decrees. . . . That may require centuries.

Peace, more or less lasting, can be made, of course, on paper, unless the Reds of Bordeaux "go for" the constituents and cut their throats. As to the future government of France, her Witenagemot will have to choose between the Empire (or an Imperial Regency) and a "Republic." Legitimists and Orleanists seem counted out of the game. . . .

February 5. . . . Symptoms of chaos in bedevilled Gaul; that is, the Paris and Bordeaux "governments" are discordant. Visionaries like Garibaldi and Victor Hugo are likely to be chosen "constituents." Victor Hugo is a compound tincture of mountebank, maniac, and monkey. Here would be an opening for George Francis Train at last, were he not a Foreign Devil and therefore "suspect."

February 7. . . . Schism between Bordeaux and Paris continues open. The Kaiser telegraphs to Berlin that he is not even yet quite confident of a speedy peace. Southern France, being as yet unharried, wants a little more war. M. Gambetta seems unwilling to disappoint it.

February 8. . . . Paris seems in what the doctors call "prostration with excitement." The Reds propound as a remedy for the present distress a revived guillotine and a second Robespierre, and that everybody not of the orthodox shade of blood-red be immediately decapitated as coward and traitor. No government of France exists. It was to be created today by election of a constituent assembly, which will meet at Bordeaux and assume supreme authority, necessarily passing over (if it be wise) many inevitable irregularities in its creation and ignoring many technical objections to its claim to represent the whole French people. What its complexion will be, we know not. The prominent candidates, whose names I recognize, are mostly littérateurs, newspaper men, and demagogues.

February 9. Have just arisen from a state dinner at John Astor's. Sat between old William B. Astor and General [Irvin] McDowell; Mrs. Astor came next, and Judge Blatchford and Dr. Markoe were opposite. Also present were Judge Pierrepont, Mr. Charles H. Russell, Mr. Ruggles, Stephen Nash, Carson Brevoort, Alexander Hamilton, Dr. Barker, and a half a dozen more; very agreeable séance. McDowell has much to say on many subjects and talks well; so does the lady of the house. People accuse her of artificiality and affectation in her mode of speech; whereas she has merely cultivated a habit of talking accurately, instead of prattling in the slipshod style prevalent among us. Blatchford, by the by, mentioned my proposed application to the U.S. Circuit on behalf of the Sanitary Commission; and John Astor, who had come around to the head of the table after Madame's withdrawal, saw at once what that meant. But he was perfectly good-natured about it, and I said that this proposed accounting being *final*, we wanted it to have a sort of judicial character.

All travel in Broadway was suspended for nearly two hours this afternoon, and half the people of New York were subjected to annoyance and inconvenience by an exasperating procession of pediculous Celtic bogtrotters, aldermen, miscellaneous blackguards, justices of the Supreme Court, roughs, deputy sheriffs, hedge priests, corner-grocery politicians, and the like scum, gathered together in honor of certain Fenians who escaped their desert of hanging at home and have come here to rule Americans. . . .

Long visit from General Dix this morning and conference about Trinity Church affairs, and especially about his position as "acting" comptroller, which he does not like. He thinks Ogden means to make a grab at the place. Like enough, for Ogden is as rapacious in pursuit of salaried office as any man outside of the "City Ring." He makes his living by securing positions as trustee of charities and then forcing himself into a well-paid treasurership or clerkship. Witness the records of Trinity Church and Columbia College. Probably the most indecent thing ever done by a member of the former corporation was his deliberately moving that it should appropriate money to pay him and William Betts for services rendered the diocese in some ecclesiastical trial of one Walker. This was some years ago. The motion was referred, if I remember aright, to the Standing Committee, which kindly allowed it to die without a formal report.

During the last six years I have read no end of pamphlets and papers about poor Fitz-John Porter's conduct in July or August, 1862, in which he was cashiered by court-martial. I talked of the matter with McDowell, who made it clear to me for the first time. I fear poor Fitz-John Porter was justly condemned.

February 14. . . . Found Morgan Dix this afternoon in high glee and giggle over a passage in somebody's [George Kennan's] *Tent Life in Siberia*—a narrative of travel among Tartar and Kirghis hordes. It seems that English and American illustrated newspapers find their way to the steppes now and then and are immensely prized. On one occasion, this traveller entered a Tartar hut or wigwam, in which an engraving from one of these papers was stuck up, with candles burning and several Tartars in their sheepskins kneeling before it, and "saying their own little private devotions." *It was a portrait of Major-General John A. Dix!* I told the Rev. Mr. Dix that I hoped canonization would be hereditary in the family. . . .

February 15. . . . News (more or less veracious) from *Gallia Infelix.* Working majority of Orleanists in the Constituent Assembly and general wish for peace at any price. Terms of peace already informally settled. Garibaldi declines his election and resigns his military command (disgusted, no doubt).

February 17. . . . Constituent Assembly has elected one M. Grévy[3] as its speaker. It's said that it will proceed to organize a provisional government and give M. Thiers[4] the presidency, and then take the sense of the

[3] Jules Grévy (1813–1891), French political leader and later President (elected 1879).

[4] Louis Adolphe Thiers (1797–1877) led the National Assembly in making peace with Germany and restoring public order; and in August of this year the National Assembly conferred on him the interim title of President of the Republic.

French people as to the form of permanent government they prefer. That the Reds are in disfavor and that a man of even Thiers's questionable sense and judgment is talked of for a provisional presidency seem to show that France is a sadder and a wiser country than she has been for several decades. . . .

February 23, THURSDAY. . . . Tuesday night the Church Music Association concert was superb and gave universal satisfaction, except to a few who came late, would not sit in the galleries, and then complained that there must have been an overissue of tickets. People were waiting at seven for the doors to open, and at ten-fifteen, when we got through, Fourteenth Street and Union Square were blocked up with carriages. Everything went delightfully. . . . Mrs. Goold Hoyt was there, Mrs. J. J. Astor, Cisco and his wife, handsome Mrs. Jem Gerard, Delano, Osten-Sacken, and others; also, poor George C. Anthon, who honored me with a salutation cool enough sensibly to affect the temperature of the crowded room. I must meet him next summer as often as I can.

March 8, WEDNESDAY. Emerged from bed at noon today, having recessed there since I don't exactly remember when—last Friday, I think. . . . I was mostly in some sort of low delirium. . . . Monday morning Peters surprised me by the statement that I was out of danger, that I had had a sharp touch of typhoid bronchitis, or typhoid pneumonia, whichever I pleased to call it, and that he had just made up his mind to call in Flint or Van Buren.

March 13. Just from Trinity Church Vestry. A certain degree of consolation for a little illness may be found in the cordiality with which one is received after it. That people should take the trouble to affect it is something. Tonight we put Drisler's name on the Easter Tuesday ticket. . . . Not a bad appointment. Also, I got General Dix's title of office changed from "acting comptroller" to "comptroller," a change to which he attached more importance than it seemed to deserve. . . .

Engaged passage last Saturday by Colden Murray's steamer, the *Virgo,* for the 21st for Johannes and myself. A run to Savannah and perhaps a glimpse of the semi-tropical scenery of the St. John's may do us both good. . . . Moreover, it seems to me as if there were still a little typhoid poison left in my blood, for I have no more stamina just now than a pint of dish water with a dirty towel in it. Therefore, this strikes me as a good thing to do. . . .

The well-spanked Gauls, in and around Paris, squirm and invite further fustigation. The poor "National Assembly" is to sit at Versailles, not at Paris. That is certainly a gleam of common sense, though Versailles is not far enough from Paris.

March 16. . . . A "Democratic" victory in New Hampshire. The quarrel with Sumner about the San Domingo project has hurt the Administration. . . .

Domestic prospects of France look very ill. Trade and business are prostrated, ruin general, political parties in acrid hostility, the popular mind filled with wild and mischievous fallacies, multitudes of nominal *Mobiles* and *Nationales* still living on the government, no signs yet of any statesman of higher grade than Thiers. Peace does not yet appear to have been formally concluded. The first three months (at least) after its conclusion promise to be tempestuous. An attack of "secondary hemorrhage" or civil war seems not unlikely.

March 17. . . . Philharmonic rehearsal at two-thirty this afternoon. The Fourth Symphony is delicious—fresh and bright and sparkling; the grand pulsating eruptive crashes of the full orchestra (in the second movement) always sinking back into the quiet melody that forms its subject are all amazingly lovely. So are the lights and shadows of the first allegro. What a contrast to Liszt's laborious bombast! Then that most precious little trio of the third movement that contrasts so charmingly with the intensely Beethovenesque setting. No trio is so exquisitely individual and refined, unless it may be that of the *Jupiter Symphony*.

March 18. . . . Proctor's book on solar physics is most interesting. . . .[5] What the spectroscope has told and is telling us about the constitution of the sun, stars, and nebulae, seemed an achievement unlikely to be surpassed for a century at least. But if the heat, light, and activism that the sun diffuses through space emanate, not from inorganic gas and vapor, but from myriads of huge organisms, each as big as the state of New York and each endowed with a light-generating power, like the firefly—but millions of millions of times more powerful; if, in other words, the sun is alive, then have the astronomers of 1871 got hold of "a big thing," which I hope they will follow up with due diligence. . . .

March 20. . . . The old Red Devil of Paris is unchained again at last. Rather remarkable he should have been kept close so long. The Thiers government undertook last Saturday to break up a sort of passive, asthenic "insurrection" that has been established in Montmartre since the city surrendered. But the *Nationales* fraternized with the people, gave up

---

[5] Two scientific books this spring made a sensation: Richard A. Proctor's *Other Worlds Than Ours*, and Darwin's *The Descent of Man*.

their arms, and gave up, also, certain unpopular generals, two or three
of whom were summarily tried "by court-martial" (or by a revolutionary
tribunal) and shot. At last accounts, the city was in the hands of the mob
and the *Nationales* (same thing). . . .

On Tuesday, March 21, Strong and his son John embarked on the Leo, *a
"propeller" ship of which his friend Colden Murray was part owner, for a
voyage south—recuperation for Strong after his illness and a needed perking up
for John. They "joined forces" with Laurent Allien, a friend and fellow-
passenger. In his brief diary notes Strong describes the rough passage; the
southern scenery, so strange to the New Yorkers; the luxuriant vegetation,
trees, birds, reptiles everywhere about them; the "poor whites" and Negroes of
the towns and open country; the evidence of war's destructiveness. Strong found
Savannah beautiful and full of life, a contrast to what was heard of its rival,
Charleston, "which is said to be utterly stagnant and dead.* Fiat Justitia."
*He attended Christ Church in Savannah, reporting a "respectable sermon;
music flashy and bad."*

*From Savannah they took a small steamer to travel through the "creeks and
inlets that separate the sea islands from the mainland." Strong found the endless salt marshes monotonous. Bad weather forced them to spend a day and
night at one of the towns where they had stopped. Ashore, they talked to local
people and observed war devastation. Sailing from Savannah, the two Strongs
went up the St. John's River to Tocoi. Having just missed the horse railroad
train to St. Augustine, they gave up seeing that city, and descended the river
to spend a day and night in Jacksonville, where Strong found a Columbia
alumnus to whom he had a letter of introduction and who showed him about.
They visited the Marquise de Talleyrand's deserted chateau. Strong commented
on the flow of Yankee capital into Florida and the prospects of growth of the
towns along the St. John's River in the next twenty years.*

*The travelers returned to Savannah and spent a few more days resting and
sightseeing there. The trip ended with the anchoring of their ship in the East
River on April 7.*

April 8. France is doing after her kind. Latest news: Thiers got
tired of singing "Red Radicals, Retire!" and gave battle at last. His
troops seem to have done their duty, for a wonder. Supported by the
heavy guns of St. Valérien, they are reported to have driven the Rouge

Dragon back upon the city after two days of hard fighting. Within the walls are murder and sudden death. Churches plundered and houses of "aristocrats" harried. *Vive la République!* Deutschland seems to be looking calmly on, prepared to "go for" Paris whenever it shall appear that the Versailles conclave is unable to assert its authority and get itself recognized as a government.

April 10. . . . Fighting around Paris continues. The Rouges are putting up barricades and, unless their provisions give out, will make a hard fight in the streets when Thiers tries to occupy the city. Notre Dame is closed. Many clerics and other "suspects" are in durance. The hornets seem to be getting up a little extra civil war of their own within their own nest while shells are dropping on the Champs Elysées and MacMahon is battering the *enceinte*. What a "sublime *peuple*"!

April 13. . . . From three-thirty to six with Ellie at Edmund Schermerhorn's; the third of his fortnightly musical afternoons under Pech's direction. . . . These performances are very nice: handsome rooms; simple and slight refreshments; only thirty or forty invited guests, nearly every one of them really appreciative of the afternoon's work; and the best chamber music—these make a truly civilized combination. This afternoon, we enjoyed Beethoven's gorgeous septuor and Hummel's septette with piano, op. 70, with the lovely trio. These (except the last two movements of Hummel) we hope to hear on these premises next Tuesday evening under Bergner's supervision. The Rev. Cooke and Mme. Clara Peel sang Meyerbeer and Verdi. . . .

Paris is said to have repulsed a serious assault on the southern forts. Her *lorettes*, *poissardes*, and other female vermin are organizing themselves into an Amazonian corps of civic defenders. "Severe measures are to be adopted against refractory *Nationales*," and so on. Should the Centre of Civilization and Metropolis of Humanity convert itself into an extensive area of ashes, brickbats, and calcined stones, I think mankind would, on the whole, be better off. . . .

April 15. . . . M. Thiers announces by circular that the recent fighting around Paris has been "unimportant" and that all is serene. The aims of these revolutionizers seem rather more definite than were those of the original Jacobins. First, an offensive and defensive alliance of all "working men," without regard to nationality, against capital, and incidentally, against hereditary privilege, and against Christianity; or, in other words, the substitution of an international trades union for all existing governments. Second, the independence of the more populous and important municipalities, especially of Paris. The votes of eight or ten great cities must no longer be swamped by those of unenlightened rustics who go to church, but each civic commune must govern itself in some sort of vague, federal league (on most flimsy paper) with the others and with the bucolic provinces that constitute the "rest of France." *Vive la République*— One and infinitely divisible!

This demonstration against capital, though likely to come to naught, may prove memorable as the first organized and violent move of any importance toward great changes. The present relations of labor and capital are not ideally perfect (though I should dislike to set about re-modeling them), and one need not be a radical or a Communist to doubt whether they will endure to the end of time. It is to be hoped that any decomposition of our present social order will not be explosive, but gradual and spread over a century or two, but the hyenas and baboons of Paris think otherwise. Whatever changes are to come, the supreme rule of trade unions would be but a brief transition stage to something else. Birmingham and Sheffield have proved that no tyranny is more un-scrupulous, narrow, brutal, sanguinary, merciless, and intolerable than theirs, and this country has furnished evidence to the same effect. Medieval robber-barons would be less oppressive. This particular outbreak will probably fail, for Paris is as yet fighting alone. But Thiers and Mac-Mahon are making no great headway just now.

April 17. . . . Paris is much the same; the devil is clearly having a good time there. The neighbourhood of the Arc de Triomphe is much infested by shells. People (priests and nuns) describing themselves as "servants of a person called God," are incarcerated as "suspects." All church property is gobbled up by the Commune. But Paris has not yet reached the temperature of 1792. She was then in violent mania, and so furious and dangerous that the neighbours had to be called in to put a straitjacket on her—and a tough job they found it. This disturbance resembles rather the low muttering delirium of extreme prostration. . . .

The Committee on the School of Mines met this afternoon at the home of William Betts. Prolixity of our excellent president is madden-ing. Profound doubts as to our right to confer degree of doctor of philos-ophy. As if anyone cared!

April 21. At Fulton Street vestry office at half-past three this after-noon. We had a vestry meeting which approved Upjohn's plans for the Trinity Church Schoolhouse on the southwest corner of Thames Street and Lumber Street (afterwards Trinity Place, and now New Church

Street). The estimated cost is not to exceed $80,000. The elevations are well enough but are marked by Upjohn's poverty of invention. Pursuant to instructions, he has given the interior plenty of light through a score or two of windows, but they are all exactly alike in dimensions and in outline; so the building will look like A. T. Stewart's big iron store, or a factory, or an ecclesiastical penitentiary. I begged the Committee on Supplies and Repairs in charge of the matter to get this monotony relieved and also to look to the subject of active ventilation. Upjohn is a fossil. . . .

Congress has adjourned, after passing the Ku-Klux Bill, from which little good is to be expected, and after a disgraceful interchange of Billingsgate between the Hon. B. F. Butler and certain other "honorable" blackguards. The state legislature is about to become inodorous and adjourn. The Ring has carried all its measures with the help of a Republican member, O. Winans of Chautauqua, who ratted opportunely (I hope he had self-respect enough to insist on a good price), and the city of New York is now at its mercy—autonomy, self-government, rights of suffrage, and "democratic principles" being ignored. "Boss" Tweed and his tail are sovereigns of this city and county. Perhaps the title "Boss of New York" will grow into permanence and figure in history like that of the doge of Venice. All titles have their beginnings, and we may be ruled henceforth by a series of bosses, hereditary or nominally elective. This may prove a degree better than the direct rule of 30,000 beastly Celtic bogtrotters.

April 25. . . . At the Church Music Association rehearsal we had the brilliant and pretty Overture to *Masaniello*, the Niedermeyer Mass, and part of the *Midsummer Night's Dream* music. I was anxious to hear Niedermeyer's orchestration, and everybody was well pleased with it. The Mass is a noble work; the Kyrie not among its strong points but effective. . . .

April 29. . . . The inveterate A. J. Bloor is out with another manifesto against Bellows, Agnew, and myself, not with a mere lettersheet, like that of last October, but a solemn octavo pamphlet of forty odd pages. It is ugly and bitter and, even to one who is intimate with Sanitary Commission affairs, extremely obscure; for example, it alludes to "real estate speculations," of which I am profoundly ignorant, and says that members of the Commission used their position to promote their "professional advancement."!!! (In my case, the reverse is sadly true.) He always mentions Agnew as the "Doctor" (in quotation marks), and Stillé's book as the so-called history and naïvely censures it for not noticing the services of him—Bloor. He seems tingling all over with wrath and spite, to the full expression of which he feels himself unequal. But the poor fellow is certainly crazy.

Nasty affair at the Four-in-Hand Club the other night over a midnight card table, at which Henry Brevoort lost some eight hundred dollars. He was stimulated by this misfortune grossly and gratuitously to insult William Jay (John Jay's son), a good-natured fellow who was innocently looking on. Jay knocked him down, the others interfered, and Brevoort carried away an ensanguined countenance and has not been heard from since. Some say that a challenge from him would be declined because his pistol discharged itself out of due time when he fought a duel with one Calhoun at Paris, which may be true or may not. All this story is printed in great detail by the scandal-mongering *Sun* newspaper. I remember Brevoort telling me last fall that he had some weighty grievance against some of the members or committees of this club; hence, probably, his bloody nose.

May 2. . . . Tonight's *Post* prints a flaming eulogy of the Church Music Association, with extracts from my little essay to which (during my absence South) my name was appended in full, instead of the "S. T. G." with which I signed the MS.

May 4. Rain set in just at the close of last evening's Church Music Association's concert, and there was much jostling confusion among the herd of carriages that filled East Fourteenth Street and Union Place. Our aristocratic sidewalk awning was useful for the first time. The concert seemed to give great satisfaction to an overcrowded house. The Goold Hoyts, George Schuylers, and other fastidious people sat in the upper gallery, listening eagerly in a steamy atmosphere of carbonic acid from eight o'clock to the end, at ten thirty-nine, and told me they were sorry it was over so soon. The chorus was perfect; the orchestra (about eighty) was not too loud. Everyone was much impressed by the Gloria, Credo, Benedictus, and Agnus of the Mass. . . .

I'm thankful that I have had something to do with getting up this Church Music Association. Besides giving thorough training to some hundreds of our best amateurs and introducing to them and to "society" people a new and most noble school of music, it has done something toward teaching New York audiences good manners. I often hear it said that the vile habit of talking and giggling is much less general than heretofore not only at our concerts but at the Philharmonic and elsewhere, and that the improvement is due to our daring handbills requesting silence and to the printed notices that have been delivered with our programmes at the door of Steinway Hall. I thought they would have been resented, but people took them kindly. I think, however, that at the February concert some silly young person sent up an anonymous pencil note to the conductor complaining of this "insult to the audience." The Philharmonic rehearsal this afternoon with Ellie was unusually satisfying. First was the delicious Mendelssohn Symphony. Then nice Miss Marie Krebs sang the *Freischütz* aria very nicely, considering that she has no remarkable amount of power; and afterwards Dachauer's setting of poor Gretchen's song in *Faust*. Remarkable that so accomplished a pianist should make a fair shew as vocalist, too. Then the newly imported Dr. Leopold Damrosch[6] did Beethoven's Violin Concerto in D, op. 61 (three movements), most brilliantly. The orchestral work is fully worthy of the composer. The performer introduced a "cadenza" of his own, creditable to his manipulation, disgraceful to him as an artist. Who is worthy to append a bit of his own writing to a composition of Beethoven's? Also played was the Overture to *Idomeneo*; also Berlioz's eructation styled *Carnival Romain*.

May 6. To Edmund Schermerhorn's this afternoon; very agreeable on the whole. Rubinstein's Trio, op. 53, is turgid, labored, and obscure. The Chopin "Polonaise" (piano and 'cello) is brilliant. Haydn's Quartette, op. 77, is full of sunshine and truth.

To Philharmonic tonight; last concert of this season. In our box were the imperial Mrs. Camilla Hoyt, William Schermerhorn, and others. The concert was charming, though the Beethoven concerto, lovely as it is, might be advantageously abridged. In the symphony, Mendelssohn seems to have boiled down all the Scotch melodies, grave and gay, that ever were written into a Caledonian beef-stock wherein the flavor of them all survives though no one of them can be identified. The Mozart overture, though comparatively slight, is very handsome. Kingsley speaks in some essay on modern poets of the time "when Alexander Pope and plain sense went out, and Shelley and the Seventh Heaven came in."

---

[6] The eminent composer and conductor (1832–1885) had been conductor of the Breslau Philharmonic Orchestra, and organizer of the Breslau Orchestra Society, a choral body. A republican by conviction, he was disheartened by the triumph of imperialism in the War of 1870. An invitation to come to New York as conductor of the Arion Society was therefore eagerly embraced. He made his first appearance in New York on May 6 of this year, the program presenting him as conductor, as composer, and as solo violinist. He soon brought the Arion Society to a high pitch of efficiency.

Substitute for Pope, Haydn or Mozart, and for Shelley, Liszt, Wagner, Berlioz, and others, and you will have a condensed bit of sound musical criticism.

May 10.   Afternoon and evening spent at Law School examination. A large class; ninety-eight go for their degree, and there are also some twenty students of but one year. I begin to tire of this annual drudgery. We cannot get Dwight to name an assistant professor or coadjutor, and he ought to have at least three to render the school an institution not wholly dependent on his life and health. Were he laid up for a month with a bad cold or a broken limb, the School would collapse and disappear. I am willing to endure much boredom for the sake of a permanent law school, but not for our eminent professor's private ephemeral academy, though it's useful in its day.

An unusual number of men in this class whose fathers I know or have known. There are sons of James W. Beekman, George Ticknor Curtis, Fulton Cutting, Henry De Forest, Denning Duer, W. M. Evarts, Foulke, Judge Hilton, the Rev. J. H. Hobart (not a shewy specimen), Judge Mitchell, Gouverneur Ogden, Judge Peabody, Bill Remsen, Dr. Tyng, Varnum, Edward A. Weeks (deceased), H. J. Raymond, and others.

May 11. . . . The Parisian chiefs are making haste to resign and get out of the way. A final assault seems close at hand. The Communists may collapse at the critical moment and bide their time for another outbreak, but it is probable they will fight like cornered sewer rats, in which case "beautiful Paris" is likely to be damaged. Streets are said to be mined. Heavy guns will have to be used against barricades, houses, palaces, and churches. Both parties have become embittered, and there will be little forbearance shewn by either.

May 13. . . . Am reading Darwin's *Descent of Man.* It is an interesting collection of physiological details but nothing more. It brings forward no new doctrine and merely discusses the application to a single race (man) of the general law sought to be established by the author in his *Origin of Species* some twelve years ago.

To me, as a "poor ignorant cretur," the popularity of Darwinism among physicists seems no less amazing than the late epidemic of so-called spiritualism among the Polloi. The theory is unscientific because it is without a scintilla of evidence. From the harmonies and analogies that underly the whole realm of organic life, Darwin infers the descent of the higher species from the lower. He might as fairly infer the descent of gold from lead from the properties they have in common. To reply that metals have no reproductive power such as animals possess is a *petitio principii*; for the question is whether species can or cannot generate new species, not whether individuals can or cannot reproduce themselves. . . .

May 17. . . . The column of the Place Vendôme *fuit*; laboriously pulled down by cables and windlass, and received on a bed of "manure" to deaden the concussion of its fall. The balconies of the Rue de la Paix crowded with lady spectators. The head of the imperial statue that surmounted the column broken off by its overthrow and was expectorated upon and kicked about by braves of the "National Guard." Cheers and music by the band—"La Marseillaise." So sublime a people never existed.[7]

Surreptitious marriage of Henry Astor (John and William's brother) to the daughter of one Dinehart, a Rhinebeck farmer. He is independent of the paternal William B. Astor and is reputed a little odd and unsocial.

An act of our last legislature substantially restores the old practice as to admission of attorneys, making three years in an office the preliminary requisite, though I believe our law school retains its privileges under the Act of April, 1860. This swing back of the pendulum is encouraging; the end of an elective judiciary looks less remote.

May 18, THURSDAY, ASCENSION DAY. Fine day. Early to church and took possession of our pew, which I held against all comers till Ellie arrived. . . . Service introduced by the fourth movement of the C Minor Symphony. . . .

Uptown with Ellie and lunched at Delmonico's. Tonight a soirée at the Rector's, 50 Varick Street. The Bishop highly approves this morning's service at which he assisted. . . . Very funny that nice people come and thank *me* for these orchestral services as they do for the Church Music Association concerts—very much as if I had written the music, drilled the chorus, and led the orchestra; whereas, my share in each has been merely the suggestion of something obviously worth doing, on which suggestion other people have acted efficiently. Mr. and Mrs. Ruggles, Miss Julia Ruggles, and Jem were at church this morning. Trinity draws people in and is a rather respectable old institution, among the most respectable in this vulgar city.

May 19. Dined here, Charles Bristed and his wife (nicest of the

---

[7] The Vendôme Column had been constructed 1806–1810, partly of the metal of captured Russian and Austrian cannon, to the glory of Napoleon Bonaparte. Rising to a height of 143 feet, it was designed in imitation of Trajan's column in Rome. An absurd figure of Napoleon as Caesar stood atop it. The Communards, ruling with a high hand in Paris while the troops of the National Assembly at Versailles labored to recapture the city, were demolishing the more important reminders of the old regime.

Sedgwicks); Dick; Colonel John Hay, poet of the Bret Harte School (which is derived from Tennyson's "Northern Farmer"); and wonderful to relate—Mr. John R. Strong. . . . Bristed seemed good enough to enjoy his dinner, and especially certain hock. I always tremble when I ask a man like him to break bread with me. Hay is decidedly clever. He was Lincoln's private secretary.[8]

Dividend to members of the Philharmonic Orchestra is $203 this year; never heretofore above $130. Good for "my administration"!

May 20. Attended a meeting tonight at a Mr. John Falconer's in East Fifteenth Street to do something about organizing a Reform Party in this corrupt city and state. Small prospect of accomplishing anything, but one forfeits his right to grumble at misgovernment by ignoring these movements or by omitting to vote. This meeting (of some twenty men—for example, William H. Neilson and little Scudder) is alleged to be in aid of a movement throughout the whole state. Were it confined to the city, it would be contemptible in its weakness; but there are in the rural districts many thousand voters who have not bowed the knee to Baal or to any ring, provincial or metropolitan, and a league among them may possibly—and only possibly—accomplish somewhat. . . .

Prussia is *not* preparing to move on Paris. The citizens of that bedeviled capital are arresting M. [Henri] Rochefort (of the *Lanterne*), suppressing the *Revue des deux Mondes*, plundering churches, and locking up priests and nuns. Paris is preaching mankind a most instructive sermon, or rather reading men an impressive commination service, to which New York may listen with advantage.[9]

May 22. Law School Committee this afternoon at Mr. Ruggles's. . . . We talked things over and all agree that there must be an addition to the force of the Law School such as shall make its existence no longer dependent on Dwight. We also approve of a third year for those who

---

[8] Charles Astor Bristed, we may repeat, represented all that was select in New York society, and everything fastidious in taste. His father was a wealthy Episcopal clergyman who had dabbled in letters, and his mother was a daughter of the first John Jacob Astor. Bristed himself studied at Cambridge, England, became an expert classical scholar, wrote books, and with his wife, the former Grace Sedgwick of Lenox, played an important rôle in social affairs. It was Hay's *Pike County Ballads* which stamped him in Strong's estimation as a poet of the Bret Harte school.

[9] The vandalism and terrorism practised by the Paris Commune were bad enough. Men were shot, churches were destroyed or plundered, newspapers suppressed, historic buildings and monuments wiped out. The press, however, tended to make them worse than they were, and said nothing about the better side of the revolt or about its partial justification.

have taken the degree of bachelor of law. A subcommittee (Mr. Ruggles, Ogden, Dwight, and Nash) was appointed to draft a scheme embodying these two changes. As to the former of them Dwight manifestly relucts, though without avowing his dislike to it. We shall have to drag him along. But the committee seems in earnest; and if he cannot find men, we will. . . .

In the last *Blackwood* appears the most striking article which that now prosy magazine has published for years, "The Battle of Dorking"—the story as told in A.D. 1925 of that disastrous battle fifty years ago by a volunteer who fought in it and of the consequent subjugation of England and her degradation to insignificance as a European Power. It is cleverly told. Sudden war with Prussia (apparently with the Czar for an ally), great enthusiasm, general arming, the English fleet disposed of (in a rather summary way), then invasion, march of an army of militia volunteers and a few regulars to repel it, want of organization, defective commissariat, brave men unscientifically handled, and a crushing defeat. I don't believe this article or a dozen like it will induce the English government to provide for national defense.

May 23. . . . Reports from Paris are cloudy but lurid. Conflagration, massacre, heavy batteries playing, magazines exploding—these are conspicuous words in more or less trustworthy telegrams. Paris seems to have fallen again. The Assembly is reported to have gained the Hôtel de Ville and Montmartre and to dominate the whole city. The Rouges have collapsed. But even assuming order is reëstablished, the real difficulties of the situation remain to be met. . . . There is no faith anywhere in the stability of the new régime, no confidence in any leader—civil or military —and above all, no belief in God and no conception of the meaning of the word law, except when represented by a gendarme.

France now had a new temporary government established by the National Assembly, with the able Louis Adolphe Thiers at its head; and this government, with its seat at Versailles, had two emergency tasks—the making of peace with Germany by acceptance of the treaty of Frankfort (May, 1871), and the quelling of the ugly revolt of the Commune in Paris (April–May). This Commune united various elements among the half-starved, long-neglected, sullen workingmen and debtor groups of the capital: Socialists, Anarchists, Republicans, Collectivists, and others. Gaining power in elections of March 28, they set up an executive council of ninety, lodged arbitrary authority in a few desperate men, such as Raoul Rigault, prefect of police, and embarked upon a series of violent measures. Among their military leaders were a Frenchman named Cluseret, and a Pole named Dombrowsky who had served in the Russian forces. They suppressed newspapers, closed churches, shot prisoners and hostages wholesale, and burned the Palais-Royal, the Hôtel de Ville, the Tuileries, and other splendid public buildings. But the government of Thiers at Versailles had almost the whole of France behind it. The national army, far superior to the forces of the Commune, broke through the city's fortifications on May 21 and entered Paris. Then ensued a series of bloody battles at street barricades, lasting for a whole week until, on May 29, the Vincennes fort was taken, resistance ceased, and Thiers was master of the whole capital. A bloody vengeance was taken upon the Communards.

At this very moment a great battle for peace was being won by the English-speaking peoples. On May 24 the Senate ratified Hamilton Fish's Treaty of Washington with Great Britain, under which a whole series of difficulties between the two nations were to be submitted to adjudication.

May 24. . . . News from Paris. The Reds still maintain their barricades in the Place Vendôme and Place de la Concorde. Mischief is going on, which the telegraphists probably exaggerate. "Great fires raging in various quarters." Tuileries[10] and Louvre fired "with petroleum" by the insurgents. The former "entirely burnt down." Hopes of saving the galleries of the latter. Halls of the Council of State and Legion of Honor (across the Seine) also fired. Hôtel de Ville believed to have been blown up, and so on. No doubt a vast amount of wanton destruction has been effected by the beastly hordes who raised such a howl over "Prussian vandalism." No doubt Victor Hugo is still proud of the noble People of Paris. May they spare Notre Dame and the Sainte Chapelle!

May 26. . . . Reports from Paris. Fighting and combustion still in progress. . . . Battle going on in Père-Lachaise. The destruction of its ugly, crowded, dingy monuments would be no loss. It's said the Rue Royale has been blown up with mines; also, that the *loups-garous* of the

---

[10] Only two small sections or pavilions of the Palais des Tuileries survived the conflagration set by the Communards. The great building, which had been begun in 1564 for Catherine de Médicis, was completely gutted; its site was later turned into a public garden.

Seine have murdered all their "hostages" in cold blood, including the estimable old archbishop and some fifty of his clerics.[11] Nothing more likely, but the report wants confirmation. Summary execution said to have been done upon Dombrowsky and sundry other vaporing Communist scum captured by the Versaillists. Very proper and creditable. From the positions still held by the insurgents, they are said to be throwing "petroleum shells" impartially into every part of Paris.

May 27. . . . Telegrams from Versailles and St. Denis are many, muddled, and contradictory. Whether the Versailles men are giving no quarter and the streets of Paris are running with blood, the Rouges are pumping petroleum out of fire engines into burning buildings, and the Palais de Justice is destroyed; or, whether the converse of all this be true, no man can tell at present. I suppose these Red gentlemen to have spared most of the churches as "of no account anyhow," and not worth the expenditure of petroleum and gunpowder.

May 29. Am just from Niblo's with Ellie and Jem. We saw *Kit*, a most melodramatic melodrama, the principal character wherein (a generous, good-hearted, reckless, rough Southwesterner) is played by Chanfrau, who made a memorable hit twenty-five years ago as "Mose," the rowdy, fireman, and b'hoy of the Bowery.[12] This part has been studied with equal care, and the result is a photograph of the fire-eater and "high-toned gentleman," who would be an utter ruffian but for his affections and good impulses. The piece is got up with expense, and many of its scenes are most elaborate in machinery and appointments: the Southern Hotel barroom, for instance; the Mississippi steamer lying at the levee; the saloon of the steamer, with gamblers roping in greenhorns; the upper deck of the steamer at night, when she is blown up and plundered. One Boniface played the Southern gambler—"gentlemanly," cool, stoical, and villainous—with great effect.

Paris: The last fires of insurrection seem to have been trampled out (for the time) yesterday morning. "Fifty thousand dead and wounded lie unburied in the cellars and the streets of Paris," say the telegraphists.

---

[11] Georges Darboy, Archbishop of Paris, a prelate of fine character, was executed by the Communards.

[12] Francis S. Chanfrau (1824–1884), character actor, was appearing in *Kit, The Arkansas Traveller*. As Strong writes, he had made his first great success in New York when he appeared in 1848 as Mose, a typical daredevil fireman of the period, in the short drama *A Glance at New York*, written by Benjamin A. Baker. *Kit* now proved equally popular, and Chanfrau kept playing the piece throughout the country for a dozen years.

Possibly it may prove that there are only forty-nine thousand. It is positively stated that Archbishop Darboy and some sixty priests ("hostages") were murdered in cold blood on Saturday. The victors gave no quarter to men, women, or children with arms in their hands during the final struggle. They are now shooting insurgents in batches of from fifty to one hundred, on summary conviction; and if the word justice mean anything, they are quite right. . . .

May 30. . . . According to official reports from Washburne[13] at Paris to the State Department at Washington, this French Assembly or Convention is intensely reactionary and Legitimist, and the ideas of its majority date back to a period before 1789. So says Bancroft Davis, who ought to know. He thinks the Comte de Chambord will come back to France and rule *jure divino*, with all the prerogatives of Louis XIV, for a certain period—longer or shorter. Perhaps he will. After the events of the last ten months, nothing can astonish me. . . . The conquerors of Paris are executing justice swiftly and sternly, by the most rigorous methods of martial law. If they overdo their fusillading, they may awaken some sort of pity for the defeated Communists now universally execrated.

May 31. Walked up to Central Park this beautiful afternoon and inspected the new Museum of Natural History in the old arsenal building. It contains much that is interesting and new (to me), but the cases seem unnecessarily crowded. There is also quite a nucleus outside of the arsenal of our zoological garden that is to be hereafter. The Park is lovely and leafy. These things should exert a civilizing and humanizing influence upon "the masses." . . . Looked into St. Thomas's Church; the interior peculiar but effective—the stained glass is very good. There is much building in progress uptown. Domestic architecture is improving.

It is just three years ago today since poor George Anthon decided to end an intimacy of more than thirty years because we differed about a question of portrait painting. A little while afterwards, he declared he was glad "we" (the College trustees) were offended, for he *meant* to offend us. When he was reminded of this remark a few months later by Charley Strong, he thought it a pity it had been communicated to me but said no word of apology or regret. We have had pleasant times together. I can't feel unkindly toward him, for he inherits his father's bad, ugly, cantankerous blood; and I think, moreover, that he was hardly in his right mind in May, 1868.

[13] Elihu Washburne, formerly Senator from Illinois and briefly Secretary of State, played an intrepid part as our Minister to France.

Nearly all the leaders of La Commune are said to have been shot, Rochefort (of *La Lanterne*) and Cluseret among the rest. As yet no mercy is shewn; perhaps it would be out of place. The victors are substituting *mitrailleuses* for musketry as more economical in the execution of justice upon their batches of convicts. The foot of the bourgeoisie is on the neck of the dreaded and hated Rouges at last, and it will stay there till they are made powerless for mischief on any large scale, if anything short of extermination can render them innocuous. . . . Victor Hugo is ordered out of Belgium and thus made to seem a person of importance.

The Orléans Prince and the Comte de Chambord, alias Duc de Bordeaux, alias Henri V, or "Dieudonné," are said to have shaken hands and to have agreed to pull together for the vacant throne of France. Henri is to take it for life, and the remainder is to go to the Comte de Paris. Henri is childless. No one believes the "Republic" will last a year. This arrangement would possibly have just the least bit better chance of stability than any other because it is founded on ancient institutions and on legal right, though such considerations have but nominal weight with Frenchmen. . . .

June 2. . . . The so-called "Democratic" Party is trying to "take a new departure"; in other words, to change front for the battle of 1872 and set up a new "platform." But it is sorely bothered by speeches of that old pirate Jeff Davis about the "cause of the South," and how it is not a lost cause at all, but will certainly triumph yet, and how the war decided nothing. What's equally embarrassing, Southerners, being more candid than politic, uproariously applaud every word he says. So the New York *World* denounces Jeff Davis as a pigheaded and conceited windbag, devoid alike of patriotism and of common sense! Sich is human friendship.

> Is all the counsel that we two have shared,
> The brothers' vows, the hours that we have spent—
> O, O, is all forgot? . . .

June 5, MONDAY.   Ben Silliman continues ill. If I had $400,000 left me by an aged and cantankerous female relative, I should expect illness in my family according to the great rule of compensation.

Columbia College sagamores met this afternoon. Recommendations of Law School Committee adopted *nem. con.* So we are authorized to appoint an adjunct professor of municipal law and to organize a third year course. Barnard produced a cord or two of closely written foolscap MS and said he would read a few brief extracts from his annual report to the trustees on which he wished to base one or two recommendations. He turned on the steam and began throwing off sheet after sheet of vehement diffuseness about "elective studies," disputes among the college authorities of Yale, and the "evidences" as part of an undergraduate course. Morgan Dix and Dr. H. J. Anderson slipped quietly away, evaded, erumped, in consternation. The rest of us sat with anguish depicted on our countenances. At last, Gouverneur Ogden got up and interrupted Barnard with the statement that, as the report would probably be printed and as some of us had urgent engagements elsewhere, it might be unnecessary to read any more of it. Ogden is useful sometimes from not possessing the delicacy of feeling that makes one unwilling to bell the cat in a case like this. But Barnard was hard to suppress. He tried to go on and lay before us just a little more of his views; and "O Ewigkeit," how he did prose! At last, Mr. Ruggles got up and objected to his criticism on the affairs of Yale, and the Bishop (in the chair) had something to say against his position that we ought to match public opinion about courses of studies and be guided by it, instead of guiding it. Very fine and grand, of course, and in a certain sense true. But we twenty-four fogies are as capable of guiding public opinion as one of our park sparrows is of modifying the course of an equinoctial storm. It resulted in an order that the report be printed for the use of the trustees. The practice has been to print one thousand copies.

Walked tonight on the west side. The viaduct railroad, Brooklyn Bridge, stone piers, and a river street 250 feet wide, the blowing up of the Hellgate reefs—these changes, all now under way, will make this a new city within ten years.

June 7. . . . Details begin to arrive of the final struggle in Paris; they are fearful. Babylon is become an habitation of devils, and there is little to choose between Communist and Versaillist. On both sides the women outdevil the men. So lively a presentation of the pit of hell has never before been got up on earth. It was produced with absolute disregard of expense and with the most refined and scientific modern machinery of death and devastation. Other like catastrophes of civil war may have called out as much fury, rancor, and cruelty, and cost as much blood, and even more; but in this the accessories were effective and terrible beyond precedent.

June 9. Law School Committee met this afternoon at the School in Lafayette Place; Mr. Ruggles, Ogden, Blatchford, and I. Dwight was absent and sent no explanation of his absence. His policy is passive resistance to any change, like the pickpocket in Dickens who bothered the policeman by lying down on his back on the sidewalk. He wants the school to be his alone, and I fear he thinks more than so able and so rich a man ought about the diminution of his income by the introduction of an adjunct paid out of the fees. We talked over matters and men for an hour. A. C. Bradley and A. R. Macdonough were suggested. Blatchford strongly recommended Charles H. Hunt. The special difficulty in the case is that Dwight will assuredly make it uncomfortable for any man we put in the place and will sooner or later squeeze him out in some subtle way. He does not understand, perhaps, that although the school is (thanks to him) most successful and useful and creditable to the College, we are perfectly ready to cut loose from it, unless we can give it a faculty and make it an institution with Dwight for its head, instead of Dwight's private legal academy.

To Society Library this evening. Re-read that admirable "Battle of Dorking" article in the May *Blackwood*. It has attracted much attention and is the best and most vivid military narrative I ever read. Some of its little touches are worthy of Swift. One believes the story as one believes Gulliver. To be sure it is without inherent improbability. The narrator's first vision of the German-spiked helmets through the pouring rain, the skirmish line halting, firing and advancing by degrees, the angry artillery general's query, "Who commands this battery?" "I do, Sir Henry"; and what follows—the piercing of the English line and the regiment finding itself "without knowing how" drawn up in the rear of its original position—are most admirable realistic pictures expressed in the simplest language. The article is said to be written by Captain Hamill, the author of *Lady Lee's Widowhood*, a novel of sixteen years ago. It might have been written by Defoe.

June 12. . . . Not much news from Paris. The *Versaillais* have introduced a new feature into the law and practise of courts-martial. Good-looking women caught with arms (or "petroleum bottles") in their hands are "degraded" before they are shot. The same braves execute both branches of the sentence. Another ingenious novelty is to *half* shoot a leader of La Commune . . . and watch him howling and kicking on the pavement for an hour or two before his brains are finally blown out. There can be no doubt that *la belle France* is Satan's country seat and summer home and that he is making quite a little visit there. These statements in the present tense relate back to the latter weeks of May, whereof we began to learn particulars by mail. Paris seems rather quiet now. The *energumen* is in comatose sleep after her last fearful paroxysm.

June 15.   Dawned with pouring rain and every portent of a wet day. But at nine, the rain abated, the carriage came, and Temple, Louis, and I set off to make a day of it at the Leake and Watts Orphan House, this being its annual festival. The Park looked lovely after its copious watering as gleams of sunshine began to brighten it. At the House were Morgan Dix and Dunscomb; Knox (our treasurer) with a lot of women; old Fred DePeyster (secretary) with another lot; Benjamin H. Field (blowing and braying after his kind), and others. Examinations, singing, callisthenics were all very nice. There are about 130 children this year—a remarkably good-looking lot for beneficiaries of a charity. It's not merely that they are rosy and plump and look jolly, but few of their faces are of the type one so often sees in such establishments—dull-eyed, prognathous, and with foreheads villainously low, as if born in cellars and reared in the gutter. The great majority of these little boys and girls are fine specimens of their race; several of the girls look vigorous and bright enough and are pretty enough to tempt a childless man of fortune to adopt half a dozen of them as pets. We came away at four after a substantial lunch, through another brief summer shower. . . .

June 17. . . . The Hon. Clement L. Vallandigham of Ohio accidentally shot himself yesterday and is dead. There was mair tint at Bull Run.

The Roman Catholics of this city . . . are celebrating the "jubilee" of Pope Pio Nono with prayer and pyrotechny. By "jubilee" is meant the twenty-fifth anniversary of his election to the pontificate by the Italian "Ring." No one of his predecessors since the mythical pontificate of St. Peter has worn the tiara so long. Pius is now aged eighty-one. Being infallible, he is, of course, guaranteed against chronic cerebral ailments, a fact which materially increases his expectation of life. Rome becomes capital of Italy next month, but it's said that when Victor Emmanuel and his court walk in, Pius IX and his cardinals will walk out and make a Pilgrimage to Ajaccio. Do desertion and non-residence vacate a see?

June 22. . . . In the Viele case, prevalent opinion seems against both parties. Can "Miss Julia D——" (a liaison with whom the defendant charges against her husband) be the nice pretty girl I met at Brattleboro last summer?[14]

June 24. . . . Prussia and England appear to have fallen out a little;

[14] General Egbert L. Viele shortly married Miss Juliette Dana. This well-known engineer, whose connection with the planning of Central Park and active Civil War career have already been noticed in this diary, still had many fruitful years before him. He was Park Commissioner in New York 1883–84 and member of Congress during Cleveland's first term.

probably about Heligoland. I do not believe Prussia wants another war just yet, but after this *annus mirabilis*, no military or political event can surprise me, not even the establishment of General von Moltke's headquarters at Windsor, the proclamation of a republic at Charing Cross, or the selection by Queen Victoria of an eligible brownstone front on Fifth Avenue for her future residence. The times are prestigious, and the Powers of this world are shaken. What single year has ever witnessed events as startling and as weighty as the ignominious overthrow of France, the destruction of half Paris, the proclamation of the infallibility dogma as *de fide*, and the downfall of the temporal power? . . .

June 25, SUNDAY. To Trinity with Temple and Louis. The Rev. Mr. Love preached. He is a deacon from Jacksonville, Florida. He called on me the other day to solicit a small donation for his church and school, and this was a begging sermon. His hue is ebony, or jet. In fact, he seemed to me the blackest black man I ever saw. "Where he gazed a gloom pervaded space." But this apparent intensity of color may have been in some degree due to contrast with his white surplice. His sermon was much too long, and a certain uniform monotonous intensity of voice and manner made it doubly wearisome. But it was better than our average sermons, and decidedly better than Vinton, as some man whom I did not know remarked to me coming home on the Fourth Avenue car. There was no peculiarity of style or accent, and the preacher's apparent earnestness and sincerity were impressive. . . .

June 27. Meeting of the Law School Committee this afternoon, with Mr. Ruggles, Professor Dwight, Judge Blatchford, and Gouverneur Ogden. Abbott's name was brought forward and generally approved. It was thought prudent, however, to let Dwight confer with him about division of duties and methods of instruction, and so on, before committing ourselves; so we adjourned to July 19. We thus enable Dwight to continue his policy of passive obstruction, if he be so disposed. But it is mere justice to say that there were no symptoms of that policy this afternoon and that he seemed cordially disposed to help the committee carry out its views. Macdonough's name being mentioned, I felt bound to say that his position during the war made it probable that his teaching on constitutional questions would not be such as members of the committee would altogether approve. If I am correctly informed, he was a most cantankerous Copperhead. It's unpleasant to have to say such things about a man behind his back. . . .

June 29. . . . A French loan ($900,000,000) is promptly taken, though this is evidently a mere lull in the storm; and the credit of France will not be firmly established until a great majority of the French people have torn out each other's throttles or blown each other away with *mitrailleuse*. But the success of this loan is to France the first gleam of light through the clouds since Napoleoniculus declared war in July, 1870. It proves that France is not so dead but that she can put her hand in her pocket—a very vital function of national life.

July 3, MONDAY.   Saturday Ellie was at Brooklyn, "Prospect Park," with Stranahan, A. A. Low, and her papa; she highly approves it. This was an occasion. A bust of Washington Irving was "inaugurated," which being interpreted from the newspaper dialect means "uncovered and displayed to the public for the first time." There were speeches by the Rev. H. Ward Beecher and others, and Irving had what is termed in the same patois "an ovation." . . .

July 4.   Saw hardly one New York face in the streets today. New York has gone out of town. There were none but detonating boys and little squads of self-evident rustics. Of the latter, a crowd was gathered around Trinity, gazing with wide-eyed wonder up at the steeple, the chimes whereof were canorous and clangorous. I spent two hours in Wall Street listening to their melody, reading morning papers, and wondering what had become of Charley Strong.

French elections indicate popular apathy. Probably a very moderate Republicanism will have a working majority in the Gallic Witenagemot. Victor Emmanuel (alias Caiaphas, Diotrephes, Nero, Judas, Herod, Pharaoh, Mahomet, Termagaunt, and others) has moved to Rome and seems inclined to stay there for the present. Poor Poppy Pio!!!

July 5.   Charley Strong sailed for Liverpool in the *China* and is to return by steamer of August 10. . . .

July 6. . . .   That gander-monkey Victor Hugo was badly beaten as candidate for the National Assembly. Sweet are the uses of adversity. It seems to have brought out glimmerings of common sense from even the French people. . . .

July 8.   Dined at five-thirty. Took the Seventh Avenue Railroad car to the Park, wherein I prowled about with satisfaction. The "playground" is very lovely in the slant afternoon sunlight, with its groups of ball players and of lazy spectators. Walked to the Mall, Ramble, and "Belvedere Hill." The new tower of grey limestone (?), not yet finished, is creditable; so are nearly all the structures of the Park. It certainly contains much that is beautiful and interesting.

Comte de Chambord, alias Henri V, is said to meditate a grand coup; not likely. The attempt would be premature and would fail ignominiously, like Louis Napoleon's experiments at Boulogne and Strassburg. The Legitimists seem weaker than I thought. The Assembly is to commit the grave blunder of moving from Versailles to Paris.

July 10. To Trinity Church vestry tonight. Our financial outlook for next year, as set forth by General Dix, is not rose colored. The assessments—heavy outlay upon the cemetery made necessary by the opening of the new boulevard and 155th Street, and the erection of our Trinity Church Schoolhouse—will probably leave us with a deficit. . . .

Prospect of a "faction fight" on a large scale next Wednesday. The Orangemen turn out in force on that day to celebrate the Battle of the Boyne with a grand procession, *more solito*. The Fenians, Ribbonmen, Greens, and miscellaneous Irish scum of the popish persuasion propose a grand target excursion and picnic for the same day and avow their design to break up the procession and to bate the skin off the ugly bones of the processionals. There is a proclamation of civil war for day after tomorrow.[15] Many of the Roman Catholic clergy mildly recommended their flocks yesterday at mass to behave dacently and to commit no breach of the peace, and (what is more to the purpose) the police and militia are said to be ready for action. I hope they are. The lawless, insolent arrogance and intolerance of these homicidal ruffianly popish Celts must be suppressed somehow. If all the braves of both factions could be brought together, well-armed, within the enclosure of the Union Racecourse and kept there to fight it out . . . until both parties were exterminated, criminal justice in New York would be administered at a greatly reduced expense next year. Sagacious old Cyrus Curtiss (this evening) thinks there will be no row, and I incline, on the whole, to think so, too. Predicted riots seldom occur. But if we experience any rumpus, it will be a rather grave one—*à la mode de Paris*. Hundreds of Irish harridans are quite equal to the rôle of a *pétroleuse*. I remember them in July, 1863.

July 11. The city government strikes its colors to *Patricino Furens*;

[15] The previous year, 1870, an Orange procession celebrating the Battle of the Boyne had been brutally attacked by Irish rioters; the police made little effort to interfere, and nobody was punished for the assault. Now the Orange Association was making large-scale preparations to test the question whether they had a right to parade, and the Irish Catholics were preparing to repeat their performance. Two prominent members of the Tweed Ring ruling the city represented the Irish Catholic element, and they gave orders to Mayor A. Oakey Hall and Superintendent of Police Kelso.

and Mr. Superintendent Kelso issues a general order to the police to stop any Orange procession tomorrow and, if possible, to prevent any assemblage for that purpose; and Mayor Hall publishes a letter setting forth the pretended reason why. . . . Most people are furiously exasperated (they'll forget their exasperation in a week and it will lead to nothing). There was an extempore meeting at the Corn Exchange this morning to denounce our politic mayor, and all the leading newspapers claw him savagely, except the clever but venial *World*, which now defends the Ring through thick and thin, though it was denouncing the same gang as utterly corrupt only fifteen months ago; so it was bought by the Copperheads in 1861. I suppose it is called the *World* because it turns around. There are strong arguments for the course taken by the authorities, but it exasperates me because I know and everybody knows that if a St. Patrick's Day procession had been threatened with lawless violence and attack, it would have been protected by the whole power of the county. But we are to Papistical Paddy as Cedric the Saxon to Front de Boeuf.

Tonight's reports are that both factions mean to turn out tomorrow in spite of the city government; that the Seventy-first Regiment is under arms tonight, and that the Seventh and other regiments will assemble early tomorrow; that Mayor Hall and Mr. Kelso are scared by the general feeling of wrath and indignation against them; and so on. I do not believe there will be any serious outbreak, but, unless tomorrow be a rainy day (of which there is hope), it may witness a sanguinary triangular duel and the gravest mischief. The trained bands of Brooklyn are said to be ready for action—"hushed in grim repose." Governor Randolph of New Jersey has put forth a sensible and manly proclamation (trouble being expected in Jersey City) to the effect that all people have the right to meet peaceably together for any purpose not unlawful, and that if any organized attempt be made to interfere with the exercise of that right, the whole power of the state must be used to repress such interference.

July 12. Everyone taken by surprise this morning. Governor Hoffman issues a masculine proclamation overruling the pusillanimous surrender of Oakey Hall and Mr. Superintendent Kelso, and announcing that any peaceable and orderly people who wish to solace themselves by parading the streets in this infernal weather are at liberty to do so and shall be protected in the enjoyment of that right by all the armies of the state, of which armies he, John T. Hoffman, is commander-in-chief. Good for Hoffman!! By this step he repudiates the Ring, of which he has been accounted the slave and tool, and leaves Hall floundering on his back in the mud. It may cost him the most sweet voices of the Irishry of New York and the cities but will strengthen him immensely throughout the country and may make him President. He saw that the Ring had made a false move and that a tempest of indignation was rising; so he cut loose (at least for the present) from his disreputable allies and made himself their master.[16]

At eleven o'clock Broadway below Union Square looked as usual, except that groups of shabby men and boys were loitering on corners and strolling about. Few roughs visible. Crowds to be seen a block or two eastward through Prince, Houston, and Bleecker streets. No shops closed. Wall Street very quiet. Extras began to appear a little after twelve and sold fast. They announced nothing important, except the muster of militia and police in great force (some thirteen thousand men), that the Orangemen meant to parade, and sundry fictions about riot and slaughter.

Uptown at one-thirty in the afternoon. Left omnibus at Bleecker Street to look after the Bank for Savings, which I thought might be in danger of molestation, as Bleecker Street was occupied by a hard-looking crowd. Within its doors all was serene, and the clerks told me the only peculiarity they had noticed was an unusual deference and civility on the part of their Irish depositors. Very significant. Then strolled uptown. Broadway was quite crowded; many laborers off duty in the crowd. Walked far down Tenth Street in quest of what seemed a great fire. Vast volumes of smoke were swelling out against the clear sky. Gave up the pursuit at last, for the sun shone intensely hot. They said the fire was at the foot of Horatio Street, but this evening's extras make no mention of it. Curious to observe how little effect this orgasm of riot and bloodshed produced in side streets. Children were playing on shady spots of sidewalks, ladies in lovely flowing summer robes fanning themselves at parlor windows or on balconies, little tradesmen pursuing their vocations. Lunched at St. Denis Hotel (Eleventh Street and Broadway).

[16] Great public indignation, as Strong notes, had greeted Mayor Hall's edict that the Orangemen should not march. Nothing since the Draft Riots had so thoroughly aroused and united the respectable population of the city. Governor John T. Hoffman responded to the wave of public anger by making a hurried night trip to the city, proclaiming that the procession would be allowed to take place, and calling out the militia to protect it. The militia regiments, especially the Seventh, responded to his call in great force. The best citizens, while regretful that an Old World quarrel had been transferred to American shores, felt that the governor had saved the community from a grave breach of civil liberty.

THE NEW YORK POST OFFICE (1875–1938)

A. B. MULLETT, ARCHITECT

CHARLES F. CHANDLER

THOMAS EGLESTON

There had been a row there an hour or two before; mob dispersed by police and a few heads broken—nothing serious. Going down Broadway again, I observed three or four rioters, more or less bloody as to their noses, escorted by veteran policemen toward the station house. At the corner of Eighth Street, there was a movement in the crowd, and presently twenty or thirty omnibuses, each densely packed with perspiring police-men, went tearing up Broadway, accompanied by a racing mob of raff, some merely running in quest of any fun that might be in prospect, and others (Celtic blackguards) "with the light of" riot and homicide "on their faces." Then to a brief meeting of Savings Bank trustees.

Thence to Eighth Avenue, which from Twenty-fourth to Twenty-seventh streets was the scene of the sharpest collision between the mob and the civil authority of which I have yet heard as occurring today. Quite a crowd, and rather a dark-looking, grim, silent crowd on both sidewalks. All shops closed. Many fresh bullet marks on brick walls and windows. Talked with many people who had seen the collision, but I could not distinctly ascertain its particulars. It would seem that Celts began firing down from roofs upon Orangemen and militia and charged the procession; that the militia returned the fire and killed some ten—some say twenty, some sixty—rioters, including (one man said) an old woman and a child; that the rioters broke and ran, but that several militia-men, including one officer, were killed.[17]

July 13.   The town has been peaceful today. Celtic laborers on the boulevards who struck work yesterday for a day's murdering have been discharged and Germans employed in their stead under protection of a small militia force. Returns of yesterday's casualties vary. Probably forty were killed and one hundred disabled. The only serious collision was that on Eighth Avenue, though there were several minor skirmishes. In every collision the Celts were as cowardly as they were brutal. They shewed far better pluck in 1863. They made no stand anywhere. Their bestiality was of the type peculiar to France, Erin, and the Carnivora; for example, a woman in the crowd waved an orange handkerchief and was instantly shot dead by a gallant Irishman who stood behind her. A little girl of fifteen or sixteen was picked up dead, with a pistol shot through her

[17] The roster of dead in the riot rose within a week to forty-seven, while scores were wounded. Governor Hoffman's unexpected display of firmness and independence had vindicated some basic American principles. The episode, however, led to much discussion of the misgovernment in New York and Albany. As the *Nation* said: "Behind the folly and wickedness of the Irish there lie American shortcoming, corruption, and indifference."

breast. She wore a yellow (or orange) and white striped sack or jacket—meaning no harm, I dare say, poor thing—and was murdered by one of these gorillas because he objected to the color of her dress. O what an amount of bosh has been written about "Erin"! For example,

> And blest forever is she who relied
> Upon Erin's honor and Erin's pride.

So sings the delectable Tommy Moore, and to do him justice, he has sung more mellifluously sometimes. For a due estimate of Erin's chivalry and honor, read the history of the Rebellion of 1698; that of the Parliament which was bought—one member after another—when England wanted the Act of Union; that of James II's Irish Parliament; and that of the narrative of the pranks played by our Irish rebels in July, 1863.

Casualties among policemen and militiamen were few. Of course a certain number of mere spectators suffered, victims of their own curiosity and desire of witnessing a possible tragedy. Some of the militia fired without orders, and of this fact an evil-disposed coroner's jury may make mischievous use. But I have heard only one sentiment expressed today—namely, gratification that the Irish roughs have had a rough lesson.

Our laudations of Governor Hoffman seem to have been a little premature. There is evidence today that he consulted with Oakey Hall and Kelso and concurred in their pusillanimous policy till he saw that it was raising a storm of popular indignation and that he was going to cut a most pitiful figure beside Governor Randolph of New Jersey. Then he ratted to the side of law and order, but too late to intimidate the beasts who had been encouraged to regard themselves as sovereigns of this city.

July 15, SATURDAY. Wednesday's savage outbreak and slaughter are not quite forgotten even yet. We have lost, I think, a good deal of sensibility and gained a certain amount of sense since the Astor Place riot of 1849. The almost universal expression as to the spectators killed on Wednesday is: "Sorry for them, but it was their own fault. People who mix with rioters or hang about the skirts of a riot in search of the picturesque and exciting must take the chance of a stray bullet." In 1849 the community seemed to half-believe, in a vague imbecile way, that the militia were to blame for taking life, though the necessity of firing in self-defense was even more urgent on that occasion than on this. But since 1849 we have passed through the Rebellion and the Irish Riot week of 1863.

Yesterday was buried a poor little Mary something; eleven years old.

The child ran out to see the procession, wearing some article of dress with yellow stripes or trimmings. One of these "ferocious human pigs" (should we not substitute Irish for human?) found his susceptibilities wounded by a color too like orange, so he put a pistol he happened to have about him to this little girl's breast and shot her dead. Erin go bragh! It's well established that a couple of Irish girls—biddies—were stationed at a window on Eighth Avenue firing down on the procession with pistols that were loaded as fast as they were discharged by men behind them. Irish chivalry![18]

July 17. To Park after dinner, and had myself rowed about on the lake in the twilight and among the swans. The Park gains on me at every visit. I have not found out half its points even yet.

Another member of the Ninth Regiment (Pryor) died today. From two till near five yesterday, a dense but perfectly well-behaved crowd occupied both sides of Fourth Avenue, spectators of the funeral (at Calvary Church) of Paige and Wyatt, Ninth Regiment men, murdered last Wednesday. Police and militia were out in force, and there was no row. But some of the militia officers on their way home were actually set upon by a party of these Celtic hog-wolves, armed with sword-canes, and narrowly escaped with their lives. The afternoon was most sultry looking and black, with an occasional premonitory sprinkling of rain, but at about five the rain came suddenly down in floods and scattered the crowd like a "whiff of grapeshot." Mr. Ruggles took refuge here. It was a most drastic thundershower. The wind swept away a fire-alarm tower on Third Avenue near Fifty-first Street, and overthrew a large tree at the southeast corner of Madison Square, which completely barricaded Madison Avenue.

Died, C. V. S. Roosevelt, a highly respectable old landmark and millionaire. His appearance always suggested to me a Hindoo idol, roughly carved in red porphyry.

July 18. Left Wall Street at two-thirty with Murray Hoffman, Jr. for an exploring expedition to Prospect Park, Brooklyn.[19] Lunched at

[18] Strong's vehement denunciation of the Irish must be read with due account of the feeling excited by the Draft Riots, the Fenian organization ("from first to last a standing outrage on the peace and dignity of the United States," wrote E. L. Godkin), the misdeeds of Tammany, and the generally high rate of violence among Irish immigrants. But his explosion is lacking in historical perspective and in tolerance.

[19] Prospect Park was new. Most of the land had been bought from the Litchfield estate just before the Civil War, at a cost of nearly four millions. The war delayed its improvement, and it was not until 1866 that development of the park began under James S. T. Stranahan, head of a city commission.

Downing's. Crossed at Fulton Ferry. Inspected the Brooklyn pier of the future bridge. It is about thirty feet high, and the great mass of granite masonry looks like business. Then a long horse railroad car ride up Fulton Street and Flatbush Avenue, and reached the "Plaza," a large open place with a most lovely fountain and a tolerable statue of Lincoln. Reservoir on the left, with a kind of observatory. The outlook thence is panoramic and most striking. It takes in New York, Brooklyn with its numerous suburbs, the Jersey hills, the Bay, Staten Island, the Navesink Highlands, an expanse of ocean, Canarsie or Jamaica Bay, and the great belt of level ground that extends eastward from the Narrows to a latitude south of Jamaica. Then explored the Park, even to "Lookout Hill," from which one gets a fine view to the south and west. We almost saw the crest of the surf breaking on Coney Island beach. We certainly rejoiced in the tonic saline air that entered our lungs only some five minutes, if so much, after contact with the sea spray. Then walked back to our point of entrance.

This Park beats Central Park ten to one in trees. Its wealth of forest is most enviable. I think we cannot match its softly undulating lawns. But we beat it in rock and the boxes of landscape. Prospect Park's attempts at rock are pitiable, most palpable piles of boulders. We beat it also in water and bridges and other like structures. But it beats us in views and is a most lovely pleasance. . . .

The ferry boats coming in as we left our car were a phenomenon. Each (six-fifteen) carried just as many men as could stand on her deck. If I wanted to buy a house in Brooklyn (and I envy residents on the Heights overlooking the Bay), the necessity of using such an overcrowded conveyance morning and evening would reduce the value of any piece of Brooklyn real estate . . . at least thirty per cent. The bridge, if ever completed, will remove this drawback.

To Delmonico's, where we dined modestly. This was a delightful expedition. . . .

July 21. . . . The orators and the editors of Erin are still doing their best to create a strong anti-Irish party. Their thrasonical huffe-snuffe is intolerable. John T. Hoffman seems to have lost the Irish vote beyond recovery. Hanging him in effigy is an innocent amusement very popular with Hibernians just now. But he has failed to secure the hearty approval of the other side, for nobody supposes he would have issued his "Proclamation" of the twelfth if he could have helped doing it. Thus do politicians without principle try to sit on two stools and tumble between them.

July 22. Uptown this evening to Central Park. . . . With the growth of this city, my evening strolls have resumed their northern or uptown direction. In old Greenwich Street days—1838–1848—they were up to Fourteenth Street. Now they are up to Seventy-ninth and Eightieth streets. . . . Entered the Park at Seventy-second Street and explored a new and lovely region in and around the Ramble. The Park is a priceless acquisition. Thank God for it. . . .

The *Times* is creating a deep sensation by detailed statements of vast sums embezzled by the Ring, with names, dates, and amounts. Some clerk in the Comptroller's office has been bought, no doubt. An unclean job, but one must fight the Devil with fire. As yet there appears no answer. But even Bill Tweed the Boss (that is, *Der Böse*), Oakey Hall, Sweeny & Co. cannot let three distinct (verifiable) charges of fraud go by default.

Abolition (by "Royal Warrant") of the purchase system in the British Army creates a certain degree of excitement throughout Albion.[20] England is drifting from her old moorings faster and faster every year, but whitherward remains to be seen.

July 26. . . . Recent evenings spent in exploring expeditions. Beekman Place, on the East River from Forty-ninth Street to Fifty-first Street, is unlike any other part of the city and dimly suggests Brooklyn Heights. Its brownstone houses look very reputable but are separated from civilization by a vast tract of tenement rookeries and whiskey mills, and streets that absolutely crawl with poor little slatternly pretty children.[21] Outlook over the East River is nice and includes a clear view of the penitentiary, the smallpox hospital, and the other palaces of Blackwell's Island. On Sunday night the Park was especially lovely. I have succeeded in discovering the Casino (where I got outside a sherry cobbler), the Morse statue, and the Schiller bust.

The New York *Times* continues its revelations, which are making an impression that I hope will last. Mayor Hall replies at last, feebly and irresponsibly, severely criticizing the motives of the editor. These disclosures of Tammany's iniquity may now be considered as taken *pro confesso.* They must tell heavily against the Democratic party at the fall

[20] Gladstone, after an Army Bill had been smothered in the House of Lords, brought about the abolition of the purchase of commissions by a shrewd manoeuvre—use of the royal warrant.

[21] At this time Beekman Place was the home of prosperous families in brownstone houses, but the northward march of the slums presently brought about its abandonment to the poor. It was not until the 1920s that a number of wealthy people, including Miss Anne Morgan and Mrs. W. K. Vanderbilt, restored the neighborhood to more than its old dignity.

elections. The Ring is said to be perturbed and wrapt in dismal thinkings. "I saw the tents of Sweeny in affliction, and the curtains of the land of Connolly did tremble."—Habakkuk. Tweed . . . is reported anxious and with a digestion impaired by forebodings.

> Instead of sweets, his ample palate takes
> Savour of poisonous brass and metal sick.

I hardly dare hope that this gang of the lowest and most vulgar swindlers that ever defrauded and misgoverned a great city is about to be broken up, but it is certainly in a bad way.

France seems in a lucid interval for the present, and is honestly hard at work repairing damages. A curious letter from "Henry V" affirming the white flag with the lilies the only French flag he can recognize. It seems to have alienated most of his friends and disbanded the Legitimist party.[22] Perhaps he is weary of fruitless intrigue, and (having no children) selects this as the most dignified mode of renouncing his "legitimate" rights to the throne of France, preferring to spend the rest of his days in repose. If so, it is a rather fine and graceful act by the last survivor of the Bourbon line. But why don't he go back to the Oriflamme?

Granite masonry of the new post office begins to shew above the fences that surround the lower end of City Hall Park.

July 27. . . . The New York *Times* revelations seem to be discussed in nearly every newspaper in the country, except the *Herald* and others of this city. They are mostly bought by the Ring. Even the *Post* and the *Tribune*, generally reputed honest, speak out less boldly than they should, because they value the advertising patronage of Tweed and Company. The feeble babbling of the *World* in defense of Oakey Hall is contemptible. "He might have been compelled to sign these (flagitious) warrants by a mandamus"; possibly. But why did he interpose no objection, make no resistance, or public protest, and at least warn the community of these enormous frauds to which he now pretends that "the law" compelled him to be an accessory?

Significant fact that $40,000 of city bonds put up at auction yesterday

---

[22] Henry, the Count of Chambord, the grandson of Charles X, had for a time seemed not unlikely to rule in France as Henry V. A childless man, he had made an agreement with his cousin, the Count of Paris, by which he was to take over the throne, and on his death it was to go to the Count of Paris as head of the House of Orleans. But Chambord now announced that he was determined to restore in France the lilied white flag of the Bourbons, and along with it their divine right principles. This was too much. The stock of the republic experienced a sudden rise.

found no bidders. But it's a great misfortune that these disclosures are made at this time; for everybody is out of town, and vigorous action is impossible. By next October everyone will have begun to think of something else, and there will be no vigorous campaign against these thieves and ruffians.

July 31, MONDAY. . . . My digestion was not much improved by this morning's papers with their sickening, heart-rending details of the frightful accident to the Staten Island ferryboat *Westfield*, which blew up at her New York dock yesterday afternoon, crowded with people—men, women, and very many little children. Very many papas and mammas were taking baby (who looked a little wilted with this sultry weather, no doubt) out of the hot city for an afternoon's breath of salt air across the bay and back again. Baby has, as a general rule, been steamed to rags, and also papa or mamma or both; but it is too horrible to write about. Such hideous details I have never read. Not less than sixty are known to have been killed. More than twice as many are badly hurt, mutilated, or parboiled. Cause of all these unspeakable horrors—at which I have only hinted—an ill patched or cheaply cobbled boiler, and the absence of the engineer from his post for fifteen minutes. But "nobody is to blame." Carlyle says that the word "assuredly" or "verily" sometimes occurs in the Koran as a sentence by itself (in *Hero-Worship*, I think). It is a pity that in our contemporaneous record of events, the words "damn," "condemn," "hang," occur so seldom, each as a sentence by itself. If this fearful tragedy be due to the parsimony of this wretched ferryboat's owner or to the negligence of her engineer, one or both should be solemnly and reverently killed within the week—solemnly and reverently, as an act of divine service. This is the worst steamboat massacre in our New York waters since the *Henry Clay* noyade of 1852.

Died, old John Slidell, the "Reineke Fuchs" of Secessia; no great loss to mankind.[23] There are predictions of a run on the Savings Bank. They hold many millions of city bonds, and depositors begin to distrust those securities after receiving recent disclosures about Tweed and Oakey Hall. . . .

August 1. Have just got in from a long stroll in the beautiful Park,

[23] John Slidell, former Louisiana Senator and Confederate representative in France, had remained in Europe after the Civil War, chiefly in Paris. His daughter had married a son of the great financier Emile Erlanger. Taking refuge in England at the fall of the Empire, he now died at Cowes. Slidell had been born in New York and was a graduate of Columbia College (1810); he was a brother of Commander Alexander Slidell Mackenzie, who added to his name.

from Seventy-ninth Street down by tortuous footpaths in which I lost myself twice. What a priceless acquisition that Park is to New York!

Life and Trust Company this morning. A fifteen per cent dividend declared. Then to the Battery. They were dragging in boats for more *Westfield* victims, and a diver was said to be at work in submarine armor. A crowd was looking on. The dead roll of that hideous catastrophe now foots up seventy-six or eight, I am not sure which. About 140 severe cases are in the hospital, and of these at least a half dozen are moribund and in such misery that the sooner they die the better for themselves and for everybody else. Such evidence as we possess tends to fix this crime on the engineer rather than on the boiler-mender. If we could but hope that *somebody* would be hanged to avenge these poor women and pretty children of whose torture we have such piteous details! . . .

Foreign news looks squally. There is another war cloud. France and Italy are on bad terms about the Temporal Power. When a big bully has been licked by a man of his own size, his natural impulse is to avenge himself by pounding some small boy. Then, Western Europe seems threatened by cholera. And there have been "Republican" demonstrations and riot in London (Trafalgar Square). England may possibly be in the first stage of a revolution and destined to come down to "Odger, First Consul." If her ruling classes do not soon begin to assert themselves a little and to treat mobs and demagogues according to their deserts, England will be a chaos and a mobocracy within a very few years.

August 3. . . . The hospital doctors say the *Westfield* death list will certainly exceed one hundred, and some of the dead will probably never be known or recorded; strangers without friends who have been blown to bits, or drowned, and drifted away. . . .

August 15. [After eight days on the Rhode Island shore.] Left Narragansett Pier yesterday at 11:45 A.M. by stage and Shore Line with Miss Rosalie, always a charming companion. She stays here a few days before going to the Charles Bristeds' at Lenox, and is nice to have in the house. . . .

Charley Strong writes from Paris on a brief shopping expedition with Miss Puss. Shops brilliant as of old. Damaged house fronts mostly repaired—an easy job with the soft Paris building-stone. His wife in much suffering. He may have sailed on the twelfth but probably will not sail till the nineteenth. Cholera reported at London and at Hull; if so, due here within thirty days.

Cornerstone of monument in Central Park to dear old Sir Walter

Scott, laid today with Gaelic solemnities, this being the centenary of Sir Walter's birth. . . .

August 17. . . . Coroner's inquest on the *Westfield* victims has brought in a creditable and masculine verdict, charging the carnage upon the president of the steamboat company (Jacob Vanderbilt), another of its officers (Braisted), and their engineer. All three have been arrested and held on this criminal charge. Even if this prosecution die out and come to naught, as I dare say it will, this finding will be a wholesome warning to all directors and managers of public conveyances. One hundred and three men, women, and children have been slain by these ogres of Staten Island. Whether the sufferers were destroyed with actual intent to kill, or merely by negligence and disregard for human life as compared with cash profits, seems a distinction without much difference.

Interest in the question about city finances and Tammany frauds seems as yet unabated. The (Democratic) Albany *Argus* has the inconceivable audacity and folly to put its defense of the Ring on the ground that these enormous stealings were needed to buy votes of "radical" senators and assemblymen in support of absolutely indispensable legislation at Albany!

August 19. Long stroll on the West Side tonight. Inspected the crowded and brilliantly lighted Eighth Avenue, which is, of a Saturday evening, one of the sights of New York.

Public anti-Ring meeting promised for September 4. The enormous iniquities of Tweed and Company must materially affect the fall election in this state. Hoffman will hardly venture to veto remedial action by the legislature. He has got all the city and the state can give him, and he dare not go before the country with the fatal ring of brass round his neck as a confessed serf of Tammany. Some say he has already mutinied against his late masters; others, that he would really rather be honest than not. He is certainly ambitious and rather shrewd. If his aspirations will be promoted by throwing our city thieves overboard, he will throw them over without wasting a thought on auld lang syne. These charges of gigantic fraud being now taken *pro confesso*, his true move is to call a special session of the legislature for October and send in a vigorous message inviting prompt action. That move might well carry him into the White House.

Forensic joke heard yesterday. Some years ago Daniel Lord was trying a case before Judge Vanderpoel in Superior Court. He became excited, his rhetoric waxed flowery (unusual with Daniel Lord), and at last (his classics being rather the worse for want of wear) he brought forward the "poisoned shirt of Nemesis" under which he alleged the other side to be suffering. Ralph Lockwood, who was lounging in the courtroom, *more suo*, wrote in pencil and passed up to the bench the following exquisite poetical criticism:

> Poor Brother Lord forgets that Nemesis,
> As Goddess, wore, not shirts, but *chemises*.

August 30, WEDNESDAY.   To Narragansett Pier, Wednesday the 23rd by Shore Line Railroad through drizzle and fog. . . . Two evenings were spent (Vinton, Ellie, Miss Margaret, Jem, and I) in the deadliest concoction of the vilest and most vapid jokes for an exhibition of "Mrs. Jarley's Waxworks" at Canonchet Hall in aid of St. Peter's Church or chapel. . . . Left Narragansett in the rain yesterday at twelve noon. The stage ride was purgatorial. Occupying a middle seat, one sweated and stewed between two human poultices; and if next the window, one was bombarded with mud and splashed with foul water. The railroad ride was much better. . . .

City news. *Vixerunt* William Irving Graham, and Scribner of Scribner & Welford, my booksellers.[24] We were schoolfellows at Holbrook's in 1828 and 1829. . . . Masonry of the west side of the new post office has risen above its enclosure of boards. That fence is illustrated every day by a new crop of advertising handbills. They call it the "New York Academy of Design." Many of these placards are curious; for example, a flagrant advertisement of somebody's cathartic pills, adorned by a rough engraving of one of the little cherubs (with his chin resting on his hand) from Raffaello's Dresden Madonna.

Strong returned to a city in the floodtide of insurrection against the Tweed Ring. This ring, composed of Boss William M. Tweed, City Chamberlain Peter B. Sweeny, Mayor A. Oakey Hall, and Comptroller Richard B. Connolly, with some minor politicians, had for several years held full control of the city, and (having made John T. Hoffman governor) partial control of the state. Since 1859 it had pocketed a large proportion of all the bills paid by the

---

[24] Charles Scribner (1821–1871) had helped establish the publishing firm of Baker & Scribner in 1846. On Baker's death in 1850 he continued the business alone. The firm of Scribner & Welford, of which Strong speaks, did a book-importing business, but at this time the publishing was done in Scribner's name. He had begun *Scribner's Monthly*, a magazine of distinguished literary and artistic quality, in 1870. The first of a line of great publishers, Charles Scribner (like his successors of the same name) enjoyed the affection of authors and the esteem of the public.

city and county; at first one-half, and later eighty-five per cent. But in 1870 Thomas Nast, the brilliant cartoonist, had begun a fierce and incessant campaign against Tweed and his associates, and late that year the New York Times, *owned by George Jones, opened an editorial cannonade. Alarmed by these attacks, the ring had dealt a masterly counterstroke by inviting a committee of able and distinguished businessmen to examine Connolly's books; and this body, after a few hours in the Comptroller's office, had issued a card certifying that the financial affairs of the city "are administered in a correct and faithful manner." The card appeared on November 5, 1870, just before election— and in the election Hall was reëlected mayor and Hoffman governor.*

Nevertheless, nemesis was at hand. Public distrust grew, as Harper's Weekly *and the* Times *continued their assaults. And suddenly the thieves fell out. Sheriff James O'Brien, obtaining from a clerk in the office of the county auditor proof of the enormous thefts that were occurring, first tried to use it to blackmail Tweed's crew into paying certain demands of his own; and when he failed in this—for O'Brien and Sweeny were enemies—he gave all his proofs to George Jones of the* Times. *The grafters, who had tried to buy off Nast with half a million, offered Jones five millions not to publish his materials. Of course these offers were spurned, and in July, 1871, the* Times *spread its sensational evidence before the city. By the end of that month every intelligent citizen knew that the ring had stolen at least six millions. Mayor Hall protested that he had been hoodwinked; Tweed maintained a brazen silence; Connolly and Sweeny were half blustering, half cowardly. At last the best men of the city were thoroughly aroused. During August legal steps were taken to prevent Connolly from paying out more fraudulent sums. Samuel J. Tilden, Joseph H. Choate, William F. Havemeyer and others, consulting together, decided to call a mass-meeting for September 4, and were ready with a program for its adoption. As Strong records below, the meeting was held; it showed a grim determination to end the era of corruption; and a committee of seventy, with Tilden its chief leader, was named to carry forward the battle.*

September 4, MONDAY. . . . Grand meeting on Tammany frauds at Cooper Institute at eight. Walked down with Murray Hoffman, Jr. Had a card for the platform, but the crowd and heat were beyond endurance; so I adjourned to the committee room awhile with Dr. Lieber, [Oswald] Ottendorfer of the *Staats-Zeitung,* Peter Cooper, and others, and then looked at the auxiliary open-air meeting. Both seemed earnest and up-roarious. Havemeyer was speaking when I left the hall, constantly inter-rupted by earnest plaudits. But the minds of a New York assemblage are as running water. The impressions of today are effaced tomorrow.

The disease of this community lies too deep to be cured by meetings, resolutions, and committees. We the people are a low set, without moral virility. Our rulers, Tweed and Company, are about good enough for us. The Alcibiades of New York is Mr. James Fisk. Mr. J. G. Bennett, Jr., who makes money by printing the advertisements of abortionists . . . is elected "commodore"—or some such thing—by the aristocratic Yacht Club of New York, and is a leader of fashion in the Belmont clique. John Astor, Willy Duncan, William T. Blodgett, and others sit in the same railroad direction with vermin like Bill Tweed.

In discourse with Astor and Mr. Ruggles in Wall Street about this meeting, I found neither inclined to be "prominent" in it. Mr. Ruggles fears these villains might take vengeance on him by stopping certain improvements now in progress to the damage of sundry uptown lots of his. But his conscience is a little uncomfortable.

Vanderbilt and others are duly indicted for the *Westfield* carnage of July 30. Two to one they are not tried. Ten to one they are not punished.

September 5. . . . Mr. Ruggles is on the Executive Committee of Seventy appointed by last night's meeting. The Seventy make their first move against the Powers of Darkness tomorrow (papers prepared in advance). Mr. Justice Barnard (!!!) is to be asked for an injunction against what Shakespeare calls the "ring the county wears," forbidding further issue of city and county bonds, and so on.[25] This does not look promising, but its result depends on the degree of importance the politic Barnard attaches to this reform movement. He will, of course, rat whenever his interests require it. This movement is formidable; its success may lead to his impeachment. These "caterpillars of the commonwealth" have done all they can for his advancement. By appearing in the new rôle of an honest and fearless judge he may escape mischief and gain much kudos with unthinking people. These considerations may lead him sorrowfully to decline the huge bribe that is doubtless within his reach and try to act with the semblance of uprightness. I have sundry intimations that he will

[25] The Tweed Ring was for the first time being brought into court. One Foley, taxpayer and member of the Committee of Seventy, was asking for an injunction to restrain the mayor, comptroller, and others from paying money to certain collusive claimants, or from issuing any more bonds.

do so. But he is an evil beast and will most probably aim at amusing the reformers, without doing substantial harm to his old allies in corruption.

September 7. This morning Justice Barnard, on motion of Barrett, granted order to show cause against perpetual injunction in the suit of John Foley against the mayor, aldermen, William M. Tweed, and others. The announcement was received with indecent but pardonable applause from a crowded courtroom. But it is a mere order *nisi*. It was very possibly agreed upon as judicious by Tweed, Oakey Hall, and Company after free consultation with the judge. It may be a mere tub prudently thrown to the anti-Tammany whale. Tammany needs some "stern and incorruptible" Democratic judge to play off against a "possibly somewhat extravagant Democratic mayor and comptroller," at least until the November election is over.

September 8. . . . Rejoicings over Barnard's order *nisi* are perhaps a little premature. But there are signs that the rural democracy begins to find the Ring a burthen too heavy to be borne. They say the unexpected Republican victory in California is due to the discredit brought on the Democratic party by these colossal frauds in New York. The whole country is ringing with them. The New York *Herald*, which has all along most stupidly ignored the whole subject, being subsidized by the Ring, comes out today on both sides. It thinks that the charges are made for political effect; also, that Tweed and Connolly ought to resign at once; also, that their manifest confederate, Oakey Hall, is the noblest and purest of men and mayors.

Philharmonic directors in session here this afternoon till near six o'clock. Much work and more talk, chiefly from our new colleague U. C. Hill, who seems a little fussy. He wanted a symphony of Haydn's struck off our programme as "obsolete." But he made no convert.

September 11. The mayor, aldermen, Oakey Hall, and others, defendants named in Foley's complaint, began shewing cause against the injunction this morning before Barnard. I believe the city demurs and Oakey Hall answers. Yesterday afternoon the comptroller's office was broken into and sundry books and vouchers carried off.[26] The burglars were doubtless employed by the malefactors at the head of the city government. We are not far from the fearful and perilous experiment of a vigi-

[26] A committee of councilmen and citizens, appointed to examine the city's finances, were to spend this day looking into the books of Comptroller Connolly, a member of the Ring. The well-arranged but stupid theft of vouchers and other papers temporarily blocked this committee. News meanwhile came from Washington that Mrs. Connolly had put one and a half millions into government bonds!

lance committee. Many people who are usually cool, sensible, and conservative declare that they are ready for it.

September 12. Things are moving. The burglarious raid on the
Comptroller's office and the abstraction of vouchers and other papers that
were to have been submitted to the Investigating Committee today have
reacted against the Ring, as might have been expected. This attempt of
these cornered and panic-stricken thieves to destroy the evidence of their
gigantic thefts is regarded as morally conclusive against the Ring by
everybody who is not paid by the Ring to think otherwise. Even Mr.
Oakey Hall sees that someone must be thrown overboard; so he writes
to Connolly (in very bad English), inviting that functionary to make a
martyr of himself for the sake of his endangered confederates and resign.[27]
This invitation is enforced by this morning's *World* with the statement
that "if the Comptroller's resignation be not received before night, New
York will be too hot to hold him." Mr. Hall makes a strong appeal to
Connolly's "magnanimity," and we have that "magnanimous" official's
response in tonight's *Post*. It is in substance thuswise. "You be d——d.
I ain't a-goin' to resign nohow. You and I are in the same boat. They
accuse me of swindling the city. How could I have done it without your
help, or connivance at least? I'm not going to be made the Jonah of this
crew, without a little fight." Good for Connolly. I feared he would help
to smooth things over by resigning and then emigrating to Paris with
his fraudulent millions.

N.B. Maine went Republican by an increased majority. Tammany is
fearfully damaging the (so-called) Democratic party.

September 15. . . . Another "accident" in Beekman Street yesterday. A
great cart-load of "union torpedoes" exploded and killed sundry people
and horses. The "formula" of these pestilent playthings is reported to be
nitroglycerine and picrate of potash and fulminate of silver. Probably it
is no such thing, but they are most dangerous and their sale is prohibited.
I hope their surviving manufacturer, who has been arrested, may be
punished. The other member of the firm was hoist with his own petard
and so thoroughly disintegrated as to be beyond reach of indictment or
identification.

I infer from an obscure paragraph in the last edition of tonight's *Post*
that Barnard has granted at least one branch of the injunction asked for

[27] The general (and correct) public assumption was that the Ring was disrupted;
that Mayor A. Oakey Hall and City Chamberlain Sweeny had determined to jettison
Tweed and Connolly in an effort to save themselves.

by Foley. Justices Barnard and Ingraham are believed to have decided on asserting their independence, but it's said that Mr. Justice Cardozo is still a slave of the Ring and is ready to grant any injunctions and stays of proceedings it may need. The New York *Herald* reluctantly abandons the Ring to its fate, all but Oakey Hall for whom it still retains some tenderness. But it thinks that even Oakey Hall had better resign. The New York *World* itself is demoralized by this suicidal burglary and by the discord among its clients. Its brazen trumpet gives forth an uncertain sound. It is understood that Hall and Sweeny are in alliance, offensive and defensive, against Tweed and Connolly—skunk *vs.* rattlesnake.

September 18. City affairs are in a complicated state. Justice Barnard granted his injunction Friday as soon as the argument was closed. The respectable [William F.] Havemeyer writes to Connolly advising him not to resign but to appoint Andrew H. Green deputy comptroller with full powers. "Slippery Dick" follows this advice and appoints Green to hold office till February 1. Thereupon, Mr. Oakey Hall (who must have lost his head altogether), forgetting that he wrote to Connolly a week ago that he had no power whatever to remove him, writes him again that he considers this appointment possibly equivalent to a resignation and that anyhow he holds the comptrollership vacant. So he invites General George B. McClellan to take that position!!! McClellan will hardly be such a fool as to take it. Connolly writes to Oakey Hall that he has not resigned and does not contemplate resigning. An opinion from Charles O'Conor is published tonight freely sustaining Connolly and A. H. Green. The case is perfectly clear without any opinion from counsel. Green has taken possession of the comptroller's office and posted a guard of policemen to prevent any more burglaries.

I believe A. H. Green an honest man. People generally think well of him. I have known him since 1844, more or less. The only person I ever heard speak ill of him was F. L. Olmsted, who had relations with him in Central Park administration, and Olmsted has a rather *mauvaise langue.*[28]

---

[28] It need not be said that Andrew Haswell Green (1820–1903), one of the men who did most to plan public improvements in New York, and the chief agent in bringing about the creation of the greater city in 1897, was a civic leader whose high abilities were complemented by his unspotted integrity. No citizen ever did more to improve and adorn the municipality. He helped plan Central Park; suggested Riverside Drive and many of the smaller parks; was for a time an efficient member and president of the board of education; established the American Scenic and Historic Preservation Society; and did much to effect the merger of the Tilden, Astor, and Lenox foundations in the New York Public Library.

Poor Professor [Dennis Hart] Mahan of West Point jumped over-board from the *Mary Powell* on Saturday in temporary insanity.

September 19. . . . That cautious campaigner, G. B. McClellan, declines the comptrollership, of course. Hall should have foreseen that he would do so. Who can be Hall's adviser? Every move of his is a gross blunder. "Slippery Dick" Connolly has turned state's evidence, they say, and dis-covered "Satan's Invisible World" to the astonished Seventy. I should not care to insure his life, though his office is garrisoned by some fifty stalwart b'hoys, armed to the teeth. Tonight's indications are that Hall contemplates a collapse.

September 20. Two cases of cholera rumored at Perth Amboy among German immigrants.

Rumor that Mayor Hall has collapsed and recalled his circular letter refusing to recognize the comptroller and deputy comptroller; also, that he has not. He has made himself supremely ridiculous and contemptible during the last ten days. Further rumor that the heart of Connolly is broken and contrite, and that he longs to disclose, confess, and make restitu-tion. *Vide* the instructive biography of Reineke Fuchs.

September 22. . . . Yesterday were arrested one Haggerty, janitor of the new court house, his wife, and Balch his assistant—all three charged with the voucher burglary of the 10th. Evidence against them seems strong. Quantities of charred and half-burned documents are found on their premises. They are defended, *more suo*, by that prodigy of impudence, Mr. John Graham.

The *World* sees at last that the wounds of the Ring are probably mortal; so it declares that they were inflicted by the Democratic party! "Lord, Lord, how this *World* is given to lying"!!! For weeks it has been denounc-ing all charges against Tweed and Company as a mere party clamor, cun-ningly devised by hungry radical office-seekers. But I fear our labor for reform will be in vain. We may succeed in breaking this Ring, but another will soon be riveted round our necks. A sordid and depraved community cannot govern itself without corruption. Cutting out a cancer or a gangre-nous spot does not *cure* a patient whose blood is thoroughly poisoned. . . . When we the people learn (among other things) to consider wealth basely acquired and ignobly enjoyed a reproach and not a glory, we shall have a right to hope for honest rulers.

September 25. . . . Church Music Association subscription $4,950. Am not confident of raising the additional $3,500 but mean to try.

They are pulling down the tall iron railings of Union Square. Posts and chains are to take their place. This is an improvement. I never understood why our public places must look like paddocks for tame kangaroos. The Battery, City Hall Park, Madison Square, and other spots have been greatly improved and embellished by this scurvy and sinful Ring, but for every dollar expended on that work, they have put five into their own filthy pockets.

Tweed "der Böse" (the Boss) convened a mass-meeting or Walpurgis Night of his *tappe-durs*, mercenaries, repeaters, and whiskey-millers, on the east side of the city on Friday. Great enthusiasm and a display of fire-works and calcium lights that cost that patriotic statesman much money. Think of this confessed thief—a thief on the largest scale—parading himself in public! Should A. H. Green, comptroller *de facto*, be made to find money for current city expenses and be forced to discharge the five thousand laborers employed on the parks and "boulevards," a great riot would probably occur. Ample funds for these purposes ought to be in the city treasury, but the Ring has stolen them in advance, relying on its unlimited power to issue city bonds. The exercise of this power is checked by Barnard's injunction. The banks are coming to Green's aid and advancing him funds which he has no legal authority to borrow. The *Herald* and the *World* denounce this remedy as irregular and as a fraud by the banks on their stockholders; and they do so, I think, in the interest of the Ring, designing to bring about a suspension of work and an outbreak of murderous incendiary Celts in support of Mr. Tweed and Company.

September 27. . . . Barnard modifies his injunction so as to enable Green to raise such funds as are urgently required—to pay workmen, and so on.

Strange news from England. At a public dinner, Mr. Disraeli makes a speech in which he states that the Queen is now physically and mentally incapable of performing the duties of her station! Extraordinary proceeding for a man in Dizzy's position, though he is not a member of government, to be sure. But it seems indecent anyhow. The Queen's hereditary tendencies and her seclusion for ten years past, under pressure of what looks like morbid grief, make the statement not at all incredible. I believe she is, or recently has been, quite gravely ill. How would England stand the rather unsavory young Prince of Wales as Regent or as King? It is fortunate for the public peace that the English republican (and atheistic) agitators seem to be, without exception, curs of low degree and likely to exert but little influence in any crisis that may follow a demise of the crown.

September 28. . . . There is dissatisfaction with Barnard's partial relaxation of the anti-Ring injunction and with the Seventy. People say the menace of a riot has enabled the Ring quietly to recover all its lost ground. I "don't see it in that light."

That irregular and dangerous demagogue Ben Butler fails to be nominated as governor of Massachusetts by the Republican Convention at Worcester.[29] Washburn prevails against him. Butler did great service at New Orleans, but his subsequent career has been more curious than useful. In the New York Republican Convention at Syracuse, Horace Greeley and his special adherents are likewise discomfited; whereupon they bolt and organize a schismatic convention. What a pity, when the Republicans had such a chance of carrying the state! . . .

September 30. . . . The "Hon." T. C. Fields publishes a letter certifying that Judge Hilton told him that he [Hilton] had inspired the infamous editorial in the *Star* recommending unpaid workmen to sack the houses of Foley and the editor of the *Times*, and kindly specifying their street numbers so that there might be no mistake.[30] Fields is not the most credible of witnesses, but his story reads as if it were true, and it is highly probable. . . . It is sweet and soothing to the humble taxpayer to sit apart and watch the split among these sons of Belial spread, widen, and ramify. Hilton's repute for honesty, once tolerably fair, has become shabby and threadbare during the last month. His influence over A. T. Stewart is supposed to prevent that millionaire from allying himself with the reformers. But his colossal job of a viaduct railway seems defunct. After the disclosures of last July, a bona fide subscription to its stock would have justified a commission of lunacy, and there have been, it would seem, no subscriptions whatever; so that bright vision of a few more fraudulent millions has faded from before the eyes of Hilton, Hall, Tweed, and Company, never, I trust, to gladden their longing optic nerves again.

October 1. . . . Heard of John R. Livingston's sudden death at Great Barrington. When I was elected to Trinity Church vestry in 1847, he was an active member. His policy was always one of lavish expenditure. Private embarrassments rather impaired his financial morale, and some of his alleged transactions were so queer that we were forced to drop him from the Easter ticket. He behaved very well about it, and was always—socially—nice, genial, and well-bred.

October 2, MONDAY. College trustees solemnized their regular monthly

[29] William B. Washburn, known for able service in Congress, defeated Ben Butler in the Republican State Convention 607 to 460, thereby much delighting friends of decent politics.

[30] The New York *Star* was the organ of Tammany Hall.

corporate doze at the Law School at two. We muttered a little in our sleep about two or three measures; but they were promptly referred and got rid of, and we slumbered again. Rutherfurd suggests the abolition of under-graduate fees. The President suggests a little educational observatory on the College grounds, to cost not more than $7,000, and also the merger of the School of Mines Library with that of the College proper.

October 3. To Trinity Church at three-thirty; meaning merely to shew myself at John R. Livingston's funeral. Attendance quite large, but the arrangements had been necessarily hurried, and there was a deficiency of pallbearers. A *tales de circumstantibus* being called for, I was summoned and could not refuse, though I objected that I was not in decorous black but in an ordinary morning suit. The others were Anthony Bleecker (Living-ston's special ally in the vestry long ago), old John Warren, Judge Roose-velt, John Astor, William Morris, Pen Hosack, and James F. DePeys-ter. A graceful feature in the service was the procession of surpliced choir boys preceding the coffin down the middle aisle and then to the vault near the southwest corner of the church and singing a processional hymn. Poor Livingston has gone where tradesmen cease from calling and the checkbook is at rest. He will have no more trouble with atrophied bank accounts and hypertrophied bills. This is a grand and solemn thought which goes far to reconcile one to the Inevitables.

It is believed at West Point that Professor Mahan walked off the deck of the *Mary Powell* accidentally and without suicidal intent.

The Seventy have opened fire on Mayor Hall with criminal proceedings for a misdemeanor.

October 5. . . . That synagogue of Satan, the Rochester "Democratic" Convention, talks bravely against corruption and fraud. But it allows the Tammany delegation from New York to be magnanimous and withdraw "so as not to embarrass the convention." It has not the courage to kick Tweed and Company into the street. It declines to admit a "reform delega-tion" claiming to represent the city "Democracy." Some think this a stun-ner for Tweed. . . . But I do not so see it. Tammany is still the vital centre of the state Democracy, and Tweed is entitled by strict Democratic rule to the votes of all true Democrats. He and his pals are not read out of the party. Perhaps it's as well. The prospect of the Republicans is brightened by Democratic tenderness for these notorious scoundrels and thieves. The convention may have slightly chilled the ardor of city rascaldom without having secured cordial support from comparatively honest rural Democrats. The party could not afford to lose the services of Oakey Hall's noble army of repeaters, or the control of city funds wherewith to buy up invertebrate Assemblymen. It could not spare the great fraudulent majorities that are rolled up at every city election; so it dared not make thorough work against corruption and goes into the fall campaign with the filthiness of Tweed and Company in its skirts just a little wiped off. . . .

Philharmonic directors held a long session here yesterday afternoon. Brooklyn means to sustain her own Philharmonic organization a little longer.

October 9.   Run on the Third Avenue Savings Bank. It was denounced in yesterday's papers and is doubtless in an unhealthy condition.

Great fire at Chicago Saturday night destroying several blocks. A second fire broke out last night at ten, and was reported still unchecked at noon today. It seems that nearly half—and the more important half—of that city is burned. It was generally a wooden city. Even its streets were paved with wood. Its hotels, churches, banks, courthouses, grain elevators, gas works, and waterworks, its Fifth Avenue, and its Wall Street, and the shipping at its wharves are destroyed. "A hundred fifty thousand people are without shelter." All this may be somewhat overstated, but the truth is doubtless bad enough. The loss must be enormous, and New York will feel it sharply. Every merchant in Chicago owes money in New York, and moreover, our insurance companies are badly hit; so Skidmore tells me. They will have to call in loans and investments, and the shrinkage will be seriously felt. This may well prove the entering wedge for the panic and crisis which people predict, and which must come before long.

City affairs: Keyser, the plumber of the new court house, denies all liability to the city, but assigns to Jackson S. Schultz assets worth $600,000 in trust to pay such liability if established! He has also made certain revelations to the Seventy. . . . Ingersoll was in court today as witness. Garvey has fled and evaded. People scrutinize the personnel of the grand jury that will have to pass on the charges against Mayor Hall and find the Ring fully represented there.

October 10.   Little talk of anything but Chicago. Found Ellie crying over the morning papers. Indeed, it is horrible to think of so many thousands suddenly evicted from their homes and sleeping under such shelter as roadside fences can give them. At noon we had news, by way of St. Louis, that the fire was probably checked at ten in the morning by help of a rainfall. But the fourth edition of this evening's *Post* says that the fire still rages in the northern part of the city, that "crowds in the streets are making turbulent demonstrations," entering houses and helping themselves, and that "two men caught in the act of firing houses" have been informally hung to lamp posts on the west side of the city. The roughs and dregs of a half-burned city become violent and mischievous, of course. Kernot (at Scribner's) tells me Ezra B. McCagg's precious library is destroyed with several other fine collections.[31] Chicago was a book-buying city. This fire has destroyed property roughly estimated at from eighty to one hundred and fifty millions. Assets to that amount cannot be annihilated without a financial shock to the whole country. It will be felt everywhere, even by, for example, the Church Music Association and the Philharmonic. People will hesitate about subscribing to concerts when a general panic and smash may be close at hand. The smoke of Chicago will penetrate every cranny of American life. Omnibus horses in New York and in 'Frisco will draw lighter loads; theatre audiences will fall off; free churches will be better attended; the professional income of street bootblacks will be reduced. . . .

October 11. . . . With all our terrible faults, I believe we are the most generous people in the world. It is lovely to behold the great torrent of money and matériel that is spouting and gushing into Chicago from every quarter. Even while the great fire was raging unchecked, message after message was flying over the wires all to the same purport, namely, "Draw on me at sight for $——"; and extra express trains were converging on the city, laden with supplies, freely given and freely transported. A. T. Stewart gives fifty thousand dollars, though he is said to lose half a million by the fire. How I envy him! Five hundred people are said to have perished in this conflagration. Their number is doubtless exaggerated. The pluck of the Chicagoners is a marvel. By the time Mr. A. B.'s store was half burned down, he had sent off orders for brick to rebuild it with.

October 13. We don't yet know how we stand. People are anxious and ripe for a panic, but there are no serious failures as yet. A few third-class brokers have succumbed, and the Stuyvesant Bank (Broadway and Astor Place) cannot pay its depositors and goes to a receiver. But it was young and weakly, and in bad and irregular standing. It's a comfort that we have not to dread the bugbear of a general bank failure, as in 1857, because our banks have been in a state of "suspension" for some nine years.

What shall we do about the Church Music Association? Our subscription is now $6,050. Last year we proceeded to business with a smaller

[31] Ezra B. McCagg, well-known Chicago lawyer and civic leader, the son of a wealthy lumber merchant, had married the sister of William B. Ogden, first mayor and for a time wealthiest citizen of the city. His Clark Street house contained one of the best private libraries in the country.

amount secured, relying, and as the event proved, reasonably, on additional subscriptions, which brought us up to $7,500 and carried us through the season. Can we venture to take the same course this year when things are so uncertain and a general smash may come next week? Strange there should be a connection of cause and effect between a kerosene lamp kicked over in a Chicago cow stable and the performance or nonperformance of Haydn's and Beethoven's church music in New York—that a careless boy should thus paralyze our orchestra and chorus!

Ruins of Chicago continue to be the target for a concentric fire of benefactions from nearly all Christendom—from San Francisco, London, Birmingham, Frankfort, Vienna. All tents and army blankets in Canada are to be handed over. There is something not utterly bad in this world after all. Meanwhile, the Chicagoners are helping themselves with amazing elasticity and vigor, and have already extemporized a new Chicago of shanties and cantonments on the circumjacent prairie, the ruins of old Chicago being still too fiery to squat upon. It's now reported that fifteen hundred people lost their lives by this conflagration! This can hardly be. But sundry thieves and incendiaries perished by the fire indirectly, having been summarily shot or hanged for practising their profession too openly. They found it impossible to resist so tempting an opportunity. Lynch law is bad, but *inter ignes silent leges*; and moreover, the Democratic vote in this city next November will be a little smaller, for among these victims were several eminent malefactors from New York.

October 14. . . . Pech and the Rev. Cooke here tonight. . . . We decided to go forward with the Church Music Association, having it in our power to stay proceedings at any time within the next month without serious expense. For the first concert, Haydn's Mass No. 2, and perhaps selections from Wallace's *Lurline*, on which Pech has set his affections. Subscriptions come in, though but slowly.

Signs of panic do not increase. The Democratic Party seems demoralized by its series of defeats. There is talk of its disbanding and allying itself under some new name with disaffected Republicans. Tammany has made its present name to stink in the nostrils of Christendom.

October 15, SUNDAY.   To Trinity Church *solus*; Ellie ritualized at St. Alban's; the Rev. Dix preached ably. His text was about "no abiding duty," but with wonderful self-control he omitted all allusion to Chicago, even though the offertory was for Chicago itself. Collection $250—large for a Trinity Church congregation. . . .

October 16.   The old Manhattan Insurance Company (W. P. Pal-

mer's) has foundered! A portent of evil. Skidmore's company (the Howard),
though severely damaged, expects to weather the storm, but Skidmore's
honest face looks rather rueful. I reinsure in the Equitable, my policy
in the Manhattan being just renewed and premium paid. So the cow with
crumpled horn that kicked over the kerosene lamp of the boy all tattered
and torn and left Chicago all forlorn, has kicked a small sum out of my
pocket at an inconvenient time.

October 17. . . . The Lorillard and Security Insurance companies are
reported to have gone down. The former, like the Manhattan, was of the
highest caste. It is painful to go into the Manhattan office that used to be so
sunshiny under the genial influence of William P. Palmer. Its atmosphere
is depressing now. Secretary and clerks are particularly civil and attentive
but in a hushed and quiet way, as if someone of their family lay dead in the
next room. Palmer didn't shew; that is, I have not happened to see him.

October 18. . . . The Attorney-General (Champlain) gives Charles
O'Conor *carte blanche* to institute proceedings in his name, or in that of the
state, against the blackguard robber barons of the City Hall and all or any
of their confederates. But some say that O'Conor will decline this office
out of his tenderness for Celts and Romanists. I think otherwise; and
General Dix, who was at Albany yesterday—a representative of the Seventy
—is confident O'Conor will undertake the work *con amore*. Mr. John T.
Hoffman was solemnly invoked and harangued yesterday by Judge Pierrepont and others on behalf of the Seventy. But he considers himself guber-
natorially impotent for good, in which opinion he is probably not far
wrong. . . .

October 20. If this fine weather holds, Chicago will be rebuilded
before 1872.

Johnny's birthday: twenty years old! . . . He's a fine manly fellow, and
the cloud that overhung him a year ago has passed away. He is now a little
reserved, certainly, and never garrulous but genial, kindly, and conversational, and no longer resembling a biped hermit crab. But I wish his eyes
were in better order. They seem to have lost ground for a day or two past.

With Ellie last evening to first private rehearsal of Church Music
Association at Trinity Chapel Schoolhouse. Attendance large; 280 according to Pech. But however that may be, the room was full. There are scores
of applicants for a seat in the chorus, but we cannot find space for them. We
have the chapel schoolhouse gratis and cannot afford to hire other and room-
ier quarters. O that I were a millionaire! . . . Haydn's Mass in C, No. 2.
was read through—and wonderfully well read for a first trial. Mrs. Bishop

was there and took the soprano solo passages charmingly. I had almost forgotten what a brilliant, vigorous, and varied work this is, and never enjoyed a private rehearsal more. Perhaps a new effect was given it by the great body of voice. When I last heard it (here, in 1868), the chorus was only a dozen or twenty. The finest movements of the Mass seem of the nature that demands performance on the largest scale to do them justice and convey their full meaning. Except always that loveliest Benedictus, which is for the soli, and which embodies somewhat of the feeling—sweet but with a shade of sadness—of an Indian summer afternoon, "when all the woods are still and twinkle in the smoky light the waters of the rill." I think, with Ellie, that Pech takes that movement too slow, though he falls back on the authority of Haydn's text. And I will make an affidavit that Haydn marked a change of time for the Hosanna that follows the Bene-dictus, though our copies omit any indication of such change. Nothing can be clearer than that the music demands it and assumes it.

Charles O'Conor with Evarts, Judge Emott, and W. H. Peckham as his staff, advertises that his "Bureau of Municipal Correction" is now open in Brown Brothers' building, Wall Street. He is understood to contemplate a vigorous campaign—civil and criminal.[32]

October 25. . . . Church Music Association is now $6,381; ahead of last year, notwithstanding Chicago.

People are looking anxiously for the Grand Duke Alexis, now behind time. I have a ticket for the "reception steamer," the *Mary Powell*, but shall not fash myself about this Muscovite.

Preparations for November 7 continue active. Reform organizations are wide-awake and make good nominations. The Democracy will lose the state, but by repeating and ballot stuffing, Tweed and Sweeny, Oakey Hall, and Mike Norton, and the other evil Jinn of the Ring will doubtless carry the city. Tweed's impudent serenity is sublime. Were he not a supreme scoundrel, he would be a great man.

Our dear, good, intelligent, efficient, loyal, and pretty Lizzie Conlon is to leave us tomorrow and marry Mr. Michael Riley, a carpenter of New Brighton, Staten Island. She has been with us for ten years, and has become

[32] James Emott (1823–1884), who had been a justice of the state supreme court (1804–1884) was special deputy attorney-general for the state in its action against City of New York, was now prominent in the effort to bring the Tweed Ring to justice. He was a member of the Committee of Seventy. The redoubtable O'Conor (1804–1884) was special deputy attorney-general for the state in its action against the Ring, and prosecuted his suits with a skill which enhanced his fame. But, opposed by David Dudley Field, he failed to obtain the sweeping victory he desired.

rather a friend of the family than a servant. We shall miss her sadly. . . .
She came to us in June or July, 1861, a mere little "slip of a girl," a child
of fifteen or sixteen, and has been steadily winning our affection ever since
with her kind helpful ways, her efficiency, and her cheerfulness. She is,
moreover, one of the prettiest girls in New York.

October 26. . . . Morning papers published full, detailed, tangible proof
of Boss Tweed's iniquities—footing up between three and four millions—
and announced that this swindler would be held to bail today in a suit
instituted by O'Conor. Bail is set at $1,000,000. The order of arrest was
granted by an Albany judge. . . . O'Conor knows what he is about, but I
cannot see that the people or the attorney-general have any standing in
court in a civil action against Tweed. Tweed has not robbed the state and
owes the state no money.

October 28.   With Sackett, General Dix, and Duncan (chief clerk of
the vestry) to the cemetery. The new boulevards and avenues north of the
Park will be magnificent some day, if New York be not swindled to death.
Inspected work in progress at the cemetery, and especially our suspension
bridge, the piers whereof, as yet unfinished, promise well. . . .

This evening, Edmund Schermerhorn, Pech, and Cooke here. We
decided upon Wallace's *Lurline* for the second part of the Church Music
Association concert. . . .

Tweed magnanimously submitted to arrest yesterday and was held on
bail for one million dollars. Respect for the illustrious defendant compelled
the sheriff to make the arrest in person and not by one of his deputies.
Tweed is a grand moral spectacle—statuesque as a demigod in Greek tragedy. Although "interviewed" and badgered at least nine times a day by
"one of our reporters" (as the vultures interviewed Prometheus), he is
always calm and great, if not perfectly grammatical—and that defect may
be chargeable on the reporters. With wise forecast, he is preparing (so far
as may be) for the struggle and for the possibility of adverse fortune by
divesting himself of his impedimenta and by transferring the spoils of
many happy years of swindling (real estate and securities) to his wife and
children and confidential pals. I wish I could hope to see the scoundrel
hanged, but he will be elected to the State Senate on November 7. . . .

November 3. . . . It is sad but true that we have made up our minds to
send Johnny to Dresden for the winter! I think it clearly best for him, but
one cannot help feeling anxious and unhappy about it. . . .

November 4. . . . Indications multiply that Oakey Hall means to promote
systematic fraud on the largest scale next Tuesday. He should be cautious.

Exasperation may be so stimulated as to endanger his precious neck. Merchants will generally close their counting houses and brokers their offices on election day by recommendation of the Chamber of Commerce and the Brokers Board, so that respectable people may be free to vote and to look after the polling places. This is unprecedented in my time. But the roughs and the repeaters and Oakey Hall's fraudulent counters will doubtless prevail. The present excitement must keep itself alive for several years, which can hardly be hoped for, to recover us the ground we have lost by neglect of city affairs.

November 6, MONDAY.   College trustees sat long this afternoon and their prosing was gruesome. The president of the College being deaf and the board blind, it is no wonder our proceedings often become a muddle.

His Lordship of Lichfield preached at Trinity yesterday morning. Crowded congregation; music decidedly good; the service unusually impressive. Four bishops were in the chancel . . . and a strong platoon of presbyters. The "prancing prelate's" sermon was simple, dignified, and earnest, but not far above commonplace.

Tomorrow will be a critical day. Its result will probably demonstrate beyond gainsaying that democratic institutions are a mischievous folly— and that, at least in crowded cities, universal suffrage leads straight to fraud and anarchy. It is a test case. There are no disturbing elements to embarrass one in drawing his inferences from the result. No question of Copperhead or Radical, of protectionist or free-trader is involved in it. The question to be decided is simply between acknowledged scoundrelism and common decency. Which will the "masses" choose? Bill Tweed has been daily denounced as a thief in every newspaper every day for months. Leaders of his own party—O'Conor, Tilden, Horatio Seymour, and others —vehemently urge his conviction as the greatest swindler of modern times. He is held on bail for a million dollars at the suit of the people for frauds committed on the city. He and his Ring are known to have stolen fifty millions. They have been conveying securities and great blocks of real estate to sons and daughters and sons-in-law during the last month. Several of Tweed's confederates have fled to parts unknown and the sheriff sighs to find them in the new City Hall no more. Neither Tweed nor any of his gang have made an attempt even to explain away the damning charges against them. But Tweed and Oakey Hall will probably be endorsed by the enlightened voters of New York tomorrow.

November 7. . . . The howl of the newsboy is now beginning to be heard, and I have sent the faithful Peter out for an extra (ten tonight).

Died, Judge Hiram Denio and Edward Slosson, a Centuriator and formerly active in the club.

Eleven P.M. An extra *Express* received. George C. Barrett probably elected to the Supreme Court and that scallywag Ledwith defeated. Tweed elected senator by 12,000 majority. He expected 30,000. . . . "Mike Norton," a shoulder-hitter and king of repeaters, elected in the Fifth District. O'Brien, endorsed by the Committee of Seventy, prevails over Bradley in the Seventh. Bradley is a notorious slave of the Ring, but I have little faith in O'Brien. S. J. Tilden probably goes to the Assembly and so (probably) does the Hon. Horatio Seymour. If so, that wretched pickpocket Thomas C. Fields is discomfited. Shandly, a Tammanite, prevails against Sigel for the registrarship. All this is much "mixed," but it looks as if the Reform party had gained more in the city than it could expect. Of the state ticket we know nothing whatever.

November 8. Election news brightens every hour. Tweed is elected, to be sure, but the Senate will probably shut the door in his face. Tom Fields will probably be in like manner received by the Assembly, and then one's regret at his election is mitigated by the thought that it is the Hon. Horatio Seymour who is defeated, though I should, of course, have voted for him in preference to a thief like Fields.

Both houses are Republican—more than two to one. The state ticket (Republican) has a majority variously estimated at from 10,000 to 20,000. Mike Norton, whose impudent ugly ("plug-ugly") countenance has glowered upon us for weeks from two banners stretched across Broadway, is beaten by a great majority. So are Gerret, Bradley, Shandly, Ledwith, and many a chief corruptionist besides. Tammany has received a shattering blow from which it will not soon recover. I suppose this result is mainly due to the success of the Reformers in securing nearly the whole German vote, hitherto blindly given, as a general rule, to the so-called Democracy. . . . The politic Peter B. Sweeny promptly resigns his commissionership of parks and announces his final withdrawal from public life—with his pockets full. He has been the sneak thief of the gang, Tweed being its Bill Sikes and head of its Bureau of Burglary. So Tweed and Oakey Hall are left alone together, the last official representatives of that goodly fellowship that had such pleasant days of peace.

Though none of the chief municipal offices was to be filled in the November elections, they were regarded as a test of feeling upon the Tweed Ring. Their outcome was eminently satisfactory. The Republicans won the legislature by almost a two-thirds majority. Every Tammany candidate for office was defeated except Tweed himself—and Tweed gained reëlection to the State Senate only by fraud at the polls. Tilden's election to the State Assembly gave a guarantee that the reform forces would be ably represented there. The bench was strengthened by the choice of a group of good new judges. By this time the authoritative estimate of sums stolen from the city had reached twenty millions. Public anger continued to run high. The best lawyers of the city had given a tremendous amount of time to exposing and denouncing the rascals—the venerable Charles O'Conor lending particularly valuable aid; many merchants had exerted themselves as devotedly; the pulpits had thundered alongside the newspapers; men had forgotten party lines in making common cause against thievery. The Nation declared that in all American history no parallel could be found for this fervid and vigorous uprising. Nevertheless, the work had only been begun. Not a single knave had yet been brought to justice; Tweed still occupied public office and still defied his foes with the demand, "What are you going to do about it?"; and it was by no means certain that the legislature would show much zeal.

News of the ruin wrought by the Chicago fire continued to harrow all sensitive people. The whole central area of this city of 330,000 had been devastated; a district a mile in breadth and four miles in length had been swept by the flames. Happily, not more than two hundred lives had been lost. Within a month brick and stone walls were going up, three hundred burnt-out businesses advertised themselves in new quarters, cargoes of goods for sale were being briskly unloaded, and a new public library—to which Queen Victoria sent a large gift of books—had been opened in a church basement.

November 11. Bell and Henry Hilton resign their commissionerships under Tammany. It is pleasing to watch the rats desert the enemy's ship. Democratic defeat in the state is more severe than at first reported.

To a private Philharmonic rehearsal yesterday with Edmund Schermerhorn and Johnny. The Sinfonia Pastorale was most refreshing, of course. An overture to Julius Caesar seems a flashy work. Wagner's Overture to the Mastersingers of Nuremberg was long and dreary and passed all comprehension. U. C. Hill and some others of the orchestra were damning it bitterly after the rehearsal. . . .

November 13, MONDAY. Auction sale of Philharmonic boxes at Academy of Music from three to four-thirty in the afternoon. A. H. Müller auctioneer; attendance large, bidding spirited; proceeds, I guess, larger than last year. To Trinity Church vestry tonight. . . . The Rev. Mr. Vinton sent in an application for $1,500 to pay poor Mrs. Vinton's expenses at Nassau this winter. The general feeling is adverse. . . . The application was declined almost unanimously. . . .

Half a dozen of one's friends, dropping in, make a pleasant evening. But these little gatherings tend, I don't know how or why, to become too loud for a Sunday evening and too long and too late for any evening. From our seven o'clock tea till near one o'clock Monday morning, is a heroic dose of even the most informal "society." But how to set about toning things down? One can't order people out of his house, or even give them to suspect that he earnestly though inhospitably wishes them to "get up and git" instanter. But last night's exertions as hostess have given poor Ellie a raging sick headache under which she has been prostrate and suffering intensely all day. It has been affected by the thought of Johnny's exodus in the *Cimbria* tomorrow. . . .

Church Music Association subscription is a little over $7,500. Better than last year.

November 15. The Law School Committee met this afternoon. Our students do not like Mr. Austin Abbott, our new adjunct professor. They think him monotonous and ungenial. . . . I cannot for a moment believe that Dwight is undermining him. I suppose him to be in fact learned . . . but quite without a trace of Dwight's magnetism. Anyone introduced into the School must suffer from contrast with Dwight.

Johnny went off at three in the afternoon yesterday in the *Cimbria.* . . .

Got home from Hoboken and the *Cimbria*'s wharf in time to dress for Mr. Ruggles's dinner in honor of his Lordship of Lichfield. There were *the* Bishop; also the Rt. Rev. Potter, the Rev. Mr. Selwyn (Lichfield's son), the Rev. Mr. Iles of Wolverhampton, and the Rev. Mr. Edwards of Trenton(?)—these three constituting Lichfield's tail. There were also Mr. and Mrs. John Sherwood, Dr. Lieber, William M. Evarts, Dr. Washburn, and nice young Willy Astor. . . . Some discourse with Lichfield himself—a courteous, dignified man, with strong symptoms of humor and geniality. This Anglican party sailed this morning.

I couldn't attend Morgan Dix's reception last evening, nor the breakfast at Delmonico's yesterday morning, nor Mr. Consul General Archibald's reception on Monday night, though asked to all three. At the

breakfast, there was a little incident worth noting, perhaps, in its sentimental aspect. The Rt. Rev. Potter presented to the Anglican prelate a
handsome copy of our prayer book with a little speech in which he declared that its text should never be changed without the consent of the
Anglican branch. To which Lichfield responded, quite gracefully, and
pledged himself that the Anglican Liturgy should never be modified
without the acquiescence of the American branch. These pledges have
no practical value, but they are agreeable symptoms of Catholic feeling.

November 16. . . . Another strong tower of the Ring has fallen. The
"Viaduct Railroad," which was to have been the most magnificent job
of larceny mentioned in profane history (the city government alone
excepted), is obliged to "reorganize." Its directors resign. They perceive with regret that there are no subscriptions to their stock. Of course,
nobody wants to put his money where Hilton, Tweed, and Oakey Hall
will have the handling of it. A new board of directors has got to be created.
Hilton, Tweed, Hall, Sweeny and Company must be counted out of the
direction before the viaduct can be resuscitated.

Abbott called on me this morning and announced his intention of
resigning his adjunct professorship forthwith. I naturally assumed that
his resignation was prompted by the state of facts which Dwight disclosed to us yesterday and was beginning to say something civil and
emollient from that standpoint, when I perceived that he did not understand me, and I was fortunately able to draw back before fully committing myself. Abbott said he was delighted with his work and with his
class and should be only too happy to go on; but lecturing so many hours
every day had revived certain symptoms of pulmonary trouble, and he
felt compelled to give it up. He will communicate his intention to Professor Dwight within a few days. Abbott seemed utterly ignorant of any
dissatisfaction with his teaching, and I think he was so. But Dwight was
instructed yesterday to inform him of this dissatisfaction and to suggest
his resignation. So I instantly wrote Dwight to withhold that mortifying
communication.

I hear that the Rev. Vinton inclines to be truculent and savage about
our action of last Monday night. If he could be inspired by his arrogance
to pick a quarrel with the vestry, we might be enabled to rid ourselves of
him. He does fearful damage to the cause of Christian faith every Sunday
at Trinity Church.

November 20. A most succulent, rainy day; so the grand parade that
was to have honored the progress of our sweet young Duck of Muscovy

up Broadway did not come off, and he drove quietly to the Clarendon Hotel. Many score of people with umbrellas were watching its windows as I omnibussed uptown at four in the afternoon under a pouring rain, hoping vainly for a beatific vision of His Imperial Highness—such snobs we be. This long expected Muscovite reached the harbor of New York yesterday. . . .[33]

The "Guardian" Bank for Savings (Bowery), William M. Tweed, president, and the "Bowling Green" Bank for Savings (Broadway), both being rotten fungi got up by members of the Ring to facilitate their swindling operations, have severally faintly exploded and have gone into the custody of receivers. Sundry other savings banks, officered by members of the same conspiracy, are reported in danger.

November 22. . . . The Grand Duke Alexis made his triumphal entry yesterday, turned all the omnibi off their established routes, filled Broadway with a dense mob of roughs, rustics, and lion-hunters, and made things generally uncomfortable. I did not use my ticket for the reception of His Imperial Majesty on board the *Mary Powell.* We are all sovereigns in America, and Alexis is a mere princeling.

Connolly has resigned in form, at last. Oakey Hall (with many a wry face, no doubt) appoints the detested Andrew H. Green in his place. He is also putting decent men upon the Park Commission—most reluctantly. He is an invertebrate rascal. But His Scoundrelism William M. Tweed holds on to his place, grim and undismayed. The basalt columns of the Giants' Causeway are not more rigid than Boss Tweed's backbone. . . .

November 30. . . . To Boston on Saturday, the 25th. . . . Eloise met me at the depot, and I never was so cuddled and made so much of as during my sojourn at 166 Charles Street. Great growth of the city on the "Back Bay" and Milldam region . . . houses on hills. But they are fine solid bricks and have a "paid-for" look. Dined with Hasket in his handsome establishment (Brimmer Street). . . . With Hasket to vespers at the Church of the Immaculate Conception, where they brag of their music. It was certainly good, but not wonderful. . . . Most admirable performance of *Judas Maccabaeus* at the Music Hall. Santley and Company were principals, and the Handel and Hadyn Society formed the chorus. The Handel and Hadyn Society beats the Church Music Association. The Museum of Natural History did not greatly impress me. Tuesday opened

[33] The Grand Duke Alexis, a modest, sensible young man in pursuit of education and amusement, was received as the representative of a reigning family and a nation which had always shown friendliness to the United States.

clear (after a spell of drizzly weather) but with a temperature of eight degrees Fahrenheit.

Yesterday morning I left Boston with dear little Lucy, the nicest, kindest, warmest-hearted of little girls, and the most unselfish and thoughtful of others in the small matters that make up the sum of common life. . . .

Trouble ahead. The Rev. Cooke tells me of charges against Dr. Pech, who is to be investigated by letters of enquiry. He is accused of assuming an academic title that does not belong to him and of marrying in America, though already married in England. I trust these charges may prove unfounded. His professional rivals and competitors hate him bitterly because he has succeeded where they have failed; and they may have convinced themselves, without due examination and enquiry, that this, that, and the other rumor is true, and committed themselves to the assertion of its truth. But I have forebodings. There has been from the first a certain mystery about this gentleman.

Connolly is in jail, for want of bail who can justify to the amount of one million.

December 2. . . . Sorry to hear that Professor Drisler is a case of severe typhoid pneumonia and quite dangerously ill. . . .

Report generally believed (but I think doubtful) that Slippery Dick Connolly has "squealed" and is preparing under O'Conor's supervision a full revelation of his own iniquities and those of his confederate malefactors. . . . Oakey Hall and Sweeny have been invited to resign as members of the Union Club. Sweeny accepted the invitation; Oakey Hall declined it, and there is a movement to expel him. The question comes up next Wednesday, and its result is doubtful, for a two-thirds vote is needed. . . . Belmont fights hard for his friend Oakey Hall. Any dirt has a fascination for Belmont.

This is a bad season for rascals. They are at least being unmasked and branded by scores. Our judicial abuses, the pet "Gratzes" of the bench, and the lamentable degradation of our courts are fully and freely divulged outside the bar, at last. Fisk and his Erie Ring are in affliction. Their bungling attempt to bribe jurors has come to light. A pioneer case growing out of the Black Friday conspiracy has gone against them, and if the verdict stand, they are lost. In the Fisk-Stokes-Mansfield battle, a special stinkpot has exploded, damaging Clarence Seward. . . . Seward mixed himself up in Jem Fisk's quarrel . . . and begged to be appointed

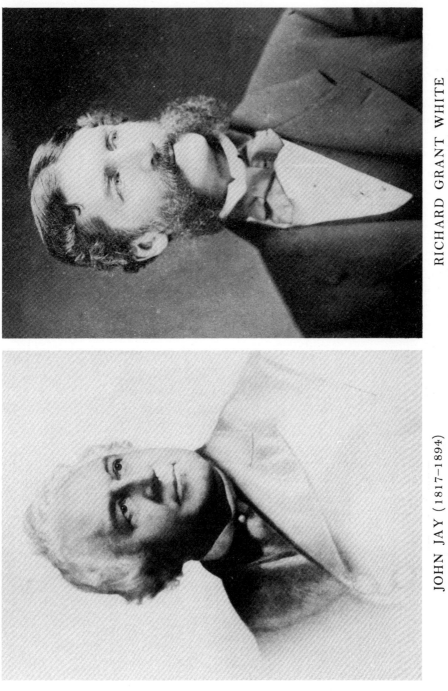

RICHARD GRANT WHITE

JOHN JAY (1817–1894)

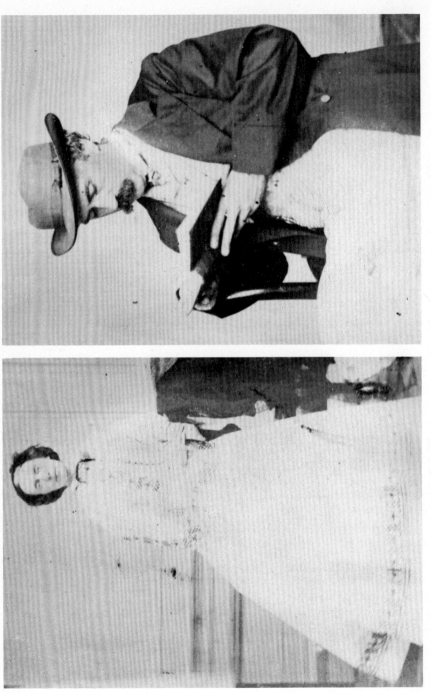

G. T. S.

ELLIE

as referee to decide it because he might thereby strengthen his chance of a Tammany nomination to a seat on the bench of the Supreme Court.

Oakey Hall, once so jaunty and cocky, is said to be sadly wilted down, like a broken lily, in fact. His wife and daughter in Europe are driven from one hotel to another by people who point at them as the family of one of the Great American Swindlers. One can't help pity the poor things. Hall himself, who had a kind of social position once, is now very generally cut, as he deserves to be. He is less callous and far less heroic than some others of his gang, and he is understood to feel this acutely. He suffers also a good deal from Nast's stinging caricatures in *Harper's Weekly*. I hope these will be republished in some permanent form.

December 5. . . . In the evening through the arctic weather to Niblo's with Ellie and Miss Lucy. . . . Sothern played Lord Dundreary in *Our American Cousin*, a most admirable and artistic performance about which one could write a great deal. I laughed till I cried. We enjoyed it much— all three of us. How that fierce wind rattles the windows! Look out for bad fires this winter.

College trustees met yesterday; several important questions "laid over." The question of a change of site had an airing, and we resolved that a change was expedient. I doubt its expediency; but it will be long before we find a new site and the money to pay for it. Professor Drisler continues very low, and Newberry's health has failed, compelling him to ask for a leave of absence. . . .

December 9. A sad piece of news. Died, at Hamburg on the eighth, of typhoid, John N. A. Griswold, Jr., son of George Griswold (the younger). He was only twenty-three, married a very pretty Miss Whitney about six weeks ago, and sailed in the *Cimbria* on November 14 with his wife, his mother, and others. What a happy little party they seemed, and what lots of friends came to see them off, bringing no end of bouquets for the pretty bride! . . .

December 11. The Rev. Edward Y. Higbee was found dead in his room at noon yesterday; apoplexy, no doubt, for he had grown positively spheroidal and had no more neck than a blackfish. He has been shelved for some years, but, while in his best estate, he was by far the most eloquent and impressive preacher I ever listened to. . . .

To Trinity Church vestry tonight. Resolutions about poor Dr. Higbee. The Rev. Vinton's application for leave of absence was granted with great cordiality. Ostrander or Arnold moved to give him $1,500 for his expenses. General Dix objected, and so did I, and the motion failed. Vestrymen who attend Trinity Church are not disposed to favor Vinton's applications for money. He has made himself uncommonly odious. . . . I think General Dix's tenure of the comptrollership will be made permanent after all. The objection that his son, the Rev. Morgan Dix, is Rector never had the least weight with me, and others begin to see that it amounts to nothing.

December 14. The Church Music Association rehearsal at three-thirty P.M., at Steinway Hall, with orchestra; attendance large but cold, like a considerable iceberg. No applause, except for the lovely Weber solo. There are felicitous and infelicitous rehearsals, and this was of the latter type. . . . The Ocean Bank, the Eighth National Bank, and the Union Square Bank—outworks of the Ring, all three—have severally been undermined by a strong current of public distrust and have sunk. "Receivers" have engulfed them and all their assets, be the same more or less.

The Prince of Wales, reported moribund for the last three days, is said to be a little better. I guess he still has a chance.

December 15. To Philharmonic rehearsal this afternoon. . . . The Raff symphony grows on one. But how infinitely below good, honest, old Joseph Haydn (Haydn in G) in freshness, "spontaneity," geniality, and inspiration! It is like a volume of Robert Browning after Shakespeare's songs, or Milton's "Allegro" and "Penseroso." Note Haydn's slow movement, and his lovely finale. Why does nobody write phrases like the opening of that finale any more? . . .

December 16. . . . Indictment for felony against Tweed, and he was lodged in the Tombs but was bailed out by Mr. Justice Barnard. He has a great array of counsel. Connolly is indicted for a misdemeanor. Judge Learned of Albany reduces Connolly's bail to half a million, but leaves Tweed's at the original amount (this in the civil suit). General Frank Barlow, who has recently had occasion to call on Tweed, says he finds that chieftain in a broken and demoralized condition, confessing that he has lost heart and quails under the concentric fire now playing on him. . . .

The Bar Association is pusillanimous; its members are afraid to get up a case against Barnard, Cardozo, and Company, though abundant proof of corruption is within their reach. If they should fail, Barnard and the others would be hostile to them, and they would lose clients. . . . I feel inclined to resign from this Bar Association. Sorry to see John Burrill among Tweed's counsel. As to the Fields (*père et fils*), Stoughton, Fuller-

ton, and that blatant beast John Graham, they would take retainers from
Satan himself. As between Michael and Satan disputing for the body (or
the assets) of Moses, they would prefer to be concerned for the latter. . . .

December 17.   Some forty people came in after tea—a few invited,
but mostly fortuitous. . . . An agreeable evening. But these Sunday
evenings have unaccountably grown into something almost oppressive.
I regret the old practice when six or eight habitués of the house happened
in. Still, the aspect of things under this new dispensation is certainly not
inelegant, and the "entertainment" is modest if not Spartan. There is
nothing snobbish—no effort, and no parade.

December 19.   A ferocious snowstorm plagued the city from noon till
nightfall. First Church Music Association concert at Steinway at eight.
With me was Ellie (on the platform), Lucy, and the two boys, who
officiated as programme distributors. The house was crowded and less
cold and undemonstrative than usual. . . . Some foolish newspaper critic
speaks of the *Preciosa* as "Weber's *weakest* opera"! If the dunderhead had
classified his ideas, he would have perceived that he meant to say "short-
est" or "least elaborate." One would hardly call Milton's "L'Allegro"
one of his weakest works. . . . A most satisfactory concert. . . . Thereafter, we all, with Phelps the Scholastic, took a little supper at Delmonico's.

December 21. . . . Letter from Johnny at Dresden, November 29. He
is having "a splendid time," but abridges his letter because his eyes are
not well enough to enable him to write at length. . . .

A general meeting of the Union Club is called for Friday night to
consider a resolution that Oakey Hall's membership is prejudicial to the
character of the club. There are sixty-five signatures. Oakey Hall feels
this very keenly and has been begging and praying O'Conor to help him
—talking about his young daughter whose prospects would be blighted
by the infliction of a social stigma on her papa, and so on. O'Conor has
been rather melted, I regret to say. Belmont's enthusiasm for Oakey Hall
seems to have cooled down a little. Hall wrote yesterday to Denning
Duer, acting president of the club, that he feels he is "unwilling the
serenity of the club should be imperiled" by differences of opinion on a
merely personal question; and that in case the proposed meeting should
happen not to take place, he would like this to be considered as his resignation.

December 22. . . . I hear from Braem that the Rev. Vinton is very
truculent and bumptious about the refusal of the vestry to give him money
for his traveling expenses. Could he be inspired by vanity and insolence

to write us a letter, such as he would like to write, we should have legitimate ground for getting rid of him. A majority of the vestry would jump at the opportunity. Those who represent Trinity Church—Ogden, Braem, Astor, and I—have long been utterly sick of him.

December 26, TUESDAY. . . . O'Conor at the office today asking Bidwell for names of trustworthy Canada lawyers. He is after Garvey and the other thieves and runagates who have fled across the border. The Union Club has accepted Oakey Hall's resignation—a judicious compromise. . . .

December 29. . . . Black Tweed . . . was invisible for a day or two. Deputy sheriffs went through the motions of looking for him and declared he was not to be found. But this morning, he appeared at the sheriff's office and surrendered in discharge of certain of his bail. He also resigned his commissionership. Alas, for the mutability of human affairs; all human grandeur is vanity.

Died, J. H. Hackett, the only Falstaff extant;[34] also, that tough old financier, Jacob Barker, and Theodore Hagen the musical critic.

Dined at John Astor's yesterday. There were the Rev. Washburn, General McDowell, and others. Young Willy Astor is a nice, refined young fellow, and his statue, "The Wounded Amazon," is a creditable work.

December 30, SATURDAY. . . . The Tammany Society itself repudiates Tweed and degrades him from his place as chief Sachem. It throws him over reluctantly, no doubt, and from an instinct of self-preservation; but that makes the blow more severe. Even Tammany cannot stand Tweed. . . .

---

[34] James H. Hackett, aged seventy-one at the time of his death, had first acted Falstaff in New York in 1828. We have encountered him earlier in this diary as manager of the Astor Place Opera House, and as the impresario who brought Mario and Grisi to sing in the United States. He was not merely an able actor, much interested in native American material, and one of the first to present Rip Van Winkle on the stage, but a student of Shakespeare, who published a correspondence between himself and John Quincy Adams on the subject.

1872

MURDER OF JIM FISK · THE LIBERAL REPUBLICAN MOVEMENT ·
GREELEY NOMINATED FOR PRESIDENT · REMOVAL OF JUDGE
BARNARD · GRANT REËLECTED · STRONG MADE
COMPTROLLER OF TRINITY

Reform was the watchword of the hour as the year 1872 opened; the attention of the entire country was occupied with the movements for reform in the city of New York, reform at Albany and other Northern state capitals, reform in the South, and reform in the national government. The fierce uprising of the previous autumn against the Tweed Ring had accomplished something, but less than most good citizens expected. A member of the Ring named Keyser had restored a few hundred thousand dollars; a civil suit had been brought against Tweed himself to recover stolen funds, and he had been arrested on a criminal charge; Connolly had fled the country. But Tweed still kept his seat in the State Senate, the confederates of the Ring maintained their influence over the legislature, and the principal rascals, defended by able attorneys, were making the most of every legal obstruction. The corrupt judges were still unharmed. The Erie Ring was still untouched. The legislature at Albany, like that at Harrisburg, yet exhaled an odor of uncleanness if not corruption. In short, there was still a great deal of work for such reform leaders as Samuel J. Tilden, Andrew H. Green, and George William Curtis to do. Equally urgent was the need for reform in the South. State after state there had been languishing under governments both inefficient and dishonest. Among the state officers whom even the most radical of Republicans could no longer defend or tolerate were Holden of North Carolina, impeached and turned out of office for dishonesty; Scott of South Carolina, one of the state's "forty thieves"; Warmoth of Louisiana, who had accumulated wealth while the people were robbed; and Reed of Florida, who was

*being put on trial for the theft of railroad bonds. The reconstruction policy of
Grant had proved a failure.*

*In national affairs, a "Liberal Republican" movement originating in
Missouri was gaining important adherents in other states. Its object was to
defeat President Grant for a second term, put an end to corruption, introduce
civil service reform and other administrative improvements, and inaugurate a
more liberal policy toward the Southern people. Carl Schurz of Missouri, Lyman
Trumbull of Illinois, former Secretary Jacob D. Cox of Ohio, and Horace
Greeley of New York were among the leaders who hoped for a brighter era in
Washington. An investigation of the New York custom house early in the year
disclosed a shocking system of blackmail and graft, while it was generally
known that other branches of the government were run by machine politicians
for selfish ends. It was already plain that the country would witness a Republican
schism and a bitter presidential campaign.*

*Strong began the new year with a lament that because of a slow omnibus
he did not reach a meeting of the Columbia trustees in time to vote to put Abram
S. Hewitt in a vacancy of the board. Had he arrived promptly he could have tied
the vote; as it was, the place went to Anthony Halsey, who lacked Hewitt's
commanding abilities. Strong recorded thirty calls on New Year's Day;
a delightful Saturday evening concert on the 6th by the Philharmonic; and that
same evening, news at the Century Club that Ned Stokes had fatally shot Jim
Fisk on the stairway of the Broadway Central Hotel, the sequel of a miserable
quarrel over a strumpet named Josie Mansfield.*

January 7, SUNDAY. . . . The great Fisk died this morning. No loss to
the community—quite the reverse—but it's a pity he should have escaped
the state prison in this way. He seems to have died surrounded by his
congeners, amid the sobbings of Tweed, David Dudley Field, Jay Gould,
and Dr. Carnochan. Stokes is in custody, and it is difficult to see on what
plea he can escape hanging.

January 8. . . . Much talk about Fisk and Stokes. The remains of the
former were conveyed to the railroad depot in great state for interment
at poor little Brattleboro. What a scamp he was, but what a curious and
scientifically interesting scamp! When he "took to the road" a very few
years ago and opened his campaign against society he was penniless. By
talent and audacity he raised himself to the first rank among business
scoundrels, and (I suppose) to great wealth—certainly to opportunities

of great wealth—but then he was reckless in spending. He was opera impresario, "commodore," financier, roué, mountebank, corrupt to the core, with great faculty of corrupting others, judges included, colonel of a regiment of militia, which he uniformed at his own cost and the splendid band of which he supported. He paid its first cornet-player $10,000 a year, it is said. Illiterate, vulgar, unprincipled, profligate, always making himself conspicuously ridiculous by some piece of flagrant ostentation, he was, nevertheless, freehanded with his stolen money, and possessed, moreover, a certain magnetism of geniality that attracted to him people who were not particular about the decency of their associates. He was liberal to distressed ballet dancers and munificent to unfortunate females under difficulties. Let us put this generosity down to the credit side of the scamp's account. The item may be more important than it seems to *us*. His influence on the community was certainly bad in every way, but it is also certain that many people, more or less wise and more or less honest, sorrowed heartily at his funeral. . . .

January 9. . . . Talk of possible war with Spain. May I see no more wars!

That beast John Graham enters an appearance before the Fisk coroner's jury, and is more blatant and insolent than ever. Before any witnesses are sworn, he makes a speech "protesting against the coroner's introducing a murderous atmosphere into the jury room." He should have been collared by policemen and dragged out of it. I am ashamed to live in a community of Fisks, Tweeds, Vanderbilts, John Grahams, and D. D. Fields. Connolly, by the by, has cut and run.

An investigating committee uncovers a most nasty mess of corruption in the custom house, with "Colonel" Frank Howe seemingly ensconced in it, like a burrowing coprophagous beetle.[1]

January 11. . . . Oakey Hall withdraws "for a few days" from malversation in office, and John Cochrane is acting mayor. Hall's private affairs require attention. This is thought a prelude to his resignation; perhaps. Prospects of city reform do not improve. A squabble between two Republican factions interests the legislature more deeply.

January 15, MONDAY. . . . Annual meeting of Century Club Saturday

[1] The principal culprit in the custom house corruption was a hanger-on of Grant's named George K. Leet, who by the President's favor obtained control of the "general order" business (the holding of certain imported goods in a general order warehouse kept by a private citizen under authorization by the government, with large fees attached). Leet made a fortune while performing no real service. But the custom house was also a citadel of machine politics in the state.

night. Edward Slosson bequeaths the Club some thirty or forty pictures, mostly by American artists. Average is fair. Election was nearly unanimous, save that Theodore Weston retained his place by only 97 to 92, which should be a warning to him. —— was there, drivelling about "art" and "tone." From a fribble he is solidifying into a bore. Also —— (Sir Mungo Malagrowther), who acts on the spirit of the rule *nil de mortuis*, and so forth, by never saying anything *de vivis nisi malum*. Also Egleston, in one of his fits of depression. Discoursed with the Rev. Mr. Osgood, William C. Bryant, and other magi, and came off before supper. . . .

They say Stokes will set up that he slew Fisk in self-defense, that he lived in hourly dread of Fisk's myrmidons, and that Fisk instigated the nocturnal assault from the effects of which D. B. Eaton has not yet recovered.[2] Then why did he not have Fisk bound over to keep the peace? Such evidence is absurdly inadmissible, as it strikes me. But it will be got in somehow and will give John Graham a field for indecent gymnastics such as he has never yet enjoyed. And the jury will disagree.

January 19. . . . Tonight with Ellie, Temple, and Louis to Booth's theatre for *Julius Caesar*. Booth as Brutus. Performance fairly good, every part rather above average merit. Perhaps Mark Antony exhibited as too enlightened to rant and roar, but he was effective in his funeral oration. So were Brutus and Cassius in the Tent Scene. So was pretty little Portia in her five minutes' work. Caesar's ghost was a good piece of supernaturalism, and the setting of the play—the *mise en scène* (I hate writing French words)—was unsurpassable.

January 25. . . . Johnny arrived Tuesday, after a voyage that was long and rough, but which he endured without seasickness. Eyes much better; general health and spirits excellent. Very fluent, unreserved, and vivacious in telling his experiences. No trace of moodiness or apathy, *laus Deo*. He went to College this morning and was cordially received by Dr. Barnard and others. He is as nice as he can be. . . .

[2] Dorman Bridgman Eaton (1823–1899), formerly a law partner of Judge William Kent, had been counsel for the Erie Railroad. As a result of that bitter controversy, he was seriously injured by unidentified assailants in the night attack Strong mentions. Upon recovery he resumed practice and threw himself into a crusade for civil service reform. In 1870 he gave up his practice to devote himself entirely to reform activities. President Grant appointed him chairman of the national Civil Service Commission in 1873. He wrote important books on municipal administration and civil service and by bequests endowed professorships of the science of government at Harvard and Columbia.

Custom House Investigating Committee drags slowly along with its work and causes much skipping in the morning papers. The New York *World* and the New York *Tribune* have entered into a partnership for the throwing of dirt at Grant. But their projectiles are so mephitic, fetid, ammoniacal, hippuric, cacodylic, and abominable that they do Grant little harm. They merely disgust and alienate the public. The specially smart malignity and virulence of the *World* must make friends for Grant every day. . . .

January 30. . . . Read Robert Dale Owen's new book on spiritualism, *The Debatable Land*. It is more readable and less irrational than most books of its very low class. His testimony as to personal experiences as to things seen, heard, and felt cannot be summarily disposed of in a lump as legerdemain or delusion, except by some ruling that would exclude all human evidence as to any new and strange occurrence. It must go to the jury for what it is worth, and I dare say cross-examination would shew it to be worth very little indeed. . . .

February 2. Philharmonic rehearsal this afternoon. Very large attendance. Sarasate [the Spanish violinist and composer] did a violin concerto by Max Bruch. . . . The Schumann symphony is really respectable. . . .

February 3. . . . The Assembly at Albany is "going for" Cardozo and Barnard at last, and its Judiciary Committee is instructed to take up the charges of the bar association against those learned judges. Only one legislator voted against the reference and that was the notorious Tom Fields, who has a natural antipathy to investigations. So far, well. We are living in a day of ruffianism and of almost universal corruption. Life and property are as insecure here in New York as in Mexico. It is a thoroughly rotten community. "The whole head is sick and the whole heart faint. From the sole of the foot even unto the head, there is no soundness in it but wounds and bruises and putrifying sores. Run ye to and fro through the streets of Jerusalem and seek in the broad places thereof, if ye can find a man, if there be any that executeth judgment, that seeketh truth." Unless some peaceful and lawful remedy be found, a dangerous convulsion cannot be far off. To degrade venal judges and restore confidence in the courts is manifestly the first step toward reform. . . .

February 6. . . . Columbia College trustees met yesterday afternoon. Mr. "Zbrowski" writes from Paris resigning his seat once more, and we accepted his resignation. So I hope we are at length finally rid of that insufferable noodle. There was considerable debate on the question of setting up an adjunct professorship in Nairne's department. Decision affirmative, and I think unwise. Anthony Halsey took his seat as trustee. Had not seen him since our college days and found him pleasant, as he was of old. He tells me that N. W. Chittenden is practising law in San Francisco. I had supposed him to have died several years ago.

February 10. . . . A little fluster about possible war with England. John Bull talks foolishly about repudiating the Treaty of Washington, because our claims under its provisions are too large. That strikes me as the very question which arbitrators were selected to decide.

Indictments brought in today against Mayor Hall, Sweeny, the Pecksniffian Nathaniel Sands, and others.

February 14, ASH WEDNESDAY. . . . Yesterday's atmosphere was succulent. Toward evening it deliquesced into pouring rain, and at about nine in the evening the Lacrymosa of Mozart's Requiem at Steinway Hall was accompanied by a vehement hailstone chorus on the roof, much more than *sotto voce*, with lightning and low thunder. Concert (Church Music Association) was crowded. I knew nearly every other person in the room. Policeman told me "with amazement and awe" that by half-past ten "there was nearly five hundred carriages in Fourteenth Street, sir, and half of them was private." Fifteenth Street also blocked with vehicles.

The *Struensee* Overture came out well, and is certainly handsome. The harp passages are fresh and effective. I like it better than any other orchestral work of Meyerbeer's. The Requiem traveled well. The Dies Irae was as impressive and aweful as anything I know in music, and the Lacrymosa embodied another sentiment with almost equal power. And then that gem of a Benedictus, so pure, sad, and elegant! . . .

February 20. . . . At Columbia College yesterday afternoon with William Schermerhorn, Barnard, Haight, and H. J. Anderson, the Doctor Angelicus, or Simplicissimus. Then we spent an hour in the cabinets of the School of Mines. The College library is now all but useless.[3] We incline to make it useful in spite of the treasurer, whose way it is to oppose

---

[3] On this subject see Brander Matthews' testimony in *These Many Years.* He writes that at this time the Columbia library was open only one or two hours a day, in the afternoon when most students had gone home; that he for one never entered it during his undergraduate career, and he thinks no classmate did so; that the collection of fewer than 15,000 volumes was kept in glazed cases all carefully locked; and that the librarian, allowed $1,000 a year for purchases, took pride in returning to the college treasury as large a part of this as possible.

every little disbursement no matter how necessary for our students, while he pants to run up a debt of a million or so for a new site and new buildings.

February 26. . . . Oakey Hall's trial began today.

Died, at Geneva, Mrs. M. H. Grinnell. . . .

The legislative committee is diligently investigating the judicial career of Judges Barnard and Cardozo. Results, if any, are kept very close. E. H. Owen (!!!) and Fullerton attend on Cardozo's behalf, and Bidwell (!!!!) is retained "for consultation."[4] This is for the sake of his white cravat and his high character, for there can be nothing to consult about, and there has been no consultation. Cardozo wants to be able to talk about "my eminently respectable counsel, Mr. Bidwell and Mr. Owen." As to Fullerton, he and his client are well suited to each other. Bidwell took this retainer reluctantly, feeling bound by the strict rule that forbids a refusal, unless there be an actual prior retainer on the other side. But I think he was wrong, and that that rule applies to none but judicial proceedings. On investigations by legislative or congressional committees, and the like, counsel do not appear professionally and as sworn officers of a court, but merely as experts in badgering witnesses; and they have a perfect right to accept or decline that function. This committee is no tribunal. I regret that Bidwell should have befouled his fingers by touching—even formally—such filth as Cardozo. The immaculate Barnard is weak enough to publish a "protest" against Mr. S. J. Tilden's acting as a member of this committee, because Tilden has publicly denounced him and is not impartial. Impartiality is the first qualification of a judge, but it is not essential to a prosecutor, or to him who collects evidence for a prosecution.

February 28. . . . Went to a state dinner at William Schermerhorn's. We were honored by none of the ladies but Mrs. Fanny Bridgham. There were Samuel, her husband, R. M. Blatchford, Alexander Hamilton, Fred Sheldon, Rives, General McDowell, Robert Hone. . . .

After three days' hard work, eleven jurors have been bagged for Oakey Hall's trial. The defendant's pertinacious fight over every minor point does not look as if he felt the confidence in his case which he pro-

---

[4] Marshall Spring Bidwell (1799–1872), who had been born in Massachusetts but reared in Canada, had been compelled to leave Upper Canada after the rebellion under William Lyon Mackenzie. He became one of the leaders of the New York bar, and a man of prominence in society and philanthropic affairs. For his long career as a member of Strong's law firm, see the earlier volumes of this diary, and the Introduction. Bidwell's integrity and standing were indeed in striking contrast with the reputation of his client.

fesses with so much flourish. . . . The case made against Judge Cardozo before the legislative committee is said to be fearfully damaging.

Yesterday afternoon a long session of Philharmonic directors at Steinway and some effusion of pepper sauce. Vocalists give us no end of bother, and we seriously incline henceforth to do without them, if we can. Remmertz, the respectable barytone, was engaged for our next (fourth) concert by Herr Rietzel as a Committee of One with power at $100. The other directors rightly thought this sum exorbitant and wanted to rescind the bargain, but I advised them that they could not do it.

March 3, SUNDAY. . . . I hear that the genial climate of Nassau has reinvigorated the Rev. Vinton and that he will inflict himself upon Trinity Church again by Easter at latest. I am glad he is better, of course, but what a pity he could not have received a loud "call" to some tropical parish in Nassau, or Tobago, or Trinidad, or Tierra del Fuego, where one would have niggers for "underlings" and could bully them at his own sweet will!

March 5. At three to the first of Edmund Schermerhorn's series of musical "matinées" in the afternoon. About fifty present, among whom were Miss Nilsson, old Robert Ray, Count Costi, Osten-Sacken, and the usual set. Edmund has advanced from the quartettes and septettes of last year to an orchestra of twenty-five! mostly Philharmonics. Pech is the leader, of course. We had Bennett's Overture to *Die Naiaden*, which is pretty; Haydn's B-flat Symphony, No. 12, a dear old friend, and one of the loveliest and healthiest orchestral works extant—sweet, sound, and simple as an oread. Then Mrs. Imogen Brown sang certain truck from *Traviata*, and we closed with a "potpourri" by some Frenchman from the *Freischütz*, which was pungent and delicious. A most brilliant afternoon. Talked with nice, kind Miss Louisa Schuyler. . . .

College trustees met yesterday. A bare quorum and a most unsatisfactory meeting. Professor Egleston had asked for another assistant for the reason, among others, that his mineralogical and metallurgical collections are growing so fast that it takes the whole time of one man to determine, arrange, and label them. The Standing Committee made a most elaborate report adverse to the application and recommended, as a remedy for the professor's difficulty, that "foreign exchanges" be stopped and our advantageous arrangement with the Smithsonian terminated! In other words, "the child is so vigorous and grows so fast that we really cannot afford to find it in clothes, and we must stunt and dwarf it by putting it on half-allowance." And this while we are saving up money for a site and for buildings and have near $200,000 already hoarded. I wonder the committee did not recommend a public notice that no contributions to the cabinets or the library will be hereafter received. I moved that consideration of the report be postponed, which passed, and I suppose it will never be called up. This seemed to me rather better than a recorded vote endorsing the positions of the committee, and it was manifest that their recommendation would have been adopted.

What a Boeotian board it is! How easy it is to see why Harvard and Yale are securing millions of new endowment from year to year almost, while we lie still, except as we are aroused by the falling in of leases.

March 7, THURSDAY. Church Music Association rehearsal tonight with Ellie; satisfactory. Evening was devoted to Kyrie of Beethoven in D, and Gloria, down to the Quoniam. These movements were worked at very hard and in detail, many passages repeated four or five times, and single parts (bassi, and so on) drilled separately. Then we tried part of the refreshing *Lorelei*. These movements of the Mass begin to glimmer out into form and comeliness as one knows them better. . . .

Wall Street is more infested than ever with roving presbyters from the ends of the earth—clerical privateers—each setting forth the claims of his own local Zion, and each declining to stop his noise and move on for anything less than a ten dollar bill. Three of these "frères mendicants" came for me this morning, and my pocketbook feels "as if an elephant had stomped on to it." I object to these centralizing tendencies. The rural districts should have the privilege of doing a little for themselves, instead of making this metropolis their foraging ground. . . .

It is a majestic spectacle, the mayor of New York on trial for stealing or for helping certain pals of his to steal, and defended by a great array of counsel, who are pettifogging their case with technical quibbles against every offer of evidence. . . .

March 8. . . . Yesterday afternoon Oakey Hall and his battalion of counsel were dumbfounded by the appearance of A. J. Garvey, the plasterer, who was supposed to be in foreign parts. He was called by the prosecution, took the stand, and was sworn. Had the late estimable Mr. Watson risen from the dead and come forth as state's evidence, he would not have struck more terror to the souls of Hall and Company. But the estimable Stoughton soon rallied, found room for an objection to a question, and then talked against time till the hour of adjournment. There was great need of consultation as to the treatment of this unexpected and most uncomfortable symptom.

This morning there were more objections and "nice sharp quillets," maintained with vehemence. But Judge Daly seems to dispose of them fairly and well. From what the respectable Garvey has said on the stand today, he would seem ready to make a clean breast of it, to reveal the "Mysteries of New York," and "display Satan's Invisible World." Slippery Dick Connolly is reported to have slipped off, leaving his bail liable for half a million and absquatulated—"G.T.T."[5]

Grand subject for a historical picture on a large scale—the Awful Apparition of Garvey, Oakey Hall turning pale, John Burrill and Stoughton and dirty Tom Buckley and others making a ghastly effort to grin and look unconcerned, Daly watching the scene with the impartial serenity of a rather sagacious old owl, a courtroom full of briefless barristers in high excitement and delight.

March 11. . . . Hall's trial suspended today because of a juror's illness. His counsel have irreparably damaged whatever breechcloth of reputation he has left by their continual objections and obstinate resistance to the admission of evidence. They love darkness rather than light, because their client's deeds are evil. A single sunbeam blackens him as certainly as it does a sensitive plate. . . .

It would seem that the Erie Ring has come to grief. A little talk with General Dix about it this evening, but I do not understand the situation precisely. There has been a conspiracy and a *coup d'état*. The General is president, and the company is rid of the scoundrelly cabals that have ruled and swindled it so long. But Jay Gould (the dethroned president) and D. D. Field will doubtless fight hard to recover their opportunities of peculation, and they will be backed by Cardozo, Barnard, and Ingraham, judges they own.[6]

March 12. . . . Died, the incendiary, agitator, and humbug, Mazzini.

[5] "Gone to Texas"; but Connolly had gone first to Canada and then Europe. Andrew J. Garvey, a plasterer, had been one of the leading rascals of the Ring, and as executive officer so-called to Tweed, had prepared a great part of the fraudulent claims which Mayor A. Oakey Hall admitted. Garvey's sudden introduction into the trial was a *coup de théâtre* indeed. When the autumn storm burst he had fled to Europe, but his wife (intent on saving part of his money) brought him back and delivered him up to the prosecutor as state's evidence. He at once began telling how the frauds were planned and the money divided.

[6] Jay Gould was president of the Erie Railroad down to March 15, 1872. In a complex series of transactions, various American and British investors anxious to place the railroad in honest hands combined forces and brought about the election of a new directorate, which chose the eminent John A. Dix as president of the road. Daniel Sickles and S. L. M. Barlow had been prominent in the change. In midsummer of this year Peter H. Watson, former Assistant Secretary of War, succeeded Dix.

Jay Gould appears to have begun the day with a notification to all agents of the Erie Company that he insisted on his rights as president and should treat yesterday's meeting of directors as illegal and its action as a nullity. But the fourth edition of the evening's *Post* announces that he resigned at two-thirty this afternoon and that the Erie Ring has finally collapsed, after doing the country infinite disgrace and mischief throughout Christendom. Fisk's sudden death seems to have destroyed it, as Watson's led to the destruction of its ally, the Tammany Ring.

March 14, THURSDAY. . . . By Mrs. John Taylor Johnston's kind invitation went this afternoon to see her husband's beautiful gallery (8 Fifth Avenue), which he liberally throws open on Thursday afternoons.[7] How superb it is, how rich he must be, and how much wiser of him to spend his money this way than on race horses, four-in-hands, and great ostentatious parties! There are Church's "Niagara," Cole's "Voyage of Life" series, several fine things from the old Düsseldorf collection of twenty years ago, Gérome's "Death of Caesar," Müller's admirable "Conciergerie" (duplicate in the Luxembourg), and many other covetable pictures. Not one of them struck me as bad. J. T. Johnston is quite an enviable person. But I dare say he has his troubles and anxieties and sore spots like other people.

The Republicans recovered New Hampshire from the Democrats on Tuesday, which victory is rather a disappointment to the anti-Grant wing of the successful party and makes Grant's renomination nearly certain. His unfriends (the *Tribune* and *World* especially, a most unnatural alliance!) have so overdone their harping and nagging that every fair man must incline to side with him. These newspapers have certainly made me quite a partisan of Grant's.

March 15. . . . Philharmonic rehearsal at two-thirty. *Eroica*, Mendelssohn's *Fingal's Cave* overture, and Bargiel's *Prometheus*. In our box, Ellie, Johnny and Temple, Mrs. Noble, Mrs. Talboys, Rosalie, Dick, Jack Ehninger. I could write an essay on the *Eroica*. It is ranked by no orchestral work except Beethoven's immortal C Minor Symphony. One feels, after hearing it, as though he had fully dined on a score of most exquisite courses, with due allowance of champagne (in the third move-

---

[7] John Taylor Johnston (1820–1893), the first president of the Metropolitan Museum, had been trained for the bar but had turned to railroading. As head of the Lehigh & Susquehanna and the Central Railroad of New Jersey, he had accumulated a large fortune. His private collection of pictures was at this time probably the best in America. Financial reverses caused him to sell most of the collection in 1876, but he remained head of the Metropolitan until 1889.

ment), the raciest old Madeira (in the fourth), and so on. One is hardly able to imbibe any more music. . . .

March 17. . . . Jay Gould has resigned from direction of the Erie Railroad.

March 21. Trinity Church Standing Committee met this afternoon. Cisco has secured for us the Barbey house (built by William T. Blodgett) on Twenty-fifth Street, west of Trinity Chapel, as a rectory. The price with furniture is $75,000; cheap, but we must ask the vestry for an additional $15,000. . . .

Bidwell was subpoenaed to attend the Judiciary Committee now investigating Barnard. With characteristic timidity, he "really could not undertake to state the general opinion of the New York bar as to Mr. Barnard," and so was not examined after all.

Owners of the fatal *Westfield* are already nearly ruined by judgments for damages growing out of the massacre of July 30. Each of their ferryboats is now placed in custody of a gallant deputy-sheriff, who should be well paid for thus facing death in the discharge of his duty, for levying on an active volcano, as it were, and going into possession.

The valiant Sir Charles Dilke has now fired off the first anti-monarchical gun in the House of Commons. He moved for an enquiry and report as to the cost of the Crown. He lost 274 to 2.[8] But this ridiculous minority will not discourage the extreme Radicals. They have certain plausible half-truths on their side. It requires no thought or study to take in their arguments. Every coal-heaver or navvy or semi-brutal agricultural laborer can understand them. The Radical movement seems to me sure to grow stronger year by year.

March 25, MONDAY. . . . Saturday evening, Edmund, Pech, the Rev. Cooke, and General C. C. Dodge were here. Dodge desires to take hold of the Church Music Association; he will be useful. A rather anxious council, followed by a deliberative and aesthetic tea, over the asperities and the arduosities of the Beethoven Mass. Agreed to introduce four experimental "saxophones," or other wind instruments, at next rehearsal to guide and steady the aberrant voice parts of the chorus. . . .

Marrin, who has been looking after our Life and Trust Company bill at Albany (the fate of which bill is as yet uncertain because certain

[8] Sir Charles Dilke had been conducting an agitation against the monarchy, in the course of which he made a violent speech at Newcastle. When he tried to carry his crusade into the House of Commons, Gladstone sternly indicted him, and the House howled down both him and his single supporter. The really strong English movement was not republican but laborite.

honorable members oppose it in the hope of being bought off) tells me
that this "reform" legislature is at least as corrupt as the worst of its
predecessors, and I believe him. Judge Barnard will, it is said, be unanimously elected colonel of the militia regiment recently orphaned by the
untimely death of James Fisk, Jr.!!! I fear our trouble lies deeper than the
venality of legislature and judiciary. I fear the community has lost all
moral sense and moral tone, and is fast becoming too rotten to live. We
are seriously threatened by social disintegration and a general smash. I
wish I could flee into the wilderness as Lot fled from Sodom and take
refuge in some dull but decent New England village. No rich and crowded
community can long survive universal suffrage.

March 27. . . . Erie stock has gone up like a balloon, and great fortunes have been made by people whom *I* think quite rich enough already.[9]

Maledictions on the memory of the doctor who steered safely through
measles and whooping cough the maternal grandfather of the man who
invented the income tax! I am engaged over those pestilent "returns."

The New York *Times* publishes transcripts of the bank accounts of
Cardozo and Gratz Nathan, and they present coincidences that are curious
and instructive. Connolly having evaporated and disappeared and his
evidence being essential to the conviction of Brady and Haggerty, the
voucher-stealers, their trial cannot be brought on, and Cardozo (perhaps
not improperly) admits them to bail. So they will go unpunished. But it
is comfortable to think that the scoundrels have been locked up for several
months.

The Rev. Vinton is not to return before the fifteenth of April, *Deo
gratias*. He will not afflict us on Easter Sunday.

April 1, EASTER MONDAY. The College trustees met this afternoon;
only a quorum. The Boeotian report . . . about Egleston's cabinet was
called up. Mr. Ruggles, the Bishop, and Dr. Haight had severally a little
to say against it, and I spoke briefly on the same side. Ogden was prolix
in its support. The result was that the more offensive recommendations
were withdrawn, especially the stolid proposition that the professors be
instructed to purchase henceforth such minerals only as are "necessary
for purposes of instruction" and to purchase no mere "curiosities." Then
the Committee on a New Site reported progress and asked for power to

[9] The spectacular rise in Erie stock, a result of the dramatic change in management,
made more than a million for Jay Gould himself. Actually the financial condition of
the road was so desperate that two million dollars had to be raised at once to save it
from bankruptcy. General Charles C. Dodge, mentioned above, was one of the sons
of the eminent merchant and philanthropist William E. Dodge.

purchase whenever they should find a site to suit them; a modest recommendation, which was objected to and laid over. . . .

March went out like a roaring and a rabid lion. A cold outrageous northeast storm poured and blustered all yesterday. Nevertheless, Trinity Church was jammed full, standing room and all, long before the service began. Morgan and Messiter had got together an orchestra from outside the Musical Protective Union (some of whose members were so disgusted with the attempt to extort money from the church last Thursday that they resigned and appeared in the organ loft yesterday). It was an excellent orchestra. . . .

April 3. . . . Died, Professor S. F. B. Morse, the Father of Telegrams, at eighty-one. Strange how little sensation was produced by the first telegram from Washington to Baltimore (or vice versa) on May 27, 1844. I have no recollection of the event. Probably book-buyers of 1480 remembered nothing about the appearance of the Mazarin Bible or the Mainz Psalter. Flags at half-mast all day and everywhere, partly for Morse and partly for General Anderson's funeral. The reliquiae of that good man and faithful soldier were removed from the Second Avenue cemetery for final interment at West Point. . . . The Republicans carried Connecticut by an increased majority.

April 8. . . . Poor Vinton returned from Nassau yesterday and had to be carried from the steamer to his house. The Rector saw him this morning and thinks badly of the case. The patient's liver is congested, and he is jaundiced. There is dropsical effusion in his legs and abdomen. He "has not slept for five weeks," and his stomach cannot retain food—all which looks rather grave. But the Rev. Mr. Vinton's stamina are iron—or brass. . . .

April 10. . . . Through the rain yesterday afternoon to a College library meeting. Long talk with Barnard and Dr. Haight. Every screw in the College is loose. Both undergraduates and faculty have slipped down far below concert pitch. I fear Barnard is a King Log.

This anti-Grant or "Liberal Republican" movement looks like fusion with the so-called "Democratic" party. Black Marble of the *World* and Goose Greeley of the *Tribune* are in sweet accord. Greeley means right, I think, but he is ruined by overweening vanity and a most plentiful lack of practical common sense. During the war, and during the period of suspense that preceded it, his paper was somehow a constant embarrassment and damage to the national cause, weakened it, and retarded its final triumph more than all the Copperhead presses of the North. Now he has allowed himself to be seduced by the old Copperheads of eight years ago and fondly hopes that they will make an honest President of him! It's a comfort to think that they will find him a very fractious and uneasy bedfellow. This bolt may prove to be a serious matter. Personal hatred of Grant seems at the root of it. I cannot understand how he has not merely alienated so many of his old supporters but converted them into bitter enemies. Mere coldness and hardness of manner, ungeniality, and taciturnity, do not justify or account for active and savage hostilities.

April 12. Meeting of the anti-Grant Republican Bolters at Cooper Institute tonight looks formidable in numbers but is doubtless strongly reinforced by Copperhead auxiliaries. General Dix and other prominent men are in the movement. Strange they take no warning by the plaudits and the caresses of the New York *World*. If they succeed, they will break up the Republican party and throw the government into the hands of the doughfaces, Copperheads, and traitors of 1860.

The first public rehearsal of the Church Music Association at Steinway yesterday afternoon, a rehearsal satisfactory beyond expectation, was devoted to Beethoven's Mass and lasted from three thirty-five until near six. That is an extraordinary work. Even those portions of it which I do not understand (and they are many) keep my attention riveted. Obscure passages in other works . . . drive my thoughts miles away. But this music, hard and unmelodic as it is, collars me with its first chord and holds me tight till its finale, as the Ancient Mariner held the Wedding Guest. It's very strange, almost uncanny. One carries away few definite memories of phrases in the Mass. I cannot now distinctly recall any part of it but the grand opening of the Kyrie, and the awful "Ante Omnia Saecula." One can find no words to define the peculiar something which distinguishes Beethoven's second from all other compositions, even from the Ninth Symphony, which belongs to the same period of Beethoven's development.

April 15, MONDAY. . . . Yesterday, Ogilby preached at Trinity—"with acceptance." The Rev. Vinton is reported rather better but extensively hydropic. In the evening, Dickon was here, Carroll, General Dix, one Hazard of Boston, [E. S.] Nadal of the *Nation*, and a dozen more. General Dix gives an appetizing account of the pickings and stealings wherein the Fields (*père et fils*) reveled while counsel for the Erie Ring, and pals of Jay Gould and the late Jem Fisk, Jr. Carroll wants the adjunct professorship of belles-lettres, and the like, in Columbia College, but he will not get it; for though he is just the man for the place, our fogies and noodles will hold his connection with the press a disqualification. . . .

Work resumed on Brooklyn Bridge tower, now eighty-five feet above tidewater.

April 19. . . . Cloud of war on the other side of the Atlantic. France is arming with all her might, and arming avowedly for a campaign of vengeance. It is *said* (and it is also denied) that Bismarck has given Thiers formal warning that unless these hostile preparations be discontinued at once, Prussia will be obliged to resume hostilities in self-defense. Like enough.

April 20. Miss Rosalie here this afternoon. The Setons' boarding-house (28 and 26 Union Square) is to be abandoned by them May 1 and converted to business uses, and the young lady does not know where she will find shelter thereafter. Another change on Union Square: the C. V. S. Roosevelt house on the southwest corner of Fourteenth Street and Broad-way is coming down to be replaced by a sewing machine warehouse.

General Vinton says his reverend uncle is "better," but the Rev. Ogilby says, with significant look and emphasis: "He's a very sick man."

Dan Sickles, by John Graham his attorney (*arcades ambo*), threatens the New York *World* with a libel suit. To which threat that newspaper makes a plucky and orgulous response. One might as well try to spoil a rotten egg as to damage Dan's character. His service during the war has inclined Republicans to speak mildly of him, or to say nothing about him. But it cannot quite blot out his infamous record, which, in the judg-ment of Copperheads, it rather aggravates. Putting Sickles forward as a chief speaker at the Grant meeting last Wednesday was a blunder, but sending him as minister to Spain was worse. I fear Grant's perceptions of propriety are a little dull. If he fail of reëlection, it will be because of a series of mistakes, mostly unimportant, which a man of delicate organiza-tion would have avoided by instinct, and which are dwelt upon and exag-gerated by his rancorous, unscrupulous enemies to his great prejudice.

In spite of all these, I expect to vote for him if I live long enough, for I believe him honest and strong, judicious *on the whole*, and certainly entitled to every honor the country can give him.

April 24. Much vexation of spirit about our programmes, which are still in the printers' hands. It's Pech's fault for writing a programme as big as a family Bible and including whole pages of musical notation. But he fumes and frets and is, generally, so uncomfortable a coadjutor that I am tempted to drop the Church Music Association after this season. If Charles Dodge would take my place, I would abdicate instanter. But the Rector is about taking certain steps that may materially modify all the future (if any) of the Church Music Association. He proposes to act *ex parte*. I wrote him sometime since that this seemed to me unfair. . . . Most clerics are the better for a little lay counsel when acting in a judicial or quasi-judicial capacity. I have a strong presentiment that no sufficient defense or explanation will be offered, but there should be an opportunity to offer it, nevertheless.

April 26. . . . Yesterday's first public orchestral rehearsal of the Church Music Association was satisfactory. The whole programme was executed, the Kyrie excepted. The Mass is prodigious. . . . Richard Grant White, to whom the Mass was new, declared it the most marvelous music he ever heard, and "the biggest thing out." . . .

Newspaper critics publish daily paragraphs about the Beethoven Mass, some of which shew thought, at least, which is seldom found in their lucubrations. For example, they say that it is not so much a church service as a cantata or oratorio with the service as its text; that a great deal of it is, strictly, choral declamation; that many of its subjects or phrases cannot be called melodies but are something transcendental, above all the melody we know, and in a higher plane.

April 29. Call from W. E. Dodge, Jr., who wants Richard Grant White made adjunct professor of English literature in Columbia College. No question as to White's great acquirements; but could such a Miss Nancy keep a class in order? Dodge has seen him tested in a somewhat similar position and thinks he could. . . .

Died, at Garrison's (opposite West Point) Nathaniel F. Moore, at ninety; a good man, an elegant Greek scholar, sometime professor of ancient languages in Columbia College, and for seven years (1842-1849) its president.[10] He retained his vigor of body and mind up to within a few months or weeks. Of the faculty of my college days, Dr. H. J. Anderson is now sole survivor. . . .

The formidable Carlist rising in Spain seems an anachronism, as if a Pharaoh were to emerge from his pyramid with a carload of galvanized mummies behind him and assert his hereditary right to the throne of Egypt. But this move against an alien king may possibly prevail. Grant is more seriously threatened by the Cincinnati "rising." But I have faith in his star. His position at Pittsburgh Landing was most critical. He seemed

[10] In the roll of Columbia's presidents, the scholarly, retiring Moore succeeded W. A. Duer and preceded Charles King. He had never married, according to one account, because in youth he fell in love with "the heavenly Ellen Conover," forbidden to him because a first cousin. He had been an enthusiastic amateur photographer in the 1850s, and Columbia preserves some of his work.

hopelessly beaten, but he won the battle at last. It's funny to see the wicked old Democratic party shamming dead, or (to be more accurate) solemnly averring that its teeth are drawn and its nails are pared and trying to seduce silly Greeley and the other vagrant Republican sheep to accompany it into the wilderness, which the confiding creatures seem not unwilling to do. Since Greeley underwent his ovidian and ophidian metamorphosis into a Copperhead, he has discovered that General D. C. Buell was abominably treated ten years ago and that it's all Grant's fault. At that period, he recommended that General Buell be shot as a traitor. Everything is Grant's fault, according to Greeley, and his main ally the New York *World*. The prevalence of smallpox in New York is due to "nepotism" and the recent baleful activity of Vesuvius is due to the "Military Ring." . . .

May 1.   The virtuous Cardozo has resigned, but I trust his impeachment will not be thereby abated. . . .[11]

May 3. . . . News tonight—scarcely credible—that the Cincinnati Convention has nominated Horace Greeley for President!!! These political experts know much more about availability than I do. Horace Greeley's name may be a word of power in Southern Niggerdom; but, availability apart, this is the most preposterous and ludicrous nomination to the Presidency ever made on this continent, except, perhaps, Mr. George Francis Train's, and that was made by himself alone. Horace Greeley's purposes are honest, but he is so conceited, fussy, and foolish that he damages every cause he wants to support. Nobody doubts his loyalty and patriotism, but he did more to weaken and embarrass the national cause during the war than any of the Copperhead editors. He deals cleverly enough with abstract questions, but he is devoid of practical common sense, the first qualification for high political place. . . .

All spring the Liberal Republican movement had grown in strength. It was based on disgust with the low moral tone of the Grant Administration, with the President's indifference to civil service reform, tariff reform, and administrative reform, with the growing power of bosses and machines, entrenched in customhouses, navy yards, and post offices, with the sterile, unimaginative Southern policy of the Administration, and with the prominence of military men in the

[11] Of the three vicious New York judges, McCunn was dead; Barnard had been impeached, and in August of this year was convicted, removed from the bench, and disqualified from holding any office; while Cardozo, though escaping impeachment by his resignation, was disgraced and forced into retirement.

government. While Carl Schurz was its most active leader, a number of other eminent Republicans gave the revolt their support. Of these, Charles Francis Adams of Massachusetts and Lyman Trumbull of Illinois were regarded as strong presidential aspirants. A brilliant group of editors were prominent in the movement—Greeley of the Tribune, *Samuel Bowles of the Springfield* Republican, *William Cullen Bryant of the New York* Evening Post, *Horace White of the Chicago* Tribune, *Murat Halstead of the Cincinnati* Commercial, *and Henry Watterson of the Louisville* Courier-Journal. *When an enthusiastic convention of volunteer delegates gathered in Cincinnati on May 1, hope of success in the national campaign ran high; for it was clear that the Democratic Party would accept any reasonable candidate and platform.*

Had Charles Francis Adams or Lyman Trumbull been nominated, Grant might well have feared the loss of the election. He had been almost a total failure as President. On the first ballot the universally-esteemed Adams was far in the lead, with 203 votes against 147 for Greeley and 110 for Trumbull. Unfortunately for the movement, a group of astute journalists (such as Whitelaw Reid) and some expert politicians succeeded in sweeping the gathering off its feet; and on the sixth ballot, Greeley was nominated. The convention no sooner realized what it had done than it was ready—too late—to undo its work. For the country, as Strong indicates, received Greeley's selection with derision.

May 6, MONDAY. On my way downtown, I found Broadway at Houston Street no thoroughfare—Niblo's Theatre was burning up. . . . Columbia College trustees at the Law School. Had a long discussion on the resolution giving the committee "on the site" power to buy land anywhere on the island in their discretion and to run the College in debt not more than half a million. I opposed any purchase as premature . . . but the motion prevailed. . . .

May 11. . . . The Rector has moved at last in Pech's case and has acted, I think, with great discretion and humanity. He wholly ignores the graver charges against Pech and invites his resignation on the ground that his duties as *Kapellmeister* have been and are grossly neglected (for example, he has absented himself from twenty-one services during the last four months without leave and with apology), and the congregation of St. John's is discontented. These graver charges therefore need not be made public. . . .

May 13. . . . Decadent, 50 Wall Street, old George Griswold's granite building in the thirty-third year of its age. Also, the buildings on the southeast corner of Fifteenth Street and Union Square, whilom Mme. Chegaray's school for young ladies, of late a second-class hotel. A first-class hotel is to be erected on their site.

May 15. . . . Pech called last evening for a painful interview. He gave me his unfortunate story with seeming frankness and in full detail. In 1849 he ran away with a woman older than himself and below him in social position and married her clandestinely, he being then nineteen. She proved vicious, false, cantankerous, and incorrigible. She threatened his life, broke up his professional engagements by malignant pranks, and so harassed and degraded him that after six or seven years of torment, he abandoned her. She stipulated not to molest him, and he has annually remitted her some fifty or one hundred pounds. Mrs. Pech No. 2 is fully aware of the premises and doesn't mind. As to his alleged Oxford degree . . . he says that having proceeded bachelor, he is entitled to the doctorate whenever he applies for it (which I do not believe to be the case), and that he therefore thought himself authorized to write himself "Doctor" of Oxford.

He is a bundle of strange inconsistencies, good points and bad, strength and weakness. I gave him a great deal of advice, such as it was, and much genuine sympathy. He must change his base and leave New York. The aggravating or irritating feature of the case is that Pech is thus destroyed by the professional envy and jealousy of his colleagues in Trinity parish. But for them (and Morgan especially) this scandal, of more than twenty years ago, would never have been forced on the Rector's notice. As an artist and a conductor Pech is worth ten dozen of them, but they found a weak spot in his armor and have killed him. He may say to Morgan, as the Scottish earl (in *Tales of a Grandfather*) said to his murderer, "You have spoiled a better face than your own."

May 17. . . . The New York State Democratic Convention declines to endorse Horace Greeley, which is a blow to the Philosopher of Chappaqua. But we cannot yet afford to laugh at his nomination. There would be at least as much tragedy as comedy in the election of that old gander, and Grant is undeniably weaker than he was a year ago. His negotiations with England hurt him. . . .

Church Music Association subscription is $1,060. I doubt whether we can accomplish a fourth season with our raised prices; and should we secure the money, I don't know where we could find a conductor as able, as indomitable, as zealous, and as disinterested as poor Pech. . . . With all his faults, his loss is irreparable.

May 20, MONDAY. . . . On Saturday had a long Law School Committee meeting. Lieber is to keep his place one year more. Mr. Ruggles insists on his putting the substance of his lectures into the form of a textbook, which Lieber is too lazy to do and which he will not do, in spite of Mr. Ruggles's adjurations.

Died, Friday evening, John David Wolfe, millionaire, at eighty; heart disease. . . . Wolfe was profusely generous to such church agencies as were managed by men like minded with himself—moderate or "dry" Low-Churchmen. In 1845 or 1848, he was "dropped" from the vestry of Trinity Church because he maintained, openly and offensively, that its endowment belonged equally to all the city parishes. This injury he never could quite forgive. . . . Mention of Trinity Church always made him look sour. But he always treated me civilly and kindly enough.

May 23. . . . Horace Greeley's letter accepting the Cincinnati nomination is a dishonest and scandalous bid for the votes of Democrats and Free-traders. It has destroyed my faith in Horace Greeley's sincerity and integrity. I have believed him honest, though without judgment and sound practical sense, but he has at last taken his place among mere trading politicians. Horace Greeley, chief captain for years of the high protectionists and fanatical in his advocacy of extreme protectionist doctrine, declares that in his judgment all questions about protection should be settled by Congress and that the President should not interfere by exercise of his veto power, or otherwise, with its decision. That is, Horace Greeley renounces in advance, as to a most important question, a most important power vested in the Executive by the Constitution in trust for the country, and pledges himself, if elected, not to exercise his official authority in certain contingencies, though profoundly convinced that the country will suffer infinite damage by his inaction. . . .

May 27. Called on this afternoon by Boehm and G. F. Bristow, committee from the Philharmonic, who presented me with a certificate, or rather a copy of a resolution, conferring on me an honorary membership, most ornamentally engrossed and handsomely framed. They said a great many civil things about the favor with which I am regarded by the Society. It's a case of manifest overestimation. But I am glad they like me. My relations with all these gentlemen are very pleasant. . . .

On Friday I presided over the annual Philharmonic meeting; about eighty present and a long session. Was unanimously reëlected president; a close vote on one or two other offices. Bernstein and Reiff are new directors. . . .

The Rev. Vinton has been convalescent for some time and driving out every day. But grave symptoms have returned, and he is again confined to his room and taking digitalis.

Stokes the Fiskicide was arraigned on Friday before Judge Ingraham. McKeon tendered a dilatory plea, an anomalous kind of plea in abatement. It was not received. Whereupon Stokes "stood mute" and the court ordered a plea of not guilty to be entered instead of subjecting him, as in the "good old times," to the *peine forte et dure*.

Mrs. Douglas Cruger leaves a large slice of her estate to the "Bible Society" and to the "Presbyterian Board" of something or other. The heirs deny her capacity, and these societies will compromise on easy terms, for the old lady had "a bee in her bonnet" this long while.

Talk with John Astor about the extreme desirableness of a cathedral. "He would give $100,000 toward it." Were churchmen generally like-minded with him, we could easily raise the sum of three or four millions such an undertaking would require. Often as I have thought of it, I never regarded the realization of such a conception as within the bounds of possibility till my casual talk with John J. Astor at the door of 68 Wall Street this morning. Why not try to make the dream a reality?

May 30. . . . The Horace Greeley hallucination does not seem contagious; it does not spread. This will be the most comic of presidential campaigns, though involving the possibility of gravest disaster.

June 1. . . . Old James Gordon Bennett is reported dead or dying. During a period of about thirty-seven years, he has done more than any living man to debase American journalism, his nose has been oftener tweaked in public, and he has been oftener kicked and horsewhipped.

Sumner, the Ciceronian Thersites of the Senate . . . devotes an entire senatorial day to the laborious pelting of Grant with all the dirt he can lay his hands on. . . . It is an erudite speech into which the Senator has emptied several pages of his commonplace book. He quotes Plato and Plutarch, the *Lives of the Popes*, Juvenal, Colonel Forney, Lord Brougham, and Shakespeare, and denounces Grant for smoking, for traveling in "Palace" railroad cars, and for going to the seaside in hot weather. . . . This hot, heavy, malignant oration will do Grant little harm.

June 3. Fine day. College trustees met at two. Endured Barnard's prosings about one thing after another for two hours and then fled, for he had before him a vast pile of manuscript. I knew it to be his annual report and that he meant to read it all—a fearful ordeal. I wanted to be the first to step off. I have no doubt many followed my example. Barnard, by the by, received certain heavy shots from the Rev. Mr. Haight (who is his special friend) about the manifest want of discipline and subordination in the faculty. Everybody takes leave of absence whenever he considers it desirable without consulting King Log or anyone else. . . .

June 5, WEDNESDAY. . . . Long talk with Pech. He is much cut up and deeply to be pitied. It is all his own fault, of course, but so are more than half the woes and troubles of humanity. . . . He will leave the country and end his days in some obscure corner. It's a dismal close to what promised to be a splendid career. Though loaded down with faults of manner and of temper, he was fast winning his way to the highest rank in his profession, and not without hope of gaining the "social position" he so longed for. . . . I dare say John P. Morgan will soon suggest himself as conductor of the Church Music Association. I should like to receive the suggestion and to give Morgan my answer.

The mass-meeting at Cooper Institute on Monday night (*Ludibrium Greeleyanum*) was large and noisy. For nearly all the roughs and bummers and repeaters and whiskey-millers and free-booters and malefactors in general who belonged to the Ring last year now hurrah for "Honest" Horace Greeley, Bill Tweed's provisional successor as Boss of New York blackguardlam. Horace Greeley might be likened to "Mr. Casby," the Patriarch in *Little Dorrit*, were not Horace Greeley so notably a boor or even a Yahoo. I used to hold him an honest but unwise philanthrope. But I can only say of him now: "Thou wretched, rash, intruding fool, farewell. I took thee for thy better."

June 6. The city is agitated by "eight-hour" strikers in all the trades, and there are symptoms of disturbance. . . .[12]

The *Evening Post* just arrived. Grant was unanimously nominated at Philadelphia and with every sign of cordiality. Henry Wilson was put up for Vice-President, beating Colfax by a few votes. I have little faith in Wilson, but hurrah for Grant!!! and also, of course, for Wilson as his appendage.

June 8. . . . The New York *Tribune* is now so vapid that I have stopped it. Horace Greeley does its editorials no longer. He is too busy intriguing for the votes of Irishmen, Copperheads, and corner-grocers. (Diogenes

---

[12] An eight-hour movement (the ordinary working day being ten hours or more) had gained strength since the Civil War under the determined leadership of Ira Steward. The federal government had just given impetus to the demand by adopting the eight-hour rule in its arsenals and workshops. This month various New York labor groups, notably the cabinet-makers, piano-makers, and employees in sewing-machine factories, were on strike for shorter hours. Before June ended most of these strikes had failed.

Slyboots would be a good name for him.) His successors, Whitelaw Reid, and others, are a feeble folk. . . .

June 10. A cloudy, sultry, oppressive day closed with a gorgeous sunset, and this evening is clear and cool. Just from a Trinity Church vestry meeting. Our parish infirmary or hospital project is successfully launched. Poor Pech's resignation is accepted. The proposition to make him a parting present was rather demurred to, but was referred at last to the Rector and the Standing Committee with power "not exceeding $1,000," which is fully up to my expectations, if not a little beyond them. . . .

The Rev. Mr. Vinton, by the by, writes Braem that he would like a basket of champagne and a few bottles of the very best old cognac (the same being good for his case) and that he expects his friends to keep him supplied with these valuable therapeutic agents. To beg, he is *not* ashamed, though so very much richer than 99 per cent of his clerical brethren.

June 13. . . . Old J. G. Bennett was buried today under a volley of eulogistic paragraphs and resolutions of dolour and deep affliction. Flags at half-mast! This community is devoid of moral sense. It has proclaimed an extra Beatitude of greater practical influence than all the others together, namely, "Blessed are the smart."[13]

The Democratic party tends more and more to Greeleyize and (so far) to justify the standing accusation against it that it cares much for place and nothing for principle. A party of cardinals running H. W. Beecher for Pope would be, in some respects, a less preposterous phenomenon; for Beecher has great ability and would, moreover, become ex officio infallibly right on all questions the moment he was installed in the Vatican.

June 20. Tonight is superlatively sultry. With Ellie . . . at nine-thirty this morning to Government Landing at the foot of Whitehall Street, where we boarded the U.S. gunboat *Frolic* . . . for inspection of

[13] As an attorney Strong could hardly be expected to do justice to the great and in the main beneficial revolution that the elder James Gordon Bennett (1795–1872) had wrought in American journalism. This Scottish immigrant had found newspapers dull, stilted, unenterprising, and dependent on political cliques. In 1835, with two empty barrels and a pine board in a chilly cellar, he founded the *Herald* as an aggressive, enterprising, independent medium for the presentation of all kinds of news—financial, social, religious, and business as well as political. The *Herald* was sensational, salacious, inquisitive, and cynical, prying into everything and sparing nobody. It made the most of crime, sex, and sports. But he made journalism democratic and sleeplessly active; if he was hated, he was also read. During the Civil War he had employed sixty-three war correspondents. In 1867 he had handed the conduct of the paper over to his son and partially retired.

the Yacht Club Regatta. There were the Secretary and Mrs. Robeson (both nice), and the little cantankerous Aulick (offspring of her first marriage), a sturdy little whelp of five in nautical costume. . . .

June 29. . . . There is such an epidemic of burglaries of late that we have for the first time sent off all the silver and Ellie's more valuable jewelry to Tiffany's for safekeeping during the summer. The valuation is much higher than I expected it to be—more than $8,000.

It is now generally thought that the "Chappaquacks" will prevail and that Horace Greeley will be nominated by the "Democracy." A most unnatural, hideous, loathsome alliance, which none but the hungriest of office-seekers can contemplate without a shudder. So much for the "principles" of the old "Democratic" party.

July 9. . . . The defense on the Stokes trial has shewn its hand. Stokes, being put on the stand, swears he saw Fisk in the act of drawing a pistol on him and that he fired in self-defense. People generally believe this a little bit of perjury. Mrs. Mansfield . . . swears that Fisk told her that he meant to kill Stokes and also that D. B. Eaton was knocked down and nearly killed (he is still disabled) by his (Fisk's) myrmidons. This will weigh with the jury, Fisk being universally conceded to have been an eminent and dangerous scoundrel. Then Dr. Carnochan (!!!) is called to find fault with Fisk's treatment after he was shot. They gave him opium too freely, and that *may* have been the cause of his death!!! As if four perforations of the intestines with a pistol bullet were not cause enough! Fisk was a portentous and mischievous caitiff; but under a healthy social system, Stokes would have been hanged within ten days after this assassination. Under our system, there is at least an even chance that he will not be found guilty. Should he be convicted, he can stave off his doom for years with exceptions and appeals, pending which he may die, as he might in his own house.

July 11. . . . The Democrats at Baltimore have swallowed Horace Greeley whole, not without a few wry faces, but with less fuss than was to have been expected; and Horace Greeley (!!!) is Democratic (!!!) candidate for the presidency. "Can such things be?" There will be no bolt. The party has not enough moral sense to produce one. Was there ever in modern politics so shabby and shameless a transaction?[14] Southern

[14] The Democratic Convention, which had met in Baltimore on July 9, was by no means happy over the prospect of nominating its ancient enemy and critic, Greeley. But it had no other course open, and the Greeley-Gratz Brown ticket received much more than the necessary two-thirds vote on the first ballot.

ruffianism and rebeldom follow the banner of Horace Greeley. Northern
"Democracy" elects the proprietor and editor of the New York *Tribune*
its representative and leader. It sounds like a grim satire on the sayings
and doings of ten years—chivalry and Copperheadism hurrahing for Horace Greeley. They are eating the biggest dish of the nastiest dirt mentioned in sacred or profane history. Southern rebels have been fearfully
punished for their great crime, but I did not suppose that this humiliation
was to be inflicted on them and that they were destined to sink beneath
contempt. Had Greeley as much grace as Falstaff, he would be ashamed
to march at the head of his renegade regiments with their ragged reputations, especially as they include Boss Tweed and the whole rabble-rout
of Tammany. . . .

The worst is that the election of this foolish old philanthropic gander
(whose philanthropy now seems mostly bogus) is horribly far from impossible. The dimensions of such a calamity cannot now be accurately
estimated, for his weakness, gullibility, and capacity for folly are unlimited. The first result of his election would be the installation of men
like Toombs and Jeff Davis and Tweed and Andrew Jackson Davis, "the
Poughkeepsie Seer," in high place at Washington. This sciolist, fool, and
quack may be enabled by his foolish countrymen to do his country the
gravest mischief.

July 12. Overcast and most sultry. This evening cooler. Saw the
Orangemen's procession—a scurvy gang, and so enveloped by policemen,
a phalanx in front and rear and a column on each flank, that it looked like
a procession in custody on its way to the Tombs. Popish Paddy glowered
at its banners with their portraitures of William crossing Boyne River,
and the like, and inwardly blasphemed but attempted no violence. . . .

July 15. Stokes's jury disagreed, as it was supposed they would;
seven were for conviction, it is said; two for acquittal; three for some
limp verdict of manslaughter. . . .

The New York *World* reluctantly supports the Chappaqua chieftain
now. It says that he left the Republican party because it denied him his
due share of "patronage" and honors, and joined the "Democratic" party
because he thought it would appreciate him more accurately and treat
him better. This is a somewhat cynical avowal that "Honest Horace" has
turned his coat and changed his note and become a renegade and a rat for
the sake of office.

N.B. The smash of poor old Stephen Cambreleng, deceased, is a most

awful smash for himself and his clients. He was trustee for no end of
wealthy people. They are left lamenting. He was prominent in that disgraceful legislative campaign against Trinity Church in 1857. That was a
bad business for all concerned in it—for Mark Spencer and others.

August 3. . . . That pedantic twaddler, Charles Sumner, declares for
Greeley, and his name will carry more weight than it deserves, especially
in Southern Niggerdom. I fear he is impelled to this mischievous folly by
a mere personal grievance. Little General Banks comes out on the same
side, but nobody cares for him, except so far as straws and feathers shew
which way the wind blows. I hope the wind that blows him may be a mere
local eddy. What is worse, the North Carolina election seems to have
resulted in a defeat to the Administration. The Maine election comes off
next (in September), and I hear of much Greeleyism in that state. But I
cannot believe we are reserved for aught so loathsome and horrible as
Horace Greeley President-elected.

The marriage announced of General E. L. Viele to Miss Juliette Dana.
What has become of Mrs. Teresa Viele? Can it be that the decree in the
divorce suit allowed *him* to marry again?

August 6. . . . Mrs. Philip Van Rensselaer (née Talmadge) died very
abruptly of apoplexy. She was a famous beauty in her day. . . .

"Democratic" gains in North Carolina seem not so very formidable
after all. Harlequin Greeley's election would be so damning a disgrace
and so dire a calamity that we may have even soared into overestimating
the probable chances of that very philanthropic old bucolical Scaramouche.
General Dix prints a forcible letter against him. I personally know no
sensible man unconnected with a shade of politics who does not denounce
Horace Greeley and deride his nomination.

August 20. . . . Exit Judge Barnard—convicted by a nearly unanimous
vote on nearly all the articles of impeachment, unanimously removed, and
disqualified from all future office 33–2. Very good, as far as it goes. But
downright Bishop Latimer would have gone a step further. "There lacks
a fourth thing to make up the mess, which, so God help me, should be
hangum tuum, a Tyburn tippet to take with him. . . . Yea, an were it my
Lord Chancellor himself, to Tyburn with him!" Latimer is right. Barnard's
skeleton neatly hung on wires in a glass case should "point a moral and
adorn" the new court house. . . .

August 22. The Republican State Convention nominates General
Dix for governor. A good choice, which will strengthen the ticket in

Wall Street and with all sensible, practical men. Some curiosity is felt about the convention of "straight-out" Democrats—Bourbons or Malignants—that is to meet at Louisville. It was thought a joke at first, but it looks like earnest now. . . . But many thousand Copperheads and ex-traitors hate Grant and cannot bow the knee to Greeley; and their appearance in the field as an organized third party will complicate the situation. They will probably nominate Charles O'Conor.[15] There might be worse Presidents. He would be better than Horace Greeley. He is honest, though his political principles are damnable, and able, though his ability is not of the kind that is useful to statesmen. . . .

August 28.   Died, at Saratoga, Henry Hall Ward, my classmate from 1834 to 1838. He has been breaking up for some time. The presidency of the old New York Club killed him. It led him to turn night into day and imposed on him much official drinking.

The frequent burglaries in this neighborhood are at last satisfactorily accounted for. The burglars were two policemen whose beat was around Gramercy Park and its vicinage. . . .

No political news. These savage, malignant, personal attacks on Grant are still poured out by the *World* and other papers. As to one branch, or class, of them, I think the temperance societies of the country are called upon to interfere and say something. If it be true that a beastly drunkard, without sense of decency, can successfully conduct great campaigns, can win great battles, and can raise himself from insignificance to be a lieutenant-general and President, what is the use of all this fuss about sobriety? Why these warnings against the "Inebriating Cup?" What teetotaller has ever achieved half as much as Grant, who is (according to these slanderous liars) always boozy and is very often troubled with snakes in his boots and with "jim-jams" and blue monkeys in his bedroom. . . . When good old sagacious Lincoln was told, during the war, that Grant drank too much, he asked: "Do you know what's his favorite brand of whiskey? I'd like to send a keg of it to each of our generals."

September 4. . . . Vermont election: cold comfort to Chappaqua! Louisville or "Bourbon" Convention: O'Conor declines its nomination in a very long letter that reads like a No question on political economy. He is keen, clear, and logical, but with as little statesmanship as Mr. Babbage's

---

[15] A discontented segment of the Democratic Party was about to meet at Louisville. It drew up a short State Rights platform, attacked the "false leadership imposed on the party by the Baltimore convention," and named Charles O'Conor of New York and John Quincy Adams II of Massachusetts.

calculating machine. I suppose he is of the class that Napoleon called *idéalogues*.

Canterbury Cathedral greatly damaged by fire yesterday.

September 5. . . . Yesterday morning at Bank for Savings (Bleecker Street) with Tappen, president of the Gallatin National Bank (the old "National") as examining committee. We manipulated and counted up twenty millions of securities, verified the statements of James F. De-Peyster, treasurer (fussiest and most fatiguing of men), and so on. With what marvellous precision and dexterity an expert like Tappen despatches business of this kind! Came straight home thereafter feeling chilly and sick.

The Greeley-Democratic coalition nominates Francis Kernan for governor. Not a strong nomination. He is a Copperhead and Romanist.

The *Bourbonidae* of Louisville nominate O'Conor and Adams for President and Vice-President. Both decline, but this Witenagemot resolves to elect them *nolens volens,* and then adjourns, decomposes, disintegrates, vanishes, and fades away into the dismal realms of chaos and of night. Faint gibberings and wailings are heard from Mr. Blanton Duncan, Brick Pomeroy, and others, but these die away in the distance. The Ku-Klux rifles and revolvers are heard snapping behind the scenes.

September 10. . . . Maine election yesterday. Result comfortable. Greeley's gains are insignificant, if any. . . .

Police have bagged one Forrester, a notable malefactor, suspected of the Nathan murder (July 29, 1870).[16] But after more than two years, it is probably impossible to make out a case against him. I have no doubt, however, that he deserves hanging and that the hanging of so dangerous and malevolent a rational animal would be salutary to society. . . .

September 13. . . . Charles O'Conor won't be a candidate. But the Louisville Bolters—the "Straight-out Democrats"—declare (through their committee) that they will vote for him just the same, and I suppose he cannot prevent them from doing so. It is not a case in which a court of equity would interfere by injunction. Never was so queer a "presidential campaign" as this. . . .

Democratic ratification mass-meeting last night on Union Square and at Tammany Hall. Crowds, of course, but no sign of enthusiasm. I think the rockets were less brilliant than those the Democracy used to send up

---

[16] The death of the rich and respected merchant Benjamin Nathan at the hands of some unidentified assailant had led to suspicion of parricide by one of his rather dissolute sons.

in the good old days when Tweed was boss—when he had his fist in the city treasury, and when he dreamed of nothing less than being called upon to support Horace Greeley as a Democratic candidate. The Hon. R. M. T. Hunter made a great speech. I like his impudence. Having taken and broken an indefinite number of oaths to support the Constitution, he turned seceder and traitor, did his best to destroy us, was Rebel Secretary of something ("State," I think) when the Confederacy collapsed, and then became a fugitive from justice.[17] And now he comes here to lecture us about the welfare of the country and to teach us our duty as patriotic citizens. It sometimes seems a sad oversight that we omitted to hang one or two of these arrogant traitors.

Last night the Philharmonicals serenaded the illustrious Rubinstein, who arrived by the *Cuba* on Wednesday. We met at eleven at a very beery and smoky lager shop in East Fourteenth Street, and proceeded thence to the Clarendon. Was introduced to the great man, a long-haired Kalmuck, who looks as if he belonged to the conservatoire of Pobolsk or Nizhni-Novgorod. But his expression and manner are kindly. He has a good brow. He speaks English quite well. I made him a remarkably brief allocution of welcome (as president), which was graciously received and answered simply and cordially. There were also some ladies, who are to assist at his concerts, I believe, and to whom I was presented. But their English was badly broken, and my German in a state of perfectly comminuted fracture, so the impressions left by our colloquy were vague. Our orchestra was quite full and did a brazen overture of Wagner's, Meyerbeer's *Fackeltanz*, and the Andante of the C Minor Symphony. A great crowd gathered in Fourth Avenue. . . . Got home very late, indeed.

September 16. . . . The Greeleyites shew a bold front still, but they rely almost exclusively on the pettiest, dirtiest, vilest personalities, generally mendacious. The other side is sufficiently malignant, too, and the whole conduct of the campaign disgraces the country. I hope and believe that Grant is rather pachydermatous. Were he in the least sensitive, he would be stung to death by the envenomed proboscises of this swarm of minute black flies, like the *World* and the *Sun*. As to the *Tribune*, once so vigorous, it now secretes no poison more potent than dish water.

September 18. The *Commercial Advertiser* and *Times* think it very

---

[17] R. M. T. Hunter, the stiff, aristocratic Senator from Virginia before the war, an authority on finance, had been Confederate Secretary of State for nearly seven months 1861–1862, then going into the Confederate Senate. He was a man of probity who had played a useful part in the reconstruction of Virginia.

hard that Grant should be held responsible and abused (by the *World* and others) for every malfeasance by any one of his friends and family connections, and enquire very pertinently how the chief editor of the *World* would like to be called to account for the conduct of one of his editorial staff in appropriating other people's chattels without paying for them. This refers to the brilliant Abbé H———, whose articles are always readily recognized by their smartness, their smooth English, and their evidence of extensive reading, and a tenacious memory.[18] The *World* has not yet noticed this home thrust. What a pretty row there would be if those old transactions of 1857 were raked up! And if I were called upon to state *why* Charles Kuhn, Lewis Jones, Frank Hampton, *et al.*, and I formally cut the accomplished H.! He is among the very few human creatures whom I loathe, as a gaudily-colored and fetid bug. My correspondence with him in August, 1857, of which I retain certified copies, proves him to be among the basest of mankind. I never read of such a combination of profligacy and insolence. First, he tried to seduce his friend's wife and nearly succeeded. Then he demanded to be made a party to any settlement between her and her husband and threatened to make the affair public ("to appeal from the narrow circle of private prejudice to the wide horizon of the public heart") unless his modest demand were granted. Then he long refused to give up her letters, and at last had the infamous audacity to name certain ladies as his backers, as cognizant of the intrigue and as his advisers and endorsers!

September 21, SATURDAY. Philharmonic directors in session here nearly three hours this afternoon. We adopted a promising programme. Tho' there is too much Liszt, there are the Seventh and Fifth Symphonies, the *Zauberflöte* Overture, and a symphony of Haydn's. Prices of reserved seats and prices of boxes were raised, against my judgment, but the rest seemed of one mind about it. The illustrious Rubinstein will probably assist at the first concert. . . .

Another stock-jobbing conspiracy has nearly produced another Black Friday. It was checked by the bold and perhaps rather questionable action of the City Bank (Moses Taylor's) and Bank of Commerce. They refused to pay their own certified checks because the greenbacks thereby demanded were to be locked up in private safes and withdrawn from circulation in

---

[18] The unprincipled William Henry Hurlbut was putting the capstone on his career by service on the *World*, of which in the days of Jay Gould's ownership (that is, just before 1883, when Pulitzer began its regeneration) he became editor-in-chief. Strong has repeatedly mentioned him in the diary, never favorably.

order to make a tight money market and help the bears! The pirates who get up these murderous "corners" may repeat the experiment once too often and may find themselves unexpectedly hung up to telegraph poles or lamp posts, as they well deserve to be. Firing a city for the sake of picking up valuables in the confusion is not one whit more flagitious than a plot like this, and if lynch law be justified in any case, it is when one of these plotters is caught red-handed. Poor Mrs. Dater, who was so pretty and gracious at Mt. Desert; her husband's long-established and most respectable firm has been forced into suspension by these *hostes humani generis,* and I dare say the poor lady may be crying her eyes out at this minute. These scoundrel "operators" might just as well form a combination to fire grapeshot into Wall Street and Broad Street at a given hour. There is bitter exasperation against them.

September 23.   To the first Rubinstein concert tonight at Steinway, Mr. Grau having been good enough to send me a pass.[19] The house was full and uncommonly demonstrative. . . . Sat with Mills and Richard Hoffman— high artistic company. They were generous in their laudations and indignant with me for saying that I didn't see why the Great Man's playing was so much finer than what I have often heard from our own resident performers. Rubinstein plays with immense brilliancy, delicacy, and force, but I am too dull to appreciate distinctions in execution that are self-evident to most lovers of music. The concert room was so hot that I left the programme unfinished. As it was, I came away limp and nearly stewed to rags. The orchestra was poor, the stringed force far too small. . . .

September 24. . . . We [Trinity Church Vestry] appointed the English Charles E. Horsley as organist at St. John's, vice poor Pech. His testimonials are of the first order and his father was an eminent composer of glees, and the like.[20] I expected an attack on our Cemetery Committee from General Dix and was ready to meet it, but it did not come and our minutes were read without hostile comment.

September 26.   In Diocesan Convention, Bishop Potter brings up the subject of a cathedral and committees are appointed. Should it be begun on any proper and worthy scale, I shall of course not live to see it finished. But I think it will be undertaken. Apropos of that, the interior of the new

[19] The brilliant Russian-Jewish pianist, Anton G. Rubinstein, had now for several years been making extensive and successful concert tours in Europe and America.

[20] Charles Edward Horsley (1822–1876), son of the composer William Horsley, had written oratorios and other music of merit, and composed the ode for the opening of the Melbourne Town Hall in 1870. His American career was distinguished, and his music for *Comus* written in the United States is still played.

St. Bartholomew's on Madison Avenue, now nearly completed, is showy and seems to me good.

"Metropolitan Gallery of Art" (Fifth Avenue near Fifty-third Street) visited for the first time.[21] Collection larger and (alleged) Old Masters are more numerous than I expected. There seems to be nearly an acre of high art. In very few of these pictures did my unskilled eye detect anything to admire; High, Old Low Dutchmen preponderate largely. Turner's famous "Slave Ship" is there, lent by its owner, John Taylor Johnston. It is certainly among the most astonishing of pictures. Such lovely and wonderful painting of sky and cloud I never beheld. That portion of it is a poem. Every detail is perfect and truthful; yet I don't believe so varied and beautiful a sunset was ever seen by mortal vision. The heaving sea appears to me to be mere lunacy and so does the foreground with its preposterous fish and the iron manacles that are floating about. But the picture, as a whole, gave me an impression of prodigious genius—of immense power manifested without effort—such as one receives from a Beethoven symphony.

September 28. Mr. Ruggles has a new hobby; he is astride the high-pitched roof of a dream cathedral and riding hard. . . . Would that his dreams had been as innocuous a few years ago when he got me into this "Minnesota Railroad" scrape! . . .

Poor Vinton is "very low" and "failing." So says the Rev. Mr. Ogilby. Last night he was thought *in extremis* but rallied. He may survive through weeks of misery; witness the dismal memories of November, 1853. I am very sorry for this. His organic disease made it impossible he should ever preach again; so his power to do mischief to the church on any large scale was ended, and I hoped he might live with comfort, though more or less an invalid, for years yet. Except when in a paroxysm of arrogance or in one of flunkeyism—when he was not playing Hildebrand or Uriah Heep—he was agreeable and well-bred. He had considerable ability of a certain kind, and he might have been valuable as a colonel of artillery, as a captain of a whaler, or as chief of police. But he had mistaken his vocation. A few shallow sisters and half-educated brethren were awed by the bow-wow of his oratory. There are silly women, I believe, who think him a Massillon and have given him money they could ill spare, for he went begging in all quarters,

---

[21] The Metropolitan Museum had been incorporated on April 15, 1870, and was launched with some gifts, a purchase of 174 Dutch and Flemish paintings, and the acquisition of the Cesnola collection of ancient materials from Cyprus. The building Strong visited was a temporary home. Not until 1880 did the city complete the first unit of the great structure in Central Park.

though his official income and his private means were exceptionally large for a clergyman. But every intelligent listener was disgusted by the superficiality, wordiness, and windiness of his sermons, by his frequent atrocious sins against reverence and decency, and by the apparent insincerity and hollowness of his manner (of his manner alone, no doubt).

His administration of the parish church caused sober-minded people much pain and annoyance in many other ways; for example, his bullying communicants and ordering them right and left as they came to the chancel rails. Then he involved himself in secular affairs, a certain guardianship, among other things, and gained himself little credit thereby. I suppose there cannot be found in the judicial records of the state a fiduciary account as audacious and shameful as that he rendered of this guardianship; and it unfortunately got into the newspapers. Thus, poor Vinton so sank during the last ten or twelve years that it seems incredible now that he should ever have been a leader in conventions and a prominent candidate for the bishop's throne. Poor old fellow; may he get out of this world with the least possible amount of suffering. What sad mistakes we all make, irreparable here!

October 1. Dr. Vinton died Sunday at two-thirty in the afternoon, aged sixty-three, having been but half-conscious for several days. When the Rector and Dr. Ogilby saw him on Friday and did their office, he knew them and knew what it meant, but kept dropping off at intervals. . . . The funeral is tomorrow. I hope my comments on him (above) are not uncharitable.[22] It is most certain that he would have done better had he stuck to the army, to the law, or to civil engineering—all which he had tried. He was not cut out for a clergyman. All the Vintons are clever, but they are mostly better fitted to be dragoons than to be deacons or presbyters.

At Life and Trust Company meeting, I congratulated Johnston on his Turner. He says he doesn't know what to do with the confounded thing, for it kills every picture he puts it near.

Mr. Ruggles (Sunday night) cathedral-mad, as though bitten by a rabid transept. So much the better. . . .

Greeleyism looks up a little. Grant's friends seem uneasy about Pennsylvania and the West. From the Pope, the Devil, and Horace Greeley, good Lord, deliver us!

[22] A more favorable account may be found in the *Dictionary of American Biography*, which specially commends Dr. Vinton's work in building up Emmanuel Church (merged with Grace Church) in Brooklyn, his "exceptional command of language," and his expertness in canon law. A memorial volume appeared in 1873, *Francis Vinton: Priest and Doctor.*

Church Music Association $3,750. Prospect doubtful. I will not go on till we are secured against the possibility of another deficit. . . .

Temple and his mamma are practising the lovely *Pastorale* in the *William Tell* Overture, piano and oboe, as arranged by Temple! He has wonderful cleverness and facility in things pertaining to music.

October 2. Brilliant fall weather. If the late Rev. Dr. Vinton, in his present "sphere," or phase of existence, retain any of his ante-mortem traits, he must be much gratified by his obsequies at Trinity Church at three this afternoon. When I entered the church at two-fifteen, I found it difficult to penetrate the crowd and reach the vestry room. Every inch of standing room was soon occupied, and I hear that very many people went away because they could not get inside the doors. The Bishop assisted, with a score or two of surpliced presbyters, and very many other clergymen occupied seats reserved for them in the body of the church. A majority of the vestry attended and entered the church together. I was pushed to the head of the column as warden. The service was elaborately rendered. Music copious but vile. There was no address or eulogy. Interment is to be at Newport, whither the Rev. Dr. Vinton's reliquiae went per Fall River boat. He is probably now off old Field Light. We shall see him in Trinity Church no more. . . .

During dinner, a message was brought from Mr. Ruggles that he wanted Rosalie to go with Temple and take his place, since he did not feel like going to the opera tonight, for he had just heard of Dr. Lieber's death!!! This is startling. Lieber must have passed his seventieth year, for he was in the Prussian ranks at Ligny, where he got a musket shot in the ankle, of which he was proud. But I had not heard of his being ill.[23] With all his foibles of egotism and vanity, he was a learned, thoughtful, and valuable man whom it would be very hard to replace. His familiarity with the details of modern history was wonderful, and so was his grasp of the laws that underlie them. But for conceit and inability to conceal it, he would have been great. Everyone has some good story to tell about his weaknesses, and but comparatively few will remember his strength, his erudition, and his earnest patriotism as a naturalized American.

Talk with Henry Dorr . . . about Vinton after service this afternoon. Never was anything so quiet, decorous, quaint, and dry as Dorr's comments on the doctor's career. He thinks Vinton had felt himself "played-

[23] Lieber had been wounded in the neck at Namur, almost mortally (1815). It is not strange that Strong had not heard of his illness; he had been slightly indisposed for a few days, and while sitting quietly with his wife, fell dead.

out" and had considered his life a failure ever since November, 1862, when
Morgan Dix was elected Rector of Trinity Church. I do not think so.
Never were bumptiousness and self-assertion more emphatic and offensive
than Dr. Vinton's during the last ten years. I may say, by the by, that when
Dr. Berrian's death left the rectory vacant (in 1862), he might have been
thought of by some of the vestry as a possible candidate for the vacancy,
but for his folly and flunkeyism on the occasion of the Prince of Wales's
attendance at Trinity Church in the fall of 1860. That performance satisfied
us all that Vinton would never do for a Rector of Trinity Church. His
memorable orgasm of flunkeyism at the end of his sermon—"On this
august and memorable occasion, the church in America prays for Queen
Victoria, the Prince Consort," and the like—blighted his hopes of succeed-
ing Dr. Berrian. When the vacancy occurred, at last, nobody thought of
voting for Vinton.

October 4.   Conference of an hour with the Rev. Cooke and Jem about
the Church Music Association. C. C. Dodge telegraphs me a subscription
of $500! How nice it must be to be rich! This carries us up to $4,280, not
far behind where we were this time last year. We have no applicants for
Pech's place. . . . I must write to Pech and invite his resignation. Wonder
whether he will turn upon us and sue for pay as conductor during these
three years. He is unlikely to do it, unless instigated by his smart little
"Mrs. Pech," who is now lecturing as "Miss Susanna Evans." Such a suit
could be successfully defended, I think, but it would be a bore. . . .

October 5.   To Century Club tonight. Dick unanimously elected at
last, after waiting his turn for a couple of years. Several others also brought
in. Notice was taken of poor Kintzing Post's death, of Lieber's, and (by
Dr. [Noah Hunt] Schenck) of Vinton's, on whom Schenck pronounced a
flaming eulogy. Mr. Ruggles's reminiscences of Lieber were interesting
and pungent. Judge Daly followed on the same side. Ye Gods, how he
did prose! Charles Bristed there; also, the Rev. Bellows, [George W.]
Cullum, General [John G.] Barnard, Rutherfurd Stuyvesant, Pete Strong,
Henry Pierrepont, and others. Talked cathedral with [Stephen P.] Nash.
Dick [Derby] was delighted to hear of his election. He will be a great
acquisition to the Club.

Saw the *Tribune* today; seldom see it now. It has degenerated into a
mere *mitrailleuse* of slander, a machine for the reckless squirting of putrid
ditch water. The Democratic party so-called, having professedly repudiated
all of its old principles, has no weapons left but the meanest and nastiest
personalities. Everybody who becomes conspicuous in Grant's support is

instantly attacked by some sneer or insinuation no matter how groundless. Burnside, for example, is hooted at by these filthy papers as "no soldier," and the like. It is enough to sicken one of his country.

Were I important enough to be worth assailing as an upholder of the Administration, the *Tribune, World,* and *Sun* would unite in saying: "This corrupt scoundrel, Strong, was treasurer of the Sanitary Commission. We have no doubt he stole a large amount of its money. If he didn't, why doesn't he *prove* that he didn't? He got up a swindling concern called the Church Music Association, and we have reason to believe that he pocketed all its funds. Somebody said so. Let him disprove it if he can!" The next day we should read: "The atrocious corruptionist, Strong, has not ventured to attempt clearing himself by any kind of positive proof from a single one of the grave accusations with which we thought it our duty to charge him. We hope the People will at last hold these proven beyond all question. We are credibly informed that this infamous minion of a perjured and profligate Administration is affiliated with the Erie Railroad, the Crédit Mobilier, and Bill Tweed; and further (*this on affidavit*) that he designs to go to Long Branch week after next and secure as the reward of his baseness from the Speechless Nullity who is reveling there with his cigars and his horses and his whiskey, the appointment of consul-general at the Galapagos Islands. *This we know.* The Hon. Snooks of Oregon has written a letter positively affirming the digraceful fact! People of America!!!! The Farmer of Chappaqua! the great and good Horace Greeley!!! Single-minded, pure, and patriotic! *Honest* Horace Greeley!" and the like.

October 7, MONDAY.   College meeting at the Law School at two this afternoon. Little more than a quorum. Many details came up for settlement. . . . Betts, now unable to read his own minutes, announced that he should resign the clerkship of the board at its next stated meeting. Someone asked me if I would take the office. I said I did not think I would. It would be too humiliating to draw a little two-penny salary from this somnolent old institution, though a little more money from any quarter would find a welcome, God knows! Question of a "new site" was ventilated on report of committee and made special order for special meeting next week. . . . Had a long talk about "new site" with Gouverneur Ogden after adjournment. He sought to convert me to his views and supported them with some force, but he did not fully convert me. Perhaps I may come round, but I am at present disinclined to move the College at all, unless the necessity of moving it be demonstrated. The proximity of railroad tracks and depots is a grave objection to our present site, but measures are in progress that will mitigate that trouble and may remove it altogether. I do not much reverence no-madic colleges or nomadic churches—colleges and churches that move every first of May (more or less).

October 8. Call from poor Pech this morning and an interview of more than an hour, during which I dealt with him very plainly. He doesn't want to give up the Church Music Association, and of course, I had to go into our reasons for making a jettison of him. He denied their sufficiency and put forward a volume of arguments and dodges. I never knew a man more deficient in moral sense or more illogical and slippery. . . .

Much depends on the state elections held today in Pennsylvania and other places. Their result will go far toward determining that of the presidential election next month and toward deciding whether we can or cannot avert the ignominy of such a President of the United States as Horace Greeley. I am not sanguine; but Johnny, who has just been out investigating, brings me certain extras fraught with first impressions of the result, and they look not unpromising. . . .

October 9. The low moaning of the "Greeley" morning papers over yesterday's elections lifted me for a moment out of my slough of despond, and I enjoyed a brief period of calm bliss. If complete returns from Pennsylvania, Ohio, and Indiana confirm the good tidings of today, then is Horace Greeley cut down as a flower. Miserable old charlatan and traitor. God grant he may be squelched indeed! And this looks very like his utter defeat and extermination. . . .[24]

Dined here, Charles Bristed and Mrs. Bristed, Mr. Ruggles and Dick; also Johnny, who appeared very well. Ellie has gone to the opera with Mr. and Mrs. Bristed and Temple. Mrs. Bristed is most uncommonly bright and clever. Mr. Ruggles is still cathedral-mad. And the cathedral project marches! Several millionaires are ready to give $100,000 each to secure a site. *Laus Deo! . . .*

October 10. . . . Seward died at Auburn at seventy-two. He has played with great ability a most conspicuous part in our affairs and has done the country great service, though I should hardly call him a great man. Died, also, old Dr. [Samuel] Seabury, a valiant champion of church principles and of Bishop Onderdonk during the long series of troublous and polemical

[24] The three great states holding October elections, Pennsylvania, Indiana, and Ohio, all gave aid and comfort to the Grant forces. Pennsylvania elected a regular Republican governor and increased its list of Republican Congressmen; Ohio gave the Republican state ticket a majority of about 16,000; and Indiana, though electing the Democrat Thomas A. Hendricks as governor, chose a legislature with a Republican majority on joint ballot. It was now certain that Greeley would be defeated.

years that followed 1843. His memory would be more fragrant had he not committed the folly of publishing an elaborate "defense of slavery" just before the war broke out and had he not been a most venomous Copperhead all through the war.

The New York *World* says "there is left but a slender chance of Mr. Greeley's election." Indiana is still doubtful, probably Democratic, but the vote is so very close that the state seems safe for Grant in November. It looks now as if New York would go the same way next month. Dix will surely run ahead of his ticket. Democrats are chopfallen and repent of having eaten so much dirt to so little purpose. Some of them say they would throw their Chappaquacker overboard were there time to choose a new captain. But let us beware of premature jubilation. Much may happen before November. The time to hurrah will come when Horatius is finally squelched and thrown into the gutter.

After my last interview with Pech, I was not much surprised by a brief note this morning purporting to be his, but manifestly copied by him from a draft furnished him by some attorney, for it was terse and clear, whereas his communications are generally diffuse and mucilaginous. It is in substance: "If I am continued as conductor of the Church Music Association, I will permit the amount already due me to remain for further consideration. If not, I expect its immediate payment. Yours truly, James Pech." The dirty dog! After insisting on our spending the amount of subscriptions on extra rehearsals and the like because he cared nothing about compensation, after parading his disinterested love of art and his gratuitous services in all our circulars and programmes, and after throwing deficits of $2,500 on us by his violation of our instructions, he now turns round and asks us to pay out of our own pockets some large sum for these "gratuitous" services. I think shrewd little Mrs. Pech has put him up to this, and I think we can beat him in the lawsuit which he evidently contemplates. After this note, we, of course, throw him over, hold no further intercourse with him, and take no further trouble to conceal his malfeasances, or promote his professional interests. I am sorry he proves so utterly unworthy and base, for I have fought his battles and maintained him against assailants almost daily for three years at least and have seriously compromised myself in thus upholding him.

October 11. . . . To Trinity Church Music Committee this afternoon. We discussed at great length a proposition to increase our musical appropriations but came to no result. We recommend that the organ of St. Paul's be henceforth blown by a galvanic battery! . . .

October 14, MONDAY. . . . Yesterday, I retired to my tents, sulked or moped, and spent the evening in the library, though there were pleasant people downstairs. Saturday evening, Jem and the Rev. Mr. Cooke were here discussing the Church Music Association affairs. Whether there will be any more Church Music Association is still doubtful. We threw Pech overboard finally and formally and elected Horsley of St. John's as provisional conductor. He called on me this morning and made an agreeable impression. . . .

October 17. This evening to the first (and perhaps last) Church Music Association rehearsal for this season. Horsley took up Haydn's third Mass and appeared well as conductor. Attendance of chorus was unexpectedly large. . . . Everything promising but the treasury. Only about $5,000 subscribed as yet. I want to back out and let the Rev. Mr. Cooke take over, as he feels sure he can, but he won't consent to my withdrawal. That wretched scallywag, Pech, has been running up a bill at Schirmer's for music we never even heard of, and it seems he has in his hands a large portion of our orchestral parts, which he will doubtless not give up, except on compulsion. . . .

October 22, TUESDAY. To Law School this afternoon for special meeting of the College trustees on the question of a new site, which was narrowed down to a choice between two purchases, namely, the "Harsen" block so-called on or about Seventieth Street and the Wheelock property about 157th Street ($800,000 and $375,000 respectively). I said I should vote against both, believing any purchase at present unwise. Robert Ray and one or two more took the same view. Gouverneur Ogden led off with a statement and explanation an hour long. He urged the Wheelock investment. Mr. Ruggles followed at length, advocating the other. Nash sided with Ogden and the Bishop with Mr. Ruggles, but deprecating any immediate action. Dr. Haight left the chair and Mr. Ruggles took it, and Haight made a speech on the Wheelock side and then resumed the chair. Some allusion of his to Mr. Ruggles as "sanguine in his views," called up the latter again, who spoke for ten minutes with an earnestness and excitement that seemed a little unnatural. He was followed by Nash, and then Mr. Ruggles rose to make some suggestion as to the form in which the question should be put (so he told me afterwards). He spoke low and with hesitation. I could not understand him, and I noticed one or two who sat near him looking at him, as I now remember, with an anxious expression. The question was taken (11 to 4 in favor of Wheelock!—monstrous folly), and then Dr. Haight said to me that he thought Mr. Ruggles seemed ill. I found him so indeed. One side of the mouth drawn down, left hand paralyzed and numb, articulation thick. But he was perfectly rational. We adjourned as soon as the question had been taken—at four-thirty in the afternoon.

I ran instantly across Lafayette Place and ordered a carriage, and returning, met him on William Schermerhorn's arm. I put him into the carriage and drove to 24 Union Square. Going up the front door steps, I found that one of his legs was not quite under his control. There were only servants in the house. He thought the trouble was "exhaustion" and that a little brandy and water would do him good. I substituted a hot cup of tea. There was at first a little difficulty in swallowing, but it was overcome, and his articulation became clearer. There was a little more freedom, too, in moving the arm. Mrs. Ruggles and Miss Mary Bostwick soon came in, and their perfect self-possession and helpfulness were beautiful. I had already sent off for Dr. White and Dr. Crane, his physicians.

I came away at six and returned at about seven and saw Jem. Mr. Ruggles was in bed. The doctor had called and prescribed. He pronounced the case paralysis, of course, but sees no immediate danger. The only fact that makes me hesitate about this is that it *seemed* to *me* that the action of the right hand was also a little impaired. I may be wrong as to the fact, but if the attack involve both sides, I suppose (in my ignorance) that it must be a grave affair. But his perfect lucidity seems a favorable indication; and there is no drowsiness.

Mr. Ruggles is seventy-two. The wear and tear of these years, from the amount of excitement, toil, brain work, and struggle against adversity concentrated in them, could not be equaled in the history of twenty common lives. All this last summer he has spent in morbid worry over the new building adjoining No. 24 and its party walls, and in anxiety about the Minnesota Railroad. Lieber's recent death was a source of intense excitement; so was Seward's. He always took such events very hard. Then he had been studying hard for a speech on "unification of the currency," delivered last week, and last night he "received" Froude at the Century Club and sat there late.[25] Jem thinks his condition has been rather abnormal for several months. I have noticed nothing of the kind, but I am not a keen observer.

[25] The eminent historian James Anthony Froude was visiting America, where he delivered some very controversial lectures upon the Irish question.

(N.B. William Schermerhorn called at ten tonight to ask after Mr. Ruggles. He told me much about George A. Jones's affairs that I did not know. It seems a fearfully bad case.)

I expect that Mr. Ruggles will be almost himself again in a week. But I fear this is the beginning of the end. Unless another shock occur within the next twenty-four hours, he will rally from this one. But in that case, he must lead an idle (at least comparatively idle) life, do no work, and adopt an ascetic regimen. Can he bring himself to this? . . . If he do not, there will soon be another and a sharper attack. He was perfectly clear this afternoon commenting on the discussion in the College board, with his usual keenness. Before I left him at six, he had evidently begun to recognize the real significance of his "seizure," and to see its probable consequences, and he did so with magnificent firmness and the fullest resignation to God's will. Would I were in his place after a life as diligent, earnest, and useful as his! . . .

October 24. In every sense, a dark and gloomy day. Entering 68 Wall Street as usual, I saw a lounge in a new position. O'Halloran and Charley, our little office boy . . . were standing about, and a sensation that "something had happened" came over me at once. O'Halloran said simply, "Mr. Bidwell is dead, sir. He has just had a stroke of apoplexy." So it was, and there he lay, his expression absolutely natural and serene, and his features without trace of distortion or pain or any suggestion of death. . . . His daughters are both at Monterey, Berkshire County, Massachusetts; his son lives at Sheffield. They were telegraphed. . . . He died at eleven-fifteen. I entered the office at eleven-thirty. . . .[26]

To Trinity Chapel Schoolhouse this evening for Church Music Association rehearsal number two. I told the Rev. W. H. Cooke finally that the event of this morning made it impossible for me to give any time to the Church Music Association this winter and that he must find another president. . . .

The horse disease spreads. Aspect of the streets is wholly changed. Hacks, omnibusses, and horsecars are reduced by more than half.

[26] This was the end of a notable career which had begun in Upper Canada in 1824, the year Bidwell was elected to the provincial legislature, and which had been transferred to New York in 1837. Bidwell's practice had specially dealt with realty, trusts, and wills; Strong had always leaned heavily upon him, and during the Civil War, when the diarist was busy with the Sanitary Commission, he was the main pillar of the firm. For thirty years he had been one of the most learned, eloquent, and persuasive attorneys of the country, greatly admired for his wisdom, logic, and copious flow of language.

October 25. . . . Bidwell's two daughters arrived this evening. I have made a long series of dreary New Year's calls on them and always found them utterly uninteresting and colorless. . . . Arrived also, Bidwell's son from Sheffield. . . . We settled funeral arrangements. . . . Silliman had called a little before, and the ladies had given him, very wisely, the will of which we had been in quest all day. I think it will be found to give the son a trifling legacy and the residuary property to the daughters. The son's marriage a few years ago without the father's consent was never forgiven. . . . Strange that this family, after so many years in New York, should have formed no positive friendships or alliances, especially considering poor, dear old Bidwell's warm-heartedness, geniality, and strong social instincts. . . . I suppose poor Bidwell's Puritanic convictions led him to look on "calls," tea parties, and all the little two-penny machinery of "social" life as of the nature of evil, in spite of his own natural impulses. . . .

October 26. . . . Strange that Bidwell's death has not yet been noticed in the courts and that there has been no meeting of the bar, for he was pretty generally conceded to be one of the ablest and most learned lawyers in the state. At No. 68 we have all leaned on him, too much for our own good. Instead of studying up a question, I usually went to Bidwell and received from him an off-hand abstract of all the cases bearing on it and of all the considerations on either side. He loved law as a pure science, and this sometimes led him to advise according to strict logical principles, when it was clear and certain that any jury and any court would assuredly declare otherwise and devise some way of getting around the letter of the law and doing plain justice. He had a kind of joy in asserting a legal principle rigorously and inflexibly in a hard case. . . .

Mr. Ruggles improves. But the facial distortion and the impeded articulation have not quite disappeared.

October 30. . . . Horse distemper rages. Saw an ox-team in Broadway. They will have to utilize the elephants and camels of Central Park. The last learned name for the disease invented by the *Herald* is the hippo-shinorshaea!!! . . .

November 2.   A bar meeting at twelve noon at the circuit courtroom. The respectability of the profession was largely represented, and the meeting was fuller (much) than I supposed it would be, for Bidwell's plane or sphere was exalted so high above that of the average New York lawyer that he was (so to speak) out of the sight of the great majority of them. Judge Ingraham presided and John P. Crosby was secretary.

Henry Nicoll moved the resolutions. Silliman seconded them, reading his address. Then Professor Dwight spoke forcibly and so did Evarts. Erastus Benedict put in his oar (uninvited), and Neilson (Judge of the Brooklyn city court, a Canadian who used often to come to see Bidwell years ago) got up, and in a plain, lumbering, earnest way made an interesting speech. He told us much that none of us knew about Bidwell's early career and the circumstances attending his departure from Canada in December, 1837. It was a satisfactory meeting.

Long conference with the Rev. Mr. Cooke, to whom I turned over the books and papers of the Church Music Association, consenting, however, to let my name stand as president. Jem Gerard, Jr., and Ben Stephens go on the committee as working members. The subscription is now nearly $6,800. . . . Active omnibi increase daily in number, but the nostrils of nearly every horse shew signs of disease.

Savage attack by the notorious Mrs. Victoria Woodhull on the Rev. Henry Ward Beecher, whom she accuses of "preaching every Sunday to twenty of his mistresses," and the like. She is probably demented, or perhaps possessed of a "spiritualistic" devil. The harridan was arrested today on a charge of libel, and being unable to find $8,000 bail was, when last heard from, incarcerated in Ludlow Street. (The charge was sending obscene literature through the mails.) . . .[27]

Ellie (piano), Johnny ('cello), and Temple (oboe) doing trios in the front parlor, and as it seems to me most charmingly. What should I have said thirty years ago had anyone told me I should ever have the blessing of such a wife and such boys and of such home music? What should I say about it now, were I in mental health and not utterly morbid and melancholic?

November 4. Horrified to find myself retained on behalf of the Associated Savings Banks in the case of the U.S. *vs.* The Dollar Savings Bank of Pittsburgh, now pending in the Supreme Court at Washington. It's an internal revenue case, and on looking into the papers this evening, I cannot see that my plaintiffs have a leg to stand on. Benjamin R. Curtis of Boston is on the same side.

Long meeting of College trustees this afternoon. Dwight had drawn

[27] Mrs. Woodhull's attack on Beecher was even more specific than Strong indicates. She had been carrying on an intrigue with Theodore Tilton, and on the basis of information from him, she accused Beecher, in the November 2 issue of *Woodhull and Claflin's Weekly*, of an intimacy with Tilton's wife. Mrs. Woodhull and her sister Tennessee Claflin were sent to jail for issuing an obscene publication, but were acquitted. The consequences of the affair to Beecher were disastrous.

certain resolutions about Bidwell, who was nominally connected with the
Law School as lecturer. . . . There were other resolutions about Dr.
Lieber, drawn and brought before us in like manner. They certainly were
too long and rather high-colored, but I never knew resolutions of this
kind to be objected to before. Their allusions to Lieber's public services
during the war, however, and to the "nationality" of his books and his
teachings, revived Betts's Copperheadism of eight years ago, and he
objected to their passage, and Ogden withdrew them. Everyone was so
tired with our long session that a debate would not have been endured,
and I did not trust myself to say anything, fearing I should say too much.
I thought it prudent not to call on Mr. Ruggles as I came home, for this
intelligence would have put him into a twitter that might have hurt
him. . . .

Now for tomorrow. The barometer promises fair weather. So far
good. Greeley's defeat is believed to be certain. Dix's chances are good.
Havemeyer's are fair. But Jemmy O'Brien will poll a very heavy vote.
From a Celtic mayor, *libera nos, Domine!* The third candidate, Abe Lawrence, is a good fellow—able, and I believe honest—but he is tainted
with Tammany and ceremonially unclean.

November 5, TUESDAY. With John to our local Temple of Liberty
(at 290 Third Avenue) where he deposited his maiden vote. Everything
was serene. There are astringent precautions against fraud, and I think
Commissioner Davenport's vigorous action will be found to have kept
from the polls not only actual repeaters but many others who are conscious that they might, could, would, or should have voted early and
voted often but for these new obstacles, and who felt a vague guilty
fear that somebody might do something to them if they came near a
ballot box, and therefore did not vote at all.[28] Comparatively few roughs
were hanging about the polling places today, so far as I saw. The New
York *World* scolds fearfully about these safeguards against fraud. . . .

Jem Ruggles came in, and I went with him at nine-thirty to Madison
Square. The New York *Times* was publishing the returns as they arrived
by means of a transparency and a magic lantern (Jem Fisk's advertising
agency) corner Broadway and Twenty-third Street. Crowd was immense
and in high good humor, cheering and singing. Returns all one way,
thank God, and transcending my hopes. Unless they are founded on a

[28] John I. Davenport was United States Commissioner supervising elections in the
Southern District of New York. This was under the so-called Enforcement Act of
May 31, 1870.

system of objectless mendacity and making allowance for partizan enthusiasm and exaggeration, Greeley's defeat is total and crushing and this state is probably safe. Of course, estimate enters largely into figures, but they are all one way. Pennsylvania has given Grant 100,000 majority (!), North Carolina 10,000, Delaware 3,000; New Hampshire, Vermont, Ohio, Indiana, Connecticut, and other states carried for Grant. Gains everywhere, the only exception being in the Ninth Ward of Louisville, where a Democratic gain of 100 and odd is reported. A hundred ninety-eight electoral votes reported securing Grant's election. As we came away at eleven, the prolonged roar of the crowd indicated another heavy instalment of good news.

In this city, the Democratic majority is reported to have been reduced from 60,000 to 22,000. It seems incredible. Great Republican gains in the interior are announced, and I have little doubt the state is safe. As to the mayoralty, "returns from 86 election districts place Havemeyer 719 ahead," which is good as far as it goes. It seems tolerably certain that the Almighty has not visited us in His wrath with a Greeley for President, for which mercy let us humbly thank Him. To take the lowest view of it, every businessman will feel easier and look brighter tomorrow if the morning papers confirm tonight's glad tidings. Gold will go down and securities and real estate will go up from Maine to Texas. What a national disgrace we are spared! And what a deathblow would have been given to all political honesty and principle by the triumph of this most cynical and shameless of coalitions!

November 6. Grant has carried about thirty states or so, generally with enormous gains in each. Georgia, Kentucky, Tennessee, West Virginia, and Maryland seem to have Greeleyized, but we can spare them. The majority in this state about 45,000. In the city, O'Brien is certainly squashed. Havemeyer and Abe Lawrence were reported all day as "about nip and tuck, Havemeyer a little ahead." Tonight Havemeyer is said to be certainly elected, but I am not quite sure. Charles Donohue is district attorney by about 1,000, the only unfortunate result of this election. He is said to be in Tweed's interest.

Where be now the goodly fellowship of rats—Carl Schurz, Doctor Charles Sumner, Charles A. Dana, Fenton, John Cochrane, Chauncey Depew, General Banks, Littlejohn, and Company? And how does the honest and genial patriot and sage of Chappaqua feel today? I doubt whether the sinful old Democratic party can long survive this blow. The *World* attributes it to the Tammany frauds; but it was during the

war that the "Democracy" gave itself the wound of which it has ever
since been languishing and is now, I hope, dying at last. It has submitted
in vain to a degrading surgical mutilation (of all its principles), or perhaps I should rather say has committed suicide by swallowing dirt under
a delusive hope of resurrection and rejuvenescence. The *Tribune*'s leading editorial is headed "The Liberal Triumph Postponed." Rather so, I
should think.

Mr. Ruggles's convalescence is a little retarded by neuralgia, but his
spirits are good. Jem and Dr. White had hard work to keep him from
going out and voting yesterday. Repose is essential but will be difficult
to secure, and opposition to his wishes may cause excitement and do
harm. His mind is always at work on the College, the projected cathedral,
"unification of the currency," or something else. Jem is not free from
anxiety. . . .

It does not yet appear that anybody has voted for O'Conor. I look
anxiously for Horace Greeley's twenty-ninth bulletin. He can hardly
hope, like Napoleon, to organize a new Grand Army after this Moscow
campaign. And to whom can he address himself? Not to the Democrats,
who took him up with loathing under the delusion that he might prove
a useful tool and have found him, to their sorrow, worse than useless;
and certainly not to the Republicans whom he so shamelessly deserted
and whom he sought to destroy. He has ruined one party and has done
his best as renegade to ruin the other. His honesty of purpose, in which
I for one used to believe, is an exploded superstition, and I see nothing
left for him but to spend the rest of his days chopping with his little
hatchet at the cherry trees of Chappaqua. *Requiescat in pace.*

November 7. Clear and blustering after a murky wet morning.
Rosalie dined here. Talk with Allan Campbell in downtown omnibus.
Standing Committee at vestry office. Congratulated General Dix, who
seems to feel pretty well and quite proud of having run only a little, if
at all, behind Grant.

Election returns. "The longer they blossom the sweeter they grow."
The overthrow of the coalition is cataclysmal. Pennsylvania's majority
is creeping up to 125,000. The aggregate of Grant's popular majorities
is from 500,000 to 700,000; amazing facts. In this city, [William F.]
Havemeyer is elected [mayor] by 8,000. B. K. Phelps and *not* Donohue
is district attorney. O'Brien is beaten out of sight. Since Boyne Water
and Vinegar Hill, Paddy has sustained no such discomfiture. Horace
Greeley "resumes the editorship of the *Tribune*, which he relinquished

on embarking in another line of business six months ago." ("And peals of devilish laughter shook the cave," that is, the editor's office.) The old boor doubtless thinks this way of putting it at once genial, facetious, and statesmanlike. . . .

Dead, General George G. Meade, to whom, under God, this country is indebted for Gettysburg and salvation from extremest disaster and for much good service besides. He was among the strongest of Grant's lieutenants. Horse disease is passing off. The *Herald* has composed another name for it: "Febrequobronchiatis." What a thing learning is!

November 9. Grant's majorities keep on growing. He has got West Virginia, it seems, and (according to the *Tribune*) Tennessee likewise. I wish the Democratic defeat were not quite so overwhelming. The Republican Party has secured such absolute control that it is not unlikely to run wild, abuse its power, disgrace itself, and fall to pieces. Somebody has said that the best and safest of all majorities is a majority of one. The prospects of Republicanism would be brighter were it watched by a strong minority in both houses and obliged to walk warily. It was the utter and total rout of General Scott in 1852 that emboldened the Democrats to open that bitter wellspring of calamity and woe, the Nebraska and Kansas question.

Since the beginning of the campaign Grant's reëlection had been certain, and the October results had shown that his majority would be large. The Union now had thirty-seven states, and for the first time in our history, all of them chose electors by popular ballot. New York went for Grant by more than fifty thousand majority, Illinois by as much, and Ohio by nearly forty thousand. In the whole nation the popular vote stood: Grant 3,597,132, Greeley 2,834,125. Great gains were made by the Republicans in Congress. They held the Senate with undiminished strength and would hold the new House with approximately a two-thirds majority. Most party leaders were astonished by the magnitude of their victory, and Grant took it as a popular endorsement of his policies and acts, which it was not. Actually the large support which Greeley received among conscientious Republicans was a rebuke which the Administration should have taken to heart. Strong was justified in scoring the editor's flippant reference to his canvass as "another line of business"; he should have spoken of the great effort to reform the national government, improve the civil service, and restore fraternal amity between North and South in more dignified terms. But Greeley deserved sympathy as he went back to his editorial chair, proclaiming that he meant to make the Tribune *"a thoroughly independent journal, treating all parties and political movements with judicial fairness and candor."*

The election was hardly over when the country was shocked by a great fire in Boston, originating nobody knew how, which laid waste much of the business district, destroying sixty acres of splendid stores, warehouses, and public buildings.

November 10, SUNDAY. Morning papers announced a very serious fire at Boston. It began between seven and eight last night on Kingston and Summer streets and gained headway before the engines could be brought into action. The fire department horses were disabled, and the "machines" had to be dragged by hand, and a half hour was thus lost. Great devastation in the business streets, and the fire is still raging. When we emerged from Trinity into Broadway, that region, commonly so quiet on a Sunday at noon, resounded with the clamor of the canorous newsboy proclaiming his "extry—an' great loss o'life." From my extra and from despatches posted at the telegraph office corner Liberty Street and Broadway, I infer that the fire was somewhat checked or brought under control at about twelve today after an (estimated) destruction of $100,000,000. Went to the Fifth Avenue Hotel after tea this evening with Murray Hoffman, Jr. The latest despatch there bore the date eight o'clock in the evening and was not definite. But it seemed to indicate that the fire was but recently subdued and was unlikely to break out again now.

This is a grave business. The New York insurance companies will suffer heavily. . . . As nearly as I can make out the principal business streets of Boston are destroyed. Whether State Street, the principal banks, the new post office, the "Old South" meetinghouse and Faneuil Hall have escaped the conflagration is not yet known. It seems to have destroyed few private dwellings; so but few people are made homeless compared with the multitudes who were burned out at Chicago last year.

November 11. . . . Received a lawyer's letter from one C. W. Brooke, attorney for James Pech, demanding $4,500 for services to the Church Music Association. He is a squirt and a geyser among squirts. . . .

Called at Mr. Ruggles's this afternoon. His progress does not seem to me satisfactory. His spirits are good and his mind and memory active, but he says it wearies him to fix his mind on anything for five minutes, and his physical strength seems all gone. His mouth is certainly a little wrong, and his articulation is not perfectly normal. All this must indicate

(I suppose) continued irritation and disease somewhere in the brain. I fear a great sorrow for poor Ellie is drawing near.

Dick came in awhile this afternoon, just from Boston, much better, and full of details of yesterday's strange phenomena. No churches are running; most of them are converted into depositaries of property saved from the fire. The Common is covered with ledgers and books of account, pianos, furniture, private libraries, bales of dry goods, boxes of boots and shoes, canary bird cages, and other things, all dumped miscellaneously together. There was another outbreak of fire at four this morning, caused by an explosion of gas, but it was suppressed with comparatively trifling loss, destroying only one or two great warehouses. Losses by this terrible fire are variously estimated at from fifty to two hundred and fifty millions. Probably about eighty is not far from the truth. When will this city have its turn? We are no better secured against conflagration than was Boston, and we have not been burned out since 1845. Mansard roofs are shewy but dangerous and should be prohibited unless built of incombustible material.

November 12. . . . Newspapers are mostly taken up with the Boston fire and dwell on the probability that like disaster or worse may befall us any windy winter night. One need only walk through, for example, Church Street from Fulton to Canal to see that probability with clearness. Or let him contemplate Drexel's immense banking house on the corner of Wall and Broad, now culminating in a vast mansard roof and towers all lath and pinewood and quite out of effective engine range. Once on fire, it would devastate the whole block. Such structures are scattered throughout the city like so many sporadic powder magazines, or fire ships permanently anchored on dry land. Dr. Nelson Borland writes that the Boston loss exceeds two hundred millions. Doubtless a great overestimate. His house . . . is packed full of rescued furniture and other chattels.

Working tonight on the Bank for Savings case and trying to frame certain dishonest forms of speech in the hope of convincing a little squad of sleepy old gentlemen at Washington that an act of Congress (a very unrighteous and impolitic act, but that makes no difference) does not mean what it says.

November 13. . . . Ellie went with Johnny to hear Rubinstein this evening and returned in rapture. . . .

November 14. . . . At Edmund Schermerhorn's at four-thirty. There were Horsley, Cooke, and our two new members, Jem Gerard, Jr. and

Ben Stephens. For the second concert they agreed on Spohr's "Last Judgment," an innovation on our usages, which goes far to destroy my interest in the Church Music Association, and reduces it from the position of an expositor of church music to the level of a common vocal society—doing oratorios. Horsley pressed the adoption of this work very strongly; the others seemed inclined to acquiesce, and I did not feel inclined to oppose. . . .

The Auchmutys, Chadwicks, and Costers, victims of George A. Jones, have finally settled with him. Under threat of criminal proceedings against him, he and his wife surrender everything, thus making good about forty per cent of his defalcations, and they retire to Bristol, Connecticut, where he is to resume the manufacture of clocks, "lamp-movements" and "walking dolls" and try to work off the balance of his liabilities. If he can endure life, I think I ought to make an effort to do so. Poor George A. Jones was first led into evil courses by losing $60,000 in a "walking doll" operation. Tragedy and farce are strangely mixed in this life.

I think I will resign from the Church Music Association positively and finally. Horsley shews an inclination to be "director" in the fullest sense of the word and to dictate what music we shall produce. And he knows nothing about the peculiarities of New York audiences.

November 16. Yesterday afternoon to a Philharmonic rehearsal with Ellie and the boys. Mrs. Harry Chapman and Miss Sarah Lazarus sat in our box. . . . The great Rubinstein did a concerto of his own and certain "preludes" by Chopin with amazing delicacy, power, and prestidigitation. He seems to me beyond all question the most skilful pianist or pianizer I ever heard. In the evening with Ellie and Louis to Academy of Music for *Nozze di Figaro,* my first operatic experience this long while. What a flood of various, delightful melody it is! . . .

November 22. . . . Wall Street convulsed today by a "corner in Northwestern" (railroad stock). But "cornered" animals are dangerous, and so Mr. Jay Gould has discovered to his cost, for the "shorts" have caused him to be held to bail in a million at the suit of the Erie Company for nine millions of money by him fraudulently engulphed, absorbed, and assimilated during the happy Fiskian "days that are no more."

November 23. . . . It is most unaccountable that Marshall (of the Seamen's Bank for Savings), who knows me well and who listened to my bungling, lifeless argument before a committee of the legislature in 1867, should have pressed me upon this committee of savings banks as the best man to be associated with the Hon. B. R. Curtis on this writ of errors and should have apologized for pressing the counsel of that bank upon the committee too earnestly. I am certainly a humbug, though against my will.

November 25. The glory of Evacuation Day has departed. I remember a remote period when it was almost a Fourth of July. But our National Fowl shrieked not from her proud perch today, and our Invincible Militia did not shew, at least "the trumpet spake not to the Armed Throng" within my hearing. . . .

The Rev. Ogilby tells me a dismal story of the late Stephen Cambreleng's embezzlements, for which there is absolutely nothing to shew. Ogilby is among the badly wounded. . . .

Found Mr. Ruggles bright this afternoon and moving about. His voice indicates weakness, and he says he cannot let his mind dwell on any one subject for ten minutes without great fatigue, and that he could not stand having *Quentin Durward* read to him. But he keeps up his spirits and told with great glee how he and Dominick Lynch took Chancellor Kent to the very first performance of opera in New York (by the Garcia troupe in 1825), and how at an early stage of the performance—I think it was "The Barber," and that Almaviva was pouring out his soul in "Ecco ridente al Cielo"—the Chancellor jumped up, ejaculated, "It's an insult to human nature," and rushed out of the house. N.B. The Chancellor was a man of strong sense and insight. Compare a note of Sydney Smith's declining Lady Holland's invitation to the opera: "The whole thing seems (I cannot help it) so childish and so foolish that I cannot abide it."

November 27. . . . No trace yet of the Church Music Association music stolen by Pech and worth $1,000 at least. It is probably pawned. Little Bower the librarian is investigating the subject with zeal and good will (for he hates Pech), but without success. The general detestation of Pech is quite remarkable. Everybody abominates him—music dealers, Philharmonic musicians, members of the Church Music Association chorus, Bohemians of the press, choristers at St. John's, and others, down to the assistant janitor of Trinity Chapel schoolhouse. Except his wife, I am aware of no one who stands by the unfortunate scamp. I never knew a man with like talent for calling forth antipathy and aversion. . . .

November 29. . . . Poor old Horace Greeley is probably dying of brain fever brought on by the loss of his wife, by the excitement and work of his late unfortunate campaign, and by the bitter disappointment and mortification of his defeat. He was reported pulseless at the wrist to-day. . . .

Here Dick comes in just from Boston, where he ate the Thanksgiving turkey. He tells me that Judge Selah B. Strong of St. George's manor, my first cousin, died this morning. He was eighty last May. Quite a clever lawyer and has filled important judicial places, and a rather credit-able Christian man. But I have not seen him for twelve years and never liked him a bit.

November 30, SATURDAY. . . . Poor Horace Greeley died at seven last evening after an illness that became manifestly formidable about a fort-night ago. Better for his good name had he died this time last year. But had God granted him a little plain practical sense, Horace Greeley would have been a great man.[29]

Died, also, Harvey A. Weed, whom I used to know well but have not seen for years. After graduating at Columbia College in 1836, he studied law and practised awhile in connection with that windbag Giles M. Hillyer. He went a little into politics also as a disinterested wor-shipper of Henry Clay. His health failed, and he flitted to Darien, Con-necticut. . . .

December 2. . . . The general wail of the newspaper press over the great newspaper man, Horace Greeley, is preposterous, especially since so much of it comes from papers that were denouncing him a month ago as the basest of mankind. . . .

December 3. Coming downtown, I was aware of a long column of foolish people in triple or quadruple queue stretching from the front door of the old City Hall to Broadway, up Broadway to Chambers Street, and how far up Chambers Street I don't know. They were slowly moving through greasy mud for two minutes and then standing fast for ten at the beck of the stern policeman, and they all wanted to see the late Horace Greeley who was "lying in state" in the Governor's Room. The same phenomenon was visible this afternoon. I suppose they were impelled

[29] Greeley was physically exhausted by his campaign tour, and by long vigils at the bedside of his sick wife. A succession of blows had fallen upon the head of the great-est of American editors. His wife died on October 30; he was deeply humiliated by the election, declaring that he was "the worst beaten man who ever ran for high office"; and when he returned to his beloved *Tribune*, he found that control of the paper had passed into new hands and that his long tenure as editor was ended in all but name. Stricken in mind and body, he died insane. Of the sincerity of the popular grief, extend-ing across the entire nation, there could be no question.

partly by morbid curiosity and partly by a vague, half-remorseful feeling that "if we had only voted for the poor old rooster, he might have been alive now." At least I heard that sentiment expressed.

To Trinity Church Cemetery Committee with Palmer and Sackett. Thereafter, John Astor spoke to me about the Trinity Church comptrollership (vacated by Dix) which he wants me to take, and to which he says they want to elect me. Rather a grave question. . . . But there are other considerations of some weight. I need not try to balance them, for I afterwards heard from an outsider that Skidmore would be a candidate, and I guess he would be elected. The Chicago fire bore heavily on his company (the Howard) and on himself, and the salary may be an object. . . .

December 7, SATURDAY. To Boston via the New Haven & Springfield on Wednesday the 4th. . . . Found my little Lucy at the Boston depot looking out for her Uncle George. At 166 Charles Street was the usual unbounded welcome. Thursday morning, Lucy and I explored the . . . smoking ruins of the great fire, and thereafter attended a very creditable "Harvard Symphony concert" at the Music Hall. . . .

Mr. Ruggles sat through the first Church Music Association rehearsal on Thursday. I could not confer with the Hon. B. R. Curtis at Boston, for he had been summoned to Washington on Monday night. The Rev. Benjamin I. Haight was elected bishop of Massachusetts, vice Right Rev. [Manton] Eastburn, deceased. His acceptance is doubtful. . . .

December 9. . . . Went to the Trinity Church vestry meeting. . . . We went into an election without nominations; twenty votes. I put in a blank, and the other nineteen were for George T. Strong!!! I said a few words of acknowledgment very sincerely, and they seemed to be well received, and my friends were most kind and cordial after adjournment. The two alternates were Benjamin Winthrop and Dunscomb. . . . I have pulled no wires and made no effort in the premises. All I have done has been to tell Cisco, Astor, Braem, Campbell, and Skidmore, and possibly one or two more, that if the vestry wanted me I would probably take the place, and this has generally been in response to enquiries from them.

December 10. Sixty-eight Wall Street seemed most unlike itself this morning after I had announced to Charley and to Drake my intention of flitting and had begun to realize that I was no longer responsible for any of the weary work of running that venerable machine. Spent the morning sorting and destroying papers. Tons of rubbish have accumulated in and around my desk, and I took a grim satisfaction in watching them burn up. But of this work I have only made a beginning. Charley and

Drake will get on quite as well without me, though they duly express civil regrets at my departure. It seems like a dream that I should be free to keep away from Wall Street tomorrow without an uneasy conscience and a feeling that someone might think me a malingerer or a shirk. I hardly recognize myself. . . .

December 11. . . . Fire at the Fifth Avenue Hotel last night. It did serious damage to the building and destroyed a score or a dozen of its woman servants. . . .

General Dix's resignation takes effect next Saturday, and I must then enter upon my duties as comptroller. How the aspect of things has changed during the last few weeks since October 22: Bidwell is dead; Mr. Ruggles is stricken by paralysis; and I am abandoning Wall Street and the practice of the law.

December 12. . . . At Trinity Church vestry office, I held a long conference with General Dix about my future duties as comptroller. Prospect not unpromising. The General already tastes the woes of high place. While I was with him, suitor after suitor called, each urging the "claims" of himself or of some friend to some two-penny office. But the General is an old hand and used to business of this kind.

Died, suddenly, Edwin Forrest, the tragedian, beloved of Bowery Boys . . . a ruffian among actors and an actor or mere histrio among his congenital ruffians and shoulder-hitters.[30]

The Bowles banking house at Paris, London, and elsewhere has come to grief. There are criminal proceedings against its members. It has made a great noise and flourish for several years, but I have always distrusted it because Charles S. P. Bowles was so prodigious a blower six or seven years ago.

Visit to Mr. Ruggles this afternoon. He seemed well but persisted in talking about "minority representation" and "unification of the currency," in spite of my efforts to change the subject. I feared he would do himself harm, so I came off abruptly, remembering an engagement.

December 13. . . . Newberry called this evening, weary of the inertia and stupidity of the College authorities and not unlikely to resign his professorship. I dissuaded him as best I could, but his premises were undeniable.

[30] For more than ten years Edwin Forrest had been in partial retirement, though making occasional—and very successful—appearances as an actor. Since 1865 he had been partially paralyzed, and his final performance in New York this fall had been merely as a reader. He died in Philadelphia, bequeathing most of his property to found a home for aged players.

This morning I signed a long batch of "consents for substitution" in cases wherein I am attorney of record. . . . I worked most faithfully for some fifteen years after my admission, or till about 1856, when the progressive debasement of bar and bench disheartened me. And then I was (professionally) demoralized by the engrossing cares of the Sanitary Commission and never got myself thoroughly into legal harness again. Signing these consents was a solemn process. It closed a long chapter of my life. Probably what may follow can be put into an appendix.

Mr. Ruggles at Philharmonic rehearsal but had to go home after some fifteen minutes, finding orchestral clang and color too much for him. His brain and nerves cannot yet endure stimulants. He chafes under his enforced inactivity but is more patient and docile than could have been expected.

December 14, SATURDAY.   At Wall Street winding up affairs and at the vestry office, which was duly turned over to me by my "illustrious predecessor," General Dix. My headquarters are now on the northeast corner of Fulton and Church streets, with a sunshiny outlook over St. Paul's churchyard. Lunched on cold turkey and pie. I never knew that we maintained a diurnal lunch for the sustentation of the comptroller and his clerks. Morgan Dix came in to make me a "visit of ceremony" on my installation, and we had a hilarious session. . . .

To Philharmonic concert this evening. In our box were Ellie and the brats, Mr. and Mrs. D'Oremieulx and their Miss Laura, and a nice Miss Meta Renwick; also for a time Herr Benno Walther, who seems nice, young, and amiable. Enjoyed the concert beyond my expectations. . . .

I am glad I had a sunshiny day for my inauguration.

December 16.   To Wall Street and thence to my new office. The Rev. Ogilby called; also, the Rev. Wiswall, with a long obscure narration of his troubles and their origin. Attended to a little routine business and gazed for some time on the snow that was whitening St. Paul's church-yard, the vivacious little sparrows, and the leafless trees. Lunched with Gouverneur Ogden. I think we shall pull together comfortably.

December 19. . . .   With Ellie and Louis after dinner to "Robinson Hall" and the Amateur Philharmonic. Room was more than full; the audience was lively and good-natured. . . . The orchestra did itself very great credit. On both these occasions Johnny was 'cello (first 'cello of the latter), and Temple the Indomitable played the second oboe. It was funny to watch him this evening with his eyes as big as saucers, or as soup tureens, and with his whole being concentrated upon his work. I am well pleased with their devotion to music. It may be somewhat excessive and draw them off a little from books; but it tends to keep them out of mischief and it secures them for all their lives a source of most intense and healthy enjoyment. The faculty of appreciating in some moderate degree the music of Handel and Beethoven, of Haydn and Mozart, of Weber and Mendelssohn is no less a subject of profound thanksgiving than the sense of sight. It is among the greatest of earthly blessings.

December 20.   Presided over the Standing Committee this afternoon. The chief subject of discussion, the affairs of the Rev. Mr. Wiswall, which are neither flourishing nor promising. Skidmore did not attend. Cisco was miserable with violent influenza. He tells me the cathedral project is not dead or even sleeping, but that a strong and carefully picked committee is in process of aggregation and will soon be ready for work. I have little hope of any result, but this is an age of marvels.

December 21. . . . Died suddenly, George P. Putnam, the publisher, whom I knew years ago when he was of Wiley & Putnam, the booksellers.[31] He was an amiable and public-spirited man, but not a successful man, if money-making be the sole test of success. He seems to have had disease of the heart.

There is a shade of anxiety at 68 Wall Street. Charley fears that one or two most important clients will withdraw their business. I trust that "the office," founded by my father and John Wells sixty years ago, may go on and prosper. As I am now without pecuniary interest in its affairs, I can without impropriety or indelicacy use any influence I may possess to send it business, and I will gladly do so if anybody will tell me how to go to work. I never had the least notion of the processes by which one "gets business."

December 22. . . . Ellie spent the afternoon with her father and dined with him. She came home depressed and tearful, poor little woman, though Mr. Ruggles was in good spirits and his convalescence is, according to Dr. White, unusually steady and promising. I did my best to comfort her, but she appreciates her father thoroughly and loves him intensely—and with good reason. So his present condition and its possible sequel cause her the deepest distress.

[31] To George Palmer Putnam (1814–1872) the literary world owed many services; he was Irving's close friend and publisher, and *Putnam's Magazine* as founded in 1855 broke new ground in its broad use of American material. After one business failure, for which the panic of 1857 was partly responsible, he had reëstablished his publishing house in 1866.

His strength is nearly restored. The only morbid indications are incapacity for sustained mental effort without fatigue and nervous irritability, by which word I do not mean crossness or anything like it, but merely a sense of annoyance from, for example, a conversation between third persons in his hearing, like the annoyance inflicted on everyone by a street hand organ or the filing of a saw. This irritability is manifested also in his intense feeling about insignificant things, such as resolutions that may or may not be passed by the College trustees about Dr. Lieber. His affections rather outvote his judgment and good sense just now. Lieber was learned and thoughtful, but it is strange to see anyone so strong and clear-headed as Mr. Ruggles worrying himself about two-penny tributes to Lieber's memory, in spite of Lieber's selfishness, indolence, and preposterous self-conceit, which no one appreciated more keenly than Mr. Ruggles did before Lieber's death.

December 24. At about four this morning, Barnum's circus and menagerie on Fourteenth Street, nearly opposite the Academy of Music, took fire somehow. The thermometer stood at about four degrees above zero; there was a strong wind, and the flimsy structure was soon past saving. Four or five giraffes perished miserably, refusing to let themselves be led out; so did a magnificent elephant. The large carnivora could not be taken out of their cages, of course. The whole collection was destroyed, except for two elephants and two camels. Then the fire took hold of the chapel of Grace Church, which was burned up, and then of Mrs. John L. Lawrence's house, which was rendered untenantable, the roof and upper story being eliminated and the rest of the house flooded with water now converted into ice. This house was one of my earliest and best remembered localities of "social" or "society" experience. The Academy of Music was saved but severely singed. . . .

December 26. . . . To Church Music Association concert. . . . Attendance was beggarly, of course, and the chorus came in so slowly and in force so small that Horsley asked me whether the concert should not be postponed, to which query I returned a prompt negative answer. To my amazement, the performance proved among the most spirited and brilliant we have ever given. . . . Pech . . . was present with one of his wives. As an article has just appeared in Watson's *Art Journal* eulogizing Pech and denouncing the Church Music Association executive committee for leaving his three years' labors unpaid, I thought it possible the cad might propose getting on his legs during the entr'acte and making a speech or some other disturbance. . . . But he kept quiet, and (to do him justice), he is said to have joined heartily in the applause, which was unusually copious. . . .

Pech's position is simply this. He pressed his gratuitous services upon us as conductor, and in that capacity became one of our managing committee. At the end of our first season, we told him that we were unwilling he should work for nothing and included in our published estimate of expenses for subsequent seasons, a conductor's salary fixed by himself. As he became more and more extravagant in his expenditures as our executive officer, we warned him verbally and in writing fifty times that he was expending money that ought to go into his own pocket and begged him to be more moderate. His answer always was that any increase in the brilliancy of the concerts would redound to his credit, improve his "social position," and be worth more to him than the money. So he not only spent all the subscriptions but ran us personally in debt some three thousand dollars besides. And now he considers himself ill treated, threatens to sue for his "salary," and attacks us in the papers for our meanness in letting him serve gratuitously. To be sure this is unimportant. Nobody sees Watson's *Art Journal*; everybody who knows Pech knows that he is a scallywag.

December 27. Two feet of snow, and the drifts are prodigious. Charley Strong spent twenty-one hours between Philadelphia and New York, stuck in the snow. . . . Mails are past due; cars and omnibi are diminished by one-half, for every team has to be doubled. The streets are ways of unpleasantness (footed it both ways today). . . . It is said to be the heaviest transaction in snow since January 1856, and it causes everyone serious and multiform discomfort. . . .

December 31, TUESDAY. . . . It is five minutes to twelve; starlight now. Much has changed since January 1, 1872. Bidwell has "joined the majority"—gone over *ad plures*; Mr. Ruggles's active career is probably closed; I have given up my profession for a salaried place.

There go the midnight bells. It is 1873. May God of His great mercy carry us all . . . safely through this new year!

1873

RUBINSTEIN · THE MODOC WAR · FAILURE OF JAY COOKE ·
PANIC AND DEPRESSION · THE *VIRGINIUS* AFFAIR ·
BOSS TWEED IN COURT

———————⟡———————

*T*he *Crédit Mobilier investigation was the sensation of the day in national
affairs, as the trial of William M. Tweed was the focus of attention in
New York. Never in American history had so great a scandal in the national
government been disclosed as that which a House committee under Luke P.
Poland of Vermont was laying before the public. The Crédit Mobilier was a
corporation promoted by Oakes Ames, a Massachusetts manufacturer and Con-
gressman, with T. C. Durant and other associates, for the purpose of keeping in
the hands of a small group all the profits derived from the building of the Union
Pacific Railroad. This road was heavily subsidized by the government, and the
Crédit Mobilier carried out the construction work in such fashion that the
federal endowment, or much of it, was drained into private pockets. In 1867–
1868 Oakes Ames, fearful that Congress might interfere with the arrangement
between the Union Pacific and Crédit Mobilier, distributed at least 160 shares
of the highly valuable Crédit Mobilier stock among fellow-members of Congress
at bargain rates—some Representatives paying for it out of the colossal divi-
dends. In January and February, 1873, the newspaper headlines were full of
revelations highly injurious to various public figures. Among the men whose
reputations suffered worst were Schuyler Colfax of Indiana, James Brooks of
New York, and Senator James W. Patterson of New Hampshire. Oakes Ames
barely escaped expulsion, and was formally censured by House vote. The affair
was a staggering blow to public faith in the honesty of the national government,
felt the more keenly because just before its adjournment in March Congress voted
itself a retroactive increase in pay for two years—the much-censured "salary*

[466]

grab." Plainly reform was needed in Washington. Just how badly it was needed other shocking disclosures in the next few years were to show. In New York, reform suffered a sharp setback when, at the beginning of February, the Tweed trial ended in a hung jury.

Strong, happy in his new salaried position, retained a keen interest in the affairs of his old law office, and was delighted when his son John entered it to begin the study of Blackstone. "He seems inclined to take hold hard," wrote the diarist. "Thank God!" The vestrymen of Trinity Church were much troubled by the case of a minor clergyman who, having speculated in real estate and lost heavily, complained that he had no money for food and fuel, and asked the parish to pay his debts. Among public events, the conviction of Ned Stokes for the murder of Jim Fisk pleased Strong, who thought that the man deserved execution. "Still I would hang him in a silken rope, as having rid this community of one of the worst and most dangerous scoundrels that ever disgraced it." Actually Stokes was to get off with a few years in jail. Mrs. Strong was giving a series of winter receptions, to the first of which came ex-Governor E. D. Morgan, the painter Eastman Johnson, and other men of distinction.

January 8. . . . Johnny and law seem to get on well together so far. McBride has shewn him through the registers' and the clerks' offices, and Drake put him through the courtroom today. He witnessed the majestic spectacle of impaneling a jury in the case of Boss Tweed this morning and saw how careful the law is to admit as jurors in an important criminal case only those who are willing to swear that they are devoid of common sense and incapable of forming an opinion as to the truth or falsehood of notorious facts. O for a day of Jeffreys or Scroggs! Only *one* day and nothing more.[1]

January 25. . . . At three-thirty to a special exhibition of the "Babcock Fire Annihilators" at the Bowling Green. It was got up for our benefit and instruction, the company having applied to Trinity Church vestry to purchase a lot of them for the churches, schoolhouses, and the like. The experiment was successful. A high pile of barrels half filled with straw was fired and allowed to burn undisturbed for seven minutes by my watch, when it was in full blaze, and reminded one of the Smithfield

[1] The Tweed case jury was of exceptionally low character. Most of its members had little education or intelligence; several were liquor dealers, one was a "bummer" from the docks, and one had been a lobbyist for Tweed in Albany. The sheriff, a Tammany henchman, was accused of failing to summon decent men.

engravings in Foxe's *Book of Martyrs.* When the combustion seemed to have reached its stage of greatest activity, I signaled (by request) to the operator; he brought his portable apparatus to bear, and in two minutes and a half, the fire was out. "Down sank the flames, and with a hiss expired." The invention seems valuable.[2]

January 27. . . . "Probabilities" (*vide* daily despatches from Washington) for the next meeting of the College trustees are falling barometer, severe gales, and rising temperature. Gouverneur Ogden tells me that his son Gouverneur has been dismissed and a son of Alfred Ogden's expelled for some boyish prank with the lock of a lecture room door. I am partial to vigor of discipline, but this looks Draconic, especially as discipline at the College has long been lax. Gouverneur Jr. is a nice boy, of remarkably good repute, and a lover of Philharmonic and Church Music Association concerts, and I incline to sympathize with him. His papa considers that the Rev. Barnard has behaved badly in the premises and that the faculty has erred grossly, and he is putting on his war paint for an attack on the Rev. Barnard at the next meeting of the board. So there will be a shindy unless Professor Drisler or someone else can arrange matters, and that is unlikely. It is dangerous and mischievous, as a general rule, for the trustees to entertain any appeal from the faculty on questions of College discipline. Such appeal should be heard only in cases of such gravity and such apparent injustice that a reversal would be equivalent to a vote of censure on some officer of the College and a call for his resignation. I have as yet heard only one side of this case. I am satisfied, however, that the Rev. Barnard is stronger as a physicist than as a college president.

January 28. . . . Ellie has gone to a big ball at Governor Morgan's. . . . Ellie has just returned and pronounces the party to have been a dense conglomeration of all sorts and conditions of men and women and an uncommonly heavy bore. People spend much money and subject themselves to much discomfort by "entertaining" on a large scale and get little thanks for their sacrifice to the Moloch of "Society."

February 1. . . . Our campaign against scoundrelism in high places makes no progress. Boss Tweed's jury disagreed, some of them being beyond all question bribed, and the report of the Bar Association in the matter of D. D. Field was a mere wordy apology for doing nothing in

[2] The Babcock fire-extinguisher had recently been invented by James Francis Babcock (1844–1897), a Boston chemist.

the premises.[3] That impudent scoundrel came here last night to Ellie's reception uninvited. Perhaps he thought that as the Cyrus Fields were invited and also his daughter-in-law, Mrs. Laura (née Belden)—his next-door neighbors on either side—he was invited by implication. I could not very well order him out, for I did not know but that Ellie might have thoughtlessly sent him a card. But I received him with sad civility, and people generally did not seem disposed to cultivate him. . . .

The reception (number two) was pleasant, though just a little too crowded for dancing. Brown reported 231. . . .

February 3, MONDAY. College trustees met at two this afternoon. After the minutes of the faculty had been read, Gouverneur Ogden opened his batteries on Dr. Barnard and made a somewhat bitter speech of an hour's duration. He professed to speak entirely on behalf of his young relative . . . and not on behalf of his son (for whom Nash had been engaged), but what he said was, of course, for the benefit of both, the two cases being identical. It was a rather intemperate speech and befitted the father and the kinsman rather than the trustee. Barnard responded at great length. He did not prose as usual, but was spirited and effective. He modified my views of the case. Then Nash said a few words for his client, Mr. Gouverneur M. Ogden, Jr., and someone moved that the subject be laid over for consideration at an adjourned meeting and be referred to a committee for a report. I moved to amend by striking out the useless machinery of a committee, and as the Bishop took the same view, this was carried and we adjourned to Wednesday week, the 12th.

From talk with certain trustees . . . I think Ogden will injure himself by pushing his aggressive movement any further and that he should try to smooth the matter over, which he can easily do. So I shall advise him if he ask my advice. The sentences on these two young boys seem severe. But Barnard avers that an epidemic of annoying pranks like theirs has just broken out, is making serious trouble, and must be crushed out. . . .

February 25. Sent copy of Müller's "Holy Family" to Dr. Ogilby

[3] David Dudley Field had been implicated by the evidence and verdict in the impeachment of Judge Barnard. When the State Senate found Barnard guilty, it implied that Field, having shared in certain acts which brought Barnard his penalty, shared also in the guilt. The new Bar Association referred the matter to its Judiciary Committee; and this body reported that a prosecution of Field before the Supreme Court would involve long hearings before a referee, which might be protracted almost forever. With some scorching words upon Field's conduct, it refrained from recommending a vote of censure.

for the parish school, to the excellent old doctor's great delectation. Our "guild" is doing much to humanize and civilize the barbarians of the First Ward, not merely by strictly church agencies, but by entertainments, lectures, private theatricals (!!!), and the like in the new schoolhouse; and I thought this picture, the beauty of which, though perhaps wholly superficial, is at once patent to everybody, would help a little. Those poor children, far downtown, are cut off from almost every refining influence through art and amusements. They have sunsets to watch on the Battery, to be sure, which we uptowners have not. . . .

February 27. . . . Standing Committee meeting met tonight at the Trinity Chapel in the vestry room. The Rector was with us. Had a long debate over an application for aid to a Western Indian bishopric. Curtiss advocated it, of course; he would bankrupt Trinity Church in six months if he had his way. So did D. H. Arnold rather petulantly, and so, to my surprise, did Cisco. Campbell, Ogden, and I opposed. Skidmore dubitated. But a recommendation to the vestry to decline the application was carried; very right. The savages and barbarians of New York have a lien on any surplus funds of ours prior to that of all the Navajoes, Arapahoes, and Modocs.

Ellie returned from Washington last night after a lovely time with heads of departments, first-class diplomats, and Chief Justice Chase. Also, with President Grant, who instantly recognized her, addressed her by name, and remarked to someone: "It was at Mrs. Strong's I had my first New York dinner after Richmond." The De Lobos have been hospitality itself. Ellie's train was forty minutes behind time, and I spent a most chilly hour promenading the Jersey City depot and wearily watching for its advent. It was midnight when we got home to a nominal supper. . . . With Ellie journeyed Miss Newbold, daughter of the late Tom Newbold and of the lady whilom known as Miss Posy Rhinelander, having been so dubbed in her babyhood by Washington Irving.

March 1. Monthly meeting of the Century Club this evening was uncommonly large, lively, and long. First came up the question of amending the constitution so as to increase our membership from 500 to 600. . . . But the proposed increase was negatived by a large majority at last. . . .

March 8. In the evening, a special meeting of Trinity Church Standing Committee "with the Rector." We reconsidered our action about the diocese of "Niobrara" and its hopeful catechumens in their war paint, and agreed to recommend a small appropriation. I acquiesced, being unwilling to seem pigheaded and opinionated, and being satisfied, moreover, that the vestry would make the grant over the heads of the committee should it adhere to its original adverse report. . . .

March 11, TUESDAY.   With Ellie, Lucy, and Temple at three-fifteen to Edmund Schermerhorn's for the first of his new series of afternoon concerts. Rietzel succeeds the pseud-oxonian Pech as conductor. Orchestra about eighteen, picked Philharmonickers. . . . Audience about fifty, nice people and remarkably sympathetic. . . . Violin solo with orchestra, Benno Walther. (He plays with spirit and fire.)

This evening, . . . little Lucy's "party" came off, the session of her little "club." Some forty assisted and seemed to enjoy themselves, though their refreshments were of Spartan simplicity, black broth being represented by chocolate. Never was so vigilant, indefatigable, and efficient a hostess as dear little Lucy. She was trotting about all the evening taking care that nobody seemed neglected and that no binary combinations endured so long as to become stale. It was an entirely new set: the Cushmans, Parke Godwins, Sedley of the *Times*, Whitelaw Reid of the *Tribune* (!), and many others; a kind of semi-literary and semi-Bohemian set. Many very pretty girls among them. There were performances; recitations by Mr. Charles Miller—"Lord Ullin's Daughter," with clothes-basket boat and broomstick oars; and a series of tableaux illustrating

> When I was a little boy, I lived by myself,
> And all the bread and cheese I had, I put upon a shelf. . . .

March 13.   Dined here Ellie's cousin Mrs. Harriet Rogers (of Philadelphia), who was a Miss Ruggles; her son, sometime of West Point, his wife, who was Miss Sue Fish and is very nice; Dick Hunt and his exuberant Sultana of a Mrs. Hunt; Colonel Hay, Lucy, and Dick.[4] I thought it an uncommonly lively symposium. John Hay is extremely agreeable, and Hunt would put life into the dullest Fifth Avenue dinner party or into a *convivium mortuorum*. . . .

March 14. . . . The *Evening Post* announces that the Governor decides not to commute Foster's sentence, so that ruffian will be hanged

[4] Richard Morris Hunt, the architect, had a studio in New York and was briskly designing buildings; he had married Catharine Clinton Howland in 1861. The lively John Hay, widely known for his *Pike County Ballads* and *Castilian Days*, was helping Whitelaw Reid run the *Tribune*. Dick (frequently Dickon) was Dr. Richard Henry Derby, the diarist's nephew.

next Friday.[5] Morgan Dix tells me tonight that his father has written an elaborate opinion, of which copies were being made yesterday for the press. All honor to the Governor's firmness. He has had to resist a pressure unprecedented even in John C. Colt's case, and most painful to him personally. . . .

Foster's friends may yet contrive a rescue or an escape, or may smuggle implements of suicide into the condemned cell. A great deal of money has been spent in manufacturing public opinion for him, and there is more to be spent if it can be used to save his comparatively "respectable" connections the disgrace of his hanging.

March 15.   General approval of the Governor's decision against Foster. Even the New York *World* approves it heartily. The only dissenting view I have heard comes from the disreputable *Sun* newspaper. . . .

March 17. . . . The "Ward" house (north corner of Bond Street) is coming down; a very venerable Broadwayian landmark, being some forty years old. It was built by Samuel Ward the First [1786–1839] and bought of his estate by Joseph Sampson who inhabited it till his death. . . .

March 20.   This afternoon to Edmund Schermerhorn's second orchestral concert, fully attended by nice people. An Abyssinian, Captain Atkinson, was astonished by this sign of civilization in the New World. . . . Mr. Ruggles was there. . . .

Seven of Foster's enlightened jurymen make and publish an affidavit that when they found him guilty of murder in the first degree, they did not believe him guilty thereof but supposed that such verdict, coupled with a recommendation to mercy, would lead to a commutation of his sentence to imprisonment for life, the penalty of murder in the second degree. They must be well paid for thus stultifying themselves. The strongest point that could be made for Foster is that a majority of his jurors have written themselves down as asses or noodles, and have solemnly sworn to their ignorance of their duties and the obligation of their oaths. It might be plausibly urged that no man should be hanged on the finding of idiots like these. But Governor Dix stands firm, notwithstanding the cackling of philanthropes and paid pettifoggers and

[5] Foster was a ruffian who, after insulting a woman passenger on a Broadway car by persistent ogling, attacked her escort with a car hook and killed him. A body of soft-hearted (some thought in this instance soft-headed) men and women, including Evarts, besought Governor John A. Dix to let Foster off easily. Several prominent attorneys and judges, two bank presidents, and eleven of the jury joined in this plea; but those who thought New York too much at the mercy of drunken toughs asked the full penalty.

weak-backed presbyters about "judicial murder." So Foster will probably be hanged tomorrow. He has been watched for a week or more,
night and day, without a moment's intermission by relays of deputy
sheriffs. Were I in his place, I should have been long ere this eager for
the gallows as a means of escaping this horrible, ceaseless surveillance.

March 21. . . . Foster *suspensus per collum* at twenty minutes after
nine this morning, according to his deservings, and with every possible
civility and attention. As might have been expected, the cowardly ruffian
wilted down under abject terror when he found himself face to face with
death, and the sheriff had to signal to the Rev. Tyng to cut short his final
prayer as the patient was manifestly just about to collapse and faint away
with fright. Everybody I meet earnestly approves the Governor's firmness in this matter and says that everybody else does likewise. The
"public opinion" in favor of a commutation was factitious and manufactured by money. Evarts, Judge Pierrepont, and the Rev. Tyng have
not raised themselves in public esteem by their interference.

March 23, SUNDAY. An unusual conglomeration of people this
evening. Miss Rosalie, Miss Lina Routh, Mrs. Talboys and her spouse,
pretty Miss Nina French, Miss Sarah Lazarus, and others. . . . Among
the others was the distinguished Sothern, creator of the illustrious and
memorable "Lord Dundreary." He seems a lively, gentlemanlike person
and "do please me much," as Mr. Pepys would say.

March 25. The Philharmonic board sat nearly two hours at Steinway; all present. I found them (Hill excepted) in high wrath. We had
arranged with that guileful Israelite, Mr. [Maurice] Grau, that Rubinstein should lead his *Ocean Symphony* at our next concert, for which loan
of that maestro and also of [Henry] Wieniawski we were to disburse
$1,000. It was one of our conditions that Rubinstein should not produce
that symphony in New York until after he had conducted it for us. Now
Mr. Grau advertises it for next Monday night at a concert speculation
of his own. The board was strongly inclined to repudiate Mr. Rubinstein
and change the whole programme, though it has been advertised and
announced. Bergmann was particularly irate, and Bergner talked more
tincture of capsicum. . . . The question was referred to a meeting of the
Society. I favored this course, for one of the points on the other side was
that the orchestra was so exasperated that it would not receive Rubinstein civilly or play with spirit under him as leader, and I wanted to see
what their temper really was. . . .

March 27. At ten o'clock this morning, a general meeting of the

Philharmonic Society at Steinway. Schaad had his resignation in his pocket ready to be presented if the Society should decide to break faith with its subscribers and to withdraw its announcement of the *Ocean Symphony* after tomorrow (thereby tempting them to give up the opportunity of hearing Rubinstein conduct the rubbish on Monday at Grau's concert). I had not put my resignation on paper, but had settled its wording in my own mind. We sat long but were spared the heated discussion I thought likely. . . . My opinion was called for and I gave it in an oration of ten minutes, which was applauded and may have done some little good. . . . N.B. I begin to perceive in the Philharmonic Society, what I suppose a shrewder person would have perceived long ago, namely, an intense jealousy of Theodore Thomas and his orchestra. . . .

March 28. . . . To Trinity Chapel tonight. Dix's deadly sin for this evening was impurity—a difficult subject to discourse of. He could not possibly go to the root of the matter as in his previous lectures, but he was most earnest and forcible, nevertheless. He touched on the new school of erotic poetry (Swinburne & Co.), on the nasty illustrated flash weeklies that are sold at every newsstand, on fast women and fast men, on innocent flirtations among married folk, on increasing facilities for divorce, on our new race of women (like Mrs. Julia Ward Howe) who are not content with being different creatures from men and far nobler and better, but seek to become second-rate men or bad imitations of men, and the like. I dare say, by the by, that Mrs. Julia Ward Howe is an excellent person. But she is a representative of a very bad lot. . . .

April 1. . . . The last of Edmund Schermerhorn's musical "afternoons" was this afternoon. Pity it should be the last, for few entertainments so refined, so civilizing, and so pleasant have ever been given in New York. . . .

April 3. . . . A most fatal shipwreck near Halifax. Steamer *Atlantic* got out of her course, struck a rock, and forthwith foundered. Out of 900 crew and passengers, 500 are reported lost. It is alleged that she ran short of coal, though only ten days out, and was thereby compelled to make for Halifax; that the captain mistook one light for another and turned in at the critical time when his steamer was approaching a dangerous iron-bound coast. So the captain and the managers of the White Star Line are the subjects of a howl just now, in which I shall not join till I have heard their side. But their case looks bad. . . .

April 4. Rather a painful interview with poor little Morgan. His confession was tearful, contrite, and ingenuous. Some little time after the investigation of our books that followed Mr. Dick's defalcations, he found that there were four items of rent unaccounted for ($250 in the aggregate) which had not been detected. Of course he should have notified General Dix or Duncan at once. But he was nervous and afraid that Dick might turn upon him and charge him with the misappropriation. So he put it off from one day to another till the annual examination by the auditing committee drew near. It was too late then to make the disclosure, so he covered it up with false entries—a terrible mistake. He had been wretched ever since thinking of it and had been made ill by it. His doctor had said "there must be something on his mind"; he could stand it no longer. So he volunteered this statement. I told him he had done very wrong, but talked to him kindly so as to mitigate his distress a little, I hope. . . .

April 5.   Called on Cisco this morning to speak of this affair of Morgan's. As I feared, he took a hard view of the subject, which I did not succeed in mollifying. He was clear that Morgan should be suspended from duty till the case had been reported to the vestry. As he is an expert in all business affairs, at the head of a heavy banking house, and formerly of the Treasury, where he had 120 clerks under him, I did not feel justified in disregarding his advice. . . .

This evening to Century Club. The case of Frederick A. Lane came up. He sent in his resignation, which was laid on the table. Then came the motion to expel, which William P. Lee opposed in a forcible–feeble way. There was no reply, and the motion was carried 85 to 3. The three were William P. Lee, Hitchcock, who is an editor of the *Sun* and therefore presumably without moral sense, and one Goodridge, said to be a personal friend of Lane's. For the charges against Lane, *vide* the proceedings and evidence on the trial of Judge Barnard.

The truth is that our excellent Governor Dix, while comptroller, was so engrossed with politics, Erie Railroad, and fifty other things, that he was little in the office and gave its business little or no personal attention. Thus things had naturally lapsed into a chaotic state, and our sinful collector, Mr. Dick, was enabled to carry on a series of petty frauds that amounted to more than $4,000 before he was found out.

April 6, SUNDAY.   At two to Dudley Field, Jr's. (127 East Twenty-first Street) for Mrs. Belden's funeral. . . . Her last two or three days were spent in most severe distress, but she took leave of her daughters, her sons-in-law, and her little grandson, severally, prescribed the method of her funeral, and named her pallbearers. Service was at the house, Morgan

Dix and a country presbyter officiated. Pallbearers were Judge Roosevelt, Mr. Ruggles, Cornelius Dubois, Harbeck, old Gerard, myself, and others; and after the service we dispersed, leaving the coffin in the back parlor, and the *raison d'être* of the pallbearers undecided.

She was a lively and eccentric old lady, of English birth, and always understood to have been the daughter of a Dr. Miles, an eminent London physician. But among her old friends and contemporaries there has long been a whispered tradition that she was the daughter of Lord and Lady Lansdowne. That illustrious couple, it is said, wanted a male heir, for some very special reason, and swapped this little girl-baby off when she came for a little boy-baby of their Dr. Miles. It is alleged in support of this theory that she was utterly unlike her so-called sister, the wife of her husband's brother Charles. The story is absurd, of course; the only argument in its favor is that it is so incredible that nobody would ever have invented it.

April 11, GOOD FRIDAY.   John Astor has presented the church with a pair of magnificent, colorful candelabra for the chancel, holding sixty lights each—a most costly gift, no doubt. Good for John J. Astor. . . .

It would seem that the inveterate practical joker Sothern got up the practical joke of Wednesday afternoon. Circulars had been distributed stating that "Professor Cantell A. Biglie of the Scientific School of the University of Wisconsin would at three that afternoon fly from the top of Trinity Church steeple to the Bowling Green and back again," and would thereafter exhibit and explain his apparatus. At that hour there was a vast gathering of geese on Broadway and Wall Street. Many of them wanted to get into the church steeple, and Augustus Meurer had to bolt the gates to keep them out and then to call their attention to the "professor's" very significant name. By help of the police the crowd was dispersed at last, most frightfully sold. It was a brilliant sell and worthy of George Anthon in his best days. . . .

April 15. . . . College Library Committee at three this afternoon. Thereafter I inspected our little new observatory and called on Newberry. There are a few interesting additions to his well-filled cases, among them a recent crinoid, dredged up from a great depth. . . .

April 17. . . . Nothing decisive yet from the "Lava Beds," where that sanguinary sagamore, Captain Jack, and his Modoc horde are grimly awaiting an assault. Their treacherous murder of General Canby and one of the government commissioners during a peace conference justifies their extermination, and they will be exterminated if the U.S. forces can get at them. But storming their fastnesses will be no child's play. The attack delivered a short time ago failed rather badly.[6] Canby's murder will probably cause the government to reconsider the rosewater Quaker philanthrope policy it has recently adopted toward these horse thieves and cutthroats. Our noble savages can be "improved," I think, only by removal to a better world. . . . The elimination of the Indian "quantity" from our social problem seems desirable. It should be eliminated gently and mercifully. . . .

April 18. To Philharmonic rehearsal this afternoon. Academy was packed. . . . The illustrious Wieniawski[7] played a prettyish concerto by Spohr quite as well as it deserved, and the illustrious Rubinstein conducted his own *Ocean Symphony* without the score. He is a most magnetic conductor. His pantomime, or gesture, expressed *p*, *pp*, *ppp*, *sf*, *fff*, staccato, and the like, more clearly than words could have done it. The orchestra was on its mettle, and never played better. But the symphony is nothing more than a piece of scholarly, careful work, never offending good taste and signifying nothing at all.

April 19. . . . After sharp fighting for two days, the Modocs are whipped, but not in the least exterminated. Though "surrounded," most of them seem to have squirmed out of their pedregal somehow and to have vanished. . . .

April 28. To the U.S. District Attorney's office (Bliss) and clerk's office (George Betts) with Charley Strong and John Cadwalader, and Cadwalader and I became sureties on the receiver's bond (Atlantic Bank) in $40,000. The U.S. judicial functionaries keep themselves in awful seclusion and inaccessibility, and the bar seems to grumble against Judge Blatchford for this and other reasons. In the clerk's office were this wretched little Taintor with his custodian and his counsel John Sherwood arranging for an offer of bail, I suppose. Taintor looked like a whipped cur, with a super-added expression of bewilderment and of extreme boredom. I thought he would prefer not to be recognized in his present estate by so very slight an acquaintance as myself. (I have not met him for many

[6] General E. R. S. Canby had been treacherously murdered on April 11 by "Captain Jack" of the Modocs while holding a conference with these Indians in an effort to bring about peace. "Thus," wrote General Sherman, "perished one of the kindest and best gentlemen of this or any other country, whose civil equalled his military virtues." The "government commissioner" was the Rev. Dr. Eleazer Cady Thomas of San Francisco. Savage fighting followed. By an early date in June the Modocs had been taught a lesson and "Captain Jack" and his confederates were prisoners awaiting trial.

[7] Henry Wieniawski (1835–1880), eminent Polish violinist and composer.

years.) Poor fellow; I am sorry for him and much sorrier for his nice wife. When the bond was approved at last, Charley went down to the bank and took possession of it and of such of its assets as its cashier has not thought worth stealing.

Left at Astor Library this morning a small cart-load of Sanitary Commission account books which Agnew tumbled in upon me without ceremony last summer and which have been greatly in my way ever since, piled on this library floor. . . .

April 30. . . . The Modocs, though surrounded, beleaguered, cornered, trapped, and so on, "still live," and have got our men into an ambuscade and cut them up terribly. This reminds one of the old story of "Hello, fellows, I've caught a splendid wild cat!" and then, two minutes later, "Halloo!! fellows!! come here quick, and help me let this pesky critter go!!!"

Died, William C. Macready, whose name will be remembered in connection with the Astor Place riots of 1849, long after the actor is forgotten. Mr. Ruggles and he were great friends.

May 2. . . . Died . . . (of Napoleon's disease), the "Hon." James Brooks, the meanest of political mankind, except his brother, Erastus, or "Rat." What floods of benumbing venom those two Copperhead reptiles injected into our veins while we were struggling for life ten years ago! The American flag, half-masted over the *Express* office, looks ashamed of its situation. . . .

May 6. . . . John L. Aspinwall died this morning. Bishop McIlvaine "lay in state" at St. Paul's this morning. Funeral services (provisional, or *in transitu*) were at three this afternoon, and the *exuviae* were then put into a freight car bound for Ohio. According to the invaluable and most accurate newspaper press (of this evening), I was present at the service, but I'm not conscious of the fact. . . .

Died of pneumonia, John Romeyn Brodhead, a clever man but wrong-headed. His special gift was that of grubbing sedulously and successfully among ancient Low Dutch documents for valuable historical information about Wouter Van Twiller and other great men.

May 8. Saw . . . Charley Strong. He is invited by Kennedy and Tappen to succeed James F. DePeyster as treasurer of the Bank for Savings, and hesitated. But he has concluded to decline. Glad of it, for I should not like to see the old office established by my father seventy years ago finally broken up.

Served with a summons and a voluminous complaint this morning.

Pech, the plaintiff, versus the members of the Church Music Association Committee. There is a claim for some $5,000 for "services." I think we can send this dirty dog out of court with his tail between his legs.

Went to the Church Music Association concert tonight; full house, and a most uncommonly sympathetic and appreciative one. Almost every movement was vehemently applauded. The third movement of the Haydn symphony was encored for the sake of Bergner's brilliant 'cello solo (the Trio). So were the Benedictus and Agnus of the Mass, and the pianissimo chorus of the Walpurgis Nacht, "Disperse, disperse, ye gallant men." (Had Pech been conductor, he would have changed "disperse" to "disburse.") Everybody seemed pleased and interested beyond all precedent in the "short and simple annals" of this association. Much trouble finding a carriage in the rain after the concert. With us were Mrs. Talboys, Graham, Mrs. Ruggles, and Louis. The most brilliant and "successful" concert yet given by the Church Music Association. . . .

Entered appearance at the Law School examination yesterday afternoon and notified Professor Dwight that I should not attend again. My first default. But so long as it continues his private school, de facto and without a faculty, I will not be bored with it further.

Died in this city, of apoplexy, Chief Justice Chase. . . . He leaves an honest record behind him, though in office nearly all his days, . . . and was an anti-slavery man long ago when anti-slavery opinions seemed an absolute bar to all hope of social or political advancement.[8]

The general term of the Supreme Court denies Stokes's motion for a new trial. His only remaining hope is in the Court of Appeals, for he has little chance of executive clemency during Governor Dix's term of office. . . .

May 10. . . . To annual Philharmonic Association meeting and election yesterday at Germania Assembly Rooms, 293 Bowery. Was reëlected president 62 to 2, and the announcement by the tellers was received with loud and long-continued applause by my good-natured German friends. These gentlemen seem quite to like me, Heaven knows why. All the others were reëlected, but by smaller majorities. . . . We made Herr Rubinstein an honorary member.

I hear that Pech's real name is Peck, and that he Germanified himself when he did this country the honor to adopt it. Also that in 1860 placards

[8] Salmon P. Chase, whose great career had filled a long chapter in American political, financial, and judicial history, had suffered a paralytic stroke in the summer of 1870 but resumed his place on the bench. He had weakened visibly during the spring of 1873. On May 6 occurred a second shock, and he died next day without recovering consciousness.

were posted in London and advertisements inserted in the London *Times* offering £5 reward for his apprehension, he having deserted his wife and children and left them chargeable to the parish—Islington or Kensington or some other parish. Pech means pitch, and my experience certainly shows that one cannot touch Pech without being defiled or at least subjected to humiliating annoyance and bother. . . .

May 13. At Law School this afternoon reëxamining three weak vessels of the graduating class, with Dwight and Gouverneur Ogden. Passed all but one hopeless ignoramus. It is a fact that Dwight is too kindly in these examinations and helps a lame candidate with leading questions beyond all reason and measure. Under fairly strict examiners, I believe a third of every graduating class would fail. . . .

May 20. . . . In the evening to the Committee on Music at Trinity Chapel vestry room. The Rector, Cisco, Palmer, Professor Drisler and I were there. . . . My plan of putting a second story over the robing rooms on the south side of the chancel of Trinity Church and opening a kind of triforium into the chancel for the orchestra on festivals seems favorably received; so I shall talk to Upjohn about it. Our Committee on the Infirmary is to hold its first meeting on the premises at 50 Varick Street on Friday afternoon. . . .

May 23. . . . In the afternoon, Morgan Dix, Ostrander, Braem, and I (of the Infirmary Committee) met at 50 Varick Street. . . . We examined the house and agreed to ask the vestry for $7,000 for alterations, furniture, and the like. We shall need a good deal more. In fact, we are spending money at a frightful rate just now. The only comfort is that nearly all goes into investments, more or less permanent, as, for example, the new organ at St. John's, work on the interior of St. Paul's ($20,000), redecorating reredos at Trinity, this Church Street lot, the fence on Tenth Avenue for Trinity cemetery ($25,000), and the like. These are not extra-parochial objects.

That little pup, Brander Matthews, son of the unsavory millionaire, Edward Matthews of Fifth Avenue, is reported to have clandestinely married Miss Ada Harland, one of Lydia Thompson's troupe of high-kilted Saltatriculae.[9]

May 26, MONDAY.   Crisis at Versailles. Thiers is out and MacMahon

[9] Why Strong called so able and likeable a young man as Brander Matthews a pup is not clear. Matthews, who graduated from Columbia College in 1871 and from Columbia Law School in 1873, married Ada S. Smith, an English actress whose stage name was Ada Harland, on May 10, 1873. His father, Edward Matthews, lost most of his fortune in the panic of 1873 and ensuing depression.

is in. All quiet in Paris. This is a reactionary step, prompted by natural dread of Communism. A small majority of the Assembly is hostile to the Republic, but that majority is made up of hostile elements—Legitimist, Orleanist, and Imperial. MacMahon is said to be Legitimist at heart, and he holds the army in his hands. . . .[10]

I should like to understand the law that governs the coming of Sunday evening visitors. Sometimes there are but one or two, and last night there were nearly forty, of whom, however, four or five had been asked to "happen in." I will try to remember some of them. Mrs. Little (no longer in the least handsome), a Miss Redmond, Mr. and Mrs. Something Stone (a pretty woman), Rosalie, Dr. Peters and wife, good Mrs. Lily Clymer, Edward Snelling and wife, Clarkson Potter, Miss Edith McVickar, Miss Lina Routh, Miss Sarah Lazarus and her brother Frank, . . . Bradley Lee, Hancock, Sothern—clever, witty, and well-bred—and Mrs. Philip Henry Lee and her husband. She is the Miss Neilson who is playing Juliet and Rosalind and the Lady of Lyons with so much approval; a most gorgeous young woman, with amazing eyes and brow and hair, who reminds me of the wood engraving of "the Fotheringay" in the English edition of *Pendennis*; very ladylike and attractive, and I believe every way nice. . . .[11] Also, there were the chevalier De Lobo and Madame, Stumm of the German Embassy with a nebulae of lesser diplomats, Charles E. Strong, little Wetmore, Phelps, Ridgway Moore, another Moore (Anglican), Jem Ruggles, Viaini, Dick, and others.

May 30. "Decoration Day," now a legal holiday. I did not open my office. . . .

Another serious fire in Boston. Boylston Street, Washington Street, and the like, suffered severely. Chickering's establishment and the Globe Theatre were burned.

May 31. . . . The gang of "Legs," commonly called "Legislators," at Albany has disbanded at last, to the great relief of all honest men. Such a crew of buccaneers has seldom been got together since the days of Captain Kidd. They were nearly all "on the make."

[10] President Thiers had declared that a republic offered the only safe future for France. Angered by this, the followers of the Count of Chambord and the Count of Paris (that is, the Legitimists and the Orleanists) united to force the resignation of Thiers and the election of MacMahon—a rigid royalist—in his place.

[11] Adelaide Neilson, of English birth and training, had made her debut at Booth's Opera House in 1872, captivating the American public; she was "ravishingly pretty," her silver-toned voice was enchanting, and she played romantic parts with more than a touch of genius.

June 2.   College trustees met this afternoon at the new Law School, Great Jones Street. After waiting an hour and sending a special messenger for the Rev. Hutton, we got a quorum. Haight was absent (quite ill), so Robert Ray was chairman. Rather an amusing session from Gouverneur Ogden's manifest purpose to make war on Dr. Barnard and avenge himself for Barnard's execution of justice upon the two little Ogden boys. Every proposition of the president was opposed by Ogden in his usual somewhat piggish way, but he failed in every instance. His objections to printing the president's annual report and to authorizing the degree of doctor of philosophy to be conferred on resident graduates of the School of Mines were overruled *nem. con.*, for he did not think it worthwhile to give a negative vote, though he had made two or three hot and blundering speeches on both questions as "involving a great principle." He fared no better with sundry other equally stolid objections. He is no match for Barnard in debates, and moreover, every trustee saw his animus and rather enjoyed his successive defeats.

But for Haight's absence, we might have had the case of the "two little Ogden, three little Ogden, four little Ogden boys" brought up once more—*ad nauseam.* This is merely an inference of mine from the fact that I received two or three weeks ago, I know not whence, a copy of what purports to be a letter from Dr. Haight to Dr. Barnard "deeply regretting" that neither president nor faculty had done anything to relieve these two contumacious young cubs from the disagreeable position in which their own folly (or that of their papas) had placed them (that is, had declined to certify that though they were expelled, the College was quite willing that they should be received by Harvard), and stating further that this had caused deep and growing dissatisfaction in the board. It seems incredible that Haight should have written such a letter. It is wholly inconsistent with the views of the case I heard him express not very long ago.

June 3. . . . Visited this afternoon the Metropolitan Museum of Art in the late Mrs. Douglas Cruger's palazzo on West Fourteenth Street. The Cesnola collection of antiquities from Cyprus is interesting and large. Some of the glass vessels are exquisitely colored with iridescence from partial decomposition or disintegration of the surface, I suppose. The gallery of "Old Masters" is not exciting to behold, Johnston has deposited Turner's "Slave Ship" there. A large quantity of "articles of bigotry and virtue"—namely, vases, arms, odd china, and the like—has also been loaned by Sam Barlow, Meredith Howland, Kennedy, and others. Some

of these things are costly and curious. The specimens of early printing are
good (there is a Caxton among them!), and there are a few little volumes
of MS *Hours*. Art treasures (so-called) are evidently accumulating in
New York, being picked up in Europe by our millionaires and brought
home. This collection promises very well, indeed. Twenty years hence
it will probably have grown into a really instructive museum.

That noble savage, Captain Jack the Modoc, who assassinated General
Canby at a peace conference, has been bagged and is not unlikely to be
hanged. The most mucilaginous philanthrope can say but little for *that*
"poor Indian."

A most uncommonly shocking murder this morning at the Sturtevant
House on Broadway and Twenty-ninth Street. Mansfield Walworth, son
of the last of the chancellors and a kind of small littérateur who devoted
himself to the concoction of dish-water little novels, received four revolver
shots from his own son and was instantly killed. They had got into a hot
discussion of some trouble between Walworth and his wife at Saratoga.
The parricide, a boy of nineteen, went coolly to the nearest station house
and gave himself up. He accounted for his indiscreet and precipitate pistol
practice by the statement that "he thought his father was going to draw
a pistol on him"! We shall have to make the carrying of concealed weapons
a felony.

June 4. . . . Upjohn sent in plans for altering the south side of Trinity
Church chancel, so as to make a place for the orchestra. They look well,
and Morgan Dix likes them. The *outsidest* estimate of cost (Upjohn's
estimate) is $15,000 (???) . . .

June 6. . . . Letter from Dr. Barnard about certain matters that came
up at the last College meeting. He fully appreciates Gouverneur Ogden's
personal hostility to him and seems to reciprocate the feeling.

June 7. . . . Strange that [Charles] O'Conor should have volunteered
his services as counsel for young Walworth. O'Conor's mental and moral
processes are past finding out by ordinary mortals. . . .

June 9. I read [at vestry meeting] a sworn petition for "pecuniary
relief" handed me this morning by Mrs. Alvah Wiswall's attorney, that
little cad Jerolomon, and it was referred to Nash, Palmer, and myself as a
committee of investigation. This will be a pleasant job! The petition
charges Alvah the impecunious with all manner of fraud and iniquity and
the little attorney "is ready to verify." . . . We approved the action of the
Standing Committee in buying the Church Street lot without any authority
whatever and appropriated $7,000 for outfit of the infirmary. . . .

June 11. . . . I fear the opinions of the Court of Appeals in the Stokes case go far toward ensuring the assassin's acquittal on his new trial. That this plain case of murder should stand now exactly where it stood seventeen months ago (except so far as the defendant's chances of escape are improved by this decision) is a disgrace to our criminal jurisprudence. Such scandalous shortcomings are tolerated only because people have lost sight of the truth that to let crime go unpunished is criminal injustice and wrong, and that the community takes on its own shoulders the guilt of the unhanged murderer.

June 12. . . . Cemetery Committee met at three this afternoon; Sackett, Palmer, and I. We must ask the vestry for a little more money at once and for a great deal more within the year. That cemetery is a bottomless pit, an insatiable consumer of money. . . .

June 13. . . . We talked this morning for the first time of the expediency of removing the Leake and Watts Orphan House to some new site—say on the North Shore of Long Island at Bayside or Great Neck. Our present site, fronting on the proposed Morningside Park, and close to Central Park, is fast becoming of such market value that we ought to put it into the market for sale or lease and move elsewhere.

June 14. Trinity Church again burglariously invaded last night. The poor boxes were violated and were quite empty this morning. Perhaps they were empty before. It was probably not a remunerative job.

Great demolition on the southeast corner of Pine and William Streets and the same on Cortlandt and New Church Streets. On the latter corner, I believe, the Delaware and Hudson Canal Company is to build.

June 16. . . . Had a visit from Schaad. My Philharmonic friends are evidently perturbed by the triumphs of Theodore Thomas. He has cut out Bergmann[12] as conductor of the Brooklyn Philharmonic, and his garden concerts are growing in brilliancy and in public favor. Schaad has at last perceived that we think a great deal too much about the amount of the annual dividend to members of our orchestra. I saw this long ago, but did not think it was for me to say it. Thomas's people rehearse daily. If our society would consent to do likewise, it could beat them out of sight, being numerically so much stronger than they; and if we would treat the candid and sagacious "critics" of the daily press a little more liberally in

[12] Carl Bergmann was sole conductor of the Philharmonic Society from 1865 to the year of his death, 1876. He was a versatile man, connected with various organizations, and interested in opera as well as orchestral concerts; but he had the reputation of not working very hard.

the matter of complimentary tickets and reserved seats, they would be more civil to us, though that is no great matter. As it is, whenever we play Beethoven or Mozart, they denounce us for producing "hackneyed" compositions, and when we bring out some "novelty" of Raff's or Rubinstein's, they deplore our neglect of the great old classical models.

June 25. . . . The political *Mare Putridum* is heaving vaguely in the calm that has followed the last grand presidential typhoon. . . . There seems to be a prevalent feeling that a new party is wanted. Republicanism has grown immoral in its old age and survived much of its usefulness. But there are many thousand disgusted Republicans who remember the war times, and would as soon vote for the Devil as with the Democracy. They have no place as yet, but there are indications (at the West especially) that a new organism may be tending toward development with free trade for its vital principle.

There are signs, also, that Grant's friends are considering whether they can venture to put him up for a third term of office, and there are signs that a certain considerable number of "Democrats" would like to change the name of their party. Not that they are ashamed of it, as they ought to be, but because it is a "Scarlet Letter," and a badge of disloyalty, *incivisme*, and infamy, which keeps them out of office and profit. New political combinations are almost certainly forming, but what they will be like no man knoweth.

June 26. . . . Evidence for prosecution in case of young Walworth, the parricide, is closed and the defense opened. His counsel will find it a hard case to befog.

The ultra "temperance" fanatics, lunatics rather, in the general asylum or unwitenagemot assembled, cut loose from the Republican party and gibber at Governor Dix. That disinterested patriot, Ben Butler, is trying to be Governor of Massachusetts and is backed by Grant's influence, which I regret for Grant's sake. Puritanism is always the same. . . . [It] may be defined as a religion or a way of thinking that can see any given question only from one single standpoint. . . .

Spain is in a curious condition that may be described as a mild, gelatinous, or albuminous anarchy. There is no government to speak of, the country seems decomposing or falling to pieces, and yet nobody is hurt, unless it may be by a few roving gangs of Carlist banditti.

June 27. . . . At 68 Wall Street this morning. Young Bache McEvers Whitlock there, having just entered as a student. He is poor Sam Whitlock's eldest son; he inherits his father's kindly pleasant manner, and, I regret to say, a little of his mamma's deafness. He and Johnny are studying law in the very same office in which their respective papas had a good time together as law students some thirty-three years ago. I don't believe a like case can be found in this city. . . .

June 28. . . . Walworth, the murdered man, seems from his own letters to have been such an unprecedented compound of lunatic, beast, and devil, that the jury may be tempted to think his son, or any one else, justified in exterminating him on sight. . . .

Mr. and Mrs. Ruggles go to Delhi next Tuesday for the summer. I fear Mr. Ruggles will perish of the vacuity and inanity of a country village, however pretty and picturesque, before two months are over. But his doctors recommend the experiment, or rather order and prescribe it. Perhaps they may not understand their patient quite so well as I do. He must have undergone a radical and probably a fatal change if he can endure six weeks of Delhi.

June 30. . . . Received a nice note from nice Mrs. William Astor enclosing a check for $300 with which she requests me to give the poor children of Trinity Church a picnic or rural holiday of some kind. Good for Mrs. William Astor! I must go to work straightway and write the lady the prettiest note I can devise. . . .

July 1. . . . The outlines of the two square wall pews on either side of St. Paul's that were respectively the President's and the Governor's in old times have come to light in the flooring, and we propose to restore, or rather to rebuild them. They used to be dignified with canopies, which may or may not be replaced.

Died, while traveling in California, Zabriskie, ex-chancellor of New Jersey; a sound lawyer and worthy man. He was a great friend of Rosalie's. His daughter married Bille, the Swedish minister. . . .

In Walworth's case, the jury is, or has been, listening to evidence (by the prosecution) of the murdered man's good character, a curious inversion of ordinary practice. O'Conor makes one point that is highly ingenious, namely, four shots were fired by the murderer, only one of which was necessarily fatal. Now the defendant remembers firing but thrice. Ergo, he was in an epileptic condition (!!!!) and unconscious when he fired the fourth. This forgotten fourth may have been *the* fatal shot, the cause of death. If it was, the defendant must be acquitted, as *non compos mentis* at the moment of the homicide, and at all events he is entitled to the benefit of the doubt whether it was or was not and therefore to an acquittal. Thus O'Conor gravely argues. He, or one of his colleagues, officers and counsellors of the court, speak of the coroner and his jury, who sat on the deceased Walworth, and the policemen who arrested the avowed parricide, as "the demons and ban-dogs of the law"; and this without any rebuke, crushing or otherwise, from the court. This makes one regret the days of Scroggs and Jeffreys. Our ways of dealing with criminal cases are marvelous and past finding out.

July 2. . . . One of the young Irvings came in with a note from his aunt, Mrs. William Astor, who wants to consult me as "the old family lawyer" . . . about certain troubles growing out of a trust deed improvidently executed. Strange how these millionaire families quarrel among themselves about money—brother alienated from brother, sister at daggers drawn with sister—and all about property, of which every one of them has more than enough.

July 3. Walworth convicted of murder in the second degree, a verdict possibly correct under our recent legislation, but then so much the worse for our recent legislators! I suppose he will be pardoned out of prison in a year or two. O'Conor's conduct of the defense is sharply criticized, and with reason. He has seemed to forget that an advocate owes anything to the court, to the community, or to his own conscience, and has defended, or rather sought to justify, his miserable client by propositions and arguments audacious and profligate beyond example. He is childless, so his sophisms cannot expose him to personal risk. But his argument in support of the praiseworthiness of parricide whenever a boy thinks his pa objectionable has been read in the newspapers by many hundred thousand people, including, doubtless, no end of ill-conditioned boys who think themselves somehow aggrieved by their respective "governors." If counsel must be allowed to eulogize crime, the courts should at least forbid the publication and general dissemination of their wicked and shameful arguments. I never had much faith in O'Conor, and what little I had is gone entirely. He began his career as a low Irishman and worked his way up by energy, industry, and a talent for bitter vituperation (which he no longer exercises); and after he had acquired wealth, by disinterestedness or indifference to money whenever he took hold of a case that enlisted his sympathies. But I fear he is a bad and mischievous man. . . .

July 15. . . . Ethelbert S. Mills of Brooklyn drowned at Coney Island, whither he used to drive every morning before breakfast for a sun bath. He was a prominent and public-spirited Brooklynite, a respectable lawyer, and a very specially favorite law student of my father's. . . .

July 19. Poor Ethelbert Mills's trust company, the Brooklyn Trust

Company, of which he was president, with a most respectable board that left him to run the machine in his own way, has come to grief and closed its doors. An investigating committee finds overdrafts by the president and investments on queer security that have sunk half its capital. Mills had been operating in real estate, not very successfully, and building fine houses near Prospect Park that would neither sell nor rent. It is suggested that he was tempted to these alleged overdrafts so that he might be saved the necessity of sacrificing this property. But I suppose the state of the case is not yet accurately understood. Of course the Mungo Malagrowthers will whisper that his accidental drowning is stuff and nonsense. All this is unfortunate. His reputation was unblemished. I never heard him spoken of but with praise. . . .

July 21. . . . There can be little doubt of Mills's suicide. Last Monday he paid off his household bills, usually settled on the first of the month, made a deposit in the bank to his wife's credit, went to Coney Island in the evening, sat up all night in his room, and proceeded to take his last surf bath early Tuesday morning. His trust company is a wreck, over which the newspapers moralize platitudinously. Even had he lived, it must have been swamped in a few days. Thank Heaven that I am a genteel pauper, and that after paying the butcher and the baker, I have nothing even distantly resembling a surplus left wherewith I might be tempted of the devil to operate in real estate or anything else.

July 22. These three cases of George A. Jones, Taintor, and Mills, all occurring within so short a time, show how thoroughly even our so-called best people are demoralized by the prevalent passion for acquiring the maximum of money in the minimum of time.[13] "*Qui volunt divites fieri, incidunt in loqueum diaboli,*" saith the Vulgate. Great wealth, unless inherited, or acquired by professional energy and industry, is now, as a general rule, presumptive evidence against the character of its owner. . . . Most of the

[13] These cases were all evidence of the speculative mania which, stimulated by the post-war inflation, had brought the country to the verge of a great panic. Taintor, the cashier of the Atlantic Bank, had embezzled $162,000 worth of securities kept on special deposit. The Brooklyn Trust Company had been similarly robbed by President Mills and its secretary. "The present time is fertile in embezzlements and peculations," grumbled the *Commercial and Financial Chronicle* of August 30, 1873. A committee representing the New York Clearing House Association shortly reported (November 11, 1873) on needed banking reforms. It condemned the "sharp and degrading competition" among metropolitan banks, and pointed out that the creation of many new banking institutions since the war and their frenzied efforts to gain public favor and amass wealth had "induced others to adopt newer methods of obtaining patronage equally pernicious."

dodges, devices, and complots which Wall Street considers legitimate and in which millions are lost and won (on paper) every day, are, of course, plainly guileful, dishonest, and wicked. But how many of our nice, fresh, ingenuous boys are plunged into this filthy pool every year at eighteen or even younger . . . though their parents can well afford them a liberal education. Each hopes to win some great prize in that great gambling house, an establishment far less honest than were those of Baden-Baden and Homburg. And so they grow up to be mere illiterate sharpers, with possible fine houses and fine horses and fine Newport cottages and without capacity to appreciate anything higher—men without culture and with damaged and dwarfed moral sense.

July 24. . . . Cholera is doing a lively business at the West and will, no doubt, soon visit New York. The board of health is getting ready for it at last with some show of vigor, to the credit of which I think our excellent Professor Chandler[14] chiefly entitled. Last night the filthy, festering, fetid booths that have been growing up unlawfully around Washington Market for years past and obstructing the adjoining streets, were summarily torn down and swept away, amid volleys of curses from the ejected squatters, who squirmed like maggots molested in a dunghill, and as vainly. I inspected the place this afternoon. A line of booths still remains on Vesey Street between Washington and Greenwich, inviting folks to purchase unripe apples and bad lobsters.

August 5, TUESDAY. . . . Left Fulton Street earlier than usual, at three this afternoon. There was a queer looking black cloud obscuring half the sky, which I took to be a new style of thunder cloud till I learned that it arose from the conflagration of a great oil factory, or oil works, at Hunter's Point.[15] I inspected it from the roof of this house. The vast column of black, ropy smoke that was rushing upward and then spreading over the heavens would have done no discredit to a second-class volcano. While I was writing (at nine tonight), I peered eastward out of the library window and saw a red glare that showed the conflagration still active. I put on my coat and

[14] The doughty Charles F. Chandler of Columbia, who had joined Egleston in establishing the School of Mines, and who became professor of chemistry in the college, was this year appointed president of the city's Board of Health by Mayor Havemeyer. He did magnificent work in stopping food adulteration, establishing tests for kerosene, attacking gas nuisances, improving plumbing, and in general lifting the city to a higher sanitary level. The Washington Market booths were destroyed under the personal supervision of Chandler in a rather daring coup.

[15] This fire in one of the great plants of the Standard Oil combination gave many New Yorkers their first understanding of the magnitude to which the oil industry had grown in fifteen years.

marched down Twenty-third Street to the East River. All the loaferism
of New York—male and female—seemed marching the same way, and the
Twenty-third Street dock or bulkhead swarmed with sweaty Teutons and
Irishmen and their womankind. To the north, the Hunter's Point ruins
still sent up a great column of dead black smoke, which hid the moon. Only
the base of the column "burned a still and awful red." A mile to the south
was another fire, and a large one, that seemed dying out. I could not learn
what it was. Some said that a "barge on fire" had drifted down there, but
the combustion was too extensive to be accounted for that way.

August 16.   John went to Long Branch this afternoon to confer with
Gerard the Venerable, who is a trustee of Gramercy Park. Mr. Ruggles
wants permission to put down a slab or tablet recording the fact that the
Park was founded or set apart by him at such a date some forty years
ago. . . .

Received from Matthews of Williamsburg, the binder, our little volume
of certificates of elections of wardens and vestrymen of Trinity Church since
1757, beautifully bound, with broad, tooled joints and silk linings and most
of its leaves extended. It is a fine piece of work, and Matthews's bill is
$100! What will our Committee of Supplies and Repairs say to that? I do
not think that any one of their number has the least appreciation of artistic
bibliopegy. But a prettier job was never turned out by an American bind-
ery, and few volumes of records belonging to any New York corporate
body deserve honorable clothing more than this. The old coarse brown
paper covers are preserved, as I directed, as is also Bishop Hobart's
memorandum, "these pages added . . . 1830, J. H. Hobart, Rector." This
little volume has been produced at every Easter election for twenty-five
years, according to my own observation and, in fact, for nearly a century
and a quarter. It was dilapidated and disintegrated, and in the spring of
1861 I asked the vestry to have it bound, and my prayer was granted. But
then came Sumter and Bull Run and the war, and trifles like this were
forgotten. Last spring I conferred with Morgan Dix, and I carried into
effect the resolution of twelve years ago. It is now the most "covetable"
little volume I have seen for years.

News from Spain is obscure but interesting. Strictly speaking, there is
no Spain just at present. Spain's place on the map is occupied by an incoherent aggregate of mobs, or clans (minus chieftains and fidelity) calling
themselves "local governments," and (at Seville, Grenada, and other
places) playing pranks which (if the newspapers tell the truth) are worthy
of hogs, he-goats, and hyenas. After all our brag about modern civilization,

it is capable of decomposing at any moment into anarchy, barbarism, and diabolism.

August 19. . . . Died old Mrs. Peter G. Stuyvesant at eighty-four. Also, the Rev. Gardiner Spring at eighty-nine. What a cool, gentleman-like, thorough old Turk of a blue Presbyterian he was! He should have been a minister in New England or in Scotland a century and a half ago.[16] His militant orthodoxy and love of ecclesiastical discipline would then have had room for development. It's said, and on good authority, that a young daughter of his many years ago was induced by some of her young friends to go with them to the Park Theatre on the sly. When she came home, her stern parent opened the street door for her in silence. Her escapade was not mentioned till the next "Sabbath morning" exercises at the old Brick Meet'n House, and then at the stage appropriated for announcements from the pulpit, the young lady heard her father proclaim that "Eliza Spring, having recently visited one of those profane and sinful places of carnal recreation, commonly called theatres, is hereby cut off from the communion of the Church of Christ. We will now sing to the praise and glory of God the —— Psalm, Common metre." If this be not true, it is well invented. I well remember the grand fight this resolute old Calvinist made against the Unitarian Wolcott Gibbs's election as professor of chemistry in Columbia College nearly twenty years ago. It was then very apparent that if the Rev. Spring could have had his own way, he would have treated Wolcott Gibbs as Calvin and the Genevan magistrates treated Servetus. He married a few years since for his second wife an ancient damsel, rich in the world's goods and daughter of the once famous Elisha Williams. They soon fell out and fell apart and she died a few days before her husband.

August 26. . . . Called on by some man who wanted me to buy the musical library of the "Harmonic Society" for $5,000, which investment I declined. He told me that the Harmonic Society and the Mendelssohn Union have severally disbanded. Their place will be filled by an "oratorio society" which Dr. [Leopold] Damrosch is organizing. I must soon take up the papers of the Church Music Association and try to fill up its subscription list. . . .

[16] See the second volume of this diary for references to Spring and his conservative position among the Columbia trustees. A powerful preacher and stern-spirited Calvinist, he had gained a commanding influence in New York. He was seventy-five years old in 1860. But since then he had brought the Old School Presbyterian Assembly into line for the Union, buried his first wife (mother of fifteen children) and married a second, published two volumes of *Personal Reminiscences*, and fought successfully for the reunion of the Old School and New School Presbyterians.

Yesterday morning I found myself evicted from my Fulton Street quarters by certain Philistines with ladders and paint pots. So I fled to Central Park and spent most of the clear, cool day there roaming about, lunching frugally at the Casino, visiting the "Belvidere" and the dairy and inspecting the animals. No man can look at a menagerie without the dim, awful perception of a great mystery. The same feeling is excited by the view of a case of stuffed birds or an entomological cabinet, but not so strongly as when you watch, for example, the cruel eyes of some living leopard or tiger, the kindly expression of some of the antelopes, the uncouth honest craving for human sympathy and affection manifested by some little black bear, or the cold-blooded cruelty embodied in the hideous form of a sleeping alligator ten feet long. The animal creation is a mystery of mysteries. . . .

August 28. . . . General B. F. Butler is stumping Massachusetts for the Republican nomination as governor with his usual audacity, impudence, and smartness. Pity he is so extremely disreputable, for he did the country good service at Baltimore and New Orleans. Defalcation in Brooklyn City treasury in which E. S. Mills, deceased, is somehow implicated. His estate is said to prove insolvent.

Alleged fusion in France of Legitimists and Orleanists. Count de Chambord, being without issue or prospect of any, to reign for life, with remainder to the Comte de Paris. A sensible programme, but Imperialists and Republicans will have somewhat to say about it.

August 30. . . . Very curious ultramontane or obscurantist reaction in rural France, with mediaeval miracles and pilgrimages. . . .

September 2. Life and Trust Company meeting at one this afternoon. Then I had a few hours to kill before keeping an appointment with Murray Hoffman, Jr. Crossed the Fulton Ferry to inspect the towers of the future (possible) suspension bridge. That on the Brooklyn side has attained two thirds of its height and is "conspicuous from afar." Its New York brother is about one-half as high. . . .[17]

September 16. . . . Father Farrell's Roman Catholic parochial school of St. Peter's on Barclay Street is giving trouble as expected. As our Trinity Church school children were peacefully marching this morning from Trinity Church to our parish school, they were set upon by some hundred of Farrell's Celtic lambs, stoned, punished, and maltreated. One or two escaped sorely hurt, their heads bathed in blood. This won't do. If we are to have a holy war downtown—a "children's crusade"—we may as well

[17] The bridge, designed in 1867 by John A. Roebling, was completed in 1883 by his son Washington. Its granite towers rise 272 feet above mean high water.

know it at once and take measures accordingly. We can to some extent
rely on the secular arm of the police. It looks a little as if these politic
shavelings might have quartered themselves and their infant Ribbonmen
and Whiteboys next door to us for the express purpose of frightening and
bullying our "Prodesan" children (so-called) from attending our school.
This may lead to a very pretty row and controversy.

September 18.   Going into Wall Street, I found crowds standing about
and general excitement. The great house of Jay Cooke & Company, with
its affiliations and auxiliaries, had hauled down its flag; so had Robinson
& Suydam—also Richard Schell. Their example will probably be followed
by many others tomorrow, and this may prove preliminary to the general
smash that must come before long. One or two gentlemen who looked as if
they came from the country and who probably had monies on deposit with
these collapsed bankers were walking about in an aimless sort of way and
talking loud to nobody in particular about "d——d infernal swindlers and
thieves." . . .

September 19.   Panic grows in Wall Street, "the hubbub multiplies,"
and indications are graver than at any crisis since 1857. The street (seen
from Broadway) was a compact mosaic of shiny umbrellas, like a bed of
mushrooms. Many notable speculators have suspended, among them Fisk
& Hatch, reputed impregnably strong. There is a run on the Union Trust
Company (Broadway and Rector Street), and another on the Fourth
National Bank, and things look squally. The failure of these great stock-
gambling concerns would be a public benefit but for its probable damage to
so many honest businessmen. All this may be a mere flurry, or may be
much more.

September 20.   To Wall Street. Nervous excitement seemed less, but
bank officers and everybody said things were going from bad to worse, and
the air was filled with prophesyings of woe. By twelve o'clock the Bank of
the Commonwealth and the Union Trust Company had stopped, and the
Stock Exchange had closed its doors. A wise measure, and would they
might never be reopened. The secretary of the Union Trust Company,
Carleton, son of a Methodist divine, is said to have vanished into Faery
Land, like King Arthur, with $250,000 of the company's assets. A run on
the 'Fourth National Bank continues unabated and seems resolutely met.
The tellers at most of the Wall Street banks seemed to be kept very busy.
At the Bank of America were more depositors than drawers. At the Me-
chanics' Banking Association, an ominous preponderance of the latter. That
concern, the Continental and the Bank of North America, are considered

shaky. The central focus of excitement was, of course, at the corner of Broad and Wall streets. People swarmed on the Treasury steps looking down on the seething mob that filled Broad Street. There was a secondary focus at Cedar and Nassau streets where folks were staring at the closed doors of the Bank of Commonwealth and at the steady current of depositors flowing into the Fourth National and then flowing out again with an expression of relief.

In Wall Street again after lunch and at the Fifth Avenue Hotel this evening. The National Trust Company . . . has stopped. Comparatively small failures are many. All this looks ill for my Minnesota Railroad bonds, wherein I was seduced to invest by——, and very ill for the nascent Church Music Association subscription list.

September 22.   In Wall Street awhile at noon. Crowd still abnormal but less feverish than it was last week. A run on the Fourth National Bank is rather tending to dry up. Stock Exchange still judiciously closed, giving brokers time to pick up their wits and cool off. Bank people, Palmer, and others thought the prognosis favorable; so it has continued. The worst is probably over, unless some new explosion take place to "fright the street from her propriety," and rekindle panic. But the next few days will be anxious. . . .

September 23.   Wall Street affairs improve, and I think the fire is got under, though Henry Clews collapsed this afternoon. Left Fulton Street early. . . . To Bleecker Street Bank for Savings; great crowd. Chiefly Italian and Irish depositors. Up to three o'clock about $125,000 was drawn out, but we can stand a drain at that rate for four weeks at least without sacrificing securities or requiring notice of drafts. Nearly all our savings banks have fallen back upon that rule and pay only in small sums to depositors who declare they need their money. . . .

September 24.   Relapse in Wall Street. Clews's failure yesterday did mischief, and so did that of Howes & Macy this morning. The street was not excited but faint, sick, prostrate, and resigned to the approach of some great indefinite calamity. My inquiries were answered: "Things look black"; "About as bad as they can look"; "No use trying to do anything," and so on. But the evening papers announce no new catastrophes, and the crowd at the Fifth Avenue Hotel this evening looked comparatively bright.

Diocesan convention at St. John's this morning. My colleagues, S. P. Nash and the Hon. [John A.] Dix, did not attend. Discoursed with Charles Swords, the Rev. Morgan Dix, Hamilton Fish, the Bishop, and others. . . . Some little routine business was done.

The great boom which followed the Civil War had ended. Ever since the failure of the Atlantic Bank the previous April, the atmosphere had been uneasy. On September 8 the New York Warehouse & Security Company suspended; Kenyon, Cox & Co., in which Daniel Drew was a partner, failed on the 13th; on the 18th Jay Cooke & Co. went down, and on the 19th Fisk & Hatch. Men had looked upon Jay Cooke's house as a financial Gibraltar. It had done more than any other agency to market the nation's securities during the Civil War, and was currently building the Northern Pacific Railroad. The panic on the Stock Exchange became so severe that before noon on the 20th its governing committee closed it for ten days. Bankruptcies became the staple of news, factories and mills shut down, railway construction stopped, and business fell to a low ebb. On the heels of the panic came a great depression, destined to last for six years— years of unemployment, widespread poverty, grave labor disturbances, and radical political movements.

At first the people called the panic "a Wall Street affair" and poured denunciation on the heads of stockbrokers and railway speculators. It soon became evident, however, that its roots went deep into the national and international situation. Over-expansion in the building of iron mills and factories in various Western lands; too rapid extension of the railway systems of Europe, the United States, and Argentina; the dislocation of trade by the new Suez Canal; the heavy losses in the Chicago and Boston fires; and above all, the cumulative evil effects of the American Civil War, the Franco-Prussian War, and other conflicts, were among the principal causes of the crisis. In Europe and America alike the speculative boom had gone to excessive lengths. On both continents banks had lent money too wildly and brokerage houses had marketed securities recklessly. A battle at once developed in Washington between inflationists and conservatives, Grant after some hesitation taking his stand with the latter. And in the era of deflation and retrenchment which now opened, an appalling list of governmental and business scandals was exposed to the public sight. Strong could be thankful for his $6,000 salary.

September 26, FRIDAY. Business active at No. 187. We must borrow $25,000 at least to carry us over November 1, and it may be hard to do it in these times. If we cannot do it, I must try to prevail on our Rector and assistant ministers to receive their salaries on the "truck system"—namely, in hassocks, surplices, prayerbooks, and the like. It is fearful to think of the vestry office besieged, and me, the comptroller, rent limb from limb by a mob of hungry and furious presbyters, deacons, organists, sextons, Sunday School teachers, and female annuitants. *Spero meliora.*

Wall Street is very quiet. No mob there and none in Broad Street or Nassau Street. Closing the Stock Exchange acts as an anaesthetic and suspends our financial convulsions. But the community cannot be kept under chloroform indefinitely.

September 27. . . . All quiet along the Broad Street sidewalks. Affairs unchanged. . . . How to move the crops is becoming a grave question. Banks are suspending throughout the land. If Trinity Church suspend, I shall be gibbeted in church history as the Romulus Augustulus of comptrollers.

September 30. . . . Most admirable sermon (published) before the alumni of the Theological Seminary by Morgan Dix. Nobody treats of Catholicism as contrasted with Romanism and with Protestantism half so clearly, forcibly, and lovingly. But there are expressions in this sermon that can be sorely misrepresented by those who wish to misunderstand and misrepresent them.

October 2. . . . Strange to say, currency is at a premium of 2 or 3 per cent. The banks pay no large checks but certify them. So he who *must* have greenbacks to any considerable amount goes to a broker with his certified check and buys them as he would buy gold. Queer, anomalous, and all wrong.

Saw Shepherd Knapp of the Mechanics Bank, who says Trinity Church shall have all the "accommodation" necessary to keep her afloat till the November rents come in. He thinks everything is serene. But Skidmore this evening prophesies hard times all winter. If not too hard, they will do us good.

October 4. . . . An "evangelical" happy family is in session here. Specimens of diverse and hostile genera and species of Protestantism waiving their mutual hates for a season and meeting under a flag of truce for the sake of a grand international talking match. There seems a "revival" of religious activity just now, notably in France, where . . . pilgrimages (of a nineteenth century type) are fashionable once more, with parlor-car pilgrims, second-class pilgrims, smoking-car pilgrims, deadhead pilgrims, and the reporters. No doubt a reaction against Communism and archiepiscopocide; and so far good.

October 6. Renovation of St. Paul's interior all but finished. It is a great improvement. . . . Columbia College trustees met this afternoon at the old Schermerhorn Great Jones Street palazzo. How odd it is that our clerk should happen to be blind, our president deaf, and our treasurer dumb (Teutonice, *dumm*). The fact is symbolical of our corporate character. Our members, myself included, are somehow assimilated to these chief vital organs and made like them. . . . We are all fogies, dullards, and fainéants together, and I see no help for it. . . .

Petition received this afternoon from a half-dozen strong-minded young ladies, chaperoned by the strong-minded "Mrs. Lillie Devereux Blake," for admission to the College classes. To my surprise, the Rev. Haight thought the petition should be respectfully considered, so it was referred to some fossil committee or other. The mere suggestion of young ladies among our Freshmen and of "sweet girl-graduates" on the stage at commencement shocks all my conservative instincts, but I cannot shut my eyes to considerations in its favor, strange as the innovation would be. Morgan Dix, by the by, says that the school of the Sisters of St. Mary finds great favor with the "strong-minded" womankind, because the "Sisters" carry out the theory of "women's rights" in doing their noble work thoroughly and well without masculine aid. This Mrs. L. D. Blake has a couple of pretty little daughters under their care. Poor old Horace Greeley's Miss Gabrielle is another of their pupils and is said to be extremely clever and nice. These young ladies submit kindly to the influences of the church. Some of them have a special talent for caricature and caricature everybody —the "Sisters" included (not so very difficult).

October 8.   Clear, cold morning, but rapidly moderating. The bloated corporation of Trinity Church got a note for $20,000 at thirty days "done" at Mechanics Bank, and was thankful for the favor. It is walking in dry places just now seeking rents and finding none, or but few, and payments on account. There will be hard times this winter. . . .

October 10. . . . Talked of the savings bank with John C. Green and finance in general with him and with Palmer of the Leather Manufacturers Bank. They think our troubles not quite over yet. Gold is down to eight and a fraction today, its lowest point for some twelve years.

Mr. Ruggles looked in on me in Fulton Street, and I exhibited to him the renovated interior of St. Paul's. He was in the best spirits, but I regret to say that he looked much thinner and older than when I last saw him in June just before he went to Delhi and fearfully changed from what he was a year ago. His brilliancy and geniality survive, in his brighter moments at least, but he is manifestly infirm and old. *Eheu*, what a loss that will be!

October 17.   Professor Van Amringe called to talk of a proposed incorporation of Columbia College alumni, with a view to the possible future concession to them of some share in the government of the College, and wanted me to be chairman of a committee. . . . I told him I would heartily give my best aid and counsel to any such movement, but that I could do so far more efficiently if I were not on the committee or in any way identified with the undertaking. Any change in the College government can hardly fail to be an improvement. . . .

October 21. Sale of Philharmonic boxes at the Academy of Music this afternoon. They brought panic prices, and many were left unsold. An additional $300 for the Church Music Association came in this morning, and "we may be happy yet." It would be a great pity to let so fine and well-trained a chorus disperse. . . . His Lordship [the Bishop] of Zanzibar attended [chorus rehearsal] and was interested. He discoursed with me during the interval (a pause for refreshment and respiration), and I found him most amiable.

October 27. . . . Wall Street continues in feverish, nervous malaise. Its pulse keeps going up to 120 under hourly rumors of defalcation in this or that great corporation, railroad, or others. Faith in financial agents is gone. Every treasurer and cashier is "suspect," and no wonder after the recent epidemic of fraud. The anticipated resumption of silver specie payments seems indefinitely postponed. Factories and employers throughout the country are discharging hands, working half time, or reducing wages. There is a prospect of a hard, blue winter. We read in the papers of a "shrinkage of values," but I see no sign of it in the bills I have to pay. Heaven help me!

October 29. . . . Visit from an infuriated lover of harmony, protesting against gross fraud in the sale of Philharmonic seats at Heuser's music shop. He proposed writing to all the newspapers and calling an indignation meeting, in which purposes I subtly encouraged him under the semblance of soothing his angry passions. . . . The more fuss about this swindle the better. Schirmer and Heuser both have acted most dishonestly and scandalously and in direct violation of their instructions. . . .

Guns are firing an accompaniment to some grand ratification meeting somewhere. But the political campaign is sleepy and apathetic, and the city registration is 25,000 short. This points to a "Democratic" victory, and the present financial distress, moreover, will tell against Administration candidates. Prospects for the coming winter look darker and darker.

October 30. . . . The great manufacturing house of the Rhode Island Spragues went down today, throwing an army of operatives out of employ-

ment. This will have consequences.[18] Taintor is convicted. His defense—
namely, that his president and directors were *particeps criminis*—was
promptly ruled out. Stokes's third trial results in a verdict of manslaughter
and a sentence of four years at Sing Sing.

"General" Wade Hampton makes a great speech at Richmond and says
the South is now where Prussia was after Jena, and that as Prussia speedily
broke her chains and smote her tyrants so will Secessia be avenged of her
enemies, both nigger and Yankee, "the blacks and their blacker allies."
It seems impossible to whip the brag out of these Gascons.

October 31.   First Philharmonic rehearsal at two-thirty; a tolerable
house. . . . Beethoven's Fourth Symphony, Max Bruch's Introduction to
Lorelei, and Liszt's "Preludes."

November 3.   Columbia College trustees met this afternoon. Not much
done. Reconsidered the reference to a committee of the application of certain young ladies to be admitted as students and unanimously agreed to
decline the honor. Barnard's proposition to enlarge the School of Mines
building (150 students now!!) was referred to the Committee on the Site,
and the question of sending a representative to see that the coming transit
of Venus is in all respects regular and decorous was similarly disposed of.
Admiral Sands and other Washington magnates wish us to do this, and it
will be a scandal to leave it undone. But what can be expected from our
board? . . .

Wall Street feels better. The Spragues (of Rhode Island) show a good
list of assets, though it does include certain "cats and dogs," and Claflin's
house is plucky still. It's notable that the five-penny and six-penny fares
on our street railroads have fallen off a third. There is an example of
retrenchment for me to follow. . . .

November 4, TUESDAY.   As it is a "legal holiday," my office did not
open. I voted. Looked in at the great Barnum show. Infinite claptrap, but
many of the animals are fine specimens, and the menagerie is worth
visiting. Barnum's shewbills, by the by, present a life-sized portrait of him
as Phoenix T. Barnum, with a pair of wings appended to his shoulders. . . .

November 5.   As I expected, there are anti-Administration gains and
victories, East and West. The New York *World* is jubilant. As Dr.

[18] Senator William Sprague, who had married Salmon P. Chase's beautiful daughter
Kate, was the most prominent figure in the textile manufacturing business founded by
his grandfather of the same name. The failure of the A. & W. Sprague Manufacturing
Co. involved about $20,000,000, and reduced the Sprague fortune to a mere remnant.

Johnson would have said, "This merriment of Democrats is mighty offensive." But the absolute Democratic gain is small, if there be any. Republicans have stayed at home disgusted, reasonably or not, and left the country to take care of itself.

Had a talk with the Rev. Haight about vacancies on the College board created by the death of good old Dr. Torrey and the Rev. Spring, especially the Rev. Spring. I vote for no Presbyterian preacher-man as trustee. . . .

November 7.   Gold is 106¼. We seem not far from specie payments. . . .

Times grow harder and harder. I think our Church Music Association concerts must be given up.

The Republican defeat is a Flodden or Bull Run. But it may scare that party into better behavior and so prove a blessing in disguise.

Died, old General Delafield, DeRham *père*, the fair Miss Laura Keene, Gaylord Clark, and at Boston, C. A. Lombard.[19] DeRham, they say, left his native Switzerland as plain Mr. Rham, but after arriving in New York, adopted a prefix as being euphonious and genteel. He always looked, though, like an old marquis of the Ancient Regime. Gaylord Clark was for many years editor of the old *Knickerbocker* magazine and was the most refined and genial of our American humorists, though not so strong in the grotesque as John Phoenix, Artemus Ward, and Orpheus C. Kerr.

November 10. . . . Vestry meeting tonight. Read comptroller's annual report. Morgan Dix nominated to the vacancy at St. Paul's the Rev. Mr. Mulchahey of Ohio, a most bog-trotting, potato-munching, whiskey-drinking, "dudeen-shoughing," shillelah-brandishing name. But the gentleman is highly spoken of. Publication of the Rector's proposed annual "Manual of Trinity Parish" was informally approved. All my motions and recommendations were adopted good-naturedly and *nem. con.* My "bosses" of the vestry certainly treat me very kindly indeed.

This afternoon, the Rev. Cooke, Horsley, Gerard, Stephens, and I took counsel together at my office in re The Church Music Association. Edmund Schermerhorn couldn't come but sent me a kind note full of timidities and nervousness. The question we had to consider was whether

[19] Richard Delafield (1798–1873) had twice been superintendent at West Point and from April, 1864, to his retirement in August, 1866, chief of the Army Engineer Corps; Laura Keene (c. 1826–1873), the beautiful English-born actress, had great comic talent, and will long be remembered as chief actress in *Our American Cousin* the night Lincoln was murdered.

the Church Music Association should be dropped and left to perish and its chorus disbanded, or should be kept alive by another "season" of concerts. When we came together, the Church Music Association was in imminent peril of dissolution. I was disinclined to undertake the pecuniary risk of running it, and Ben Stephens was of the same mind. But it appeared that our subscriptions suffice to carry us through the season with strict economy. Probably the "shrinkage of values" will enable us to secure our soli and others, possibly even our orchestra, at reduced prices. There is a chance that some of our subscribers may repudiate. If so, we shall know it when the first instalment is called in, and we must then issue a circular to our honest and solvent subscribers, tell them why we can give but one concert or two (as the case may be), report to them the names of the defaulters, and return to them whatever little dividend may be left of their respective subscriptions. . . . I hope I shall not be saddled with another deficit.

November 13. . . . Great wrath over the capture of the *Virginius* and the summary execution of her filibustering crew by Cuban volunteers. "A speck of war."[20] Strange we should be nearly ready to make war on Spain for the summary execution of people who were proceeding to Cuba with homicidal intent and who went forth taking their lives in their hands. For only last Tuesday a pretty girl of seventeen, a couple of children, and a half-dozen poor laboring men, all pursuing their lawful avocations on the public highway, were massacred by the engineer of a steam hoisting machine at Harlem without notice, without provocation, and without even the formality of a drumhead court-martial. And nobody seems indignant or excited over this butchery.

November 15. Philharmonic concert this evening. . . . The house was very full. It would be indiscreet to enquire what was the percentage of deadheads. I gave away some half dozen boxes, thereby, I think, gratifying sundry nice people. Concert was delightful. . . .

Naval preparations are active. Gold rises from 107 to 110. If war

---

[20] American indignation over the *Virginius* affair was not, as Strong at first supposed, exaggerated. The filibustering vessel was captured by a Spanish gunboat, taken into Santiago harbor, and held there. Her crew of Americans and Britons were landed, and without proper trial fifty-three of them were shot. It was doubtful whether the Spaniards had any right to capture a vessel flying the American flag when on the high seas. Certainly they had no right to shoot the captured Americans as if they had been pirates; they were at worst prisoners of war. The British warship *Niobe* hastily steamed into Santiago harbor and forbade further executions. Only Secretary Fish's astute management of the crisis prevented war.

come, we shall probably gobble up Cuba at last, and what should we do with it? We certainly do not want these bloodthirsty little blackmuzzled Cubans as fellow citizens. As well annex and try to adopt and assimilate a large nest of lively black and yellow hornets. . . .

Mr. Ruggles was at the concert this evening. I talked with him during the entr'acte. I fear infirmity is gaining on him. He is five years older than he was six months ago.

November 17.   Work at the Navy Yard is lively. A Spanish war is not improbable. The slogan of "Free Cuba" would rally many waverers around the Administration flag, where they are wanted in time for the next election. Waiving the technical questions raised by the capture of the *Virginius* under American colors on the high seas, there have been wars on slighter provocation than ours. Alva's style of work is so obsolete as to have become offensive, and one doesn't want a slaughterhouse set up next door and under his very nose. Poland had to be abated as a nuisance, and Cuba may require the same treatment.

November 19.   Everyone expected Boss Tweed's jury to disagree— they were out so long—but they brought that scoundrel in guilty this morning; thank Heaven. Sentence is postponed till Friday. Pity he can't be hanged. But he'll get a new trial, I suppose, and probably get off altogether, the rank, old felonious dog-fox!

War-jaw is still loud in all the newspapers.

November 21.   Most belligerent despatch from Madrid. Our blameless representative there (the delectable Dan Sickles) has been threatened by a mob of truculent Jack Spaniards. Between the Carlists and the *Intransigentes* and the ignorant, arrogant, savage plebs of Spain, the Republican chiefs are in a tight place. Having two civil wars on their hands already, they want nothing less than a foreign war besides. But any concession to us may raise a storm that would blow their heads off. The greatest activity continues at our Navy Yards, and a rather formidable fleet will soon be ready for business. God avert war! I have seen quite enough of war times to last me my life.

November 22.   Boss Tweed the *Meister-Dieb* sentenced to twelve years and a moderate fine. Good as far as it goes.[21]

[21] This was Tweed's second criminal trial. The sentence was to twelve years in prison and a fine of $12,750; but the court of appeals shortly reduced the sentence to a year and a fine of $250! Thus Tweed was enabled to leave Blackwell's Island penitentiary in January, 1875. But he had other gauntlets to run, and finally died in the Ludlow Street jail (1878).

Active preparations for war continue, including measures for harbor defense—New York harbor included—mounting heavy guns and setting torpedoes. These proceedings bring the impending trouble home to us. A squadron of hostile ironclads anchored off the Battery and swarms of black Spanish spiders roaming up and down Broadway demanding your garlic or your life, would be annoying.

Visit this morning from Gracie King and William H. Macy on behalf of the joint Committee of Savings Banks. They were most kindly urgent that I go to Washington next month and argue the savings banks case in which I had prepared the brief of plaintiffs in error just before I evacuated Wall Street a year ago. They had taken the trouble to call on Cisco, Nash, Palmer, and others to ask that no objection to my going would be interposed by the vestry, and they were assured there would be none. This strong preference of theirs is unaccountable, by the by. I told them I couldn't do it, and I won't. In the first place, there are at least two habitual growlers in the vestry who would whisper, "We pay Strong a salary for looking after our affairs. What right has he to go off for a week on a money-making, professional job?" And I don't clearly see the answer to that query. Then the case would be sure to be reached on the last day of the month, or the second Monday of the month, when I must be here, for Dunscomb, the other warden, cannot attend a vestry meeting. Moreover, my case would be defeated. The bill of exceptions is bungled and defective, and judgment below must be affirmed, I think, though its practical effect is most inequitable.

November 25. . . . In the evening at the Rev. Mr. Bellows's, where we had a meeting as of the olden time. There were Van Buren, Newberry, Agnew, Blatchford, and Stillé of Philadelphia. We are trying to close up the Sanitary Commission affairs at last, and I must get up a treasurer's report covering receipts and payments of some years past—a great bore. Fortunate that Lathrop is in my office.

The Cuban fever is going down a little. The war dance of the editorial corps grows less maenadic.

November 26. In Wall Street awhile. It has suddenly dawned on the Hon. B. R. Curtis that there is nothing to be said for defendants in error in that great savings bank case, and so he writes Charley Strong. I never advised the writ of error and have always been of the Hon. Curtis's opinion, except that I have thought that the inequitable operation of the act might be made so manifest that the court would try to nullify it.

Boss Tweed is still in the Tombs, "setting up his private affairs," but must soon be on Blackwell's Island, unless some bribed Supreme Court justice grant a stay of proceedings. Ingersoll is now on trial, a subordinate forger, swindler, and thief.

November 29. . . . Official report that Spain very genteelly agrees to surrender the *Virginius,* apologize, and so on. But it's said that the truculent Volunteers of Cuba will refuse to let the *Virginius* go and that they are mounting heavy guns for defense against Spaniard and Yankee alike.

Mr. Attorney-General Barlow writes to ask Mr. Sheriff Brennan why Boss Tweed still lingers in the Tombs and is not consigned to the penitentiary. Mr. Brennan replies that he is waiting for an "intimation" from Judge Davis or the district attorney. Mr. Barlow rejoins that the sentence might be considered a sufficient intimation to the sheriff of his official duty in the premises, and that if he, the sheriff don't do it rather promptly, the Governor will know the reason why. So Mr. Tweed was this afternoon translated from the Tombs to Blackwell's Island—the "Isle of Sinners"—cropped, shaved, washed, and arrayed in his penitential garment of many stripes. "For this and for all other mercies," and so on! Mr. Frank Taintor "goes up" to the Albany penitentiary for seven years; Ingersoll, the Ring forger, to Sing Sing for five. One of the Stokes's jurors is fined and imprisoned for misconduct during the trial. John Graham (Front-de-Brass) and his disciples, Fullerton and Bartlett, are reprimanded and fined by Judge Davis for their unprofessional and indecent attempt to bully him off the bench when he opened Tweed's trial. There is certainly an epizooty (why not epizoic?) among scamps and thieves and thieves' lawyers just now, and Judge Davis has justly earned much praise by his vigorous action against the crew.

December 1. Sad news from the great deep. The *Ville du Havre,* screw-steamer, which left this port on November 15, "collided" on November 23 at two in the morning with the iron ship *Loch Earn* and sank in twelve minutes. Some twenty passengers and fifty of the crew and officers were saved. About 200 passengers were lost.[22] Among these would seem to be Mrs. Herman Le Roy Edgar, and one of her two daughters (the other, Miss Cornelia, saved), Hamilton Murray, Mrs. A. Bininger, and sundry delegates returning home from the Evangelical Council of last fall. Few particulars as yet.

December 8. . . . Complications with Spain are not yet straightened out. "They look more serious than ever," says the last Washington

[22] The *Ville du Havre,* a splendid ship of the French line, collided squarely on a bright moonlight night with the sailing ship *Loch Earn,* which had the right of way.

despatch in the *Evening Post*. If the Lord permit us to drop a few regiments of hungry wild Mississippians and Arkansawyers on the Cuban coast, Santiago will have his saintly hands rather full.

The Rev. Bellows, who was a little under the weather when I last saw him, has broken down entirely and gone away for some months of leisure and recuperation. So his son tells me. . . .

December 12. . . . Philharmonic rehearsal this afternoon. Ellie was not well enough to attend. In my box were Temple, Mr. Ruggles, the Lord Bishop of Zanzibar, and, for a season, Carroll. Mr. Ruggles pumped national statistics into the Bishop during pauses. The Bishop seems genial and nice and says that the name of his first native convert was a mere monosyllable, but that he has been vainly trying to pronounce it for years. Sorry to see that Mr. Ruggles tended to doze off a little now and then while the music was going on. I fear that one of the most powerful and magnificent brains in the country has never recovered from the shock it suffered a year ago and probably never will.

December 15. . . . Died, at Cooperstown, without a minute's warning, the ancient Mr. Justice [Samuel] Nelson, late of the Supreme Court of the United States. His judicial career was long and most honorable. I feel grateful to his memory for sundry kind words of his, worth a good deal, coming from him. Died, also, Professor Agassiz last night after a brief paralytic seizure. My recollections of him are few but pleasant, especially pleasant that of an afternoon spent on the "sunken ledge" at Nahant at low water, when I learned more about marine polyps and the whole pecus of Proteus than ever before or since. He was a good man and strong against Darwinism. . . .[23]

Gouverneur Ogden tells me that his Committee on the College Site will report in favor of building at once on the uptown property, somewhere between Central Park and Albany. It is monstrous folly, but why should I "fash my thumb" about it, or get myself into a fidget over any blunder this stolid board may contemplate?

December 18. . . . Dined here the Right Rev. Tozer of Zanzibar, Morgan Dix, Mr. Ruggles (who was in the best of spirits but took leave before the ceremonies of deglutition were concluded), Dick, and nice Mr. and Mrs. Handcock. Johnny and Temple honored us with their presence. Session was agreeable and abundant in good talk. His Lordship is genial and cultivated and has seen much. His talk is of hippopotami; he enjoys

[23] Jean Louis Rodolphe Agassiz (b. 1807) had suffered an apoplectic seizure in 1869, but lectured as usual at the Harvard Museum of Comparative Zoölogy this fall.

a joke and seems a thoroughly nice person. They stayed pretty late, which looks as if they enjoyed themselves.

December 22. Columbia College trustees had a special meeting at two this afternoon to receive the report of the Committee on the Site. After many sessions and much debate, they had agreed on a report, but members of the committee "went back on it," and it went for nothing. There was an hour's prosing talk, and the committee was authorized to expend $150,000 on the present College buildings.

Mr. Harry Genet, a notable though subordinate and second-class Ring thief, was just convicted of forgery, has fled to parts unknown, and left the sheriff lamenting. For the sheriff, trusting the parole of his friend and congener, had allowed him freedom and opportunities of escape— altogether irregular—and is now expecting to be attacked for a contempt, indicted for a misdemeanor, and otherwise hatcheted and bedeviled. Messrs. "Mike" Norton, Coman, and Walsh seem also to have cut and run. They were among the minnows whose Triton was Tweed. Their bereaved bail are seeking them diligently but in vain.

The streets were never so crowded with Christmas shoppers. The interior of Tiffany's shop was jammed full this afternoon. Navigation on Broadway is impeded by the great raft of carriages before Stewart's store. All which looks unlike present pauperism, whatever it may point to as coming hereafter.

December 23. . . . To Trinity Church at three-thirty this afternoon for rehearsal of the Christmas service. All the music is from Mozart's Mass No. 1, except the offertory, Benedictus of Beethoven's in C, which seems cold when contrasted with the music of the most intense and brilliant of Mozart's Masses. Messiter has converted the gorgeous Quartette and Chorus of the Dona Pacem into an anthem. The exquisite Agnus Dei solo, which ought to immediately precede the superb Dona Pacem, was well rendered by one of our little boys. Singing against an orchestra frightened the child; his heart was in his mouth as he sang. . . .

December 24. . . . I saw the "Children's Service" and Christmas tree at Trinity Church at three this afternoon. A great crowd there. The Rector officiated with the Lord Bishop of Zanzibar and others. The procession of 500 children, with the bright banners of their classes and their little "guilds," singing as they marched, was very pretty. Trinity parish is a great institution. I grow more and more patriotic over it and feel more and more as some verger feels toward his grand old cathedral. Would that it made me as much better as it ought! Ellie was there, Jem, old Adam Norrie, Cook Rogers, and lots of people beside. The service was hearty and genial.

The small ruffians of the streets began to blow the trumpet in Zion at an early hour this morning. It's a tin trumpet, and its brayings are now rising and falling outside. I remember no Christmas eve when the outward and visible and audible signs of the Christmas feast have been more prominent. Only drawback is Ellie's depression. Her father and mother cannot dine here tomorrow. Both are well on in life and both seem failing. Mrs. Ruggles is now suffering from nephritic disease, which Ellie fears is formidable. . . .

December 26. Trinity Church is rather hard up, which is due mainly to unavoidable expenditures on that insatiable cemetery. Probably $100,000 will not pay for work hereafter to be done on 155th and 153rd streets. We are now paying for work on the Boulevard and on Tenth Avenue. I must look about for ways and means to provide for our monthly $15,000 of ordinary expenditure on January 1.

Everybody regards Oakey Hall's acquittal as equivalent to a verdict of not proven, but it was rather a verdict (right or wrong) of not guilty on the ground of imbecility. If he did not see that the preposterous vouchers he approved were fraudulent on their face, he was an idiot. The jury seems to have been charitable enough to think so.[24] I don't, for one. I cannot doubt that he knew what he was doing and conspired with Tweed and Company to swindle the city. That he got none of the money is likely enough. His corrupt inducement may well have been merely the implied promise of political promotion. He was to have been governor and that miserable John T. Hoffman President. But he has come very near joining his politic ally Tweed, the vanished King Arthur of their shattered Ring, for whom civic scoundrelism weeps and wails and looks out in vain.

December 27. . . . Caleb Cushing succeeds the virtuous Dan Sickles at Madrid.

December 30. Clear and tolerably cold. Trinity Church is hard up. After selling our last 5/20 ($10,000), we shall barely be able to meet our payments, and our receipts for the next following week will be but a trifle. I hope we may not die of atrophy before the February rents come in.

---

[24] The brassy A. Oakey Hall had conducted his own defense. He was utterly discredited; but he lived to spend active years in New York journalism, to get admitted to the English bar and practise in London courts, and to sue James Bryce for libel after Bryce published a chapter on the Tweed Ring in his *American Commonwealth.*

The vagabond *Virginius* has foundered on Frying Pan Shoals, off Cape Fear. A good riddance, but Cuba will swear she sank it on purpose.

December 31, WEDNESDAY. . . . The clock kindly given me by Mary at Christmas now ornaments the second landing on the stairs, just by the window, and it is a great acquisition. It is an old-fashioned Londoner, seven feet high, tells the day of the month and something about the moon, and tells the hours as if from a cathedral tower.

Governor Dix appointed Professor Dwight a commissioner of appeals. His acceptance would kill the Law School, but it is unlikely; not that he loves professional honor less, but money more.

God carry us well through A.D. 1874!

1874

———&———

*T*he bleak early months of 1874 were marked by demonstrations of the
unemployed in many cities, by a sharp struggle in Washington between
inflationists and anti-inflationists, and by largely futile efforts on the part of
businessmen to get the wheels of industry turning faster. Strong recorded in his
diary for January 8 that Union Square had been filled with a mob of laborers
demanding that the city find them work. "Why should not our horde of briefless
and poverty-stricken lawyers require the public to get up suits for their benefit
and relief?" he asked—for many fellow-attorneys were suffering severely. The
efforts of the inflationists to increase the stock of paper money at first met some
success, but when they pushed their movement too far, trying by a Finance Bill
to raise the amount of greenbacks to $400,000,000, with a corresponding
increase in National Bank bills, President Grant on April 29 met them with a
veto. For this act all "sound money" men enthusiastically praised him. Industrial
conditions continued bad, however, with general lack of confidence, a weak
market for goods, and a high bankruptcy rate. In the Middle West the Granger
movement for drastic state regulation of railroads succeeded in passing some
highly controversial laws; that of Wisconsin, signed in March, provoked much
protest in the East.

Strong was now admitting that Grant was a very poor President. His
efforts to get various unfit men into the Chief Justiceship, rendered vacant by the
death of Salmon P. Chase, disgusted the diarist. He named and then withdrew
Attorney-General George H. Williams, who was not only incompetent for the
post, but open to charges which affected his financial integrity. Strong dealt

[509]

with this misstep in emphatic language. It was "a nomination that should never have been made," he wrote; "Williams is a tenth-rate man." Then Grant startled the country by nominating for the Chief Justiceship none other than Caleb Cushing, a learned but crafty, erratic, and time-serving politician and jurist widely hated and generally distrusted. When Cushing's enemies showed that he had written in 1861 to "my dear friend" Jefferson Davis, recommending another friend to the Confederate President, this nomination was crushed. Grant then turned to Morrison R. Waite of Ohio, who as E. L. Godkin put it, was in the front rank of second-rate lawyers. The "moiety scandal" in the Treasury Department was laid bare early this year, showing that Ben Butler had used Secretary of the Treasury Richardson (a henchman of Butler's Massachusetts machine) to make large sums out of the government.

January 15, THURSDAY. . . . Died yesterday in Washington, Charley Bristed! His last letter to me not a fortnight ago, I think, spoke of his being unwell. . . . In spite of certain foibles and oddities, "Carl Benson" is a great loss. We have few such scholars, and nobody more honest of purpose and resolute in expression. Hatred of snobbery, and especially of Southern swagger and presumption, was one of his strong points. He was partial to me, and I infer from things I have heard of his saying that he strangely overestimated me, though he was somewhat disposed to criticize people sharply.[1]

January 16. . . . "O Cupid, king of gods and men," what have I heard today!!! First, from Gouverneur Ogden at lunch; second from Duncan, who had it as a matter of incontrovertible verity from Cisco; and third from Miss Mary Bostwick (who called to ask after poor Ellie) and had it from Mr. Tom Ogden—Morgan Dix is engaged to Miss Soutter, Mrs. Ned Bell's younger sister.[2]

January 17, SATURDAY. . . . To Philharmonic concert; only Temple, Johnny, and Louis, and a couple of Temple's and Johnny's musical pals in our box. There was a full house. The *Melusine* Overture was played, and a long piano concerto by Hanselt, performed by Mills, which was melodic but protracted. Schubert's "Fantaisie," orchestrated, is very

[1] Charles Astor Bristed, frequently mentioned heretofore, was not yet fifty-four. He had published several books in recent years, including *The Interference Theory of Government* (1867) and *On Some Exaggerations in Comparative Philology* (1873). A man of wealth and leisure, he had of late spent most of his time in Washington.

[2] Morgan Dix was to marry Emily W. Soutter, daughter of James T. Soutter, on June 3 of this year.

melodic and brilliant but excessively protracted and full of damnable iteration. Phrases so lovely are outraged and insulted by being rubbed into one over and over again. Then there was some Chopin played by Mills. Chopin is wholly beyond me. During the second part of the program, the Schumann symphony was played. Schumann's diction is masterly; pity he has nothing new to say.

Morgan Dix's engagement is the town talk. The fact rests not on Ned Bell's authority alone, but on that of the lady's brother; so I suppose it must be admitted. Opinions differ about it (if that be of any consequence). There are some who say "how very injudicious; disparity of age (twenty-three and forty-five). It will destroy his usefulness," and the like. Others dwell on his lonely life and his genial instincts, his fondness for young people and children, and so on. I prefer to side with the latter. The disparity of age is nothing. As to the young lady, I know that her sister, Mrs. Bell, is charming and kindly, with the special attractiveness that belongs to the best Southern women, or women of Southern descent. . . .

January 20. . . . Chang and Eng, the Siamese twins, died last week at their home in North Carolina, surrounded by their wives and children. One died of paralysis, it would seem, and the other, though in good health, survived but a couple of hours. Their physician, if they had any, did not venture on amputation, cutting the Mezentian bond. . . .

One Waite of Ohio nominated for chief justice, a respectable nobody. What has got into Grant?

January 22. . . . Standing Committee tonight. After our calendar was cleared off, Ogden suggested that I withdraw for a little, and when I returned, I was informed that the committee had agreed to recommend an increase of the comptroller's salary from $6,000 to $8,000 (very acceptable, Heaven knows!). I returned thanks and the committee "made compliment," and I said with great sincerity that I hoped the increase might take effect from a future day—say May 1—and not immediately. I had two reasons for this: first, we are hard up and in debt and shall be so till we get our May rents; and second, it's my business to oppose all increase of expenditure, and so I have been doing. Tonight, several applications were laid over indefinitely, on my suggestion, because we are short of funds. I thought that common fairness required me to apply the same principle in my own case, and also that I should be able to fight propositions for extravagant and improvident outlay more effectively hereafter if it were known to the vestry that I had demurred to a grant in my favor. But Cisco, Skidmore, Arnold, and others "shut me up," said I had nothing to do with it, and insisted on their recommendation that the increase take effect from the first of January. I have to thank Gouverneur Ogden for this. He undertook the measure without the slightest suggestion from me, and has been extremely kind and unselfish about it.

Waite is confirmed as chief justice. "Now God be with him," saith Uncle Sam; "since better mote not be. But I think we have in this our realm five hundred good as he." Waite may make his mark yet, however. . . .

January 23. . . . Died at London, Mme. Parepa Rosa, a magnificent singer and greatest in the best music—Handel, Haydn, and Mozart.

January 24. Orders were sent out from police headquarters last night to all the station houses that the police keep an eye on the churches. The German and French Communists or "free-thinkers" (calling themselves unemployed workmen) were said to have designs on them. We were called upon this morning at No. 187 by policemen enquiring about St. Paul's and Trinity.

January 26, MONDAY. . . . Trinity Church has become, not exactly a den of thieves, but a "fence" or receptacle of stolen goods. A certain young man . . . has long been a devout and punctual worshipper there, and specially edifying in his outward demonstrations of reverence. . . . Saturday, he asked Augustus Meurer, the sexton, to lock up a little satchel or traveling bag for him till he should call for it. Yesterday, a detective intervened and requested Augustus to submit the same to his inspection. It was found to contain about $1,000 worth of jewelry, burglariously abstracted from the safe of the youthful saint's former employer, and the saint was incarcerated. . . .

February 6. A Philharmonic rehearsal tonight. In the Strong box were Temple and Louis, Rosalie, Miss Sarah Lazarus, and Dick. He returned this morning from Cleveland, where he "stood up with" Col. John Hay, who has married a Miss Stone.[3]

February 7. . . . Edwin Booth has gone into bankruptcy (!!!), whither I must expect to follow him. But I hear vague and second-hand rumors concerning "Minnesota." It will certainly begin paying up "next summer," which is, being interpreted, at the Greek Kalends. Such is Mr. Ruggles's report.

[3] Hay married Clara Stone, daughter of Amasa Stone, railway builder and for a time managing head of the Lake Shore & Michigan Southern.

February 9. Vestry meeting tonight was brief. I retired and was promoted from six (thousand) to eight (thousand), *nem. con.* I am very much obliged. Cisco, by the by, though a very good friend of mine, grows more and more arrogant and censorious, and finds fault with everything and everybody. . . .

Died, Saturday evening, old James W. Gerard. He had been failing for at least a year. In spite of much flippancy and a profusion of bad jokes, he used to be a most dangerous antagonist, especially before a jury. As a low comedian, he would have rivaled the late Mr. Burton, but he was a learned lawyer and a potent advocate, nevertheless. He loved music with all his heart and was among its chief patrons and promoters here thirty years ago. But his zeal was not always according to knowledge—witness his frequent strident ejaculations: "Ah, bravo, bravo, very fine, very fine indeed; brav-iss-i-mo! Bra-a-ah! Extremely staccato!" Witness also his fatal liberality to organ-grinders, so often productive of torture to other residents on Gramercy Park. He was thoroughly public-spirited. Even before he left the bar (in 1868), he was active and useful in public school affairs and in other civic matters, and to him, I believe, we are indebted for valuable improvements in the police department.[4] In all this work he sought neither place nor profit, nor even notoriety or distinction, but the general good alone. Strange that so honest and sagacious a man should have gone so far astray during the war. But he is entitled to be forgiven that one grave error.

February 11. . . . Died yesterday at Rome, Mrs. Arabella Mott, wife of Dr. Aleck B. Mott, much to be regretted. That pestilent Roman fever, I suppose. The lady was always nice to me, though she had a sharp tongue. . . .

Last night's Church Music Association concert went off well. The house was full and good-natured. It seemed to like parts of the Schumann Mass. I am glad to have heard the last of that leaden work. Weber's Jubel Overture and Gade's "Erl-König's Tochter" were delightful, of course.

February 13. Philharmonic rehearsal at two-thirty this afternoon. In my box were Rosalie, Mrs. Newman (who was Miss Ellen Rogers), Mrs. DeNeufville, Mrs. Harry Parker, Charles Carroll, and Temple.

---

[4] James W. Gerard, eighty years old at the time of his death, had been not only one of the best lawyers of the city, but an unwearied worker to aid juvenile delinquents and paupers, and (as school trustee and school inspector) a vigorous advocate of better education.

Wieniawski did a brilliant and beautiful Mendelssohn concerto, and a dry, hard, scrapy something by Bach. Then a director's meeting. The projected performance of Beethoven's Ninth Symphony with the Church Music Association chorus seems likely to fall through. The two hundred members of that chorus want two reserved seats each. We have not a quarter of that number to give them. Were this difficulty got over, two of the directors (at least) are unwilling to give the Ninth Symphony at all. It will involve expenses, and they think, moreover, that the Church Music Association chorus cannot do it. Possibly they are right. . . .

February 17. Spent last evening at the rectory on Twenty-fifth Street at a "reception" for the Rev. Mulchahey (a nice person, it would seem). Present were the Bishop, a dozen of the vestry, and a half-dozen of the clergy of the parish. O how slow it was!

Died, at two-thirty in the afternoon on Sunday, Dunscomb, aged eighty-six. He was taken ill on Friday and retained consciousness, though without speech, till Sunday morning. He had belonged to Trinity Church vestry as vestryman, warden, clerk, and comptroller for forty-four years but had been unable to attend a meeting since December, 1872. He was, I think, the most impenetrably dense, wooden, and stolid old gentleman I ever knew, but he was painstaking and thoroughly honest and served Trinity Church faithfully and did his duty doggedly, according to the very best of his perception and judgment. More can be said of no man. I wish one-tenth as much could be said of me. As I am now sole warden, the capacity of the vestry to meet and transact business depends on my life; so I have called a meeting for Thursday to fill the vacancy. I tell the Rector that my precious life should be watched and protected night and day till Thursday by a powerful bodyguard of sextons and lay visitors. After Thursday, I shall relapse into my original insignificance.

Bristed leaves his "adopted" daughter, Miss Cecile, the income of $41,000. That rather odd and self-willed young lady has left Mrs. C. A. Bristed and gone to Mr. and Mrs. Frank Weeks. Poor Johnny, the eldest son, is still insane.

Novel epidemic running through Western towns and spreading eastward. It suggests the "Childrens' Crusade" a little and also the viragoes of Paris marching on Versailles eighty odd years ago. Its symptoms are bands or mobs of pious women who run to and fro, hold prayer meetings, and sing psalms in grog shops or before the doors thereof, warning off thirsty customers and "wrestling with" the proprietor. These evangelical monads sometimes so work on the dispenser of drinks that he staves his lager-bier barrels and retires or even catches the infection, joins the train of anti-Bacchantes, and howls with the loudest of them. While these orgies are in progress, the meetinghouse bells are tolled, business is suspended, and folks come into town from all the countryside to witness the "function," or pilgrimage, as it were. The phenomenon is working on a large scale, but I think its effects will be transient. We must not speak *too* disrespectfully, however, of any movement however grotesque and ungraceful that is directed against the terrible mischief of drunkenness.

February 18. Dunscomb's funeral was at Trinity Church at three-thirty this afternoon. The attendance was very much larger than I expected. I was pallbearer with Curtiss, Sackett, Cisco, and others. Dix officiated with six other of our clergy. Interment was in the vault under the floor of the north robing room. The service was choral. . . .

The Philharmonic directors met here and smoked at five-thirty this afternoon. We agreed to abandon the Ninth Symphony for this year. There is not time for thorough choral rehearsals. Moreover, its announcement at the beginning of next season might increase our subscriptions, whereas its production at the end of this would profit us nothing.

February 20. . . . Special vestry meeting yesterday afternoon. Skidmore was unanimously promoted to be warden. We provided that plans and estimates be obtained for the new additional Trinity Church schoolhouse on 56 New Church Street and that action be taken against Erben for his failure to complete the organ for St. John's, now two months past due. Thereafter a Standing Committee meeting. There was the question whether we shall oppose or agree to opening of Desbrosses Street. So am I "King of the Cats" (*vide* Grimm's *Märchen*), that is, first on the vestry list. Of the twenty-three gentlemen who constituted the vestry in November, 1847, only two survive—William Moore (resigned) and Bleecker (extruded).

February 24. . . . The skeleton of a great dome is slowly developing above the north front of the new post office. Its arching iron supports, with their elaborate braces, look like the remains of some huge fossil radiate.

February 26. . . . Referee's office, one P.M., for Pech's case. The hour came but not the man, but at half-past there appeared unto us a scrub of a little Jew office boy, who said that plaintiff's counsel were "drying a gace in the sessions" and couldn't come. So we dispersed. . . . Standing Committee meeting tonight; chief business—the proposed opening of Desbrosses Street, which we agree to oppose—wisely, I think.

Through the snow yesterday to a Leake and Watts meeting at the garrulous Frederic De Peyster's. As usual, no quorum. Only the Dutch De Witt and the Presbyterian Paxton attended, besides Knox the treasurer, who don't count. For practical purposes, that board is nearly null. The mayor and recorder (ex officio trustees) never attend. It's hardly possible they should, and the rest are very uncertain. The orphan house runs of itself somehow, but I fear it may suddenly come to grief sooner or later for want of due supervision and disgrace us all.

March 2. . . . College trustees met at two this afternoon at Great Jones Street. The large Committee on the Site reported progress and certain resolutions concerning alterations and enlargements of the existing college buildings, the accommodations for the School of Mines, and the like. The first of these resolutions was in substance that the growth of the School be stopped should the School outgrow its proposed enlarged accommodations and that we would do no more for it in any event. On this we had a lively debate. Ogden and Barnard talked at great length pro and con. The Rev. Mr. Haight left the chair, put old Robert Ray into it, and let off one or two vehement little anti-science speeches that were founded on half truths and did his judgment little credit. I thought the resolution sure to pass, but I was resolved to bear my testimony against it; so when everyone else had got through, I spoke for three minutes about my willingness to limit the number of School of Mines students by raising the standard of qualifications for admission and about my unwillingness to be a party to putting on our minutes a resolution deliberately and avowedly dwarfing either the undergraduate corps, the Law School, or the School of Mines. I said I thought such a resolution without precedent in the history of any American college, and I might have said much more about it. That our board listened to the proposition for five minutes is quite enough to account for the fact that Columbia College lies still while Yale and Harvard and Amherst grow. The resolution was lost, and some of them said its loss was due to my little speech. I hope they were right.

The *World* and *Times* call attention to the disgrace brought on this city and on the state by the public funeral honors lavished on that corner grocery politician and swindler of savings banks, Mr. "Hank Smith," late police commissioner, and among the nastiest of the larvae that have lived by burrowing in the great dunghill of our civic corruption and have fattened thereon. There is a plentiful lack of moral sense in this community.

March 4. . . . Yesterday, the Leake and Watts board took a little doze at the Rev. De Witt's in Ninth Street. First step toward the inevitable removal of the orphan house to Westchester County or Long Island. A committee was appointed to enquire and report anent the expediency of such removal. In the afternoon (very hot) with Morgan Dix, Braem, and Ostrander, at 50 Varick Street, conferring with "Mother Harriet" and "Sister Eleanor" about the infirmary. (I can't yet make these new titles fit my tongue quite readily, and I say "Madam" when I should say "Mother.") These seem nice, kindly, efficient women, wholly free from Pharisaism and ostentation of sanctity and quite capable of enjoying a small joke.

March 6. . . . Her Majesty's Ashantee expedition seems in a doubtful sort of way. Prayers put up for it in all London churches. I guess it will come out all right.[5] But we have not forgotten England's attitude toward us ten years ago in our time of trouble. We should shed few tears over the failure of this foolish foray into the malarious swampy fastnesses of a horde of howling, gibbering savages with whom England and English soldiers have no legitimate business at all. We should be honestly and heartily sorry were England visited by famine or pestilence or harried by a Prussian invasion. But that she should be mortified and humiliated just a little would not afflict us a bit.

March 8, SUNDAY. . . . Temple and a select party of his friends were doing wind quartettes all the afternoon. That boy's musical talent is remarkable. Here has he been instrumenting for full orchestra the accompaniment to Schubert's *Erl-King* ballad!!! I don't doubt that his score bristles with blunders, but as Dr. Johnson says somewhere, "You are not surprised that a dog dances badly; you wonder that he dances at all." If I had but a little more money for Temple and his brothers, how happy I should be with them. They are three noble fellows.

March 9. . . . Died, at Buffalo, old Millard Fillmore. There was "mair tint" at Bull Run.

March 11. . . . New Hampshire elections and opposition gains. Though this result is complicated with local issues, Grant's administration is losing ground, I fear. We are dissatisfied with many things, with corruption, extravagance, and Ben Butlerism at Washington, with the currency, the tariff, and the disgraceful customhouse spy system. Staunch Republicans

[5] The Ashanti tribesmen had begun hostilities against the British early in 1873; a small force under Sir Garnet Wolseley, after some severe fighting, occupied their capital early in 1874, and compelled them to sue for peace.

would go over to the opposition in battalions if the opposition bore another name, but they cannot shake hands and rub noses with "Democrats" of 1860–65.

Died, Charles Sumner, an able, accomplished, and unwise man. The bludgeon of that caitiff and ruffian "Bully Brooks" made him a first-class confessor in the anti-slavery cause and has now promoted him to the dignities of martyrdom, for they say that memorable brutal assault was the remote cause of his death. But he never had much hold on the people. He was too self-conscious and, perhaps, too cultivated and scholarly for the American people. Ever since he deserted his party in 1872 he has been a lone man, out of humor with everyone, himself included. . . .

March 12. Flags at City Hall and everywhere else at half-mast in honor of Sumner. Who could have predicted this fifteen years ago? To do him justice, he shewed immense pluck in his fight for a principle when he seemed in a hopeless minority, and in enduring obloquy and hatred for its sake from all the South and half the North. . . .

March 16. . . . "Temperance" crusade, so-called, continues active and abundant in spasm. Query: if there be not in this, as in other developments and vagaries of ultra Protestantism, something inherited from the Manichaeans and Paulicians. . . . Manichaeans, sixteenth century Puritans, and modern Evangelicals clearly agree in regarding all enjoyments derived from matter as of the nature of evil, and the old Manichaeans justified their view by attributing the creation of matter to Ahriman. . . .

March 17. . . . The New York *Herald* reports "Bald Mountain" in western North Carolina setting up as a volcano. Probably a canard or sell.

March 18. . . . Rumors continue of subterraneous singults and borborygmi in North Carolina. That region of tar and turpentine would be much endangered by a volcanic outbreak. The rebel eruption, checked by external applications of cold steel, must have struck in. Or perhaps the buried fire-eaters are uneasy in their graves and seek to convert their conquered pine woods and plantations into *campi phlegraei.* . . .

March 19. Wet morning; evening oppressively warm. Wrote Governor Dix about certain crude, mischievous legislation wherewith we are threatened by Albany. Nash, Palmer, and I took counsel together and agreed on the outline of our report upon Wiswall—in substance, that his wife's allegations are not proven, but that his indiscretions in financial and other matters have impaired his usefulness. The lady is now suing for divorce by little Jerolomon, her attorney.

Dinner at John Astor's in his usual regal style. Besides our host and hostess and nice young Willy Astor, there were Carson Brevoort, South-mayd, Judge Brady (funniest of convives), . . . John Cruger, Mr. Ruggles, the Rev. Mr. Montgomery, Dr. Flint, Professor Drisler, Professor Dwight, and others—twenty-two, I think.[6] Cruger introduced himself to me very amiably, said he was a student in my father's office in Pine Street 1828-9, and well remembered me as a bit of a boy coming in of a fine afternoon for a long walk. Mr. Ruggles prophesied pleasant things of Minnesota Railroad, but I am of little faith.

March 21. At the referee's office, Pech made default again, but Mr. Brooke (his counsel) will positively be ready next Tuesday. Pech's Harlem Music Hall has collapsed, and the local press calls him a swindler. Meantime, Miss Susannah Evans, alias Mrs. Pech No. 2, is "lecturing on temperance"; poor little woman. . . .

The quakings and eructations of "Bald Mountain" have produced a quite powerful revival in those parts. There was probably room for it.

March 23. Tonight at the Rev. Mr. Haight's (West Twenty-sixth Street) on a College committee. With him were Barnard and Nash. We discussed the question about suppressing the "preparatory" year of the School of Mines course. We decided to ask the opinion of the faculty. Barnard's prolix prosing nearly gave me a mild fit of apoplexy. . . .

I am more disgusted every day with the inflationism, Butlerism, corruption, and fraud that rule at Washington. Grant is in bad hands. Were there an election tomorrow, I wouldn't vote at all.

March 24. . . . The House of Representatives by 168 to 77 inflates up to four hundred millions of greenbacks. Heaven help us!

March 26. . . . Long session of Supplies and Repairs Committee this afternoon with the Rector. Upjohn, Jr., submitted his designs for the schoolhouse (New Church Street), which are not bad at all. After some demur, chiefly from Cisco, I got authority to procure plans and estimates for the gallery or triforium on the south side of the chancel. Now at last there is a prospect of being able to effect that improvement, unless the estimates be too large. It will be a vast improvement.

Yesterday afternoon at the Columbia College Library Committee meeting. Then with Newberry and Chandler at the School of Mines,

[6] Charles F. Southmayd was a member of the great legal firm of Evarts, Southmayd & Choate, and one of the most learned and clear-headed lawyers of his time. John R. Brady, a brother of the more famous James T. Brady who had run for governor on the Douglas ticket in 1860, was judge of the Supreme Court in New York 1869–1891, and a great wit.

where there is always something new and instructive. The professors seem "well pleased" with the proposed extension of their buildings. Charles Haight is architect.

March 28. . . . After many delays, Pech appeared at the referee's office this afternoon an hour behind time ready for battle at last. Mr. Brooke did not shew, and the plaintiff was represented by a little ignoramus . . . of a clerk. Of course, the plaintiff was his own witness, and so bungling, incoherent, irresponsive a witness I never listened to. Drake gave him full swing and allowed him placidly to swear away nearly his whole case. His inaccuracy in immaterial statements, which he could have no motive for misstating, was marvelous. As to material points, he was utterly loose and vague. But his direct examination was not closed, and he may be better doctored a week hence. . . .

March 31. The ancient and garrulous U. C. Hill tells me the peace of the Philharmonic Society is disturbed. The late panic interfered with the sale of seats and boxes, so the next dividend will be but small. Hence grumblings and caucussings, and talk of putting in a new board of directors at the annual meeting. If this purpose be entertained by any considerable number of members, I shall make my bow and decline another "presidential term." Another cause of dissatisfaction and desire for change is that Carl Bergmann is said to be lazy and negligent and always overcharged with lager; and I guess, moreover, that the Society feels sore because of Theodore Thomas's triumphs and of the praises showered on him by the newspaper critics whom he knows how to manipulate. I don't care what the Society does, being sick of everything just now from myself up.

We are traveling toward repudiation, national bankruptcy, and the old scratch as fast as the government can drive us.

April 2. At Trinity Church at four this afternoon for rehearsal of Easter music. The church was quite full. Temple and his oboe were in the organ loft. There were the first movement of Beethoven's D Symphony (for final Voluntary); Anthem (from Handel's *Saul*) . . . ; Offertory, Twelfth Chandos Anthem—"O praise the Lord, Ye Angels of His." The rest of the music was from Mozart's beautiful First Mass. The rehearsal was pretty rough, but not so rough as some rehearsals I have known. The Handel compositions are more interesting than I expected, but so dry, chippy, and full of meaningless, florid, old-fashioned vocalization as to be out of place.

April 3, GOOD FRIDAY. Sunshine and moderately warm. March wind was raw and dirt-laden. The sands raised by the winds of the Sahara are cleaner than our street dust. Went to St. Paul's to hear our new man, Mulchahey. This was my first experience of morning service at St. Paul's since the spring of 1846, when Trinity Church was consecrated. From my earliest recollection of time, I had gone to St. Paul's regularly with my mother and Aunt Olivia. The interior of the chapel, though renovated and improved, is essentially the same, except that the pews are comfortable and wide now. But of the old familiar faces, not one was left, except old Miss Mary Jones in her old pew. The Reverend Messrs. Haight, Mulchahey, and Crapsey marching up to the reading desk and chancel from the robing room near the west entrance awakened associations. How the Rev. Mr. Schroeder used to strut and swagger up that same south aisle in the old times! Mulchahey preached quite respectably, was earnest, unaffected, and perhaps thoughtful. . . .

April 4. The infirmary on Varick Street has opened. The first patient was a little girl. . . .

April 6. . . . Died, John W. Edmonds, father of "Spiritualism."[7] I think he was foolish and sincere. According to his own pneumatology, he must be drumming under Miss Fox's dinner table before this.

April 7. Called on by some man who wanted me to be president of another musical society, an "oratorio society," of which Dr. [Leopold] Damrosch is conductor. I respectfully declined the honor, being quite tired of musical presidencies.

The Administration was badly beaten in Connecticut. This is called a "ga-lorious Democratic victory," but I am not inconsolable. . . .

April 13, MONDAY. . . . At three this afternoon at the office of Scribner, referee. Pech did not shew his ugly face. After a long delay, a clerk appeared from the office of his attorneys, asking an eleventh adjournment— "counsel being engaged." The referee, on motion, struck out Pech's direct examination because he did not appear for the cross-examination and then dismissed the complaint, but with the understanding that Pech have till Saturday to move to open his default. I may be sanguine, but I think we shall hear no more of Pecus. His lawyers, being probably without the stimulus of a retainer, have never much troubled themselves about his case. They won't get up affidavits to open the default unless they are paid for it. The default will not be opened except on terms, including

[7] See various references in the second volume of this diary; ex-Judge Edmonds had done valuable work since 1860 in compiling the best edition of the *New York Statutes at Large* (five volumes, 1863), and *Reports of Select Cases* heard by him in circuit court (1868).

payment of cost, and Pech can no more pay them than he can pay the national debt. . . .

April 15. . . . Cardinal Weld served Wiswall today with a copy of our resolution of exorcism, having been unable to find him yesterday.

April 16. Nothing from Wiswall the Decapitated, except that he tells Craig the sexton that he "means to make Rome howl."

Horsley, the Rev. Cooke, Ben Stephens, and I, as the Executive Committee of the Church Music Association, met at my office this afternoon, and an unexpected piece of news came out—to wit, that if we go on with the third concert and its rehearsals we shall be saddled with a deficit of $1,000 and upwards. Stephens the treasurer ought to have told us this a month ago. The trouble is that so many of our subscribers ("our best people") have neglected to pay their subscriptions, though often requested so to do. We must send out a circular tomorrow announcing that there will be no rehearsal Tuesday and stating the reason why. I am sorry the Church Music Association should die thus ignominiously, but I can afford to pay no more money to meet its deficits. And I don't think any of us need feel ashamed of having depended on subscriptions from men like Mr. C. C. Dodge, which they have failed to meet. However that may be, I'll have nothing more to do with musical societies.

April 18. . . . After thirty-three ballotings, the Hon. Washburn is Senator from Massachusetts, vice the late Sumner.[8] What there is of him is anti-Butler and so far good. Hopes of a veto from Grant are fading, and my faith in Grant is fading, too.

Cold storm yesterday, and I was corroded by dyspepsia. Conference with the Rev. Cooke and Ben Stephens *de rebus* Church Music Association and decided that by snipping off expenses and by selling our library for whatever it will bring, we can much reduce our deficit. So we suppressed the circular I had drafted, thus sparing ourselves a deep mortification at a cost that I trust will not prove serious. . . .

April 20. The *World, Sun,* and Sunday *Mercury* open fire on us in Wiswall's cause. The last is very scurrilous, after its kind. Little Jerolomon says he is prepared with conclusive proof in his divorce suit; perhaps. The Rev. Wiswall is a fool to open a newspaper war upon us. He may possibly compel us to reply and to hurt him, which we do not wish to do.

April 21. Conferred with the Rector and with sundry St. Johnians about the Rev. Mr. Wiswall and his malcontent backers. There was to be

[8] This was William B. Washburn (1820–1887), a former Representative, who resigned the governorship to take Sumner's vacant seat.

a meeting of St. John's Guild tonight, the Rector was to preside as "visitor," and a grand fracas, shindy, scrimmage, or muss is probably in progress this minute. He (the Reverend) consulted me as to certain points of parliamentary law.

April 23. . . . The meeting of "St. John's Guild" on Tuesday night was overwhelmingly and obstreperously Wiswallite. It passed resolutions (by acclamation), endorsing Wiswall and demanding explanations from the vestry. Only Frazer and two others opposed the *civium et foeminarum ardor prava jubentium*, and this small minority seems to have been howled down or coughed down. The harder these foolish people blow the sooner they will blow out and blow over. Our course is to be perfectly quiet, to "jouk and let the jaw gae by," as a Scotsman would say. To publish anything would be just to play into their hands.

Vivat Grant! He has vetoed the inflation bill. This veto will rank in his record with Vicksburg and Appomattox.[9] Some say this will split the Republican party and destroy it. Never mind if it does. We want a new party founded on hard money, free trade, and home rule. Only let it *not* be called Democratic.

April 24. Long call from that worthy, prosing old Mr. Bloomfield, one of Wiswall's counsel. He wanted copies of certain papers, which I declined to give him. He seems a most estimable old gentleman, a survivor of the second-grade gentlemen of the bar of fifty years ago. There are no gentlemen of the bar any more.

Visit also from U. C. Hill. It seems settled that Bergmann will rule over the Philharmonic Society no more. What Hill wants of *me* I cannot make out. It seems, sometimes, as if he wanted me to decline a re-election, which I am sure I am very ready to do. . . .

April 25. . . . Judgment entered against Pecusculum with costs, which are not worth the trouble of filling up a blank form; poor Pech! . . .

April 26, SUNDAY. Progress of the Great Parish Insurrection—latest news. St. John's Guild met Saturday night and cut itself wholly adrift from Trinity parish. Dix presided as visitor, and before putting the question on the proposed amendments to the "canons," he read a brief paper setting forth the effect of their passage and shewing that it would detach

---

[9] Grant's veto, an act of signal courage, was the more gratifying to conservatives because it was unexpected; he had leaned in the other direction. Ben Butler, John A. Logan, Oliver P. Morton and other inflationists were supposed to control his views. In his veto message he declared that he had always been opposed to irredeemable paper money, and that he had been elected on the pledge of a speedy return to a gold-based currency.

the guild from the church. The amendments were carried. Whereupon Dix "involved himself in his virtue," put on his hat and avoided the premises, expressing his best wishes for the guild on its new footing and receiving much compliment and regret from that body. I think his decisive action took them by surprise. Alvah Slyboots was thereupon elected "Master."

April 28. Here is a bill introduced to restore that iniquitous, unconstitutional, demoralizing, infernal income tax. It's supported by the spite of Western and Southern inflationists against the East. If it pass, I'll expatriate myself. . . .

Church Music Association concert tonight. House fairly full in spite of tempest. Stayed through the lovely, healthy Haydn Mass. I guess this will be the last Church Music Association concert, under its original regime, at least. Working to get up fine renderings of Haydn and Beethoven for a New York audience is like diving for pearls to be thrown before swine. The majority of our concert-goers have neither culture enough to enjoy the music nor good breeding enough to let others enjoy it uninterrupted by gabble. . . .

Wiswall is intriguing and operating and trying to make capital, but I think he begins drifting to leeward already. He is said to meditate some sort of pamphlet. I hope he may publish.

April 29. Bleakest of mornings, with great patches of snow on roofs and sidewalks. At four this afternoon, it was "spitting snow," with a freedom that amounted at last to absolute ptyalism. The thermometer registered 36°, and a wind blew that nearly took one's ears off. Tonight is clear and cold.

Had conference with the Rev. Dix. The Rev. Wiswall is writing letters, in one of which he speaks of being "ex-honorated" from all charges. The Rev. Dix sent me the draft of his answer tonight. I always itch to correct and improve anything written by anybody else, but in this I could find not a single word that I could change for the better, and I sent it back intact. I guess the Rev. Wiswall will put it in his pocket and say nothing more about it.

April 30. . . . Engaged, the Rev. [Henry W.] Bellows (!!!) to a Miss Peabody of Boston, whose sister married Eliot of Harvard.[10] The

[10] Dr. Bellows's first wife had died in 1869; in June of this year he married Anna Huidekoper Peabody of Boston. Mr. Eliot's wife, Ellen Derby Peabody, died the month he was elected president of Harvard (March, 1869).

wooing was down in Florida and pastoral—among flocks of bleating moccasins and herds of lowing alligators.

May 6. Wrote up the long minutes of yesterday's committee. Had a conference with Cisco. I think we shall soon have to appoint an assistant rector for six months or so. Unfortunately, such appointment must be for life under the charter; so we must take from the appointee a stipulation to resign. Who shall it be? Haight and Weston are physically disqualified. Cisco favors Swope. . . .

Notice from Schaad that I am re-elected president of the Philharmonic. Am undecided about accepting.

May 7. Yesterday's *Commercial* publishes a long diatribe against Wiswall and St. John's Guild—most damaging to both. It charges them with swindling on a great scale, obtaining money under false pretences, and so forth, and gives names, amounts, and details with awful precision. I knew nothing of the transactions it sets forth, and the story may be a base fiction, but Wiswall must meet it somehow forthwith or resign himself to becoming a lost Wiswall. A more devastating and destructive article could hardly be written.

Protracted meeting of Supplies and Repairs Committee this afternoon with the Rector. Much business done. My pet plan of an orchestral gallery or triforium came up and was killed, I fear, by Cisco's prejudices and ignorance. He knows no more of church music than a cow and cares no more for it than a cat, but he thinks the orchestral services are "very good as they are," and doesn't approve them, nevertheless, because they draw such crowds to the church. The question "lies over," but the proposition is moribund.

Pulling down on Broadway, southeast corner of Fulton Street, for a new office of the *Evening Post,* and northwest corner of Walker Street for some bank. The new post office nears completion. Since Solomon's Temple, no great building has ever grown so silently. . . . All hewing and stonecutting has been done miles away at the quarry, and it's strange how seldom one sees any workmen. But it has thus quietly expanded and amplified into a huge pile, and perhaps there will be legends two hundred years hence as how the Devil built it in a night.[11]

May 8. . . . Died, John Hecker, father of farina-fracturers and whilom a special friend and fantom of the late Dr. Seabury and Bishop B. T. Onderdonk; "cardiac apoplexy." . . .

[11] Happily, "Mullett's Monstrosity," one of the masterpieces of the supervising architect of the Treasury, endured only until 1938.

May 11. . . . Schaad writes in answer to my enquiry that the votes for the Philharmonic president were 66—namely, blank 10, Doremus 7, scattering 9, George T. Strong 40; and for vice-president, Reiff 45 out of 59. Schaad and old U. C. Hill both write begging me to accept. I think the politic U. C. Hill tried to elect Doremus. He is a slippery fish. The dissentient minority is of respectable dimensions, and I shall decline.

May 12. Columbia College Library Committee met this afternoon with the Rev. Mr. Haight and Barnard and the Rev. Mr. Betts, our mucilaginous librarian. . . . We took an order for printing the library catalogue!!! . . .

May 13. . . . The naked iron ribs and tendons of the new post office dome begin to be covered by healthy granulations, apparently of slate. An anomalous iron structure, hybrid of dome and steeple, is sprouting at the south end of the building. . . .

May 14. Ascension Day. Trinity was fearfully crowded and hot. It was a close day of dull, dead heat. The service was, I thought, the smoothest and cleanest we have yet had, and most effective and noble. Bishop Tozer "assisted" with nearly all the clergy of the parish and sundry outsiders. I begin to be reconciled to the departure from usage and traditional form in the opening of the Gloria. The final voluntary was the fourth movement of the *Jupiter Symphony.* All the music was good and fairly done. Ellie was at Trinity for the first time this year, also Rosalie.

Dix preached magnificently and at some length on a favorite theme of his—namely, sectarianism (why not "sectishness"?), including High Churchism and Low Churchism as compared with Catholicism. Some of his phrases might be misinterpreted and give offense, . . . but good work has seldom been done in the church without offending somebody, and I want this sermon printed, though I fear some of the learned theological critics of the vestry will rather demur to that proposition.

May 25. Wet morning, doubtless to the malignant delight of the omnibus drivers, who are all on strike because of the new fare-collecting machines that stop their little stealings. No omnibi running, and I cabbed it downtown and up again, for the weather was filthy and the cars were crowded. . . .

May 26. Vacillating weather; tonight clear as crystal. Omnibus drivers still on strike, and Broadway looks strangely vacuous. . . .

May 28. A few omnibi crawl out, guided by raw recruits from Boston. As these novices have to keep their eyes fixed on their horses' noses, the weary pedestrian signals them from the sidewalk in vain. . . .

May 30. "Decoration Day," and my office is closed. Clear and very warm. At eleven this morning, with Lucy, Ellie, and Louis to Prospect Park, Brooklyn. A beautiful drive through the sun and shade and fine bits of old woodland. Lunched at the Park restaurant, which is not quite up to our Casino or Stetson's.

June 1. Vestry meeting tonight. Many matters harmoniously disposed of: $1,500 appropriated for overhauling and cleaning Trinity Church organ and putting in two new reed stops; erection of a dead-house for the infirmary, to cost about $1,000; 5,000 copies of the Rector's Ascension Day sermon to be printed. Dr. Haight nominated and confirmed as assistant rector, the Rector stating that he had an understanding with Haight as to his resignation on the Rector's return from the six months' leave of absence we gave him. Haight, as assistant rector, put on all committees of which the Rector is a member. Cisco moved a gift of $5,000 to the Rector, which he accepted with some little demur in a very artless, straightforward, little speech, expressing his thanks and his good will to all of us and his "gratitude" for the cordial sympathy and support he had always received from the vestry. It was very nice. Mrs. Wiswall's application for pecuniary relief, with Mrs. Ulman's "sifflication" to the same effect, were referred to the Standing Committee. Mrs. Wiswall is penniless, and Mrs. Ulman has already on her hands the children of her brother, Hobart Berrian, who died insolvent, one of them an idiot. Dr. Berrian's progeny has not prospered on the earth. . . .

Died, old Sam Jaudon, a brilliant financier of other days. Thirty years ago his house was one of the gayest and most brilliant in New York. But he has long been played out and broken. His memory is unfragrant and his children have nearly sunk out of sight. Poor Mrs. Julia Van Rensselaer, whom I take to be altogether the best of the batch, keeps a little school. . . .

June 2. Morgan Dix deputizes me to pass upon admissions to St. Luke's Hospital and the infirmary—applications for free interments and the like—during his six months' leave. So I cannot hope for much summer holiday.

Dick and Hengelmüller, the Austrian attaché (whom Temple calls "Hunglebungle"), dined here very pleasantly. He is a student not merely of Shakespeare, Schiller, and Goethe, but of the *Nibelüngen* and the *Minnesänger*. His talk was interesting and instructive.

June 3. . . . To 17 East Twenty-second Street (Mrs. Soutter's) with Ellie at twelve.[12] Broun the Magnificent officiated on the sidewalk, and

[12] For the wedding of Dr. Morgan Dix; next day occurred Jem Ruggles's.

Bishop Potter in the middle room under a great hanging canopy of flowers. Nash asked me whether the Rector had a "faculty" for that "baldaquin." Attendance was small but "select." As all the clergy of the parish and nearly all the vestry were on duty, I felt quite at home. Mrs. Ned Bell received in her own kindly, hearty way. Morgan Dix looked like a beatified saint and, as it were, phosphoresced from brow to boots. The bride is brunette and looks intelligent and interesting rather than pretty. Everything went off nicely. The Governor seems a little worn with cares of state. . . .

Came off immediately after the ceremony and "compliments" and was forthwith tackled by a youthful but intelligent agent of the indefatigable daily press, who demanded information as to all the particulars of the wedding, whither the happy couple had gone, and when they were coming back. My answer was condensed and curt.

June 4. With Ellie, Lucy, and Louis to Jem's wedding at Mrs. Baldwin's (13 East Thirty-fourth Street) at one in the afternoon, where Johnny and Temple joined us. The gathering was large and included all the magnates of what's called "society"—for example, all the Astors, including old William B. Astor who seldom goes out, lots of Joneses and Schermerhorns, Mrs. Belmont, and many swells beside. Mrs. William Astor was very kind and polite to me. The reception and general atmosphere were most genial. The Bishop welded the chain. He reads that lovely service most simply, earnestly, and impressively. The principals did their parts audibly and looked very happy. Dear Mrs. Grace was the prettiest of brides and received my congratulations like a little sister. God bless her. This looks like a very nice arrangement.

Two weddings on two consecutive days! A novelty in my experience. I am very sorry neither was sunshiny, for I dislike clouded wedding days. That young monkey, Temple, contrived to kiss his new young aunt three several times.

June 8. . . . Grant permits the publication of a memorandum or informal statement of his views about a return to specie payments, which is a clear and vigorous paper, so vigorous that there are earnest advocates of hard money who think his proposed treatment too drastic and heroic. But this has raised Grant 100 per cent in my estimation.

June 9. To Columbia College Library Committee at three in the afternoon. There were Haight, Duyckinck, and I. We ordered a copy of the *Acta Sanctorum* ($800), a book I have long wished to see. Work on the new School of Mines buildings is in active progress. The rising walls look substantial and creditable. The outlay is over $125,000! Who would have thought that the little egg that was laid in this very room twelve years ago could hatch out so big a bird? . . .

June 10. . . . Bank for Savings trustees met this afternoon. The chairman (John C. Green) put me on a most important special committee, charged with the duty of enquiring into our way of doing business and the examination of accounts that foot up some hundreds of millions. I mildly suggested that several other trustees then present were better qualified for the work—for example, the presidents of the Bank of New York and of the Bank of Commerce—and I submitted that I should be excused. But Green remarked with semi-ironical suavity that the comptroller of Trinity Church was ex officio a financial magnate of the first order, and so "I will not excuse you; you shall not be excused; excuses shall not be admitted; there is no excuse shall serve," and the like.

June 13.   Died, old James F. De Peyster, one of the best of men and bores. . . .

With dear Lucy and Louis last night to Booth's Theatre to see Salvini's *Othello.* He is excellently well supported, and his is a wonderful piece of acting. Nobody ever made such play with his eyes or converted himself into so close a semblance of Satan.[13] It's a muscular performance. Of course, he overacts a good deal, condescending to the taste of an uncultured audience. I fear I quite cut myself out of dear little Lucy's good graces by humbly submitting that I rather thought so, in reply to her query. . . . In the finale, Othello turns from the audience and saws away like fury at his own throat with a great snickersnee he happens to have about him, an improvement on the obviously innocuous dagger of the ordinary stage suicide, and drops very handsomely. As the curtain descends, he is heard to gurgle or wheeze, as his breath escapes through the lacerated larynx, and he is seen to be kicking tremulously with his left leg. All which is powerful and *magnifique,* but not art. It was a very fine and telling impersonation, nevertheless. The house was jammed and enthusiastic. . . .

June 16.   Busy day at 187 Fulton Street. Dined here Bagnotti (Italian vice-counsul, I believe); also, the great Salvini, Mr. Ruggles, and Dick. . . . Salvini is genial and gentlemanlike. I gave him my thanks as a commentator on Shakespeare, which he received simply and nicely. There is no pretension about him, nor any affectation of grandeur.

[13] Tommaso Salvini, the great Italian actor, made the first of five spectacularly successful tours of America in 1873–74, producing a special impression as Hamlet and Othello.

June 25. . . . The pragmatical Pharisees of prohibitionism and sabba-tarianism have set up Myron H. Clark (!) against Governor Dix (who will doubtless be the Republican candidate), because Dix has room in his brains for more than one idea at a time and does not believe the enforce-ment of total abstinence to be the sole end and aim of civil government. . . .

June 30.   Less scorching than yesterday, when Fahrenheit reached three figures, and I nearly exuded into nonentity. George Carleton the publisher dined here. We perspired terribly. He is a clever man and an observant traveler. . . .

July 15.   The other half of the inflammable city of Chicago is burned up. Another Indian War is setting in. The "Black Hills" are to be invaded, and the Sioux braves are mustering in great force to defend that sacred soil as yet unprofaned by palefaces. . . .

July 17.   No letter from Ellie, who doubtless spent yesterday with the 24,999 other "fash'nables" (the newspapers report them 25,000) assisting at the Saratogian Collegiate Boat Race which didn't come off because of high wind and rough water. . . .

July 19, SUNDAY.   The great "intercollegiate" race, postponed for two successive days, was run yesterday morning, and Columbia came in first by several lengths, undisputed victor. I hoped for nothing better than a second or third place. Grand row and jubilation at Saratoga, and flags hoisted all over the city—City Hall included—as soon as the tidings came. Even the Brokers' board hurrahed and carried on like mad. The trustees have never given the sleepy College such an advertisement as it has received from these half-dozen undergraduates and "Miners." Their suc-cess is an interesting physiological fact, moreover. It shews that the kid-gloved boys of Fifth Avenue can develop better muscles than the rustics of Vermont and Maine. Perhaps diet has something to do with it. The former live on beef and mutton; the latter eat a good deal of salted meat, salt fish, things fried, corn bread, hot cakes, and heavy pies, like their fathers before them. . . .

July 21.   No letter from Ellie today. I fear the dinner she was to have given on Sunday to the College victors may have proved too much for her. John Astor enthuses about these athletes and wants to get up some testimonial for them. They were received in grand style at the Forty-second Street depot at two-forty this afternoon. I would have liked to be present, but there was to be a banquet or collation at the Windsor Hotel, and as I am among the few trustees in town, I should have been imperatively called upon for "a few remarks" and should have seen my dinner-table brayings reported at length in all the morning papers.

July 23. . . . After many dark insinuations and innuendoes, Mr. Theodore Tilton publishes in form and at great length his charge against the Rev. H. W. Beecher—namely, the seduction of Mrs. Theodore Tilton, with specification of time, place, and circumstance. Tilton is probably a cad or *vaurien*, certainly a goose, and his word counts for little with me. He prints a letter from the Rev. Mr. Beecher, expressing profound penitence for some wrong or other, but the letter is written under manifest excitement, and its language may be exaggerated and hyperaesthetic and refer to something far less grave than the alleged crime to which Tilton makes it apply. Most people incline toward Beecher's side, those excepted who always wish to believe anything against a notable preacher. But his abominable misconduct in the Richardson and McFarland case is now remembered, to his grave prejudice. As to Tilton, nobody has anything to say for him. His own statement befouls him beyond disinfection by chlorine or carbolic acid. He is a cur of low degree.

I guess the investigation now in progress under direction of the authorities of "Plymouth Meet'n House" will shew that Mrs. Tilton is a gushing pietist and pulpit worshiper over whom Divus or Sanctus Beecher secured a sort of influence which rather alienated the lady from an uncongenial husband who was tending toward spiritualism and free-love-ism, and writing about the communications of Mrs. Victoria Woodhull with the spirit of Demosthenes. Probably Beecher did not seek this influence and went in merely for a little pious evangelical flirtation and fun. But it would seem that Tilton, having found out the state of affairs, pitched into St. Beecher and shed tears, and the Saint said and wrote that he was very sorry and shed tears, and the lady did the same. At that point the whole nasty business should have been wiped up and never mentioned again, but Tilton is a fool. Though most erratic and unsound, Beecher is manly, able, and eloquent and many silly women besides Mrs. Tilton have made an idol of him. There are those who say he is a bad man and that he "keeps" a batch of "singular Christian women," but I do not believe it.

July 25. . . . And now comes Mrs. Theodore Tilton, puts in her appearance, and gives her tale to the newspapers, with much of the high-flavored cant and high-falutin' verbiage to which the Chosen People of Brooklyn seem partial. But it reads rather like a true story. If it be true and if her husband's recent sayings and doings be truthfully reported, he is either a "looney" or an even shallower fool than I thought him, and a malignant, mischievous fool, moreover. But the whole case is not yet disclosed. Tilton's talk about what he means to prove against Beecher is orgulous and minatory, but it is probably mere "thrasonical huffe-snuffe." If Beecher has recruited a little harem for himself from among the Plymouth sisterhood (as many believe—I *don't*, for one), he has doubtless manoeuvred too warily to be caught by a feather-brained coxcomb like Theodore Tilton.

July 28. These days are doleful. Mr. Ruggles returned from Saratoga yesterday, improved in health and spirits, and reports Ellie stronger and every way better. He proposes to take up the Life & Trust Company loan. To help him do so I endorsed his note in the Bank of Commerce, due January 20, a proceeding not at all to my taste. . . .

The Beecher pot still boils. People begin to say that whether Tilton be lying or not, Plymouth Church is a cage of unclean birds. Beecher's profound abasement for some wrong or other by him done to Tilton is the ugly feature of Beecher's case. But for that, no one would listen to the brayings of Tilton or the gabble of the drabs who uphold him. Beecher explains it by the fact that he advised Mrs. Tilton to separate from her husband, and then he discovered that he had been misinformed and had advised her wrongly. But Mrs. Theodore Tilton avers in her manifesto that her life was embittered by Theodore's "free-love" affiliations, teachings, and practices, and that he caused her home to be infested by vermin of the Victoria Woodhull species whom he patronized and cultivated. Now would any clergyman, or layman either, declare himself humiliated, prostrated, driven to despair, and ready to welcome death by learning that when he advised a separation for reasons like these, he had been misinformed as to some detail or other? The Rev. Mr. Beecher is not reputed a hysterical patient. Till this mystery be cleared up, he must be content to rest under a cloud of suspicion. His political record in the "bleeding Kansas" times and his sermons about Sharps' rifles are remembered against him now. Many Southern and Western newspapers take his guilt for granted.

July 29. . . . Tilton is arrested for libel. . . .

July 31. . . . The general character of the Beecher-Tilton stench continues the same. Newspapers still reek with it, and everyone dwells darkly on the mystery of Beecher's contrition and attrition and longings for death. People don't get themselves up in sackcloth and ashes and scrape themselves with potsherds for any small matter. Every day that passes without satisfactory explanation of this phenomenon does Beecher irreparable damage and lessens the chance of any explanation being generally received at last.

It will be remembered that in the autumn of 1872 Victoria Woodhull had published in Woodhull and Claflin's Weekly *an article accusing Henry Ward Beecher of improper relations with the wife of Theodore Tilton; she was a member of Beecher's congregation, and Tilton had succeeded Beecher as editor of the* Independent. *The great preacher took no immediate notice of the charges, but as ugly rumors and stories continued to circulate he finally, on June 30, 1873, issued a formal denial. Still Victoria Woodhull continued her campaign, and the accusations gained national currency. Beecher then, in 1874, appointed a committee of six members of Plymouth Church to conduct an investigation of the charges. Efforts were made to get Mrs. Tilton to repudiate her husband and to give the committee a denial of the Woodhull story. Tilton himself had long kept silence, but he now made a drastic move: On July 20, 1874, he appeared before the authorities of Plymouth Church and made a sworn statement of Beecher's adultery, supporting it with much documentary evidence. This statement, as Strong notes in his diary for the 23rd, was at once published in the press, and one of the most famous scandals in American history became full public property. Mrs. Tilton, always emotional and now quite distracted by the crisis into which she was plunged, deserted her husband and took her stand by the side of her pastor. A storm of denunciation from Beecher's innumerable admirers beat upon Tilton's head. As noted above, he was charged with libel. In this extremity, he brought suit against Beecher for criminal conversation, demanding damages of $100,000; and his friend Frank Moulton (another member of Beecher's congregation) supported him, both Moulton and Mrs. Moulton swearing that Beecher had confessed his guilt to them. This trial, which began on January 11, 1875, lasted until July 2 of that year, with the whole country hanging on the evidence and arguments. It ended in a division of the jury, nine to three in favor of acquittal. Students of the trial have shown this same general division of opinion.*

The Nation, *in its incisive article on the scandal in the issue of August 20, 1874, took the view that Mrs. Tilton, maltreated by her husband, had contracted an affection for Beecher which presently seemed to her overwrought mind to be unlawful, and that she made a hysterical confession of this over-fond-*

ness for Beecher in a way which Tilton, his fortunes declining, could and did use in virtual blackmail of the pastor. But in a supplementary article on August 27, E. L. Godkin added: "The lying in every direction seems to be tremendous and unblushing. . . . It has come to be a 'conflict of veracity' between people whose moral standard is evidently not that of respectable men, and the best thing the public can do is let it drop."

August 5. . . . Poor Mrs. Theodore Tilton, being examined by the Plymouth investigators, tells a most pitiful story of neglect, insult, and outrage passively endured for years. She may or may not be the patient Griselda she describes herself, but she is evidently a weak vessel, perhaps badgered, bullied, and tormented into something approaching imbecility by the pranks of her demented husband. . . . Theodore Tilton now declines the jurisdiction of the Plymouth committee and means to take his case into the courts, a sensible proceeding if he have any case to take there. The Rev. Mr. Beecher continues silent as the Sphinx. This remarkable Mrs. Theodore Tilton seems to admit having written letters or certificates affirming the Rev. Mr. Beecher's criminal intimacy with her. But she says (or seems to say) that they were written at her husband's dictation for the sake of peace and because he had a kind of mesmeric influence over her. They are all lunatics together.

August 6. . . . The mystic and enigmatic Mr. Moulton consents at last to appear unto Plymouth and to open his budget. He is said to have acted as confidant and adviser of both parties while this mess was brewing, and to be an exceptional case of sanity. He required the consent of both as a condition precedent to his appearing. It has been given, and he may throw some light on the doings of these very queer people.

August 9. . . . Forster's life of Charles Dickens does not raise the "inimitable" in my estimation. With all his endearing and charming philanthropic sentiment, he seems to have been personally egotistical, self-conscious, and far from unselfish.

August 22, SATURDAY.   Home again [from Mt. Desert]. . . .The can-can *à l'église de Plymouth* is not yet danced out but grows faster and more furious. Tilton has sued the Rev. Mr. Beecher (that great gospel-gun) for criminal conversation, damages at $100,000. Doesn't he wish he may get them? Moulton publishes a statement damaging the Rev. Mr. Beecher. Unless Moulton be a loud liar, the Rev. Mr. Beecher is a convicted Tartuffe. But these saints of Plymouth Church and their friends act and talk so unlike common low-caste Christians that one can't be quite sure they mean what they seem to say. Strange that the New York *World* after reviling the Rev. Beecher so long and so savagely should now be defending him through thick and thin. As to the gushing, saintly, "white-souled" epistolographic Mrs. Tilton, she hardly seems an accountable being. . . .

Architectural Notes: Roof of the hideous, top-heavy Union Telegraph building, corner of Dey Street and Broadway, is now sheathed in iron scales, and the huge brick and granite nightmare seems nearly complete. The metal skeleton of the hybrid between the dome and steeple at the south end of the new post office ("mulatto monkeyshines," they call it) begins to be likewise clothed upon. The Delaware & Hudson Company's building (R. M. Hunt's, corner Cortlandt Street and New Church Street) advances and promises pretty well. The grand tower of the new *Tribune* edifice has made no progress. In our old Trinity school building all the new tracery is set up and looks well enough. The new building rises slowly. Erben has nearly finished his work on the Trinity Church organ, but the *vox humana* as yet "speaks not to the goose-fleshed throng."

August 27. . . . The *Nation* prints a sensible article on Beecher and Tilton convicting the Rev. Mr. Beecher of fatuity, timidity, and foolish faith in Tilton and Moulton, but acquitting him of Tilton's charges. Though not quite conclusive, it is weighty. But I fear we have not yet got to the bottom of this most noisome mess. The present aspect of the Rev. Mr. H. W. Beecher is certainly undignified, at least, just now. It reminds one of Mr. Chadband, Mr. Pickwick, and Mr. Augustus Moddle (in *Chuzzlewit*), combining certain traits of all three. But however the case may turn out, the Rev. Mr. Beecher has Brooklyn worshippers who will continue to bow down before him.

August 29.   The Plymouth committee read to a crowded meeting of Plymouthers last night a long report or judgment, whitewashing the Rev. Mr. Beecher, of course, but so unjudicial and partisan in tone that it will do him more harm than good. Outsiders will resent its unfairness and lean against him because of it, however illogically. These committeemen are, of course, disqualified from trying this case, not only as being Beecher's special liegemen and fautors, but also as holders of costly pews that would lose half their value were Beecher ousted from his platform. The precious report was received by a great audience with laughter and triumphant cheers. The somewhat questionable Mr. Frank Moulton was so rash as to attend the meeting and to signify his dissent as a minority of one from its prevailing sentiment. He was hissed and hooted down; and after the proceedings were closed and after the Plymouth saints had sung the doxology, they "went for" Moulton with pious ejaculations of "Give him H——!"—much as Cyril's deacons and Parabolani and Nitrian monks used to go for Jews and pagans. The police saved Moulton's bones. Beecher should pray to be saved from his friends.

August 30, SUNDAY. . . . It seems that some of Beecher's shoulder-hitting saints, or progressive Christian b'hoys, brought carnal weapons —to wit, revolvers— with them to the Plymouth meet'n house on Friday night, and that Moulton escaped with his life rather narrowly. The Rev. Mr. Beecher may be innocent; he is certainly not proven guilty. But his preaching and influence had certainly raised up around him a crop of scallywags, snobs, cads, and liars that it would be hard to match.

August 31. . . . Political skirmishing is active. "Democrats" are sanguine. But I think that Dix, the probable Republican candidate for governor, will run well, in spite of the 30,000 anti-lager fanatics who will do their devilmost to defeat him.

September 2. . . . Omens of "Democratic" gains this fall. God forbid the restoration of that party to power. But I should like to see the Republicans watched and menaced by a strong minority. They have enjoyed absolute undisputed control too long for their own good. Sporadic riots and lynchings among Southerners are exaggerated by the newspapers into a war of races and a reign of terror for effect on the fall elections.

In poor sorely-punished South Carolina, the doctrine of the rights of man and universal suffrage is settled by a *reductio ad absurdum*. Semi-brutal black voters are in a great majority and, under the leading of knaves and carpet-baggers, control the state and are sinking it into deeper ruin every day. Perhaps the unfortunate result of this experiment may open people's eyes and sooner or later bring about reaction at the North where it is sorely needed. As to South Carolina, it seems as if her white folks would have to emigrate in a body unless they can save themselves by a revolution. The nigger majority is confiscating all their property by fraudulent taxation for the benefit of political operators and demagogues, or rather "zoogogues." It may come to a war of races in bitter earnest.

September 4. . . . More bills! *Billi et billiores, etiam billissioni!!!* I had to draw upon my poor little Trust Company reserve fund, and how I am to pay my taxes and the doctors, *non constat.* Thought of absconding, but it is better to stick to the comptrollership, "though billmen ply the ghastly blow." With $18,000 a year and a house, it is wonderful I should be always hard up. I spend very little on myself. Probably our housekeeping may be too loose and lavish.

Southern symptoms are bad. Black spirits and white refuse to mingle for any political purposes. They distrust and hate each other worse and worse as time goes on, far worse now, I think, than nine years ago. An explosion may come any day and a social war. United States troops are ordered down to keep the peace, but they can't garrison the whole Southern country and watch thousands of square miles of powder magazine.

September 8. Ellie returned from Cornwall last evening for a couple of days in town, and she was much better, stronger, and more cheerful, at least till dinner time today, when the fact that I have resigned the Philharmonic presidency seemed to produce a depressing effect. . . .

The catalogue of the Columbia College library is printed and is on sale; a goodly volume, but the collection includes tons of rubbish. . . .

Horsley opens an active Church Music Association campaign and hopes for another season. May he succeed! Cooke, Edmund, and I are out of that boat now, thank Heaven!

Died, Peter Remsen Brinckerhoff.

September 11. Letter from Mr. Ruggles today. Glad to see that his handwriting, which has been shakey ever since his illness, is now clear and firm. . . .

Newspapers are full of politics and nothing else. For governor, the Republicans probably put up Dix and the Democrats Tilden. Not a bad nomination, but the shattered Tammany Ring will recalcitrate.[14] The "Liberal Republicans" make no nominations. The hydrocephalites or hydromaniacs run the Hon. Myron H. Clark, I believe. He is a nonentity, a mere aquatic larva. Dix is very strong, but Republicans are languid and there is disaffection in the ranks, so the result is doubtful.

September 14. . . . F. Moulton prints another long statement—diffuse, irrelevant, and unclean—doing as much damage to himself as to Beecher, and that is saying a good deal. Were Beecher strong in conscious virtue, he would make haste to get Moulton and Tilton indicted for libel or for conspiracy.

September 15. Disturbances at New Orleans that may be premonitory of the gravest mischief.

September 16. . . . Visit . . . from the Rev. Mr. Cooke. The Rev. Wiswall means to make war on Trinity Church vestry next Easter Tuesday. An

[14] The nomination of Samuel J. Tilden, chief hero of the successful fight against the Tweed Ring, was one of the highest merit, and proved the reformation of the Democratic Party in the state.

obscure Sunday newspaper, the *Call,* prints a column of scurrility about the expected campaign. . . .

Died, the Hon. B. R. Curtis of Boston, a lawyer of the first grade. . . .

Order reigns at New Orleans, the bogus state government (so-called) having collapsed before the "White League," which will not much help the Northern "Democracy." The governments of South Carolina and Louisiana are, I fear, mere nests of corrupt carpet-baggers upheld by a brute nigger constituency. But have we here in New York any right to look down on them? Our civic rulers are, as a class, utterly base, and a Celtocracy is as bad as a niggerocracy, and in some respects worse. "When God will devast and punish a people or a kingdom . . . He bereaves them of wise, honest, and godly rulers and counsellors . . . then are the common people secure and merry, and they go on in all wilfulness. . . . Therefore, I fear the axe is laid to the root of this tree that it soon must be cut down. God of His infinite mercy, take us graciously away that we may not live to see such calamity!" Amen.

September 17. . . . Trouble not yet over in Louisiana, if it be true that Grant sides with the collapsed government and intends employing horse, foot, and dragoons to reinflate it. I don't clearly see how he can do otherwise, and there is probably not much to choose between the two gangs or factions, but we are steering close to another civil war, big or little as the case may be.

Tilden is "Democratic" candidate for governor. I thought this a strong nomination that would give Dix trouble, but Cisco pooh-poohs it and says a weaker man could not have been put up. Cisco knows more than I do, but his political prophesyings fail sometimes. Tilden's record during the black winter of 1860-61 is against him, and he will get no cordial support from the scoundrelly survivors of the Tammany Ring which he helped to smash in November, 1871. But I should hate to see even a Democrat defeated because of that good service to the city.

September 23. Radiant weather continues. No news except that General Dix is nominated by acclamation. I sent the Rev. Mr. Morgan Dix quite a long letter. . . .

Horsley has secured one Sanford for president of the Church Music Association. He is said to be rich, unemployed, and an earnest lover of music. Richard Grant White and one or two more are to be vice-presidents. Another season seems probable. I hope so. I should be sorry to see that fine chorus collapse and disintegrate. Horsley evidently means to run the machine himself, with these laymen as ornamental assessors. He is likely to blunder in his choice of music. English audiences and American audiences differ in taste. We can't stand much Handel, the *Messiah* excepted. Horsley proposes bringing out the Dettingen "Te Deum." I predict it will be pronounced a bore.

October 1.   At Diocesan Convention all day. . . . Little or nothing done outside of the annual routines. The "regular" tickets for the Standing Committee and the Missionary Committee prevailed, with but two or three scattering votes in opposition. I think Morgan Dix was scratched by four malcontents. I was made a trustee of the Episcopal fund. The Bishop's address was two hours long, mainly devoted to the inculcation of tolerance and the mischief of "restrictive" legislation on questions of ritual and things indifferent. It was Dix's Ascension Day sermon, *cum commento*, capable of great compression, like sponge. I won't say like gas, for it was thoughtful, scholarlike, and wholesome. But it might all have been said in half the time. I rather protested against being made trustee as aforesaid, for there are plenty of people who grumble about Trinity Church having too much to say and to do in the diocese.

Discoursed nice old Prof. Bartlett, whilom of West Point, Gen. Morell, the ophidian Honorable Henry E. Davies, the Honorable Hamilton Fish, Bishop Tozer, Bishop Young of Florida, the Right Rev. Horatio Potter of New York, and others. And who should appear but my old classmate, the Rev. William E. Snowden, whom I have not seen since 1838! He has been settled all this time in North Carolina, but has now come North.

October 3. . . . Much arranging for the General Convention next week. It will cost Trinity not less than $8,000—feed included.

October 4, SUNDAY. . . . The Rev. Mr. Beecher has got Tilton and Moulton indicted for libel—a sensible proceeding.

Mr. Ruggles means to take his seat in the General Convention, in spite of remonstrances and entreaties. The session promises to be stormy. He will be sure to speak and excite himself, and there is an even chance of his bringing on a second seizure like that of October, 1872.

October 8. . . . I resigned from the American Geographical Society, since I am unable to perceive the advantage of paying certain annual dues for nothing at all.

The General Convention met yesterday. Much clack and waste of time over rules of order and much grumbling over the acoustic (or dys-acoustic) properties of St. John's. Cambridge Livingston's cunningly devised system of crosswires to destroy reverberation by breaking the sound waves seems a total failure.

The "church congress" met and has, I believe, adjourned. It looks like a fizzle. But it was a happy provision for the harmless discharge of peccant wind, which, if confined and pent up, might cause distress and incite to mischievous action.

October 13. . . . Much evolution of gas at the Convention; salutary. The more they talk, the less they will legislate. Mr. Ruggles does his share, of course, and most imprudently. But he is wholly irrepressible. . . .

October 15. Went through the workshops and manufacturing lofts of Tiffany's Union Square house with the intelligent Magauran. About five hundred men and women are employed there. Processes and apparatus interesting; some of the products are artistic and splendid. . . .

The Convention went into secret session yesterday—hammer and tongs—over Seymour, bishop-elect of Indiana, and have been at it, I believe, all today. I guess his election will be confirmed.

I signed a petition with Cisco, Nash, J. P. Pirsson, Edward Matthews, *et multis aliis,* praying for deliverance from legislation on ritual. . . .

Democrats claim great gains in Ohio and Indiana. Discouraging for Dix.

October 17. The General Convention is still within the veil dissecting Dr. Seymour and clapperclawing over ritualism. . . .

Horsley has filled up his Church Music Association subscription list. His new president, S. S. Sanford, led off with a subscription of $1,500. Good for Sanford! The vice-presidents (there is no committee) are a queer assortment: General Barnard, Richard Grant White, Clarence Seward, the Rev. Mr. Stanton, and J. Wrey Mould(!). I am glad the Association has passed safely through the critical process of casting its skin.

October 19. The General Convention thinks its oysters too small. So I assumed the responsibility of ordering bigger oysters and also of issuing them daily instead of every other day. Anything to inspire the Council of the Church with the spirit of peace and harmony, which is the fruit of good living and eupepsia.

Western elections have disheartened the Republicans and also the third-termites, whoever they are. I never saw any of them. General Dix's prospects are not brilliant. . . .

October 26, MONDAY. I became a borrower today for the first time in my life. Loan of $3,000 from Charley Strong on the pledge of the Bank of New York stock. There have been unusually heavy demands on me this year, but I must economize in earnest, and I have begun clipping and trimming my little personal expenses.

Total lunar eclipse Saturday night. The sky was veiled with inopportune cirri, and the orb was visible only as through a glass darkly; so I went to bed without waiting for the phenomenon.

November 2.   College trustees took their monthly nap this afternoon, and it lasted two hours and a half. Betts, now almost quite blind, resigned the clerkship, and Halsey was elected clerk. Poor Betts is so infirm and his sight so bad that I had to give him my arm down the stairs and help him into his carriage. Barnard mumbles and maunders worse than ever.

November 4, WEDNESDAY.   Yesterday's election was a Waterloo or Sedan to the Republicans. Total rout, North and South. General Dix was badly whipped. Some 80,000 votes changed in this state since 1872. Wickham is mayor, of course. New Jersey is Democratic, and so is the governor of Massachusetts! There has been no such discomfiture since Bull Run. One consolation is that Ben Butler's Massachusetts constituency invites him to try how the door of the house shuts from the outside and then to resume his seat by the domestic hearth. This revolution does not mean that people have changed their principles and gone over to Democracy so-called. It means that people are bored by the dullness of business ever since the panic of last year, that they are disgusted by abuses of power and bad management in Louisiana and other Southern states, by stories (half true, at least) of corruption and extravagance at Washington, and they are nervous about a "third term" and "Caesarism.". . .

November 6. . . . Mr. Ruggles brought in Hunt of New Orleans, who might fill Lieber's place. He seems well read and scholarly, is a churchman, national as to his politics, a gentleman, of good family, and looks just like Mephistopheles.

The insatiate General Convention devoured, absorbed, ingulphed, ingested, bolted, gobbled, munched, masticated, ingurgitated, deglutinated, and, I hope, digested and assimilated 80,000 oysters!!! And the Rev. Mulchahey tells me that the "Hospitality Committee" expects the long-suffering corporation of Trinity Church to pay its deficit of some $7,000 (hotel bills).

Election returns are painfully monotonous. As they come in more fully, they merely magnify the revolution of Tuesday. Some Northern Democrats and many downtrodden Southerners will probably misunderstand it. They will fancy that the good old days of 1860 have come back, and they will put on airs, exalt their horn, sharpen their bowie knives, and oil their revolvers. The amiable Isaiah Rynders, who crawled out into the light the other day, gave us a specimen of this kind of thing in certain rhetorical and parabolical allusions to "niggers." Very little of this would suffice to stir up an intense anti-Democratic reaction, which might possibly—and only possibly—carry Grant into a third term if he would take it.

The Republican defeat this fall was indeed overwhelming, constituting the greatest party overturn since 1860. The Democrats swept Samuel J. Tilden into the governorship of New York by a majority of about 50,000, thus almost reversing the vote which had made John A. Dix governor in 1872 by 55,000. New Jersey went Democratic, and Massachusetts chose a Democratic governor, partly by way of rebuke to the Republicans for nominating the impudent Ben Butler. In the South new gains were made by the Democratic or Conservative Party, presaging a return to full white supremacy. The Senate remained Republican, but the new House would be Democratic—and its investigating committees were certain to make the most of the opportunity to explore Republican misconduct and corruption. A remarkably able group of Democrats were chosen to the House, including Abram S. Hewitt of New York, Julius H. Seelye of Massachusetts, and Henry B. Payne of Ohio. It was evident that the Democratic Party, under such men as Tilden and Allen G. Thurman, had a great opportunity. If it could prove its adherence to reform it stood a handsome chance of carrying the country in the presidential election of 1876.

November 11. . . . Morgan Dix returned today on the Cunarder *Russia* with the Frau Rectorinn. While in London, he went to the illustrious Poole's to order some clothes. The urbane salesman said, "Certainly, sir, with great pleasure, sir; but then we don't take orders, sir, from strangers, sir, without some kind of reference, sir." "Oh-ah—of course, very proper," said the Rev. Morgan Dix, and produced from his pocket a letter of introduction from Bishop Potter to the Archbishop of Canterbury. The salesman hummed and hesitated and then said: "Yes, sir, a most flattering endorsement, sir. It would carry great weight, sir, in clerical circles, sir, but it won't do here, sir." So the Rev. Mr. Dix had to go into the City and get a letter from his banker. . . .

November 12. . . . In the evening to the Law School; Mr. Ruggles, Nash, Ogden, and I, with the professors. Sundry radical changes in the organization of the School were discussed, and sundry unpleasant truths spoken out at last as to the great dissatisfaction of many trustees with our present arrangements. The School has proved too successful and has grown far too unwieldy for any one professor, however able, but Dwight cannot bear to have anyone associated with him. . . .

November 16, MONDAY. . . . Died Billy Wilson, colonel in 1861 of the "Billy Wilson Zouaves," a most debauched regiment. The Philharmonic season opens dull. I fear my friends of that Society have not the vigor and enterprise to hold their own against Theodore Thomas. Horsley is in affliction. Mr. Samuel S. Sanford withdraws from the presidency of the Church Music Association, taking with him his subscription of $1,500 because some of the "fashionable" patrons of the Association have not renewed their subscriptions. Rather a snobbish reason for withdrawing. But so it is, and the Church Music Association probably exhales altogether from the face of the earth, . . . which is rather a pity.

November 18. . . . Ellie and I dined yesterday at Mrs. Farnum's (Ned Bell's sister), a dinner for the Rector and Mrs. Dix. Altogether were the Rev. Potter of Grace Church and his spouse, Mr. and Mrs. Aleck Hamilton, Mr. and Mrs. John Astor, Mr. and Mrs. Sidney Webster, and John J. Cisco; a satisfactory symposium. I was put at the foot of the board between Mrs. A. Hamilton and Mrs. Dix and found the "exercise" pleasant, of course. The Frau Rectorinn seems supremely nice. She has great charm of manner, including the agreeable gift of implying things complimentary and flattering, without expressly saying them. Her tastes and turn of mind seem in harmony with her husband's, and I guess she just suits his cases.

November 20. . . . Ellie and Temple went to the theatre to see *Jane Eyre* and Louis to see *Rip Van Winkle.*

November 23, MONDAY.   Ogilby preached at Trinity [yesterday]. He is never brilliant but always simple, earnest, and effective. In the evening, we had here Rosalie, the Colden Murrays, Handcocks, Phelps, Fales, Charley Strong, and Miss Puss (plumpest of little damsels), and others. Murray's story of the Suffolk County fishermen just before last election is instructive. "Wa-al, General Dix is a fine man, and he's made a fust-rate governor, and he's a very fine man, and we all like him. But fishin' has been damn' bad this season, and we hain't averaged more'n half an eel to a pot, and I think we'd better have a change."

November 25.   Wintry but clear. Leake and Watts trustees were to have met at Frederic De Peyster's in University Place at ten in the morning, but I found him quite ill, invisible, and forbidden to talk, which is, in his case, most heroic treatment. His remarkable son, General John Watts De Peyster, had been sitting up with him all night. Only Nox was there (Erebus), and there was no meeting. . . .

Horsley still hopes to keep the Church Music Association alive by a reorganization under the auspices of C. C. Dodge and John Stephenson, the car builder, and Charley Strong hopes that something will be got out of the Minnesota Railroad. . . .

November 30. Busy day. Died, Jonathan Sturges, aged seventy-three, a retired merchant, whom every one liked and respected; pneumonia. And at a little after twelve today, Mayor Havemeyer was stricken by apoplexy and died almost instantly. He was in his office in City Hall. He was a rather dense but worthy old citizen, obstinate but without force to save himself from being made a catspaw by political scallywags. . . .

Sunday opened with a rampacious, truculent tempest of wind and rattling sleet and flooding rain. This operated as a *ne exeat* on most churchgoers, myself included. Evening was clear, and a mob invaded us.

December 1. Law School Committee this evening at the School on Great Jones Street. Mr. Ruggles, Dwight, Nash, Ogden, and I. Two hours of close, relevant, businesslike talk. We recommend a third year and a test for admission—namely, either a college diploma or an examination, including Latin. This will keep out the little scrubs (German Jew boys mostly) whom the School now promotes from grocery counters in Avenue B to be "gentlemen of the bar." Dwight relucts at anything that tends to diminish the number of students and the aggregate of fees, but he was tractable and reasonable.

December 4. . . . We construe the rule *nil de mortuis,* and so on, most absurdly. Poor old Havemeyer's coffin is copiously beslobbered with maudlin eulogies by the very men who were raving at him only a week ago as a pig and a mule and a mischievous idiot. Should Ben Butler die tomorrow, Congress would resolve unanimously and with effusion that the country had sustained an irreparable loss by the translation to a better and a brighter world of so pure a patriot and so eminent a Christian.

December 5. . Fourth Avenue and Broadway thronged with vacuous people loafing and lounging and waiting for the funeral pomp of Havemeyer to pass by. Bells of Grace Church, St. Paul's, and Trinity were tolled. It was announced that the fire bells would also be rung, which occasioned unpleasant observations. It was near three o'clock when the head of the procession reached St. Paul's, a long way from Greenwood. . . .

December 22. Dullish and thawing. Rainy evening. Streets are lamentably obstructed. Loafed about Trinity Church. Tested chimes. Meneely's new bell won't do. Its tones suggest a summons to dinner rather than to prayer. The new school building grows but slowly.

Rehearsal for Christmas music at three-thirty. Did not stay it through.

Mostly Schubert's Mass in B-flat. The Offertory, by Bach, was very long, and I fled from it. The first allegro of Mozart's B-flat Symphony, for the final Voluntary, was not at all appropriate. Also, there was the Gloria Tibi, which made me jump, for it was part of the dearly beloved Kyrie of Haydn's First Mass, whereof the leading phrase has been my pet of pets for thirty years and which I never heard with orchestra. If the shade of dear old Joseph Haydn will pardon the criticism, it is certainly fitter for a Gloria than for a Kyrie.

December 25, FRIDAY.   Christmas. Seldom a brighter or better Christmas. Sky crystalline and temperature just chill enough to be seasonable and befitting the day. To Trinity at nine-thirty, where I was joined by Ellie an hour later. I conferred with policemen and gave directions against overcrowding, which worked well. The morning service was at ten and communion was at eleven. With us were Mr. Scharfenberg and two young people, Rosalie and Murray Hoffman, Jr. The Schubert music was beautiful and well rendered. Haydn's Gloria Tibi (that is, the Kyrie) is most Christmasesque, joyous and lovely. The Bach Offertory was botched and bad. Why will the greatly daring Messiter attempt such things? Were this crabbed, fuguey music perfectly rendered, it would still be a wearisome, dull puzzle to nine-tenths of the congregation. . . .

A dangerous innovation!!! Choir and clergy marched to the chancel doing their pretty processional hymn as usual. But they were preceded by a white banner inscribed with the words, "We praise Thee, O God." I thought it graceful and nice. But I shall hear of it from —— tomorrow. "These ritualistic novelties are very alarming." "Romanistic (!) influences are gaining ground in Trinity parish," with much *dummheit* besides, to which no answer is possible. . . .

December 28.   Professor [William G.] Peck's house was robbed yesterday, at ten-thirty in the morning, in the coolest and openest way. A dissolute young gambling son of the professor's being a confederate of the thieves, admitted them to the premises. Booty, $40,000.

December 31. . . . Died old Gerrit Smith, who gloried in calling himself an Abolitionist (and behaving as such) in the good old days when that epithet was equivalent to leper, pariah, mad dog, or *hostis humani generis,* and when the whole country was cringing under the plantation whip.

Farewell 1874; may 1875 be more prosperous and more fruitful of good works.

1875

LABORS FOR TRINITY CORPORATION · THE BEECHER-TILTON TRIAL · COLUMBIA AFFAIRS · FINAL ILLNESS

Strong began the last year of his diary in apparent good health and good spirits. New Year's Day, clear, chill, and windless, fell on Friday. He made a fair number of calls, going to the houses of Mrs. John Sherwood, Mrs. William Schermerhorn, Mrs. Morgan Dix, and others. He enjoyed Mrs. Strong's party that night for "Miss Puss," Charley Strong's pretty daughter. At the Trinity Corporation office he was active as ever. His interest in public affairs continued strong, and he was outraged by the arrogant conduct of the Grant Administration in New Orleans. The recent election had left the control of the lower house of the legislature in doubt, and the President had resolved on heroic measures. He ordered General Sheridan to the state; on the 4th of January, some 1800 federal troops were posted about the State House; and at a critical juncture, General R. de Trobriand marched in, seized five objectionable members—objectionable, that is, to the Grant party—and expelled them from the chamber. Everyone recalled that even Charles I had not been able to deal quite so highhandedly with Parliament. While a wave of indignation swept over the North, the Cabinet itself took a stand against Grant, Secretary Fish and others being ready to resign if the President persisted in his course.

January 2, SATURDAY. Nothing very new, except that the Spanish Republic is dead, and Alfonso XII sits on the uneasy throne of Spain—poor young gentleman. . . .

January 7. Grant's Louisiana blunder is doing him and his friends great harm. Prominent Republicans denounce it, and indignation meetings are to be called here and elsewhere, "without distinction of party." Strange that the canny and politic Hamilton Fish can acquiesce in the wild capers of the Administration! That bold dragoon, Gen. Philip Sheridan, wants the President to proclaim all the white folk of Louisiana (except the carpet-baggers) "banditti" and to let him, General Phil, dispose of them as he did of Early and his men and afterwards of the Pi-egans. But I don't think a *la stoccata* will so carry it away quite yet. I have stood up for Grant through evil report and good report for ten years, but he is "coming it rather too strong" now. There are reasonable people who think it Grant's deliberate purpose to stay in the White House after his term expires, if he can do so, *per fas aut nefas*, but it seems preposterous.

January 9. . . . Signed (at the *Evening Post* office) the "Indignation Meeting" call. I am sorry to do it after swearing by Grant so long. Grant is said to be "not at all scared" by the storm he has raised. He is not easily scared by anything. Whatever may go to smash, *impavidum ferient ruinae*. His heart is hardened, and he "will fight it out on this line" as he once did in a better cause. As old Pepys, my prototype, says, "Pray God send all well!" . . .

January 11. . . . I hear that George Anthon, at Yonkers, has had a small boy added unto him, and to Mrs. Constance Harrison a little girl. May they thrive and prosper!

Tonight's vestry meeting was of brevity unprecedent—only forty minutes! But we gave the committees many "chores" to do. General Dix was with us for the first time in two years, and we added him to the Standing Committee, making it nine instead of eight. But this does not increase the *quorum*. In discourse with a half dozen of us, the General remarked: "It's only the other day that they murdered a score or two of niggers at Vicksburg. Why didn't these gentlemen get up an indignation meeting about *that*?" Which was a rather fatuous remark, methought. But our dear, good, astute, old sagacious General likes to be on good terms with administrations and remembers the teaching of his catechism about "honoring the civil authority," which has foreign missions and other good gifts for its friends.

January 13. . . . Mr. Morris's opening in Tilton *v.* Beecher reads like a summing up and consumed two days and a half. The look of the case may change and probably will when Evarts has his innings, but Beecher's contrite and despairing letters can never be so explained away as to free him from the gravest weight of suspicion.

January 15. . . . Grant's Louisiana message is less truculent than was expected, but palliating and trying to excuse what seems a great wrong.

Tilton *v.* Beecher. Frank Moulton was on the stand and his direct examination is not yet closed. He testifies to full and free admissions by the defendant. This threatens to be as protracted as the Tichborne case, and it is watched with something like the same interest. Plymouth Church will stand by its shepherd whatever the trial may disclose and whatever be the verdict. But outside that fane, opinion sets strongly against Beecher, and no wonder. To use his own cant or peculiar religious patois, he put too much "inwardness" into these fatal letters of his and recorded his "heart-experiences" too copiously. Unprejudiced people can give them only one construction. The plaintiff's position is, however, so assailable and his record so bad that he can expect only nominal damages in any event. Were he seeking a divorce, he would fail.

January 17, SUNDAY. . . . Two long grave conferences with Temple. I didn't scold a bit, though I was fairly entitled to do so, for Temple has been behaving ill and in an underhand, tortuous way; but I read him several fine moral lessons. I was much discouraged at first, for I could elicit nothing but a tendency to sulk, to invent plausible excuses, and to find fault with everybody. The radical cause of his troubles, of his "playing hookey" and shirking work at Mr. Everson's and now at George Anthon's, was but too apparent. He does not recognize the unpleasant truth that it generally devolves on every son of Adam to do work he doesn't like. My parenthetical suggestion of calling in grandpapa and Uncle James as a *conseil de famille* to advise me as to what the deuce I should do with him produced considerable effect, I thought. He was silent for a time and then remarked that he "didn't see the use of that." I thought he would not. At last, to my great joy, he volunteered a suggestion, or proposition, that he should do his Greek with me in the afternoons or evenings and pledge himself to regularity and effort, and I promised to watch him and see that he shirked school no longer. On these terms a treaty was concluded. I may find my share of its obligations a bore, but it looks like Temple's last chance.

January 18. . . . School work tonight with Temple. The young scapegrace knows more Greek and far more algebra than I. He's as bright as he can be. All he needs is perception of the duty of work.

January 19. Died William H. Aspinwall, at sixty-seven, whom I regret.[1] They say he never got over the death of his brother John, and he

[1] The eminent merchant had been still active in business. Probably no man had done so much to build up the Pacific and Latin-American trade of the United States. During the Civil War he had given vigorous support to the Union, and had gone to England to urge the British to stop the building of the Laird rams.

has suffered for several months under a complication of disorders, including disease of the heart, which seems to have been the immediate cause of his death. He was always particularly civil and good to me, and while I was in college, he offered to take me into the countinghouse of Howland & Aspinwall—a most special favor and distinction. Perhaps I should have become a partner and blossomed into a millionaire.

January 20. . . . Grant has blundered again: "Federal myrmidons," that is, a squad of U.S. infantry, summarily eject the sheriff of Vicksburg from his shrievalty and install somebody else in his place. This is a cheap and easy substitute for the costly, tedious, and antiquated machinery of a *quo warranto.* But unless Grant is careful, he will be outflanked by an impeachment.

January 22. Visit from Egleston—in his usual nervous, perturbed, and *wronged* condition. He *will* order work done at the School of Mines without the least authority and then wonder that there should be any demur about paying the bills; he is confident that he will die soon.

January 23. Whom can we trust, and who can feel sure of even his own honesty? Henry Nicoll, after forty years of honorable practice, after having won the unquestioning confidence of every businessman in New York, after coming to be universally regarded as the embodiment of old-fashioned integrity, caution, and conservatism—Henry Nicoll is in every man's mouth today and in the newspapers, besides, as having used, or embezzled, several hundred thousand dollars of the trust funds in his keeping!!! Townsends, Bradhursts, and Hickson Fields are among the chief sufferers. This is a public calamity, weakening everybody's faith in anybody. The Devil must certainly be unchained in these days. What will come next? Will Bishop Potter pocket the fund "for the relief of decayed and insolvent clergymen," and run away?

January 24. . . . Bad account of the Nicoll case; assets doubtful. W. H. Aspinwall is said to have lost a great deal of money during the last year or two. . . .

January 25. Died Charles Kingsley, also Maunsell Field, who worked with me in my father's office in 1842.[2] I liked him greatly then, but he underwent a kind of fatty degeneration afterwards and became heavy, pompous, oedematous, and puffy, though always quite efficient in business. His marriage turned out ill, and I don't think his life was prosperous or

---

[2] Maunsell B. Field, who had held minor diplomatic posts before the war and risen to be assistant secretary of the Treasury under Chase, left a volume of *Memories* which was published posthumously.

very happy. He had a passion for knowing notable people, not with ulterior designs, but for their own sake, and I suppose the crowning mercy of his life was his accidental presence when Mr. Lincoln died.

January 27. Two College committees met today; namely, the School of Mines this afternoon, at William Betts's (Betts, the president, Agnew, and I), and "On the Course," at the Bishop's this evening. . . . Our excellent president's prosing grows more and more afflictive. He prosed tonight a full hour on a matter as to which we were all of one mind. When he dried up and ceased at last, we were all in a kind of magnetic trance, and nobody seemed able to say anything. I broke the spell by a motion that was unanimously adopted at once (I had some difficulty in rousing myself to move it) and then came away as fast as I could. . . .

January 28. My auditing committee finished its labors and signed its report. Its examination has been searching—thank Heaven. An annual examining committee would probably have saved George A. Jones and Henry Nicoll from misapplication of trust funds and from disgrace and ruin. But I confess that as our Fulton Street office is organized I do not see how I could steal a dollar if I wanted to. I was much flattered and gratified by a casual remark of Cambridge Livingston's: "Why, I thought Henry Nicoll was like Edgar S. Van Winkle, and *you,* and a few other people about whom nobody has any doubt at all." God keep me from falling!

February 1, MONDAY. . . . College trustees met at two this afternoon. Judge Blatchford was in the chair, and Mr. Ruggles was present for the first time (I think) since October, 1872. A proposition was made by Barnard to suspend chapel services during examinations. Spirited speech by Mr. Ruggles against that proposition, and it was lost, *nem. con.* Barnard's position on the board is painful. He is prime minister and chief administrative officer, but he can never count on a majority and is constantly thwarted and snubbed by adverse votes. He doubtless wishes he could afford to resign, and I, for one, wish so, too.

Certain recommendations from the Law School Committee were carried, and I moved a resolution which I had promised Dwight to move, though expressly declining any promise to vote for it. It was to diminish the amount of Latin hereafter to be required as a condition of admission to the School. I moved it, stating that I should vote against it, and it was lost, Mr. Ruggles making another quite brilliant little speech against it and in maintenance of classical culture.

We went into an election to fill a vacancy on the board. There were twelve votes, and James W. Beekman was unanimously elected. This lay dissenter takes the place of some deceased Presbyterian or Dutch Reformed cleric—whom precisely, I don't remember. I want the College made a church college, and with that view I vote for the promotion of dissenting laymen to places long filled by dissenting parsons, quasi ex officio. As these laymen die off, they can be easily and silently replaced by churchmen. When Halsey, our clerk, read the names of men who had been nominated for the vacant trusteeship, it was sad to hear him slur over Henry Nicoll's name as being a name, strictly speaking, before us but for which, of course, nobody could vote. I should have voted for him a month ago.

February 3. . . . Tilton *v.* Beecher. Tilton still on the stand. The drift of public opinion seems setting more and more decidedly against Beecher.

Our grand little dinner for the Rector and the Rectoress yesterday was rather pleasant. Ellie knows how to entertain. People seemed to enjoy themselves and talked like ten square miles of tropical forest full of parrots and parroquets. I was glad to have John Astor here, to whom I'm indebted for many sumptuous dinners. I fear their splendors have deterred me from asking him. A half-conscious but wholly snobbish feeling that I could not rival the gorgeousness of his dinners has interfered with the performance of my "social obligations." But our table was handsome enough for any reasonable Christian, and nobody seemed to feel the absence of a service of gold plate. I don't believe that John Astor himself missed it much. The dinner was quite good enough, too. . . .

February 8. Continued monotony of rancorous cold, aggravated by the mockery of brilliant but lifeless sunshine. Many seals reported in the Lower Bay, and their visit is attributed to this severity of the winter. If it last much longer, we shall be invaded by walruses and polar bears. . . .

February 10, ASH WEDNESDAY. . . . Henry Nicoll resigns from the Bar Association. Poor Henry Nicoll!

February 12. . . . The long record of the Astor House is closed. They are selling off its gear and plenishing at auction, and it will be converted to business uses.

February 13. . . . Dined here, Hamilton Fish, Jr., and the Austrian Fritsch; both pleasant.

Died, Major Joseph Delafield, aged eighty-five, one of our vestry. He had been confined to his room for many months, but the immediate cause of his death was this lethal pneumonia, of which everybody seems to die now-a-days.

February 14, SUNDAY. . . . Dr. Edward Delafield died last night, eighty-one, brother of Major Joseph D. . . .

February 15. . . . Henry Delafield died last night. An unusual coincidence—three brothers, living apart, each confined to his own house for months and all dying of the same acute disease within little more than forty-eight hours.

February 20. . . . Tilton *v.* Beecher. The evidence begins to pinch Monsignor Beecher very hard. He is probably ruined by his utterly fatuous confidences and confessions. But Plymouth Church is a nest of "psychological phenomena," *vulgo vocato* lunatics, and its chief Brahmin is as moonstruck as his devotees. Verily they are a peculiar people. They all call each other by their first names and perpetually kiss one another. The Rev. Beecher seduces Mrs. Tilton and then kisses her husband, and he seems to acquiesce in the osculation. One of the ladies of Beecher's flock testifies that Beecher expressed to her his regret that "Elizabeth" (Mrs. Tilton, to wit) had done nothing to "repair her sin" in confessing her adultery with him and does not testify that she thereupon turned him out of her house. They all seem, on their own shewing, to have been behaving like bedlamites and to have been afflicted with both moral and mental insanity. . . .

February 23. . . . Yesterday being Washington's birthday and a holiday, I took Ellie to the Metropolitan Museum of Art (Fourteenth Street) and spent an hour there. The observance of the feast seemed slack—no parade and no circuses of any kind. . . .

March 5. . . . The Rev. Alvah Wiswall is . . . inducing sundry young scrubs of his St. John's Guild to take the communion at the church or at the chapel, fondly deeming that they thereby become corporators.[3] I don't know where he can find the men to make up a reputable opposition ticket, and I doubt whether he can drum up an omnibus load of seedy voters. But we must take every reasonable precaution, for the Rev. Mr. Wiswall is not only most vindictive, but uncommonly active, cunning, and plausible. He's a slippery enemy and dangerous, considering his scanty resources. Perhaps he may confine himself to assailing Nash, Palmer, and myself—the committee which judged him. . . .

Last night with Ellie to Booth's to see the "Grand Shakesperian Revival" of *Henry V*, which still draws crowded houses. It is mainly a costume performance, and the costumes and tableaux are carefully studied

[3] Some nervous parishioners of Trinity feared that Wiswall would try to carry the coming Trinity Corporation election by a surprise coup.

from miniatures in Froissart and Monstrelet. But it was fairly acted; Rignold as King Harry was more than tolerable; Fluellan and Ancient Pistol were excellent, and the Princess was very pretty, naïve, and taking. It was the largest and most shewy stage pageant I ever saw, especially King Harry's triumphant entry into London.

Congress adjourns and the sceptre departs from the hands of the Republican party. I bear the blow with resignation, for my faith in the party and in the Administration has been cooling off for some time.

March 8.   A rather brief vestry meeting today. Cisco, Astor, and two or three others presented us with a portrait of the late Rev. Frank Vinton, by LeClear. It's a good picture and lifelike and has one great advantage over its reverend original, namely, that it preaches not. One doesn't feel the least disposition to say, "O that those lips had language!" . . .

Died, Mrs. Henry Field, wife of a Presbyterian divine.[4] She was the Mlle. de Luzy whose name appears on the record of the De Praslin tragedy of 1846 or 1847. I knew her at one time quite well, and she was universally liked, being uncommonly clever and cultivated. Her plainness made it incredible that the Duc de Praslin should have been in love with her. Nobody ever remembered this unhappy scrape against her, except that racy and high-flavored old boar, the Count Gurowski, who, one night at a Century Club reception, hissed through his set teeth: "Murdee-ress, Mur-dee-ress," until he was invited either to stop doing it or to leave the room through the window.

March 11. . . . The newspapers still give us each morning our daily Beecher, but we no longer read the long, weary columns of irrelevant bosh. We are satisfied with a glance. Kenyon or Ellenborough would have finished off the case in three days.

March 19.   Gloomy and cold with a snow flavor. Randolph Robinson called. The sensibilities of the Century Committee on Admissions are governed by the fact that Burton Harrison (whom General Greene nominated and I seconded) was Jeff Davis's private secretary, and so they are likely to blackball him; in fact, they have blackballed him, and his name was restored to the list with difficulty. People are a little provoked because Wickham, the new mayor, made Harrison his private secretary and, still more, at his appointing Fitz-John Porter commissioner of public works. But Harrison merely went with his people, wrongly enough, of course. He has lived here as a loyal and reconstructed citizen for ten years

---

[4] Henry M. Field had married Laure Desportes, who had been involved in the Praslin murder trial.

and, I believe, voted and worked for Grant in 1872. Is the day of forgiveness never to come?[5]

March 20. The dreary monotony of the evidence in Tilton *v.* Beecher is lightened up for the moment by glimpses of brilliant absurdity. The rather pert and forward "Bessie Turner" is on the stand, and she tells how the high-souled and intellectual Theodore Tilton wandered habitually about his house in his nightgown all night "hanging pictures," how he knocked her down and thought she must have fallen somehow, how he swore at Mrs. Tilton, and the like. This trial is Bedlam's Invisible World Displayed.

March 23. . . . For safety's sake, we are busily sending out circulars to corporators, reminding them of Easter Tuesday. Henry Erben came to see me yesterday, skirling like a Chinese gander before a storm. "Had heard a story that what d'ye callum—Wiswall—was going to get some shysters together and attack the vestry. He, Erben, would be on hand at the opening of the polls, and would put a stop to anything of the sort." The chances of this scallywag Wiswall being able to effect any mischief, with all his cunning and all his spite, are exceeding small, but we must be on our guard. The consequences of his success would be disastrous. It's an awful and a saddening thought that even the august vestry of Trinity Church is subject to mutability, like other things temporal, and that even a comptroller of Trinity Church may be overthrown by politic devices and complots. . . .

March 24. A reconnoitering party (Duncan, to wit) reports all is serene at St. John's and no signs of a parochial popular uprising. If Wiswall the deacon and his picaroons be lying in wait for us, they contrive to keep wonderfully close. May they dream of evil bogies tonight! Wiswall makes a grand fanfaronade in the newspapers about his St. John's Guild and has persuaded many reputable people to let their names be used as its endorsers. They generally know nothing of its work; but it is a quack charity. I have reason to believe that Wiswall lives on it (which may be right enough) and that he draws from its funds the instalments of money with which he quiets a certain Mrs. H—— and keeps her from publicly denouncing him for having swindled her out of nearly all her property. St. John's Guild will probably collapse suddenly someday and leave a smell—and that "not a pretty one"—behind it.

[5] Burton Harrison, at this time practising law in New York, was not elected to the Century. He is best remembered as the husband of Constance Cary Harrison, author of some novels and *Recollections Grave and Gay*.

March 27. . . . It's said that Fitz-John Porter's application for a rehearing is denied. I fear this is just.

Scribners—A. and W.—have got up their new shop. It's doubtless the largest and shewiest bookstore in America, probably in the world.

March 30. Easter Tuesday. Clear and un-springlike. I found an unusual confluence of voters at Trinity Church. The polls closed at one; result: 189 votes unanimous, and *not a single name scratched*!!! . . . So the politic machinations of Wiswall prove a mare's nest. So I expected, but it was right to take precautions. Wiswall and Mrs. L—— tell Henry Erben that they are too busy just now for anything but floating hospitals and "tea-parties" at the academy; but *next* year they will try to attend to the vestry. . . .

March 31. . . . I spent most of the morning, after signing checks for April 1, pasting newspaper cuttings into a big scrapbook—materials for future memoirs of Trinity Parish. I have a vast mass of newspaper cuttings, besides, from poor old Dunscomb's desk, and Henry Dorr called this morning with a great bundle of like matter. So I have enough to keep my paste pot busy to the end of my days. Dorr is a most loyal parishioner of Trinity; he's our antiquarian. He has rummaged in the Historial Society and in the Society Library for material that appears in the appendix to Dix's sermon on the centennial of St. Paul's and in the last year book of the parish. Pity he is the ideal of a bore.

April 2. . . . The vestry met this afternoon and organized. Contoit was put on the Cemetery Committee—vice Swift disappeared; otherwise, there was no change. Then we organized a Standing Committee meeting. Our new colleague, Dr. Wilkes, took his seat. He is a descendant, or else a great-something-nephew of the London John Wilkes—a connexion of the Scotch Lord Jeffrey—and a gentlemanlike person.

One or two of my friends have set their hearts on buying lots near Central Park for $360,000 to build a new chapel for parishioners who have moved uptown, and incurring a debt of three-quarters of a million dollars. *Das geht nicht.* The strongest point made against us in 1856 and 1857 was that we built Trinity Chapel for wealthy people who ought to provide themselves with churches. It could readily be answered, but it was a telling *ad captandum* criticism. We had much better add transepts to Trinity and increase our church accommodation downtown.

Interest in that weary Tilton *v.* Beecher revives a little, the reverend defendant having taken the stand himself. He is a cool and powerful witness. Fullerton's examination will not shake him; but it will tax even his subtlety, unction, and histrionism to produce an exculpatory commentary on his *epistola poenitentialis*.

April 6. Died, the Hon. James J. Roosevelt, aged eighty. His gross personal prejudices and partialities spoiled him for a judge of the Supreme Court; and he was too servile a white nigger not to disgrace the U.S. district attorneyship, even in the days of Buchanan and the plantation whip. He slipped and fell some little time since, breaking the neck of the thigh bone. For some reason or other his stomach thereupon refused all food, and he literally starved to death. So one of his nephews tells me.

April 9. Went to Cemetery Committee meeting this afternoon. Cisco called, eager for the purchase of a dozen lots on Fifty-ninth and Fifty-eighth Streets for a new chapel. It's the finest situation in the city, just west of Fifth Avenue and fronting the Park, and we may secure them for $300,000 and build at our leisure. But I look with trepidation on a new debt of near a million, especially while a couple of hundred thousand dollars must soon be laid out on that insatiable cemetery. Our building Trinity Chapel was one of the chief and the heaviest weapons used against us in 1855–57. It was a costly church for rich, uptown people who ought to build their own churches. "But we must retain our corporators." Answer: We had 189 of them last Easter Tuesday, but I fear Cisco will push this through; he says the Rector is with him. . . .

The *Tribune* tower is finished off at last with a jaunty little steeple, like a seventeenth century peaked hat. Our Trinity Church School house tower looks well, though the gargoyles at its angles are hypertrophied. When a new idea has forced its way into the head of Upjohn, Jr., he is apt to "run it into the ground," or (as in this case) into the air.

April 26, MONDAY. At daybreak Sunday morning, the Union League Club house took fire. The storm retarded the fire signals, and the combustion was not suppressed till this costly building was denuded of its roof and every storey singed and soaked. . . .

Dick [Derby] came in at noon with sad news from Boston. George [Strong Derby] died Sunday afternoon at five P.M. . . . His father and mother were telegraphed at Norfolk on their way home from Florida. They did not even know that poor George was ill. He was one of the nicest and best fellows that ever lived.

May 1. . . . In Tilton *v.* Beecher, the defense rests from its labors at last, and there will probably be a few months of rebuttal. Fullerton, for the plaintiff, offers to waive all objections to Mrs. Tilton if called by the defense. Evarts replies from a high moral standpoint. He cannot possibly call Mrs. Tilton because it would be against the policy of the law, and so on. This affords food for meditation, but I am too tired of the case to care anything about it any more.

May 3.   To the University Place meeting house for John C. Green's funeral. . . .

A dozy meeting of the College trustees began at two o'clock—two hours in Boeotia. Amazing, how some of us dread and shrink from any profaning contact of the College with the community. Here have the board of health and one or two equally respectable bodies been allowed the use of a room in the School of Mines for evening meetings at a cost of gas amounting to less than $6.00 all told. One would think the news-paper reports of these meetings an advertisement of the School and that we should seek to make the College buildings a center for all the repu-table scientific and literary organizations of the city. But ——— demurs and objects, and the Standing Committee will doubtless agree with him. . . .

May 7. . . . In Tilton *v.* Beecher, Mrs. Tilton makes an appeal to the court—quite spontaneously and *not* on the suggestion of the counsel—to be allowed to take the stand and vindicate her reputation. To which Judge Neilson, of course, replies, *"Non possumus"*—a good dodge but rather thin. H. C. Bowen's rebutting evidence hits the Rev. H. W. Beecher very hard; while the Rev. Mr. Beecher has sworn that his deep contrition for injuries to Theodore Tilton, his wish for death, and all that, were founded on his having advised Bowen to divest Tilton from his editorship of the *Independent*. And now comes Bowen and swears that Beecher never gave him any advice or suggestion of the kind.

May 13. . . . Johnny has passed his [bar] examinations with flying colors. . . .

June 12, SATURDAY.   I finally broke down two days after my last entry, Saturday, the 15th, being unable to eat, hardly able to stand, and suffering constant sharp pain. I authorized Ellie to send for Dr. Peters, which I should have done a month before. Peters appeared and forthwith told me frankly that I was in very considerable danger, and that if I had delayed sending for him another week, he could probably have done nothing in the premises. The trouble was not dyspepsia but a liver en-larged to about three times its normal bulk, like that of a Strassburg gander, and threatening "induration," cirrhosis, and dropsy. I don't think the danger of all this quite over yet, but Peters thinks it diminishing and that, though I'm still on a lee shore, I am slowly clawing off in a hopeful way. He continues vigilant and most vigorous in his requirements as to diet and medicine.

So for the last month I have been in a state of combined torpor and medication, sustaining a passive or negative existence on pills and milk. The former were and are blue and cannabis, the latter (I believe), the "sincere milk" of the cow, furnished by an honest purveyor. Both my front and rear elevations have been tastefully frescoed with tincture of iodine; but I laid it on too freely, and the result was a pustular eruption that nearly drove me mad with itching. I longed to denude myself of all my clothes and all my flesh; and had that been practicable, I should probably have been found actively going over my ribs with sandpaper. My principal bother is now weakness, with a constant sense of almost intolerable fatigue. A few days ago, I tried for a drive in the Park with Ellie; but the vile pavement of Fifth Avenue caused me such pain that I had to turn about, and I got home feeling faint and prostrate. . . .

Jem's baby was baptized by Morgan Dix last Sunday at Trinity chapel, "James Francis Ruggles, Jr." Johnny was one of its godfathers. He—Johnny, not the baby—has gone in for a season with E. H. Owen, as he is thirsting for work in court. He is ambitious to be an advocate, not a mere conveyancer, and is full of ardor for any fray that may turn up.

I have had as many visitors as I wanted, including several of my bosses; for example, Gouverneur Ogden, Morgan Dix and the Governor, Cisco, and others.

Edmund Schermerhorn is president of the Philharmonic, an admirable choice for the Society but bad for Edmund, who will worry and fidget himself into a serious fit of illness before his first term is ended.

The case of Tilton v. Beecher is nearly run out at last. Beach is closing for the plaintiff. . . .

A weighty discovery is said to have been made by one Crookes of London, namely, that light has motive power, not of attraction, but of repulsion. Perhaps. If this discovery hold water, light will prove the centrifugal force and the cause of the behavior of comets' tails when near the sun.

Strong's physical suffering in these days was sharpened by an estrangement between him and his son Temple that became acute in the early part of April. The cause and progress of the difficulty cannot be known because the pertinent passages have been obliterated from the diary. Temple left home to earn his own livelihood with only vague prospects. Though he saw his mother daily, the rebellious youth avoided his father, who wrote on April 30: "Strange he should prefer a garret to the luxury and the indulgence of home. But I suppose it is the same feeling that makes boys long to be Robinson Crusoes and get shipwrecked on desert islands. Were he not a Bohemian to the backbone I should be sure he would sicken of this experiment within a month. Strange and sad that this unforeseen rupture should have occurred and should have become something very like permanent, incurable schism in less than thirty days. I fear I shall never hear poor obstinate, ungrateful, disobedient Temple's oboe tootling up-stairs any more."

June 16.   Warmer, but this summer is thus far backward and not torrid. I am still stupefying in this library (the Gandercoop or New Strassburg), weak as a baby and regaining strength imperceptibly, if at all. I made a sortie Monday night to a vestry meeting—only a short drive—where I was cordially received by my colleagues, the pillars of the church. A leave of absence was voted for me till October 15—a very kind deed. If I could lay my hands on a few hundred dollars, wouldn't I spend the summer in England! Dix is acting comptroller during my hypothetical absence. Our excellent old ex-Governor, ex-Major-General, ex-Secretary, ex-Ambassador, and the like, can no more live without some office, little or big, than a pagurus without his univalve. An order was taken for the purchase of land for a chapel on the south side of Houston Street, just east of the Bowery. It's the ancient Quaker burying ground, but I believe all the old Quakers have been dug up and transplanted. Our offer is $80,000 for the land, but we must probably pay a little more.

June 23.   Much warmer. I have been losing ground this last week, am as weak as I was a month ago, and have lost taste for all food save milk, of which emollient fluid I ingurgitate two full quarts per diem. Peters is to bring Dr. Alonzo Clark to inspect me tomorrow.

June 25, FRIDAY.   A hot day. Peters brought the great Dr. Alonzo Clark yesterday, who manipulated my liver with great energy but pronounced no definite judgment that I heard of. I have been improving the wrong way, like bad fish in warm weather. One day last week, I had a woeful day of headache, nausea, and malaise, which left me as weak as a sea anemone at low water. Since then, there has been no improvement.

This was the diarist's last entry; he died on July 21.

INDEX

Abbott, Austin, 366, 399, 400
Abolitionism and abolitionists, 12 n., 33, 130, 155, 213, 216, 252 n., 545
Abt, Franz, 332
Abyssinian church, 151
Academic costume, 219, 220
Academy of Design, 189
Academy of Music, N.Y., 13, 38, 54, 154, 166, 207, 236, 245, 257, 281, 317, 332, 333, 340, 341, 399, 457, 464, 498; burning of, 86–87
Acquapendente, Italy, 152
Acta Sanctorum, 528
Adams, Charles Francis, 167, 168, 190, 425
Adams, John Quincy (1767–1848), 406 n.
Adams, John Quincy (1833–1894), 434 n., 435
Adler, Isaac, 45
Aeschylus, 293
Affre, Denis Auguste, 316
Agassiz, Jean Louis Rodolphe, 10, 278, 505
Agnew, Cornelius Rea, 4, 10, 16, 19, 20, 23, 49, 54, 56, 71, 81, 100, 120, 124, 134, 159, 165, 186, 188, 214, 230, 274, 303, 319, 320, 337, 352, 478, 503, 550
Ahriman, 518
Aiken, William, 10
Ajaccio, 365
Alabama, 8, 41, 73, 175, 188, 338; elections, 157
Alabama, C.S.S., 80, 162, 244
Alabama claims, 179, 186–187, 238, 268, 339
Alaska (Russian America), 178, 185; purchase of, 129, 130
Albany, 31, 32, 92, 109, 126, 163, 164, 222, 229, 328, 404, 407, 418; G.T.S. in, 127–128
Albany *Argus*, 379
Albany Penitentiary, 504
Albert, Prince Consort, 148 n., 442
Albert Edward, 227
Aldus Manutius, 53
Alexander, Unionist of Baltimore, 213

Alexander ab Alexandro, 279
Alexandria, Va., 14
Alexis, Grand Duke of Russia, 394, 400–401
Alfonso XII, 546
Algeria, 164
Alice's Adventures in Wonderland (Dodgson), 181
Allen, Miss, 225
Allen, Horatio, 225
Allen, William F., 65–68
Allien, Laurent, 349
Alsace, 298, 305–307, 331, 343
Alston, William Algernon, 94
Alva, Duke of, 502
Amalgamated Bank, N.Y., 326 n.
American Association for the Advancement of Science, 98
"American Bastilles," 12
American Bible Society, 428
American Church Union, 176
American Geographical Society, 539
American Institute Fair, 156
American Museum of Natural History, 361
American Revolution, 199
American Scenic and Historic Preservation Society, 385 n.
Americana, 187–188
Ames, Oakes, 466
Amherst College, 516
Amiens, 227
Anderson, Charles Edward, 149
Anderson, Henry James, 9, 74, 112, 140, 176, 177, 219, 221, 340, 363, 412, 423
Anderson, Louisa, 149, 231
Anderson, Robert, 51, 420
Andersonville prison, 6, 44, 47, 61, 62, 179
Andrew, John Albion, 102, 158
Animal magnetism, 25
Annapolis, 61
Anthon, Caroline Graves (Mrs. G. H. Houghton), 143
Anthon, Charles, 119, 120, 124, 134–136, 138, 140, 143–146, 149, 160, 194,

[561]

GENEALOGICAL NOTE

George Templeton Strong was in the seventh generation of descent from Elder John Strong, a tanner, one of the hundred and forty passengers of the *Mary and John* from the counties of Somerset, Dorset, and Devon, who arrived in New England in May 1630 and settled the town of Dorchester, Massachusetts. John Strong's first wife died on the passage or soon after landing, leaving two children, and before the year was out he married Abigail Ford, a fellow-passenger, by whom he had sixteen children; at the time of his death in 1699, in his nineties, he could count 160 descendants. John Strong moved to Hingham in 1635, and by 1638 was a resident of Taunton; he later emigrated to Windsor, Connecticut, and in 1659 finally settled in Northampton, Massachusetts, as one of the founders of that town. He was ordained ruling elder of the church there in 1663.

The diarist's line of descent comes down through Thomas[2] Strong of Northampton, and his wife Rachel Holton; Selah[3] Strong of Setauket, L.I. and Abigail Terry; Thomas[4] Strong of Brookhaven, L.I. and Susannah Thompson; Judge Selah[5] Strong of Setauket, L.I. and Anna Smith; and George Washington[6] Strong.

George Washington Strong (Yale 1803), father of the diarist, was born 20 January 1783 at Setauket, L.I., and died in New York City, 27 June 1855. He married first, 8 July 1809, Angelina Lloyd of Lloyd's Neck, L.I., daughter of John Lloyd II and his wife Amelia, daughter of Rev. Ebenezer White (Yale 1733). Angelina Lloyd Strong was born 12 September 1785 and died 20 September 1814; she was the mother of Eloise Lloyd Strong, born 13 May 1810, and Mary Amelia Strong, born 25 August 1813, who died unmarried. Eloise Lloyd Strong married Elias Hasket Derby (1803–1880) of Boston, Harvard 1824; they were the parents of Dr. Hasket Derby (1835–1914), Amherst 1855; George Strong Derby (1838–1875), Harvard Law School 1861; Dr. Richard Henry Derby (1844–1907), Harvard 1864; Nelson Lloyd Derby (1846–1888), Harvard 1867; Lucy Derby, and two children who died young.

Eliza Catharine Templeton, the mother of George Templeton Strong, was the daughter of Oliver Templeton, merchant of New York who had

come from the north of Ireland, and Catharine Brownejohn, daughter of
Dr. William Brownejohn of New York (born Massey). George Washington Strong and his second wife Eliza Catharine Templeton, whom he
married 22 May 1819, had two sons, George Templeton Strong, born
26 January 1820, and John Wells Strong, who was born 3 December 1822
and died 14 December 1824.

George Templeton Strong (Columbia 1838) was married 15 May 1848
to Ellen Caroline Ruggles, daughter of Samuel Bulkley Ruggles (1800–
1881), Yale 1814, and Mary Rosalie Rathbone. Mr. Ruggles was the son
of Hon. Philo Ruggles of New Milford, Connecticut, and Poughkeepsie,
New York (1765–1829), Hon. M.A. Yale 1800, and Ellen Bulkley, "the
indomitable grandmamma" of the diary (1779–1865), daughter of Captain
Joseph Bulkley of Greenfield Hill, Connecticut. The children of Samuel B.
Ruggles and his wife were: John Rathbone Ruggles (Columbia 1841;
Harvard Law School 1846), who was born 15 March 1823, and died at sea,
6 May 1850; Ellen Caroline Ruggles (Mrs. George Templeton Strong),
who was born 30 July 1825 in New York City, and died 6 June 1891 in
Paris; and James Francis Ruggles (Columbia 1847), who was born 16
October 1827, and died 19 September 1895, and who married 4 June 1874,
Grace Baldwin, daughter of the late Hon. Harvey Baldwin, sometime
mayor of Syracuse, N.Y.

John Ruggles Strong, eldest son of the diarist, was born 20 October
1851 in New York City, and died there 6 February 1941. He received
the A.B. degree at Columbia in 1872 and the LL.B. in 1875, and began the
practice of law in New York. He was a man of brilliant mind, but was
afflicted with prostrating headaches of such intensity and frequency that he
was forced to give up his legal work. In 1885 he married Laura Coster
Stewart, daughter of Alonzo Cushman Stewart, M.D. and Laura C.
Barretto, and they went to live in Cambridge, Massachusetts, in 1892. Mr.
Strong devoted himself largely to music; he was a cellist, his wife a
pianist. After his wife's death, 26 September 1906, he came back to New
York, where he lived with his son, George Templeton Strong III.

George Templeton Strong, Jr., the second son, known as Templeton
Strong, was born 26 May 1856 in New York, and died 27 June 1948 at
Geneva, Switzerland. A tall, powerful man with a fine, ascetic face, and a
temperamental person with firm convictions, he broke with his father and
left home at nineteen. He devoted himself to the oboe and went to Europe
in 1879, where he studied for seven years at the Leipzig Conservatory;
during this period he frequently visited Liszt at Weimar. Moving to

Wiesbaden in 1886, he became a friend of Edward MacDowell. In 1891 he returned to this country and taught harmony and counterpoint for a year at the New England Conservatory of Music in Boston; at the end of that time he left the United States permanently, protesting that America neglected its composers. Settling in Vevey, Switzerland, he founded a watercolor painting society and devoted himself to musical composition. American recognition was belated but satisfactory: in 1926 the Philharmonic played his "D'une vie d'artiste," for violin and orchestra with Joseph Szigeti as soloist. In 1935 and 1936 Strong's Paraphrase on a Chorale by Leo Hassler was played in New York by the Philadelphia Orchestra and by the Philharmonic-Symphony Orchestra, and this work was played again by the N.B.C. Orchestra, conducted by Ernest Ansermet, a Swiss friend, in January 1948. Arturo Toscanini conducted his orchestral work, "Die Nacht," played by the N.B.C. Symphony in October 1939. Strong's compositions included three symphonies, "Sintram," "In den Bergen," and "An der See," the tone poems "Undine" and "Le Roi Arthur," and numerous other works; in 1930 he presented many of his manuscript scores to the Library of Congress. Templeton Strong was married three times, and was the father of five children: John Sintram Strong, Percy Templeton Strong, Richard Templeton Strong, George Templeton Strong, and Olivia Templeton Strong.

Lewis Barton Strong, the third son, was born 7 May 1860 and died 21 December 1908. He was a bachelor and a member of the Knickerbocker and Calumet Clubs; he followed no regular profession, but divided his time between New York, where he was a popular member of society, and the palatial Flagler hotels in Florida.

M.H.T.